MINNESOTA ARROWHEAD REGION

COVERAGE

MINNESOTA ARROWHEAD REGION COVERAGE

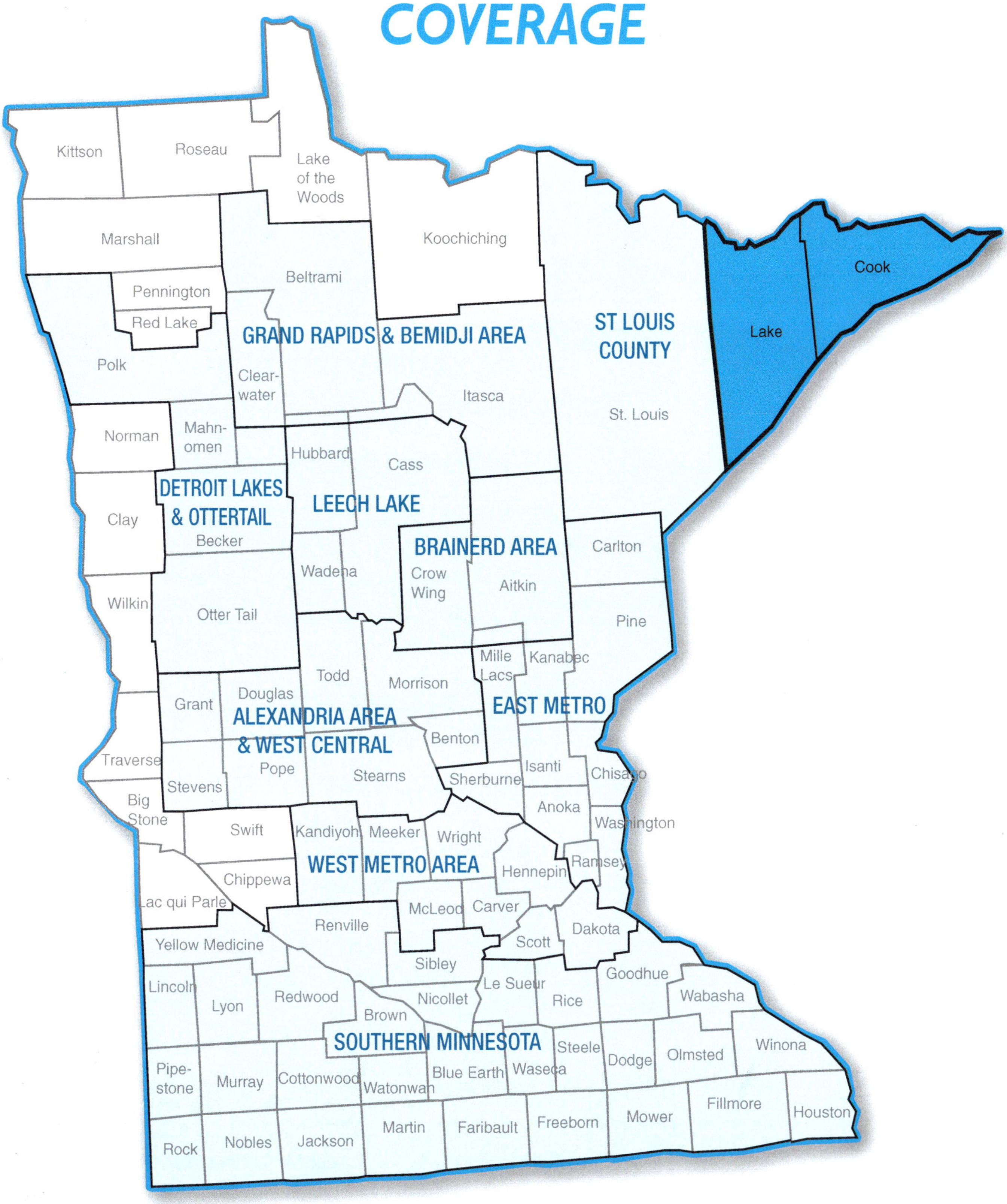

Kittson
Roseau
Lake of the Woods
Marshall
Koochiching
Beltrami
Pennington
Red Lake
Polk
GRAND RAPIDS & BEMIDJI AREA
ST LOUIS COUNTY
Lake
Cook
Clear-water
Itasca
St. Louis
Norman
Mahn-omen
Hubbard
Cass
DETROIT LAKES & OTTERTAIL
Clay
Becker
LEECH LAKE
BRAINERD AREA
Carlton
Wadena
Crow Wing
Aitkin
Wilkin
Otter Tail
Pine
Todd
Morrison
Mille Lacs
Kanabec
Grant
Douglas
ALEXANDRIA AREA & WEST CENTRAL
EAST METRO
Benton
Traverse
Stevens
Pope
Stearns
Sherburne
Isanti
Chisago
Big Stone
Anoka
Swift
Kandiyohi
Meeker
Wright
Washington
WEST METRO AREA
Chippewa
Hennepin
Ramsey
Lac qui Parle
McLeod
Carver
Renville
Dakota
Yellow Medicine
Scott
Sibley
Goodhue
Lincoln
Le Sueur
Lyon
Redwood
Wabasha
Nicollet
Rice
Brown
SOUTHERN MINNESOTA
Steele
Winona
Pipe-stone
Dodge
Olmsted
Murray
Cottonwood
Blue Earth
Waseca
Watonwan
Fillmore
Houston
Freeborn
Mower
Rock
Nobles
Jackson
Martin
Faribault

TABLE *of* CONTENTS

See back cover for alphabetical listing of lakes

MAPS IN THIS GUIDE ARE NOT FOR NAVIGATION

See back cover for alphabetical listing of lakes

MAPS IN THIS GUIDE ARE NOT FOR NAVIGATION

TABLE of CONTENTS

Minnesota Arrowhead Region Fishing Map Guide
by Sportsman's Connection

Editor and Publisher *Jim Billig*
Managing Editor *Todd Whitesel*
Senior Editor *Joe Shead*
Associate Editor *Cody Gilbert*
Editorial/Research *Mike Billig, Paul Howard, Scott Mickelson, Andy Scribbins, Ryan Stovern, Jon Wisniewski*
Creative & Production Director *Kurt Mazurek*
Production Coordinator *Shelly Wisniewski*
Senior Cartographer/GIS Specialist *Eric McPhee*
Cartographer *Linda Crandall, Tyler*
Information Systems Manager *Jon Fiskness*
Information Specialist *Daine Billmark*

ISBN-13: 978-1-885010-40-7

Sportsman's Connection
259 Main Street
Superior, Wisconsin 54880

www.scmaps.com

FOREWORD

Many books have been written about fishing. Most are of the "how-to" variety, focusing on certain species, offering tips regarding the best lures or baits and the best techniques for using them. Few books focus on the fishing waters, offering not just information on how to catch a particular fish species, but on where to catch them.

Where to catch fish in Minnesota's Arrowhead region is what this book is all about. We've attempted to be as comprehensive as possible, giving readers an in-depth view of the area's best and most notable fishing prospects. Included is information on more than 230 significant fisheries outside or bordering the Boundary Waters Canoe Area Wilderness.

This, of course, is not a complete picture of the region, or any given body of water. Nor, probably, should it be. Our purpose in publishing this book is to serve the angling public. We've tried, first and foremost, to give our readers information on waters they can use. And we've avoided, we believe, those waters that the public cannot fish.

As we've compiled this book, we've tried to be as accurate as possible in our depiction of each lake, stream or river. Within the limits of the source materials we were able to locate, we believe we have been. We have, in fact, relied not only upon our own expertise, but on the experience and knowledge of many others.

In all cases, we've used the best and most-recent data available. In some instances, however, the available data are several years old and may not accurately reflect the current situation. Readers should bear this in mind before relying solely on the information given for a lake; check the date provided with each table.

Regulations change from year to year. Be sure to consult current state and site-specific regs before fishing any new lake or river.

Readers should also be aware that data tables and management information focus primarily on the sport fishery. We believe this emphasis accurately reflects the interests of our readers. However, maintaining this focus has sometimes meant that data on less-desirable species has been sacrificed in order to present more comprehensive information on game species. The absence of rough fish or other less-desirable species in the information presented, therefore, does not mean these species are not present.

Refer to the "Reader's Guide to Using this Publication" (facing page) for terminology definitions and a map legend that will help you maximize the practical use of this publication.

We've received considerable assistance from a number of public and private agencies, each of which generously and courteously contributed material or knowledge to our work. These people help us develop a better understanding of the region and the resources. Thanks to the U.S. Geological Survey, National Oceanic and Atmospheric Administration and the Minnesota Department of Natural Resources.

Be respectful, please, of the fishery and the land, both public and private. Be especially aware of the growing problem the spread of exotic fish, plants and other aquatic species has on our fisheries, many of which are changing with alarming speed and irreversible consequences. Remove all vegetation from boats and motors, drain live wells and take other precautions before you leave the lake or river. Preserve the recreational opportunities lands, lakes and rivers offer for us all to enjoy.

Special thanks to all agencies, businesses and individuals who contributed to this effort:

Minnesota Department of Natural Resources

Maggie Gorsuch (DNR Fish & Wildlife, data manager)

Allen Stevens (fisheries program consultant)

Alan Anderson (former fisheries mgr.), Greg Berg (fisheries specialist), Steve Persons (fisheries mgr.)

Devils Track Resort, 205 Fireweed Lane, Grand Marais, MN 55604, (218) 387-9414

Knotted Pine Inn & Tavern, Dan & Paige Pasch (owners), 9702 Hwy. 1, Isabella, MN 55607, (218) 323-7681

Skube's Bait & Tackle, Cliff Noble (owner), 1810 East Sheridan St., Ely, MN 55731, (218) 365-5358

Muskie Doom Guide Service, 1517 Hwy. 61 Two Harbors, MN (218) 491-3277 www.muskiedoom.com

Thank you to our fellow sportsmen who contributed their knowledge and expertise:

David Yapel (Woods & Waters), Jeff Herrick (Superior Bakery in Tofte Holiday Station)

READER'S GUIDE *to* USING *this* PUBLICATION

Your fishing map guide is a thorough, easy-to-use collection of accurate contour lake maps along with geographic and biologic statistical information to help you locate a lake and enjoy a successful day out on the water of one of Minnesota's excellent fisheries.

The heart of this book is the **contour lake map**. Copyrighted maps are used with permission from the Minnesota Department of Natural Resources and are not intended for navigation. The lakes selected for this guide are confined to those that are accessible to the public.

Each map is accompanied by a **detailed write-up**. In each piece, you'll find fishing tips and hot spots specific to the body of water you're planning to fish.

Lake **stocking records** and **population survey statistics** are provided courtesy of the Minnesota Department of Natural Resources and summarized to reflect management trends and objectives for each fishery represented. Please keep in mind that annual fish stocking aspirations are directly affected by state hatchery production levels and sometimes the numbers available for stocking fluctuate considerably.

Detailed **area road maps** (1:160,500 scale) and **lake access** information is provided to help you plan your route to the lake. If there is more than one access point on a body of water, the GPS coordinates refer to the primary access. To locate a lake on these road maps, simply use the alphabetical lake listing on the back cover. Turn to that page to find the area road map page and coordinates for the lake. As a cross-reference, the area road maps include numbers on or adjacent to featured lakes, which designate the pages of the lake maps and information. Streams and rivers are also referenced in these area road maps.

While every effort is made to create the most accurate maps possible, the process of merging existing DNR maps with the latest GPS information will cause some slight differences to occur. (Especially on larger, more complicated lakes.)

GLOSSARY OF TERMS

Electrofishing: This is a specialized type of equipment that is most often used for sampling largemouth bass, smallmouth bass, and young of the year walleye. A boat-mounted generator is used to induce electrical current into the water that stuns the fish, allowing fisheries workers to net the fish for placement in live wells. Most of the fish caught by electrofishing recover rapidly and are promptly returned to the water after the necessary biological data is recorded.

Gill net: This is the main piece of equipment used for sampling walleye, northern pike, yellow perch, cisco, whitefish, trout, and salmon. The standard gill net is 6 feet tall by 250 feet long, with 5 different mesh sizes. Gill nets are generally set in off shore areas in water deeper than 9 feet. Nets are fished for a period of 24 hours. Fish are captured by swimming into the net and becoming entangled. Fisheries workers record length and weight data from each fish, determine the sex, look for parasites or disease, and remove several of the fishes scales for determining the fishes age. Most of the fish taken in gill nets are killed, but only a small portion of the lakes fish population is sampled during an individual survey event. The number of gill nets set during a survey is dependant on the lake acreage.

Number of fish caught (Net Catch Data): The catch is reported separately by gear type (gill net or trap net). The numbers presented are the average number of fish per net set. For example: If there were 10 nets set during a survey and 40 walleye were caught, the net catch would be reported as 4.0 fish/net.

Secchi Disk: Used in measuring water clarity, it is a white-colored, plate-size device submerged on the end of a line until it reaches a point where it's no longer visible; the depth at which this occurs is measured and recorded. In this book, secchi disk readings are given in English measure. Of course, many factors influence water clarity, and secchi disk readings vary according to season, growth of vegetation, weather, location in a lake, even human activity. Hence the readings given are approximations for any lake — snapshots of the water clarity at a given time and in a given location.

Shoreland zoning class: Minnesota's lakes range from the sterile, rock basin lakes of the Arrowhead region to the naturally fertile, shallow lakes of the southwest prairie region. These different types of lakes require different development standards. A classification system was developed so that the appropriate development standards could be applied. Lakes are divided into the following classes based on a combination of factors:

- **Natural Environment Lakes** usually have less than 150 total acres, less than 60 acres per mile of shoreline and less than 3 dwellings per mile of shoreline. They may have some winterkill of fish; may have shallow, swampy shoreline; and are less than 15 feet deep.
- **Recreational Development Lakes** usually have between 60 and 225 acres of water per mile of shoreline, between 3 and 25 dwellings per mile of shoreline, and are more than 15 feet deep.
- **General Development Lakes** usually have more than 225 acres of water per mile of shoreline and 25 dwellings per mile of shoreline, and are more than 15 feet deep.

Trap net: This is the main piece of equipment used for sampling bluegill, crappie, and bullheads. The standard trap net is 4 feet tall by 6 feet wide with a 40 foot lead. Trap nets are generally set perpendicular to shore in water less than 8 feet in depth. Nets are fished for a period of 24 hours. Fish are captured by swimming into the lead and following it towards the trap. Most of the fish collected in trap nets are returned back to the water as soon as the necessary biological data is recorded. The number of trap net sets during a survey is dependant on the lake acreage.

LEGEND

Boat Ramp
Carry Down Access
Access by Navigable Channel
Portage Access
Access Information Marker
Campground
Picnic Area
Fishing Dock (Pier)
Shore Fishing
Fish Attractors
Boat tie-up

Marina
Lily Pads
Submergent Vegetation
Emergent Vegetation
Stumps
Flooded Timber
Rocks
Submerged Culvert
Submerged Ruins

Marsh
Emergent Vegetation
Manmade Canal
Marked Fishing Spots
Submerged Rail
Submerged Road
Bridge
Submerged Riverbed
GPS Grid

Red & Green Channel Buoys
White Hazard Buoy
River Mile
Daymarker
Light & Daymarker
County Road
State Highway
US Highway
Interstate

MINNESOTA STATE RECORD FISH

Species	Weight (lbs. - oz.)	Length/girth (inches)	Lake where caught	County	Date
Bass, Largemouth	8 lbs., 15 oz.	23.5 / 18	Auburn Lake	Carver	10/05/2005
Bass, Rock (tie)	2 lbs., 0 oz.	13.5 / 12.5	Osakis Lake	Todd	05/10/1998
	2 lbs., 0 oz.	12.6 / 12.4	Lake Winnibigoshish	Cass	08/30/2004
Bass, Smallmouth	8 lbs., 0 oz.	n/a	West Battle Lake	Otter Tail	1948
Bass, White	4 lbs., 2.4 oz.	18.5 / 15.1	Mississippi River Pool 5	Wabasha	05/04/2004
Bluegill	2 lbs., 13 oz.	n/a	Alice Lake	Hubbard	1948
Bowfin	12 lbs., 9 oz.	31.5 / 18	Mississippi River	Wabasha	09/14/2012
Buffalo, Bigmouth	41 lbs., 11 oz.	38.5 / 29.5	Mississippi River	Goodhue	05/07/1991
Buffalo, Black	20 lbs., 0.5 oz.	34.2 / 20	Minnesota River	Nicollet	06/26/1997
Buffalo, Smallmouth	20 lbs., 0 oz.	32 / 23-3/4	Big Sandy	Aitkin	09/20/2003
Bullhead, Black	3 lbs., 13.12 oz.	17.17 / 14.96	Reno Lake	Pope	06/08/1997
Bullhead, Brown	7 lbs., 1 oz.	24.4 / n/a	Shallow Lake	Itasca	05/21/1974
Bullhead, Yellow	3 lbs., 10.5 oz.	17 7/8 / 11 3/4	Osakis Lake	Todd	08/05/2002
Burbot	19 lbs., 8 oz.	36.5 / 24	Lake of the Woods	Lake of the Woods	02/24/2012
Carp	55 lbs., 5 oz.	42 / 31	Clearwater Lake	Wright	07/10/1952
Carpsucker, River	4 lbs., 6 oz.	21 5/8 / 16	Minnesota River	Carver	11/19/2012
Catfish, Channel	38 lbs., 0 oz.	44 / n/a	Mississippi River	Hennepin	1975
Catfish, Flathead	70 lbs., 0 oz.	n/a	St. Croix River	Washington	1970
Crappie, Black	5 lbs., 0 oz.	21 / n/a	Vermillion River	Dakota	1940
Crappie, White	3 lbs., 15 oz.	18 / 16	Lake Constance	Wright	07/28/2002
Drum, Freshwater (Sheepshead)	35 lbs., 3.2 oz.	36 / 31	Mississippi River	Winona	10/05/1999
Eel, American	6 lbs., 9 oz.	36 / 14	St. Croix River	Washington	08/08/1997
Gar, Longnose	16 lbs., 12 oz.	53 / 16.5	St. Croix River	Washington	05/04/1982
Gar, Shortnose	4 lbs., 9.6 oz.	34.6 / 10	Mississippi River	Hennepin	07/22/1984
Goldeye	2 lbs., 13.1 oz.	20.1 / 11.5	Root River	Houston	06/10/2001
Hogsucker, Northern	1 lb., 15 oz.	14.25 / 7 1/8	Sunrise River	Chisago	08/16/1982
Mooneye	1 lb., 15 oz.	16.5 / 9.75	Minnesota River	Redwood	06/18/1980
Muskellunge	54 lbs., 0 oz.	56 / 27.8	Lake Winnibigoshish	Itasca	1957
Muskellunge, Tiger	34 lbs., 12 oz.	51 / 22.5	Lake Elmo	Washington	07/07/1999
Perch, Yellow	3 lbs., 4 oz.	n/a	Lake Plantaganette	Hubbard	1945
Pike, Northern	45 lbs., 12 oz.	n/a	Basswood Lake	Lake	05/16/1929
Pumpkinseed	1 lbs., 5.6 oz.	10.1 / 12 1/8	Leech Lake	Cass	06/06/1999
Quillback	7 lbs., 4 oz.	22 5/8 / 18	Upper Red Lake	Beltrami	08/09/2010
Redhorse, Golden	3 lbs., 14 oz.	20 / 12.1	Bigfork River	Koochiching	04/26/2003
Redhorse, Greater	12 lbs., 11.5 oz.	28.5 / 18.5	Sauk River	Stearns Wing	05/20/2005
Redhorse, River	12 lbs., 10 oz.	28.38 / 20	Kettle River	Pine	05/20/2005
Redhorse, Shorthead	7 lbs., 15 oz.	27 / 15	Rum River	Anoka	08/05/1983
Redhorse, Silver	9 lbs., 15 oz.	26.6 / 16 7/8	Big Fork River	Koochiching	04/16/2004
Salmon, Atlantic	12 lbs., 13 oz.	35.5 / 16.5	Baptism River	Lake	10/12/1991
Salmon, Chinook (King) (tie)	33 lbs., 4 oz.	44.75 / 25.75	Poplar River	Cook	09/23/1989
	33 lbs., 4 oz.	42.25 / 26.13	Lake Superior	St.Louis	10/12/1989
Salmon, Coho	10 lbs., 6.5 oz.	27.3 / n/a	Lake Superior	Lake	11/07/1970
Salmon, Kokanee	2 lbs., 15 oz.	20 / 11.5	Caribou Lake	Itasca	08/06/1971
Salmon, Pink	4 lbs., 8 oz.	23.5 / 13.2	Cascade River	Cook	09/09/1989
Sauger	6 lbs., 2.75 oz.	23 7/8 / 15	Mississippi River	Goodhue	05/23/1988
Splake	13 lbs., 5.44 oz.	33 1/2 / 19	Larson Lake	Itasca	02/11/2001
Sturgeon, Lake	94 lbs., 4 oz.	70 / 26.5	Kettle River	Pine	09/05/1994
Sturgeon, Shovelnose	6 lbs., 7 oz.	33 / 13 3/4	Mississippi River	Goodhue	02/09/2012
Sucker, Blue	14 lbs., 3 oz.	30.4 / 20.2	Mississippi River	Wabasha	02/28/1987
Sucker, Longnose	3 lbs., 10.6 oz.	21 / 10.25	Brule River	Cook	05/19/2005
Sucker, White	9 lbs., 1 oz.	24.25 / 16.25	Big Fish Lake	Stearns	05/01/1983
Sunfish, Green	1 lbs., 4.8 oz.	10.25 / 10.625	North Arbor Lake	Hennepin	06/14/2005
Sunfish, Hybrid	1 lb., 12 oz.	11.5 / 12	Zumbro River	Olmsted	07/09/1994
Trout, Brook	6 lbs., 5.6 oz.	24 / 14.5	Pigeon River	Cook	09/02/2000
Trout, Brown	16 lbs., 12 oz.	31.4 / 20.6	Lake Superior	St. Louis	06/23/1989
Trout, Lake	43 lbs., 8 oz.	n/a	Lake Superior	Cook	05/30/1955
Trout, Rainbow (Steelhead)	16 lbs. 6 oz.	33 / 19.5	Devil Track River	Cook	04/27/1980
Trout, Tiger	2 lbs., 9.12 oz.	20 / 9 5/8	Mill Creek	Olmsted	08/07/1999
Tullibee (Cisco)	5 lbs., 13 oz.	20 3/4 / 16 3/4	Sybil Lake	Otter Tail	03/09/2015
Walleye	17 lbs., 8 oz.	35.8 / 21.3	Seagull River	Cook	05/13/1979
Walleye-Sauger Hybrid	9 lbs., 13.4 oz.	27 / 17 3/4	Mississippi River	Goodhue	03/20/1999
Whitefish, Lake	12 lbs., 4.5 oz.	28.5 / 20	Leech Lake	Cass	03/21/1999
Whitefish, Menominee (Round)	2 lbs., 7.5 oz.	21 / 9.1	Lake Superior	Cook	04/27/1987

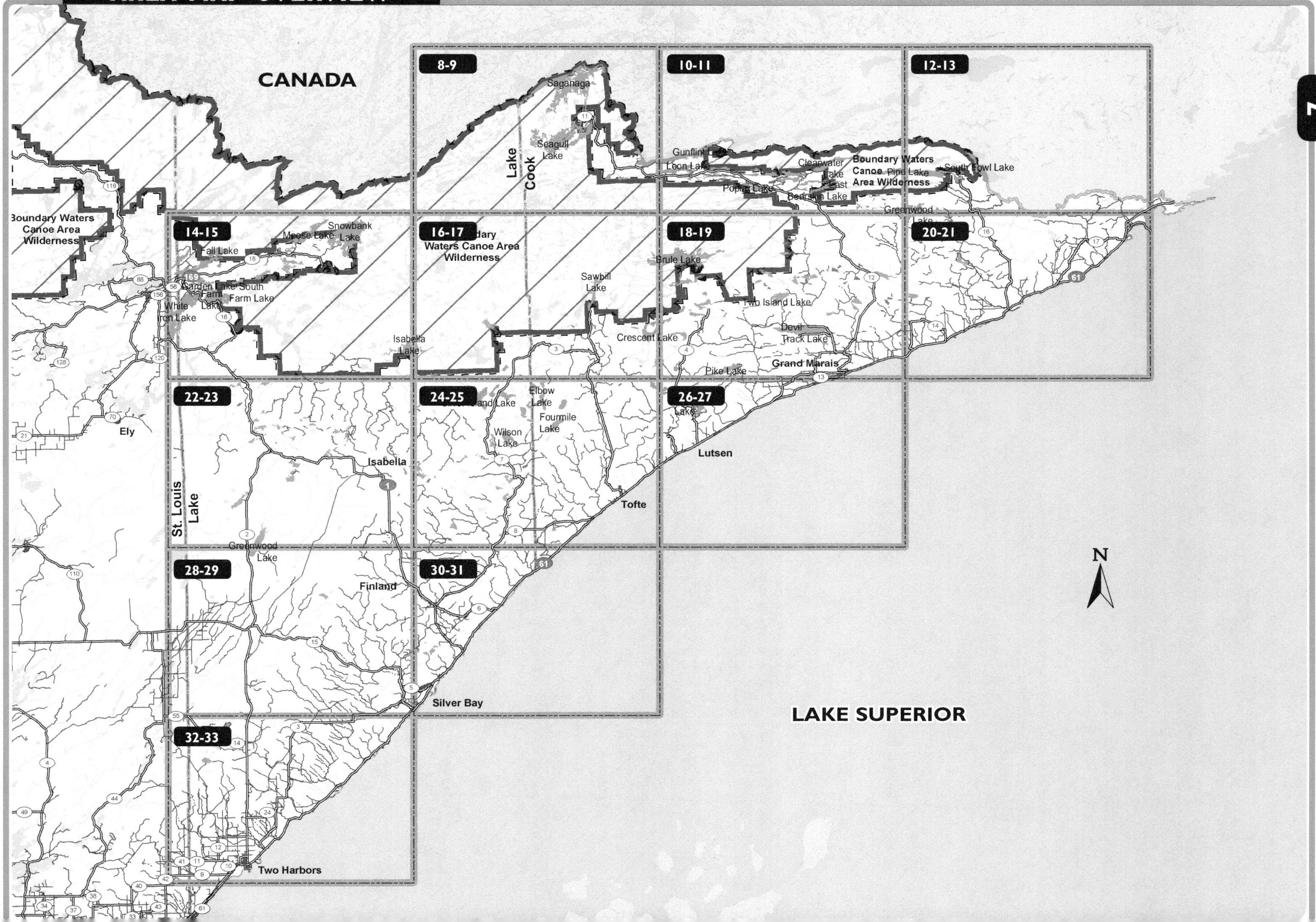
CANADA
Boundary Waters
Canoe Area
Wilderness
8-9
10-11
12-13
14-15
16-17
18-19
20-21
22-23
24-25
26-27
28-29
30-31
32-33
Saganaga
Seagull Lake
Lake Cook
Gunflint Lake
Leon Lake
Clearwater Lake
East Bearskin Lake
Poplar Lake
Pine Lake
South Fowl Lake
Greenwood Lake
Boundary Waters Canoe Area Wilderness
Snowbank Lake
Moose Lake
Fall Lake
Garden Lake
South Farm Lake
Farm Lake
White Iron Lake
Sawbill Lake
Isabella Lake
Brule Lake
Two Island Lake
Devil Track Lake
Crescent Lake
Pike Lake
Grand Marais
Elbow Lake
Fourmile Lake
Wilson Lake
Lutsen
Tofte
Ely
Isabella
St. Louis Lake
Greenwood Lake
Finland
Silver Bay
Two Harbors
LAKE SUPERIOR
N

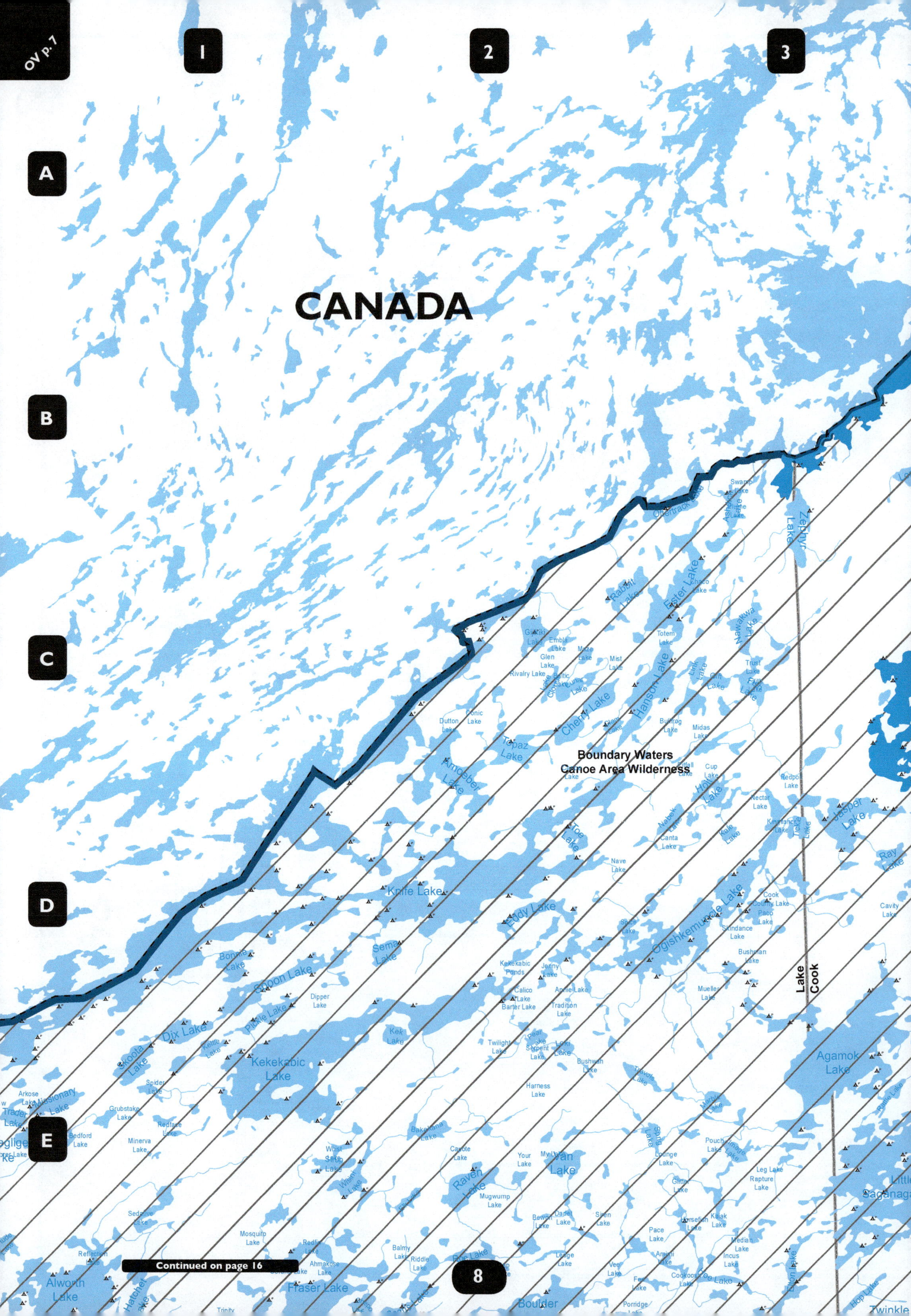

Continued on page 16

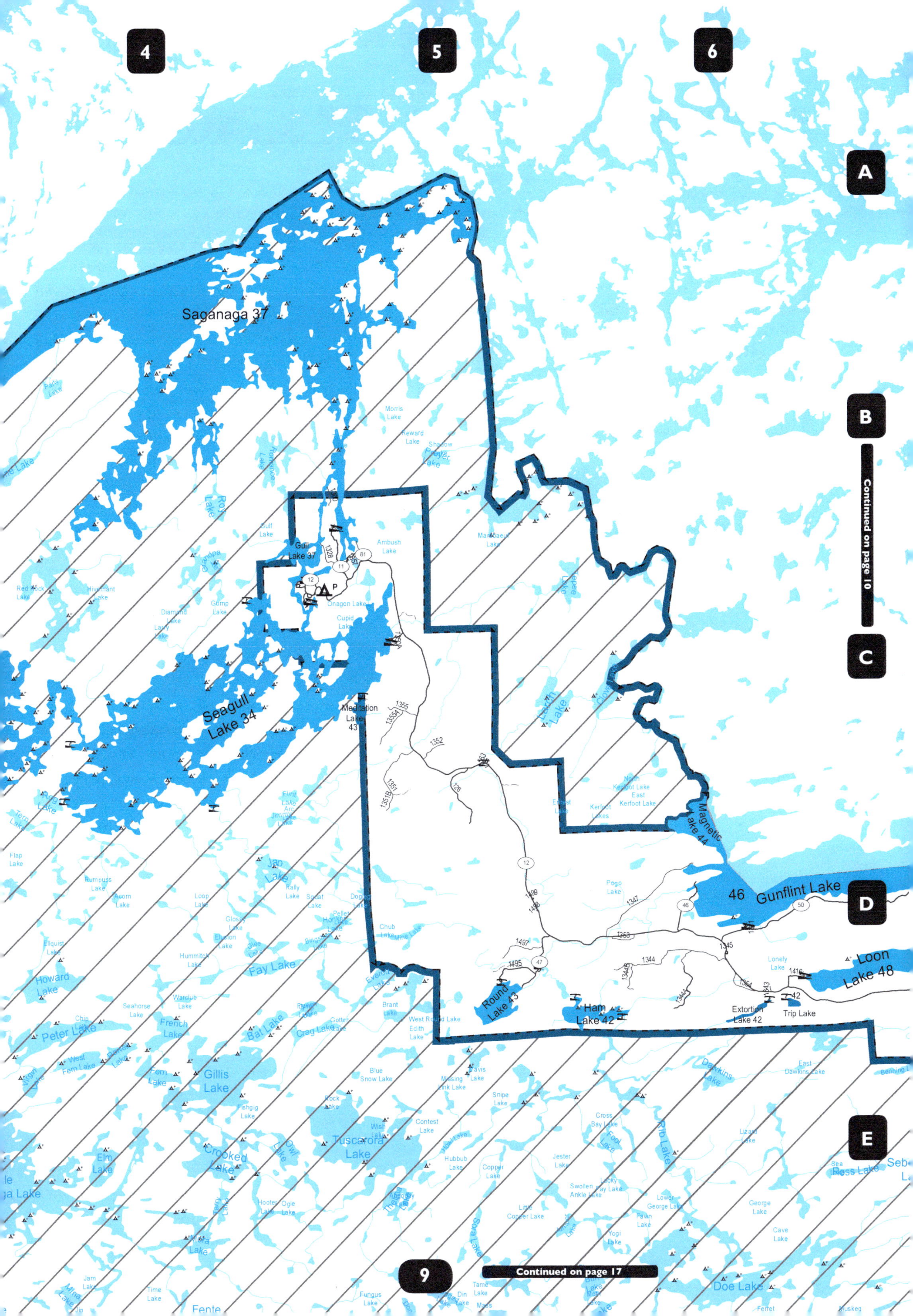

Continued on page 10

Continued on page 17

OV p.7

1 2 3

A B C

Continued on page 9

Boundary Waters Canoe Area Wilderness

The scenic beauty of the BWCAW – with its quintessential northwoods landscape of tall white pines, spruce, fir, aspen, and birch; exposed rock formations; and deep, blue lakes – rivals any wilderness in the world. And then there's the wildlife: For many BWCAW visitors, seeing a moose feeding in a lake in the evening, watching a bald eagle soaring overhead, or hearing the cry of a loon or wolf is the highlight of the trip. Whatever your interest, a trip to the BWCAW is sure to provide memories for years to come.

SPRING

Spring – when ice is off lakes and snow has melted – can come late to the BWCAW, sometimes not until May. Late May and June usually offer the best fishing. Smallmouth bass, northern pike, walleye, and lake trout are the "big four" of the Boundary Waters' fishery. Lake trout, usually deep-water fish, can be found in the shallows. Smallmouth bass will rise to a topwater plug or popping bug. Pike will chase spoons and other shiny lures. Walleyes can be tempted with jigs, spinners, and crankbaits. Unfortunately, the best fishing occurs when biting insects are often at their worst. Stories of clouds of mosquitoes and black flies thick enough to carry off an unsuspecting canoer are legion. Bugs can indeed be troublesome in spring, and visitors should be prepared to deal with them. On still, humid days, these critters can try the patience of the most hardened backcountry camper. Dry, breezy days can often keep bugs at bay. During the still of the night, however, expect to hear the whining of mosquitoes outside the tent.

SUMMER

The BWCAW receives the heaviest recreational traffic in summer, when visitors enjoy long days, warm weather, and good swimming. By early July, biting bugs have abated and fishing can still be good. As summer goes on, fish retreat to deeper water and can be more difficult to find. Raspberries and blueberries can be found along many portages and even at some campsites. Look for these tasty wild treats in July and August, when they are at their peak.

FALL

Autumn can be a great time to visit the BWCAW. The bugs are usually gone, the weather is comfortable – crisp days and cool nights – and the fall foliage can be spectacular. Fishing can be very good in September. By mid-October, the deciduous trees have shed their leaves, the first skeins of ice are forming on lakes, and snow may fly anytime.

WINTER

In winter, the canoe country becomes a mecca for cross-country skiing, snowshoeing, dogsledding, winter camping, and ice fishing. Many visitors are taking advantage of this, the longest season, when the land wears a white blanket of snow and clear, sunny days are buoyed by brilliant, blue skies.

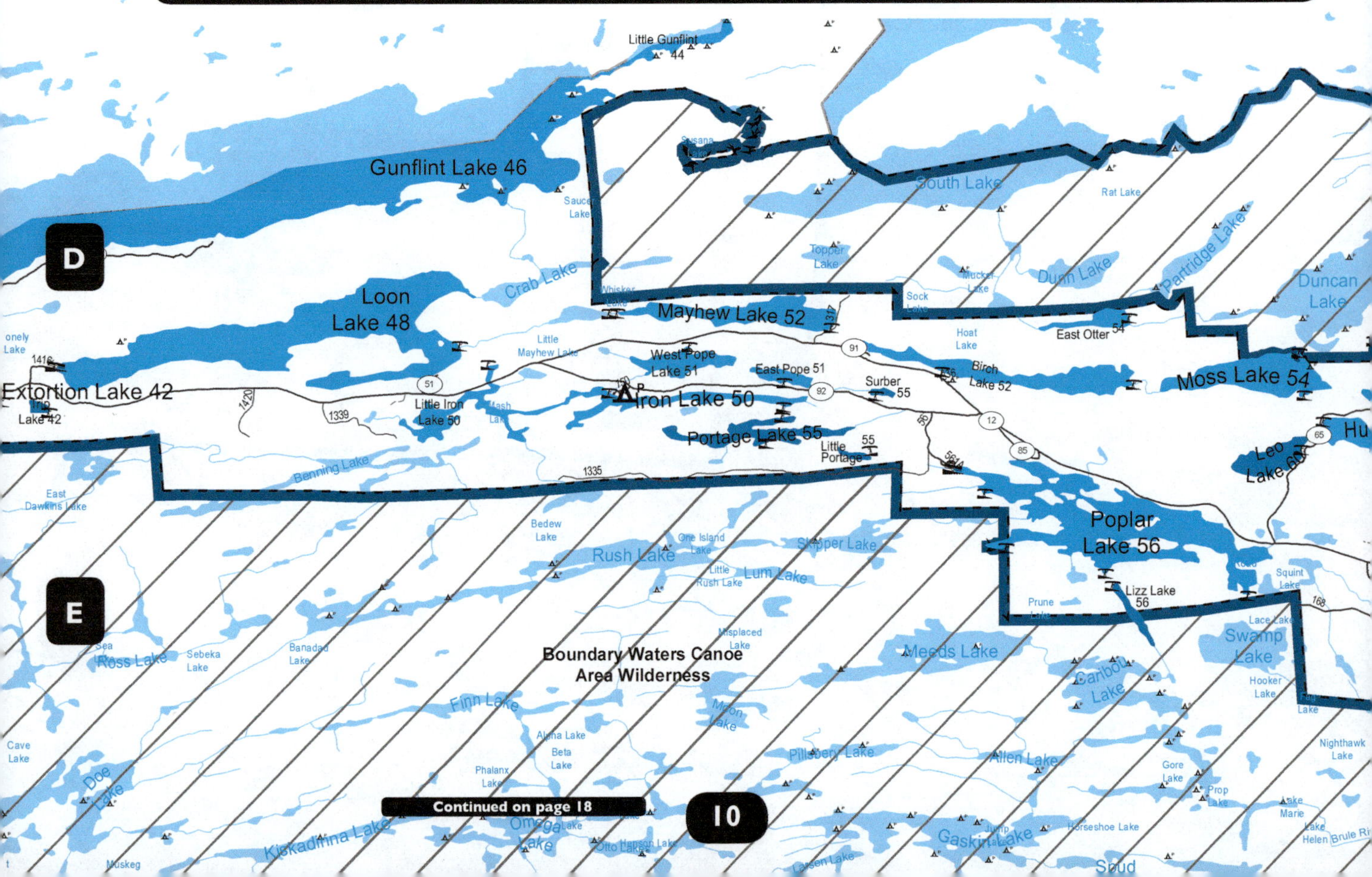

Continued on page 18

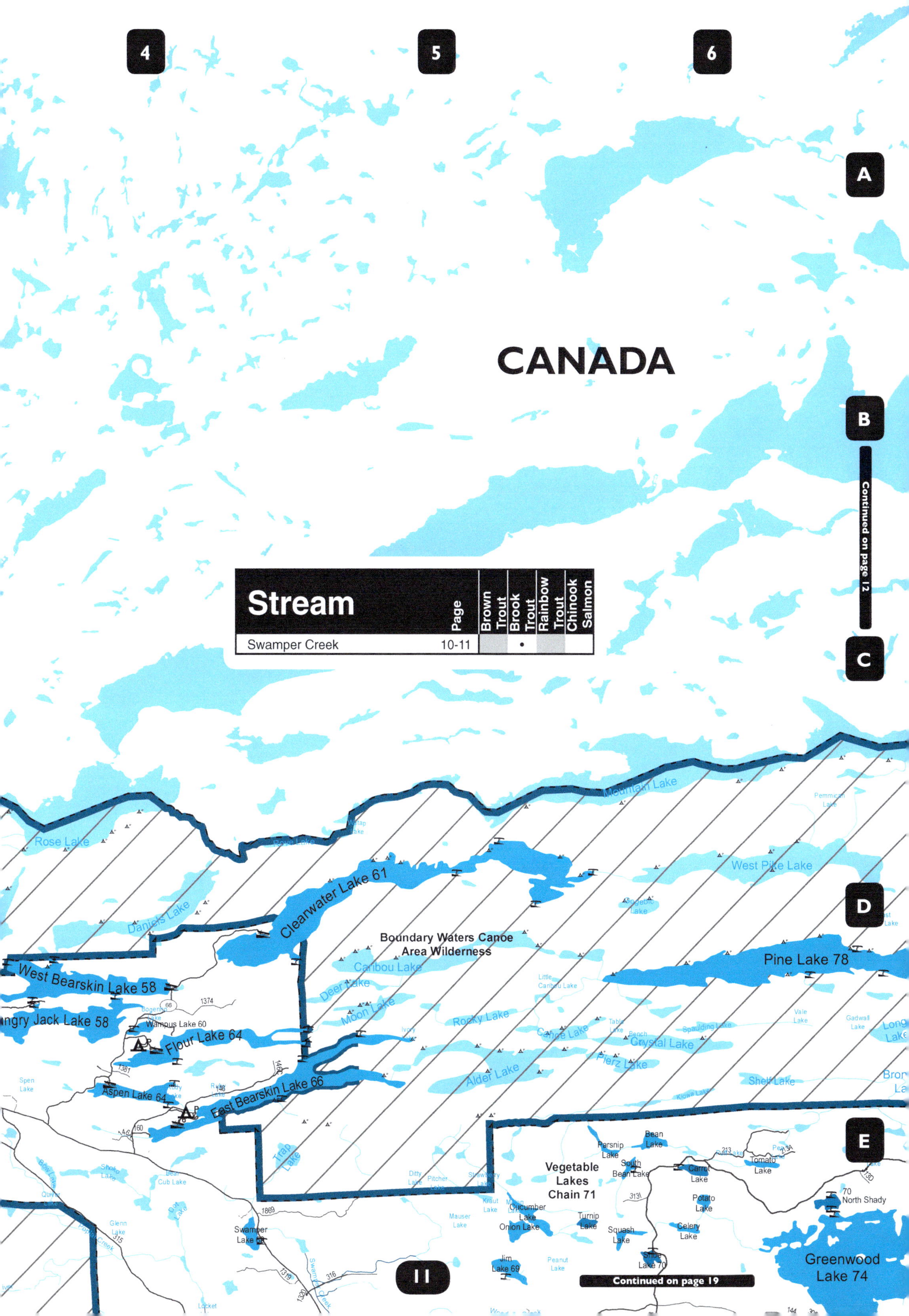

Stream	Page	Brown Trout	Brook Trout	Rainbow Trout	Chinook Salmon
Swamper Creek	10-11		•		

Continued on page 12
Continued on page 19

OV p.7

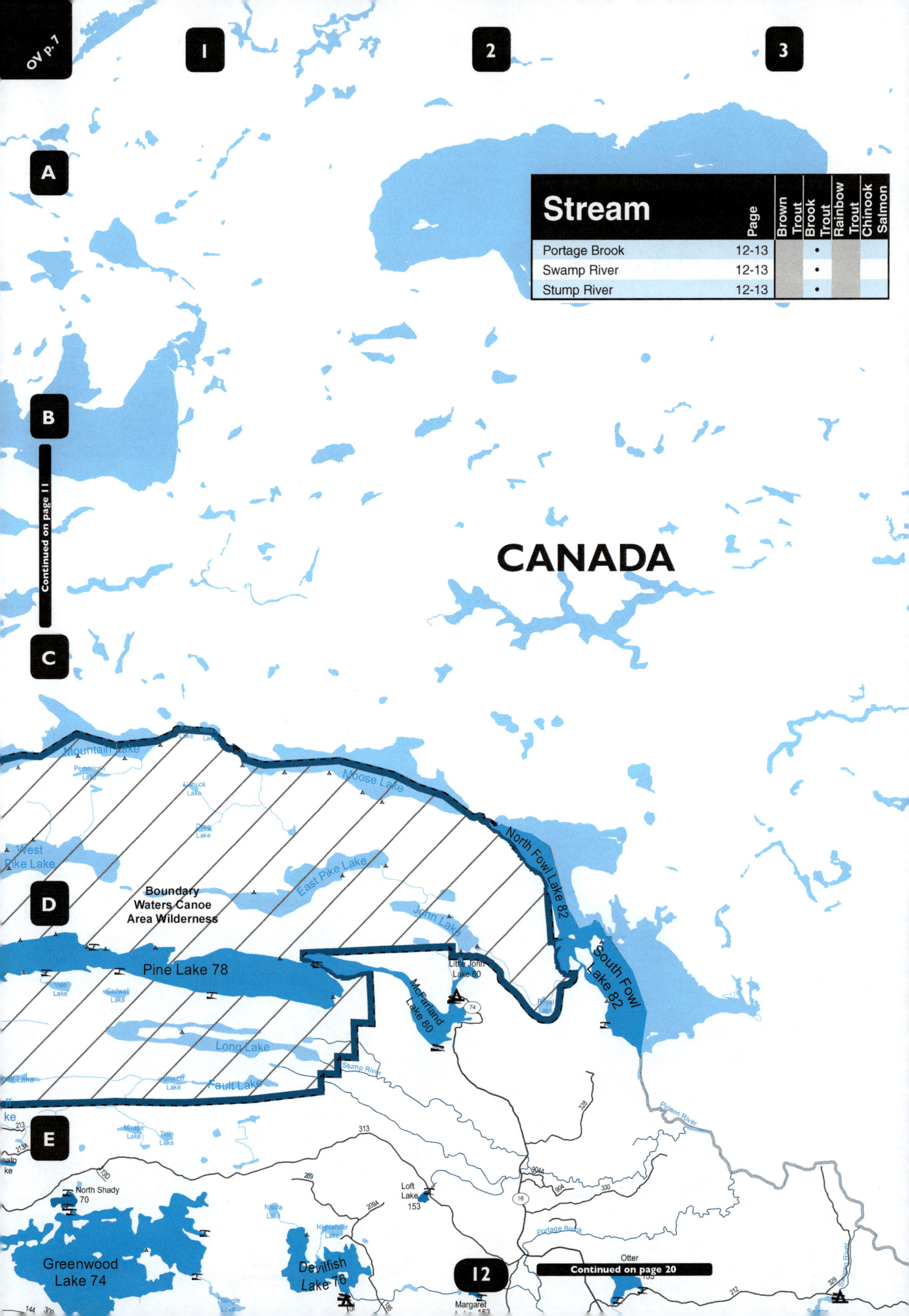

Stream	Page	Brown Trout	Brook Trout	Rainbow Trout	Chinook Salmon
Portage Brook	12-13		•		
Swamp River	12-13		•		
Stump River	12-13		•		

Continued on page 11

Continued on page 20

Minnesota Arrowhead Streams	Page	Brown Trout	Brook Trout	Rainbow Trout	Chinook Salmon
Amenda Creek	24-25		•		
Arrowhead Creek	14-15		•		
Arrowhead Creek	22-23		•		
Assinika Creek	18-19		•		
Bally Creek	18-19		•		
Baptism River	30-31	•	•	•	•
Baptism River, E. Branch	30-31	•	•		
Baptism River, W. Branch	22-23	•	•		
Baptism River, W. Branch	28-29	•	•		
Baptism River, W. Branch	30-31	•	•		
Barker Creek	24-25		•		
Beaver Dam Creek	20-21		•		
Beaver River	28-29	•	•	•	
Beaver River	30-31	•	•	•	
Beaver River, E. Branch	28-29		•		
Blind Temperance Creek	24-25		•		
Brule River	18-19		•	•	
Brule River	20-21		•	•	
Brule River, South	18-19		•		
Budd Creek	32-33		•		
Burnt Creek	16-17		•		
Caribou Creek	26-27		•		
Caribou River	24-25		•		
Caribou River	30-31		•		
Carlson Creek	20-21			•	
Cascade River	18-19	•	•		
Cascade River	26-27	•	•		
Cascade River, N. Branch	18-19		•		
Cedar Creek	24-25		•		
Cliff Creek	18-19		•	•	
Cliff Creek	20-21		•	•	
Cloquet River	28-29		•		
Cloquet River, Little	32-33		•		
Cloudy Spring Creek	28-29		•		
Cross River	24-25		•	•	
Crown Creek	22-23		•		
Crown Creek	28-29		•		
Cut Face Creek	18-19			•	
Cut Face Creek	26-27			•	
Dago Creek	32-33		•		
Devil Track River	18-19		•	•	
Devil Track River, Little	18-19		•		
Dumbbell River	24-25		•		
Egge Creek	30-31		•		
Elbow Creek	18-19		•		
Encampment River	32-33		•	•	
Fall River	18-19		•		
Fall River	26-27		•		
Falls Creek	18-19		•		
Fiddle Creek	18-19		•	•	
Flute Reed River	20-21		•	•	
Fortythree Creek	28-29		•		
Fortythree Creek, E. Br.	28-29		•		
Fortythree Creek, W. Br.	28-29		•		
Fredenberg Creek	24-25		•		
Fry Creek	18-19		•		
Gauthier Creek	20-21		•	•	
Gooseberry River	32-33		•	•	
Greenwood River	20-21		•		
Heartbreak Creek	24-25		•		
Hockamin Creek	28-29		•		
Hockamin Creek	30-31		•		
Honeymoon Creek	24-25		•		
Houghtaling Creek	24-25		•		
Indian Camp Creek	26-27			•	
Indian Creek	28-29		•		
Inga Creek	14-15		•		
Inga Creek	22-23		•		
Isabella River	14-15		•		
Isabella River	14-15		•		
Isabella River, Little	14-15		•		
Isabella River, Little	22-23		•		
Jackpot Creek	22-23		•		
Junction Creek	24-25		•		
Kelly Creek	22-23		•		

Minnesota Arrowhead Streams	Page	Brown Trout	Brook Trout	Rainbow Trout	Chinook Salmon
Kimball Creek	18-19		•	•	
Kimball Creek	20-21		•	•	
Kinney Creek	28-29		•		
Kit Creek	28-29		•		
Knife River	32-33	•	•	•	•
Knife River, Little	32-33	•	•	•	
Koski Creek	16-17		•		
Leskinen Creek	30-31		•		
Lullaby Creek	18-19		•		
Maki Creek	28-29		•		
Manitou River	24-25		•	•	
Manitou River	30-31		•	•	
Manitou River, Little	30-31			•	
Marais River, Little	30-31		•	•	
Mark Creek	18-19		•		
Mary Ann Creek	28-29		•		
McCarthy Creek	32-33	•	•	•	
McDonald Creek	18-19		•		
Mississippi Creek	18-19		•		
Missouri Creek	16-17		•		
Mistletoe Creek	18-19		•		
Mistletoe Creek	26-27		•		
Mitawan Creek	14-15		•		
Mitawan Creek	22-23		•		
Mons Creek	20-21		•		
Moose Creek	24-25		•		
Nine Mile Creek	24-25		•		
Nip Creek	22-23		•		
Nira Creek	22-23		•		
Onion Creek	24-25		•	•	
Onion River, W. Branch	24-25		•		
Pancake Creek	24-25		•		
Pine Mountain Creek	18-19		•		
Plouff Creek	16-17		•		
Poplar River	16-17		•	•	
Poplar River	24-25		•	•	
Poplar River	26-27		•	•	
Portage Brook	12-13		•		
Portage Brook	20-21		•		
Robin Creek	22-23		•		
Rollins Creek	24-25			•	
Rollins Creek	26-27			•	
Sawmill Creek	30-31		•		
Scott Creek	24-25		•		
Section Thirty Creek	14-15		•		
Sixmile Creek	24-25		•		
Skunk Creek	32-33		•		
Snake Creek	22-23		•		
Snake River	14-15		•		
Snake River	22-23		•		
Split Rock River, West	28-29		•		
Split Rock River, West	32-33		•		
Spruce Creek	26-27		•		
Stanley Creek	32-33		•		
Stewart River	32-33	•	•		
Stewart River, Little	32-33	•	•		
Stickle Creek	18-19		•		
Stumble Creek	24-25			•	
Stump River	12-13		•		
Sullivan Creek	28-29		•		
Sundling Creek	18-19		•		
Swamp River	12-13		•		
Swamp River	20-21		•		
Swamper Creek	10-11		•		
Swamper Creek	18-19		•		
Swanson Creek	16-17		•		
Temperance River	16-17	•	•	•	
Temperance River	24-25	•	•	•	
Thirtynine Creek, Big	28-29		•		
Thompson Creek	18-19		•		
Torgenson Creek	24-25		•		
Two Island River	24-25		•	•	
Wanless Creek	24-25		•		
Whyte Creek	28-29		•		
Wilson Creek	24-25		•		

Continued on page 21

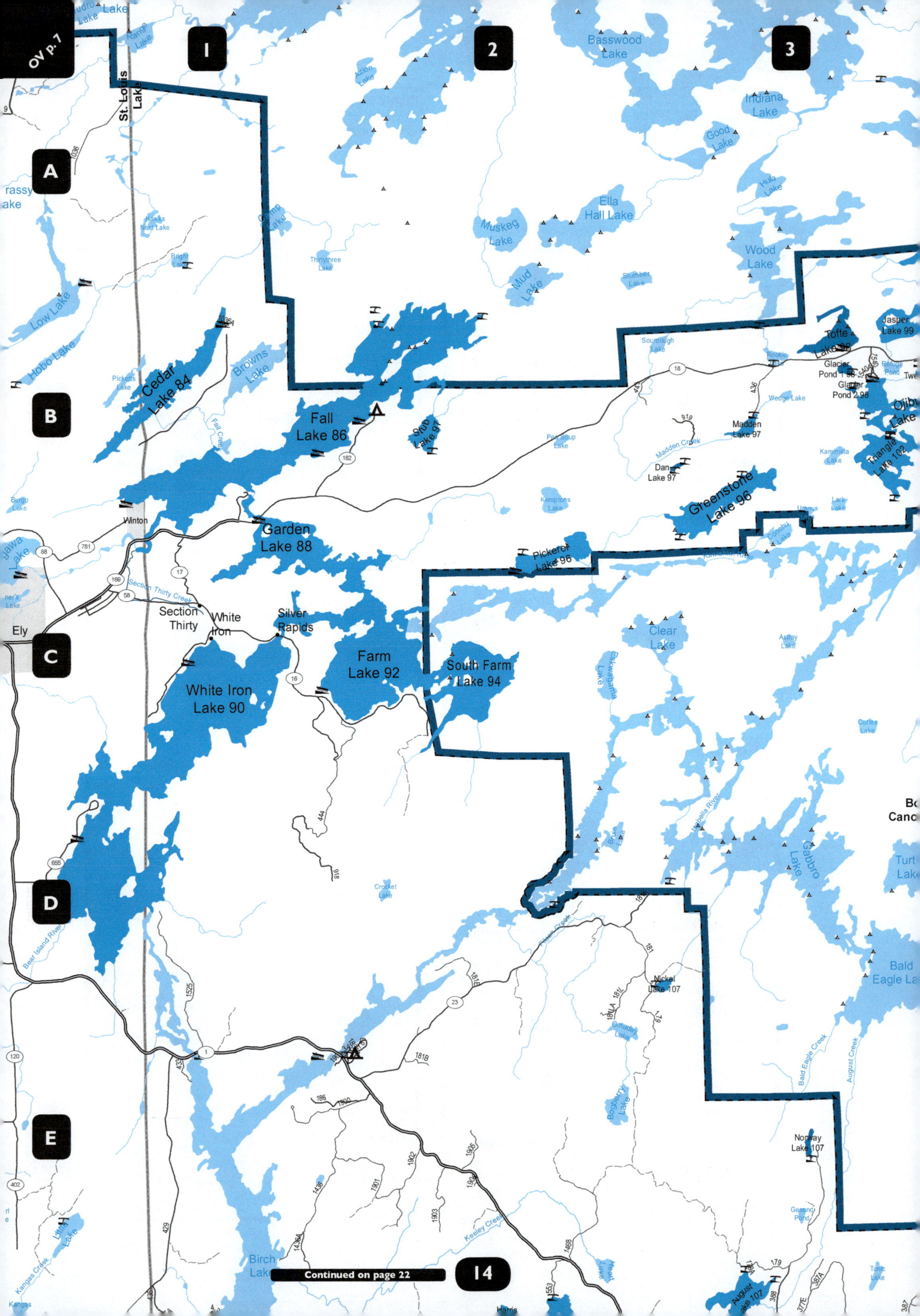

Continued on page 22

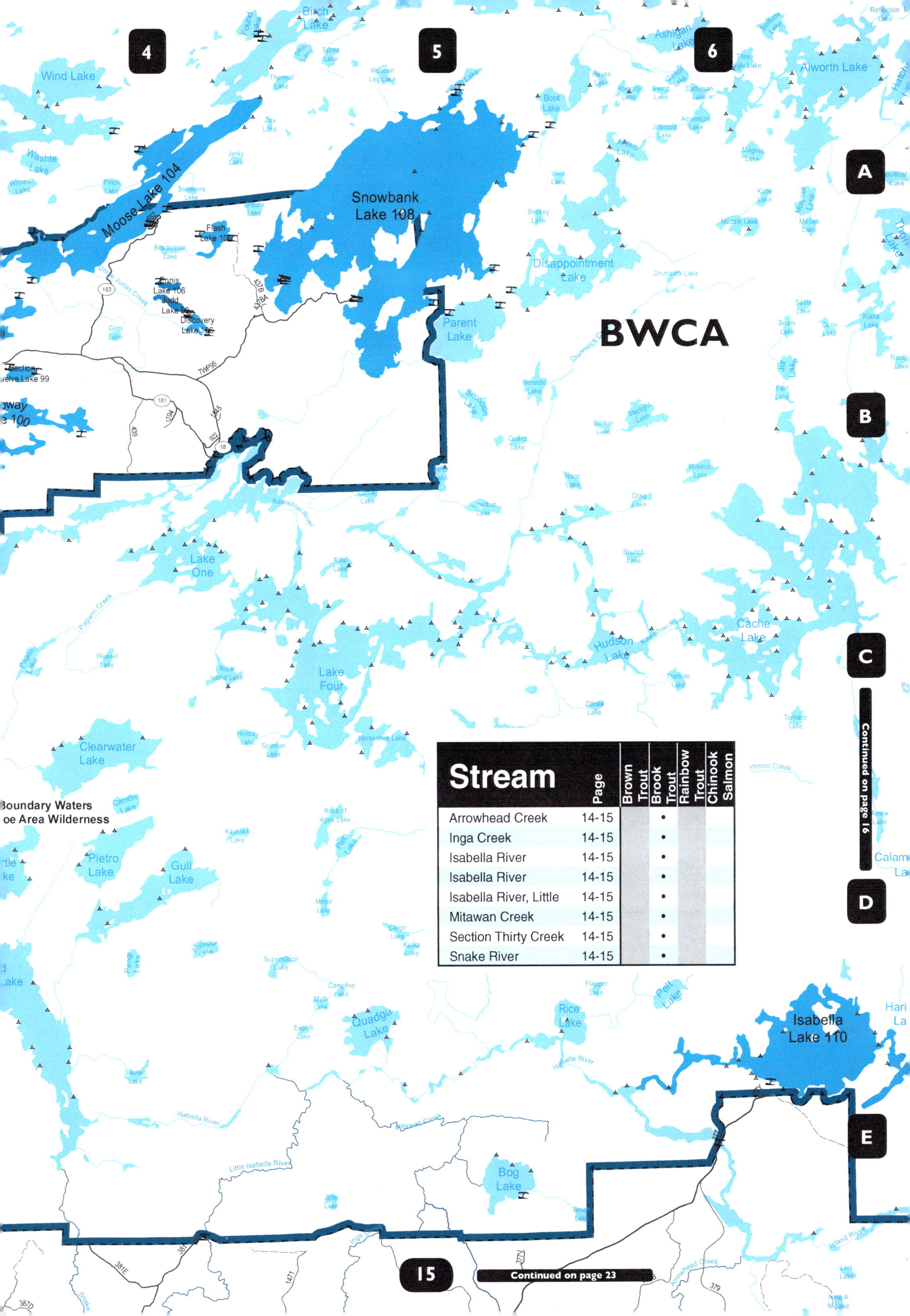

Stream	Page	Brown Trout	Brook Trout	Rainbow Trout	Chinook Salmon
Arrowhead Creek	14-15		•		
Inga Creek	14-15		•		
Isabella River	14-15		•		
Isabella River	14-15		•		
Isabella River, Little	14-15		•		
Mitawan Creek	14-15		•		
Section Thirty Creek	14-15		•		
Snake River	14-15		•		

Continued on page 16

Continued on page 23

Continued on page 8

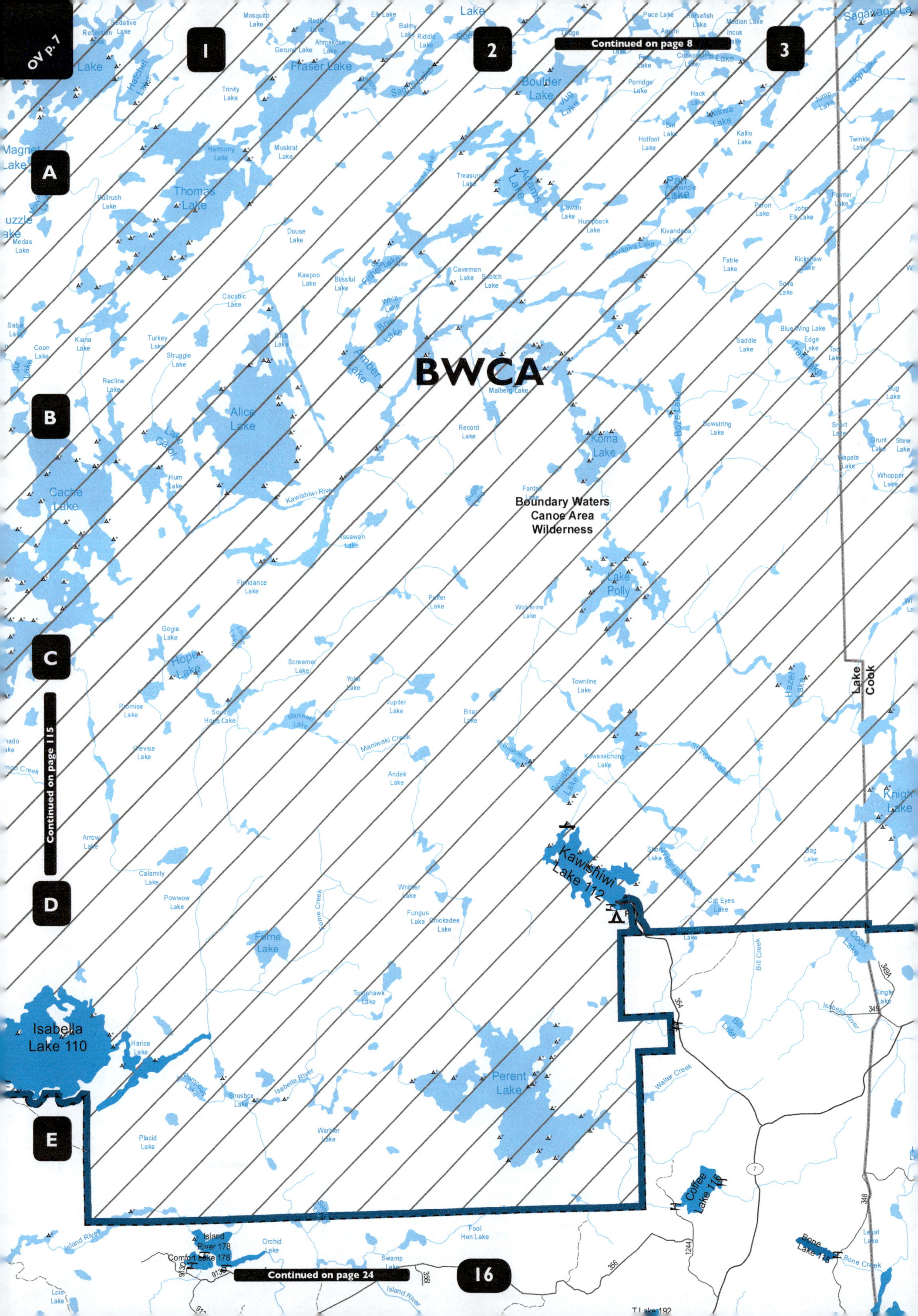

Continued on page 115
Continued on page 24

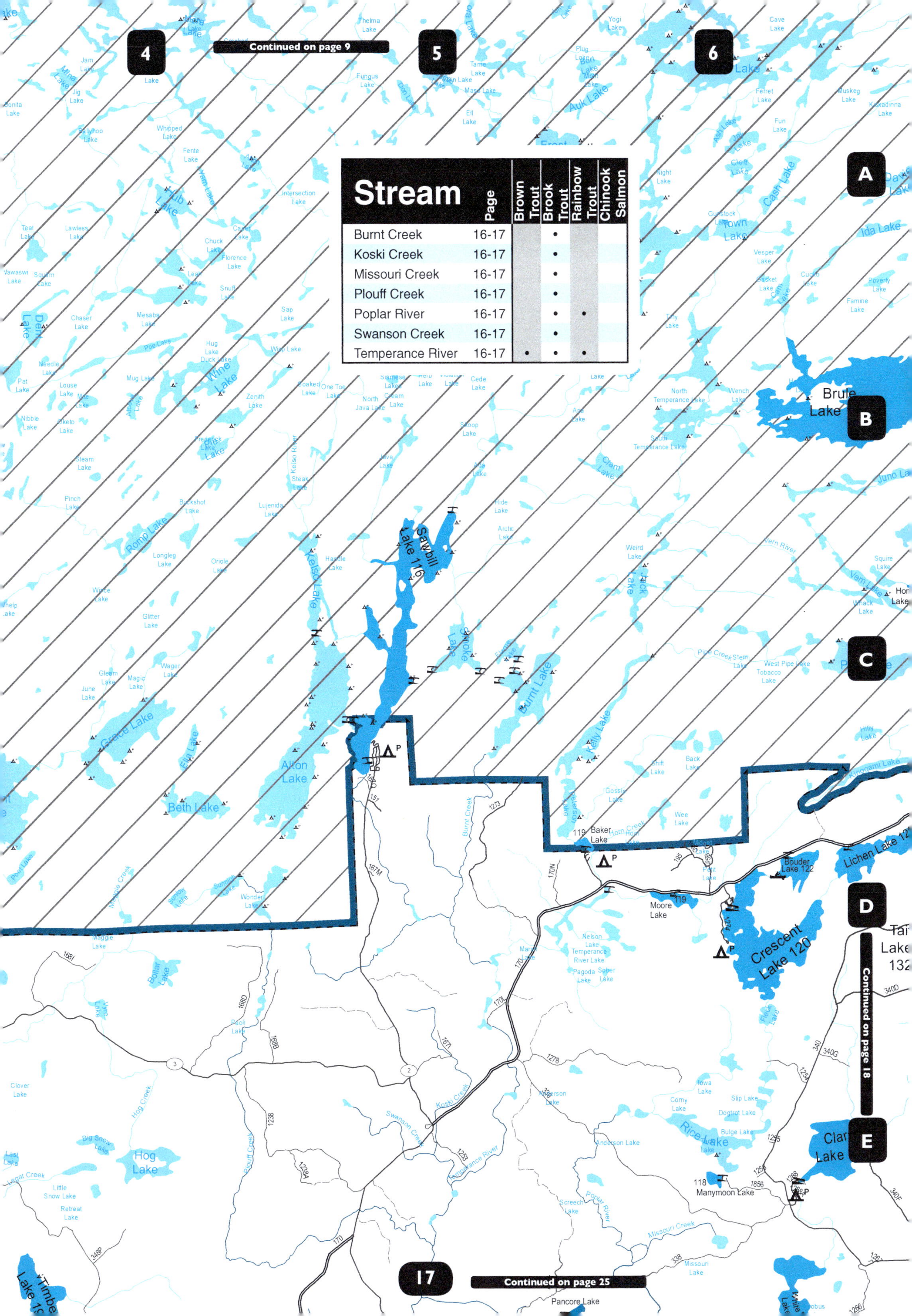

Stream	Page	Brown Trout	Brook Trout	Rainbow Trout	Chinook	Salmon
Burnt Creek	16-17		•			
Koski Creek	16-17		•			
Missouri Creek	16-17		•			
Plouff Creek	16-17		•			
Poplar River	16-17		•	•		
Swanson Creek	16-17		•			
Temperance River	16-17	•	•	•		

Continued on page 9
Continued on page 18
Continued on page 25

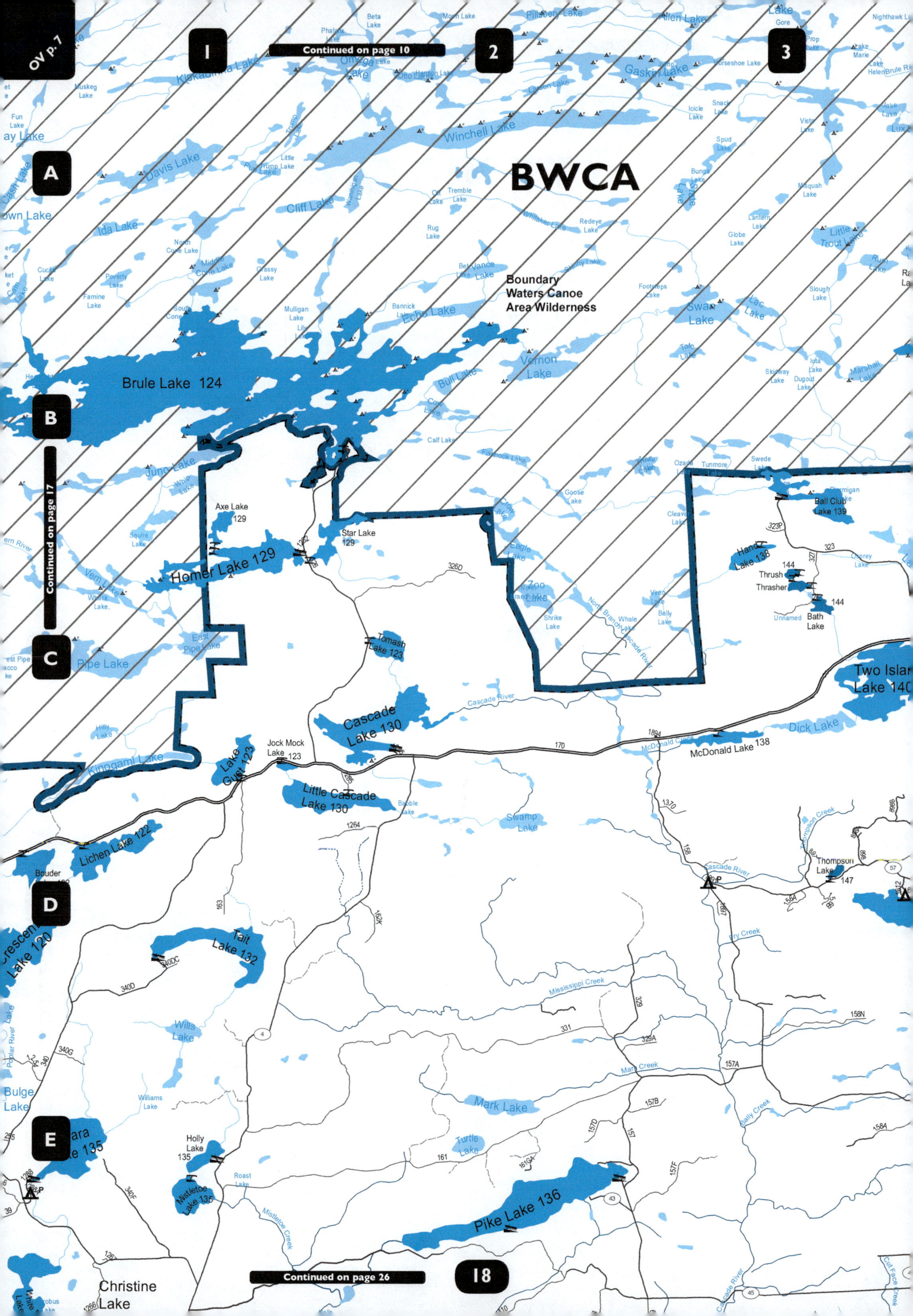

Continued on page 10
Continued on page 17
Continued on page 26

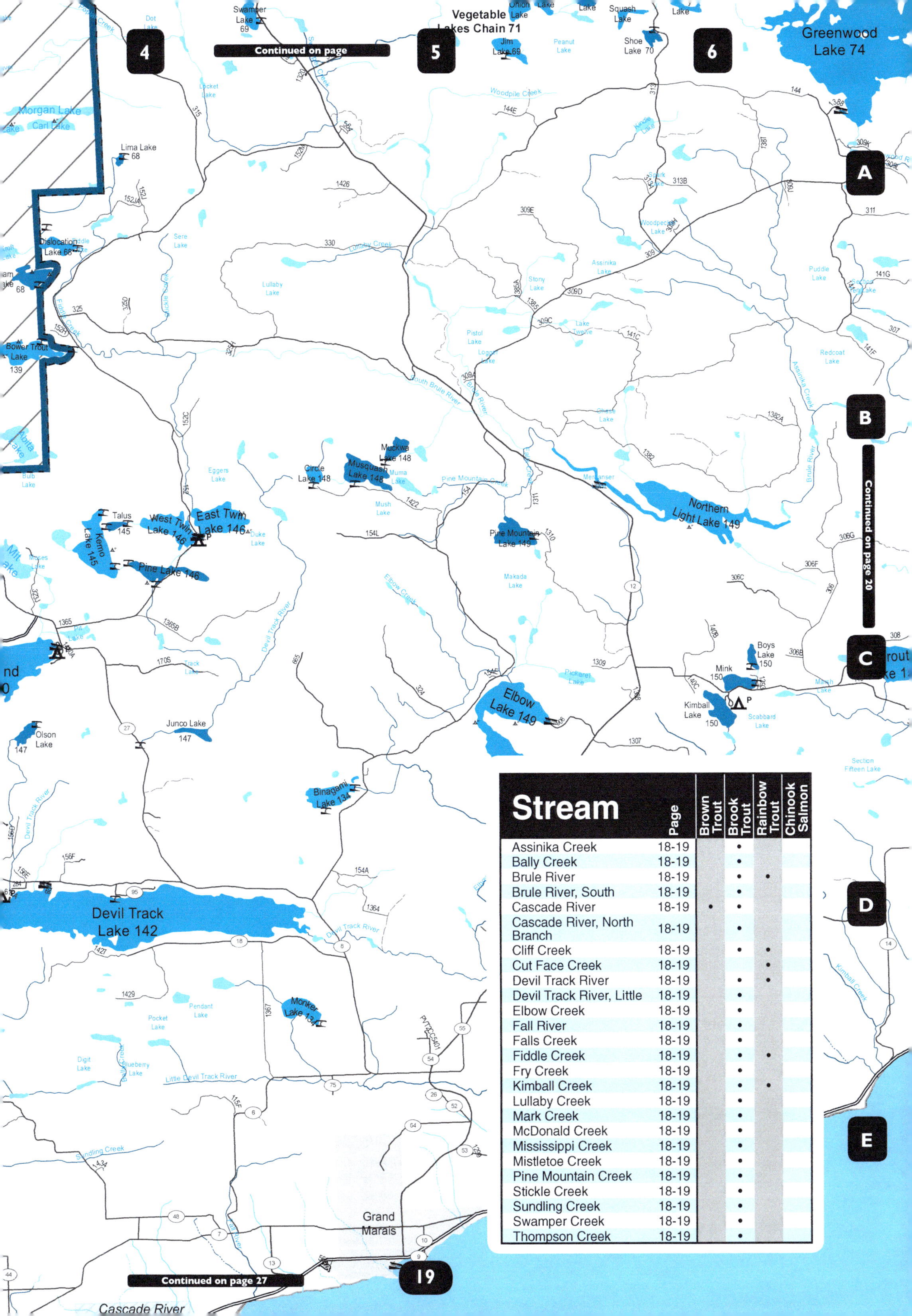

Continued on page

Continued on page 20

Continued on page 27

Stream	Page	Brown Trout	Brook Trout	Rainbow Trout	Chinook Salmon
Assinika Creek	18-19		•		
Bally Creek	18-19		•		
Brule River	18-19		•	•	
Brule River, South	18-19		•		
Cascade River	18-19	•	•		
Cascade River, North Branch	18-19		•		
Cliff Creek	18-19		•	•	
Cut Face Creek	18-19			•	
Devil Track River	18-19		•	•	
Devil Track River, Little	18-19		•		
Elbow Creek	18-19		•		
Fall River	18-19		•		
Falls Creek	18-19		•		
Fiddle Creek	18-19		•	•	
Fry Creek	18-19		•		
Kimball Creek	18-19		•	•	
Lullaby Creek	18-19		•		
Mark Creek	18-19		•		
McDonald Creek	18-19		•		
Mississippi Creek	18-19		•		
Mistletoe Creek	18-19		•		
Pine Mountain Creek	18-19		•		
Stickle Creek	18-19		•		
Sundling Creek	18-19		•		
Swamper Creek	18-19		•		
Thompson Creek	18-19		•		

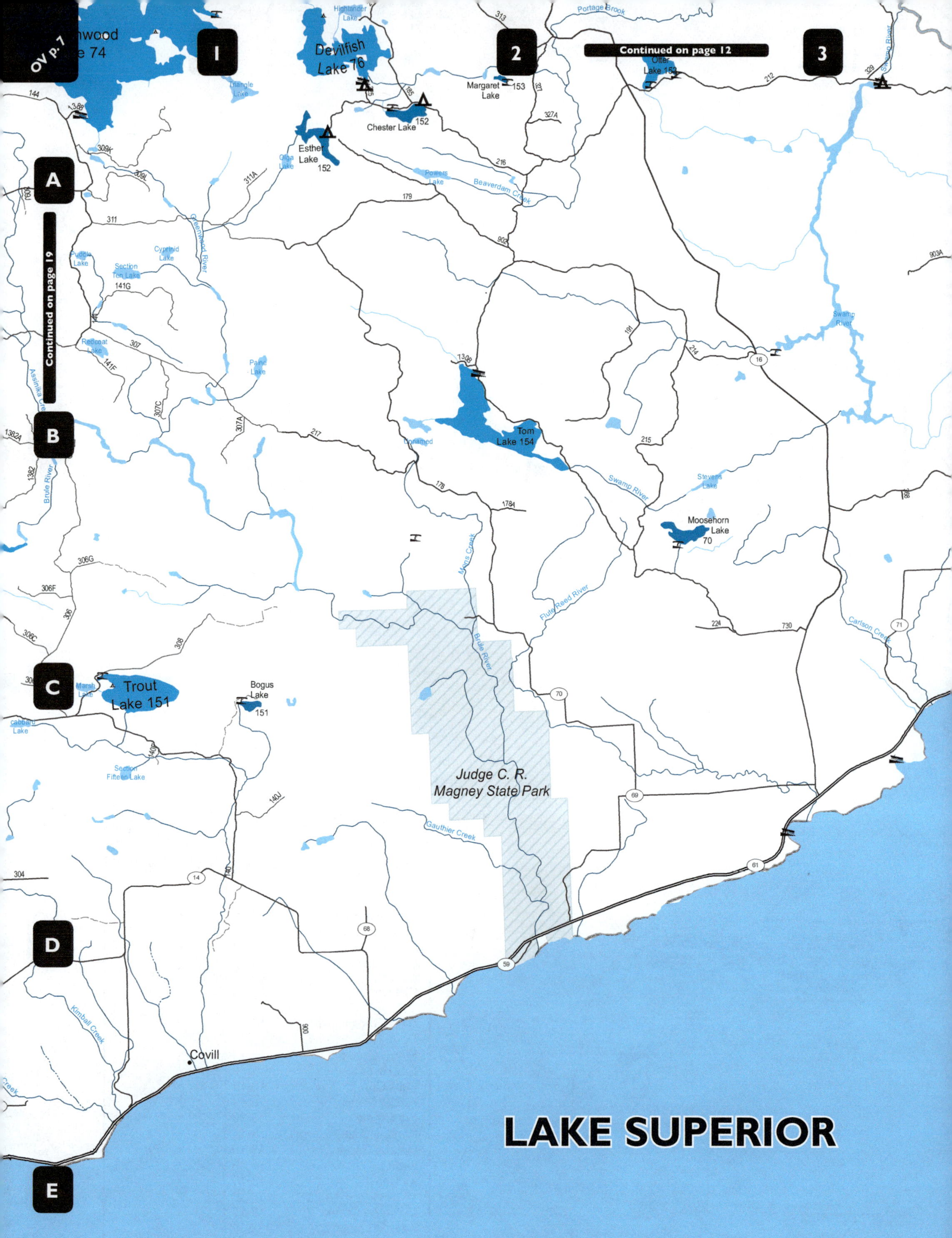

Continued on page 12
Continued on page 19

Continued on page 13

Stream	Page	Brown Trout	Brook Trout	Rainbow Trout	Chinook Salmon
Beaver Dam Creek	20-21		•		
Brule River	20-21		•	•	
Carlson Creek	20-21			•	
Cliff Creek	20-21		•	•	
Flute Reed River	20-21		•	•	
Gauthier Creek	20-21		•	•	
Greenwood River	20-21		•		
Kimball Creek	20-21		•	•	
Mons Creek	20-21		•		
Portage Brook	20-21		•		
Swamp River	20-21		•		

FISHING TROUT STREAMS

In trout streams, brook trout will be found in the cool headwaters. As the rivers continue, they often warm slightly, and this is where you'll find brown trout. The biggest browns are found in marginal trout habit, where the water is seemingly too warm to support trout. Browns tolerate warmer water than brookies, and the increased temperature produces more forage. Many Lake Superior rivers and streams receive spawning runs of trout and salmon in both spring and fall. Fishing near the mouth of these rivers during spawning season provides a unique opportunity to catch salmon and steelhead.

One of the attractions of river and stream fishing is the ability to enter a fish's world. Standing knee-deep in a clear, rushing stream, hearing the water pulsate through the bends, over rocks and fallen brush is music to the ears. Casting to a riffle or eddy where a trout lies lurking, awaiting a minnow or fallen insect to pass by, is sure to get any angler's heart pumping faster.

When fishing in rivers, keep in mind that the fish don't want to work any harder than they must to maintain their position. In other words, they generally don't like to fight the current. Therefore, look for them in places that break the current flow. Rocks, root balls, fallen trees, and even garbage carelessly thrown in the river can all break the current flow. This creates a calm "eddy" both down stream and upstream of the structure, and this is where fish lie. You'll also find fish hiding below undercut stream banks and in deep holes.

C

D

E

Continued on page 14

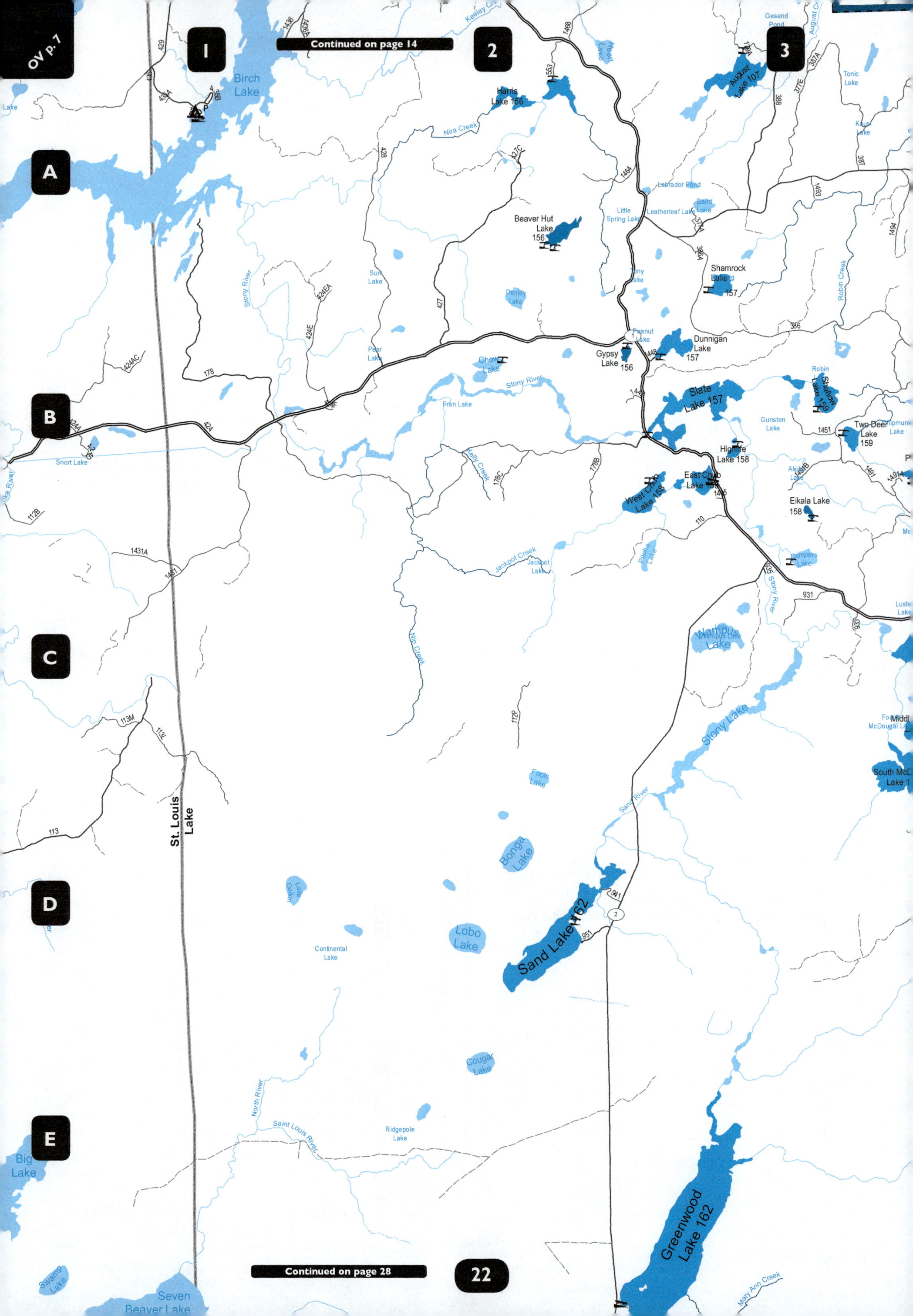

Continued on page 28

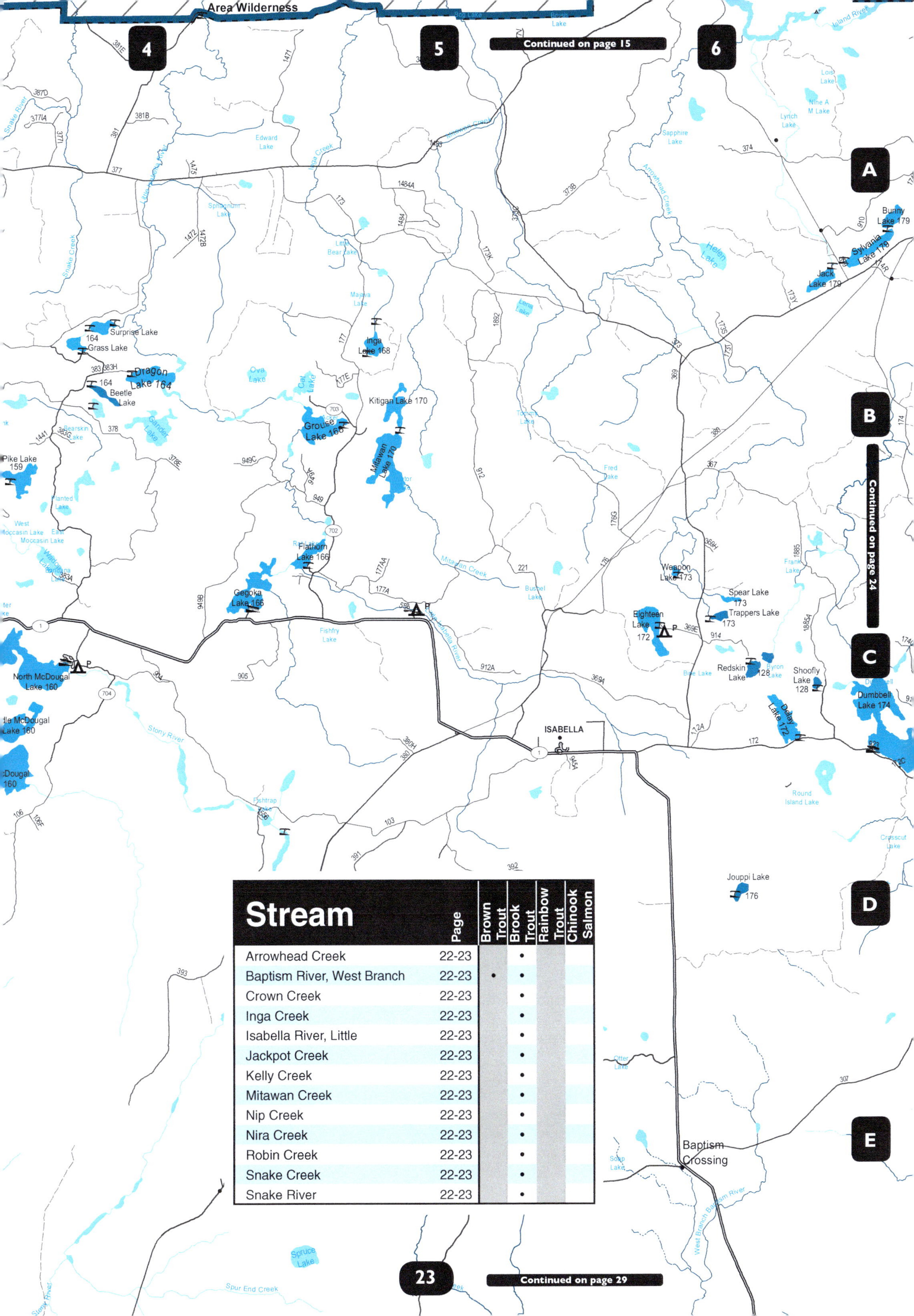

Continued on page 15

Continued on page 24

Stream	Page	Brown Trout	Brook Trout	Rainbow Trout	Chinook Salmon
Arrowhead Creek	22-23		•		
Baptism River, West Branch	22-23	•	•		
Crown Creek	22-23		•		
Inga Creek	22-23		•		
Isabella River, Little	22-23		•		
Jackpot Creek	22-23		•		
Kelly Creek	22-23		•		
Mitawan Creek	22-23		•		
Nip Creek	22-23		•		
Nira Creek	22-23		•		
Robin Creek	22-23		•		
Snake Creek	22-23		•		
Snake River	22-23		•		

Continued on page 29

OV p.7
Continued on page 16

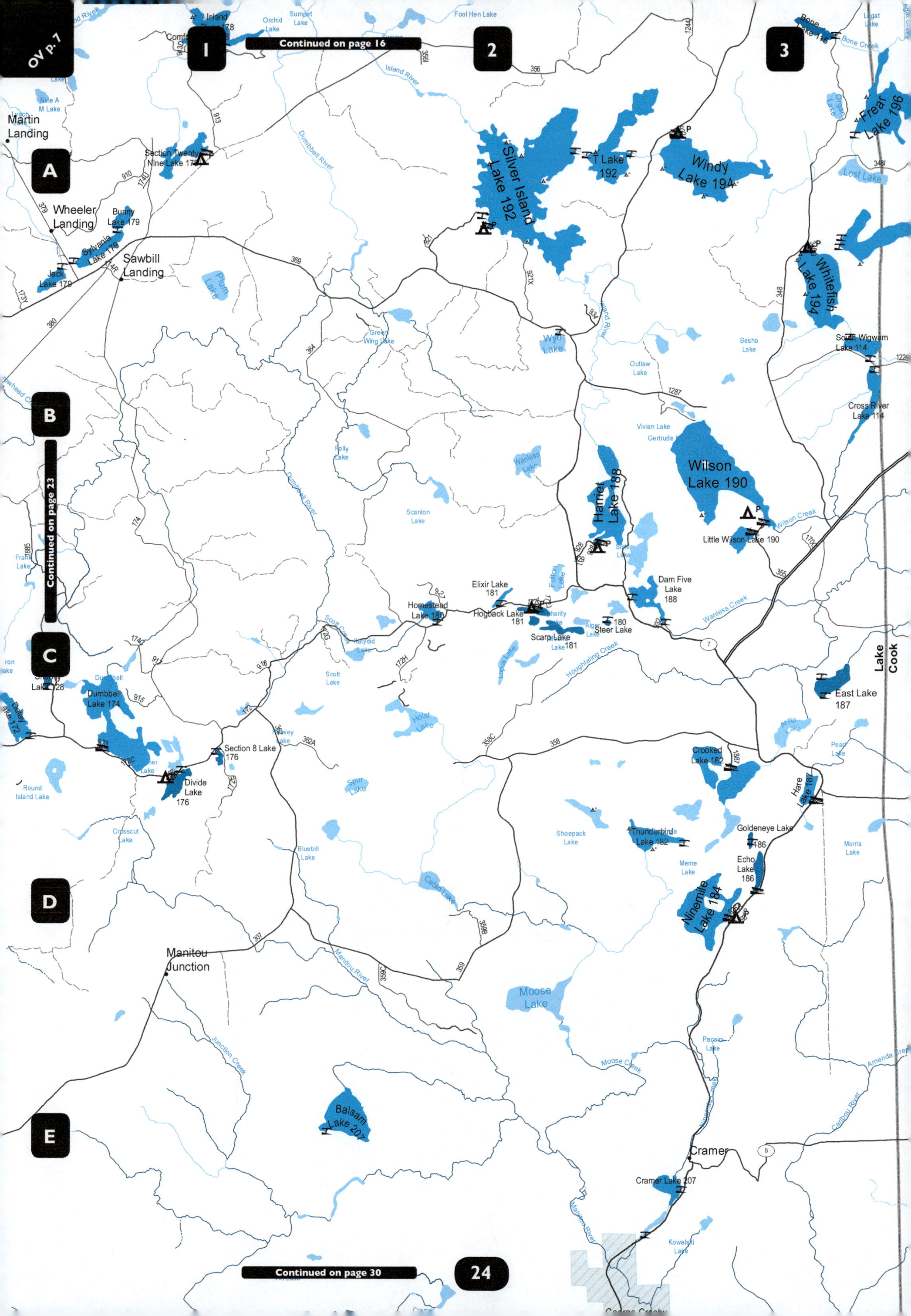

Continued on page 23
Continued on page 30

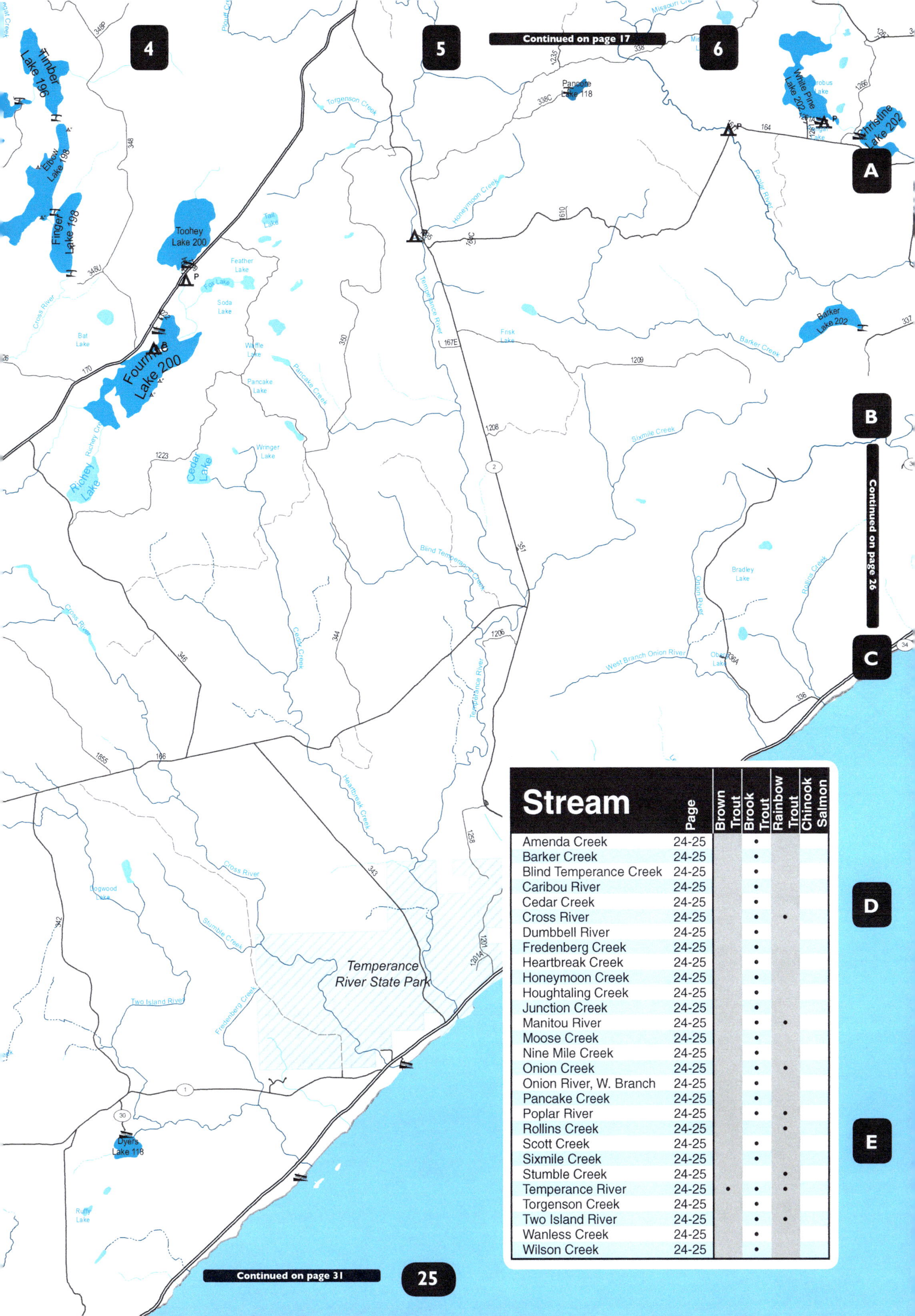

Continued on page 17

Continued on page 26

Stream	Page	Brown Trout	Brook Trout	Rainbow Trout	Chinook Salmon
Amenda Creek	24-25		•		
Barker Creek	24-25		•		
Blind Temperance Creek	24-25		•		
Caribou River	24-25		•		
Cedar Creek	24-25		•		
Cross River	24-25		•	•	
Dumbbell River	24-25		•		
Fredenberg Creek	24-25		•		
Heartbreak Creek	24-25		•		
Honeymoon Creek	24-25		•		
Houghtaling Creek	24-25		•		
Junction Creek	24-25		•		
Manitou River	24-25		•	•	
Moose Creek	24-25		•		
Nine Mile Creek	24-25		•		
Onion Creek	24-25		•	•	
Onion River, W. Branch	24-25		•		
Pancake Creek	24-25		•		
Poplar River	24-25		•	•	
Rollins Creek	24-25			•	
Scott Creek	24-25		•		
Sixmile Creek	24-25		•		
Stumble Creek	24-25			•	
Temperance River	24-25	•	•	•	
Torgenson Creek	24-25		•		
Two Island River	24-25		•	•	
Wanless Creek	24-25		•		
Wilson Creek	24-25		•		

Continued on page 31

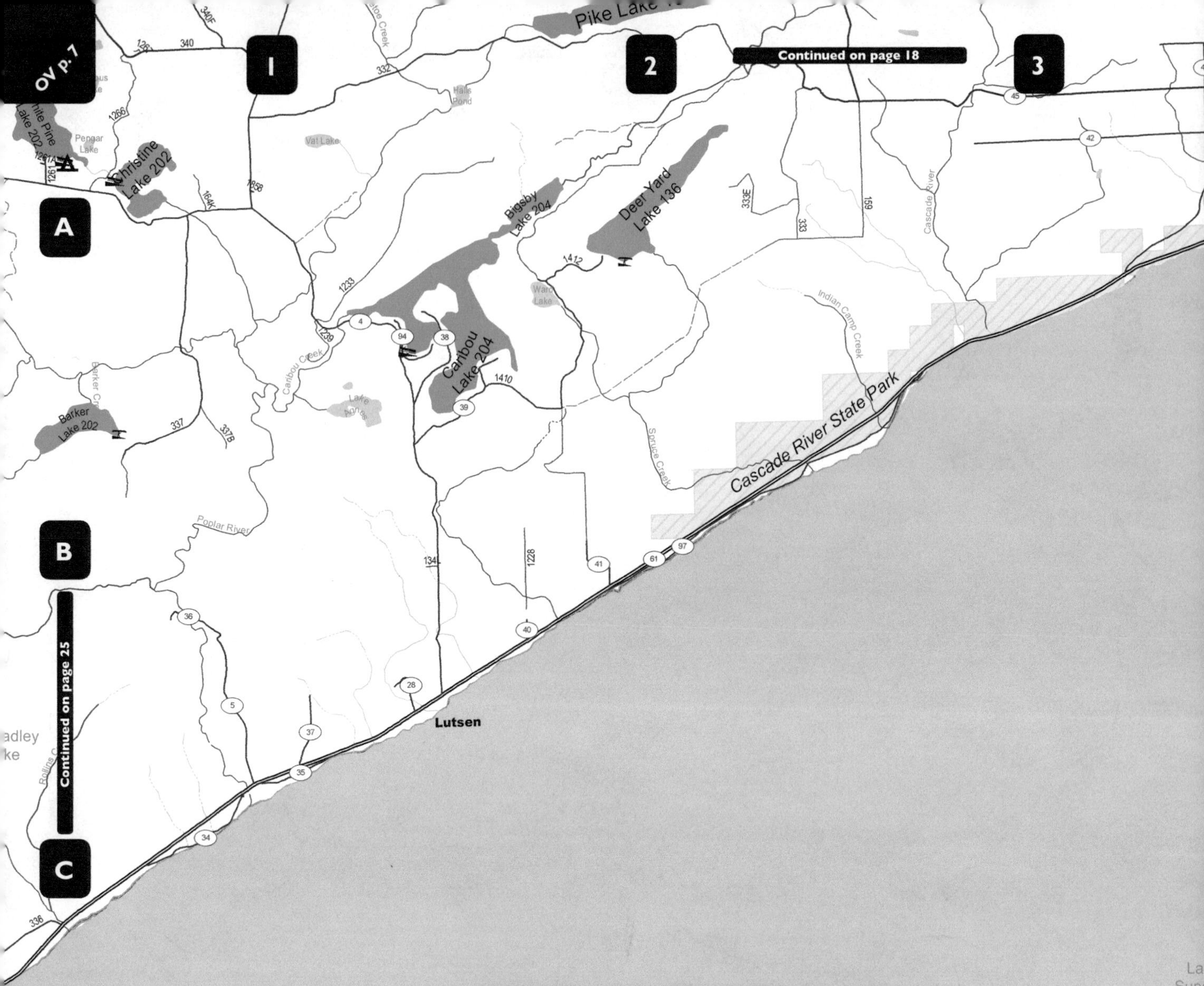

D

E

Stream	Page	Brown Trout	Brook Trout	Rainbow Trout	Chinook Salmon
Caribou Creek	26-27		•		
Cascade River	26-27	•	•		
Cut Face Creek	26-27			•	
Fall River	26-27		•		
Indian Camp Creek	26-27			•	
Mistletoe Creek	26-27		•		
Poplar River	26-27		•	•	
Rollins Creek	26-27			•	
Spruce Creek	26-27		•		

4 5 6

Continued on page 19

A

LAKE SUPERIOR

B

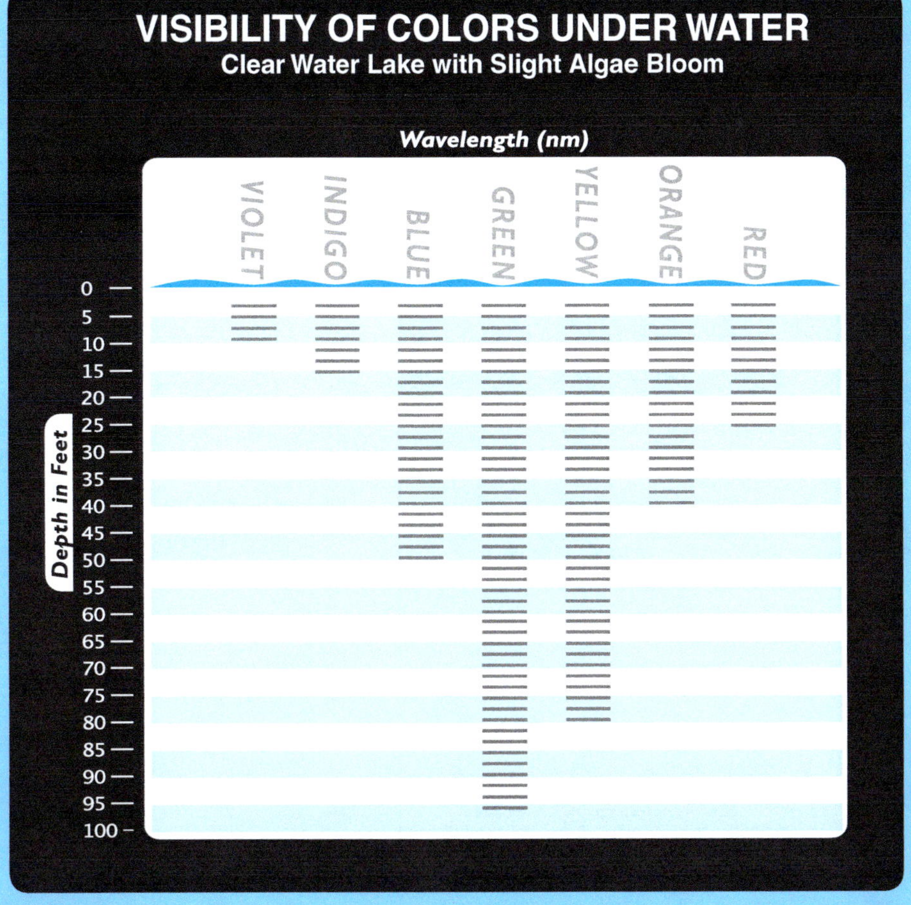

C

D

E

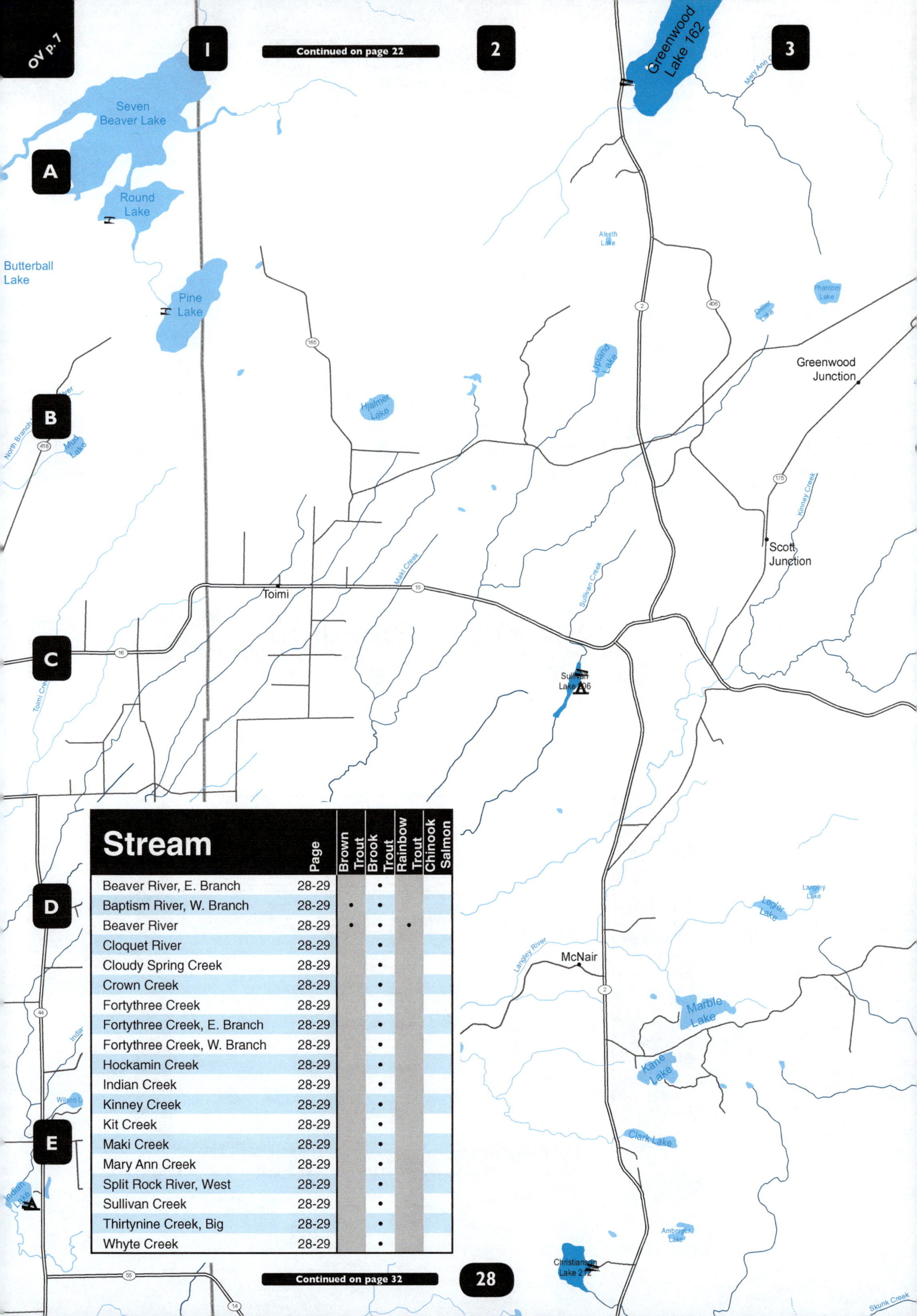

Continued on page 22

Stream	Page	Brown Trout	Brook Trout	Rainbow Trout	Chinook Salmon
Beaver River, E. Branch	28-29		•		
Baptism River, W. Branch	28-29	•	•		
Beaver River	28-29	•	•	•	
Cloquet River	28-29		•		
Cloudy Spring Creek	28-29		•		
Crown Creek	28-29		•		
Fortythree Creek	28-29		•		
Fortythree Creek, E. Branch	28-29		•		
Fortythree Creek, W. Branch	28-29		•		
Hockamin Creek	28-29		•		
Indian Creek	28-29		•		
Kinney Creek	28-29		•		
Kit Creek	28-29		•		
Maki Creek	28-29		•		
Mary Ann Creek	28-29		•		
Split Rock River, West	28-29		•		
Sullivan Creek	28-29		•		
Thirtynine Creek, Big	28-29		•		
Whyte Creek	28-29		•		

Continued on page 32

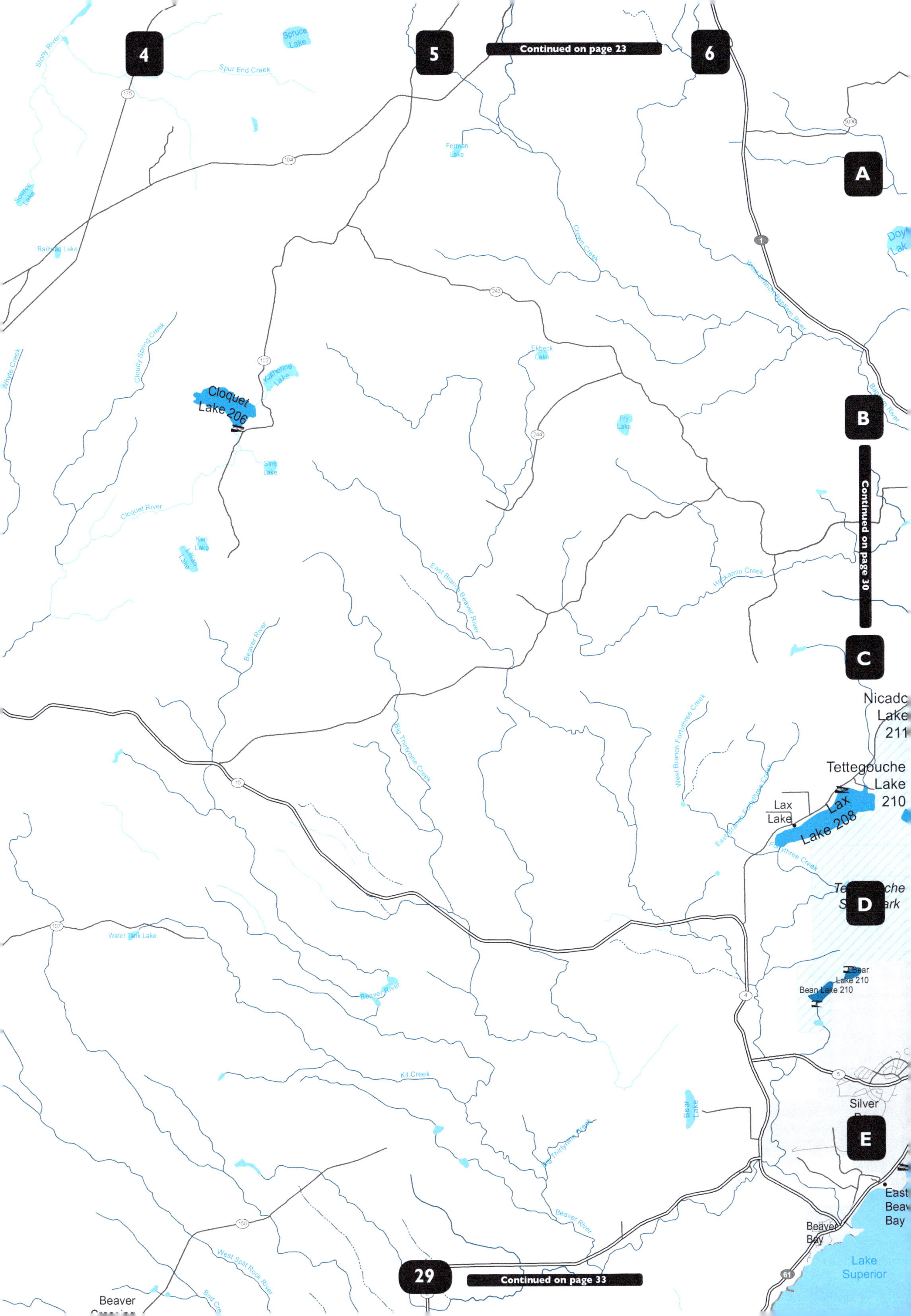

4
5
6
Continued on page 23
A
B
C
D
E
Continued on page 30
29
Continued on page 33
Stony River
Spruce Lake
Spur End Creek
Ferman Lake
Crown Creek
Railroad Lake
Ekbeck Lake
Fry Lake
Cloquet Lake 206
Katherine Lake
Sink Lake
Cloquet River
Cloudy Spring Creek
Whyte Creek
Kari Lake
Lillian Lake
East Branch Beaver River
Beaver River
Hockamin Creek
Big Thirtynine Creek
West Branch Fortythree Creek
East Branch Fortythree Creek
Fortythree Creek
Nicado Lake 211
Tettegouche Lake 210
Lax Lake
Lax Lake 208
Bear Lake 210
Bean Lake 210
Water Tank Lake
Beaver River
Kit Creek
Bear Lake
Big Thirtynine Creek
Beaver River
West Split Rock River
Silver Bay
East Beaver Bay
Beaver Bay
Lake Superior
Beaver

Continued on page 24
Continued on page 29

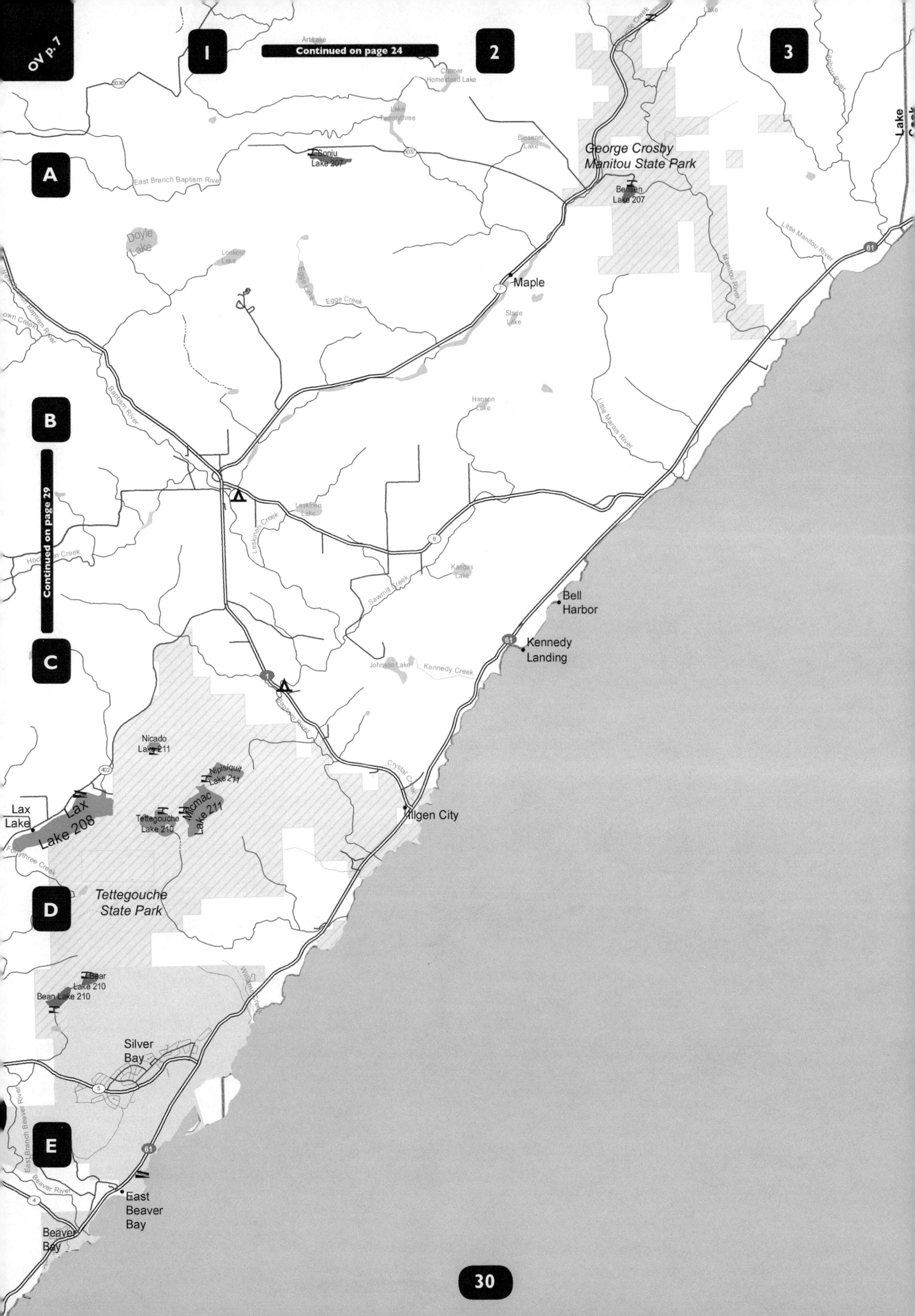

4 5 6

Continued on page 25

A

Stream	Page	Brown Trout	Brook Trout	Rainbow Trout	Chinook Salmon
Baptism River	30-31	•	•	•	•
Baptism River, E. Branch	30-31	•	•		
Baptism River, W. Branch	30-31	•	•		
Beaver River	30-31	•	•	•	
Caribou River	30-31		•		
Egge Creek	30-31		•		
Hockamin Creek	30-31		•		
Leskinen Creek	30-31		•		
Manitou River, Little	30-31			•	
Manitou River	30-31		•	•	
Marais River, Little	30-31		•	•	
Sawmill Creek	30-31		•		

Cook

B

Lake Superior

C

LAKE SUPERIOR

D

E

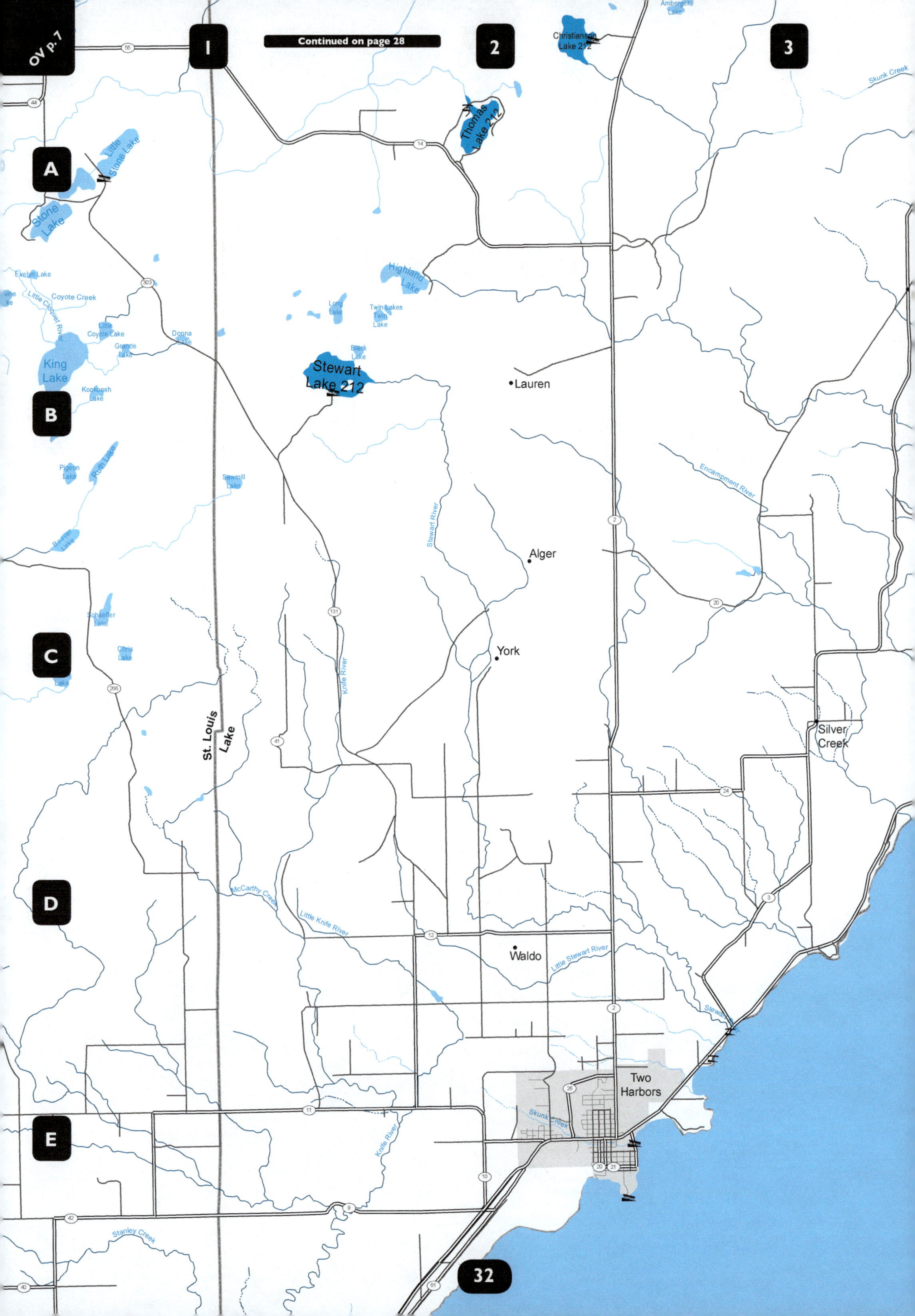
OV p. 7
1
2
3
Continued on page 28
Christianson Lake 212
Skunk Creek
Thomas Lake 212
Little Stone Lake
Stone Lake
A
Evelyn Lake
Coyote Creek
Little Cloquet River
Little Coyote Lake
Grande Lake
Donna Lake
King Lake
Kookoosh Lake
B
Highland Lake
Long Lake
Twin Lakes
Twin Lake
Black Lake
Stewart Lake 212
Lauren
Pigeon Lake
Ruth Lake
Sawmill Lake
Beaver Lake
Encampment River
Stewart River
Alger
Schaeffer Lake
Chris Lake
C
York
Knife River
St. Louis Lake
Silver Creek
D
McCarthy Creek
Little Knife River
Waldo
Little Stewart River
Two Harbors
Skunk Creek
E
Knife River
Stanley Creek
55
44
14
303
2
131
20
266
41
24
3
12
26
11
10
21
9
42
40
61

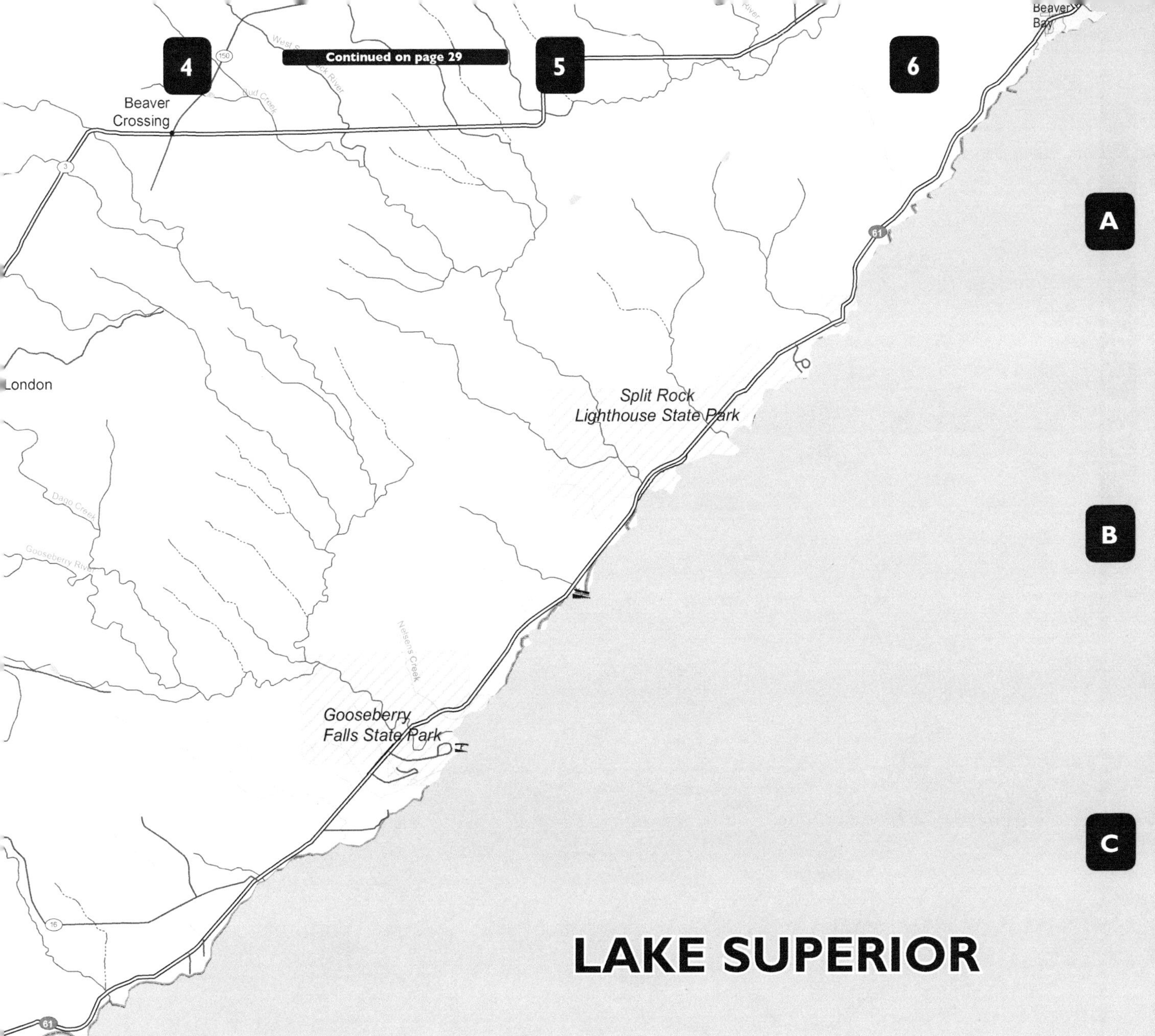

Stream	Page	Brown Trout	Brook Trout	Rainbow Trout	Chinook Salmon
Budd Creek	32-33		•		
Cloquet River, Little	32-33		•		
Dago Creek	32-33		•		
Encampment River	32-33		•	•	
Gooseberry River	32-33		•	•	
Knife River	32-33	•	•	•	•
Knife River, Little	32-33	•	•	•	
McCarthy Creek	32-33	•	•	•	
Skunk Creek	32-33		•		
Split Rock River, West	32-33		•		
Stanley Creek	32-33		•		
Stewart River	32-33	•	•		
Stewart River, Little	32-33	•	•		

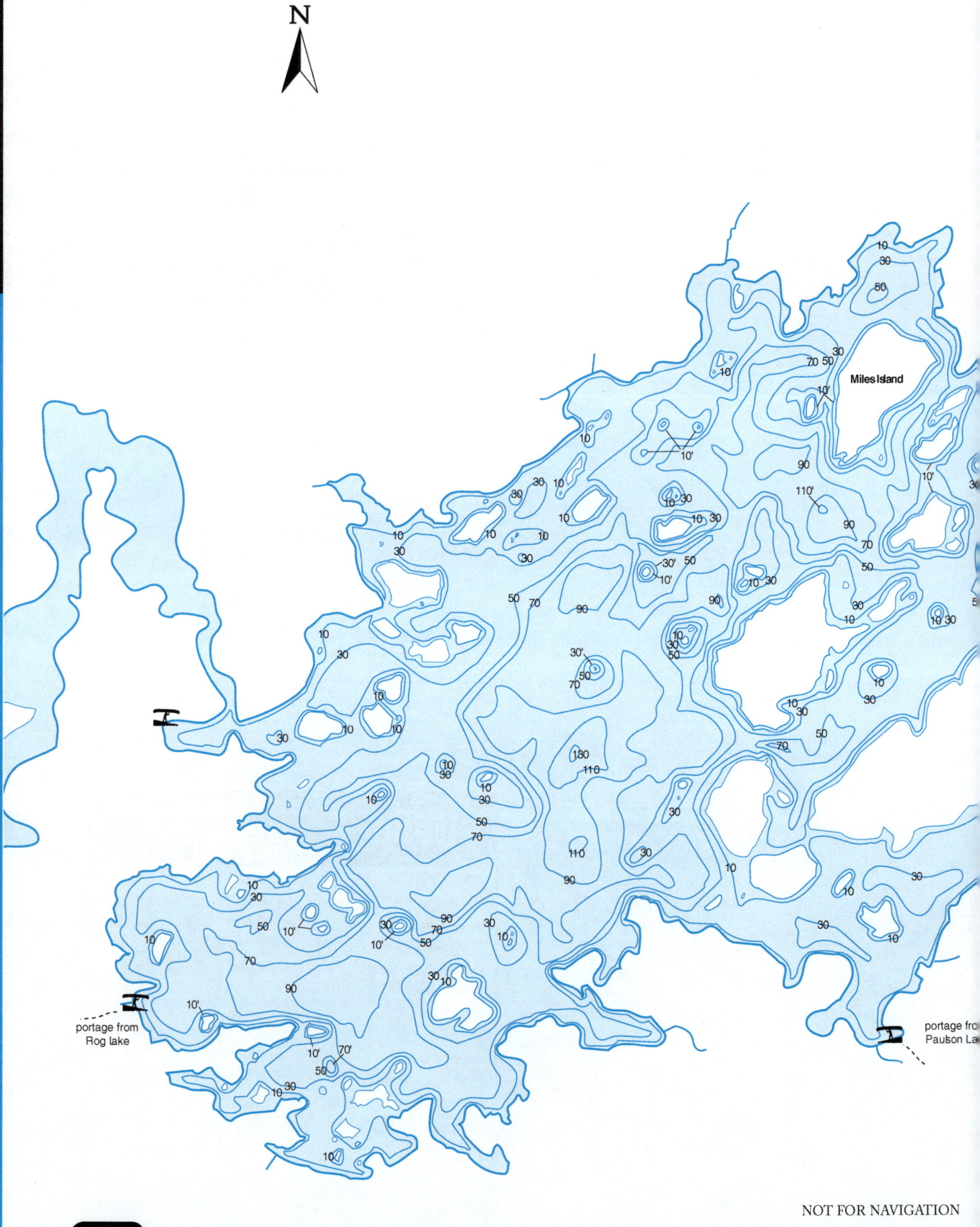

Miles Island

portage from Rog lake

portage fro
Pauson La

NOT FOR NAVIGATION

Source: Minnesota Department of Natural Resources, USGS

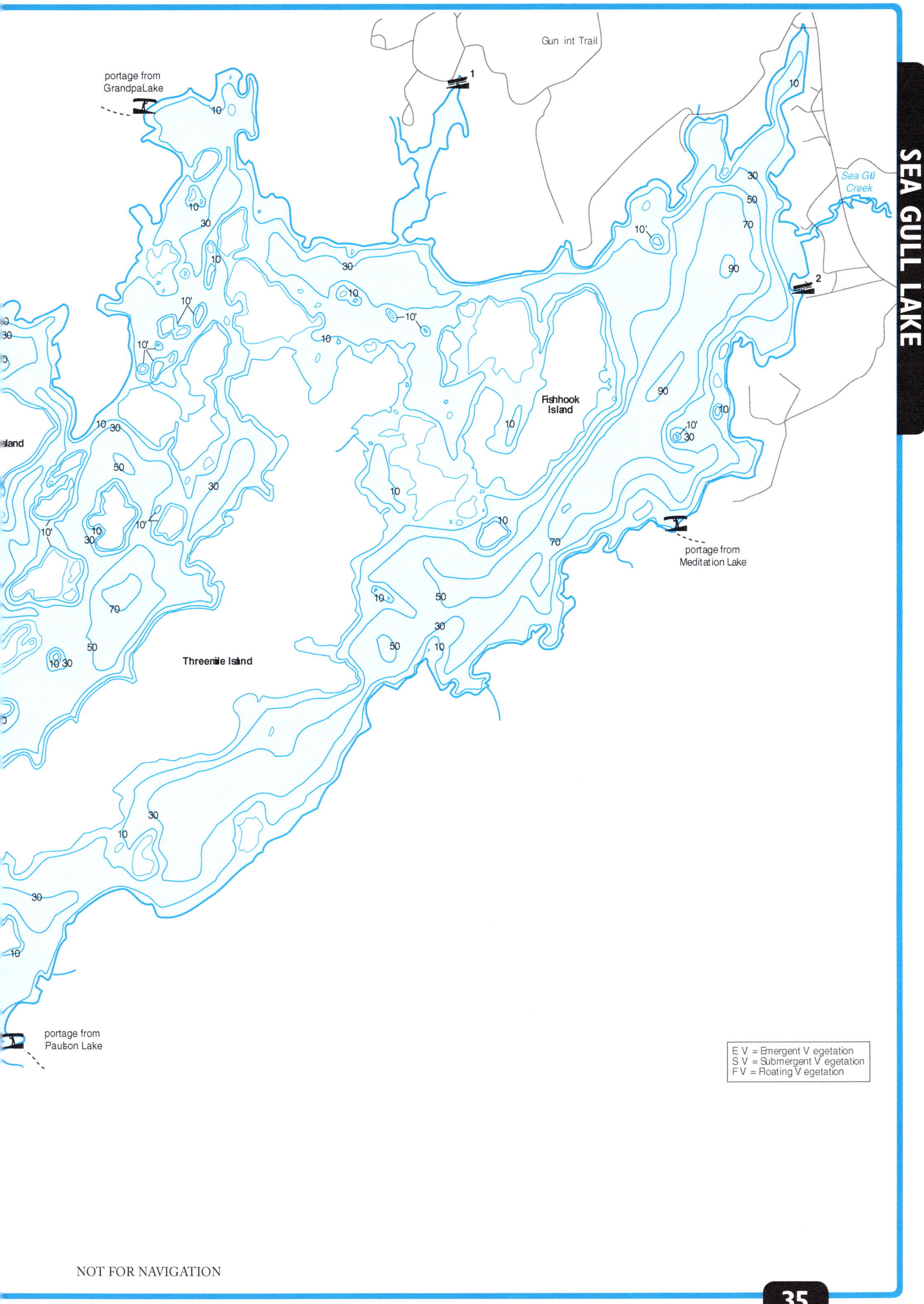

NOT FOR NAVIGATION

Source: Minnesota Department of Natural Resources, USGS

SEA GULL LAKE *Cook County*

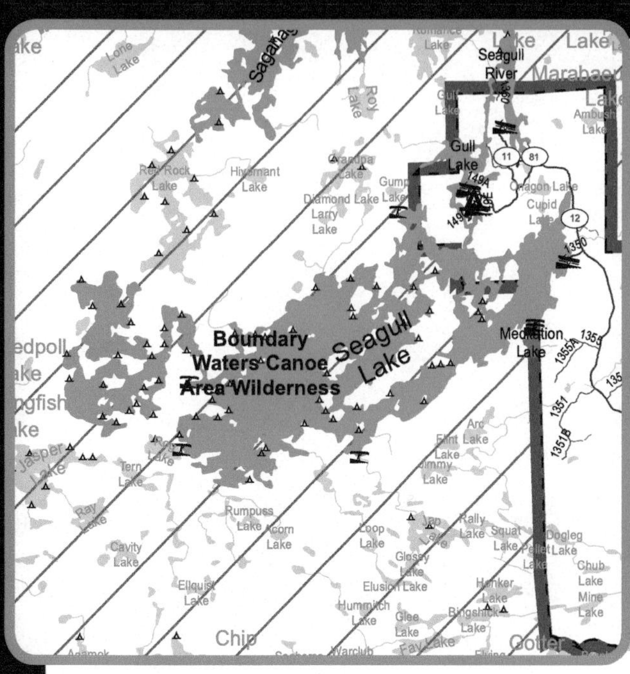

Area map page / coordinates: 8, 9 / C,D-3-5

Watershed: Rainy headwaters

Surface water area / shorelength: 3,958 acres / NA

Maximum / mean depth: 145 feet / NA

Water color / clarity: Clear / 12.3 ft. secchi (2012)

Shoreland zoning classification: NA

Management class / Ecological type: NA / NA

Accessibility: Public access with gravel ramp

1) 90° 53' 38" W / 48° 9' 24" N

Accessibility: USFS-owned public access with concrete ramp on east shore of northeast lobe; parking for 30 vehicles

2) 90° 52' 9" W / 48° 8' 48" N

Accommodations: Resort, camping, outfitters

FISHING INFORMATION

Sea Gull is one of those lakes you have to fish at least once in your life. At about 4,000 acres, it can get rough, but the fishing is well worth it. The lake boasts decent lake trout numbers, a good walleye population, smallmouth bass, northern pike, whitefish and ciscoes. The cisco and whitefish forage base helps walleyes, lake trout and northern pike achieve faster-than-normal growth rates.

Lake trout are the main draw for most anglers here. Current lake trout numbers are about normal for Sea Gull's long-term average. All the fish are entirely sustained by natural reproduction. Growth for these fish remains on the fast side of normal.

Northern pike aren't overly abundant, but trophy-size fish are available, again, because of that high-fat forage base.

Walleye numbers are generally low, which is not unexpected for such a deep, nutrient-deficient lake. Still, this is the exact recipe for producing big fish: a low-density walleye population, coupled with fatty forage. Don't expect to catch a lot of eaters, or to catch a lot of fish for that matter, but the next walleye you hook could be the fish of a lifetime. Don't hesitate to leave traditional shallow, rocky walleye structure and troll through schools of tullibees with crankbaits. That's where some of the largest walleyes may be feeding. There is a 17-inch minimum size limit on walleyes with a daily bag of three.

Smallmouth bass have been sampled in low numbers. Some quality-sizes smallies inhabit Sea Gull.

When it comes to fishing this lake, a local angler says there's so much structure it's tough to mark spots – the map would be covered by them. For lakers, he suggests jigging the humps in the spring, when the fish are in shallow. Later, the lakers will head deep, and that's the time to look for depths of 60 feet or so. Troll with downriggers and expect some action. In the winter, use a 3-inch white tube jig or an airplane jig fished in deep water. Don't be afraid to move around.

In the early part of the open-water season, look for walleyes in the shallows near the boat landing. Later, work the points and the wind-blown shorelines. The islands also offer good opportuni- ties. Jig/minnow combinations will work well until July, then bring alon some leeches or crawlers when the bite gets tougher. First ice will fin these fish moving up shallow, hunting aquatic life around weedbeds. Fis anywhere from 7 to 20 feet of water using jigs and shiners or jiggin spoons. These fish are night feeders, so a glow hook or spoon could b the ticket.

You'll find small northerns at the weedlines in the summer. In th spring, stick to the areas around the creeks and near the inlet from Gul Lake. For big pike in mid-summer, locate schools of tullibees and tro spoons and crankbaits near the schools in colors that imitate this fatt fish. In winter, check shallower areas for pike and all other species. At tha time, with cooler water temps, even lake trout can find adequate oxyge and cool enough water to go shallow.

NO RECORD OF STOCKING

NET CATCH DATA

Date: 6/25/2012	Gill Nets		Trap Nets	
species	# per net	avg. fish weight (lbs.)	# per net	avg. fish weight (lbs.
Burbot	0.70	1.50	-	-
Lake Whitefish	6.70	1.54	-	-
Northern Pike	0.87	3.82	-	-
Smallmouth Bass	0.30	1.97	-	-
Walleye	0.65	2.90	-	-

LENGTH OF SELECTED SPECIES SAMPLED FROM ALL GEAR

Number of fish caught for the following length categories (inches):

species	0-5	6-8	9-11	12-14	15-19	20-24	25-29	>30	Total
Burbot	-	-	1	7	4	3	1	-	16
Cisco Species	1	-	2	-	-	-	-	-	3
Lake Trout	-	2	1	-	3	8	-	-	14
Lake Whitefish	-	10	32	16	87	9	-	-	154
Northern Pike	-	-	-	1	1	10	5	3	20
Smallmouth Bass	-	-	-	2	5	-	-	-	7
Walleye	-	-	1	5	3	4	2	-	15
White Sucker	-	1	6	1	22	10	-	-	40
Yellow Perch	1	-	-	-	-	-	-	-	1

SAGANAGA LAKE

Cook County

Area map pg/coord: 8,9 / A,B,C-4,5

Watershed: Rainy headwaters

Surface area: 17,593 acres

Shorelength: 49.0 miles

Max / mean depth: 280 feet / NA

Water color / clarity: Yellow tint/12.6 ft. secchi (2014)

Shoreland zoning class: Rec. dev.

Mgmt class / Ecological type: Trout

Accessibility: Via navigable channel from Gull Lake; fee access with concrete ramp at south end of Saganaga Narrows (parking for 20 vehicles); fee access (county) with concrete ramp on west side of Saganaga Narrows, parking for 30 vehicle

Accommodations: Camping, outfitters

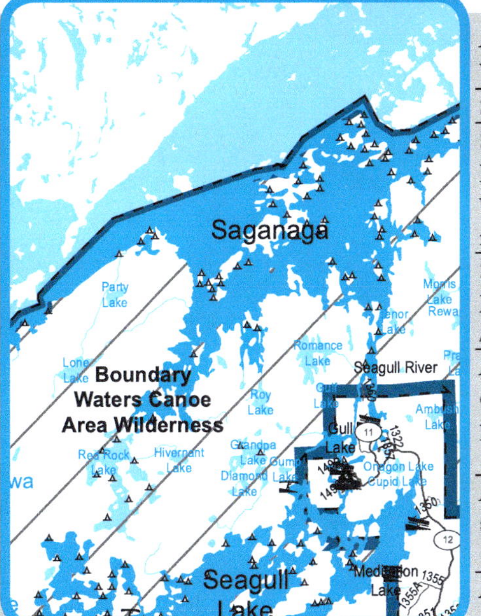

GULL LAKE

Cook County

Area map pg / coord: 9 / B,C-4,5

Watershed: Rainy headwaters

Surface area: 183 acres

Shorelength: NA

Max / mean depth: 40 feet / 14 feet

Water color / clarity: Green tint / 10.2 ft. secchi (1998)

Shoreland zoning class: Rec. dev.

Mgmt class / Ecological type: Walleye / soft-water walleye

Accessibility: USFS-owned public access with concrete ramp on south shore; parking for 30 vehicles

1) 90° 53' 47" W / 48° 9' 37" N

Accessibility: Gravel ramp on west shore of Seagull River flowage

2) 90° 53' 10" W / 48° 10' 16" N

Accommodations: Camping

SAGANAGA LAKE

FISH STOCKING DATA

year	species	size	# released
09	Walleye	Fry	4,250,000
10	Walleye	Fry	5,200,000
13	Walleye	Fry	5,400,000
14	Walleye	Fry	4,500,000

LENGTH OF SELECTED SPECIES SAMPLED FROM ALL GEAR

Number of fish caught for the following length categories (inches):

species	0-5	6-8	9-11	12-14	15-19	20-24	25-29	>29	Total
Black Crappie	1	-	1	-	-	-	-	-	2
Burbot	-	-	-	2	2	1	-	-	5
Cisco Species	2	74	147	28	6	-	-	-	257
Lake Trout	-	1	1	2	16	2	2	-	24
Lake Whitefish	-	2	6	5	25	46	-	-	84
Northern Pike	-	-	-	1	11	27	9	-	48
Pumpkinseed	1	1	-	-	-	-	-	-	2
Smallmouth Bass	-	2	1	3	5	-	-	-	11
Walleye	-	7	37	33	10	5	1	-	93
White Sucker	-	1	3	-	22	5	-	-	31
Yellow Perch	4	5	-	-	-	-	-	-	9

GULL LAKE

NO RECORD OF STOCKING

NET CATCH DATA

Date: 08/24/1998	Gill Nets		Trap Nets	
species	# per net	avg. fish weight (lbs.)	# per net	avg. fish weight (lbs.)
Green Sunfish	0.3	0.10	-	-
Lake Whitefish	6.8	2.81	-	-
Northern Pike	1.5	4.12	trace	0.58
Smallmouth Bass	0.3	0.89	-	-
Tullibee (Cisco)	2.0	1.40	-	-
Walleye	2.7	1.07	0.3	1.00
Yellow Perch	0.2	0.24	-	-

LENGTH OF SELECTED SPECIES SAMPLED FROM ALL GEAR

Number of fish caught for the following length categories (inches):

species	0-5	6-8	9-11	12-14	15-19	20-24	25-29	>29	Total
Green Sunfish	1	1	-	-	-	-	-	-	2
Lake Whitefish	-	-	2	1	23	15	-	-	41
Northern Pike	-	-	-	2	1	2	2	3	10
Smallmouth Bass	-	-	1	1	-	-	-	-	2
Tullibee (Cisco)	-	-	-	6	6	-	-	-	12
Walleye	1	3	10	3	-	2	1	-	20
Yellow Perch	-	1	-	-	-	-	-	-	1

FISHING INFORMATION

You can't schedule a fishing trip to the Gunflint area without stopping in at Saganaga and Gull. These are simply "must-visit" lakes for any angler.

Saganaga is a consistent producer of big lake trout and numbers of good-sized walleyes. Just don't overlook smallies, some large northern pike and all the whitefish and cisco you'd care to smoke. In 2009, the DNR began walleye fry stocking as a result of the relatively low catch observed in 2008. A local angler says walleye action is usually hot and heavy on opening weekend in Red Rock Bay **(Spot 1)** in the lake's southwestern arm. Locals occasionally take 'eyes to 34 inches in this area, and there are numerous catches of fish in the 21- to 26-inch range. James Bay **(Spot 2)**, just east of the Saganaga Corridor, up toward the international boundary, is another springtime hotspot, as are many of the other shallow bays. As the water warms, try around the islands **(Spots 3)** with jig/minnow combos, or troll with crankbaits. There is a 17-inch size limit on walleyes with a daily limit of three.

Lake trout numbers were on par with past survey numbers but low in comparison to other lakes in the area. A local angler suggests trolling the shoreline of Long Island **(Spot 4)** early in 20 to 30 feet of water. The western tip of Horseshoe Island **(Spot 3)** is another spring hotspot for lakers, as are many of the small islands and reefs south of Clark Island **(Spot 3)**, which lies just west of the "Sag" Corridor. Honeymoon Reef, near Rocky point, over toward the lake's western end, yields some nice lakers as well. Look for whitefish in the same area.

Gull Lake offers pretty decent numbers of walleyes, along with nice northerns and good numbers of whitefish. Fish the 'eyes around Memorial Day near the narrows along the Saganaga Corridor and in the Sea Gull River heading down into Gull Lake. Don't try here earlier, as this area has a late opener and is closed to angling during and just after the spawn. The state record walleye, which tipped the scales at 17 pounds, 8 ounces, was caught in this area some years back. There is a 17-inch size limit on walleyes with a daily limit of three. Later in the season, walleyes will leave the river. Then, you'll want to switch to the island shoreline, trolling crankbaits or a minnow on a spinner rig. The lake's numerous points are good places to try as well, and don't neglect the windward shorelines. For northerns, try the shallows in the back bays; some work these with suckers and a slip bobber, while others prefer casting spoons or trolling spinner rigs. Cast a small crankbait or jig and grub near the shorelines for smallies.

Source: Minnesota Department of Natural Resources, USGS

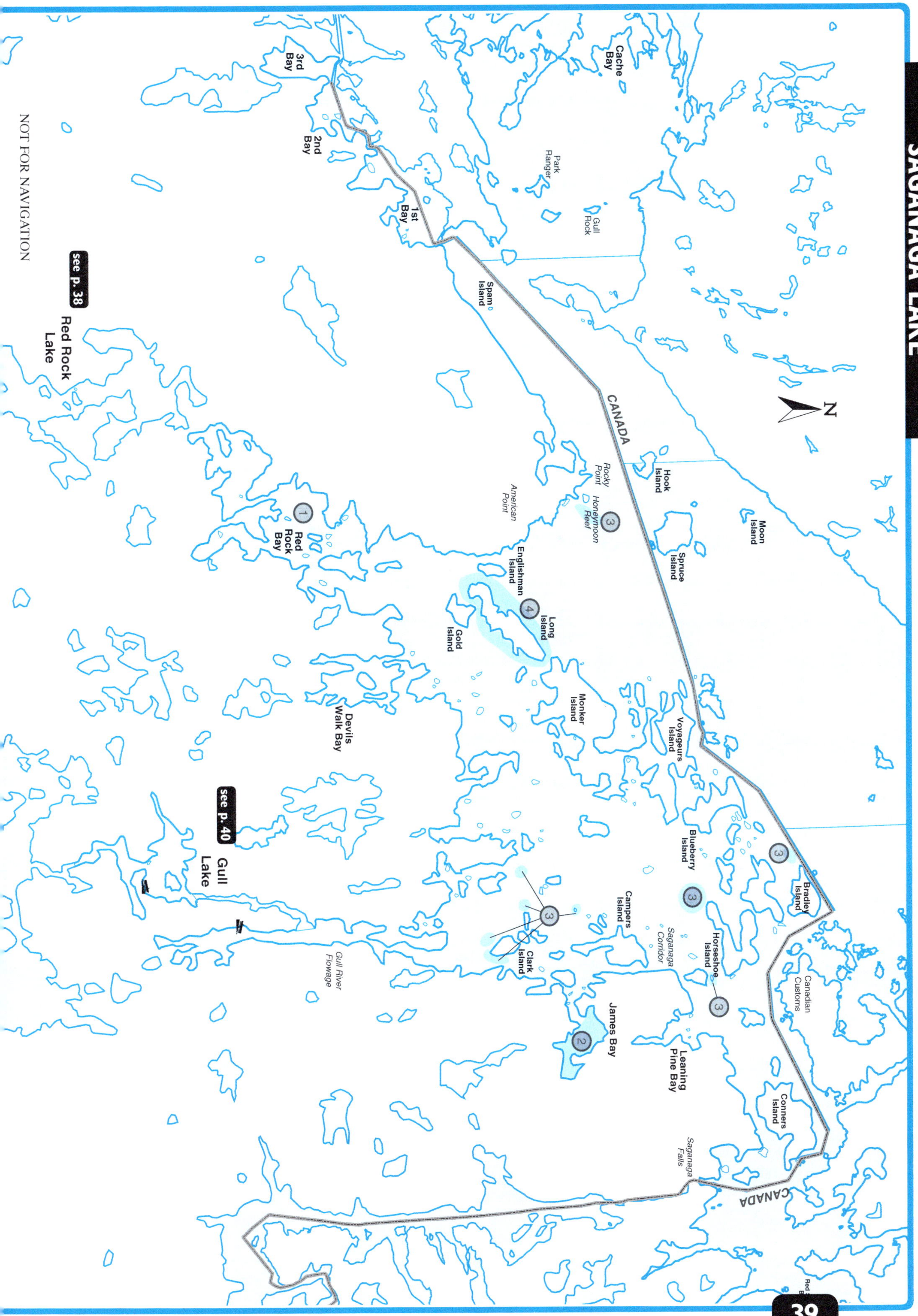

see p. 40

see p. 38

Source: Minnesota Department of Natural Resources, USGS

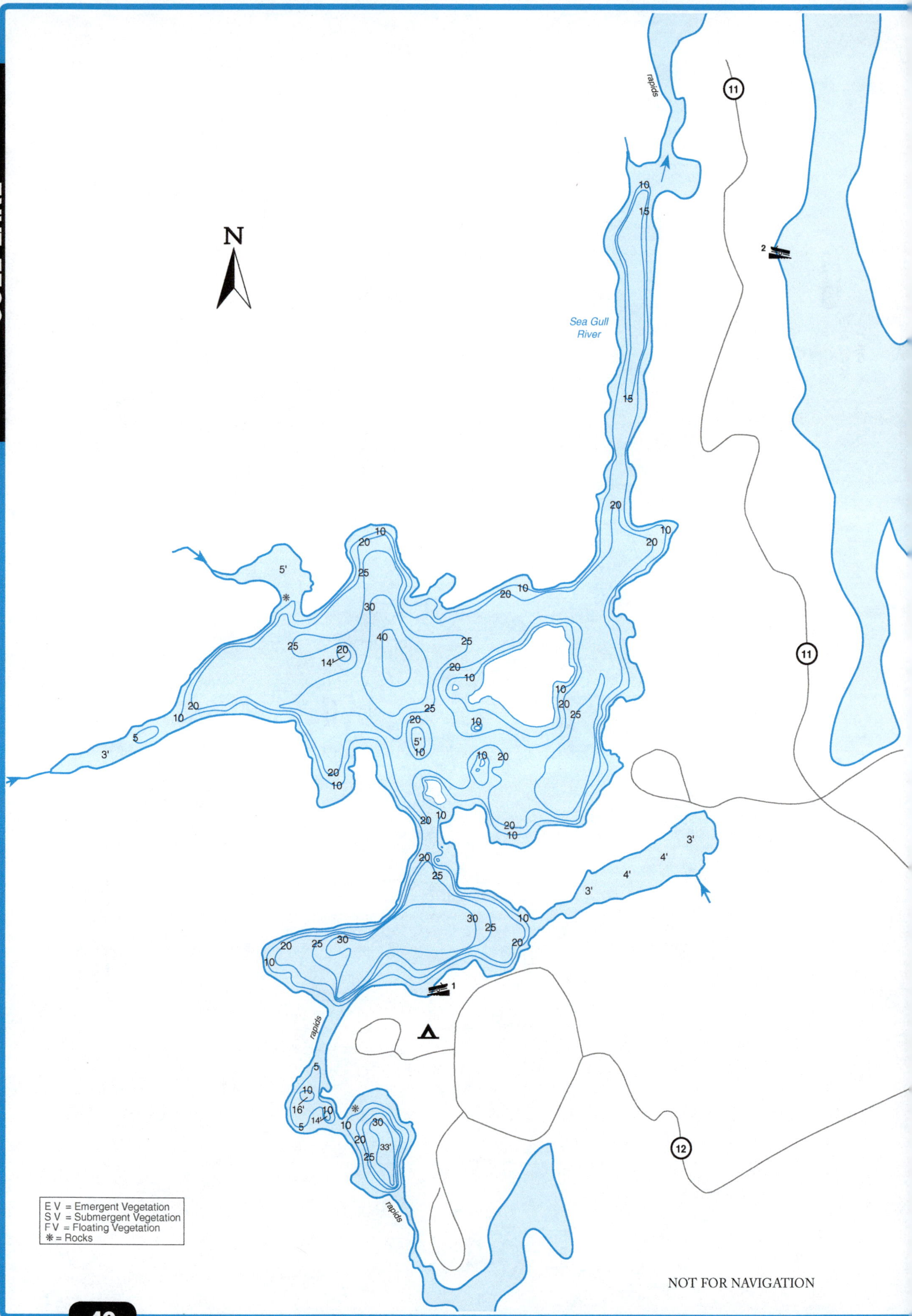

Source: Minnesota Department of Natural Resources, USGS

LENGTH TO WEIGHT CONVERSION SCALE

Average Weight (pounds)

Inches	Inland Lakes & Rivers Species								Inland Trout (Lakes)				Great Lakes Species				
	Largemouth Bass	Smallmouth Bass	Walleye	Northern Pike	Muskellunge	Channel Catfish	Flathead Catfish	Black Crappie	Rainbow Trout	Lake Trout	Brown Trout	Brook Trout	Atlantic Salmon	Chinook Salmon	Coho Salmon	Lake Trout	Steelhead
3.5	.0186	.0212	.0132	.0072	.0041	.0082	.0132	.0198	0.015	0.011	0.018	0.014					
4.5	.0409	.0454	.0282	.0158	.0098	.0188	.0292	.0441	0.032	0.023	0.039	0.030					
5.5	.0765	.0834	.0519	.0297	.0197	.0362	.0551	.0835	0.059	0.044	0.071	0.056					
6.5	0.129	0.138	0.086	0.050	0.035	0.063	0.094	0.142	0.097	0.075	0.118	0.095					
7.5	0.202	0.213	0.133	0.079	0.057	0.100	0.147	0.224	0.148	0.118	0.181	0.148					
8.5	0.299	0.311	0.195	0.117	0.088	0.151	0.219	0.333	0.220	0.175	0.264	0.220					
9.5	0.423	0.436	0.273	0.165	0.129	0.217	0.311	0.475	0.306	0.250	0.369	0.312					
10.5	0.578	0.590	0.369	0.226	0.182	0.302	0.427	0.653	0.411	0.343	0.498	0.427					
11.5	0.77	0.78	0.49	0.30	0.25	0.41	0.57	0.87	0.54	0.46	0.66	0.57					
12.5	1.00	1.00	0.63	0.39	0.33	0.53	0.74	1.14	0.70	0.60	0.84	0.74	0.58	0.67	0.71	0.51	0.65
13.5	1.27	1.27	0.79	0.50	0.43	0.69	0.95	1.45	0.87	0.76	1.06	0.94	0.72	0.90	0.90	0.65	0.81
14.5	1.59	1.57	0.98	0.62	0.55	0.87	1.19	1.82	1.08	0.96	1.32	1.18	0.90	1.09	1.05	0.85	1.08
15.5	1.95	1.92	1.21	0.77	0.70	1.08	1.46	2.25	1.33	1.18	1.61	1.45	1.11	1.32	1.26	1.06	1.24
16.5	2.38	2.32	1.46	0.94	0.86	1.33	1.78		1.60	1.44	1.94	1.77	1.35	1.59	1.57	1.28	1.57
17.5	2.86	2.77	1.74	1.13	1.06	1.61	2.15		1.90	1.74	2.32	2.12	1.62	1.89	1.71	1.59	1.79
18.5	3.40	3.28	2.06	1.34	1.28	1.93	2.56		2.26	2.08	2.74	2.53	1.90	2.24	1.98	1.91	2.15
19.5	4.01	3.84	2.42	1.58	1.54	2.29	3.03		2.64	2.46	3.21	2.98	2.25	2.63	2.21	2.29	2.50
20.5	4.68	4.47	2.82	1.85	1.82	2.70	3.55		3.08	2.88	3.73	3.49	2.60	3.06	2.52	2.67	2.81
21.5	5.44	5.17	3.26	2.15	2.15	3.16	4.13		3.54	3.35	4.30	4.05	3.02	3.54	2.89	3.14	3.32
22.5	6.27	5.93	3.74	2.48	2.51	3.66	4.76		4.05	3.87	4.93	4.68	3.51	4.07	3.22	3.63	3.70
23.5	7.18	6.76	4.26	2.85	2.92	4.22	5.47		4.63	4.45	5.62	5.36	3.99	4.64	3.64	4.18	4.20
24.5	8.18	7.67	4.84	3.24	3.37	4.84	6.24		5.25	5.08	6.37	6.11	4.52	5.31	4.01	4.90	4.70
25.5	9.27	8.66	5.46	3.68	3.87	5.52	7.08		5.92	5.76	7.19	6.93	5.11	5.95	4.42	5.57	5.39
26.5			6.14	4.15	4.42	6.26	8.00		6.65	6.51	8.07		5.77	6.68	4.86	6.35	6.06
27.5			6.87	4.66	5.02	7.07	8.99		7.44	7.33	9.02		6.45	7.47	5.35	7.30	6.82
28.5			7.66	5.22	5.67	7.95	10.07		8.28	8.21	10.05		7.35	8.24	5.89	8.00	7.49
29.5			8.50	5.81	6.39	8.90	11.23		9.18	9.16	11.14		8.02	9.30	6.35	9.00	8.23
30.5			9.41	6.46	7.16	9.92	12.48		10.15	10.19	12.32		8.95	10.28		10.20	9.10
31.5			10.40	7.10	8.00	11.00	13.80			11.30	13.60		9.85	11.40		11.30	10.01
32.5			11.40	7.90	8.90	12.20	15.30			12.50	14.90		10.85	12.51		12.50	11.02
33.5			12.50	8.70	9.90	13.50	16.80			13.70	16.30		11.85	13.62		13.90	12.04
34.5			13.70	9.50	11.00	14.90	18.40			15.10	17.80		13.10	14.88		15.40	13.11
35.5			14.90	10.40	12.10	16.30	20.20			16.50	19.50		14.35	16.25		16.80	14.21
36.5				11.40	13.30	17.90	22.00			18.00			15.77	17.62		18.70	
37.5				12.40	14.60	19.50	24.00			19.60			16.85	19.16		20.10	
38.5				13.40	16.00	21.30	26.10			21.40			18.30	20.55		22.00	
39.5				14.50	17.50	23.20	28.30			23.20			19.59	22.21		24.10	
40.5													21.60	24.10		26.12	
41.5													22.92	26.12		28.20	
42.5													24.70	28.05		31.00	
43.5													26.80	30.10		33.10	
44.5													28.65	32.21		36.10	

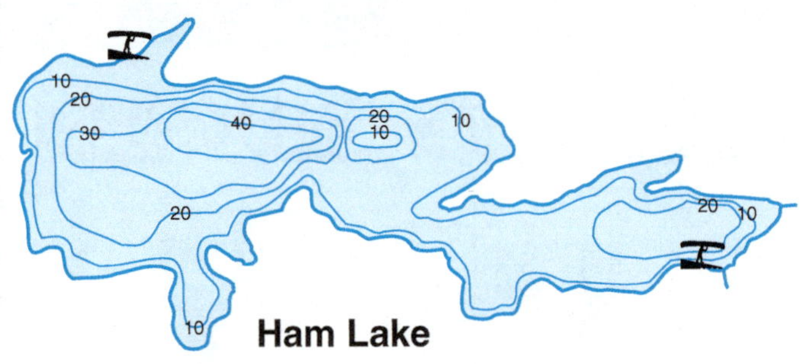

Ham Lake, Cook County

Area map page / coordinates: 9 / D,E-5,6
Surface area / max depth: 100 acres / 40 feet
Accessibility: Carry-down access to northwest shore from Co. Rd. 47; parking for several vehicles

NO RECORD OF STOCKING

LENGTH OF SELECTED SPECIES SAMPLED FROM ALL GEAR
Survey Date: 08/27/1998
Number of fish caught for the following length categories (inches):

species	0-5	6-8	9-11	12-14	15-19	20-24	25-29	>30	Total
Northern Pike	-	-	-	-	1	2	1	-	4
Smallmouth Bass	-	-	1	-	-	-	-	-	1
Walleye	-	1	2	9	10	-	-	-	22
Yellow Perch	-	8	-	-	-	-	-	-	8

Extortion Lake, Cook County

Area map page / coordinates: 9 / D-6
Surface area / max depth: 16 acres / 36 feet
Accessibility: Carry-down access (steep trail) to northeast shore, from Co. Rd. 12; parking for three to four vehicles

FISH STOCKING DATA

year	species	size	# released
10	Rainbow Trout	Fingerling	1,000
11	Brown Trout	Fingerling	1,000
12	Rainbow Trout	Fingerling	1,032
13	Rainbow Trout	Fingerling	1,000
15	Rainbow Trout	Fingerling	1,022

LENGTH OF SELECTED SPECIES SAMPLED FROM ALL GEAR
Survey Date: 9/19/2013
Number of fish caught for the following length categories (inches):

species	0-5	6-8	9-11	12-14	15-19	20-24	25-29	>30	Total
Brown Trout	-	-	-	1	3	1	-	-	5

Trip Lake, Cook County

Area map page / coordinates: 9 / D-6
Surface area / max depth: 11 acres / 19 feet
Accessibility: Carry-down access to east shore (0.2 mile) from Banadad Road off Gunflint Trail

FISH STOCKING DATA

year	species	size	# released
02	Brook Trout	Fingerling	1,002
06	Brook Trout	Fingerling	1,004
08	Rainbow Trout	Fingerling	1,000
10	Rainbow Trout	Fingerling	1,000
12	Rainbow Trout	Fingerling	1,000
14	Rainbow Trout	Fingerling	1,000

LENGTH OF SELECTED SPECIES SAMPLED FROM ALL GEAR
Survey Date: 9/18/2014
Number of fish caught for the following length categories (inches):

species	0-5	6-8	9-11	12-14	15-19	20-24	25-29	>30	Total
Rainbow Trout	-	-	-	-	2	-	-	-	2

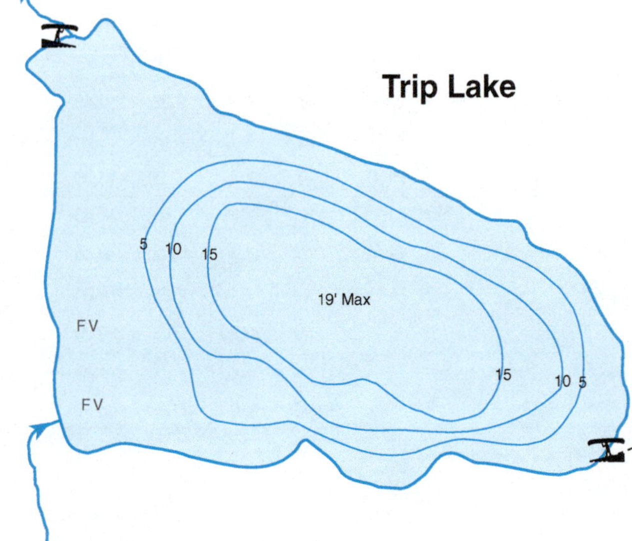

NOT FOR NAVIGATION

Source: Minnesota Department of Natural Resources, USGS

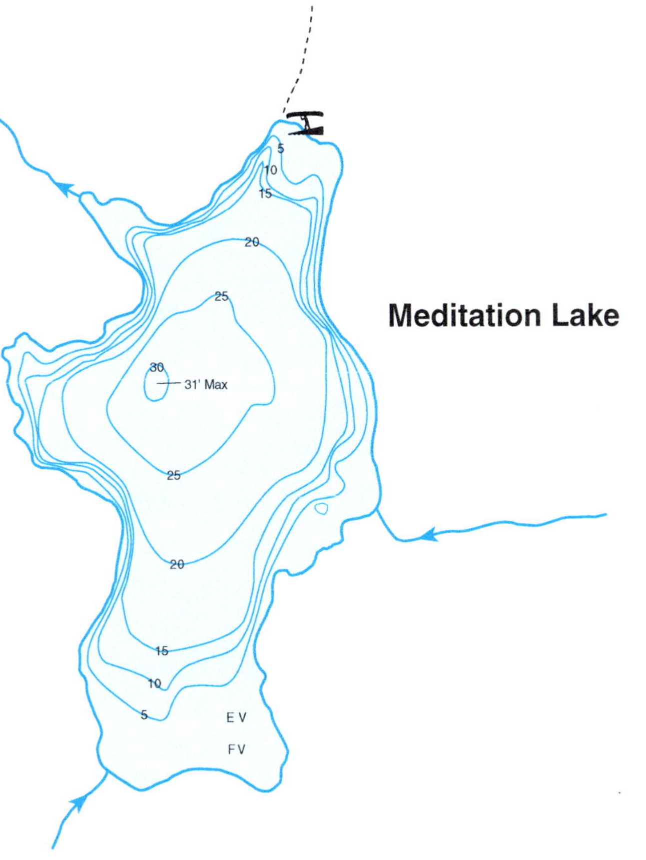

Meditation Lake

Meditation Lake, Cook County

Area map page / coordinates: 9 / C-5
Surface area / max depth: 28 acres / 31 feet
Accessibility: Portage (35 rods) from Sea Gull Lake

FISH STOCKING DATA

year	species	size	# released
07	Brook Trout	Fingerling	1,000
08	Brook Trout	Fingerling	1,000
09	Brook Trout	Fingerling	1,000
10	Brook Trout	Fingerling	1,000
11	Brook Trout	Fingerling	1,000
12	Brook Trout	Fingerling	1,000
13	Brook Trout	Fingerling	1,000
14	Brook Trout	Fingerling	1,105
15	Brook Trout	Fingerling	1,001

LENGTH OF SELECTED SPECIES SAMPLED FROM ALL GEAR

Survey Date: 9/11/2012

Number of fish caught for the following length categories (inches):

species	0-5	6-8	9-11	12-14	15-19	20-24	25-29	>30	Total
Brook Trout	-	3	8	-	2	-	-	-	13

Round Lake, Cook County

Area map page / coordinates: 9 / D-5
Surface area / max depth: 154 acres / 45 feet
Accessibility: Carry-down access to north shore

FISH STOCKING DATA

year	species	size	# released
09	Walleye	Fingerling	3,564
10	Walleye	Fingerling	2,175
13	Walleye	Fingerling	4,191
14	Walleye	Fingerling	3,606

LENGTH OF SELECTED SPECIES SAMPLED FROM ALL GEAR

Survey Date: 07/15/2008

Number of fish caught for the following length categories (inches):

species	0-5	6-8	9-11	12-14	15-19	20-24	25-29	>30	Total
Northern Pike	-	-	-	1	4	6	3	-	14
Smallmouth Bass	-	1	-	-	1	-	-	-	2
Walleye	-	1	2	3	5	3	-	-	14
White Sucker	-	-	7	2	15	7	-	-	31
Yellow Perch	10	24	2	-	-	-	-	-	36

Round Lake

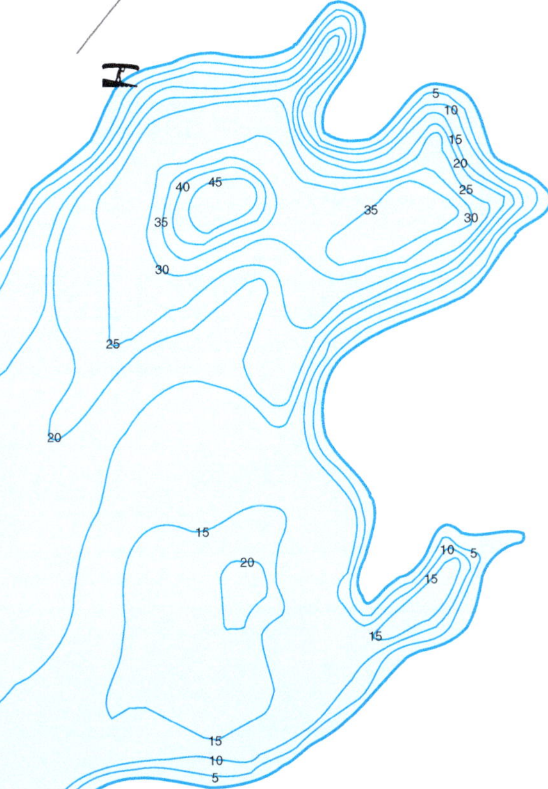

E V = Emergent Vegetation
S V = Submergent Vegetation
F V = Floating Vegetation

MAGNETIC LAKE
Cook County

LITTLE GUNFLINT LAKE
Cook County

Area map pg / coord: 9 / D-6

Watershed: Rainy headwaters

Surface area: 431 acres

Shorelength: 6.9 miles

Max / mean depth: 90 feet / 37 feet

Water color / clarity: Clear / 17.0 ft. secchi (1991)

Shoreland zoning class: Rec. dev.

Mgmt class / Ecological type: Lake trout / trout

Accessibility: Via navigable channel from Gunflint; portage trail from Pine River

Accommodations: None

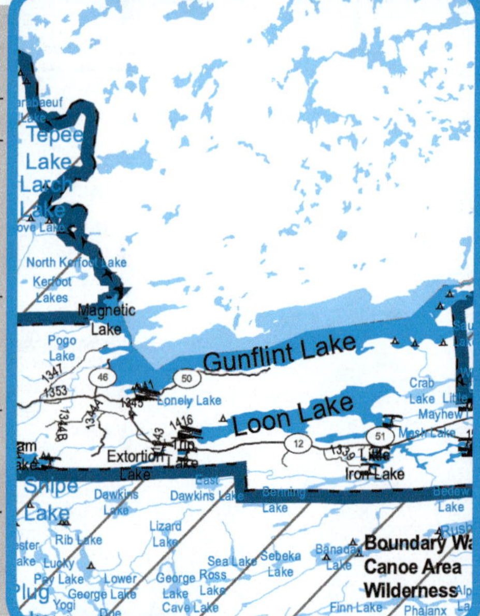

Area map pg / coord: 10 / C,D-2

Watershed: Rainy headwaters

Surface area: 95 acres

Shorelength: 2.7 miles

Max / mean depth: 16 feet / 7 feet

Water color / clarity: Clear / 15.0 ft. secchi (1990)

Shoreland zoning class: Nat. envt.

Mgmt class / Ecological type: Walleye-centrarchid / northern pike-sucker

Accessibility: Via navigable channel from Gunflint Lake; portage from Little North Lake

Accommodations: None

Magnetic Lake

NO RECORD OF STOCKING

NET CATCH DATA

Date: 08/07/1991	Gill Nets		Trap Nets	
species	# per net	avg. fish weight (lbs.)	# per net	avg. fish weight (lbs.)
White Sucker	0.7	1.56	-	-
Walleye	0.2	6.44	-	-
Tullibee (Cisco)	0.7	0.13	-	-
Smallmouth Bass	0.2	1.50	-	-
Lake Trout	1.0	2.25	-	-
Burbot	1.5	1.07	-	-

LENGTH OF SELECTED SPECIES SAMPLED FROM ALL GEAR

Number of fish caught for the following length categories (inches):

species	0-5	6-8	9-11	12-14	15-19	20-24	25-29	>29	Total
Walleye	-	-	-	-	-	-	1	-	1
Tullibee (Cisco)	-	4	-	-	-	-	-	-	4
Smallmouth Bass	-	-	2	-	-	-	-	-	2
Lake Trout	-	-	-	-	4	2	-	-	6

Little Gunflint Lake

NO RECORD OF STOCKING

NET CATCH DATA

Date: 07/23/1990	Gill Nets		Trap Nets	
species	# per net	avg. fish weight (lbs.)	# per net	avg. fish weight (lbs.)
Yellow Perch	16.7	0.37	-	-
White Sucker	5.7	1.14	1.4	1.57
Walleye	4.7	0.95	0.2	0.75
Northern Pike	11.3	0.75	-	-
Smallmouth Bass	-	-	0.4	0.38

LENGTH OF SELECTED SPECIES SAMPLED FROM ALL GEAR

Number of fish caught for the following length categories (inches):

species	0-5	6-8	9-11	12-14	15-19	20-24	25-29	>29	Total
Northern Pike	-	-	3	4	25	2	-	-	34
Smallmouth Bass	-	1	1	-	-	-	-	-	2
Walleye	-	-	1	13	1	-	-	-	15
Yellow Perch	2	26	19	3	-	-	-	-	50

FISHING INFORMATION

These Boundary Waters lakes are overshadowed by their much more famous neighbor, Gunflint Lake, which they flank on the east and west.

Magnetic Lake is a deep lake trout lake, half in the U.S. and half in Canada. This is a border water, so check for special regulations.

One local angler says the lakers are pretty decent in Magnetic. Jig around the large island early, switching to trolling the depths with downriggers later in the season. There are a few walleyes in this lake as well. Try the bays and shorelines with a jig and minnow or leech. Pay attention to the wind direction, as wind-blown shorelines are the places to fish. Another option is to just hire a guide; there are lots of resorts on Gunflint Lake, and all have guides on their staff who'll be glad to reveal their fishing spots – for a fee, of course.

Maxing out at 16 feet, **Little Gunflint** is far shallower than its page-mate. This lake also resides partly in Canada, so border water regulations apply. Expect to find decent walleyes, some fair northern pike, a few smallies and a good population of keeper-sized yellow perch. It's known as a good producer all season, so don't worry about fishing this lake early; it should provide a bite throughout the year.

Local anglers prefer to fish with slip bobbers and leeches or minnows for walleyes. Jig/minnow or jig/leech combos will work equally as well. Wind-blown points and shorelines are key. Trolling crankbaits early in the year over emerging weeds may also produce. In the winter, try drilling holes early in the season along weedlines or near humps using live minnows on a glow hook or a minnow head on a jigging spoon.

Early in the season, northern pike can be taken shallow on crankbaits. Move deeper as the water temperatures increase. Winter will produce these fish in much the same areas, with shallows being productive at first ice and deeper drop-offs getting the nod as the season advances.

Don't forget to try for hefty perch here as well. Jigging spoons intended for walleyes will also take jumbo perch.

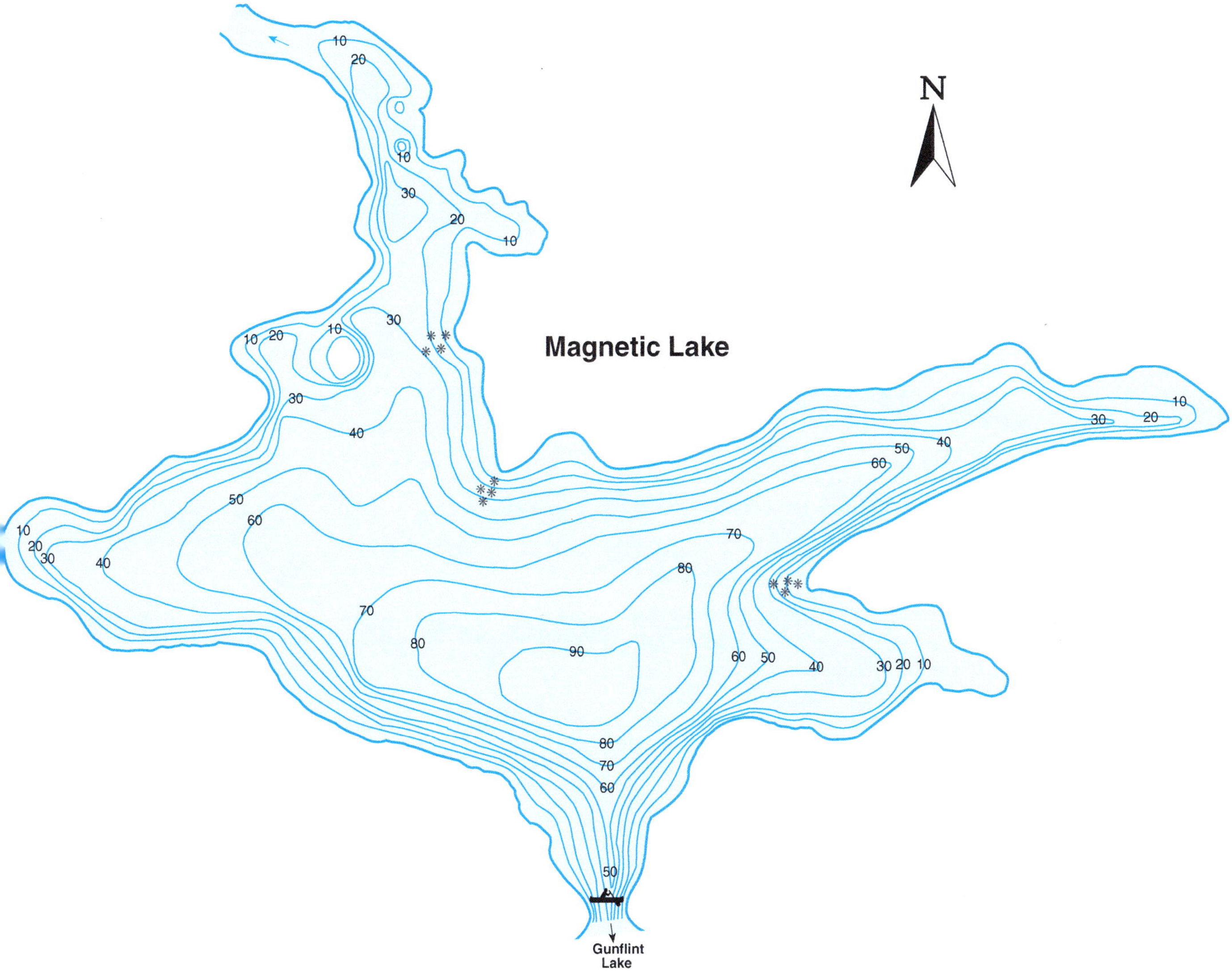

N
Magnetic Lake
Gunflint Lake

Little Gunflint Lake
17' Max
16'
11'
3'
Gunflint Lake

NOT FOR NAVIGATION

Source: Minnesota Department of Natural Resources, USGS

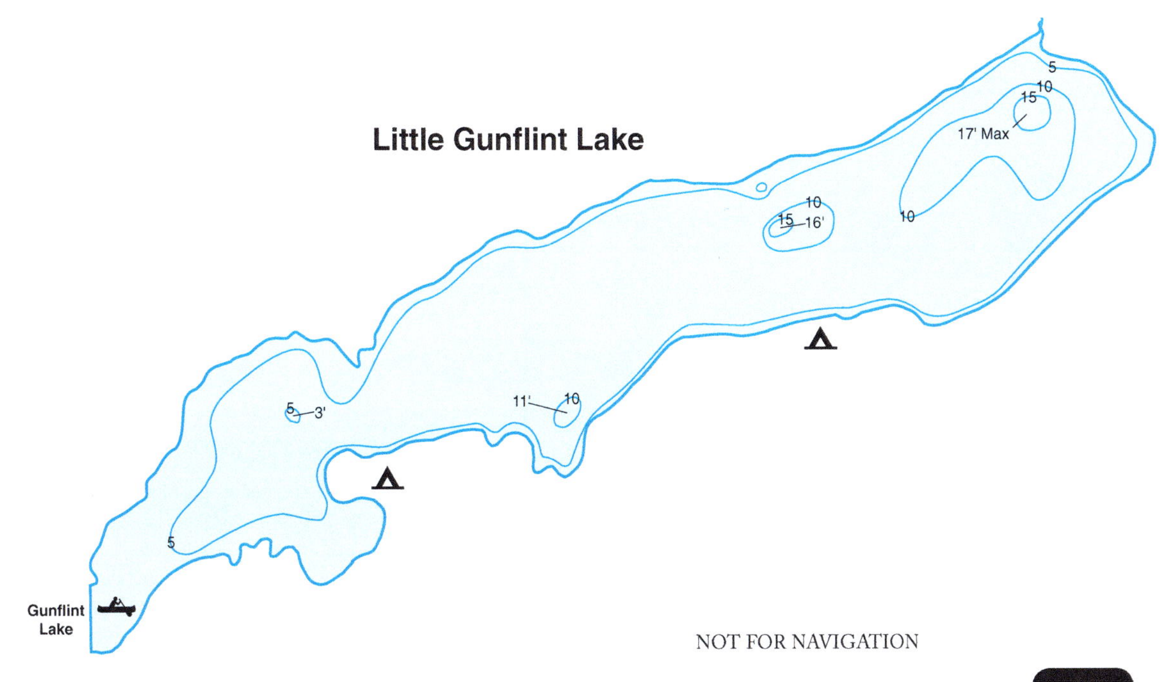

GUNFLINT LAKE *Cook County*

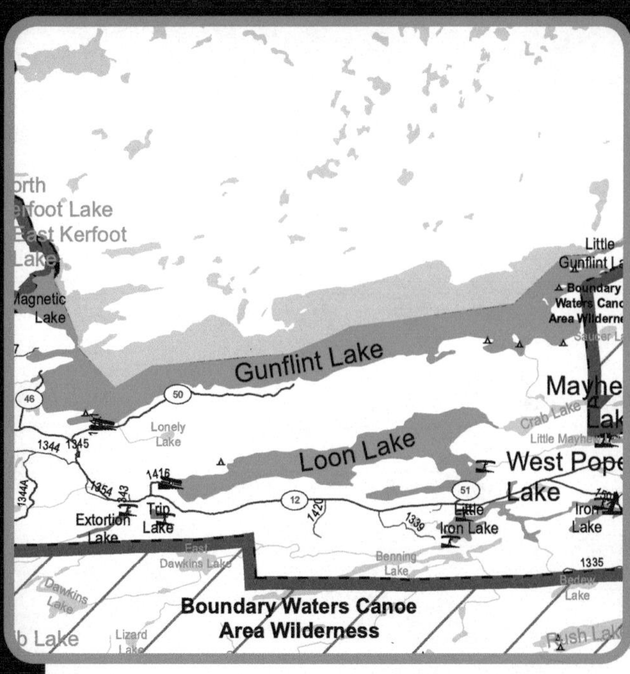

Area map page / coordinates: 9 / D-6 & 10 / D-1,2

Watershed: Rainy headwaters

Surface water area / shorelength: 4,009 acres / 18.0 miles

Maximum / mean depth: 200 feet / 99 feet

Water color / clarity: Light green / 16.0 ft. secchi (2011)

Shoreland zoning classification: Recreational development

Management class / Ecological type: Trout / trout

Accessibility: USFS-owned public access with concrete ramp on south shore of western lake; parking for 15 vehicles

90° 45' 18" W / 48° 5' 4" N

Accommodations: Resorts, boat rental, outfitters

FISHING INFORMATION

This is one of the most famous lakes in northern Minnesota, ranking right up there with Rainy, Lake of the Woods and of course, Lake Vermilion. It should be. Its fishery is excellent and it offers an outdoor experience that's usually remembered for a long, long while. It's a Canadian border lake, which means permits are required for entry and border water fishing regulations apply.

You'll find nice lake trout in this deep, 4,000-acre lake with good populations of walleyes and smallmouth bass. Lake trout numbers are on par for lakes of this type and fish are growing faster than average. This is likely attributed to the robust forage base the lake contains. The lake has a good population of older fish, which also equates to large fish.

Early in the season you can find these fish at the reefs and humps. So that's a good time to drag a cisco on a spinner at, say, 20 feet down, over structure. Later, you'll have to vertical jig the shorelines with ciscoes or "anything shiny," according to one local angler. Spoons trolled on downriggers is also a favored mid-season method.

Walleye numbers have been low, so for about the last decade, the DNR has been stocking fingerlings every few years. Walleyes have an excellent forage base consisting of rainbow smelt, ciscoes and a few yellow perch. For walleyes, try the wind-blown shorelines and points. Crankbaits in cisco patterns or minnows under a slip bobber will usually get some attention. You can also jig the breaks with a minnow or leech.

Smallies are fairly numerous, and there are some 2- and 3-pounders out there. There is certainly plenty of good rocky shoreline for these fish to inhabit. Small crankbaits or spinners will get some attention if tossed to the steep, rocky shorelines.

Northern pike are found in low numbers, like many similar deep, rocky Canadian Shield lake trout lakes. However, the ones you do find tend to be on the large side, due to the presence of rainbow smelt and tullibees. The trophy potential is certainly there.

FISH STOCKING DATA

year	species	size	# released
08	Walleye	Fingerling	67,939
11	Walleye	Fingerling	46,972
14	Walleye	Fingerling	51,157

NET CATCH DATA

Date: 8/22/2011

	Gill Nets		Trap Nets	
species	# per net	avg. fish weight (lbs.)	# per net	avg. fish weight (lbs
Burbot	0.50	1.03	-	-
Cisco Species	1.30	0.32	-	-
Lake Trout	1.00	3.46	-	-
Northern Pike	0.30	5.28	-	-
Rainbow Smelt	0.10	0.02	-	-
Smallmouth Bass	1.40	0.95	-	-
Walleye	3.25	1.16	-	-
White Sucker	1.55	2.00	-	-
Yellow Perch	0.15	0.13	-	-

LENGTH OF SELECTED SPECIES SAMPLED FROM ALL GEAR

Number of fish caught for the following length categories (inches):

species	0-5	6-8	9-11	12-14	15-19	20-24	25-29	>30	Total
Burbot	-	-	-	4	5	1	-	-	10
Cisco Species	-	4	18	4	-	-	-	-	26
Lake Trout	-	-	2	4	3	7	3	1	20
Northern Pike	-	-	-	-	-	2	1	3	6
Rainbow Smelt	2	-	-	-	-	-	-	-	2
Rock Bass	5	75	-	-	-	-	-	-	80
Smallmouth Bass	3	2	7	12	4	-	-	-	28
Walleye	-	-	6	39	17	1	2	-	65
White Sucker	-	-	4	9	15	3	-	-	31
Yellow Perch	-	3	-	-	-	-	-	-	3

An under-utilized fish species present in Gunflint Lake is the burbot or eelpout. These fish are probably most commonly caught by ice fishermen. They prefer to feed at night, and a large minnow fished on the bottom at the base of sharp breaks may draw strikes. Walleye anglers often catch them while jigging a spoon tipped with a minnow head as well. Although unsightly, eelpout are excellent table fare.

NOT FOR NAVIGATION

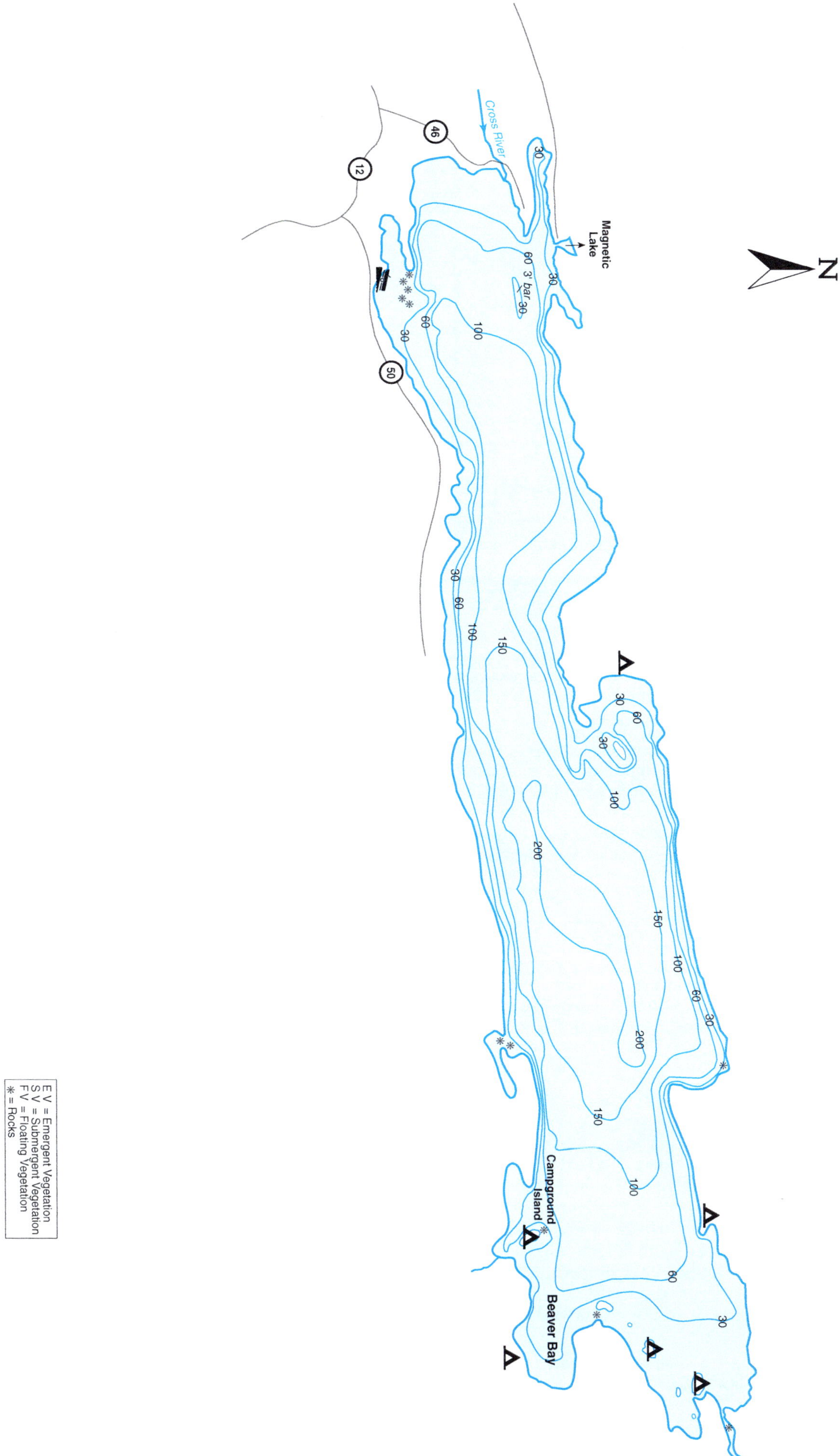
N
Cross River
46
12
50
Magnetic Lake
3' bar
Campground Island
Beaver Bay
30
60
100
150
200
E V = Emergent Vegetation
S V = Submergent Vegetation
F V = Floating Vegetation
✳ = Rocks

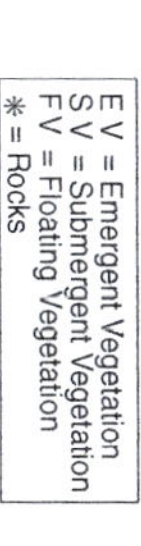

Source: Minnesota Department of Natural Resources, USGS

LOON LAKE Cook County

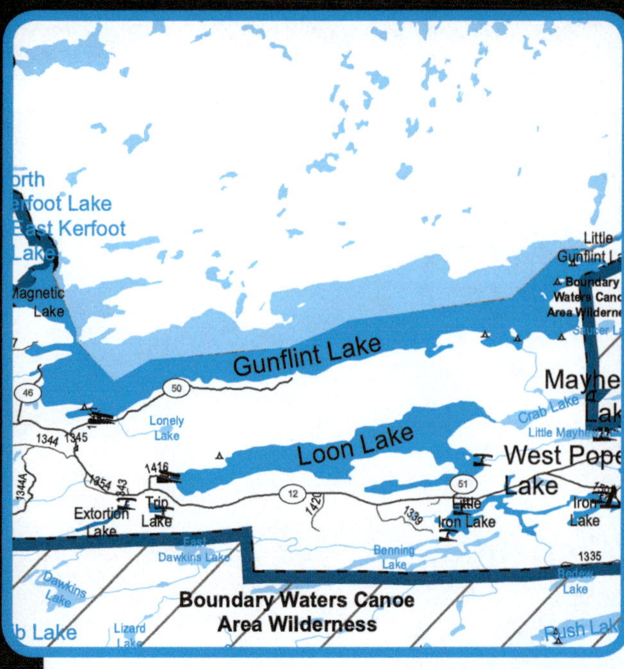

Area map page / coordinates: 10 / D-1,2

Watershed: Rainy headwaters

Surface water area / shorelength: 1,095 acres / 17.8 miles

Maximum / mean depth: 202 feet / 70 feet

Water color / clarity: Very clear / 19.8 ft. secchi (2011)

Shoreland zoning classification: Recreational development

Management class / Ecological type: Lake trout / trout

Accessibility: USFS-owned public access with concrete ramp on west shore, off the Gunflint Trail; parking for ten vehicles

90° 44' 14" W / 48° 4' 25" N

Accommodations: Resort, camping

FISHING INFORMATION

Loon Lake is in pretty wild country, only a couple of miles south of the Canadian border, just off the Gunflint Trail. Its 1,095 acres of crystal-clear water are home to a reasonably good fishery. Lake trout top the list, followed closely by walleyes, northern pike and smallmouth bass.

The lake trout and other gamefish feed on the cisco forage base, which helps them grow large. However, growth rates are below average, at least for young lake trout. The DNR believes this is because young lakers have to compete with a large tullibee populations for insect life in their early years, before their diet switches more heavily to fish. Despite that, locals say there are some real wall-hangers out there just waiting for someone to catch them. Unfortunately, as with any large fish, they can be tough to find and even harder to catch. The lake's infrequent humps **(Spot 1)** can be tried early in the year and again later in the fall. This large lake warms slowly, so it may be a while before the lake gets too warm. Then, try jigging the shoreline palisades. One local angler also says he just puts a cisco on the bottom off these steep cliffs and just lets it rest there all day in hopes that a laker will happen by.

Northern pike also get big in Loon. These fish are slow-growing and long-lived. Despite that, their average size remains high. To preserve this population of large northern pike, there is a 30-inch size limit on pike, with one allowed in the daily bag. Of course, releasing even legal fish is the best way to preserve this quality fishery. Try for jumbo northerns at the inlets and back bays in the spring **(Spots 2)** with ciscoes and suckers or large crankbaits. In the winter, place tip-ups in 4 to 12 feet of water, preferably along any weeds you can find. Use live bait early in the season, switching over to dead smelt or ciscoes as the season advances. In the summer, trolling crankbaits around schools of tullibee can produce trophy-sized fish.

Loon Lake walleyes aren't all that numerous, but the ones you find are often large. One local angler says a 16-1/2-pound specimen was caught here some years back and now resides on a nearby wall. He recommends trolling the shorelines and the bay on the lake's east end for walleyes.

Anglers can also find some smallmouth bass in Loon Lake. These fis grow very slowly, so don't expect to catch anything of even mediocre siz Their population is fairly low.

Ciscoes are found in Loon and many other area lakes. They are th primary forage species for the lake's large predators. However, they ca achieve sizes that are large enough to merit fishing for them as wel They are probably most often targeted through the ice. Look for then along drop-offs to deep slots or holes. They wander around, so eithe keep searching or plop down and wait for them to come to you. A goo technique is to fish them with a silver spoon above a small dropper ji and waxworm. These fish have small mouths and prey predominantly o aquatic insects, thus the small jig, but the spoon is necessary to call then in from long distances.

NO RECORD OF STOCKING

NET CATCH DATA

Date: 08/29/2011	Gill Nets		Trap Nets	
species	# per net	avg. fish weight (lbs.)	# per net	avg. fish weight (lbs
Bluegill	0.08	0.65	-	-
Cisco Species	6.67	0.38	-	-
Lake Trout	1.50	1.11	-	-
Northern Pike	0.58	5.67	-	-
Rock Bass	1.83	0.16	2.25	0.14
Smallmouth Bass	0.17	0.36	-	-
Walleye	0.17	3.41	-	-

LENGTH OF SELECTED SPECIES SAMPLED FROM ALL GEAR

Number of fish caught for the following length categories (inches):

species	0-5	6-8	9-11	12-14	15-19	20-24	25-29	>30	Total
Bluegill	-	-	1	-	-	-	-	-	1
Cisco Species	-	-	48	32	-	-	-	-	80
Lake Trout	-	-	2	9	7	-	-	-	18
Northern Pike	-	-	-	-	-	2	3	2	7
Rock Bass	25	23	-	-	-	-	-	-	48
Smallmouth Bass	-	1	1	-	-	-	-	-	2
Walleye	-	-	-	-	1	1	-	-	2

LOON LAKE

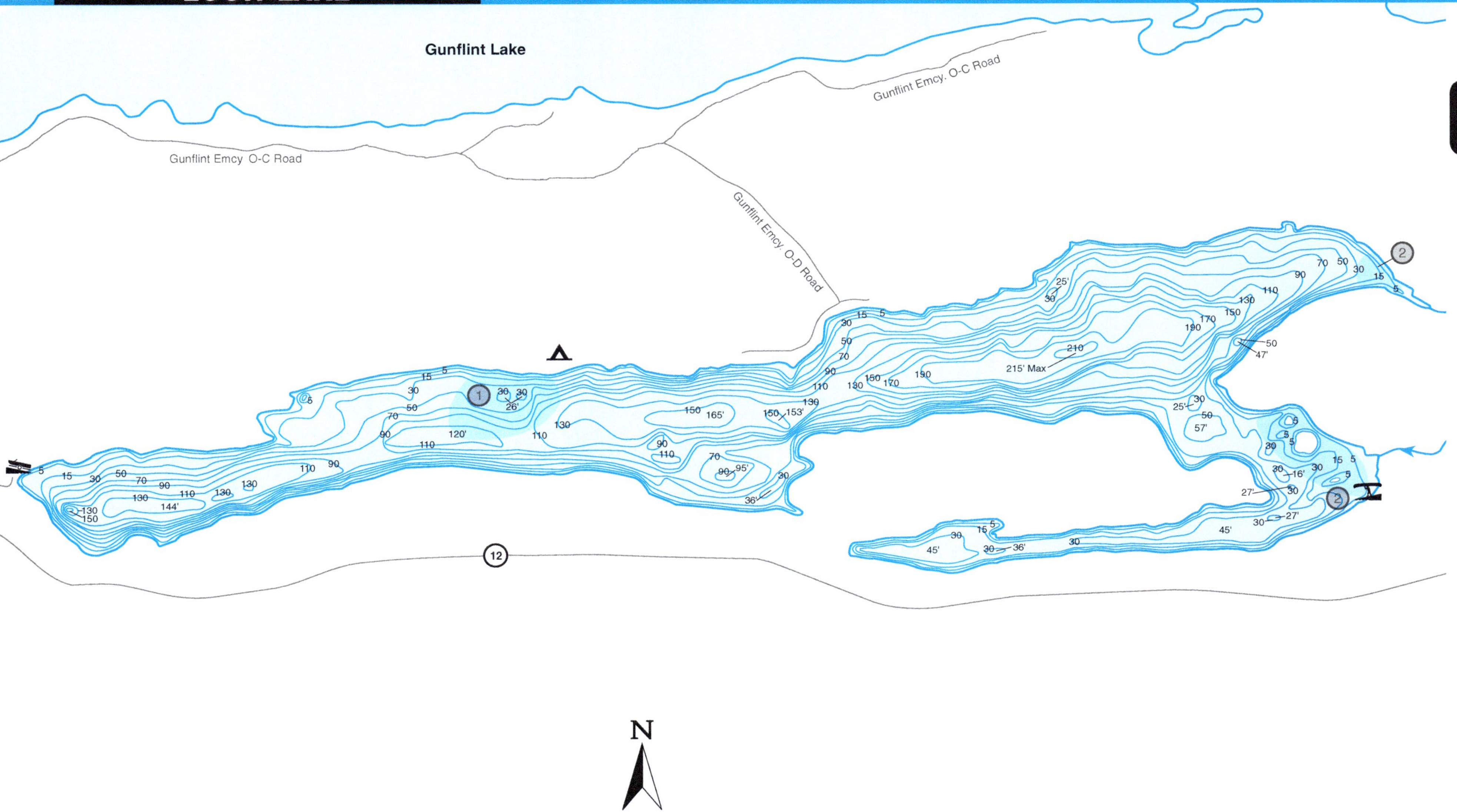

E V = Emergent Vegetation
S V = Submergent Vegetation
F V = Floating Vegetation

NOT FOR NAVIGATION

Little Iron Lake, Cook County

Area map page / coordinates: 10 / D,E-1,2
Surface area / max depth: 105 acres / 18 feet
Accessibility: Carry-down access to northeast corner; navigable channel from Iron Lake

FISH STOCKING DATA

year	species	size	# released
10	Walleye	Fingerling	2,530
12	Walleye	Fingerling	3,198
14	Walleye	Fingerling	4,034

LENGTH OF SELECTED SPECIES SAMPLED FROM ALL GEAR
Survey Date: 06/25/2012
Number of fish caught for the following length categories (inches):

species	0-5	6-8	9-11	12-14	15-19	20-24	25-29	>30	Total
Bluegill	11	2	3	-	-	-	-	-	16
Northern Pike	-	-	1	3	23	10	-	1	38
Splake	-	-	-	1	-	-	-	-	1
Yellow Perch	3	1	-	-	-	-	-	-	4

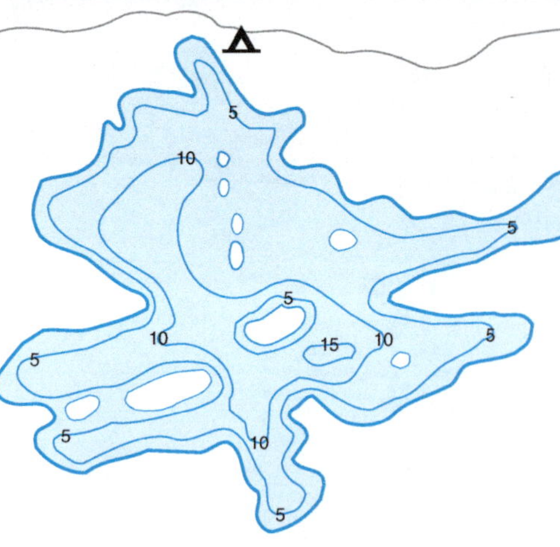

Little Iron Lake

Iron Lake, Cook County

Area map page / coordinates: 10 / D-2
Surface area / max depth: 125 acres / 19 feet
Accessibility: Steep, short carry-down from campground on north shore; portage from Portage Lake

FISH STOCKING DATA

year	species	size	# released
10	Walleye	Fingerling	2,482
12	Walleye	Fingerling	2,993
14	Walleye	Fingerling	3,624

LENGTH OF SELECTED SPECIES SAMPLED FROM ALL GEAR
Survey Date: 06/18/2012
Number of fish caught for the following length categories (inches):

species	0-5	6-8	9-11	12-14	15-19	20-24	25-29	>30	Total
Bluegill	18	3	-	-	-	-	-	-	21
Northern Pike	-	-	-	2	14	8	-	-	24
Walleye	-	-	-	-	-	-	1	-	1
Yellow Perch	4	1	-	-	-	-	-	-	5

Iron Lake

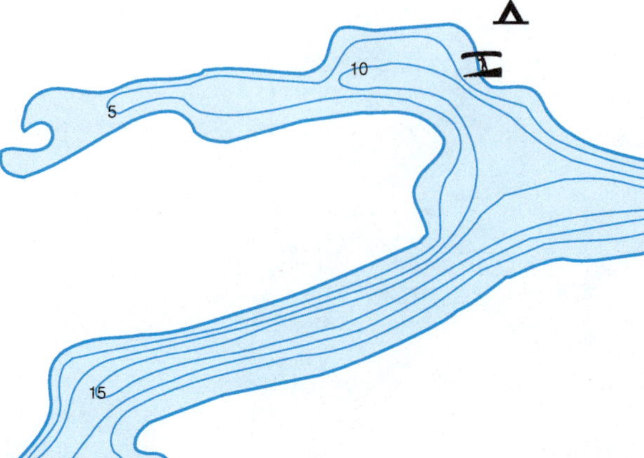

NOT FOR NAVIGATION

Source: Minnesota Department of Natural Resources, USGS

West Pope Lake

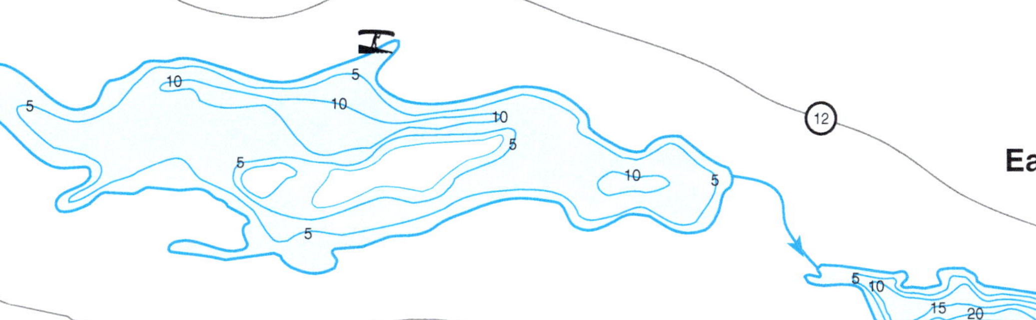

East Pope Lake

West Pope Lake, Cook County

Area map page / coordinates: 10 / D-2
Surface area / max depth: 71 acres / 14 feet
Accessibility: Carry-down access from Gunflint Trail to north shore

FISH STOCKING DATA

year	species	size	# released
00	Walleye	Fry	70,000
02	Walleye	Fingerling	1,189
04	Walleye	Fry	70,000
08	Walleye	Fry	70,000

LENGTH OF SELECTED SPECIES SAMPLED FROM ALL GEAR
Survey Date: 08/30/2004
Number of fish caught for the following length categories (inches):

species	0-5	6-8	9-11	12-14	15-19	20-24	25-29	>30	Total
Northern Pike	-	-	-	-	3	21	-	-	24
Walleye	-	-	2	-	10	3	-	-	15
Yellow Perch	4	8	-	-	-	-	-	-	12

East Pope Lake, Cook County

Area map page / coordinates: 10 / D-2
Surface area / max depth: 35 acres / 28 feet
Access: Carry-down access to south shore from Co. Rd. 92

FISH STOCKING DATA

year	species	size	# released
08	Walleye	Fingerling	2,043
11	Walleye	Fingerling	710
14	Walleye	Fingerling	1,260

LENGTH OF SELECTED SPECIES SAMPLED FROM ALL GEAR
Survey Date: 06/12/2013
Number of fish caught for the following length categories (inches):

species	0-5	6-8	9-11	12-14	15-19	20-24	25-29	>30	Total
Bluegill	-	1	1	-	-	-	-	-	2
Northern Pike	-	-	-	-	4	14	-	-	18
Smallmouth Bass	-	-	-	1	-	-	-	-	1
Walleye	-	-	-	-	2	2	-	-	4
Yellow Perch	-	1	-	-	-	-	-	-	1

Iron Lake

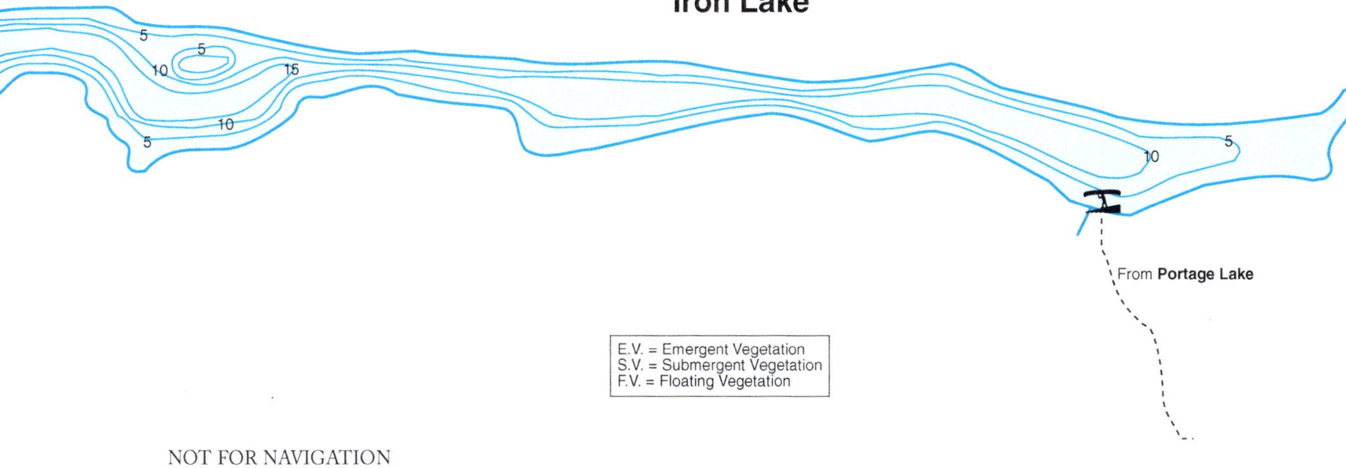

MAYHEW LAKE

Cook County

Area map pg / coord: 10 / D-2

Watershed: Rainy headwaters

Surface area: 221 acres

Shorelength: 4.9 miles

Max / mean depth: 84 feet / 33 feet

Water color / clarity: Clear / 18.0 ft. secchi (2009)

Shoreland zoning class: Rec. dev.

Mgmt class / Ecological type: Lake trout / trout

Accessibility: Carry-down access to southeast shore from FR 317; parking for two vehicles

Accommodations: None

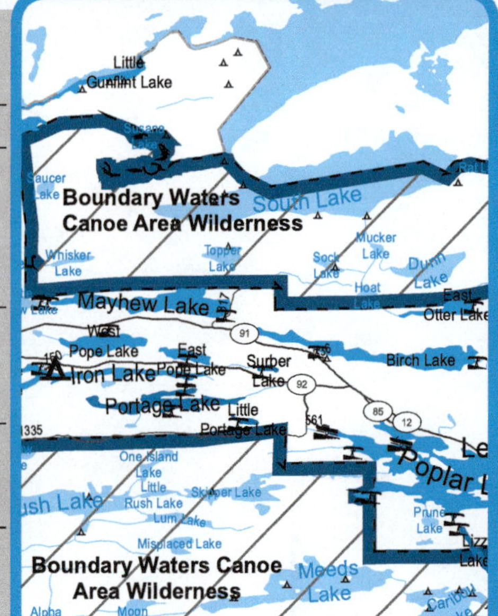

BIRCH LAKE

Cook County

Area map pg / coord: 10 / D-2,3

Watershed: Baptism-Brule

Surface area: 236 acres

Shorelength: 6.7 miles

Max / mean depth: 69 feet / 20 feet

Water color / clarity: NA / 17 ft. secchi (2012)

Shoreland zoning class: Rec. dev.

Mgmt class / Ecological type: Lake trout / trout

Accessibility: Carry-down access to southwest shore from scenic overlook on Gunflint Trail; parking for five vehicles

Accommodations: Resort

MAYHEW LAKE — FISH STOCKING DATA

year	species	size	# released
10	Brown Trout	Yearling	3,200
12	Brown Trout	Yearling	3,200
12	Lake Trout	Yearling	3,034
14	Brown Trout	Yearling	3,200
15	Lake Trout	Yearling	3,300

NET CATCH DATA

Date: 07/06/2009

species	Gill Nets: # per net	Gill Nets: avg. fish weight (lbs.)	Trap Nets: # per net	Trap Nets: avg. fish weight (lbs.)
Brown Trout	0.67	2.93	-	-
Green Sunfish	0.50	0.05	2.17	0.05
Lake Trout	3.33	1.79	-	-
Yellow Perch	1.83	0.08	2.17	0.08

LENGTH OF SELECTED SPECIES SAMPLED FROM ALL GEAR

Number of fish caught for the following length categories (inches):

species	0-5	6-8	9-11	12-14	15-19	20-24	25-29	>29	Total
Bluegill	3	-	-	-	-	-	-	-	3
Brown Trout	-	-	-	-	1	3	-	-	4
Green Sunfish	16	-	-	-	-	-	-	-	16
Lake Trout	-	10	3	3	-	-	3	1	20
Northern Pike	-	-	-	-	1	-	-	-	1
Yellow Perch	7	17	-	-	-	-	-	-	23

BIRCH LAKE — FISH STOCKING DATA

year	species	size	# released
08	Rainbow Trout	Yearling	3,500
09	Brook Trout	Yearling	4,980
10	Brook Trout	Yearling	1,692
10	Rainbow Trout	Yearling	3,199
11	Brook Trout	Yearling	5,206
12	Rainbow Trout	Yearling	5,000
13	Brook Trout	Yearling	5,000
14	Rainbow Trout	Yearling	5,018
15	Brook Trout	Yearling	4,107

NET CATCH DATA

Date: 09/04/2012

species	Gill Nets: # per net	Gill Nets: avg. fish weight (lbs.)	Trap Nets: # per net	Trap Nets: avg. fish weight (lbs.)
Brook Trout	0.44	1.23	-	-
Lake Trout	0.11	16.81	-	-
Rainbow Trout	4.78	1.14	-	-
Smallmouth Bass	0.22	0.52	-	-
White Sucker	2.67	3.12	-	-
White Sucker	2.00	2.80	-	-

LENGTH OF SELECTED SPECIES SAMPLED FROM ALL GEAR

Number of fish caught for the following length categories (inches):

species	0-5	6-8	9-11	12-14	15-19	20-24	25-29	>29	Total
Brook Trout	-	-	-	2	2	-	-	-	4
Lake Trout	-	-	-	-	-	-	-	1	1
Rainbow Trout	-	-	2	38	-	3	-	-	43
Smallmouth Bass	-	-	2	-	-	-	-	-	2
White Sucker	-	-	-	2	16	6	-	-	24

FISHING INFORMATION

Mayhew Lake's lake trout fishery consists of stocked fish from recent years as well as some naturally reproducing trout. The older fish were all naturally produced. The lake also has some large brown trout. The mid-lake hump is a good spot for early season lakers **(Spot 1).** Jigs work best in this location. When the water's still cold, troll the south shoreline, near the lake's east-end access **(Spot 2).** As the water warms, troll the depths with cowbells, spoons or crankbaits. The area around the cabin on the north-shore point can also produce. This lake also offers some winter lake trout action. The folks at Devil Track Resort say the small point that flanks the bay near mid-lake on the south shore produces well on occasion **(Spot 3).**

Birch Lake contains modest numbers of lake trout, which includes some of impressive size, according to the folks at Devil Track Resort, 205 Fireweed Lane, Grand Marais, MN 55604, (877) 387-9414. Low oxygen levels may restrict lake trout populations or eventually eliminate them entirely. The lake is managed for rainbow trout and brook trout. Rainbows are present in good numbers and are faring better than brookies. Stream trout are probably targeted most heavily during the winter. Small spoons tipped with waxworms fished near shoreline points can be effective. If you're trying for the remaining lakers, fish the shorelines early with crankbaits, heading deeper later in the season. Lakers can be found early on the lake's humps and reefs. The first is near the lake's eastern end, where the water shoals to less than 10 feet **(Spot 1).** Another area is along the south shore, about three-fourths of the way toward the east end **(Spot 2),** and a third spot is off the broad point on the north shore, about two-thirds of the way to the west end **(Spot 3).**

Access to Birch is a bit tough. There's a steep carry-down access from the Gunflint Trail.

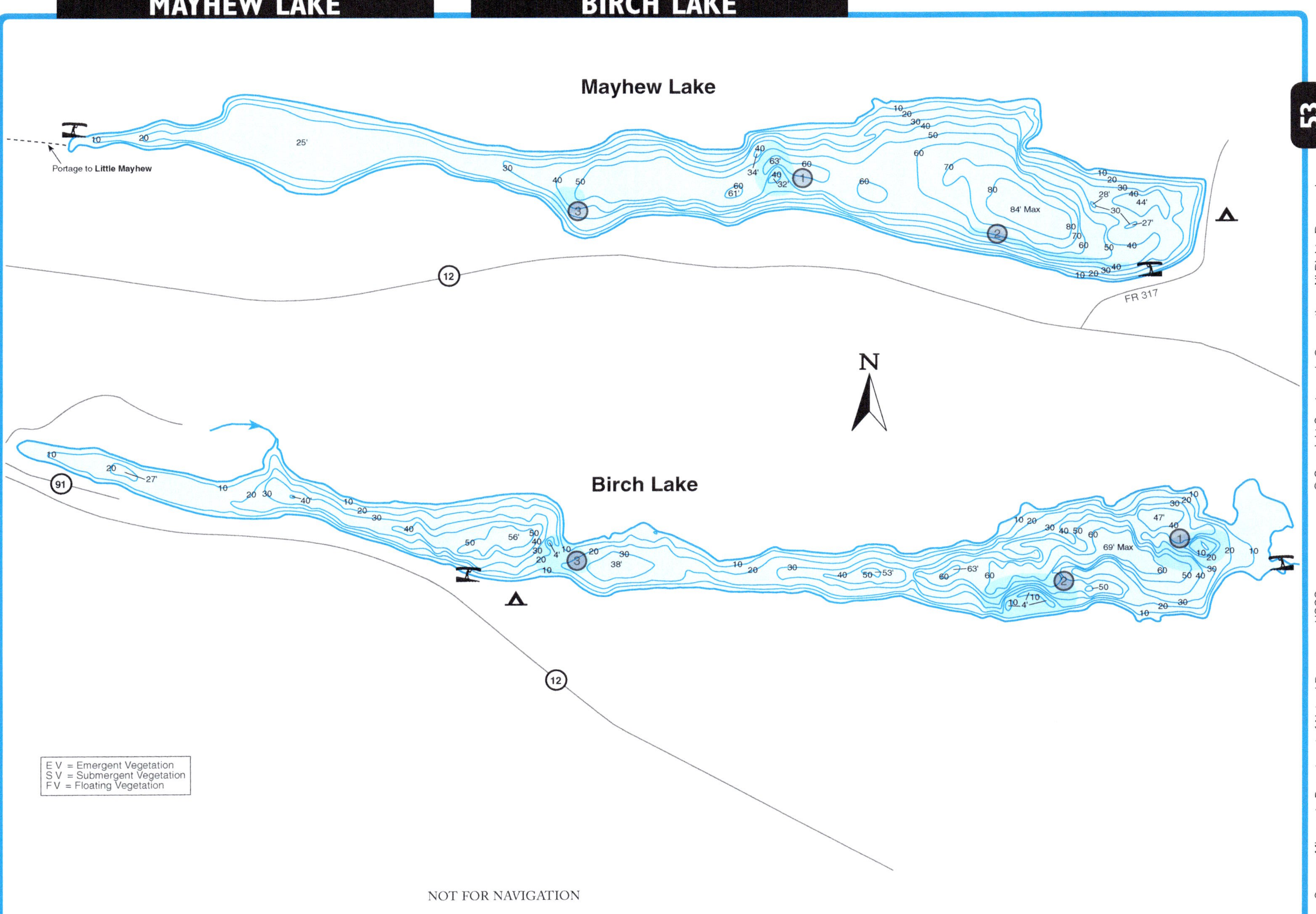
Mayhew Lake
Portage to Little Mayhew
84' Max
FR 317
N
Birch Lake
69' Max
E V = Emergent Vegetation
S V = Submergent Vegetation
F V = Floating Vegetation
NOT FOR NAVIGATION

East Otter Lake

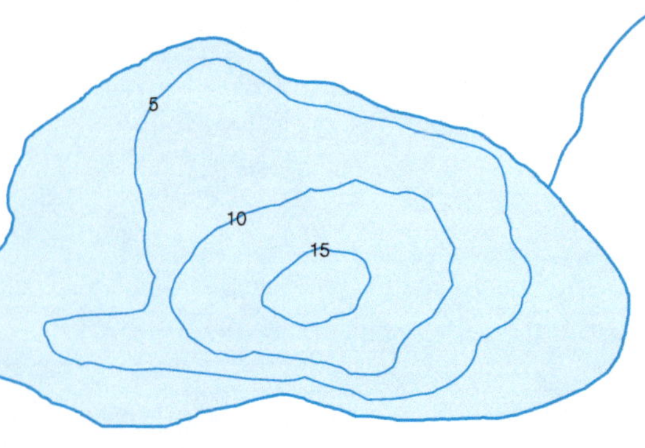

East Otter Lake, Cook County

Area map page / coordinates: 10 / D-3

Surface area / max depth: 46 acres / 15 feet

Accessibility: Carry-down access to east shore

NO RECORD OF STOCKING

LENGTH OF SELECTED SPECIES SAMPLED FROM ALL GEAR

Survey Date: 09/03/1986

Number of fish caught for the following length categories (inches):

species	0-5	6-8	9-11	12-14	15-19	20-24	25-29	>30	Total
Brook Trout	-	-	-	-	1	-	-	-	1

Moss Lake, Cook County

Area map page / coordinates: 10 / D-3

Surface area / max depth: 254 acres / 86 feet

Accessibility: Portage access to north shore from Duncan; portage access to west shore from Birch

FISH STOCKING DATA

year	species	size	# released
05	Lake Trout	Fingerling	10,271
08	Lake Trout	Fingerling	10,264
11	Lake Trout	Fingerling	10,182

LENGTH OF SELECTED SPECIES SAMPLED FROM ALL GEAR

Survey Date: 09/21/2009

Number of fish caught for the following length categories (inches):

species	0-5	6-8	9-11	12-14	15-19	20-24	25-29	>30	Total
Brook Trout	-	-	-	-	1	-	-	-	1
Lake Trout	-	2	3	4	24	1	-	-	34
Smallmouth Bass	1	5	1	-	-	-	-	-	7
Splake	-	-	-	-	1	-	-	-	1
White Sucker	-	-	1	-	3	2	-	-	6

From Duncan Lake

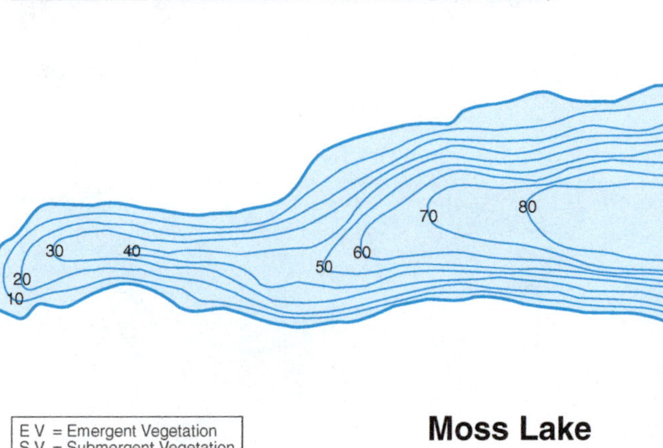

90 80 70 60 50 40 30 20 10

NOT FOR NAVIGATION

Source: Minnesota Department of Natural Resources, USGS

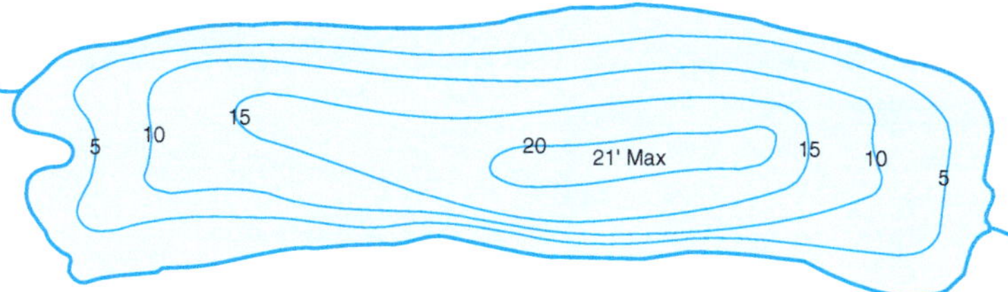

Surber Lake

Surber Lake, Cook County

Area map page / coordinates: 10 / D-2
Surface area / max depth: 7 acres / 21 feet
Access: Carry-down access to south shore from Co. Rd. 92

FISH STOCKING DATA

year	species	size	# released
10	Brook Trout	Fingerling	713
11	Brook Trout	Fingerling	500
12	Brook Trout	Fingerling	500
13	Brook Trout	Fingerling	500
14	Brook Trout	Fingerling	648
15	Brook Trout	Fingerling	500

LENGTH OF SELECTED SPECIES SAMPLED FROM ALL GEAR
Survey Date: 10/03/2011
Number of fish caught for the following length categories (inches):

species	0-5	6-8	9-11	12-14	15-19	20-24	25-29	>30	Total
Brook Trout	-	-	7	5	-	-	-	-	12

Portage Lake

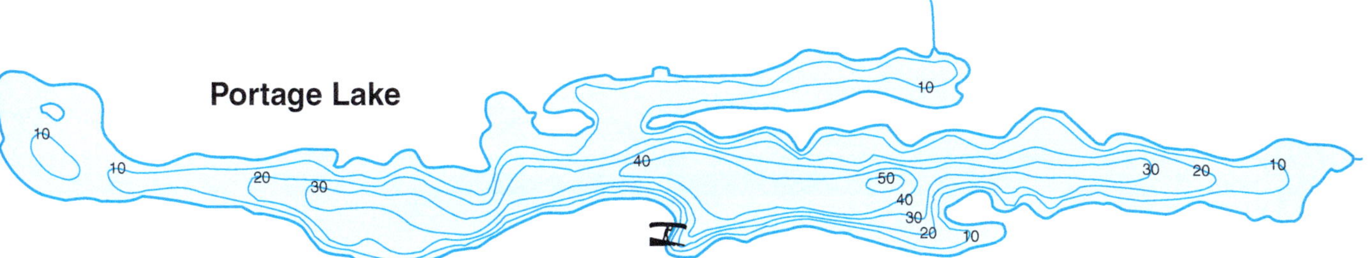

Portage Lake, Cook County

Area map page / coordinates: 10 / D,E-2
Surface area / max depth: 128 acres / 55 feet
Accessibility: Portage access to north shore from Iron; portage access to south shore from One Island

FISH STOCKING DATA

year	species	size	# released
08	Splake	Fingerling	6,000
09	Splake	Fingerling	6,000
09	Brook Trout	Fingerling	500
10	Splake	Fingerling	6,000
11	Splake	Fingerling	8,000
13	Splake	Fingerling	7,175
15	Splake	Fingerling	8,000

LENGTH OF SELECTED SPECIES SAMPLED FROM ALL GEAR
Survey Date: 06/02/2010
Number of fish caught for the following length categories (inches):

species	0-5	6-8	9-11	12-14	15-19	20-24	25-29	>30	Total
Splake	1	3	4	3	1	-	-	-	12
White Sucker	-	14	60	27	6	-	-	-	107

N

Little Portage Lake, Cook County

Area map page / coordinates: 10 / E-2
Surface area / max depth: 10 acres / 27 feet
Accessibility: Portage to west shore from Poplar Lake access road; portage from logging road off Poplar Lake landing

FISH STOCKING DATA

year	species	size	# released
Annual	Brook Trout	Fingerling	~ 500

LENGTH OF SELECTED SPECIES SAMPLED FROM ALL GEAR
Survey Date: 06/18/2014
Number of fish caught for the following length categories (inches):

species	0-5	6-8	9-11	12-14	15-19	20-24	25-29	>30	Total
Brook Trout	-	1	5	7	-	-	-	-	13
Green Sunfish	1	-	-	-	-	-	-	-	1
White Sucker	-	-	1	3	1	-	-	-	5

Little Portage Lake

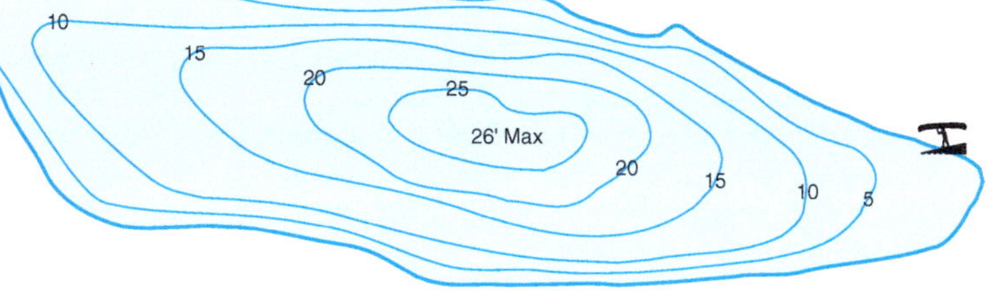

E V = Emergent Vegetation
S V = Submergent Vegetation
F V = Floating Vegetation
⁎ = Rocks

NOT FOR NAVIGATION

SURBER LAKE · PORTAGE LAKE · LITTLE PORTAGE LAKE

POPLAR LAKE

Cook County

Area map pg / coord: 10 / E-2,3
Watershed: Baptism-Brule
Surface area: 764 acres
Shorelength: 20.1 miles
Max / mean depth: 73 feet / 20 feet
Water color / clarity: Light green tint / 10.4 ft. secchi (2012)
Shoreland zoning class: Rec. dev.
Mgmt class / Ecological type: Walleye / trout
Accessibility: Public access with concrete ramp on west shore
1) 90° 32' 38" W / 48° 3' 19" N
Accommodations: Resort, outfitters

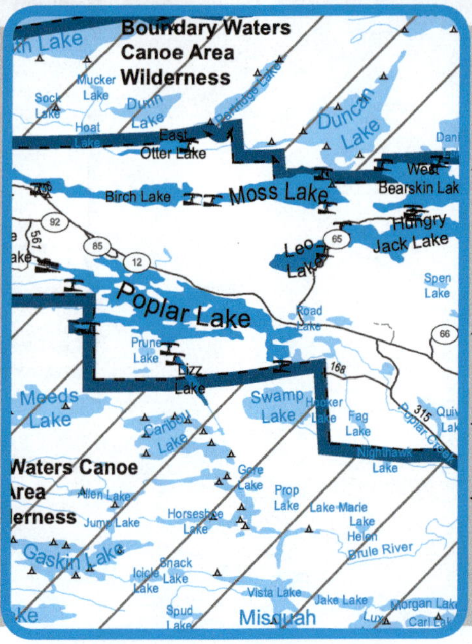

FISH STOCKING DATA

year	species	size	# released
08	Walleye	Adult	15
08	Walleye	Fingerling	14,404
11	Walleye	Fingerling	10,138
13	Walleye	Fingerling	16,351
15	Walleye	Fingerling	10,428

NET CATCH DATA

Date: 07/09/2012	Gill Nets		Trap Nets	
species	# per net	avg. fish weight (lbs.)	# per net	avg. fish weight (lbs.)
Black Crappie	0.12	0.68	0.75	0.14
Burbot	0.69	1.23	-	-
Lake Whitefish	2.06	0.84	-	-
Northern Pike	1.00	1.23	0.33	1.79
Pumpkinseed	0.06	0.02	0.17	0.11
Smallmouth Bass	-	-	0.17	1.74
Walleye	0.31	1.00	0.50	0.67
White Sucker	2.06	2.00	0.33	1.78
Yellow Perch	0.12	0.09	0.08	0.08

LENGTH OF SELECTED SPECIES SAMPLED FROM ALL GEAR

Number of fish caught for the following length categories (inches):

species	0-5	6-8	9-11	12-14	15-19	20-24	25-29	>29	Total
Black Crappie	6	2	3	-	-	-	-	-	11
Burbot	-	-	-	3	6	2	-	-	11
Lake Whitefish	-	2	11	9	11	-	-	-	33
Northern Pike	-	-	-	9	5	5	1	-	20
Pumpkinseed	2	1	-	-	-	-	-	-	3
Smallmouth Bass	-	-	-	1	1	-	-	-	2
Walleye	-	1	1	7	2	-	-	-	11
White Sucker	-	4	7	5	17	4	-	-	37
Yellow Perch	1	2	-	-	-	-	-	-	3

FISHING INFORMATION

Poplar Lake holds respectable populations of walleyes and northern pike. However, despite stocking, average walleye numbers are low for a lake of this type. The DNR is trying to fix this, but it appears lack of forage may be a limiting factor. Perhaps that means the fish are willing to bite? Northern pike numbers weren't overly high and their size was small. Smallmouth bass numbers were low, although anglers report decent smallie fishing. There are some crappies worth fishing for here. They are slow-growing, but some live long enough to reach keeper size. Anglers may also tie into a lake whitefish for the smoker. Some netting of this species is done in the fall.

LIZZ LAKE

Cook County

Area map pg / coord: 10 / E-3
Watershed: Baptism-Brule
Surface area: 23 acres
Shorelength: NA
Max / mean depth: 30 feet / NA
Water color / clarity: Clear / 8.5 ft. secchi (2013)
Shoreland zoning class: NA
Mgmt class / Ecological type: NA
Accessibility: Portage access to north shore from Poplar Lake
Accommodations: None

FISH STOCKING DATA

year	species	size	# released
06	Brook Trout	Fingerling	1,300
07	Brook Trout	Fingerling	1,300
08	Brook Trout	Fingerling	1,300
09	Brook Trout	Fingerling	1,300
10	Brook Trout	Fingerling	1,300
11	Brook Trout	Fingerling	1,300
12	Brook Trout	Fingerling	1,300

NET CATCH DATA

Date: 10/03/2013	Gill Nets		Trap Nets	
species	# per net	avg. fish weight (lbs.)	# per net	avg. fish weight (lbs.)
Brook Trout	0.50	4.21	-	-
Northern Pike	3.00	2.64	-	-
White Sucker	1.00	0.94	-	-
Yellow Perch	1.5	0.18	-	-

LENGTH OF SELECTED SPECIES SAMPLED FROM ALL GEAR

Number of fish caught for the following length categories (inches):

species	0-5	6-8	9-11	12-14	15-19	20-24	25-29	>29	Total
Brook Trout	-	-	-	-	1	-	-	-	1
Northern Pike	-	-	-	-	1	5	-	-	6
White Sucker	-	-	1	1	-	-	-	-	2

Lizz Lake was reclaimed as a brook trout lake back in the mid-1980s and for years had been managed as such. However, northern pike made their way into the lake, evidently from Caribou Lake. They pretty much devoured all the brookies and in the last DNR sampling, only one large brook trout was found, as well as several northern pike. It appears the pike may already be reproducing. The DNR reports that it would be foolish to just keep feeding the pike by stocking the lake with more brook trout, so that program has been discontinued. Because the lake is partly in the Boundary Waters, the DNR says it likely will not poison the lake again to manage it as a trout fishery. Rather, it appears the lake may go back to its natural state. The lake originally held walleyes, northern pike, suckers and perch. The DNR suspects if pike could make it back, perhaps walleyes will in time as well. As of this writing, the DNR was going to revise its management plan for Lizz Lake. So the current status of the fishery, as well as its future, is a mystery.

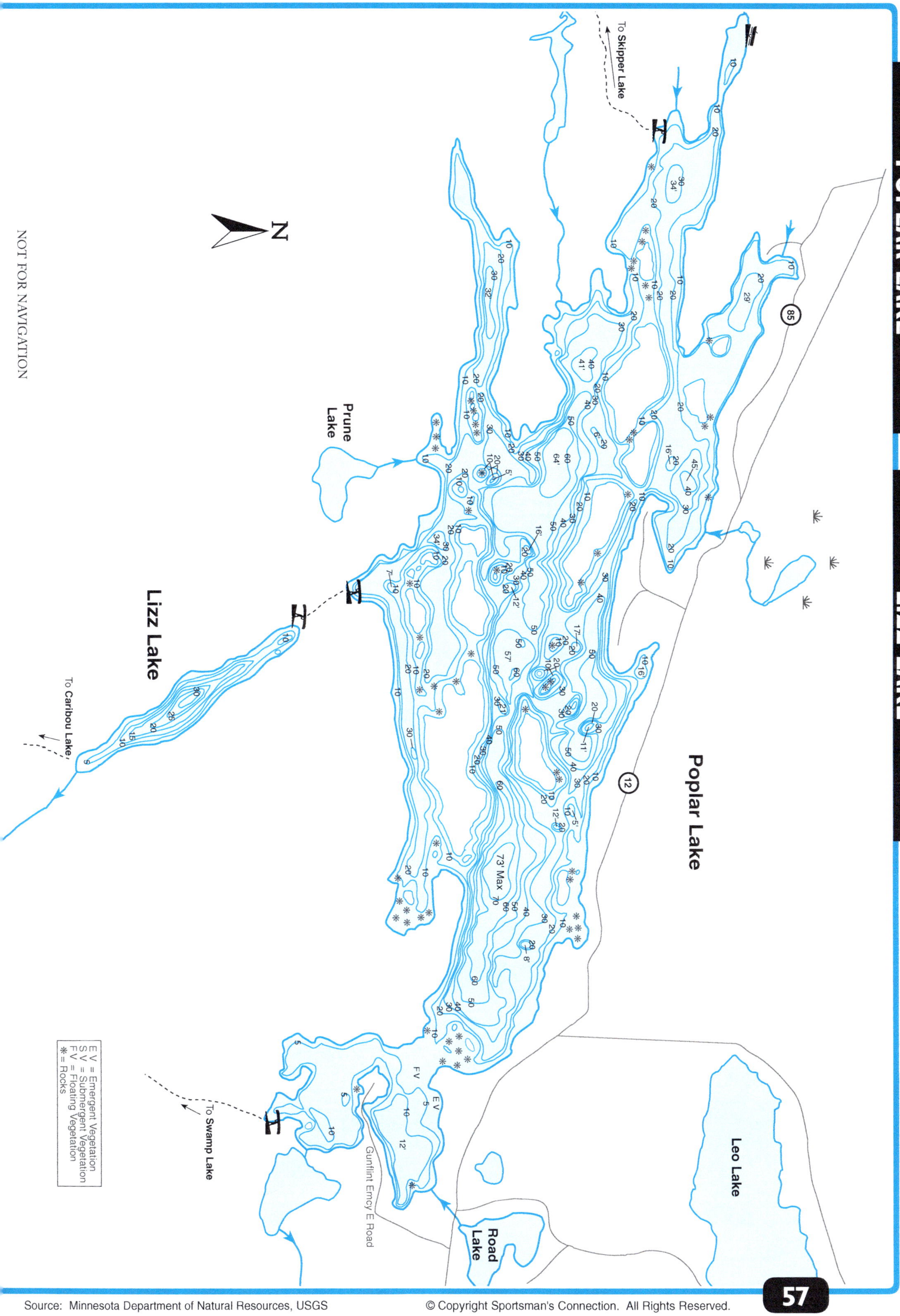

POPLAR LAKE

LIZZ LAKE

NOT FOR NAVIGATION

N

Poplar Lake

Lizz Lake

Prune Lake

Leo Lake

Road Lake

To Skipper Lake

To Caribou Lake

To Swamp Lake

Gunflint Emcy E Road

85

12

73' Max

EV = Emergent Vegetation
SV = Submergent Vegetation
FV = Floating Vegetation
✳ = Rocks

Source: Minnesota Department of Natural Resources, USGS

WEST BEARSKIN LAKE

Cook County

Area map pg/coord: 10/D-3 & 11/D-4

Watershed: Baptism-Brule

Surface area: 493 acres

Shorelength: 7.2 miles

Max / mean depth: 78 feet / 25 feet

Water color / clarity: Clear / 15.0 ft. secchi (2008)

Shoreland zoning class: Rec. dev.

Mgmt class / Ecological type: Lake trout / trout

Accessibility: State-owned public access with gravel ramp on northeast shore; parking for four vehicles

90° 23' 54" W / 48° 3' 53" N

Accommodations: Resort, camping

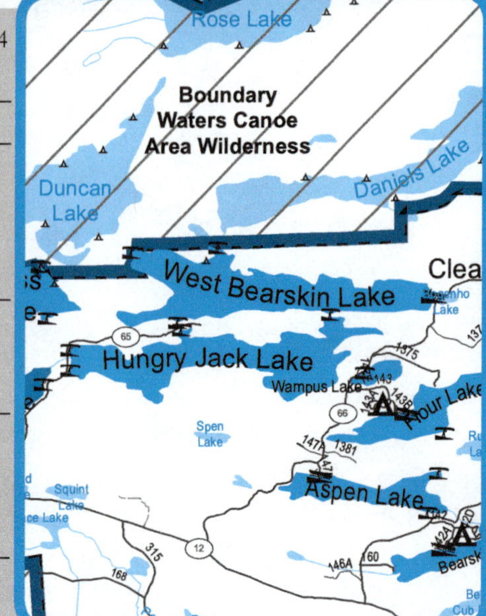

HUNGRY JACK LAKE

Cook County

Area map pg / coord: 10 / D,E-3,4

Watershed: Baptism-Brule

Surface area: 468 acres

Shorelength: 7.8 miles

Max / mean depth: 71 feet / 20 feet

Water color / clarity: Clear / 12.0 ft. secchi (2012)

Shoreland zoning class: Rec. dev.

Mgmt class / Ecological type: Walleye / trout

Accessibility: Carry-down access to small bay on north shore off Co. Rd. 65; carry-down access to west shore off Co. Rd. 65

Accommodations: Resort, outfitter

West Bearskin Lake

FISH STOCKING DATA

year	species	size	# released
05	Lake Trout	Yearling	2,575
05	Lake Trout	Yearling	2,594
07	Lake Trout	Yearling	2,579
07	Lake Trout	Yearling	2,550
09	Lake Trout	Yearling	2,527
09	Lake Trout	Yearling	2,574

NET CATCH DATA

Date: 08/25/2008

	Gill Nets		Trap Nets	
species	# per net	avg. fish weight (lbs.)	# per net	avg. fish weight (lbs.)
Bluegill	-	-	1.50	0.13
Green Sunfish	1.22	0.07	1.33	0.11
Lake Trout	3.44	2.39	-	-
Northern Pike	0.22	7.06	-	-
Rainbow Smelt	7.11	0.10	-	-
Smallmouth Bass	0.78	0.87	0.92	0.81
White Sucker	0.11	2.36	-	-

LENGTH OF SELECTED SPECIES SAMPLED FROM ALL GEAR

Number of fish caught for the following length categories (inches):

species	0-5	6-8	9-11	12-14	15-19	20-24	25-29	>29	Total
Bluegill	11	6	-	-	-	-	-	-	17
Green Sunfish	22	2	-	-	-	-	-	-	24
Lake Trout	-	-	-	-	16	15	-	-	31
Northern Pike	-	-	-	-	-	1	-	1	2
Smallmouth Bass	-	4	9	2	3	-	-	-	18
White Sucker	-	-	-	-	1	-	-	-	1

Hungry Jack Lake

FISH STOCKING DATA

year	species	size	# released
07	Walleye	Fingerling	13,107
07	Walleye	Yearling	239
09	Walleye	Fingerling	9,475
11	Walleye	Fingerling	6,241
13	Walleye	Fingerling	11,155
15	Walleye	Fingerling	6,993

NET CATCH DATA

Date: 07/09/2012

	Gill Nets		Trap Nets	
species	# per net	avg. fish weight (lbs.)	# per net	avg. fish weight (lbs.)
Bluegill	0.25	0.08	6.50	0.13
Hybrid Sunfish	-	-	0.50	0.19
Northern Pike	0.38	6.39	-	-
Pumpkinseed	-	-	0.42	0.15
Rainbow Smelt	0.50	0.10	-	-
Smallmouth Bass	0.12	0.42	0.33	0.83
Walleye	1.75	1.39	0.33	1.21
White Sucker	1.00	2.54	-	-
Yellow Perch	2.12	0.12	0.75	0.09

LENGTH OF SELECTED SPECIES SAMPLED FROM ALL GEAR

Number of fish caught for the following length categories (inches):

species	0-5	6-8	9-11	12-14	15-19	20-24	25-29	>29	Total
Bluegill	54	26	-	-	-	-	-	-	80
Green Sunfish	20	2	-	-	-	-	-	-	22
Hybrid Sunfish	3	3	-	-	-	-	-	-	6
Northern Pike	-	-	-	-	-	-	1	2	3
Pumpkinseed	2	3	-	-	-	-	-	-	5
Rainbow Smelt	-	4	-	-	-	-	-	-	4
Smallmouth Bass	2	-	2	-	1	-	-	-	5
Walleye	-	2	-	8	7	1	-	-	18
White Sucker	-	-	-	1	6	1	-	-	8
Yellow Perch	10	16	-	-	-	-	-	-	26

FISHING INFORMATION

West Bearskin offers good fishing for lake trout, but also has smallmouth bass, northern pike and some panfish. Lake trout grow faster than average here, thanks to a diet of rainbow smelt, and their numbers are consistently higher than most lakes of this type. Fish the lakers primarily early in the year. Try the humps along the north shore, east of the small islands in the lake's center **(Spot 1)**. In summer, look for lake trout along breaklines in deep water. Trolling spoons with downriggers is probably the best way to cover water and find fish. The two islands at the lake's center offer good angling opportunities for smallies **(Spot 2)**.

Hungry Jack, named for a survey crewman who ran short of food while at the lake, is known for walleyes and smallmouth bass. Walleyes are generally small. The DNR has amped up the stocking program a bit in an attempt to improve walleye numbers. One local angler says you can do pretty well for 'eyes 14 inches or larger. Recommended walleye spots include the humps in the lake's eastern lobe. These can be worked successfully with a jig/minnow or jig/leech combination. The DNR is trying to improve the smallmouth bass fishing here as well. There is now a special regulation in place that protects smallies from 12 to 20 inches. One bass over 20 inches is allowed. Few lakes in Cook County have much of a bluegill population, but Hungry Jack is an exception to the rule. Pike are found in low numbers, but when found, they're often large.

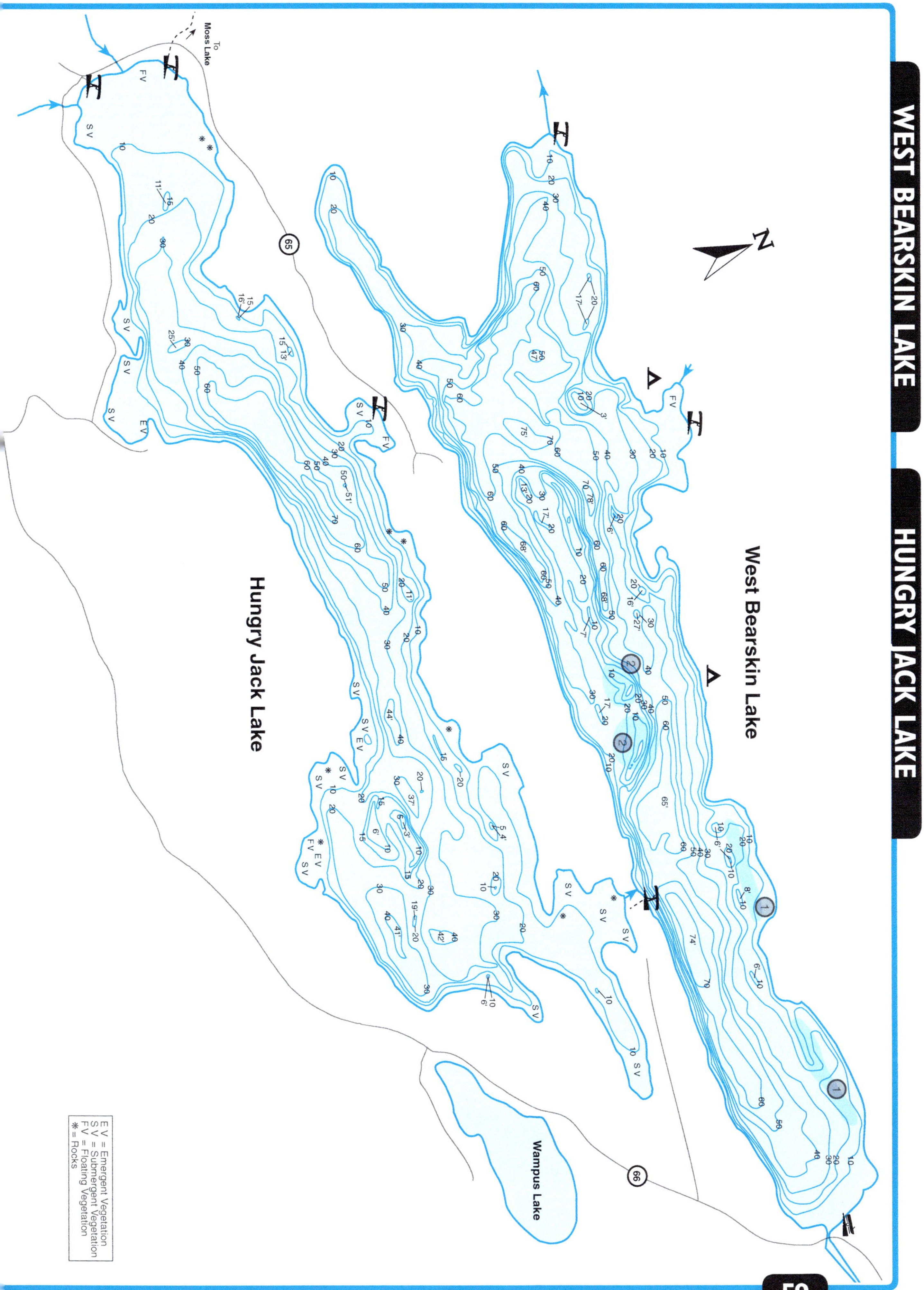

West Bearskin Lake

Hungry Jack Lake

Wampus Lake

To Moss Lake

65

66

E V = Emergent Vegetation
S V = Submergent Vegetation
F V = Floating Vegetation
✱ = Rocks

Source: Minnesota Department of Natural Resources, USGS

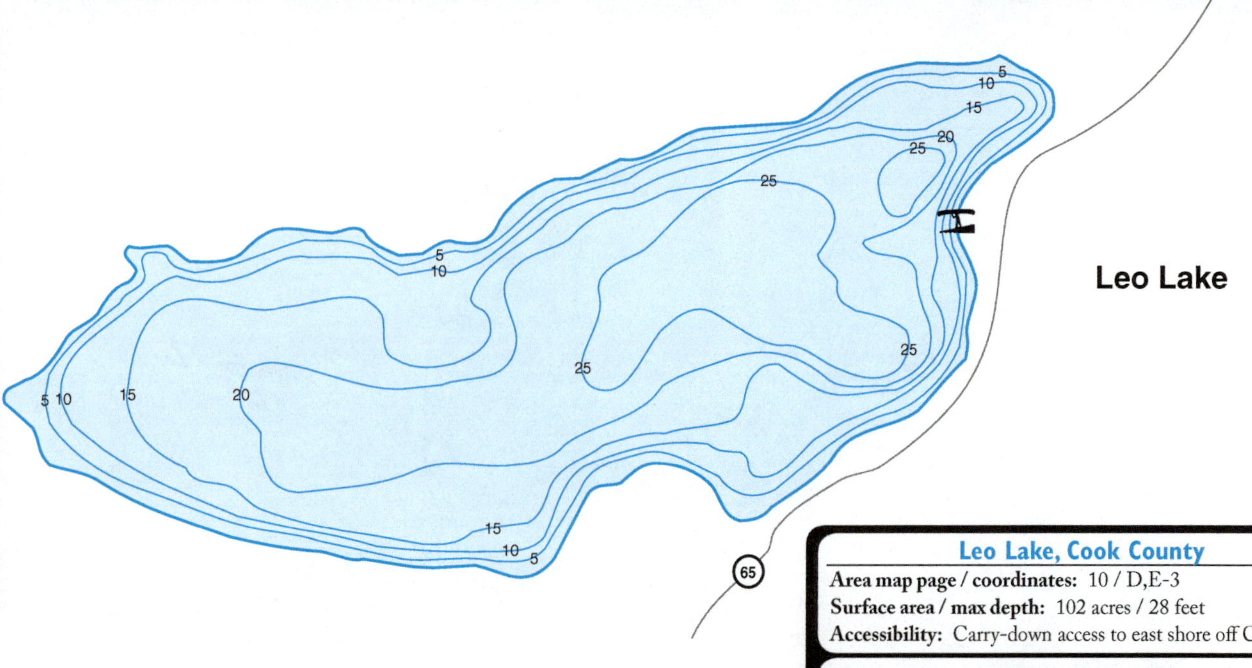

Leo Lake, Cook County

Area map page / coordinates: 10 / D,E-3
Surface area / max depth: 102 acres / 28 feet
Accessibility: Carry-down access to east shore off Co. Rd. 65

FISH STOCKING DATA

year	species	size	# released
07	Rainbow Trout	Yearling	5,000
08	Rainbow Trout	Yearling	5,000
09	Rainbow Trout	Yearling	5,000
10	Rainbow Trout	Yearling	4,997
11	Rainbow Trout	Yearling	5,000
12	Rainbow Trout	Yearling	5,000
13	Rainbow Trout	Yearling	5,009
14	Rainbow Trout	Yearling	5,730
15	Rainbow Trout	Yearling	2,855
15	Rainbow Trout	Yearling	2,145

LENGTH OF SELECTED SPECIES SAMPLED FROM ALL GEAR

Survey Date: 09/24/2010

Number of fish caught for the following length categories (inches):

species	0-5	6-8	9-11	12-14	15-19	20-24	25-29	>30	Total
Green Sunfish	12	-	-	-	-	-	-	-	12
Rainbow Trout	-	-	4	13	1	-	-	-	18
Smallmouth Bass	-	-	-	1	-	-	-	-	1
Walleye	-	-	1	-	3	4	1	-	9

Wampus Lake, Cook County

Area map page / coordinates: 11 / D,E-4
Surface area / max depth: 30 acres / 18 feet
Accessibility: Carry-down access to west shore from Co. Rd. 66; parking for two vehicles

FISH STOCKING DATA

year	species	size	# released
09	Bluegill	Adult	1,000
15	Black Crappie	Adult	418

LENGTH OF SELECTED SPECIES SAMPLED FROM ALL GEAR

Survey Date: 07/02/2012

Number of fish caught for the following length categories (inches):

species	0-5	6-8	9-11	12-14	15-19	20-24	25-29	>30	Total
Black Crappie	-	2	-	-	-	-	-	-	2
Largemouth Bass	-	-	1	-	-	-	-	-	1
Northern Pike	-	-	-	-	-	1	2	-	3
Yellow Perch	19	22	-	-	-	-	-	-	41

66

18' Max

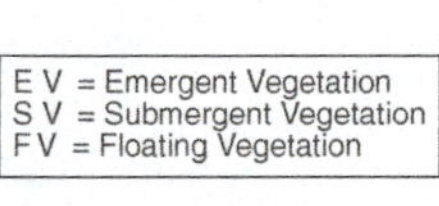

NOT FOR NAVIGATION

Source: Minnesota Department of Natural Resources, USGS

Area map page / coordinates: 11 / D-4,5,6

Watershed: Baptism-Brule

Surface water area / shorelength: 1,344 acres / 16.8 miles

Maximum / mean depth: 130 feet / 42 feet

Water color / clarity: Clear / 23 ft. secchi (2014)

Shoreland zoning classification: Recreational development

Management class / Ecological type: Lake trout / trout

Accessibility: USFS-owned public access with gravel ramp on north shore off Co. Rd. 66; parking for 10 vehicles

90° 22' 3" W / 48° 4' 30" N

Accommodations: Resort, outfitter, camping, picnicking

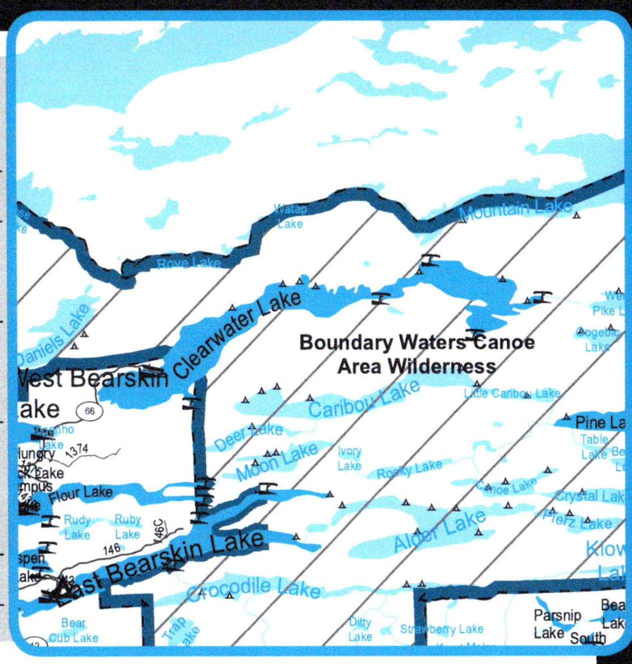

NO RECORD OF STOCKING

NET CATCH DATA

Date: 07/21/2014

species	Gill Nets # per net	Gill Nets avg. fish weight (lbs.)	Trap Nets # per net	Trap Nets avg. fish weight (lbs.)
Burbot	0.19	4.09	-	-
Cisco Species	8.56	0.42	-	-
Lake Trout	2.94	2.17	-	-
Smallmouth Bass	0.31	1.12	0.33	0.33
White Sucker	1.50	1.74	0.25	1.79
Yellow Perch	2.69	0.18	-	-

LENGTH OF SELECTED SPECIES SAMPLED FROM ALL GEAR

Number of fish caught for the following length categories (inches):

species	0-5	6-8	9-11	12-14	15-19	20-24	25-29	>30	Total
Burbot	-	-	-	-	1	1	-	1	3
Cisco Species	-	1	10	95	31	-	-	-	137
Green Sunfish	7	2	-	-	-	-	-	-	9
Lake Trout	-	-	5	5	31	3	-	3	47
Smallmouth Bass	-	2	4	1	2	-	-	-	9
White Sucker	-	-	-	11	15	1	-	-	27
Yellow Perch	1	36	4	2	-	-	-	-	43

FISHING INFORMATION

Located just south of the U.S.-Canadian border, this long, narrow body of water is a destination fishing lake in northern Minnesota. Lake trout are the foremost draw, and a trip with a guide on this 1,344-acre lake is one of the hottest tickets in the Northland. One look at the contour map of the lake and it is easy to see why, for it is filled with deep lake trout water. This vast expanse provides good habitat for these fish, but all that abundance of good water can frustrate anglers as they try to decide where to start their search for these desirable predators.

Clearwater has a good lake trout population. These fish were formerly stocked, but they are doing fine on their own and the stocking program was discontinued long ago. A variety of sizes show up in catches, with some trophies over 30 inches available. Smallmouth bass are common in the lake, however, most of them are small. Yellow perch are found here in good numbers - far higher than most area lakes. Few anglers target them, but perhaps they should. Foot-long perch are out there for the catching. Clearwater also has an excellent tullibee population. These fish play an important role as a prey species for lake trout. However, they get plenty big enough for anglers to try for them as well. Interestingly, no northern pike have ever been found in the lake, and walleyes haven't been seen since the 1980s.

Smallmouth bass are abundant in Clearwater, although not as popular as lake trout. Although the smallmouth population is predominated by small fish, they do provide lots of action and there is the chance to tie into a decent bass as well. The rock cliffs are one spot to try for them with jigs and twister tails or crankbaits. Much of the shoreline is good smallie country.

Most fishermen here are after lake trout, and local anglers say there are some big lakers in Clearwater. A sharply dropping rock wall forms the southern shoreline east of the small bay toward the lake's west end. This can be jigged successfully for lakers in the spring with smelt or ciscoes or with tube jigs or airplane jigs. The two small points just west of the landing on the lake's north shore guard a flat that offers good summer jigging possibilities **(Spot 1)**. And the same area produces well in winter on spoons, jigs or tip-ups baited with dead ciscoes. Local anglers say your best bet in summer is trolling the deeper water. Deep-diving crankbaits may work early in the season, but when fish go deeper as the water warms, you'll have to go after them. Your best bet is a downrigger. It will quickly take your spoon to any depth. If that's not in your budget, there are other options, although they won't work quite as well or get your lure down as fast. Plus, the actual depth you're fishing at will be just a guess. Still, it's better than nothing. Keel sinkers can help your spoons and crankbaits go deeper, but probably your best bet is a Dipsy Diver or a similar device. Like a large crankbait lip, these divers get your spoon down deep. When you hook a fish, they plane for minimal resistance as you retrieve your fish.

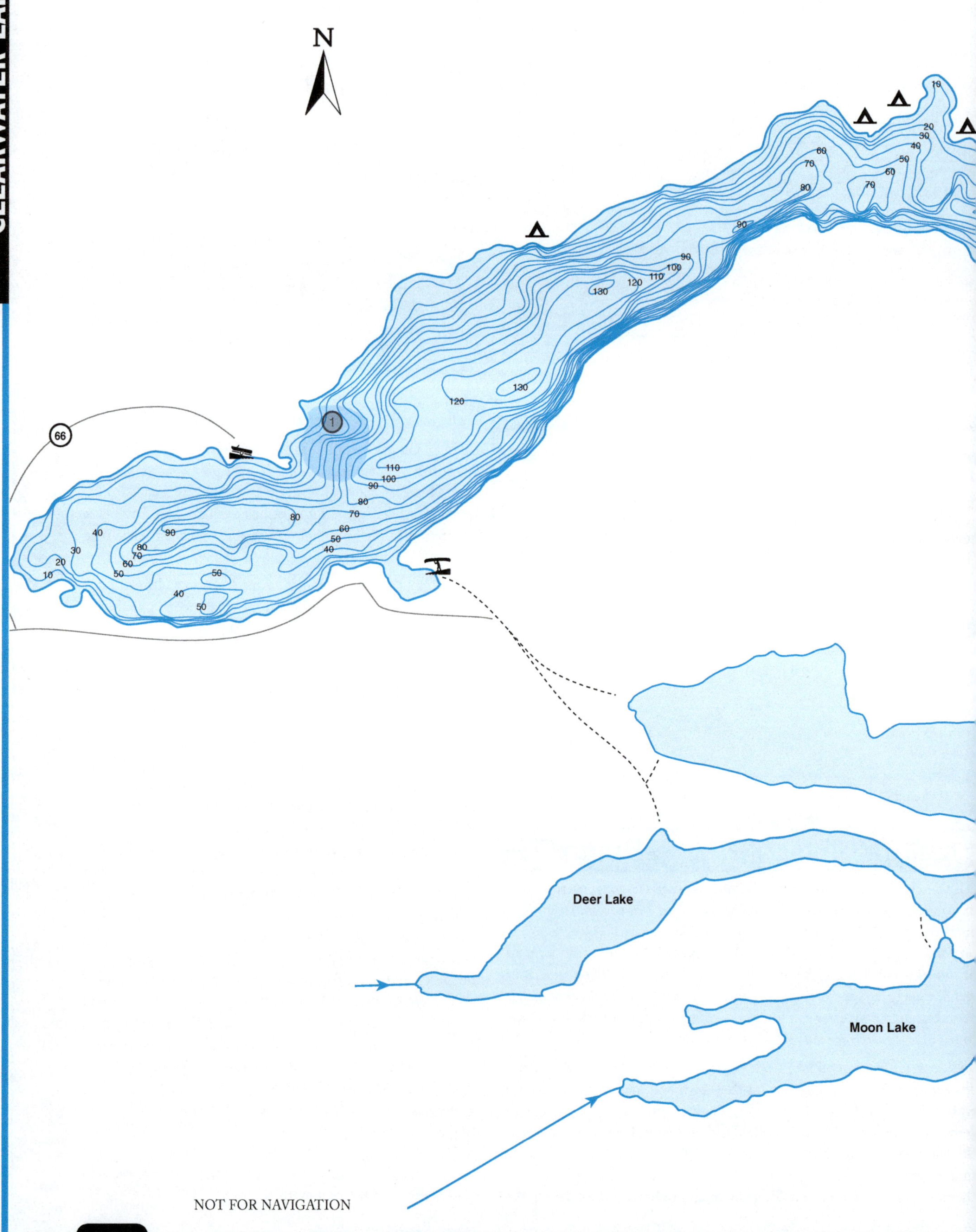

Source: Minnesota Department of Natural Resources, USGS

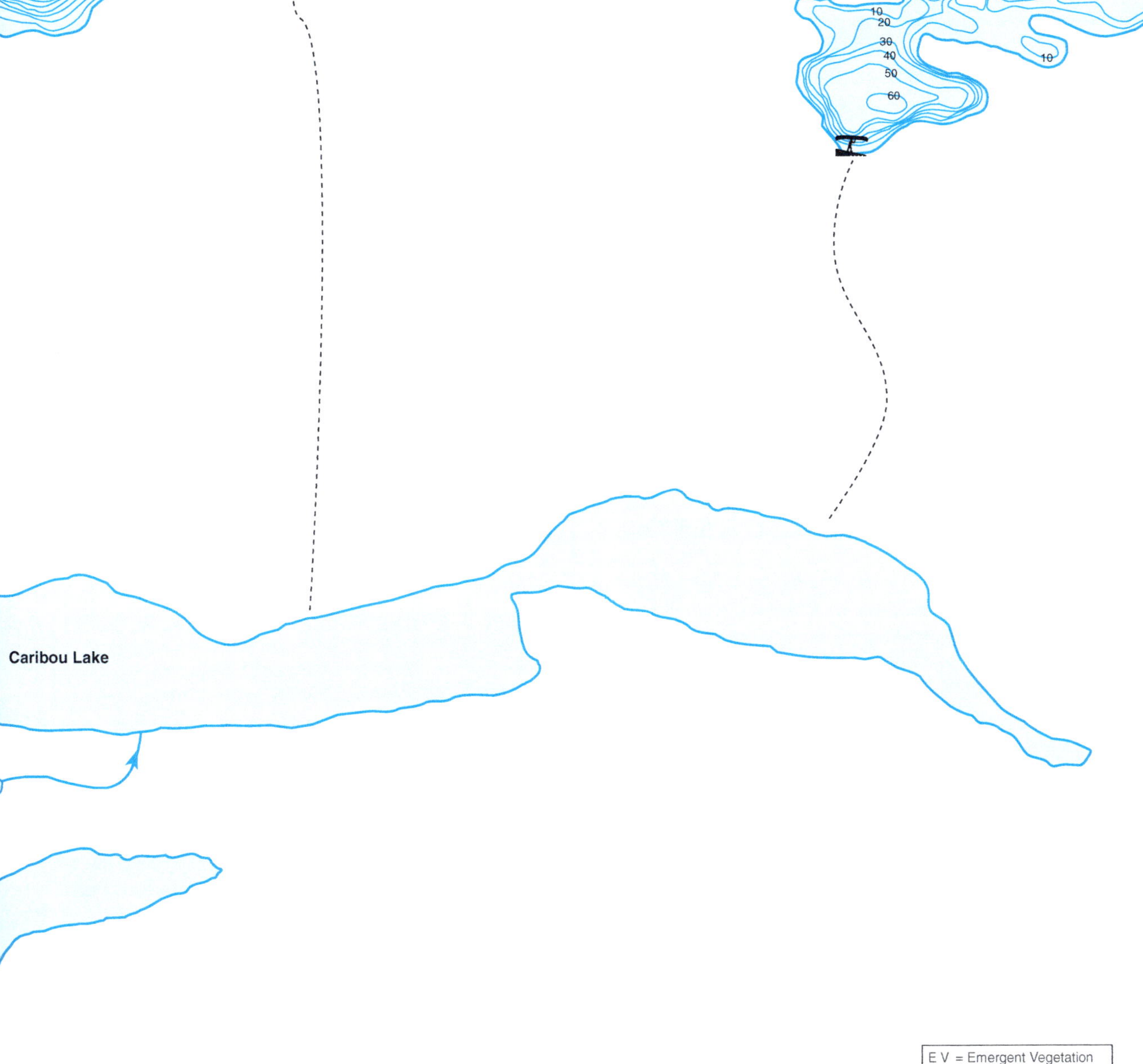

E V = Emergent Vegetation
S V = Submergent Vegetation
F V = Floating Vegetation
✻ = Rocks

NOT FOR NAVIGATION

Source: Minnesota Department of Natural Resources, USGS

ASPEN LAKE
Cook County

Area map pg / coord: 11 / E-4

Watershed: Baptism-Brule

Surface area: 141 acres

Shorelength: NA

Max / mean depth: 29 feet / NA

Water color / clarity: Green tint / 7.3 ft. secchi (2012)

Shoreland zoning class: NA

Mgmt class / Ecological type: NA

Accessibility: USFS-owned public access with concrete ramp on north shore off Co. Rd. 66; parking for 10 vehicles

90° 25' 10" W / 48° 2' 40" N

Accommodations: None

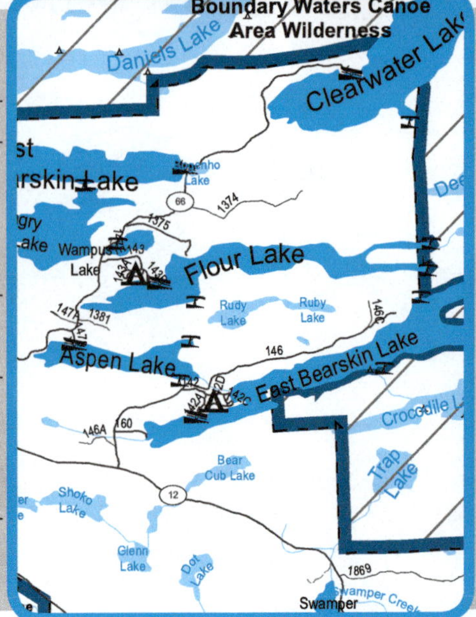

FLOUR LAKE
Cook County

Area map pg / coord: 11 / E-4,5

Watershed: Baptism-Brule

Surface area: 330 acres

Shorelength: 8.0 miles

Max / mean depth: 75 feet / 27 feet

Water color / clarity: Clear / 13.0 ft. secchi (2012)

Shoreland zoning class: Nat. envt.

Mgmt class / Ecological type: Walleye / trout

Accessibility: USFS-owned public access with concrete ramp on northwest shore in campground; parking for 15 vehicles

90° 24' 13" W / 48° 3' 5" N

Accommodations: Camping, resort

ASPEN LAKE — FISH STOCKING DATA

year	species	size	# released
08	Walleye	Fry	90,000
11	Walleye	Fry	90,000
12	Walleye	Fry	90,000
15	Walleye	Fry	150,000

NET CATCH DATA

Date: 07/16/2012

	Gill Nets		Trap Nets	
species	# per net	avg. fish weight (lbs.)	# per net	avg. fish weight (lbs.)
Black Crappie	-	-	0.55	0.96
Northern Pike	3.50	1.72	0.82	1.61
Smallmouth Bass	1.25	1.10	0.27	0.26
Walleye	3.00	1.15	1.00	1.29
White Sucker	0.25	2.38	-	-
Yellow Perch	0.25	0.09	-	-

LENGTH OF SELECTED SPECIES SAMPLED FROM ALL GEAR

Number of fish caught for the following length categories (inches):

species	0-5	6-8	9-11	12-14	15-19	20-24	25-29	>29	Total
Black Crappie	-	1	2	3	-	-	-	-	6
Northern Pike	-	-	-	-	12	10	1	-	23
Smallmouth Bass	2	2	1	2	1	-	-	-	8
Walleye	-	2	3	5	12	1	-	-	23
White Sucker	-	-	-	-	1	-	-	-	1
Yellow Perch	-	1	-	-	-	-	-	-	1

FISHING INFORMATION

The **Aspen Lake** fishery may be mostly for walleyes and northern pike, but there's also smallmouth bass, crappies and yellow perch. Walleyes are stocked here and the catch includes both stocked and naturally produced fish. The shallows on the west end off the inlet and on the east end **(Spots 1)**, are the places to try early with minnows on a slip bobber. Later, shift attention to the sharp break off the south shoreline **(Spot 2)** and to the gentle bar protruding from the blunt point on the lake's north shore **(Spot 3)**. Of course, keeping wind direction in mind and targeting the windward shoreline is always a sound plan. There aren't a lot of crappiakes in the area, so crappie anglers can get their fix here. For crappies, the shallows will work nicely early in the season. Later, soak a small minnow under a slip bobber near the lake's central trench. Northern pike will be near the shorelines hunting for a meal. In this lake, that means perch. Find the perch, and you'll probably find the pike.

FLOUR LAKE — FISH STOCKING DATA

year	species	size	# released
09	Walleye	Fingerling	5,641
10	Lake Trout	Yearling	1,600
10	Lake Trout	Yearling	1,600
10	Walleye	Fingerling	4,140
12	Lake Trout	Yearling	3,238
12	Walleye	Fingerling	3,703
14	Lake Trout	Yearling	3,240
14	Walleye	Fingerling	5,582

NET CATCH DATA

Date: 07/16/2012

	Gill Nets		Trap Nets	
species	# per net	avg. fish weight (lbs.)	# per net	avg. fish weight (lbs.)
Cisco Species	14.83	NA	0.33	NA
Green Sunfish	-	-	0.33	0.06
Lake Trout	0.83	2.05	-	-
Northern Pike	0.42	3.66	0.17	3.47
Smallmouth Bass	1.58	1.47	0.92	0.21
Walleye	0.83	1.29	0.33	0.67
White Sucker	0.42	2.69	-	-
Yellow Perch	0.42	0.08	-	-

LENGTH OF SELECTED SPECIES SAMPLED FROM ALL GEAR

Number of fish caught for the following length categories (inches):

species	0-5	6-8	9-11	12-14	15-19	20-24	25-29	>29	Total
Cisco Species	-	2	85	19	72	-	-	-	178
Green Sunfish	4	-	-	-	-	-	-	-	4
Lake Trout	-	8	-	-	-	-	2	-	10
Northern Pike	-	-	-	-	-	6	1	-	7
Smallmouth Bass	6	9	3	4	8	-	-	-	30
Walleye	-	-	2	9	1	2	-	-	14
White Sucker	-	-	-	-	3	2	-	-	5
Yellow Perch	5	-	-	-	-	-	-	-	5

Flour Lake has low walleye numbers and low reproductive rates. The walleye fishery is largely maintained through stocking. Smallmouth bass numbers are good, although you'll find a lot of small bass. A slot limit on smallmouth bass protects fish from 12 to 20 inches, with one over 20 inches allowed. The lake trout population is in good shape and some natural reproduction takes place. Try the shallow bays early for the 'eyes, later switching your attention to the small island **(Spot 1)** near the campground. The broad point **(Spot 2)**, where the lake narrows as it enters the middle section is another good place to try.

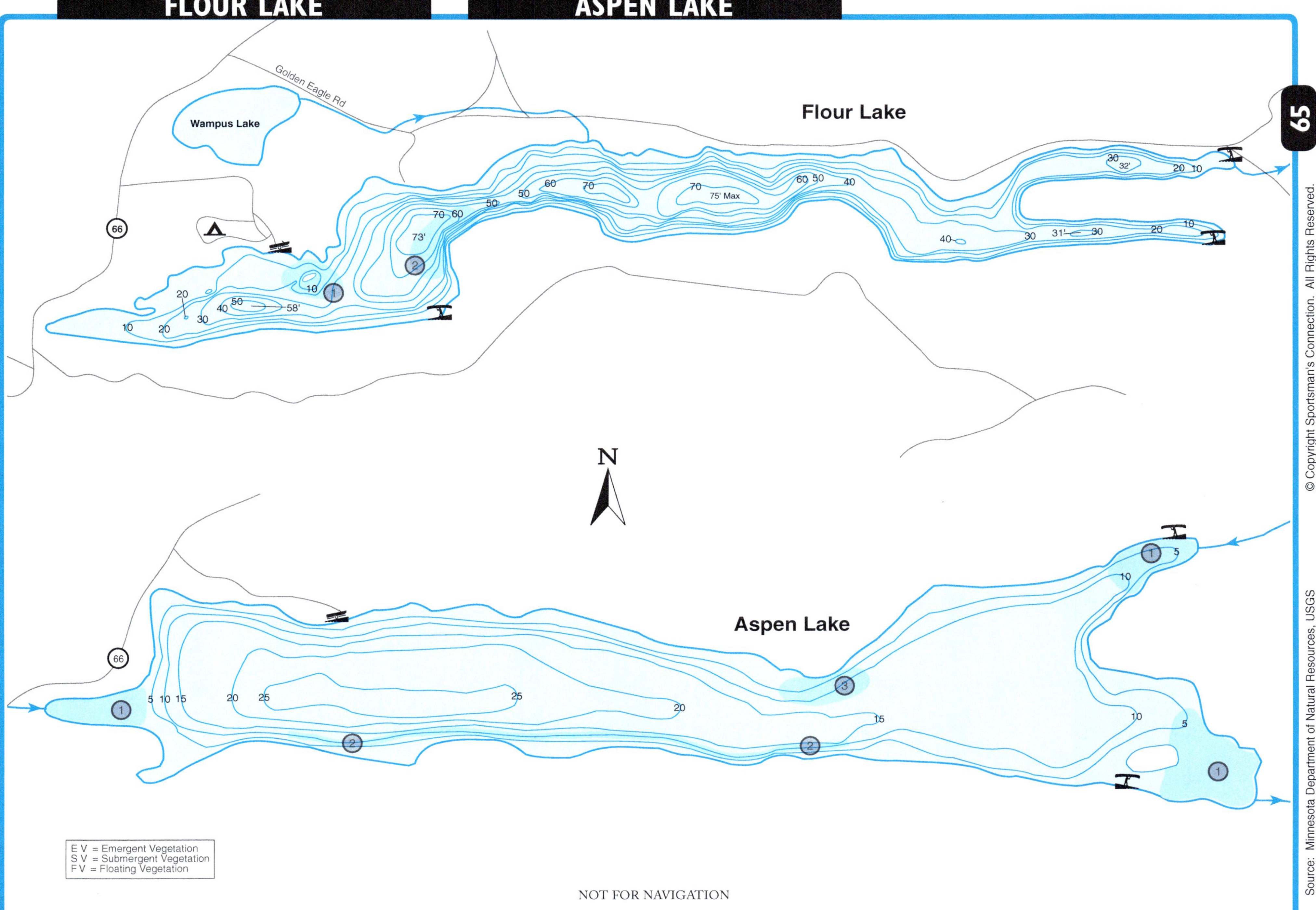

Golden Eagle Rd
Wampus Lake
Flour Lake
66
73'
58'
75' Max
31'
32'
N
Aspen Lake
66
E V = Emergent Vegetation
S V = Submergent Vegetation
F V = Floating Vegetation
NOT FOR NAVIGATION

EAST BEARSKIN LAKE *Cook County*

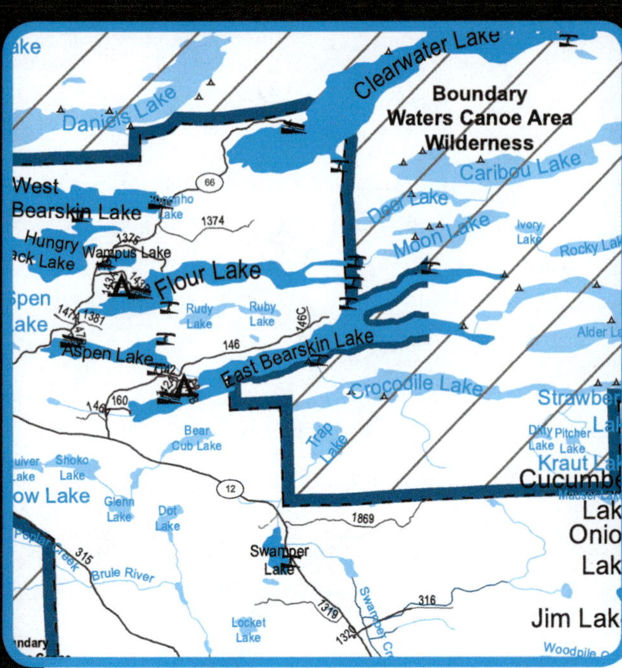

Area map page / coordinates: 11 / E-4,5

Watershed: Baptism-Brule

Surface water area / shorelength: 593 acres / 12.8 miles

Maximum / mean depth: 66 feet / 26 feet

Water color / clarity: Light brown / 9.3 ft. secchi (2012)

Shoreland zoning classification: Recreational development

Management class / Ecological type: Walleye / trout

Accessibility: USFS-owned public access with gravel ramp on north shore of western lake; parking for 15 vehicles

90° 23' 52" W / 48° 2' 8" N

Accommodations: Resort, camping, picnicking

FISHING INFORMATION

East Bearskin has had a reputation as a walleye fishery. Walleye numbers are about average and they are sustained both through stocking and natural reproduction. Walleyes have a fair size structure, with a mix of both eaters and larger fish present.

Smallmouth bass also prowl this lake. You'll find a lot of small bass, typical of many lakes in the area, but you may find some larger fish if you put in your time. The DNR has a goal of improving smallmouth bass size structure on East Bearskin.

Lake trout were not native to the lake, but owing to its deep water and rocky habitat, it seemed like a good candidate for a stocking program, which the DNR implemented in the early 1990s. However, the latest survey found only one lake trout. This may be due to inadequate oxygen levels. Whether or not lake trout will continue to be a viable fishery remains to be seen, but so far the DNR is committed to the program, still listing lakers as a primary management species and continuing the stocking program.

Northern pike have always been present in low numbers here. They are primarily caught accidentally by anglers pursuing walleyes or smallmouth bass.

Walleyes can be fished with some success most of the year around the reef structure at the entrance to the northern arm and at the lake's center. The folks at Devil Track Resort say wind is important on this lake. The best walleye fishing is on the points and bays that have good wind action. Fish the windward sides and shores of these, and you'll likely find fish. A simple jig with a minnow, crawler or leech is effective. Crankbaits can produce in the morning and evening when fish are up shallow.

Smallmouths are aggressive and getting them to bite isn't too hard once you've found them. A spinner or small crankbait should work and they won't hesitate to take a jig with live bait or artificials. The same reefs that hold walleyes should hold bass as well.

If you're after lake trout, your best bet might be to try a different lake at least until more is known about how well this species can survive in East Bearskin. If you've got your heart set on them, flat-lining crankbaits over 20-foot reefs can take fish early in the year when the water is cool but you'll need to look for deeper, cooler water as the season progresses. Helpful hint: the DNR found the best oxygen levels from 35 to 45 feet down in the last survey, so that would be a good place to look.

FISH STOCKING DATA

year	species	size	# released
09	Lake Trout	Yearling	2,267
09	Walleye	Fry	300,000
10	Walleye	Fry	300,000
11	Lake Trout	Yearling	4,399
13	Lake Trout	Yearling	4,398
13	Walleye	Fry	300,000
14	Walleye	Fry	300,000
15	Lake Trout	Yearling	4,840

NET CATCH DATA

Date: 07/30/2012

	Gill Nets		Trap Nets	
species	# per net	avg. fish weight (lbs.)	# per net	avg. fish weight (lbs
Lake Trout	0.08	3.55	-	-
Northern Pike	1.25	2.92	-	-
Pumpkinseed	0.08	0.08	-	-
Smallmouth Bass	0.50	0.88	-	-
Walleye	2.75	1.48	-	-
White Sucker	0.50	2.62	-	-
Yellow Perch	0.75	0.08	-	-

LENGTH OF SELECTED SPECIES SAMPLED FROM ALL GEAR

Number of fish caught for the following length categories (inches):

species	0-5	6-8	9-11	12-14	15-19	20-24	25-29	>30	Total
Green Sunfish	4	-	-	-	-	-	-	-	4
Lake Trout	-	-	-	-	1	-	-	-	1
Northern Pike	-	-	-	-	3	8	3	1	15
Pumpkinseed	1	-	-	-	-	-	-	-	1
Smallmouth Bass	-	3	-	2	1	-	-	-	6
Walleye	-	4	3	9	13	4	-	-	33
White Sucker	-	-	-	1	4	1	-	-	6
Yellow Perch	6	3	-	-	-	-	-	-	9

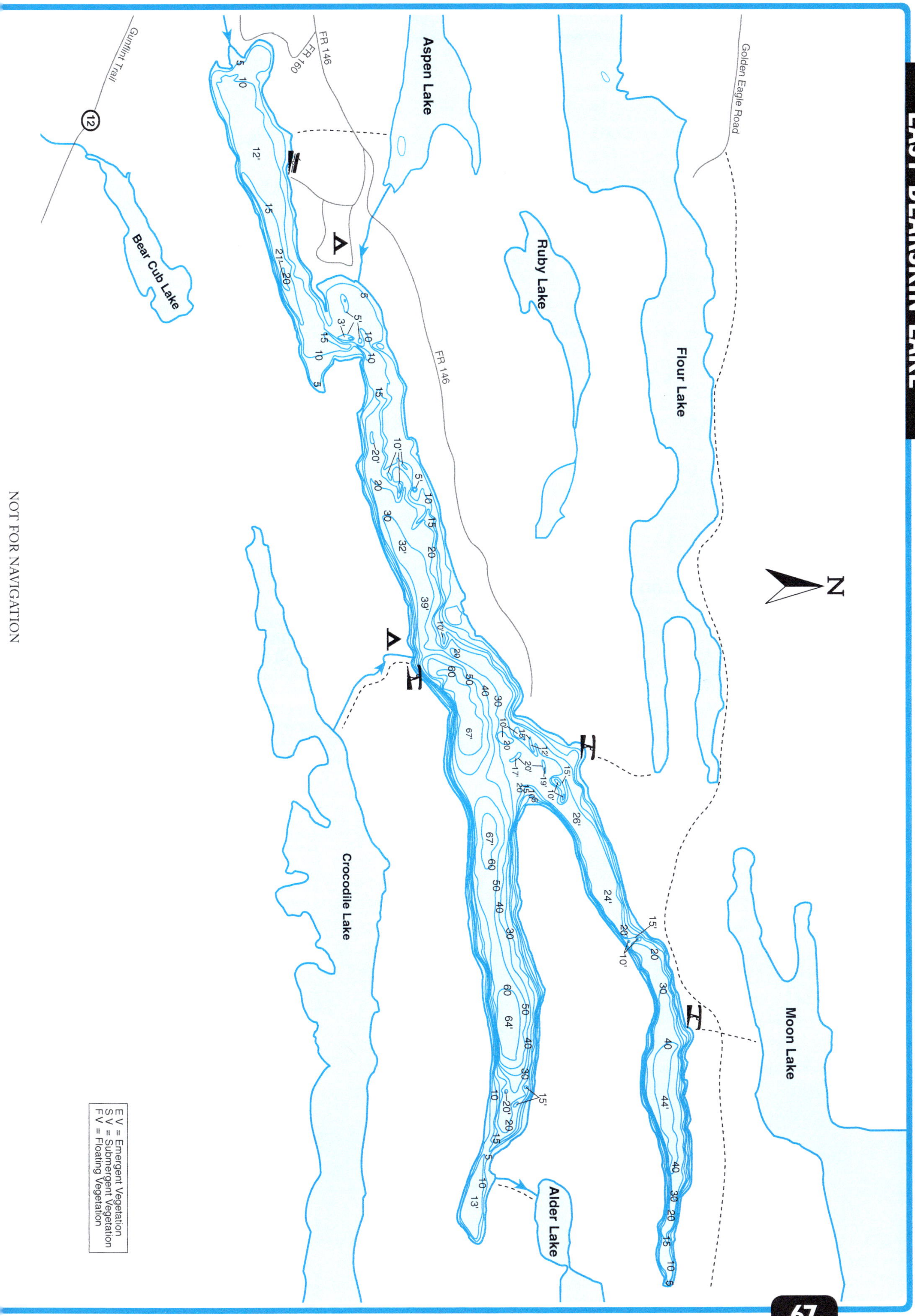

EAST BEARSKIN LAKE

Aspen Lake
Ruby Lake
Flour Lake
Bear Cub Lake
Crocodile Lake
Moon Lake
Alder Lake

Gunflint Trail
12
FR 146
FR 160
Golden Eagle Road

N

NOT FOR NAVIGATION

EV = Emergent Vegetation
SV = Submergent Vegetation
FV = Floating Vegetation

Source: Minnesota Department of Natural Resources, USGS

LIMA LAKE

Lima Lake, Cook County

Area map page / coordinates: 19 / A-4
Surface area / max depth: 10 acres / 25 feet
Accessibility: Carry-down access to northeast shore off FR 315

FISH STOCKING DATA

year	species	size	# released
07	Brook Trout	Fingerling	1,000
08	Brook Trout	Fingerling	1,000
09	Brook Trout	Fingerling	1,000
10	Brook Trout	Fingerling	1,000
12	Brook Trout	Fingerling	1,000
14	Brook Trout	Fingerling	1,105

LENGTH OF SELECTED SPECIES SAMPLED FROM ALL GEAR

Survey Date: 09/13/2004

Number of fish caught for the following length categories (inches):

species	0-5	6-8	9-11	12-14	15-19	20-24	25-29	>30	Total
Brook Trout	-	-	3	4	5	-	-	-	12

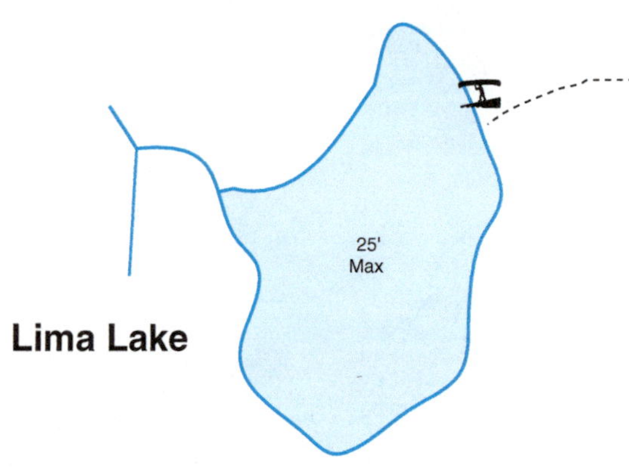

N

DISLOCATION LAKE

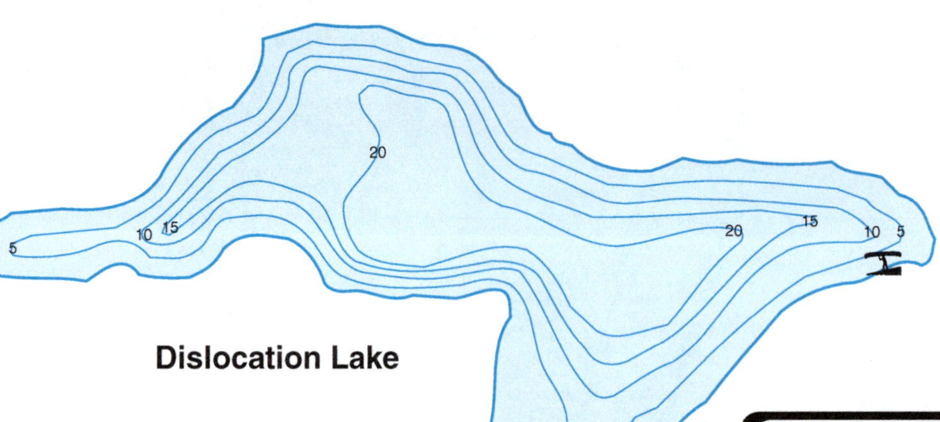

Dislocation Lake, Cook County

Area map page / coordinates: 19 / A-4
Surface area / max depth: 41 acres / 22 feet
Accessibility: Carry-down access to east shore off FR 152; roadside parking for one or two vehicles

NO RECORD OF STOCKING

LENGTH OF SELECTED SPECIES SAMPLED FROM ALL GEAR

Survey Date: 06/07/2010

Number of fish caught for the following length categories (inches):

species	0-5	6-8	9-11	12-14	15-19	20-24	25-29	>30	Total
Brook Trout	-	-	6	6	2	-	-	-	14
White Sucker	-	1	13	4	6	2	-	-	26
Yellow Perch	-	4	-	-	-	-	-	-	4

RAM LAKE

Ram Lake, Cook County

Area map page / coordinates: 19 / A-4
Surface area / max depth: 68 acres / 40 feet
Accessibility: Carry-down access to east shore from FR 152

FISH STOCKING DATA

year	species	size	# released
09	Lake Trout	Fingerling	1,536
09	Lake Trout	Fingerling	1,539
10	Rainbow Trout	Fingerling	2,905
11	Lake Trout	Fingerling	3,055
12	Rainbow Trout	Fingerling	3,015
14	Rainbow Trout	Fingerling	3,238

LENGTH OF SELECTED SPECIES SAMPLED FROM ALL GEAR

Survey Date: 06/15/2009

Number of fish caught for the following length categories (inches):

species	0-5	6-8	9-11	12-14	15-19	20-24	25-29	>30	Total
Lake Trout	-	3	9	7	12	1	1	-	33
Rainbow Trout	-	-	-	-	7	-	-	-	7
White Sucker	-	2	3	-	5	-	-	-	10

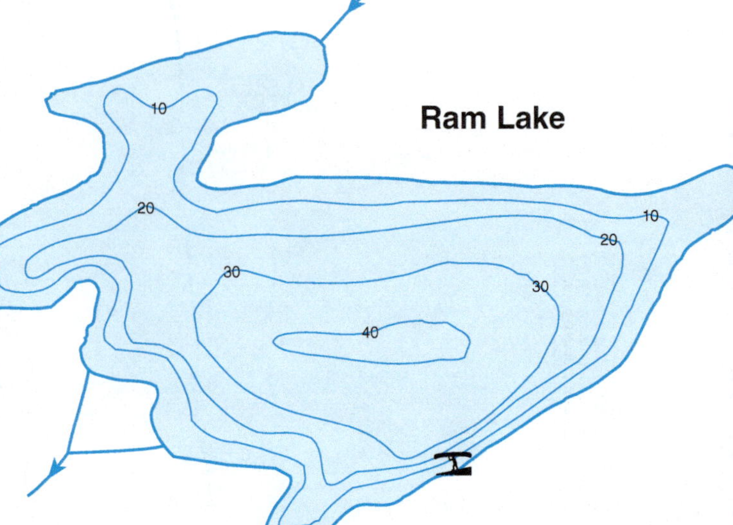

NOT FOR NAVIGATION

Source: Minnesota Department of Natural Resources, USGS

Swamper Lake, Cook County

Area map page / coordinates: 11 / E-4
Surface area / max depth: 51 acres / 9.5 feet
Accessibility: Carry-down access to southeast corner from Co. Road 12; parking for two vehicles

FISH STOCKING DATA

year	species	size	# released
07	Bluegill	Adult	200

LENGTH OF SELECTED SPECIES SAMPLED FROM ALL GEAR
Survey Date: 06/19/2013
Number of fish caught for the following length categories (inches):

species	0-5	6-8	9-11	12-14	15-19	20-24	25-29	>30	Total
Northern Pike	-	-	-	1	7	6	-	-	14
Pumpkinseed	1	-	-	-	-	-	-	-	1
Rock Bass	1	-	-	-	-	-	-	-	1
Walleye	1	1	-	8	16	4	-	-	30
White Sucker	-	1	-	1	5	2	-	-	9
Yellow Perch	1	2	-	-	-	-	-	-	3

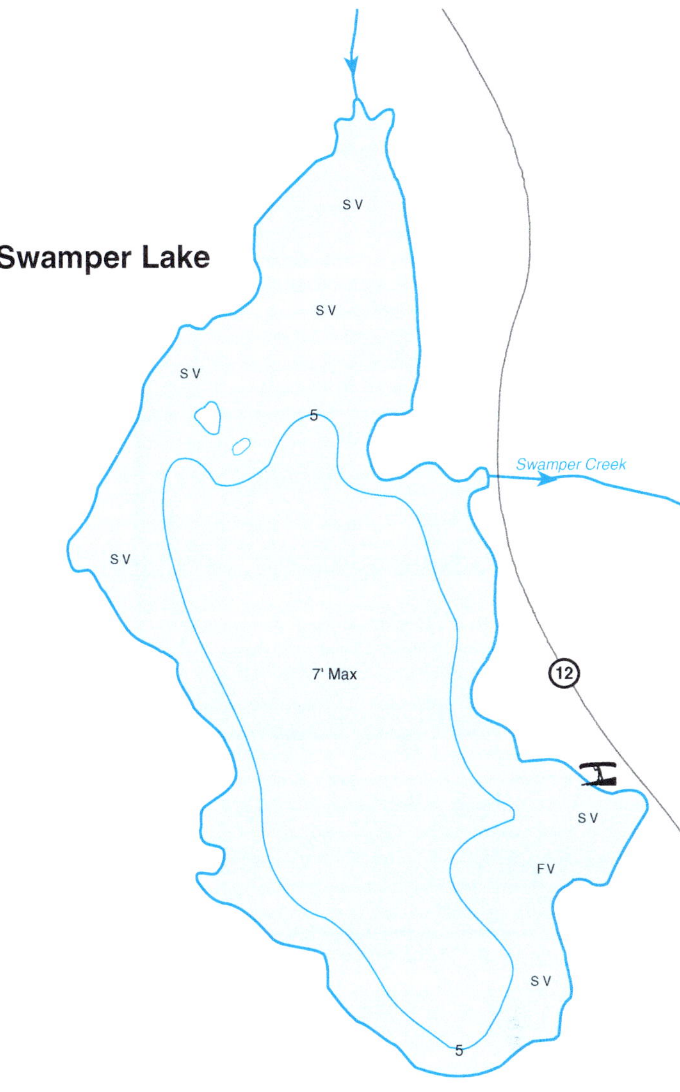

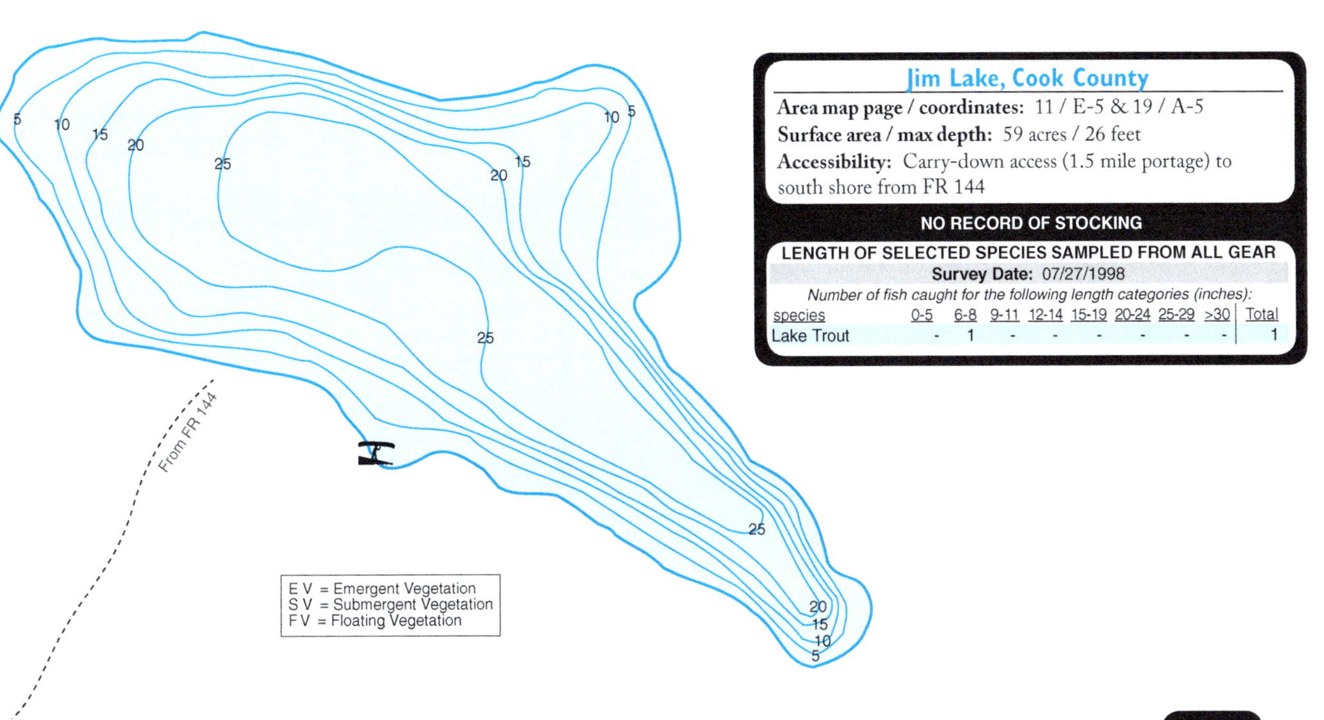

Jim Lake, Cook County

Area map page / coordinates: 11 / E-5 & 19 / A-5
Surface area / max depth: 59 acres / 26 feet
Accessibility: Carry-down access (1.5 mile portage) to south shore from FR 144

NO RECORD OF STOCKING

LENGTH OF SELECTED SPECIES SAMPLED FROM ALL GEAR
Survey Date: 07/27/1998
Number of fish caught for the following length categories (inches):

species	0-5	6-8	9-11	12-14	15-19	20-24	25-29	>30	Total
Lake Trout	-	1	-	-	-	-	-	-	1

Moosehorn Lake

Moosehorn Lake, Cook County

Area map page / coordinates: 20 / B-2,3
Surface area / max depth: 66 acres / 9 feet
Accessibility: Carry-down access to south shore from Tom Lake Road

FISH STOCKING DATA

year	species	size	# released
07	Splake	Fingerling	6,000
08	Splake	Fingerling	6,000
09	Splake	Fingerling	6,000
10	Splake	Fingerling	6,000
12	Splake	Fingerling	6,916
14	Splake	Fingerling	6,000

LENGTH OF SELECTED SPECIES SAMPLED FROM ALL GEAR
Survey Date: 10/20/2010
Number of fish caught for the following length categories (inches):

species	0-5	6-8	9-11	12-14	15-19	20-24	25-29	>30	Total
Splake	-	1	18	7	8	-	-	-	34

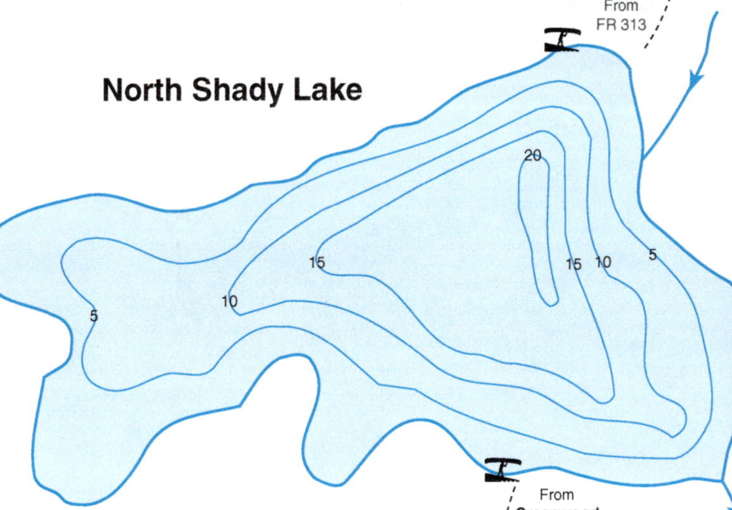

North Shady Lake, Cook County

Area map page / coordinates: 11 / E-6 & 12 / E-1
Surface area / max depth: 33 acres / 20 feet
Accessibility: Carry-down access to north shore from FR 313; roadside parking is limited

FISH STOCKING DATA

year	species	size	# released
08	Rainbow Trout	Fingerling	1,700
10	Rainbow Trout	Fingerling	1,700
12	Rainbow Trout	Fingerling	1,700
14	Rainbow Trout	Fingerling	1,700

LENGTH OF SELECTED SPECIES SAMPLED FROM ALL GEAR
Survey Date: 10/01/2014
Number of fish caught for the following length categories (inches):

species	0-5	6-8	9-11	12-14	15-19	20-24	25-29	>30	Total
Golden Shiner	-	24	-	-	-	-	-	-	24
Green Sunfish	2	1	-	-	-	-	-	-	3
White Sucker	-	2	4	24	13	-	-	-	43
Yellow Perch	21	216	6	1	-	-	-	-	244

N

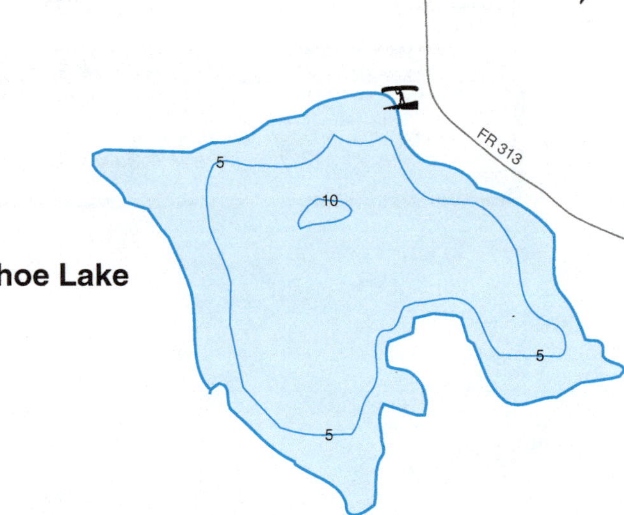

Shoe Lake, Cook County

Area map page / coordinates: 11 / E-6
Surface area / max depth: 30 acres / 10 feet
Accessibility: Carry-down access to northeast shore off FR 313; parking for four vehicles

FISH STOCKING DATA

year	species	size	# released
10	Splake	Fingerling	2,000
11	Brook Trout	Fingerling	2,000
12	Splake	Fingerling	2,000
13	Brook Trout	Fingerling	2,000
14	Splake	Fingerling	2,000
15	Brook Trout	Fingerling	2,000

LENGTH OF SELECTED SPECIES SAMPLED FROM ALL GEAR
Survey Date: 10/08/2012
Number of fish caught for the following length categories (inches):

species	0-5	6-8	9-11	12-14	15-19	20-24	25-29	>30	Total
Brook Trout	-	-	1	2	1	-	-	-	4
Splake	-	-	-	14	11	-	-	-	25

NOT FOR NAVIGATION

Source: Minnesota Department of Natural Resources, USGS

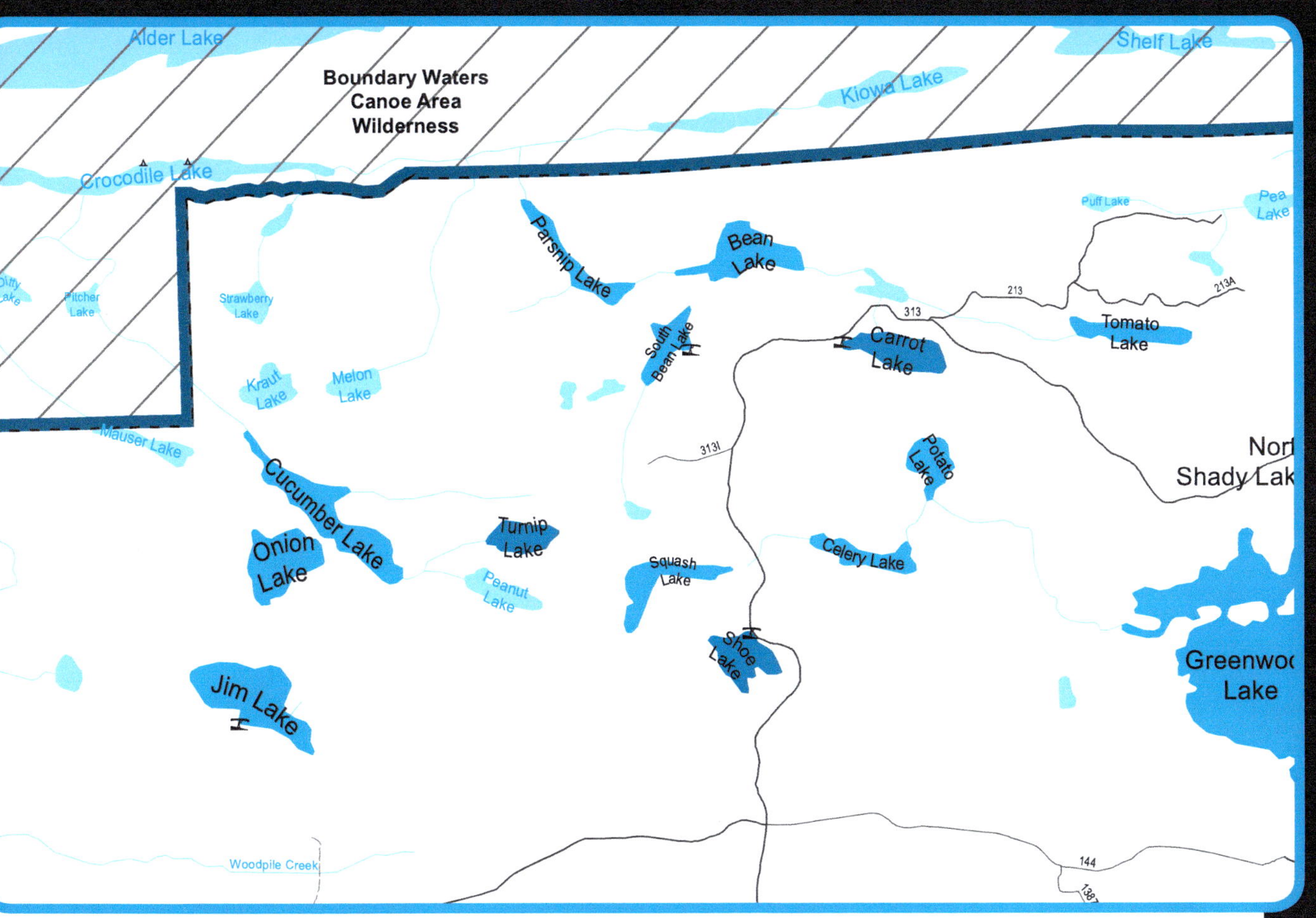

VEGETABLE LAKES

Area map page / coordinates: 11 / E-5,6

Lake Surface Area and Access Info

lake	acreage	max. depth
Bean	37 acres	10 feet
Bean, South	17 acres	14 feet
Carrot	27 acres	17 feet
Celery	16 acres	10 feet
Cucumber	54 acres	26 feet
Onion	31 acres	4 feet
Parsnip	27 acres	25 feet
Potato	16 acres	5 feet
Squash	23 acres	11 feet
Tomato	27 acres	19 feet
Turnip	18 acres	30 feet

FISH STOCKING DATA

year	species	size	# released
Carrot Lake			
Annual	Brook Trout	Fingerling	~ 2,500
Cucumber Lake			
00	Walleye	Fry	50,000
Tomato Lake			
10	Rainbow Trout	Fingerling	1,300
Turnip Lake			
Annual	Brook Trout	Fingerling	~ 1,200

FISHING INFORMATION

Although not a botanist, Steve Persons of DNR Fisheries, 1356 Hwy 61, Grand Marais, MN 55604, (218) 387-3056, sure knows a lot about the Vegetable Lakes, which are clustered together northwest of Greenwood Lake in Cook County.

Bean Lake is a shallow body of water that holds mostly white suckers, but also has some largemouth bass.

South Bean Lake is much the same as Bean. It is shallow, warm and inhabited primarily by suckers, with some largemouth bass.

Carrot Lake is a medium-sized body of water, at least when it comes to the Vegetable Lakes. The lake is stocked annually with brook trout, but unlike its neighboring trout waters, it doesn't have special regulations.

Celery Lake is a shallow, warm-water lake that is dominated by white suckers.

Cucumber Lake is the giant of the bunch at 54 acres, but it's not the deepest. The lake holds an average number of walleyes for lakes of this type. The yellow perch population provides forage for the walleyes, and some of them are big enough to interest fishermen as well.

Onion Lake won't make you well up in tears when you land a fish, or perhaps it will because small perch, sunfish and suckers are the only fish species known to be present.

Parsnip Lake contains suckers and some largemouth bass.

Potato Lake is a small 16-acre body of water with a maximum depth of 5 feet. That's about all that is known about Potato Lake.

Squash Lake has recently been stocked with rainbow trout and is subject to special fishing regulations. It is managed as a trophy trout lake. Only artificial lures with single hooks are allowed and the fishery is catch-and-release only. No winter fishing is permitted.

Tomato Lake is managed for rainbow trout. It is catch and release only, with only artificials permitted and there is no winter angling allowed. Despite this, the last survey found only largemouth bass and suckers; no trout.

Last is **Turnip Lake**. Even though this 18-acre body of water may be one of the smaller lakes, it is the deepest. Perhaps this is why it is stocked annually with brook trout fingerlings. Before you scoff, know that a 2005 DNR lake survey turned up a brook trout measuring 20 inches. The lake also has the same special regulations: catch and release, artificials only, closed in the winter.

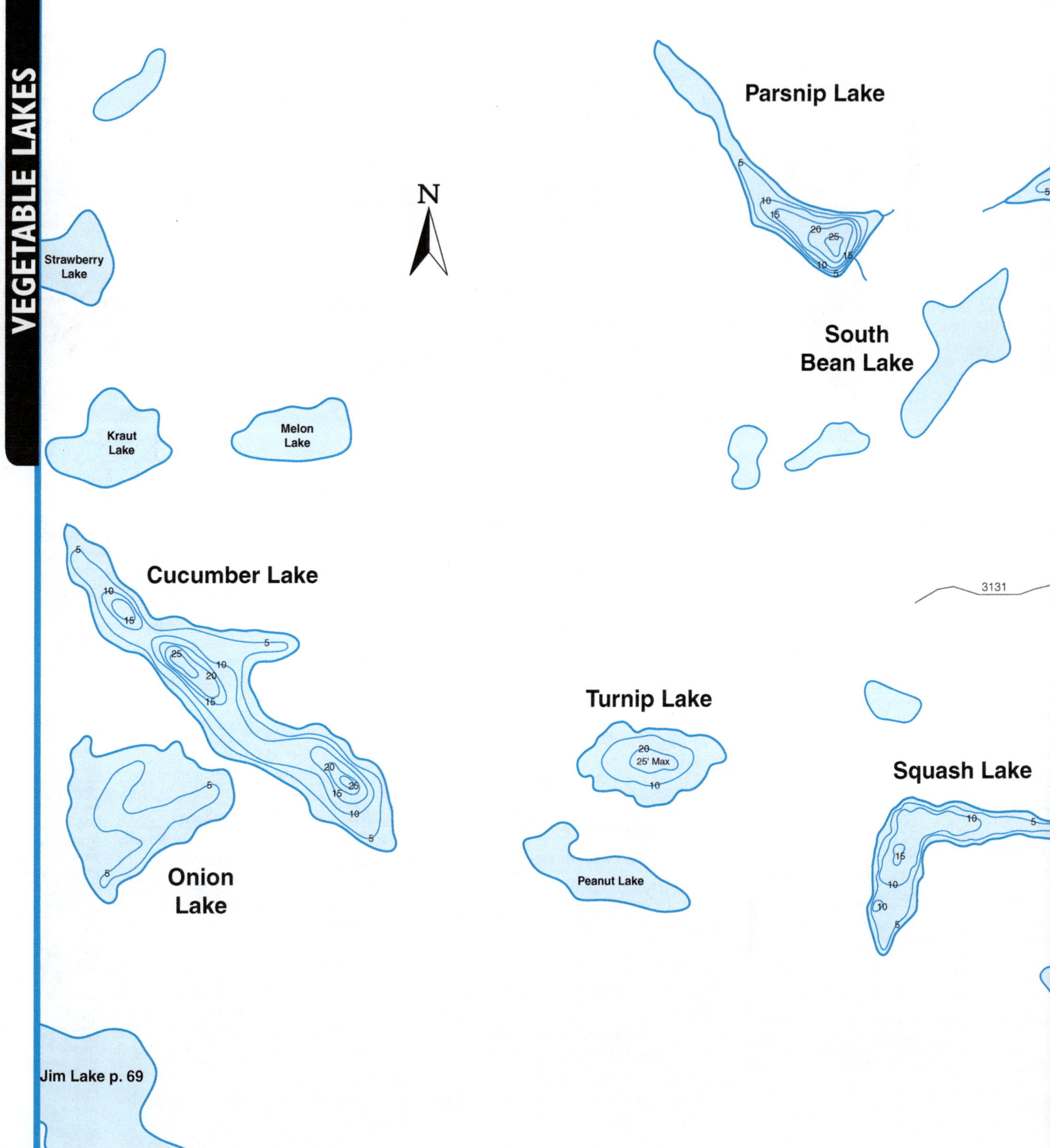

NOT FOR NAVIGATION

Source: Minnesota Department of Natural Resources, USGS

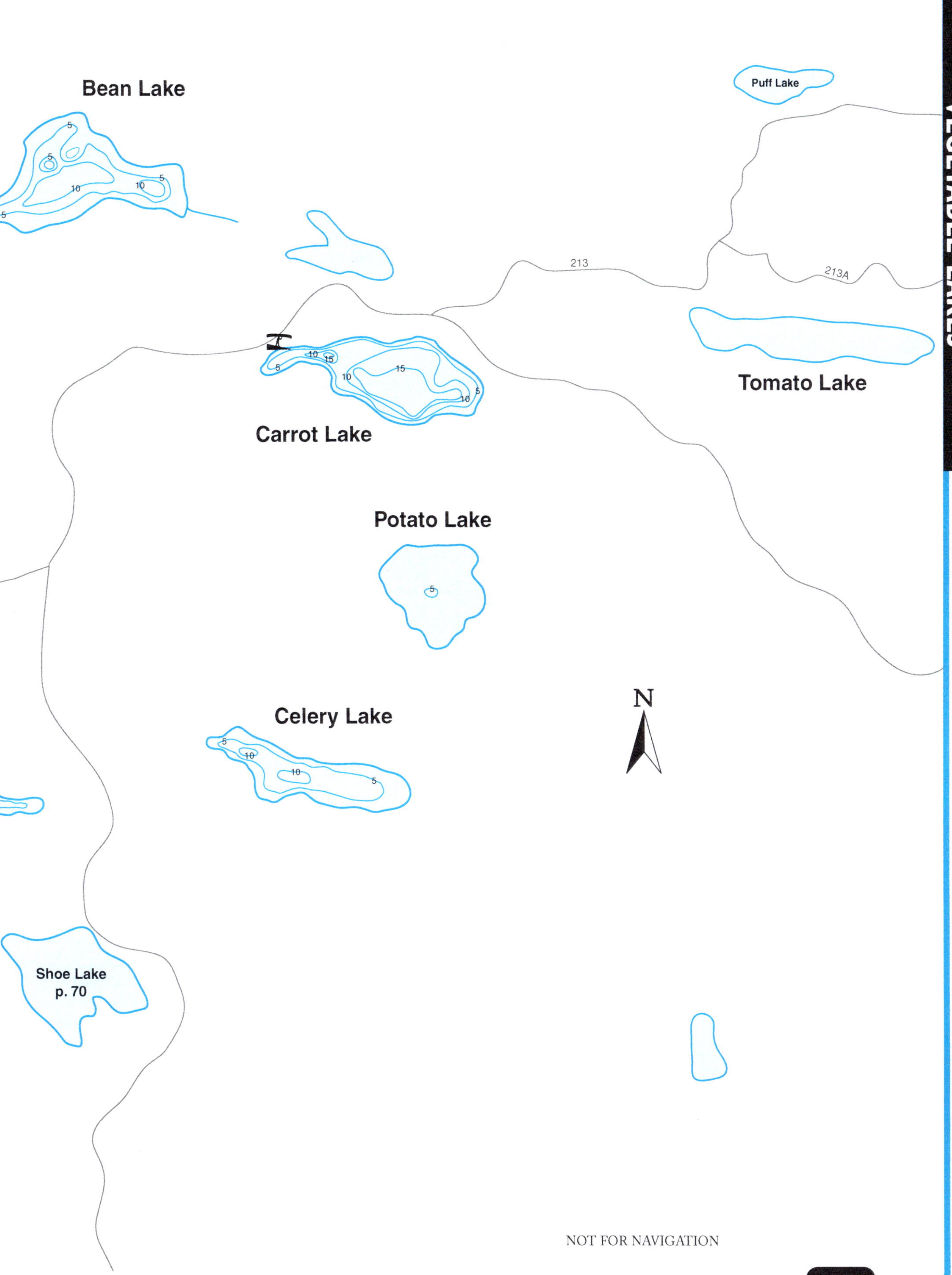
Bean Lake
Puff Lake
213
213A
Tomato Lake
Carrot Lake
Potato Lake
Celery Lake
N
Shoe Lake
p. 70
NOT FOR NAVIGATION

GREENWOOD LAKE *Cook County*

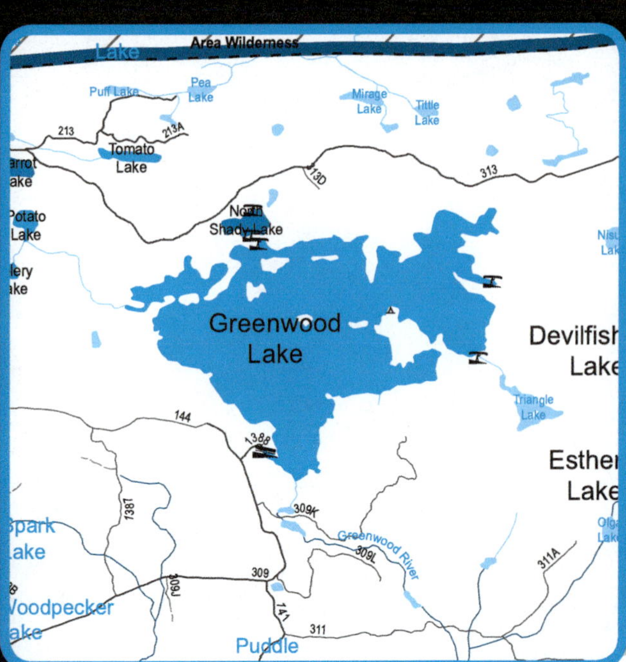

Area map page / coordinates: 11/E-6, 12/E-1, 19/A-6, 20/A-1

Watershed: Baptism-Brule

Surface water area / shorelength: 2,043 acres / 27.6 miles

Maximum / mean depth: 112 feet / 29 feet

Water color / clarity: Clear / 12.2 ft. secchi (2013)

Shoreland zoning classification: General development

Management class / Ecological type: Lake trout / trout

Accessibility: USFS-owned public access with concrete ramp on west shore of south bay; parking for ten vehicles

90° 11' 2" W / 47° 59' 13" N

Accommodations: Camping, picnicking, restrooms

FISHING INFORMATION

This large Cook County lake, just south of the Boundary Waters Canoe Area Wilderness, is the answer to a structure-fisherman's dream. It has just about everything you could ask for: islands, reefs, humps, points, fingers, inside turns, deep holes – you name it, it's down there. Therefore, it's not surprising that the lake contains a pretty good fishery. Lake trout can be found in good numbers, and thanks to a cisco forage base, there is some trophy potential. Unfortunately, the abundance of cisco also keeps the big lakers well-fed and the bite is said to be tough.

Smallmouth bass are abundant but small. You're likely to find a lot of 6- to 8-inchers, but there are fish pushing up into the high teens.

Ciscoes are present in abundance, which is good news. The trend in many waters is for declining populations. This species comprises a major part of a lake trout's diet. What's more, Greenwood has some absolute monster ciscoes! There are plenty of fish topping 15 inches, with one giant showing up in the last DNR survey that broke the 20-inch mark. This is an exceptional fishery, and one that very few anglers take advantage of.

Brook trout show up in surveys from time to time, apparently coming from the lake's outlet stream, which supports a brook trout fishery. Some surprisingly large brookies occasionally show up in Greenwood.

The latest DNR survey found northern pike for the first time, although anglers had been reporting them infrequently for years. The population is currently low. If it remains that way, there will be plenty of room for growth for the existing pike, and given the large amount of ciscoes, there is an excellent chance that Greenwood could become a trophy pike lake in time.

Local anglers like to fish for lakers along reefs in about 20 feet of water early in the season. The areas off the north side of the lake's main lobe are obvious places to try. Later, break out the downriggers and work the depths, trolling spoons in deeper, cooler water. Be careful though. With all those humps, snagging a downrigger ball wouldn't be hard to do on Greenwood.

The whole southeast shoreline is a hotspot for smallies. A small crankbait or jig will get some attention. Also try for them among the islands on the north side and in the rocks off the peninsula toward the lake's eastern shore. You might try using larger lures or fishing slightly deeper water to avoid all the small smallies.

The good news about cisco fishing is there are a lot of these fish present. The bad news is they are tough to find. Use electronics to locate schools suspended over deep water, then try jigging for them with small but heavy spoons with waxworms.

NO RECORD OF STOCKING

NET CATCH DATA

Date: 08/19/2013

species	Gill Nets # per net	Gill Nets avg. fish weight (lbs.)	Trap Nets # per net	Trap Nets avg. fish weight (lbs.)
Cisco Species	11.33	0.36	-	-
Lake Trout	1.92	1.83	-	-
Lake Whitefish	0.08	5.30	-	-
Northern Pike	0.17	2.90	0.42	2.54
Smallmouth Bass	0.25	0.87	3.92	0.34
White Sucker	0.83	2.29	-	-
Yellow Perch	0.17	0.43	-	-

LENGTH OF SELECTED SPECIES SAMPLED FROM ALL GEAR

Number of fish caught for the following length categories (inches):

species	0-5	6-8	9-11	12-14	15-19	20-24	25-29	>30	Total
Cisco Species	-	-	3	82	50	1	-	-	136
Green Sunfish	2	-	-	-	-	-	-	-	2
Lake Trout	-	-	3	10	8	-	2	-	23
Lake Whitefish	-	-	-	-	-	1	-	-	1
Northern Pike	-	-	-	-	2	4	1	-	7
Smallmouth Bass	5	28	9	7	1	-	-	-	50
White Sucker	-	-	-	1	8	1	-	-	10
Yellow Perch	-	1	1	-	-	-	-	-	2

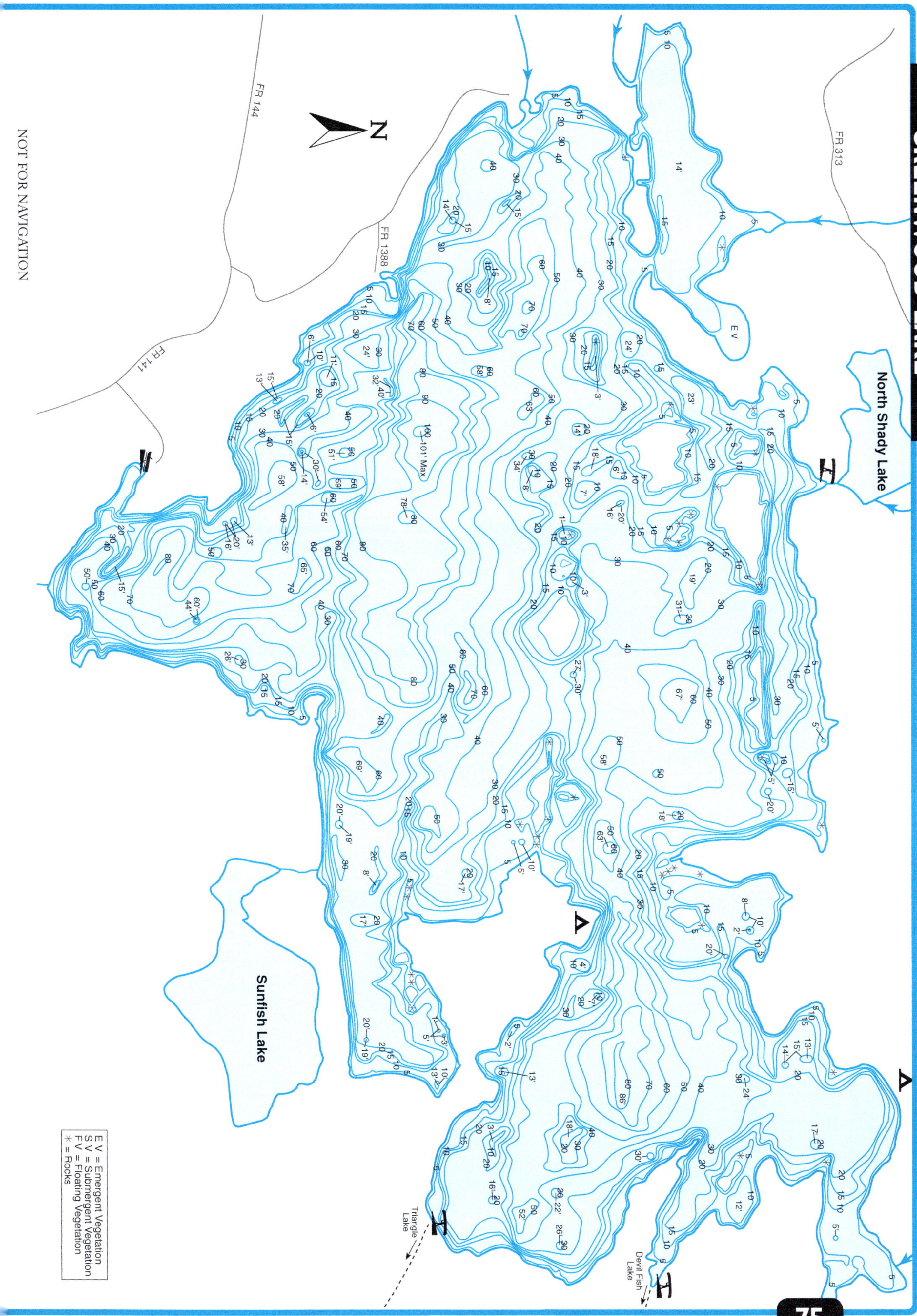

GREENWOOD LAKE

NOT FOR NAVIGATION

N

FR 144

FR 1388

FR 141

FR 313

North Shady Lake

Sunfish Lake

Triangle Lake

Devil Fish Lake

EV

101' Max

E V = Emergent Vegetation
S V = Submergent Vegetation
F V = Floating Vegetation
✳ = Rocks

Source: Minnesota Department of Natural Resources, USGS

DEVILFISH LAKE *Cook County*

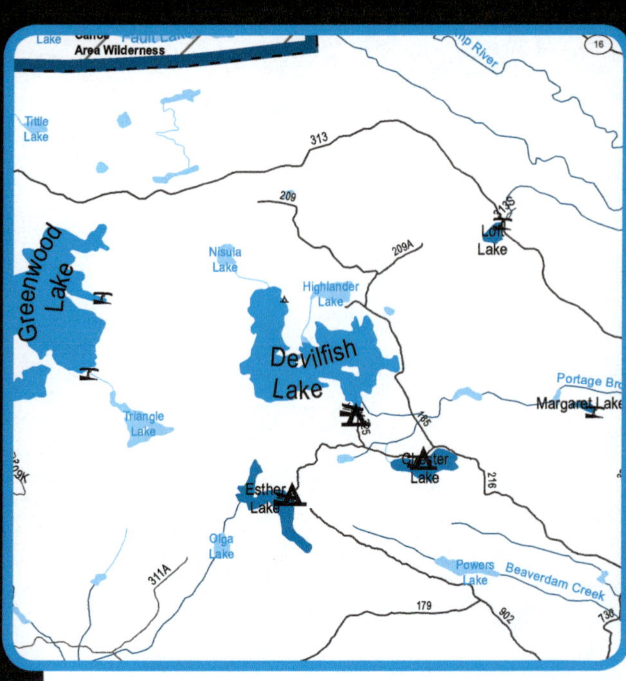

Area map page / coordinates: 12 / E-1,2 & 20 / A-1,2

Watershed: Baptism-Brule

Surface water area / shorelength: 405 acres / 6.9 miles

Maximum / mean depth: 40 feet / 13 feet

Water color / clarity: Light brown / 9.5 ft. secchi (2012)

Shoreland zoning classification: Natural environment

Mgmt. class / Ecological type: Walleye / soft-water walleye

Accessibility: State-owned public access with concrete ramp on south shore; parking for ten vehicles

90° 5' 46" W / 47° 59' 30" N

Accommodations: Informal camping area

FISHING INFORMATION

At slightly more than 400 acres, Devilfish isn't the largest lake north of Grand Marais. Just the same, it fishes well. The Minnesota DNR has been stocking this lake regularly with walleye fry. Stocking goes a long way toward supporting the walleye population, although natural reproduction does occur. Most of the walleyes you'll find here are on the small side, with an occasional large fish caught. It's hard to produce big fish when they grow slowly, and that's exactly what happens here. That may be for a couple of reasons. For one thing, perch numbers are very low; to the point they may no longer even exist in Devilfish. Secondly, smallmouth bass showed up in the lake a few years back and their population is growing exponentially, competing with walleyes for the available forage.

Although the walleyes are having problems finding food and adding growth, the opposite apparently is true for smallmouth bass. Their population is quite robust. Normally, when you've got a high fish population, growth is slow because there's not enough food to go around for all the hungry mouths. Not in this case. Not only are the smallmouths present in high numbers, but they are also growing faster than average! They're obviously finding food the walleyes aren't. Perhaps they're eating crayfish?

There's no big secret to fishing this lake, say the folks at Devil Track Resort, 205 Fireweed Lane, Grand Marais, MN 55604, (218) 387-9414. They urge: "Troll till you find fish; then go to a slip-bobber rig. When you find fish here, you find a bunch of them, so stick around and enjoy the action." That action is pretty decent all year.

The small island, attendant break and inside turn **(Spot 1)** is a good starting point. Don't overlook the bar on the island's west side. Work your way around to the inside turn on the southeast. The shoreline, bars and bay **(Spot 2)** around the two points on the lake's north side often present good walleye opportunities, particularly if the wind's been blowing across the points or into the bay. In the first part of the season, minnows on a Lindy rig or under a slip bobber should work. As the water warms and the fish begin feeding more aggressively, use leeches and nightcrawlers. Crankbaits can also produce in the shallow water in areas where walleye seem to be active. From the small island **(Spot 1)**, you might also want to head southeast to the big island and troll its shoreline, just as you did around the smaller one. The sharp break leading to the deep hole off the island's eastern tip is the spot to concentrate on. Heading from there to the southeast shore, give a look to the inside turn in the squared-off bay or explore a similar turn in the next bay southwest.

Pay attention to wind direction. This lake contains many other points, bays, inside turns and sharp breaks that can be good at one time or another. When the wind roils the water, stirring up nutrients, it concentrates the baitfish, which in turn attract gamefish. If you give this lake's walleyes a little work, chances are you'll be well rewarded. Odds are, if you're using live bait, you'll probably tie into quite a few of those pesky smallmouths as well.

FISH STOCKING DATA

year	species	size	# released
03	Walleye	Fry	400,241
06	Walleye	Fry	400,000
07	Walleye	Fry	400,000
10	Walleye	Fry	400,000

NET CATCH DATA

Date: 09/04/2012

	Gill Nets		Trap Nets	
species	# per net	avg. fish weight (lbs.)	# per net	avg. fish weight (lbs.)
Smallmouth Bass	0.56	0.77	3.67	0.45
Walleye	3.89	0.77	0.50	2.71
White Sucker	6.00	1.50	1.08	1.16

LENGTH OF SELECTED SPECIES SAMPLED FROM ALL GEAR

Number of fish caught for the following length categories (inches):

species	0-5	6-8	9-11	12-14	15-19	20-24	25-29	>30	Total
Smallmouth Bass	2	20	17	9	1	-	-	-	49
Walleye	-	4	6	17	12	1	1	-	41
White Sucker	-	-	5	39	23	-	-	-	67

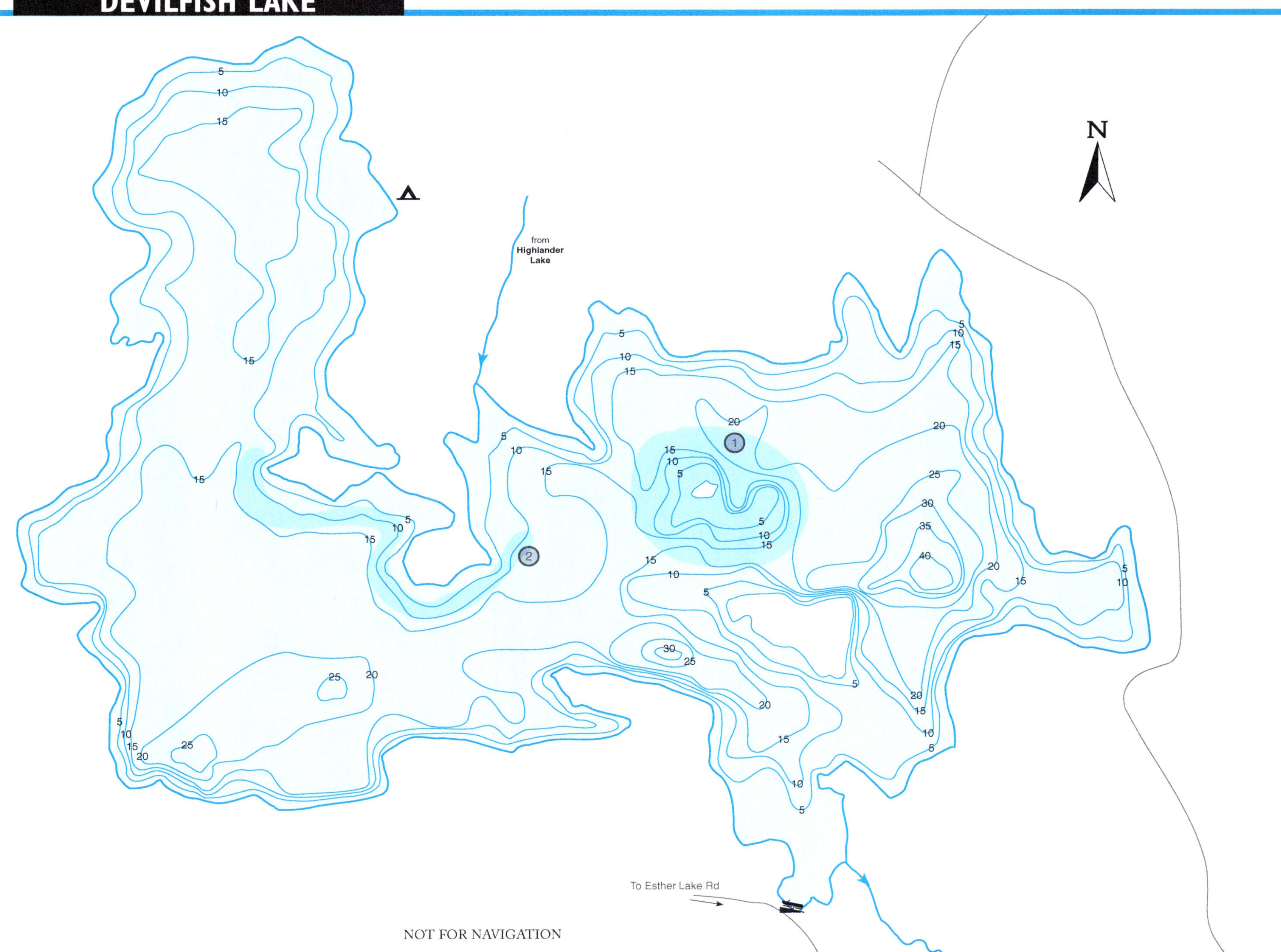

Source: Minnesota Department of Natural Resources, USGS

PINE LAKE *Cook County*

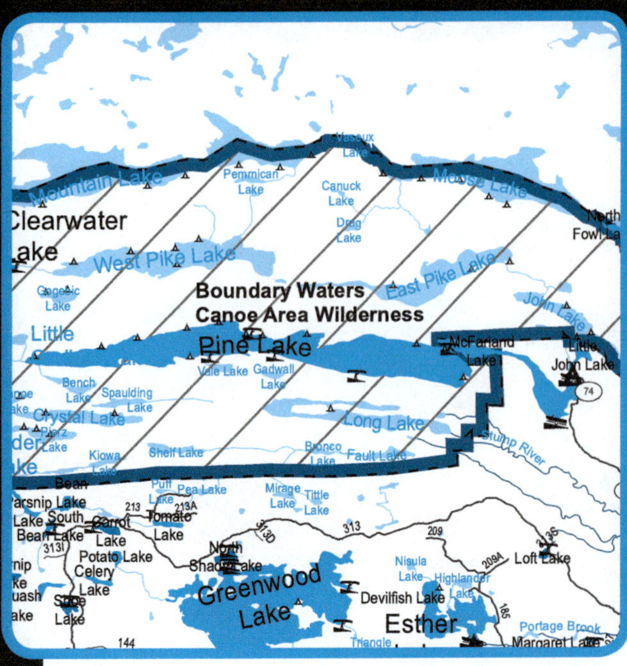

Area map page / coordinates: 12 / D-1,2

Watershed: Baptism-Brule

Surface water area / shorelength: 2,122 acres / NA

Maximum / mean depth: 113 feet / NA

Water color / clarity: Clear / 18.0 ft. secchi (2011)

Shoreland zoning classification: NA

Management class / Ecological type: NA / NA

Accessibility: Portage access from surrounding lakes

Accommodations: Camping, picnicking, restrooms

FISHING INFORMATION

Pine Lake, near Hovland, is truly a "don't-miss" lake in Cook County. It's long, skinny and picturesque, with steep banks and clear water that provides ample room for the lake's fine fisheries.

Here, you'll find a good supply of walleyes, smallmouth bass, whitefish, a few large northern pike and perhaps a lingering lake trout.

The Minnesota DNR stocked lake trout here back in the 1990s. The latest survey was aimed at seeing if any of these long-lived fish still existed in Pine Lake. None appeared in nets. It is quite possible they are gone, or at best, there might be a few large, old fish left. If you want to find out for yourself, try off the point **(Spot 1)** and the humps **(Spots 2)** off the north shore, toward the lake's eastern end. These spots would be worth a look in summer or winter. The steep-dropping shoreline breaks, **(Spots 3)**, would be worth trolling early in the year.

Now, on to fish that for sure are still in the lake. Walleye numbers are very respectable and you'll find walleyes across the board, from large to small. Walleyes grow pretty slowly here, but there are definitely a few old, large fish present. For walleyes, troll the steep shorelines with a minnow on a Lindy rig, or cast jigs to the humps. The point on the lake's southeast shore, near the campsite, **(Spot 4)** is also deserving of a few casts.

Smallmouth bass numbers just keep rising, with each survey surpassing the previous one. Despite the high numbers, growth is fast as well. And although a lot of lakes in the area are filled with those pesky 6-inch smallies that are constantly latching onto your walleye jig, there actually seems to be a pretty good population of respectable-sized bass on Pine Lake. Any of the lake's abundant points would be worth a look. A jig with a plastic grub is always a good bet, and you may even pick up an occasional walleye while you're fishing for smallmouths.

NO RECORD OF STOCKING

NET CATCH DATA

Date: 09/12/2011	Gill Nets		Trap Nets	
species	# per net	avg. fish weight (lbs.)	# per net	avg. fish weight (lbs
Burbot	0.25	1.44	-	-
Lake Whitefish	9.75	2.44	-	-
Northern Pike	0.42	5.39	-	-
Smallmouth Bass	3.17	1.69	-	-
Walleye	3.33	3.20	-	-
White Sucker	0.33	0.37	-	-
Yellow Perch	0.58	0.10	-	-

LENGTH OF SELECTED SPECIES SAMPLED FROM ALL GEAR

Number of fish caught for the following length categories (inches):

species	0-5	6-8	9-11	12-14	15-19	20-24	25-29	>30	Total
Burbot	-	-	-	1	1	1	-	-	3
Lake Whitefish	-	-	8	29	30	49	1	-	117
Northern Pike	-	-	-	-	1	2	1	1	5
Smallmouth Bass	-	-	7	17	14	-	-	-	38
Walleye	-	-	1	3	15	19	2	-	40
White Sucker	-	1	3	-	-	-	-	-	4
Yellow Perch	4	3	-	-	-	-	-	-	7

Traditionally, Pine Lake has a low number of northern pike. Althoug the most recent DNR survey didn't find a lot of them, the numbers wer higher than normal for this lake. Like walleyes, they seem to have goo size structure, with some larger fish present.

The lake whitefish population is in excellent shape, and there are a lo of these fish roaming the lake's deep, open expanses. Some of the white fish are of impressive size.

Pine Lake is located just inside the Boundary Waters. There are several portages leading into the lake from various lakes, but the easiest wa in is to paddle down a short, shallow channel from McFarland on th east end. There are plenty of campsites along the shore here, with on waiting to greet you as soon as you paddle through the channel fron McFarland.

PINE LAKE

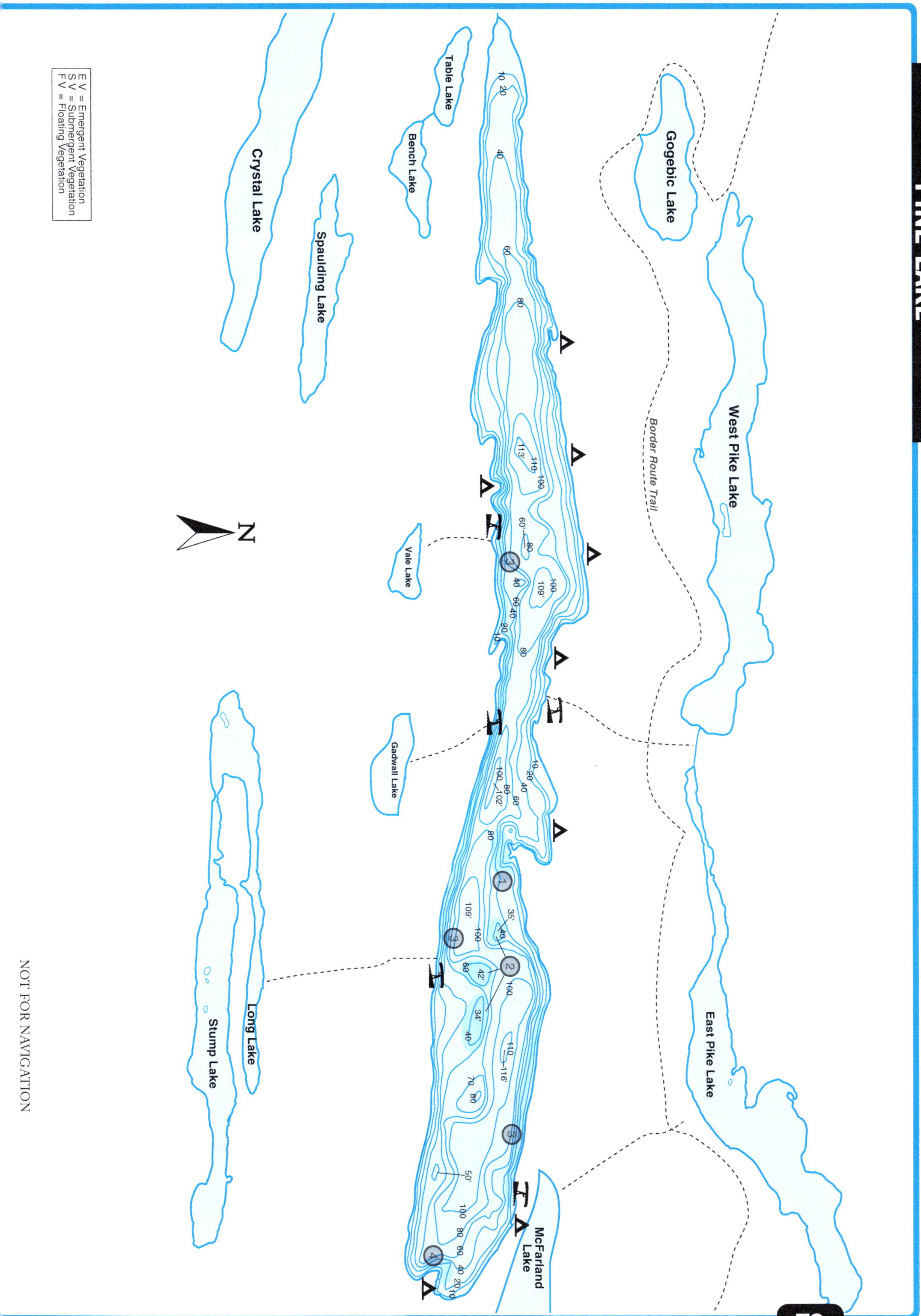

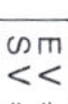

E V = Emergent Vegetation
S V = Submergent Vegetation
F V = Floating Vegetation
Crystal Lake
Table Lake
Bench Lake
Spaulding Lake
Gogebic Lake
West Pike Lake
Border Route Trail
Vale Lake
Gadwall Lake
Long Lake
Stump Lake
East Pike Lake
McFarland Lake
N
113'
109'
102'
116'
35'
42'
34'
50'
NOT FOR NAVIGATION

MCFARLAND LAKE

Cook County

LITTLE JOHN LAKE

Cook County

Area map pg / coord: 12 / D,E-1,2

Watershed: Baptism-Brule

Surface area: 386 acres

Shorelength: 8.3 miles

Max / mean depth: 49 feet / 15 feet

Water color / clarity: Clear / 15.5 ft. secchi (2003)

Shoreland zoning class: Rec. dev.

Mgmt class / Ecological type: Walleye / soft-water walleye

Accessibility: State-owned public access with concrete ramp on east shore

90° 3' 24" W / 48° 3' 12" N

Accommodations: None

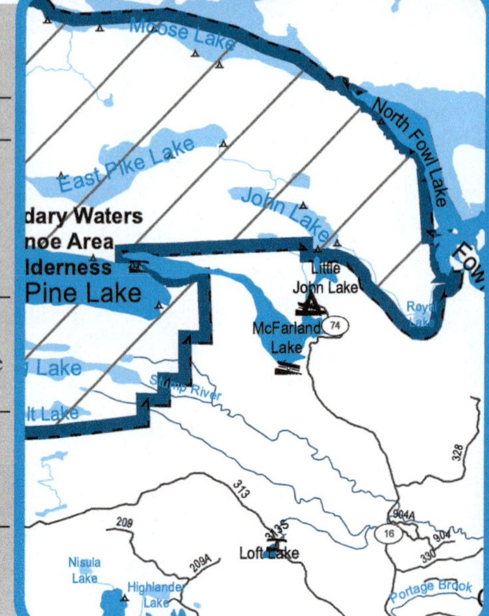

Area map pg / coord: 12 / D-2

Watershed: Baptism-Brule

Surface area: 40 acres

Shorelength: 1.7 miles

Max / mean depth: 8 feet / 4 feet

Water color / clarity: Brown stain / 8.0 ft. secchi (2011)

Shoreland zoning class: Nat. envt.

Mgmt class / Ecological type: Walleye / northern pike-sucker

Accessibility: State-owned public access with gravel ramp on south shore

90° 3' 25" W / 48° 3' 15" N

Accommodations: None

McFarland Lake

NO RECORD OF STOCKING

NET CATCH DATA

Date: 08/18/2003	Gill Nets		Trap Nets	
species	# per net	avg. fish weight (lbs.)	# per net	avg. fish weight (lbs.)
Lake Whitefish	3.0	2.97	-	-
Northern Pike	1.5	2.30	0.3	1.37
Smallmouth Bass	2.3	1.47	0.2	0.13
Tullibee (Cisco)	0.3	0.25	-	-
Walleye	6.3	0.93	0.8	0.87
White Sucker	0.3	2.86	-	-
Yellow Perch	1.2	0.18	-	-

LENGTH OF SELECTED SPECIES SAMPLED FROM ALL GEAR

Number of fish caught for the following length categories (inches):

species	0-5	6-8	9-11	12-14	15-19	20-24	25-29	>29	Total
Lake Whitefish	-	1	5	-	4	6	1	-	17
Northern Pike	-	-	-	1	-	9	1	-	11
Smallmouth Bass	-	2	1	11	1	-	-	-	15
Tullibee (Cisco)	-	1	1	-	-	-	-	-	2
Walleye	-	5	13	9	14	2	-	-	43
Yellow Perch	4	2	1	-	-	-	-	-	7

Little John Lake

NO RECORD OF STOCKING

NET CATCH DATA

Date: 06/08/2011	Gill Nets		Trap Nets	
species	# per net	avg. fish weight (lbs.)	# per net	avg. fish weight (lbs.)
Northern Pike	5.67	2.29	1.50	1.10
Smallmouth Bass	2.33	1.79	-	-
White Sucker	0.33	3.11	-	-
Yellow Perch	4.67	0.24	1.33	0.28

LENGTH OF SELECTED SPECIES SAMPLED FROM ALL GEAR

Number of fish caught for the following length categories (inches):

species	0-5	6-8	9-11	12-14	15-19	20-24	25-29	>29	Total
Northern Pike	-	2	2	1	6	13	1	1	26
Smallmouth Bass	-	-	-	5	2	-	-	-	7
White Sucker	-	-	-	-	1	-	-	-	1
Yellow Perch	3	12	7	-	-	-	-	-	22

FISHING INFORMATION

Even though walleyes have not been stocked in **McFarland** for many years, their population appears to be in good shape. Although walleyes are common, many of them are small, and not surprisingly, growth rates are on the slow side. This is possibly linked to low yellow perch numbers. Smallmouth bass are doing well in McFarland. They are present in abundant numbers and good sizes. In fact, growth rates show the fish are growing much faster than smallies in other area lakes. There are some northern pike here as well, although not in great abundance. Their size is fairly decent. Lake whitefish inhabit the depths here, with smaller fish of this species providing food for large walleyes and northern pike. There are some really large whitefish here as well that might be fun to try fishing for.

The folks at Devil Track Resort, 205 Fireweed Lane, Grand Marais, MN 55604, (877) 387-9414, suggest fishing the lake's walleyes early in the year and again in the fall. You don't need anything fancy here. The classic jig and minnow or minnow under a slip bobber will produce. The channel to Pine Lake is a good spot to try for 'eyes, as is the channel to Little John. Later, move to the fast-dropping shorelines on the northeast end. For smallies, try a small crankbait, jig or even a crawler. Look for water that drops quickly and cast to the shallows, retrieving slowly. Cast spoons or spinners to the shallows for a chance at a northern pike.

Small, 34-acre **Little John** doesn't receive much fishing pressure. In fact, the people who visit the lake are usually just trying to get out of it. That's because it is a popular BWCAW entry point, so paddlers are just trying to get to their destination. The lake does contain low numbers of walleyes, which swim in from connecting lakes. Northern pike are well fed on the lake's yellow perch, some of which are large enough to become shore lunch if you choose. Smallmouth bass also inhabit the small, shallow lake. They grow fairly quickly and reach decent sizes, so they could be worth the effort of making a few casts before you get on up to John Lake and further destinations.

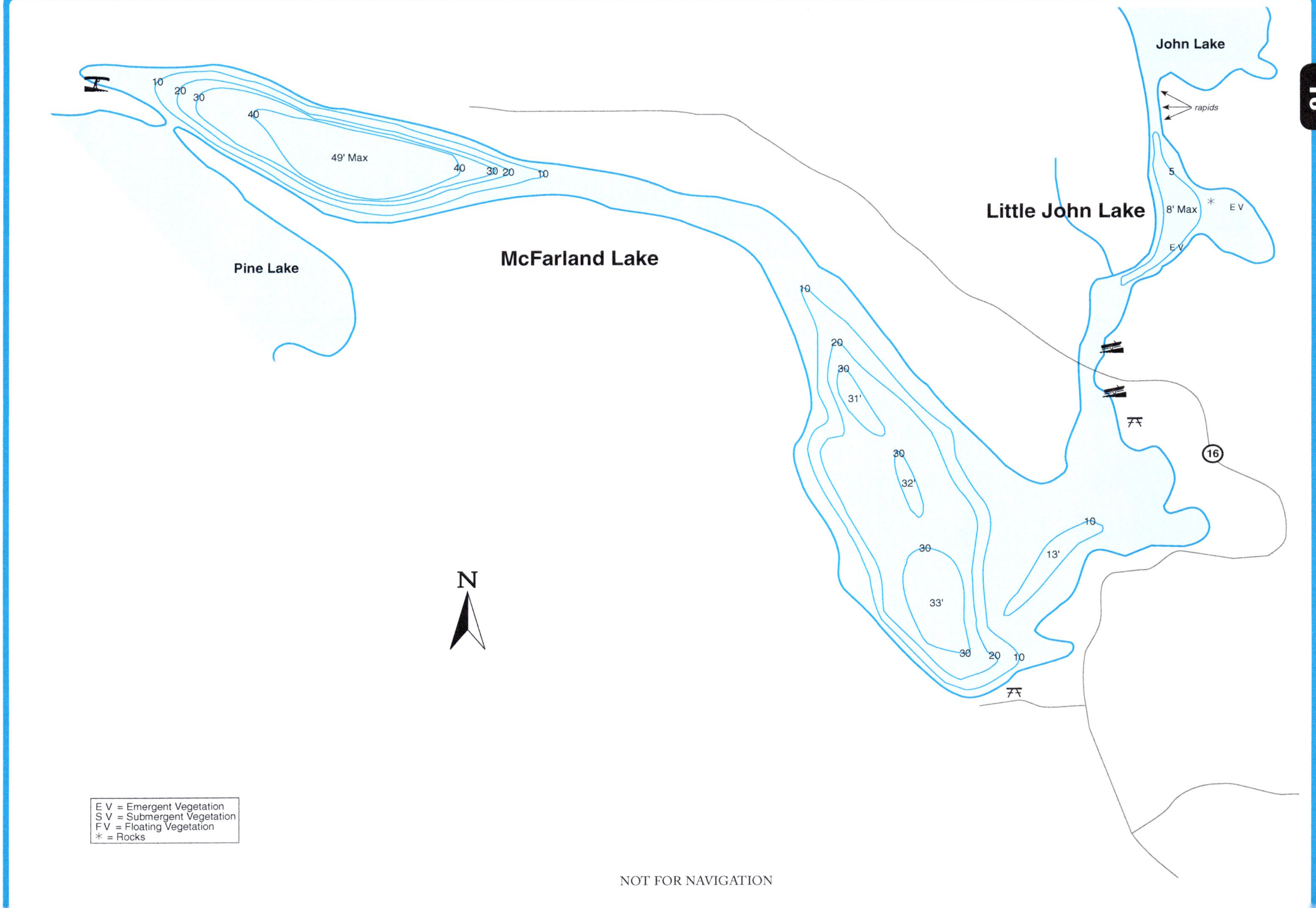

John Lake
rapids
5
8' Max
E V
E V
Little John Lake
McFarland Lake
Pine Lake
10
20
30
40
49' Max
40
30
20
10
10
20
30
31'
30
32'
30
33'
30
20
10
10
13'
16
N

E V = Emergent Vegetation
S V = Submergent Vegetation
F V = Floating Vegetation
* = Rocks

NOT FOR NAVIGATION

Source: Minnesota Department of Natural Resources, USGS

NORTH FOWL LAKE

Cook County

Area map pg / coord: 12 / D-2

Watershed: Baptism-Brule

Surface area: 1,020 acres

Shorelength: 8.6 miles

Max / mean depth: 10 feet / NA

Water color / clarity: Brown stain/ 7.0 ft. secchi (1998)

Shoreland zoning class: NA

Mgmt class / Ecological type: NA

Accessibility: Via navigable channel from South Fowl; portage access from McFarland, Little John, John to Royal River

Accommodations: None

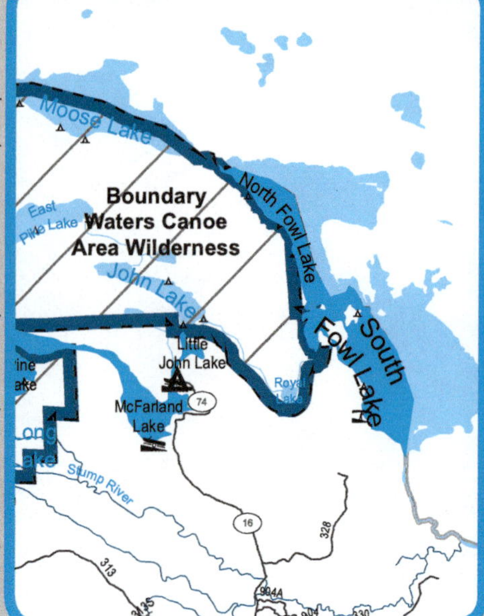

NO RECORD OF STOCKING

NET CATCH DATA

Date: 07/22/98

species	Gill Nets # per net	Gill Nets avg. fish weight (lbs.)	Trap Nets # per net	Trap Nets avg. fish weight (lbs.)
Northern Pike	3.0	1.67	-	-
Walleye	16.2	1.13	-	-
White Sucker	3.6	2.61	-	-
Yellow Perch	27.0	0.45	-	-

LENGTH OF SELECTED SPECIES SAMPLED FROM ALL GEAR

Number of fish caught for the following length categories (inches):

species	0-5	6-8	9-11	12-14	15-19	20-24	25-29	>29	Total
Northern Pike	-	-	1	4	4	3	3	-	15
Walleye	-	4	7	47	19	3	1	-	81
Yellow Perch	5	55	67	8	-	-	-	-	135

SOUTH FOWL LAKE

Cook County

Area map pg / coord: 12/D,E-2,3

Watershed: Baptism-Brule

Surface area: 1,440 acres

Shorelength: 9.8 miles

Max / mean depth: 10 feet / NA

Water color / clarity: Brown / 7.0 ft. secchi (1998)

Shoreland zoning class: NA

Mgmt class / Ecological type: NA

Accessibility: Access via navigable channel from North Fowl Lake; carry-down access via logging road / snowmobile trail off Co. Rd. 16 (Arrowhead Trail)

Accommodations: None

NO RECORD OF STOCKING

NET CATCH DATA

Date: 07/20/1998

species	Gill Nets # per net	Gill Nets avg. fish weight (lbs.)	Trap Nets # per net	Trap Nets avg. fish weight (lbs.)
Northern Pike	3.2	1.27	-	-
Smallmouth Bass	0.4	1.58	-	-
Walleye	21.0	1.10	-	-
White Sucker	5.6	2.39	-	-
Yellow Perch	14.2	0.45	-	-

LENGTH OF SELECTED SPECIES SAMPLED FROM ALL GEAR

Number of fish caught for the following length categories (inches):

species	0-5	6-8	9-11	12-14	15-19	20-24	25-29	>29	Total
Northern Pike	-	1	1	2	7	4	1	-	16
Smallmouth Bass	-	-	-	2	-	-	-	-	2
Walleye	-	7	18	48	24	8	-	-	105
Yellow Perch	-	25	40	6	-	-	-	-	71

FISHING INFORMATION

North Fowl and **South Fowl** are two Canadian border lakes that don't have much depth, and given their slightly murky water, they don't appear to be the most pristine. But don't let that fool you. They have downright good fisheries for perch, walleyes, northern pike and smallmouth bass. North and South Fowl are essentially one large lake, with the bulk of it lying across the border in Canada. However, if you like chasing perch and walleyes, the portion of the lakes lying within the United States is definitely worth a visit.

The walleyes here grow fast, likely because of strong yellow perch numbers. The folks at Devil Track Resort, 205 Fireweed Lane, Grand Marais, MN 55604, (877) 387-9414, say North and South Fowl are good early season walleye lakes, and they offer some fine winter fishing opportunities as well. Trolling is the way to go during the open-water season, they say. Try slowly trolling with a minnow on a Lindy rig early in the spring. Crankbaits also work, just experiment with different lures, trolling speeds and colors to find what the fish are particular to on that day.

These lakes have fairly dense weedbeds and are home to a decent northern pike population. There isn't a lot of size to most of the pike, but every once in awhile you'll tie into something large.

Both North Fowl and South Fowl support good perch populations, and the folks at Devil Track Resort say the only word that adequately describes them is "jumbo." These fish also experience fast growth rates and there are fair numbers of large fish present. Fish for them with small minnows on a spinner or jigs with plastic tails. You may even be able to pull early season perch out of shallow water on small spinners. There are bona-fide 12-inch perch here, and fish of that size will easily grab lures intended for walleyes, so a mixed bag of both species is a real possibility.

These lakes are border waters, and special fishing regulations apply. Be sure to check your current Minnesota fishing regulations book before heading out to fish these waters. Also, keep in mind you'll need to stay on the U.S. side of the lake, unless you've got a remote border crossing permit. Even if you do, you'll need a Canadian fishing license to fish the Canadian side of these lakes.

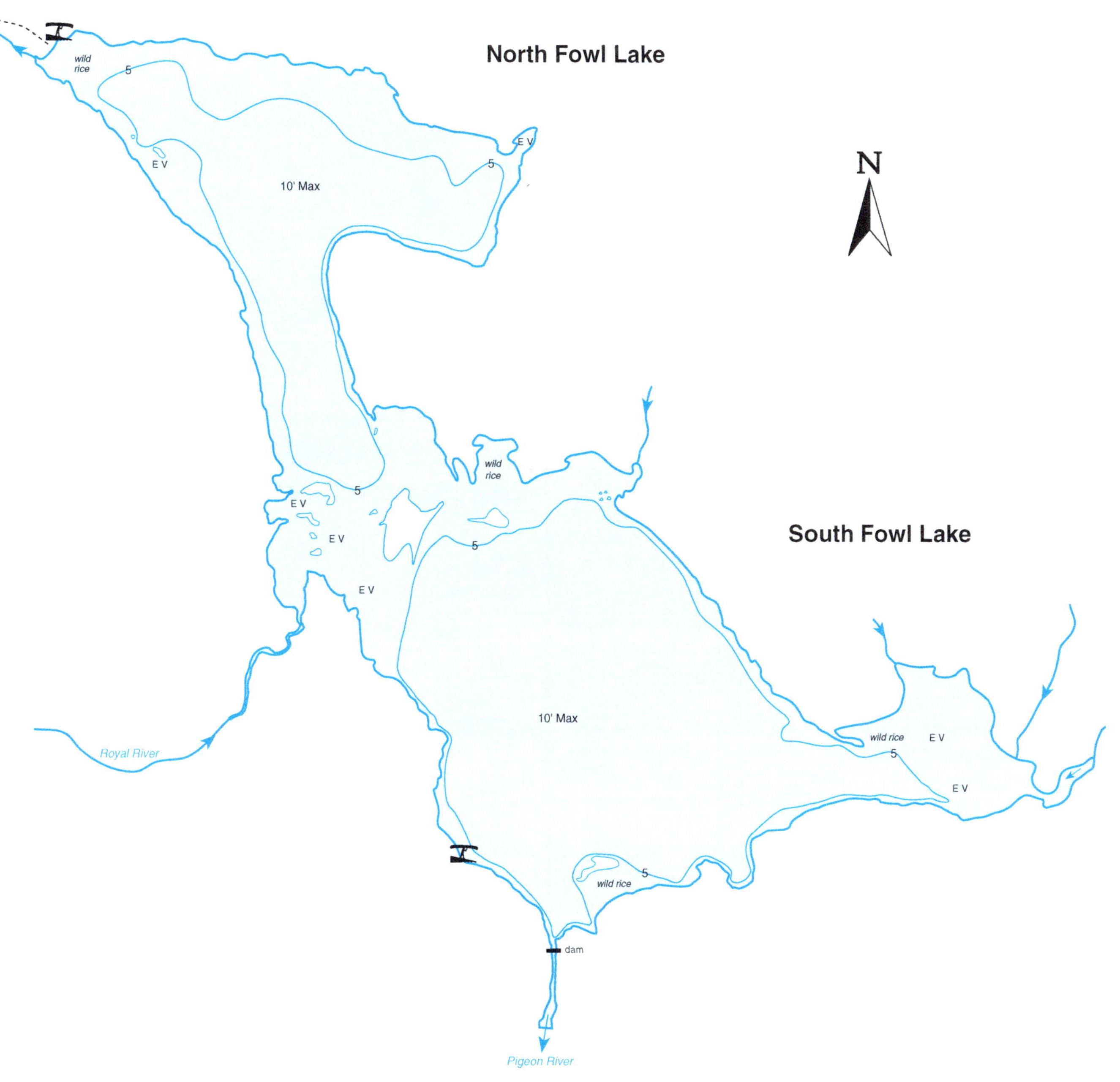

E V = Emergent Vegetation
S V = Submergent Vegetation
F V = Floating Vegetation

NOT FOR NAVIGATION

Source: Minnesota Department of Natural Resources, USGS

CEDAR LAKE *Lake County*

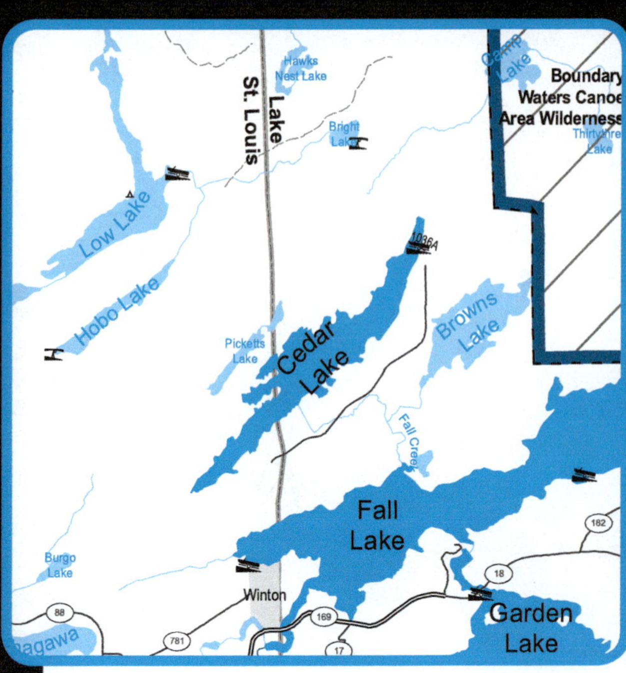

Area map page / coordinates: 14 / B-1

Watershed: Rainy Headwaters

Surface water area / shorelength: 465 acres / 8.2 miles

Maximum / mean depth: 45 feet / 22 feet

Water color / clarity: Clear / 11.0 foot secchi (2012)

Shoreland zoning classification: Recreational development

Management class / Ecological type: Walleye /soft-water walley

Accessibility: USFS-owned public access with concrete ramp on north shore off USFS Road 1036 (Cloquet Line)

91° 46' 16" W / 47° 58' 10" N

Accommodations: None

FISHING INFORMATION

Although it frequently gets overlooked by anglers headed for better-known Shagawa, White Iron and Burntside lakes, Cedar is one of the Ely's better lakes. Here, you'll find 465 acres of clear, soft water with a bottom of rock, rubble and sand that creates a quality fishery.

Cedar Lake is probably best known for its good walleye fishing. You'll find plenty of eaters here, and the occasional trophy. However, most of the ones you'll encounter are in that perfect 14- to 17-inch range; just the right size for the frying pan.

The latest survey found northern pike numbers down a bit compared to the lake's long-term average, but that isn't all bad because the ones that did turn up had a pretty decent average size. Fewer hungry mouths likely equates to more food for the existing fish.

Yellow perch inhabit Cedar Lake in moderate numbers. They likely provide the bulk of the diet for walleyes and northern pike. Some large perch are out there waiting to hit your jig as well.

Smallmouth bass showed up in the lake some years back and apparently found all the rocky areas to their liking because they have now become established. There are some decent-sized bass out there, with sizes running into the mid- to high teens.

A few black crappies are out there as well, but they don't turn up too often in the DNR's survey nets.

A small tullibee population rounds out Cedar Lake's fishery.

Cliff Noble, owner of Skube's Bait & Tackle, 1810 E. Sheridan St., Ely, MN 55731 (218) 365-5358, says the walleyes are usually pretty nice, averaging maybe 14-1/2 inches, with some fish as large as 27 or 28 inches being caught occasionally.

To catch walleyes, you'll want to try the shallow spots in the spring, using minnows, says Noble. Later in the year, these fish will move to deeper water, seeking some shade for their highly light-sensitive eyes. However, they'll return to shallow structure like the humps **(Spots 1)**, at night to feed. A leech or nightcrawler on a jig or Lindy rig fished early in the morning or near dusk is often a poten combination during the summer..

Pike can also be found in the shallows early. The inlet from Picketts Lake on the north side is a good spot to try. Any weedbeds you can find should hold pike later in the year, where they can be taken on perch-pattern stickbaits.

Fish for perch at the weed edges using small minnows or worm chunks.

There are plenty of good-looking smallmouth spots. Those same humps that hold walleyes in low-light hours may hold smallies by day. Also, try any rocky shoreline points. Where there are rocks, there are usually smallies.

NO RECORD OF STOCKING

NET CATCH DATA

Date: 07/03/2012	Gill Nets		Trap Nets	
species	# per net	avg. fish weight (lbs.)	# per net	avg. fish weight (lbs.
Black Crappie	0.11	0.29	-	-
Northern Pike	1.33	2.60	-	-
Smallmouth Bass	0.78	2.61	-	-
Tullibee (Cisco)	0.11	0.23	-	-
Walleye	10.56	1.14	-	-
White Sucker	3.67	2.59	-	-
Yellow Perch	1.44	0.18	-	-

LENGTH OF SELECTED SPECIES SAMPLED FROM ALL GEAR

Number of fish caught for the following length categories (inches):

species	0-5	6-8	9-11	12-14	15-19	20-24	25-29	>30	Total
Black Crappie	-	1	-	-	-	-	-	-	1
Northern Pike	-	-	-	-	1	9	2	-	12
Smallmouth Bass	-	-	-	3	4	-	-	-	7
Tullibee (Cisco)	-	-	1	-	-	-	-	-	1
Walleye	-	1	33	28	23	10	-	-	95
White Sucker	-	1	2	2	23	5	-	-	33
Yellow Perch	3	8	2	-	-	-	-	-	13

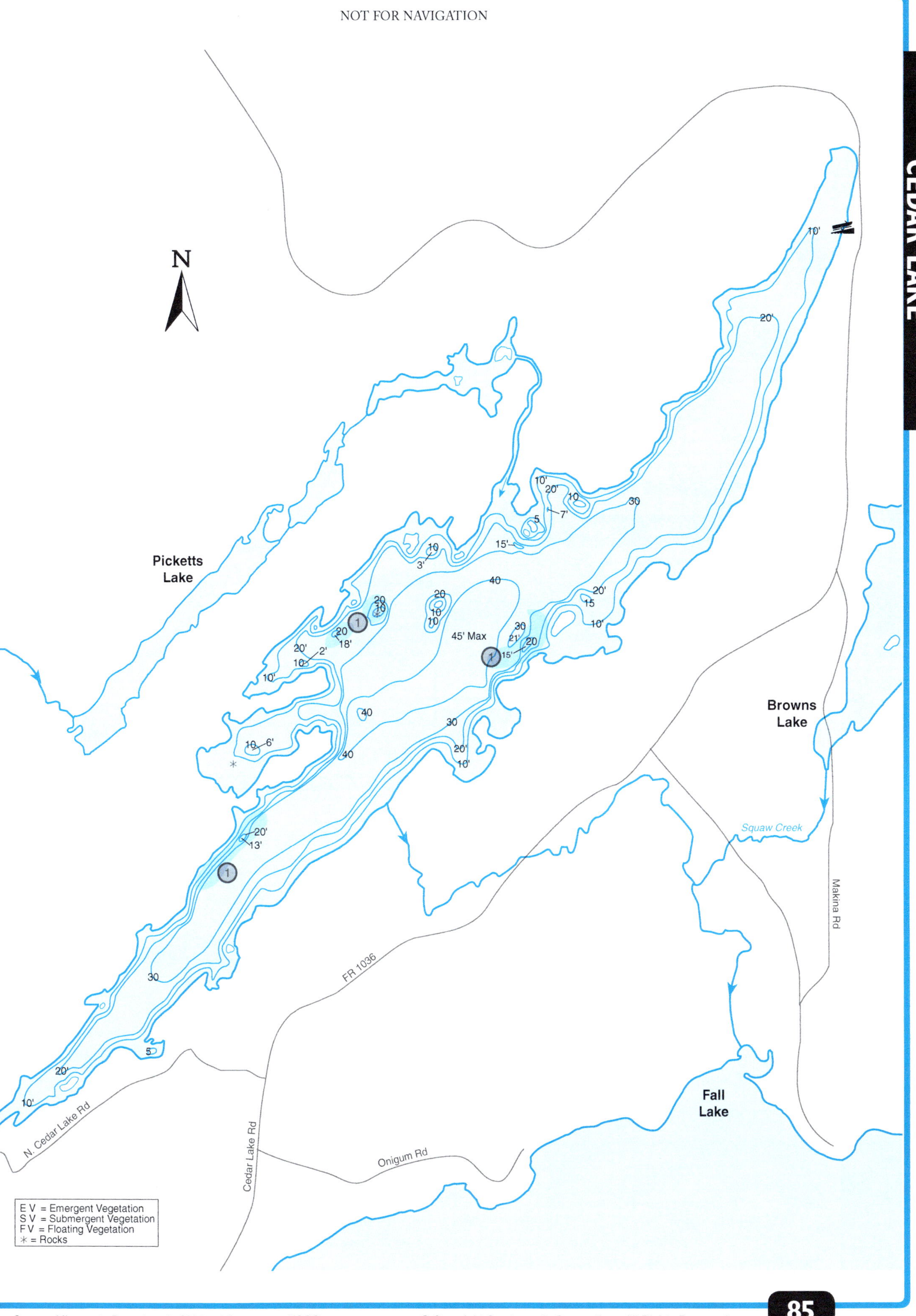

Source: Minnesota Department of Natural Resources, USGS

FALL LAKE *Lake County*

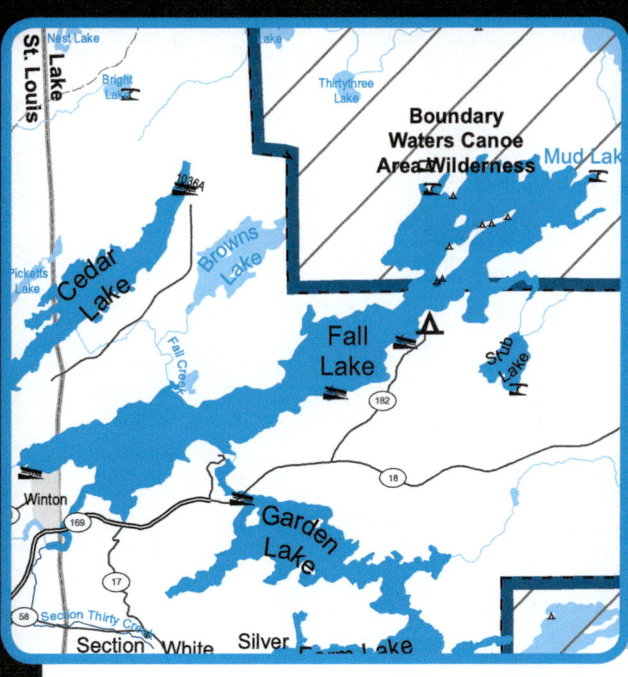

Area map page / coordinates: 14 / B,C-1,2

Watershed: Rainy headwaters

Surface water area / shorelength: 2,258 acres / 22.5 miles

Maximum / mean depth: 32 feet / 14 feet

Water color / clarity: Brown, bog stain / 4.3 ft. secchi (2012)

Shoreland zoning classification: Recreational development

Management class / Ecological type: Walleye /soft-water walley

Accessibility: 1) Public access with concrete ramp in Winton; 91° 48' 12" W / 47° 55' 55" N

2) Public access with gravel ramp on south shore; 91° 44' 28" W / 47° 56' 31" N

3) Public access with double concrete ramp on south shore; 91° 42' 51" W / 47° 57' 16" N

Accommodations: Camping, resorts, boat rental

FISHING INFORMATION

Dark, brooding and big, Fall Lake stretches over some six miles of land northeast of Winton. The lake is easily accessible, with several different launches. Amenities are available, whether you're there for a day of fishing or starting a week-long trip into the Boundary Waters.

The fishing on Fall Lake is pretty good. Cliff Noble, owner of Skube's Bait & Tackle, 1810 E. Sheridan St., Ely, MN 55731, (218) 365-5358, says walleye fishing has been picking up in recent years, but folks also do well for smallmouth bass, northern pike, perch and rock bass.

Walleyes are the big-ticket item in Fall Lake, and the population of this tasty fish species is in good shape, with lots of small- to medium-sized walleyes out there. Although catching small fish can be irritating, it just means that there will be bigger fish in a few years, although you might have to wait longer than usual because Fall Lake's walleyes often grow slowly.

Northern pike numbers have been increasing, but the average size is still good, with some decent eaters as well as some quality-sized pike.

Panfish action can be good here as well. Yellow perch are the primary panfish species here, and they grow large, with over half of them in the last DNR survey measuring 9 inches or better. Rock bass, bluegills and crappies are found here in lower numbers, but they, too, grow large, with both rock bass and bluegills sometimes topping 9 inches and foot-long crappies.

Smallmouth bass are swimming around in Fall Lake too and some of them are of quality size.

When looking for walleyes, a few key areas stand out. Among the best early in the year are the shorelines around the Shagawa River inlet **(Spot 1)** in the southwest corner and the creek inlet **(Spot 2)** north of Winton. The steep shoreline northwest of Mile Island **(Spot 3)** is a good spot later in the year, as are the small, rocky islands and humps **(Spots 4)** toward the lake's western end.

Despite the amenities and good fishing, recreational pressure is only moderate.

Anglers should be aware that part of Fall Lake, essentially everything north of the southern tip of Mile Island, is located within the Boundary Waters. Although motorboats are allowed in that portion of Fall Lake lying within the BWCA, there is a 25-horsepower limit. Boaters should be careful because lake levels fluctuate, due to a dam upstream on Garden Lake.

NO RECORD OF STOCKING

NET CATCH DATA

Date: 06/25/2012	Gill Nets		Trap Nets	
species	# per net	avg. fish weight (lbs.)	# per net	avg. fish weight (lbs
Black Crappie	0.09	0.25	0.53	0.67
Bluegill	0.09	0.03	1.33	0.48
Northern Pike	3.45	2.18	0.47	1.74
Rock Bass	0.36	0.53	0.40	0.45
Smallmouth Bass	0.36	2.37	0.07	0.85
Walleye	11.18	0.56	0.67	1.13
White Sucker	1.73	1.47	0.47	2.64
Yellow Perch	3.91	0.46	0.47	0.52

LENGTH OF SELECTED SPECIES SAMPLED FROM ALL GEAR

Number of fish caught for the following length categories (inches):

species	0-5	6-8	9-11	12-14	15-19	20-24	25-29	>30	Total
Black Crappie	-	4	3	2	-	-	-	-	9
Bluegill	1	18	2	-	-	-	-	-	21
Northern Pike	-	-	-	5	19	13	6	2	45
Rock Bass	2	4	3	-	-	-	-	-	9
Shorthead Redhorse	-	-	1	-	8	5	-	-	14
Smallmouth Bass	-	-	1	2	2	-	-	-	5
Tullibee (Cisco)	-	19	29	20	21	-	-	-	89
Walleye	7	44	20	35	26	1	-	-	133
White Sucker	-	2	3	2	19	-	-	-	26
Yellow Perch	8	11	22	4	-	-	-	-	45

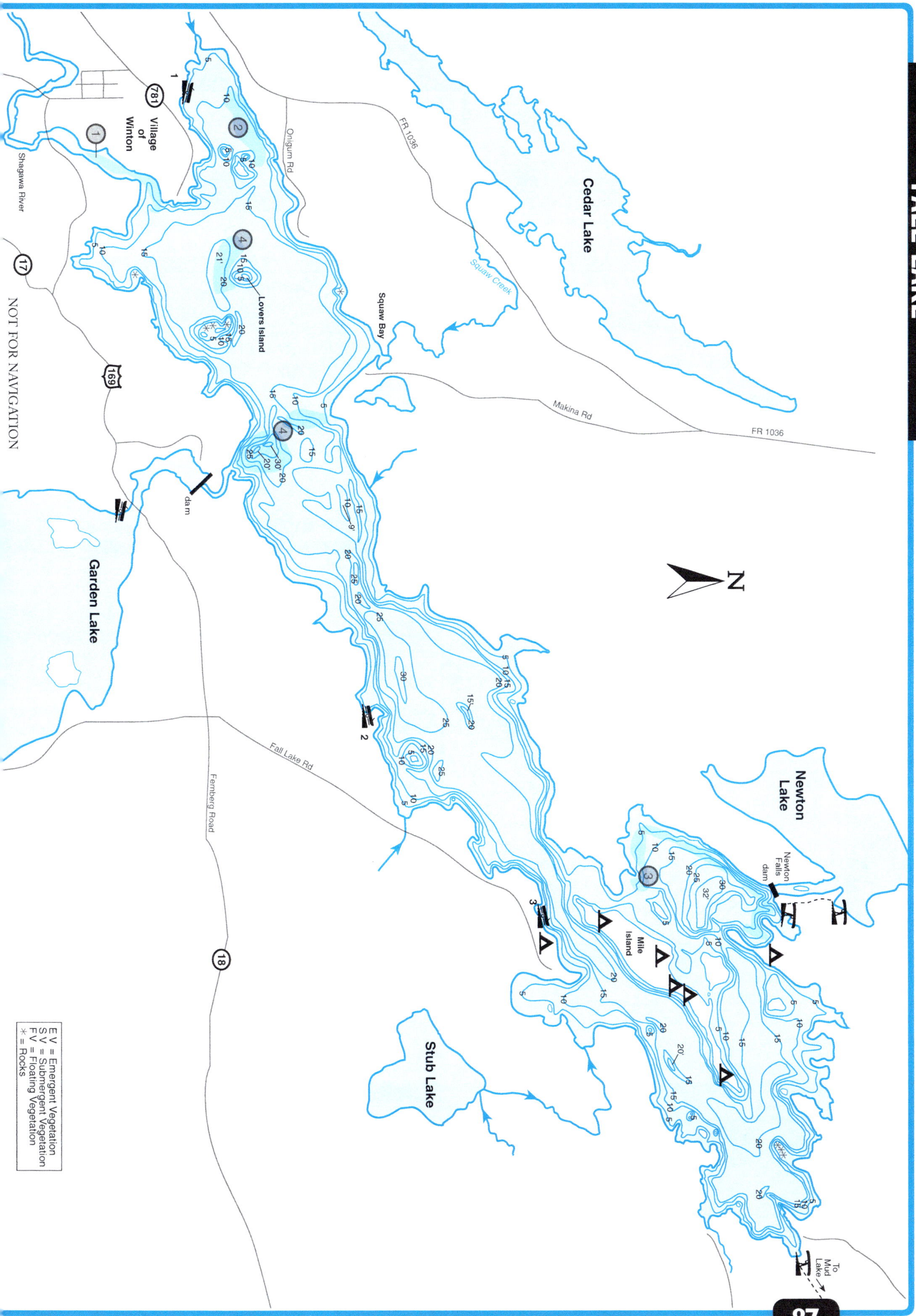
Cedar Lake
Village of Winton
781
Shagawa River
17
Onigum Rd
FR 1036
Squaw Creek
Squaw Bay
Lovers Island
169
Makina Rd
FR 1036
NOT FOR NAVIGATION
dam
Garden Lake
N
Fall Lake Rd
Fernberg Road
Newton Lake
Newton Falls dam
Mile Island
18
Stub Lake
To Mud Lake
EV = Emergent Vegetation
SV = Submergent Vegetation
FV = Floating Vegetation
* = Rocks

Source: Minnesota Department of Natural Resources, USGS

GARDEN LAKE *Lake County*

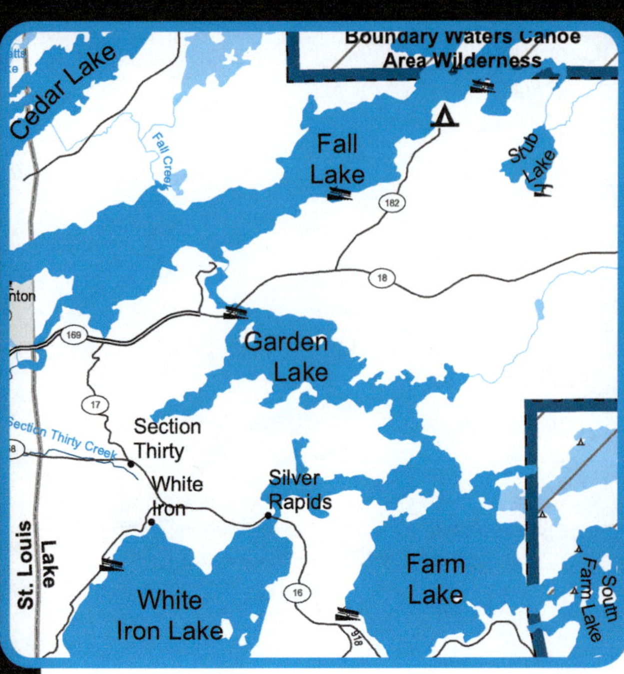

Area map page / coordinates: 14 / B,C-1,2

Watershed: Rainy headwaters

Surface water area / shorelength: 653 acres / 12.9 miles

Maximum / mean depth: 55 feet / 18 feet

Water color / clarity: Brown, bog stain / 5.0 ft. secchi (2012)

Shoreland zoning classification: Recreational development

Management class / Ecological type: Walleye /soft-water walley

Accessibility: Public access with concrete ramp on northwest shor at the bridge off Fernberg Trail; 91° 45' 38" W / 47° 55' 41" N; also via navigable channel from Farm Lake or White Iron Lake

Accommodations: Resorts, boat rental

FISHING INFORMATION

This moderate-sized, dark-water lake is another of Ely's "jewels." This one isn't quite as precious as others in the area; nonetheless, it's well worth an afternoon of exploration. Expect to find decent numbers of walleyes, average northern pike, a fair bluegill population and some decent black crappies.

Garden Lake has a low walleye population compared to similar lake types. However, the latest DNR assessment found walleye numbers to be up, at least by Garden Lake standards. The lake is stocked with walleye fingerlings every other year, which supplements the lake's natural reproduction. The fish are slow-growing. To help improve walleye size structure, the DNR implemented a protected slot on walleyes from 17 to 26 inches, with one fish over 26 inches allowed. DNR figures show the regulation is producing the intended results, with surveys since the regulation was enacted showing triple the number of walleyes over 17 inches and double the number over 26.

Northern pike are present in low numbers in Garden Lake and size structure is good, with some nice-sized fish available. Northerns, too, have a protected slot limit. Anglers must release pike from 24 to 36 inches. One pike over 36 inches may be kept.

Although there isn't a high population, bluegills are present in Garden, and they grow fast and large. Average size for this hard-fighting panfish is over 7 inches, with some fish exceeding 9 inches.

Anglers will also find black crappies, smallmouth bass, yellow perch, tullibees and a few other fish species in Garden Lake.

Cliff Noble, owner of Skube's Bait & Tackle, 1810 E. Sheridan St., Ely, MN 55731 (218) 365-5358, says leeches and minnows are the ticket for the lake's walleyes. Live bait does just fine for pike, as well. The lake's best spots, says Noble, are in the main lobe, up toward the public access and the dam. Th islands **(Spots 1)** are the main fish-holding attractions in this area, bu don't overlook the deep hole **(Spot 2)** and its steeply sloping sides. Yo might want to check out the nearby hump **(Spot 3)**, as well. Its 3-foot to juts up steeply from a bottom that's around 20 feet.

Fluorescent or even glow colors are the best way to attract attentio to your fishing lures in this moderately dark water, as visibility is onl about 5 feet.

FISH STOCKING DATA

year	species	size	# released
11	Walleye	Fingerling	4,230
13	Walleye	Fingerling	6,686
15	Walleye	Fingerling	6,952

NET CATCH DATA

Date: 06/11/2012	Gill Nets		Trap Nets	
species	# per net	avg. fish weight (lbs.)	# per net	avg. fish weight (lbs
Black Crappie	-	-	0.50	0.59
Bluegill	0.33	0.24	1.67	0.39
Northern Pike	1.11	2.67	1.00	1.31
Rock Bass	0.44	0.62	1.08	0.40
Smallmouth Bass	0.22	0.69	-	-
Walleye	3.00	0.51	0.50	0.71
White Sucker	2.11	1.53	1.42	3.15
Yellow Perch	2.56	0.22	1.58	0.31

LENGTH OF SELECTED SPECIES SAMPLED FROM ALL GEAR

Number of fish caught for the following length categories (inches):

species	0-5	6-8	9-11	12-14	15-19	20-24	25-29	>30	Total
Black Crappie	1	-	5	-	-	-	-	-	6
Bluegill	8	14	1	-	-	-	-	-	23
Northern Pike	-	-	-	3	10	5	3	1	22
Rock Bass	1	12	4	-	-	-	-	-	17
Smallmouth Bass	-	-	2	-	-	-	-	-	2
Tullibee (Cisco)	-	45	13	8	-	-	-	-	66
Walleye	3	9	7	7	6	-	-	-	32
White Sucker	-	3	3	2	24	4	-	-	36
Yellow Perch	15	16	11	-	-	-	-	-	42

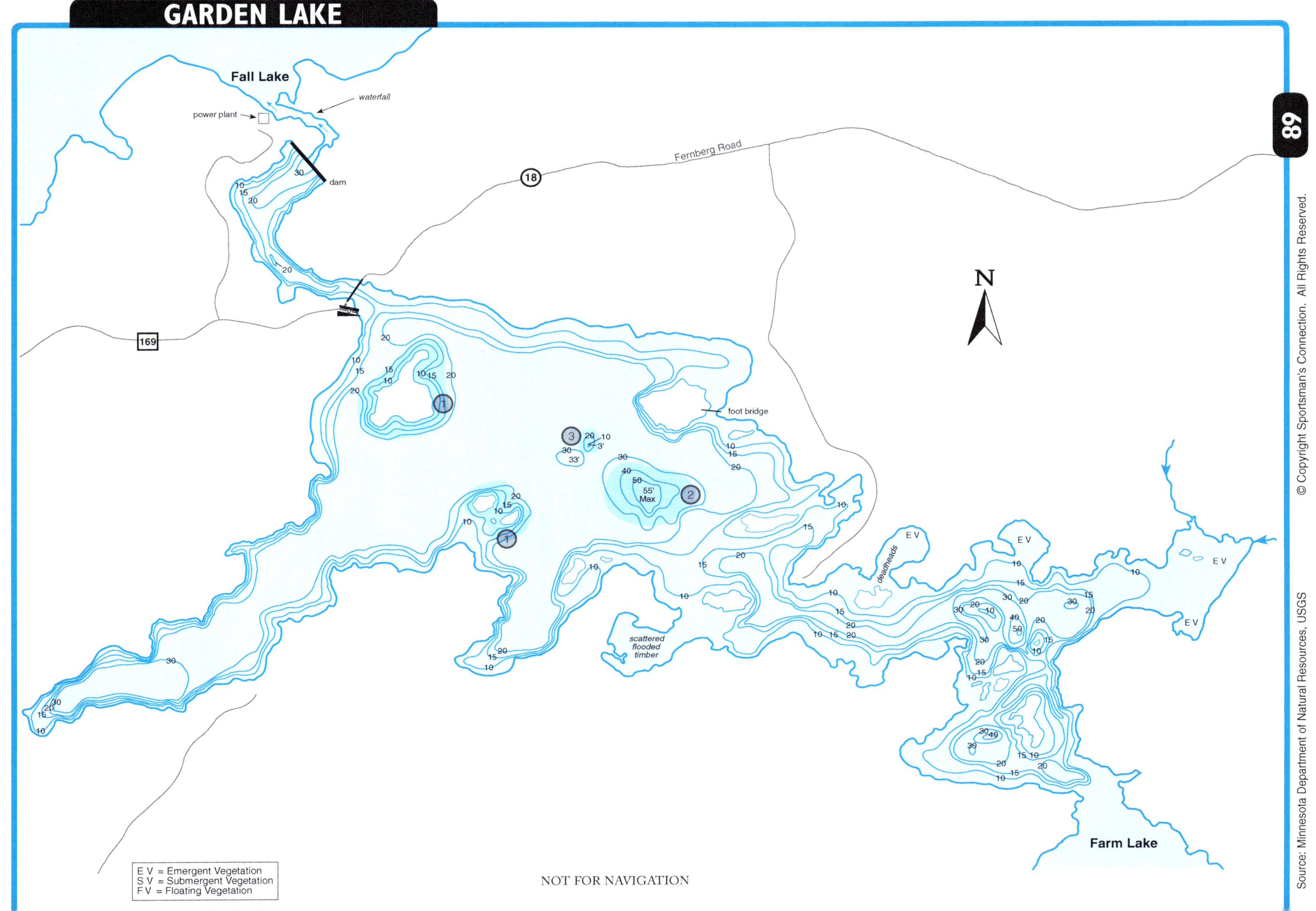

Source: Minnesota Department of Natural Resources, USGS

WHITE IRON LAKE *St. Louis County*

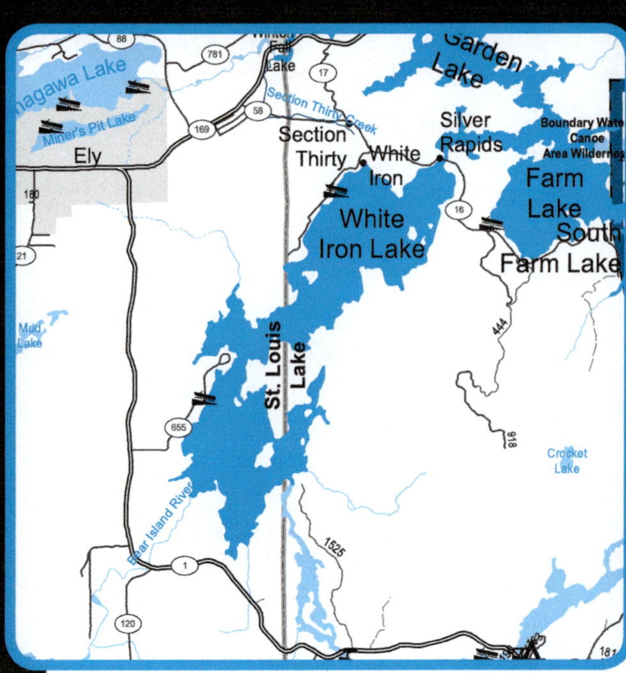

Area map page / coordinates: 14 / C,D-1

Watershed: Rainy headwaters

Surface water area / shorelength: 3,246 acres / 26.0 miles

Maximum / mean depth: 47 feet / 16 feet

Water color / clarity: Brown, bog stain / 5.5 ft. secchi (2014)

Shoreland zoning classification: Recreational development

Management class / Ecological type: Walleye /soft-water walley

Accessibility: 1) State-owned public access with concrete ramp or northwest shore; 91° 47' 2" W / 47° 53' 54" N

2) County-owned public access with concrete ramp on west shore of south basin; 91° 49' 14" W / 47° 51' 42" N

Accommodations: Resorts, boat rental, camping

FISHING INFORMATION

Located not far southeast of Ely, White Iron Lake is moderately bog-stained with limited weed growth. The lake boasts healthy populations of walleyes, northern pike, smallmouth bass, tullibees and a few nice black crappies.

Although White Iron was stocked with walleyes once upon a time, the lake's walleyes reproduce quite effectively on their own and stocking was discontinued. There is an average number of walleyes in White Iron, although the last DNR survey showed numbers were just a little lower than what is typical for the lake. Still, numbers were good, as is size structure. There is a protected slot on walleyes from 17 to 26 inches here, with one allowed over 26, and there are certainly walleyes here large enough to fall into - and above - that slot.

White Iron may be the place to go if you are looking for that northern pike of a lifetime. There are fish here topping 40 inches, thanks mostly to a good forage base of yellow perch, white suckers and tullibees. Pike also have a slot limit to protect large spawners and focus harvest on smaller fish. Anglers must immediately release all pike between 24 and 36 inches. One trophy over 36 inches is allowed, but of course, catch and release is encouraged for large fish.

Anglers will find some smallmouth bass on White Iron, and there are some quality fish here capable of reaching 20 inches.

Perch, crappies and bluegills all grow fairly large as well, providing good catches for panfish fans.

Dave DuFresne, former tackle shop owner in Ely, says there's one hotspot that has to be pointed out: it is known as Silver Rapids and is the outlet of the Kawishiwi River. This is located on the northeast side, where a slow current passes through narrow Silver Rapids, often attracting northern pike and walleyes. The fish are fairly easy to catch there, says DuFresne, and many of those landed are big, including walleyes of 3 or 4 pounds and northerns up to 20 pounds or more. Not all the action is around the river, though. There are plenty of other good early season walleye spots. Look for points and small islands in the north bay for early season walleyes and smallmouths. The same is true of the south bay, particularly th east side, which is loaded with islands, reefs, breaks, points and bars. Liv bait – shiners, leeches and nightcrawlers – is good early in the season, say DuFresne, although Rapalas are also popular.

Because of the strong forage base, a few walleyes attain lunker siz but because of heavy fishing pressure, you're more likely to find eaters Northerns are also on the large side in White Iron, where they hav good weedbeds to patrol for suckers and deep water to roam for tullibees Spoons, spinnerbaits and crankbaits fished at the outside weed edges ca be very effective.

NO RECORD OF STOCKING

NET CATCH DATA

Date: 08/11/2014	Gill Nets		Trap Nets	
species	# per net	avg. fish weight (lbs.)	# per net	avg. fish weight (lbs
Black Crappie	0.17	0.12	1.80	0.39
Bluegill	-	-	1.13	0.33
Northern Pike	1.00	3.34	1.87	2.66
Rock Bass	1.75	0.57	1.13	0.23
Smallmouth Bass	0.08	2.15	-	-
Tiger Muskellunge	0.08	5.26	-	-
Walleye	4.67	0.69	0.47	0.87
White Sucker	2.17	1.70	0.33	2.38
Yellow Perch	6.75	0.17	1.13	0.12

LENGTH OF SELECTED SPECIES SAMPLED FROM ALL GEAR

Number of fish caught for the following length categories (inches):

species	0-5	6-8	9-11	12-14	15-19	20-24	25-29	>30	Total
Black Crappie	5	13	10	1	-	-	-	-	29
Bluegill	2	15	-	-	-	-	-	-	17
Northern Pike	-	-	6	6	8	8	7	5	40
Rock Bass	9	17	12	-	-	-	-	-	38
Smallmouth Bass	-	-	-	1	-	-	-	-	1
Tiger Muskellunge	-	-	-	-	-	-	1	-	1
Tullibee (Cisco)	-	29	16	9	1	-	-	-	55
Walleye	1	15	31	4	7	5	-	-	63
White Sucker	-	1	3	8	19	-	-	-	31
Yellow Perch	38	55	5	-	-	-	-	-	98

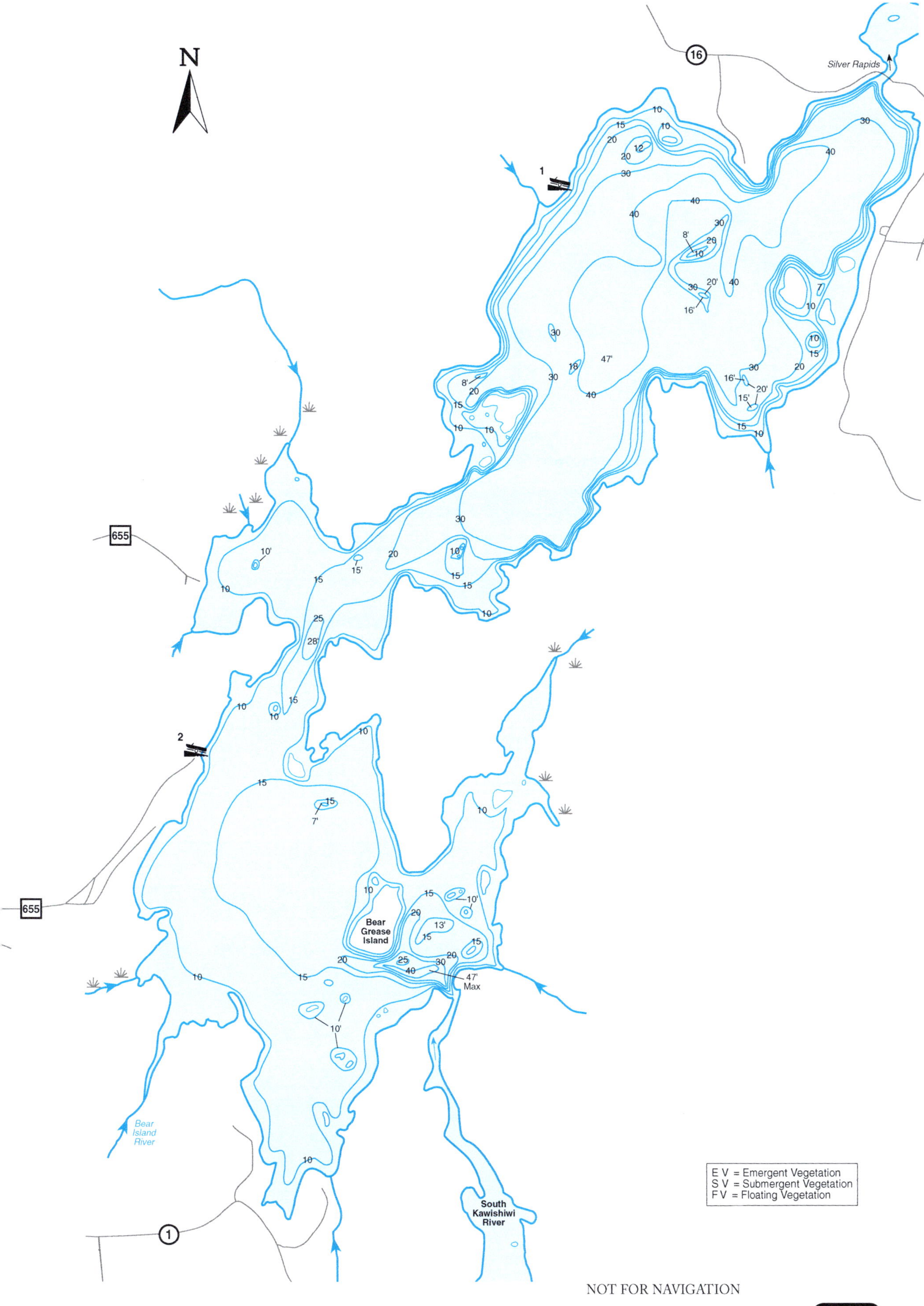

N

Silver Rapids

16

655

1

2

Bear Grease Island

47' Max

Bear Island River

South Kawishiwi River

E V = Emergent Vegetation
S V = Submergent Vegetation
F V = Floating Vegetation

NOT FOR NAVIGATION

Source: Minnesota Department of Natural Resources, USGS

FARM LAKE *Lake County*

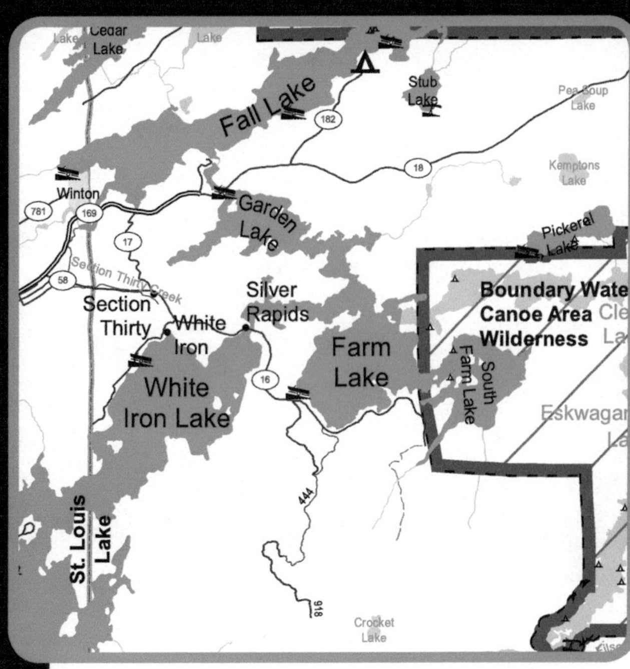

Area map page / coordinates: 14 / C-1,2

Watershed: Rainy headwaters

Surface water area / shorelength: 1,292 acres / 16.5 miles

Maximum / mean depth: 56 feet / 20 feet

Water color / clarity: Brown, bog stain / 6.0 ft. secchi (2012)

Shoreland zoning classification: Recreational development

Management class / Ecological type: Walleye /soft-water walley

Accessibility: USFS-owned public access with concrete ramp on west shore; 91° 44' 27" W / 47° 53' 31" N

Also accessible via navigable channel from Garden, South Farm, White Iron and North Kawishiwi River

Accommodations: Resorts, boat rental

FISHING INFORMATION

Stained by bog runoff, Farm is one of a group of fair-sized lakes east of Ely. This lake is very much like the others; a basic walleye fishery with northern pike, yellow perch, some smallmouth bass and a cisco forage base. Aquatic plants aren't very prevalent, as the bottom substrate is mostly boulder, rubble, sand and muck.

The last DNR survey showed walleye numbers to be at an all-time high, although most fish tended to be on the smaller side. Years in which stocking occurred accounted for a disproportionate amount of the fish sampled, although natural reproduction is certainly taking place as well. Like other lakes in the system, Farm Lake walleyes have a protected slot from 17 to 26 inches, with one fish over 26 inches allowed in the daily bag.

Northern pike are found in moderate numbers here, with definite trophy potential. The low density means more food to go around, and there are plenty of perch, suckers and tullibees to feed on. Pike have a protected slot from 24 to 36 inches, with one over 36 inches allowed.

Smallmouth bass numbers are marginal, but there are some hefty smallies lurking here, with an honest chance at a 20-incher.

Tullibee numbers have been in a downward trend in Farm for decades, but this prey species is still out there, feeding big pike and walleyes and providing good sport for the few anglers who pursue them.

Yellow perch numbers are about average. There are definitely some eaters, which are probably most frequently caught accidentally by walleye anglers.

Farm Lake bluegill numbers are about average and although the latest survey found a lot of young fish, there are a few big ones to be found.

Crappies are not super-abundant here, but they have the ability to grow large and are not often targeted.

Cliff Noble, owner of Skube's Bait & Tackle, 1810 E. Sheridan St., Ely, MN 55731, (218) 365-5358, says anglers do well on eater-size walleyes, and they take some larger ones as well.

Walleye hunters have a lot to choose from on Farm Lake, but a fe areas top the list. The big point near the Garden Lake channel **(Spot 1** is one of the best spots to try for walleyes. Directly east of the point i a nice shoreline with a steep break and inside turn **(Spot 2)**. The broa point and bar **(Spot 3)** on the lake's southwest side offer good mid-seaso angling and the islands off the long point **(Spot 4)** on the southeast sid should be explored during the summer.

year	species	size	# released
09	Walleye	Fingerling	4,688
11	Walleye	Fingerling	8,078
13	Walleye	Fingerling	12,832
15	Walleye	Fingerling	13,508

NET CATCH DATA

Date: 06/13/2012	Gill Nets		Trap Nets	
species	# per net	avg. fish weight (lbs.)	# per net	avg. fish weight (lbs
Black Crappie	0.44	0.22	0.75	0.48
Bluegill	1.78	0.15	3.67	0.15
Northern Pike	1.00	3.86	0.83	3.28
Rock Bass	0.78	0.49	1.42	0.37
Smallmouth Bass	0.22	1.32	-	-
Tullibee (Cisco)	4.89	0.35	-	-
Walleye	10.00	1.03	0.75	1.07
White Sucker	1.89	1.36	0.75	3.64
Yellow Perch	2.78	0.23	1.25	0.29

LENGTH OF SELECTED SPECIES SAMPLED FROM ALL GEAR

Number of fish caught for the following length categories (inches):

species	0-5	6-8	9-11	12-14	15-19	20-24	25-29	>30	Total
Black Crappie	3	4	6	-	-	-	-	-	13
Bluegill	43	14	1	-	-	-	-	-	58
Northern Pike	-	-	1	2	6	2	3	5	19
Rock Bass	4	19	1	-	-	-	-	-	24
Smallmouth Bass	1	-	-	-	1	-	-	-	2
Tullibee (Cisco)	-	32	4	8	-	-	-	-	44
Walleye	-	32	18	21	19	8	1	-	99
White Sucker	-	5	3	1	11	6	-	-	26
Yellow Perch	11	17	12	-	-	-	-	-	40

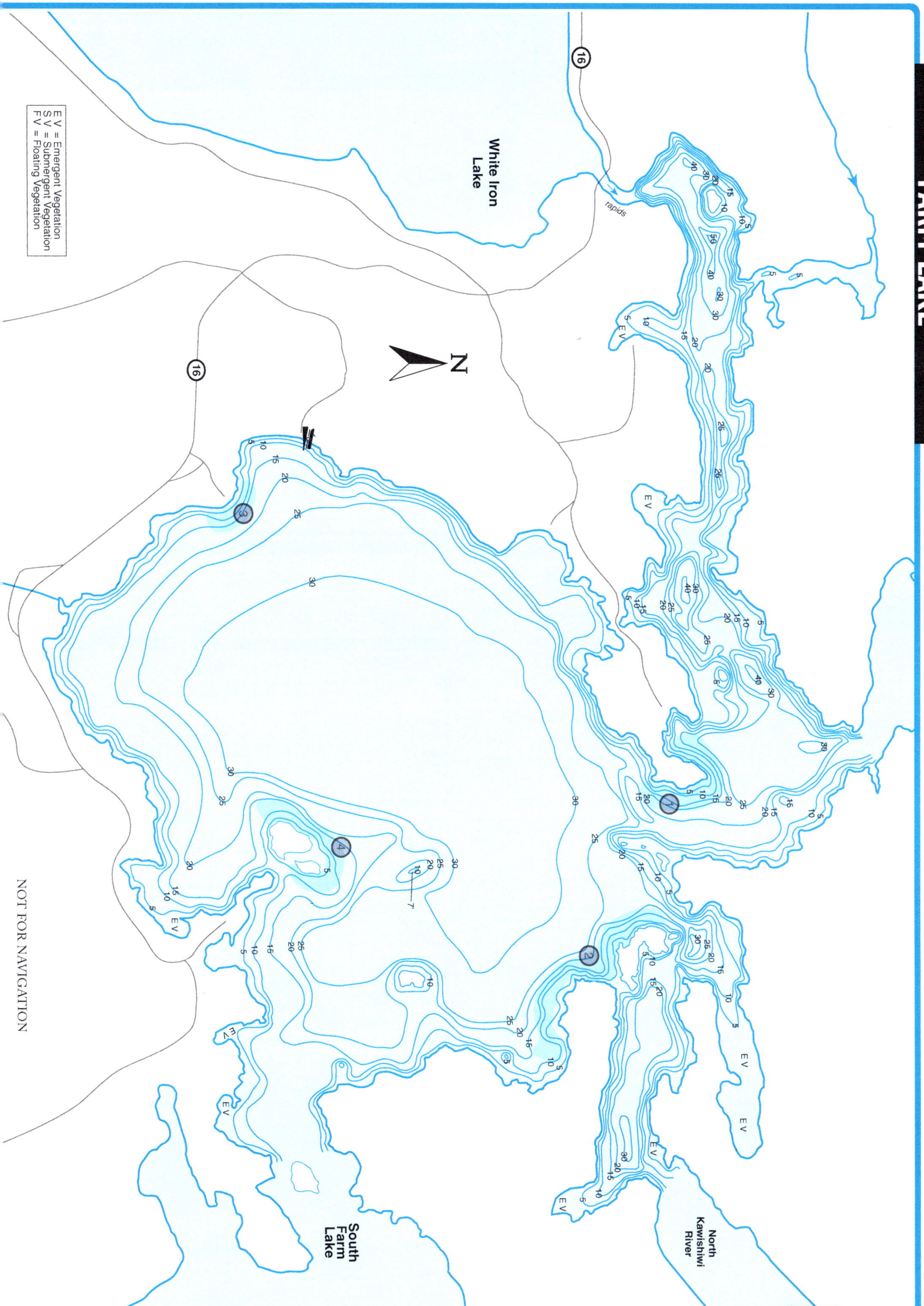

E V = Emergent Vegetation
S V = Submergent Vegetation
F V = Floating Vegetation

White Iron Lake

rapids

South Farm Lake

North Kawishiwi River

NOT FOR NAVIGATION

Source: Minnesota Department of Natural Resources, USGS

SOUTH FARM LAKE *Lake County*

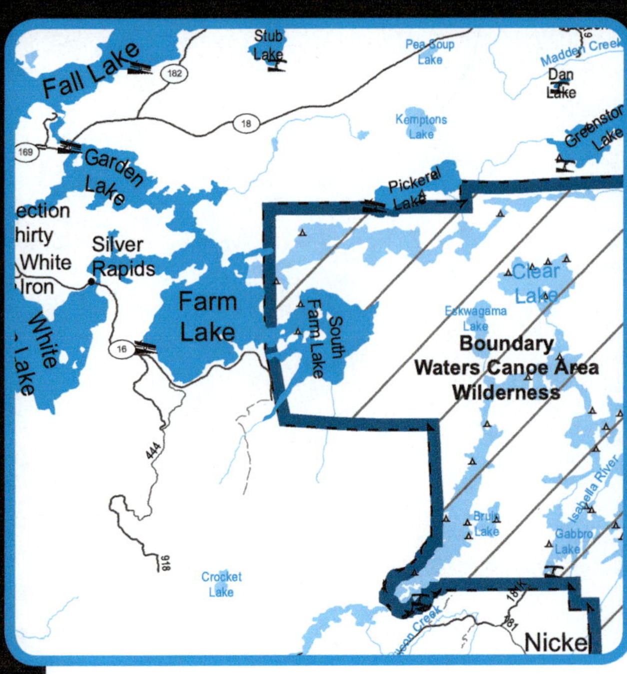

Area map page / coordinates: 14 / C-2

Watershed: Rainy headwaters

Surface water area / shorelength: 564 acres / 7.8 miles

Maximum / mean depth: 30 feet / 13 feet

Water color / clarity: Brown, bog stain / 5.5 ft. secchi (2012)

Shoreland zoning classification: Recreational development

Management class / Ecological type: Walleye /soft-water walleye

Accessibility: Via navigable channel from Farm Lake

Accommodations: Camping

FISHING INFORMATION

South Farm's 564 acres of moderately stained, mesotrophic water hold a lot of walleyes. South Farm is an entry point to the Boundary Waters Canoe Area Wilderness. That means day-use permits are required. But it's well worth picking one up to visit this lake, as the fishery is definitely something special.

During the last DNR survey, walleye abundance was at an all-time high in Farm Lake. Ditto for South Farm, not surprisingly, since the two are connected. Although there are a lot of walleyes, many of them are small. Still, small walleyes can eventually become big walleyes, and there are definitely some nice fish out there. Like the other connected lakes in this system, South Farm has a protected slot on walleyes from 17 to 26 inches, with one allowed over 26 inches in the daily bag limit.

Northern pike are present in moderate numbers in South Farm and size structure is good, with few fish of the "snake" variety sampled. Most pike are at least decent, running 20 inches or more. There are some real brutes out there as well, capable of reaching 40 inches. Fish over 40 have even turned up.

There are a few smallies hanging around the islands and rock reefs, and they grow to pretty decent size.

Panfish numbers are decent, with more crappies showing up in the South Farm survey than in the adjoining lakes. Whether that means anything or is just sampling bias is hard to say, but it is evident crappies are out there, and you'll find some good keepers. Perch and bluegills reach decent size as well.

So what about fishing on South Farm? Cliff Noble, owner of Skube's Bait & Tackle, 1810 E. Sheridan St., Ely, MN 55731, (218) 365-5358, says leeches and minnows are the preferred bait for the lake's walleyes. Fish for them in the shallows and back bays early in the season and follow them to deeper water later in the year. At that time you'll want to try the steep breaks off the shorelines and the islands. Jigging is the preferred mid-season method. Choose bright or fluorescent colors to get noticed in the relatively dark water. Smallies will hit in the same areas on live bait, spinners and small crankbaits. You'll find northern pike at the weedlines. Bluegills are in the shallows all over the lake. Fish them with worm chunks.

Motorboats are allowed in South Farm Lake, but there is a 25-horsepower limit. There are a couple campsites on this lake if you want to make your trip into a weekend outing.

FISH STOCKING DATA

year	species	size	# released
11	Walleye	Fingerling	6,480
13	Walleye	Fingerling	10,077
15	Walleye	Fingerling	10,440

NET CATCH DATA

Date: 06/13/2012

species	Gill Nets # per net	Gill Nets avg. fish weight (lbs.)	Trap Nets # per net	Trap Nets avg. fish weight (lbs.)
Black Crappie	1.00	0.49	1.58	0.62
Bluegill	2.83	0.18	7.00	0.19
Northern Pike	1.83	3.02	1.42	4.30
Rock Bass	-	-	0.08	0.31
Smallmouth Bass	1.00	1.62	-	-
Walleye	8.00	0.65	0.58	2.00
White Sucker	6.33	1.36	0.17	4.24
Yellow Perch	5.00	0.13	3.08	0.18

LENGTH OF SELECTED SPECIES SAMPLED FROM ALL GEAR

Number of fish caught for the following length categories (inches):

species	0-5	6-8	9-11	12-14	15-19	20-24	25-29	>30	Total
Black Crappie	2	4	18	1	-	-	-	-	25
Bluegill	52	46	-	-	-	-	-	-	98
Northern Pike	-	-	-	1	2	15	5	4	27
Rock Bass	-	1	-	-	-	-	-	-	1
Smallmouth Bass	-	-	1	4	1	-	-	-	6
Tullibee (Cisco)	1	60	21	3	-	-	-	-	85
Walleye	-	18	13	11	9	2	2	-	55
White Sucker	-	5	9	9	13	4	-	-	40
Yellow Perch	32	29	6	-	-	-	-	-	67

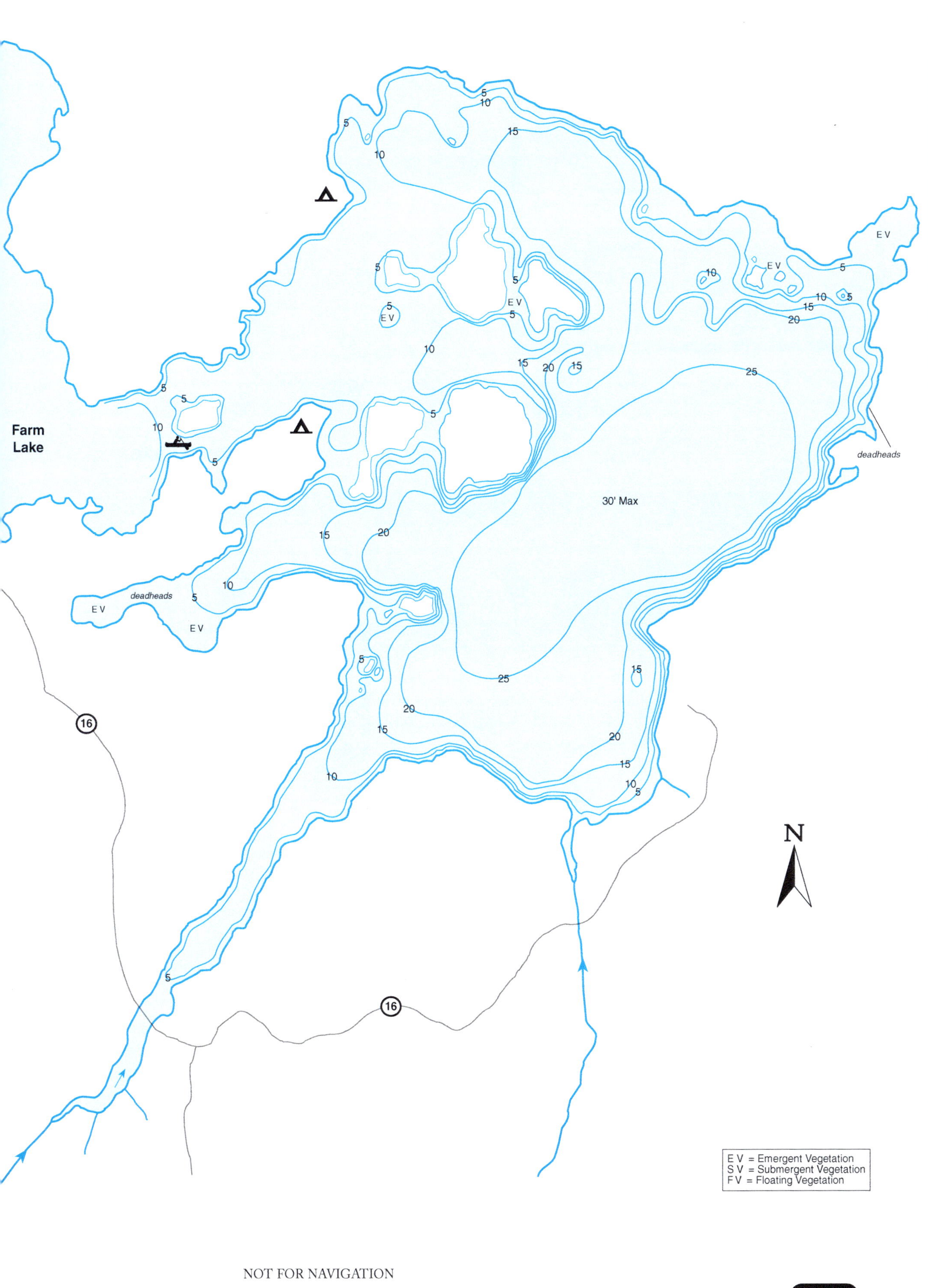

NOT FOR NAVIGATION

Source: Minnesota Department of Natural Resources, USGS

Greenstone Lake, Lake County

Area map page / coordinates: 14 / B,C-3
Surface area / max depth: 332 acres / 72 feet
Accessibility: Portage from Madden Lake to north shore; portage from Kawishiwi River to southwest shore

FISH STOCKING DATA

year	species	size	# released
06	Walleye	Fry	335,000
09	Walleye	Fry	345,000
12	Walleye	Fry	345,000

LENGTH OF SELECTED SPECIES SAMPLED FROM ALL GEAR
Survey Date: 08/11/2014
Number of fish caught for the following length categories (inches):

species	0-5	6-8	9-11	12-14	15-19	20-24	25-29	>30	Total
Bluegill	13	-	-	-	-	-	-	-	13
Northern Pike	-	-	-	-	2	7	7	1	17
Rock Bass	8	3	-	-	-	-	-	-	11
Walleye	-	1	3	7	11	7	-	-	29
White Sucker	-	1	7	-	2	5	-	-	15
Yellow Perch	1	13	-	-	-	-	-	-	14

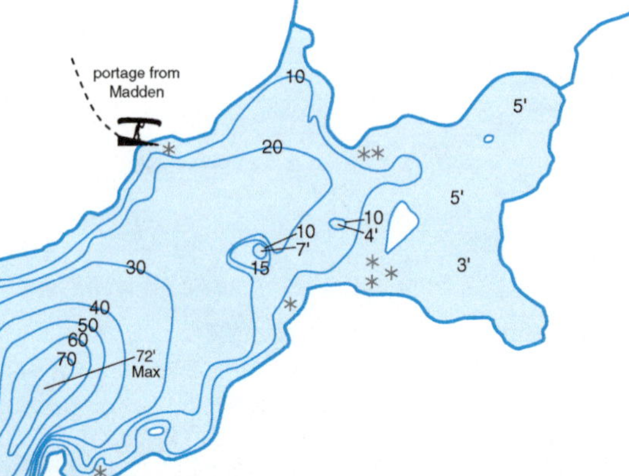

Greenstone Lake

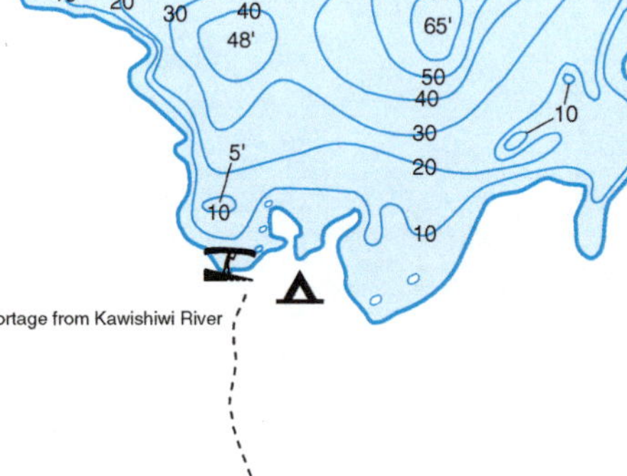

Pickerel Lake, Lake County

Area map page / coordinates: 14 / B,C-2
Surface area / max depth: 184 acres / 13 feet
Accessibility: Portage (1/4 mile) from North Kawishiwi River to southwest shore; portage (100 yards) from Glippi Forest Mgmt. Road

NO RECORD OF STOCKING

LENGTH OF SELECTED SPECIES SAMPLED FROM ALL GEAR
Survey Date: 07/14/2014
Number of fish caught for the following length categories (inches):

species	0-5	6-8	9-11	12-14	15-19	20-24	25-29	>30	Total
Northern Pike	-	-	-	-	15	17	4	-	36
Smallmouth Bass	-	-	-	1	1	-	-	-	2
Walleye	-	2	3	17	14	8	-	-	44
White Sucker	-	-	1	1	21	5	-	-	28
Yellow Perch	-	1	-	-	-	-	-	-	1

N

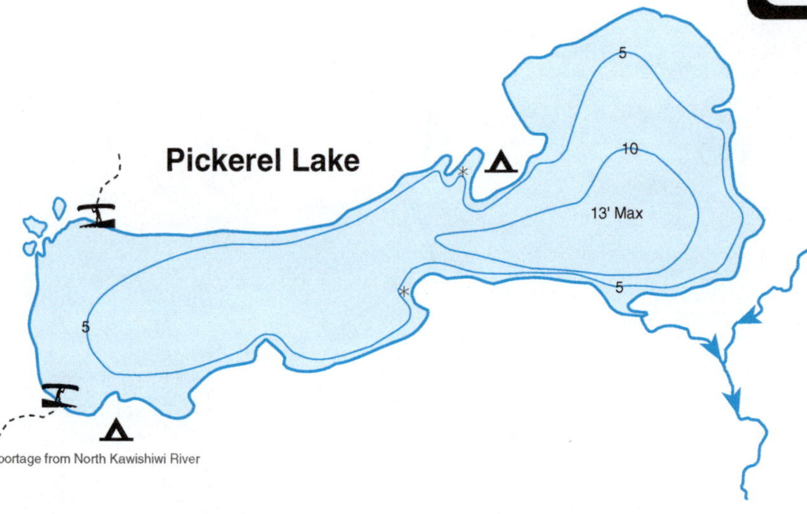

NOT FOR NAVIGATION

Source: Minnesota Department of Natural Resources, USGS

NOT FOR NAVIGATION

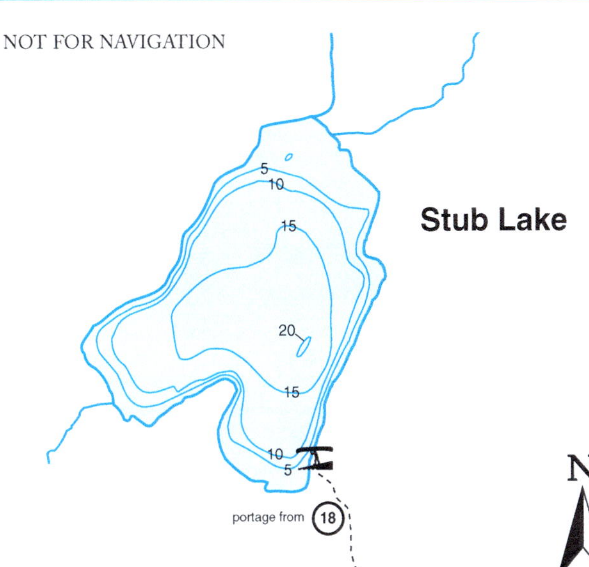

Stub Lake, Lake County

Area map page / coordinates: 14 / B-2
Surface area / max depth: 89 acres / 20 feet
Accessibility: Portage from Cty. Rd. 18 to southeast shore

NO RECORD OF STOCKING

LENGTH OF SELECTED SPECIES SAMPLED FROM ALL GEAR
Survey Date: 06/28/2012
Number of fish caught for the following length categories (inches):

species	0-5	6-8	9-11	12-14	15-19	20-24	25-29	>30	Total
Black Crappie	1	20	15	-	-	-	-	-	36
Bluegill	683	459	30	-	-	-	-	-	1172
Largemouth Bass	-	5	-	-	-	-	-	-	5
Northern Pike	-	-	-	2	2	1	1	-	6
Rock Bass	2	8	-	-	-	-	-	-	10
Yellow Perch	10	30	1	-	-	-	-	-	41

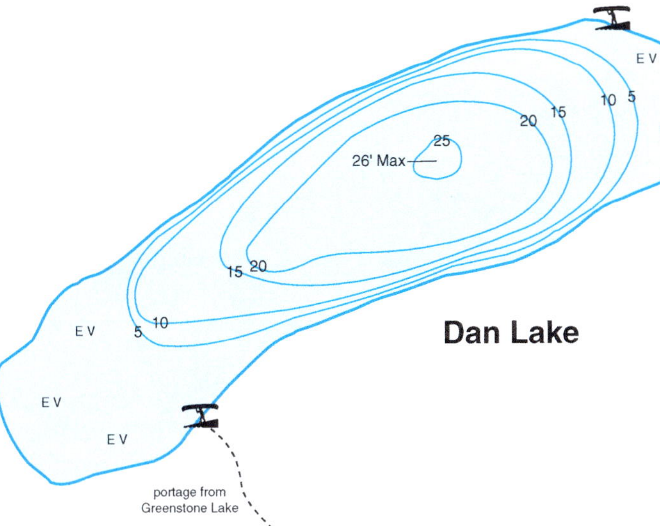

Dan Lake, Lake County

Area map page / coordinates: 14 / B-3
Surface area / max depth: 8 acres / 26 feet
Accessibility: Portage from Greenstone Lake to south shore

FISH STOCKING DATA

year	species	size	# released
05	Brook Trout	Fingerling	915
06	Brook Trout	Fingerling	831
07	Brook Trout	Fingerling	1,075
08	Brook Trout	Fingerling	990
09	Brook Trout	Fingerling	840
10	Brook Trout	Fingerling	869

LENGTH OF SELECTED SPECIES SAMPLED FROM ALL GEAR
Survey Date: 05/29/2003
Number of fish caught for the following length categories (inches):

species	0-5	6-8	9-11	12-14	15-19	20-24	25-29	>30	Total
Brook Trout	-	1	-	1	-	-	-	-	2

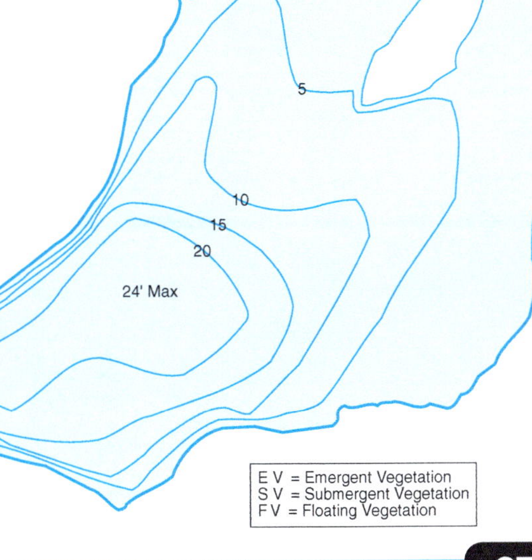

Madden Lake, Lake County

Area map page / coordinates: 14 / B-3
Surface area / max depth: 34 acres / 24 feet
Accessibility: Carry-down access from Fernberg Trail to north shore

FISH STOCKING DATA

year	species	size	# released
13	Walleye	Fry	30,000
14	Walleye	Fry	45,000

LENGTH OF SELECTED SPECIES SAMPLED FROM ALL GEAR
Survey Date: 07/11/2012
Number of fish caught for the following length categories (inches):

species	0-5	6-8	9-11	12-14	15-19	20-24	25-29	>30	Total
Green Sunfish	3	-	-	-	-	-	-	-	3
Northern Pike	-	-	-	-	-	2	8	-	10
Yellow Perch	-	6	1	-	-	-	-	-	7

Source: Minnesota Department of Natural Resources, USGS

NOT FOR NAVIGATION

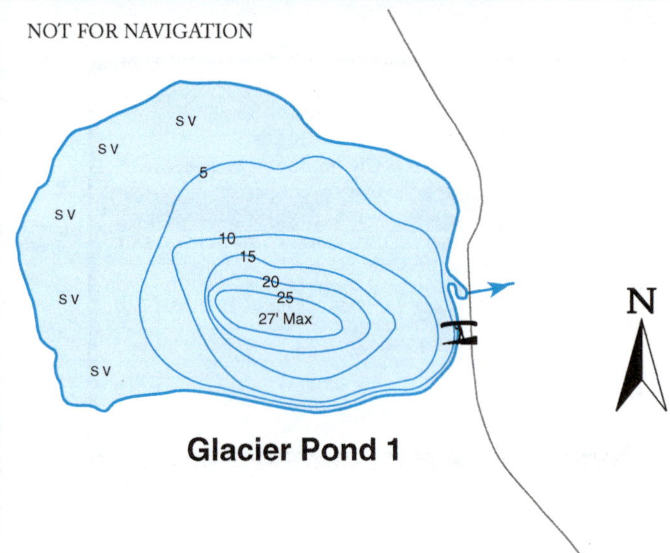

Glacier Pond 1

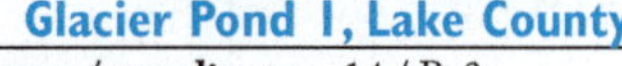

Glacier Pond 1, Lake County

Area map page / coordinates: 14 / B-3
Surface area / max depth: 18 acres / 27 feet
Accessibility: Carry-down access (100 yards) from Ojibway Lakes Summer Homes Road off Fernberg Trail to east shore

FISH STOCKING DATA

year	species	size	# released
08	Rainbow Trout	Yearling	850
09	Rainbow Trout	Yearling	850
11	Rainbow Trout	Yearling	850
12	Rainbow Trout	Yearling	850
13	Rainbow Trout	Yearling	850
14	Rainbow Trout	Yearling	850
15	Rainbow Trout	Yearling	1,275

LENGTH OF SELECTED SPECIES SAMPLED FROM ALL GEAR

Survey Date: 05/05/2004

Number of fish caught for the following length categories (inches):

species	0-5	6-8	9-11	12-14	15-19	20-24	25-29	>30	Total
Rainbow Trout	-	-	-	2	-	-	-	-	2

Glacier Pond 2

Glacier Pond 2, Lake County

Area map page / coordinates: 14 / B-3
Surface area / max depth: 6 acres / 32 feet
Accessibility: Carry-down access (100 yards) from Ojibway Lakes Summer Homes Road off Fernberg Trail to east shore

FISH STOCKING DATA

year	species	size	# released
10	Brook Trout	Fingerling	540
11	Brook Trout	Fingerling	889
12	Brook Trout	Fingerling	500
13	Brook Trout	Fingerling	500
14	Brook Trout	Fingerling	690
15	Brook Trout	Fingerling	500

LENGTH OF SELECTED SPECIES SAMPLED FROM ALL GEAR

Survey Date: 05/23/2013

Number of fish caught for the following length categories (inches):

species	0-5	6-8	9-11	12-14	15-19	20-24	25-29	>30	Total
Brook Trout	-	8	9	4	-	-	-	-	21

Tofte Lake, Lake County

Area map page / coordinates: 14 / B-3
Surface area / max depth: 134 acres / 73 feet
Accessibility: USFS-owned public access with concrete ramp on south shore; restrooms available, campsites
91° 34' 14" W / 47° 57' 43" N

FISH STOCKING DATA

year	species	size	# released
10	Rainbow Trout	Yearling	5,750
11	Rainbow Trout	Yearling	5,500
11	Splake	Fingerling	2,500
12	Rainbow Trout	Yearling	5,750
13	Rainbow Trout	Yearling	5,738
13	Splake	Fingerling	2,437
14	Rainbow Trout	Yearling	5,750
15	Rainbow Trout	Yearling	5,750
15	Rainbow Trout	Fingerling	1,560
15	Splake	Fingerling	3,035

LENGTH OF SELECTED SPECIES SAMPLED FROM ALL GEAR

Survey Date: 09/22/2008

Number of fish caught for the following length categories (inches):

species	0-5	6-8	9-11	12-14	15-19	20-24	25-29	>30	Total
Rainbow Trout	-	-	10	4	1	-	-	-	15
Splake	-	16	-	-	7	-	-	-	23

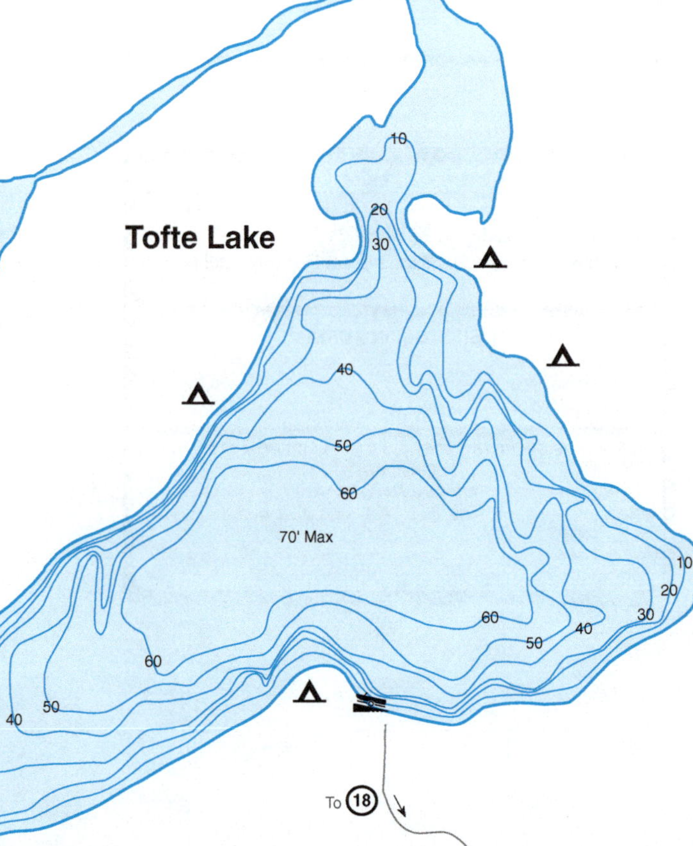

E V = Emergent Vegetation
S V = Submergent Vegetation
F V = Floating Vegetation

Source: Minnesota Department of Natural Resources, USGS

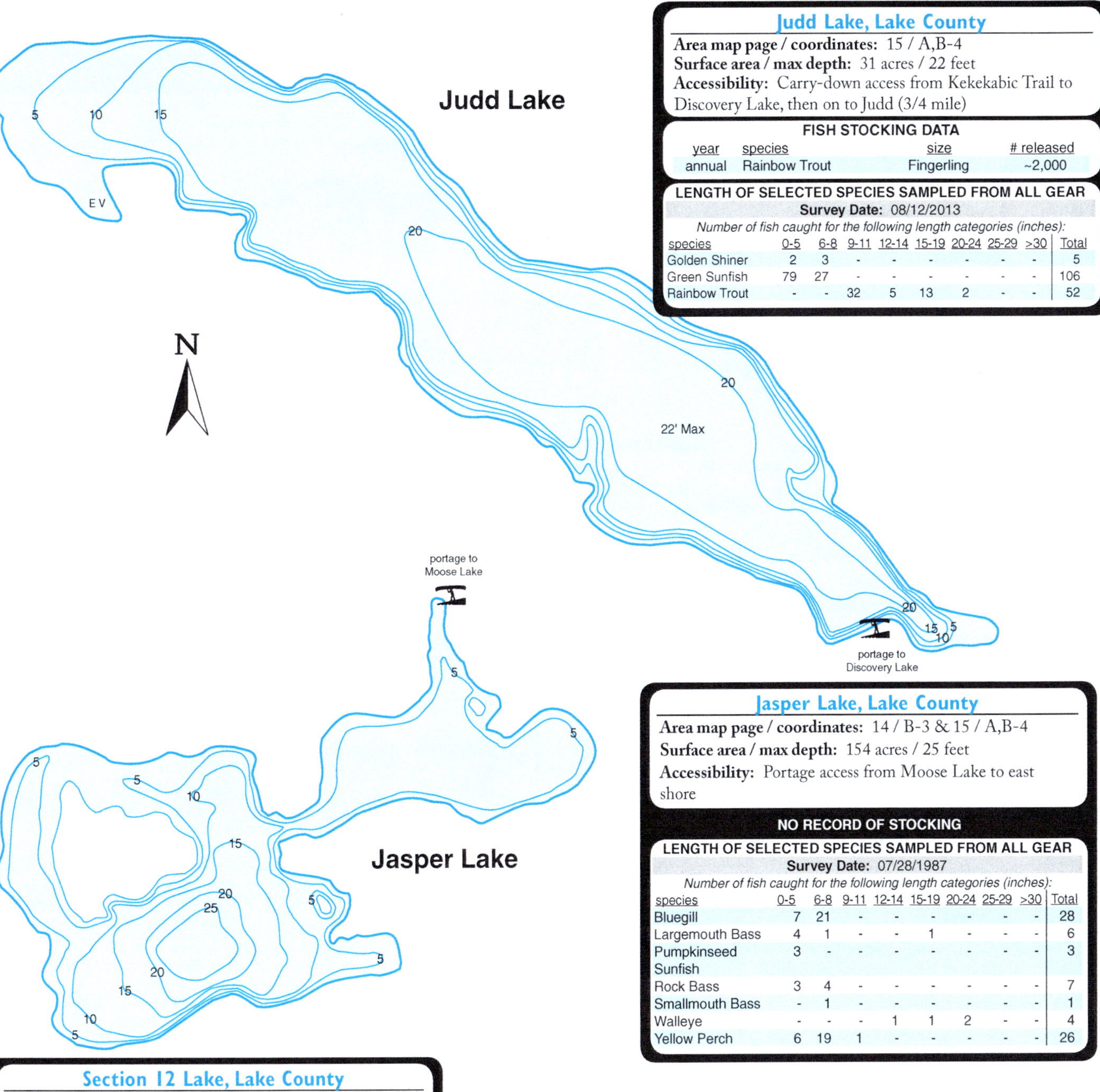

Judd Lake, Lake County

Area map page / coordinates: 15 / A,B-4
Surface area / max depth: 31 acres / 22 feet
Accessibility: Carry-down access from Kekekabic Trail to Discovery Lake, then on to Judd (3/4 mile)

FISH STOCKING DATA

year	species	size	# released
annual	Rainbow Trout	Fingerling	~2,000

LENGTH OF SELECTED SPECIES SAMPLED FROM ALL GEAR
Survey Date: 08/12/2013
Number of fish caught for the following length categories (inches):

species	0-5	6-8	9-11	12-14	15-19	20-24	25-29	>30	Total
Golden Shiner	2	3	-	-	-	-	-	-	5
Green Sunfish	79	27	-	-	-	-	-	-	106
Rainbow Trout	-	-	32	5	13	2	-	-	52

Jasper Lake, Lake County

Area map page / coordinates: 14 / B-3 & 15 / A,B-4
Surface area / max depth: 154 acres / 25 feet
Accessibility: Portage access from Moose Lake to east shore

NO RECORD OF STOCKING

LENGTH OF SELECTED SPECIES SAMPLED FROM ALL GEAR
Survey Date: 07/28/1987
Number of fish caught for the following length categories (inches):

species	0-5	6-8	9-11	12-14	15-19	20-24	25-29	>30	Total
Bluegill	7	21	-	-	-	-	-	-	28
Largemouth Bass	4	1	-	-	1	-	-	-	6
Pumpkinseed Sunfish	3	-	-	-	-	-	-	-	3
Rock Bass	3	4	-	-	-	-	-	-	7
Smallmouth Bass	-	1	-	-	-	-	-	-	1
Walleye	-	-	-	1	1	2	-	-	4
Yellow Perch	6	19	1	-	-	-	-	-	26

Section 12 Lake, Lake County

Area map page / coordinates: 14 / B-3 & 15 / B-4
Surface area / max depth: 43 acres / 54 feet
Accessibility: Carry-down access from Old Fernberg Road to northwest corner of lake

FISH STOCKING DATA

year	species	size	# released
08	Walleye	Fingerling	194
10	Walleye	Fingerling	396
12	Walleye	Fingerling	663
14	Walleye	Fingerling	804

LENGTH OF SELECTED SPECIES SAMPLED FROM ALL GEAR
Survey Date: 07/12/2010
Number of fish caught for the following length categories (inches):

species	0-5	6-8	9-11	12-14	15-19	20-24	25-29	>30	Total
Bluegill	159	22	-	-	-	-	-	-	181
Green Sunfish	1	-	-	-	-	-	-	-	1
Largemouth Bass	2	5	2	2	-	-	-	-	11
Northern Pike	-	-	-	-	2	-	1	-	3
Rock Bass	22	18	-	-	-	-	-	-	40
Smallmouth Bass	4	11	4	-	-	-	-	-	19
Tullibee (Cisco)	-	-	-	1	8	2	-	-	11
Walleye	-	-	2	5	10	4	-	-	21
Yellow Perch	2	2	-	-	-	-	-	-	4

Section 12 Lake

18

FV
38'
54' Max

E V = Emergent Vegetation
S V = Submergent Vegetation
F V = Floating Vegetation

NOT FOR NAVIGATION

OJIBWAY LAKE *Lake County*

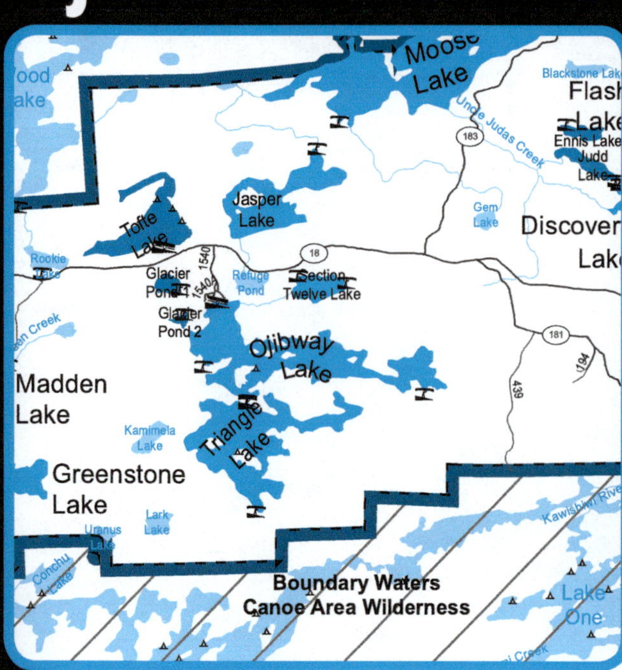

Area map page / coordinates: 14 / B-3 & 15 / B-4

Watershed: Rainy headwaters

Surface water area / shorelength: 367 acres / 8.0 miles

Maximum / mean depth: 115 feet / 24 feet

Water color / clarity: Clear / 17.0 ft. secchi (2007)

Shoreland zoning classification: Recreational development

Management class / Ecological type: Lake trout / trout

Accessibility: USFS-owned public access with ramp on north shore of western lake; parking for 12 vehicles

91° 33' 40" W / 47° 57' 19" N

Accommodations: Camping, roller portage between Ojibway and Triangle Lakes

FISHING INFORMATION

Some nice lake trout are pulled out of this lake's clear water each year, says Cliff Noble, owner of Skube's Bait & Tackle, 1810 E. Sheridan St., Ely, MN 55731, (218) 365-5358. Lake trout numbers aren't all that high, but there's certainly a fishable population within the depths of this crystal-clear lake. The DNR has been stocking yearling lake trout, and the most recent survey aimed to find out how well this species is doing. It appears oxygen levels to support this species may be marginal, still, some lakers are surviving here. In fact, some natural reproduction is even taking place. Lake trout always grow slowly, but especially so in Ojibway. If you've really got your heart set on catching a lake trout, you may be better off trying Burntside or Snowbank.

If you're willing to try fishing Ojibway's lakers, try around the islands and mid-lake rocks early in the year, says Noble. Later, they'll head for the depths. During this time anglers use downriggers to get spoons down deep.

Tullibees are present in moderate numbers and provide food for Ojibway's lake trout. The survey didn't turn up any big tullibees, but there was a good number of smaller fish, which is encouraging, as tullibee populations are struggling in many areas.

Walleyes and crappies showed up in a fisheries survey a few years back. It looks like these fish may have migrated in from Triangle Lake. Northern pike and burbot are native to the lake.

When fishing Ojibway, look for pike in the backs of the lake's small bays using weedless spoons or spinnerbaits. Some anglers report catching walleyes in Ojibway. Noble says they have their success on the steep breaks and ridges **(Spots 1)** around the center islands or near the channel to the unnamed lake on the east **(Spot 2)**. Leeches and minnows seem to work best.

FISH STOCKING DATA

year	species	size	# released
04	Lake Trout	Yearling	1,930
04	Lake Trout	Yearling	1,930
06	Lake Trout	Yearling	3,911
08	Lake Trout	Yearling	1,900
08	Lake Trout	Yearling	1,900
10	Lake Trout	Yearling	1,940
10	Lake Trout	Yearling	1,940

NET CATCH DATA

Date: 08/13/2007

	Gill Nets		Trap Nets	
species	# per net	avg. fish weight (lbs.)	# per net	avg. fish weight (lbs.
Lake Trout	0.33	1.58	-	-
Tullibee (Cisco)	16.42	0.33	-	-

LENGTH OF SELECTED SPECIES SAMPLED FROM ALL GEAR

Number of fish caught for the following length categories (inches):

species	0-5	6-8	9-11	12-14	15-19	20-24	25-29	>30	Total
Lake Trout	-	-	1	1	1	1	-	-	4
Tullibee (Cisco)	-	66	118	13	-	-	-	-	197

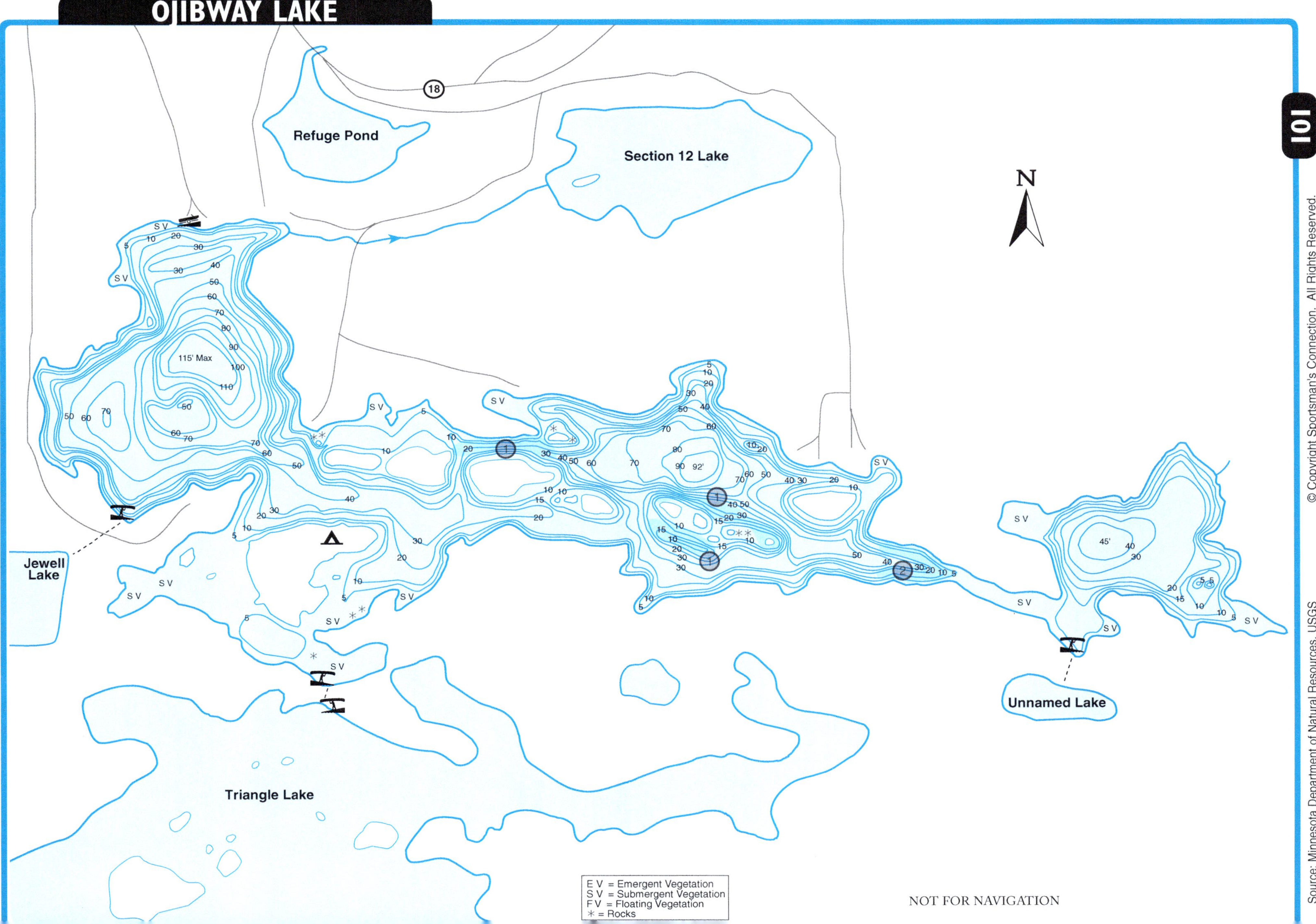

Refuge Pond
Section 12 Lake
18
N
Jewell Lake
115' Max
92'
45'
Unnamed Lake
Triangle Lake
E V = Emergent Vegetation
S V = Submergent Vegetation
F V = Floating Vegetation
✳ = Rocks
NOT FOR NAVIGATION

TRIANGLE LAKE *Lake County*

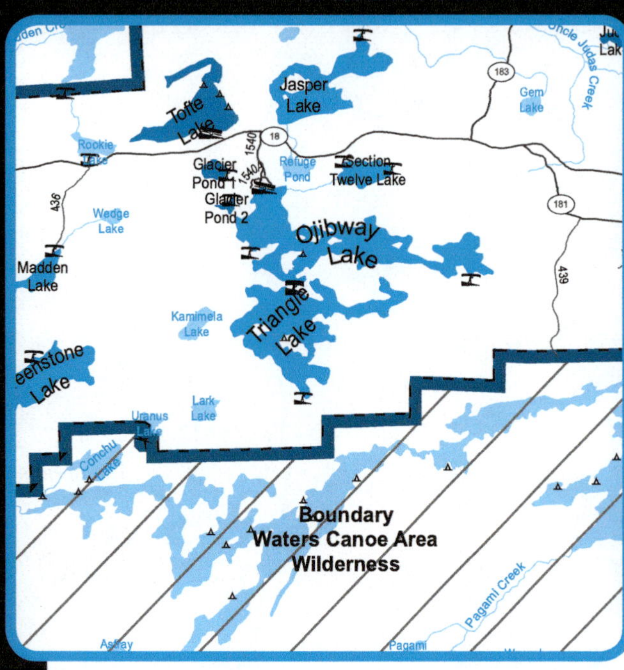

Area map page / coordinates: 14 / B-3 & 15 / B-4

Watershed: Rainy headwaters

Surface water area / shorelength: 300 acres / 7.0 miles

Maximum / mean depth: 43 feet / 14 feet

Water color / clarity: Clear / 12.0 ft. secchi (2014)

Shoreland zoning classification: Recreational development

Management class / Ecological type: Walleye /soft-water walley

Accessibility: Roller-portage between Ojibway Lake and Triangle Lake; USFS-owned public ramp on north shore of Ojibway Lake

91° 33' 40" W / 47° 57' 19" N (ramp on Ojibway Lake)

Accommodations: Camping, resort, roller portage between lakes

FISHING INFORMATION

Triangle Lake, located east of Ely, off the Fernberg Trail, is an all-around good fishing lake, particularly for walleyes, smallmouth bass and northern pike. It is relatively hard to get to, but a roller portage greatly assists those trying to reach the lake.

Cliff Noble, owner of Skube's Bait & Tackle, 1810 E. Sheridan St., Ely, MN 55731, (218) 365-5358, says anglers have excellent success fishing for northern pike, but walleyes shouldn't be overlooked, either. Average walleye length is about 13 inches, and there are fish up around 30 inches waiting for someone to catch them. Locals do best for walleyes with minnows on a Lindy rig early; switching to jig/leech combinations later.

Angler Dave Yapel says he has some success with walleyes in the first part of August using a jig/minnow combination in 12 to 20 feet of water. Yapel's focus has been on reefs, islands and prominent points.

Triangle's rocky structure provides plenty of cover for smallmouth bass and there are a lot of quality-sized fish. Although the latest DNR survey didn't find an abundance of smallies (which is normal because smallies are usually smart enough to avoid DNR nets) the ones that showed up were mostly from 12 to 15 inches long. You won't tire of tangling with these fish.

The shaded areas on the map depict some of the better spots to try for smallmouth bass in Triangle Lake. Live bait, small crankbaits or jigs with plastic tails will do nicely for these feisty fighters.

Northern pike size in Triangle is impressive. That could be because the lake isn't easy to get to. You'll find the average size to be quite high - 28 inches in the last DNR survey. One fish topped 40 inches! You'll have to do some searching to find these fish. Weedbeds are the logical starting point, but the lake isn't nearly as weedy as it was before rusty crayfish made their way into the lake decades ago. Start near any weeds you find, then work your way toward adjacent deep water, which could hold tullibees and large, hungry pike. Although tullibee numbers have been much lower than they were decades ago, they are sti present and still provide food for Triangle's large pike and walleyes.

The best access to Triangle is via a short portage from Ojibway Lak to the north. Make sure to bring a small boat or canoe, as there is special roller portage maintained by locals. Larger vessels have damage this equipment in the past. There's a single campsite, but that's enoug as this little lake doesn't get hit all that hard. That just means you migh have this quality fishery all to yourself.

FISH STOCKING DATA

year	species	size	# released
09	Walleye	Fry	400,000
12	Walleye	Fry	400,000
15	Walleye	Fry	400,000

NET CATCH DATA

Date: 07/28/2014

species	Gill Nets # per net	Gill Nets avg. fish weight (lbs.)	Trap Nets # per net	Trap Nets avg. fish weight (lbs
Burbot	0.11	0.21	-	-
Bluegill	-	-	2.78	0.08
Largemouth Bass	0.11	1.37	-	-
Northern Pike	2.56	5.17	0.56	1.59
Rock Bass	0.67	0.19	6.11	0.10
Smallmouth Bass	0.78	1.51	0.11	0.46
Walleye	5.00	1.34	1.22	1.48
White Sucker	2.22	2.62	0.11	2.92
Yellow Perch	1.33	0.11	0.11	0.09

LENGTH OF SELECTED SPECIES SAMPLED FROM ALL GEAR

Number of fish caught for the following length categories (inches):

species	0-5	6-8	9-11	12-14	15-19	20-24	25-29	>30	Total
Bluegill	25	-	-	-	-	-	-	-	25
Burbot	-	-	1	-	-	-	-	-	1
Largemouth Bass	-	-	-	1	-	-	-	-	1
Northern Pike	-	-	1	1	-	10	10	6	28
Rock Bass	54	6	-	-	-	-	-	-	60
Smallmouth Bass	-	-	1	7	-	-	-	-	8
Tullibee (Cisco)	-	4	1	3	2	-	-	-	10
Walleye	-	1	35	2	9	4	4	-	55
White Sucker	-	-	-	3	9	9	-	-	21
Yellow Perch	3	10	-	-	-	-	-	-	13

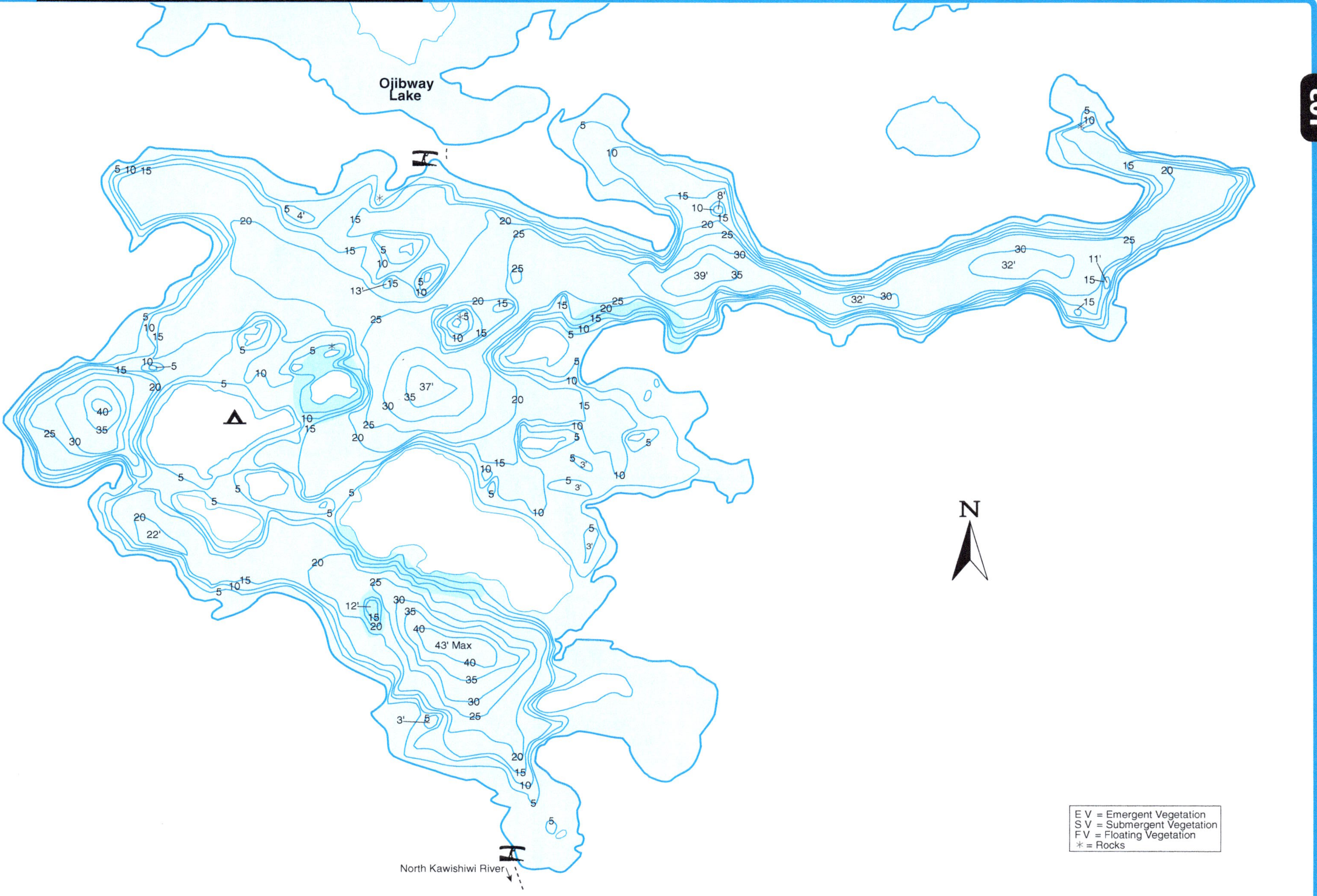

TRIANGLE LAKE

NOT FOR NAVIGATION

Ojibway Lake

North Kawishiwi River

43' Max

N

E V = Emergent Vegetation
S V = Submergent Vegetation
F V = Floating Vegetation
* = Rocks

MOOSE LAKE *Lake County*

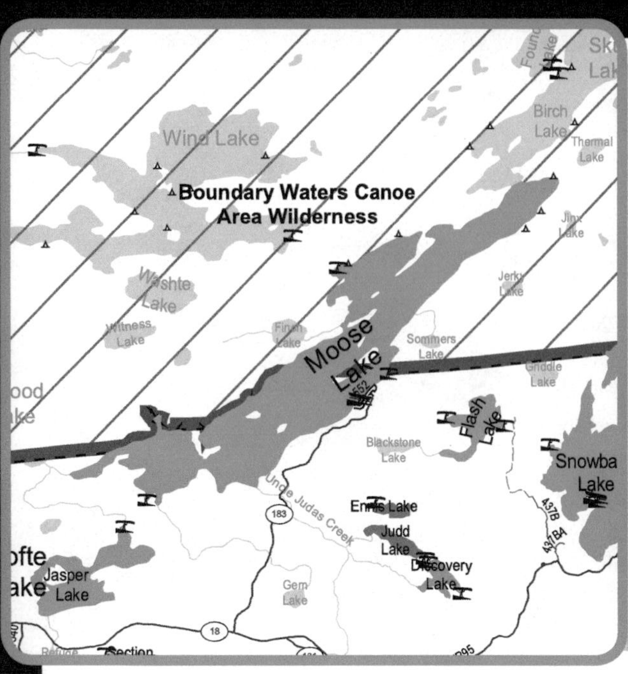

Area map page / coordinates: 14 / A-3 & 15 / A-4

Watershed: Rainy headwaters

Surface water area / shorelength: 1,301 acres / 13.5 miles

Maximum / mean depth: 65 feet / 32 feet

Water color / clarity: Clear / 13.0 ft. secchi (2010)

Shoreland zoning classification: Recreational development

Management class / Ecological type: Walleye /soft-water walley

Accessibility: USFS-owned public access with concrete ramp on south shore, mid-lake at the end of Moose Lake Road

91° 29' 56" W / 47° 59' 17" N

Accommodations: Camping, resorts, outfitters, boat rental, picnic

FISHING INFORMATION

Moose Lake is the largest entry point into the Boundary Waters Canoe Area, so it gets a lot of boat traffic, both from canoes and motorboats transporting canoes up to Prairie Portage. But don't worry about all that traffic. Most folks are just passing through, leaving the lake's fish largely unpressured.

The lake has a pretty decent fishery. Expect to find lots of northern pike – some of them pretty big, fair numbers of walleyes, a few largemouth bass, a good population of smallmouth bass and a growing bluegill population.

Cliff Noble, owner of Skube's Bait & Tackle, 1810 E. Sheridan St., Ely, MN 55731, (218) 365-5358, says locals consider this mostly a bass lake, but many fish it for 'eyes and northerns as well.

You'll find good numbers of smallmouth bass here, with lower numbers of largemouth bass present. Both bass species grow well here, with quality-sized fish measuring in the upper teens present in the lake.

The walleye population has remained steady in Moose Lake, both in terms of average size and number. Walleyes averaged over 16.5 inches in the last DNR survey, with some large fish present. These fish grow fast in Moose and the population is in good shape.

Northern pike have a decent average size at 22 inches in the last assessment. Although pike are slow-growing, there are some hefty specimens swimming around here, pushing the 40-inch mark.

Bluegill numbers have been on the rise in Moose Lake. You won't find any real giants here, but their size is respectable, averaging 6.5 inches in the last survey, with the largest measuring 8 inches.

If you cast a jig and twister tail into Moose Lake, you have a fair chance of catching just about anything that swims here. If you're after northerns, stick close to the shallows, tossing

NO RECORD OF STOCKING

NET CATCH DATA

Date: 08/23/2010	Gill Nets		Trap Nets	
species	# per net	avg. fish weight (lbs.)	# per net	avg. fish weight (lbs.)
Bluegill	0.50	0.22	11.42	0.21
Lake Whitefish	0.08	3.25	-	-
Largemouth Bass	-	-	0.33	1.09
Northern Pike	5.75	2.51	1.83	1.43
Pumpkinseed	-	-	0.08	0.05
Rock Bass	1.83	0.19	2.25	0.13
Smallmouth Bass	0.75	1.44	1.00	0.76
Walleye	4.42	1.98	0.58	1.01
White Sucker	1.92	2.26	0.42	3.14
Yellow Perch	0.08	0.11	1.25	0.17

LENGTH OF SELECTED SPECIES SAMPLED FROM ALL GEAR

Number of fish caught for the following length categories (inches):

species	0-5	6-8	9-11	12-14	15-19	20-24	25-29	>30	Total
Bluegill	37	106	-	-	-	-	-	-	143
Lake Whitefish	-	-	-	-	-	1	-	-	1
Largemouth Bass	1	-	1	1	1	-	-	-	4
Northern Pike	-	1	1	3	33	38	13	2	91
Pumpkinseed	1	-	-	-	-	-	-	-	1
Rock Bass	24	23	-	-	-	-	-	-	47
Smallmouth Bass	-	2	10	5	4	-	-	-	21
Tullibee (Cisco)	-	1	1	-	-	-	-	-	2
Walleye	-	2	5	20	16	16	1	-	60
White Sucker	-	1	2	2	18	5	-	-	28
Yellow Perch	1	13	2	-	-	-	-	-	16

spoons and spinnerbaits. Look for walleyes on the reef on the northeas part of the lake **(Spot 1)** or try the two islands **(Spots 2)** on the southwes end. However, don't overlook the northern bay **(Spot 3)** as it is a consistent producer as well.

There is a good concrete boat launch on the lake's south shore witl ample parking day or night. Be warned that the northeastern half of th lake lies within the BWCA. Motors are allowed, but they are limited t 25 horsepower or less.

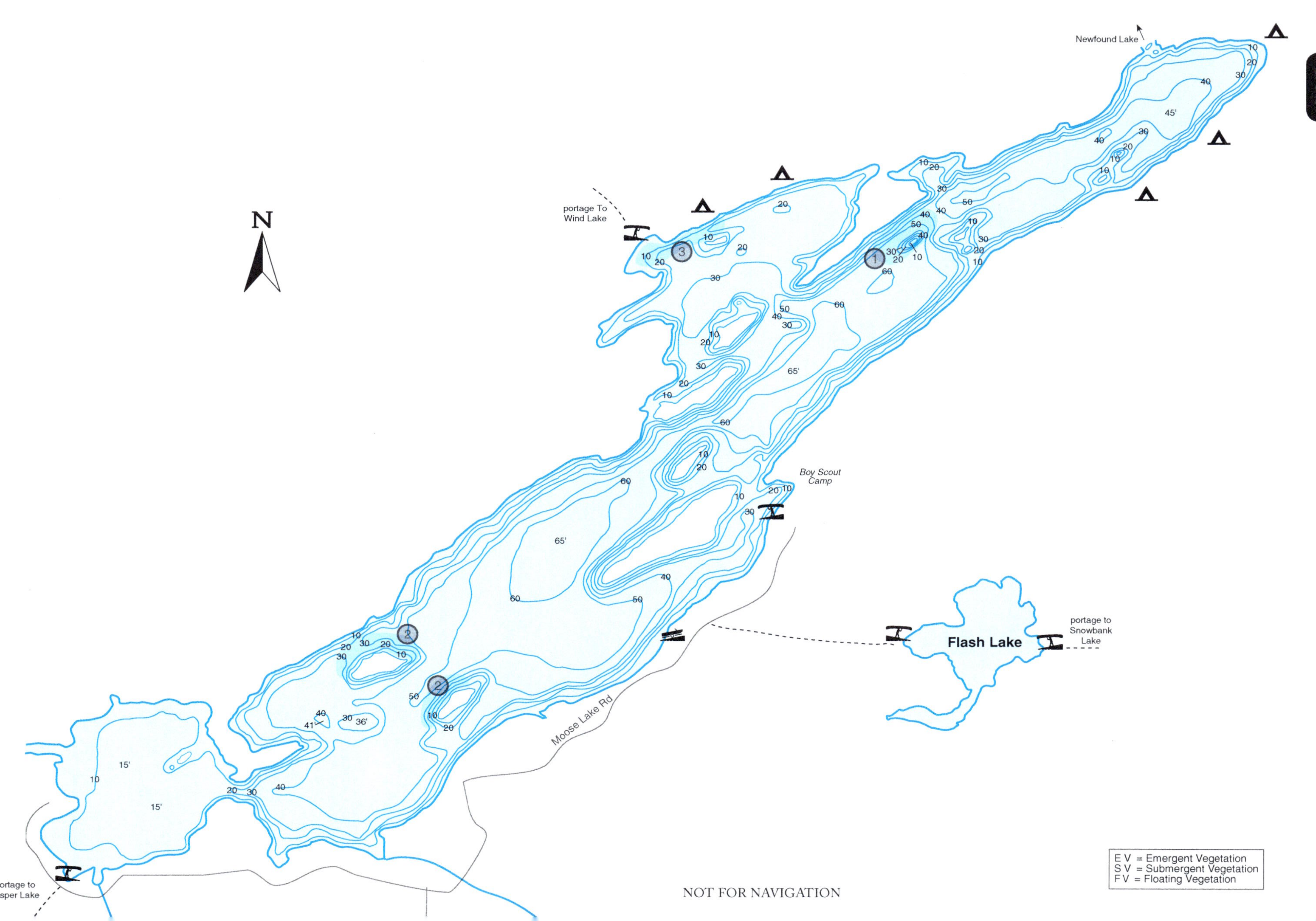

Source: Minnesota Department of Natural Resources, USGS

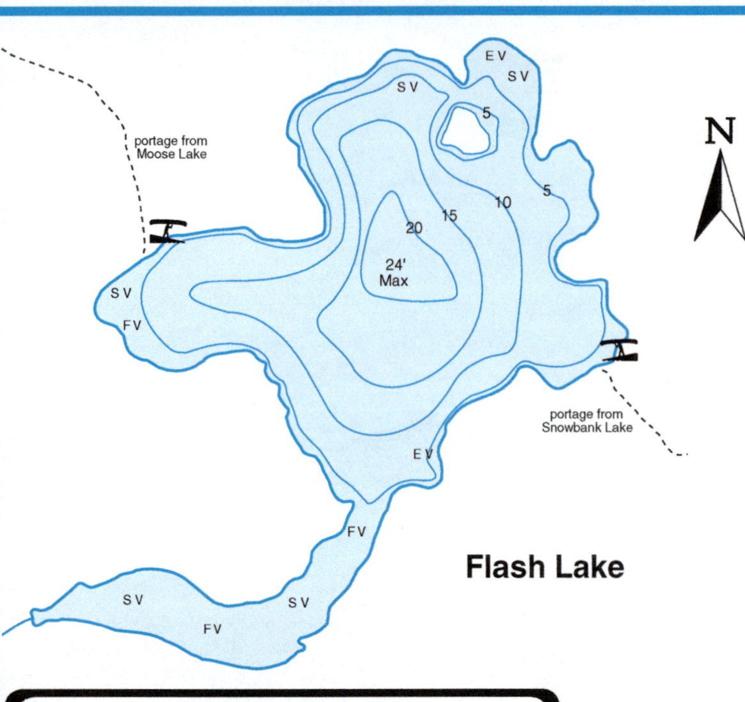

Ennis Lake, Lake County

Area map page / coordinates: 15 / A-4
Surface area / max depth: 21 acres / 42 feet
Accessibility: Carry-down access from Secret/Blackstone Trail off Moose Lake Road, past Flash Lake portage approximately one mile

FISH STOCKING DATA

year	species	size	# released
10	Brook Trout	Fingerling	1,587
11	Splake	Fingerling	1,773
12	Brook Trout	Fingerling	1,500
13	Splake	Fingerling	1,462
14	Brook Trout	Fingerling	2,071
15	Splake	Fingerling	1,600

LENGTH OF SELECTED SPECIES SAMPLED FROM ALL GEAR
Survey Date: 05/29/2003
Number of fish caught for the following length categories (inches):

species	0-5	6-8	9-11	12-14	15-19	20-24	25-29	>30	Total
Brook Trout	-	2	-	1	-	-	-	-	3
Rainbow Trout	-	-	-	-	-	1	-	-	1
Splake	-	7	-	-	8	1	-	-	16

Flash Lake, Lake County

Area map page / coordinates: 15 / A-4
Surface area / max depth: 83 acres / 24 feet
Accessibility: 1/2-mile portage from Snowbank Lake; 3/4-mile portage from Moose Lake Road

NO RECORD OF STOCKING

LENGTH OF SELECTED SPECIES SAMPLED FROM ALL GEAR
Survey Date: 06/23/2014
Number of fish caught for the following length categories (inches):

species	0-5	6-8	9-11	12-14	15-19	20-24	25-29	>30	Total
Northern Pike	-	-	-	-	2	7	1	-	10
Walleye	-	-	24	6	13	6	-	-	49
White Sucker	-	-	-	-	3	-	-	-	3
Yellow Perch	2	5	-	-	-	-	-	-	7

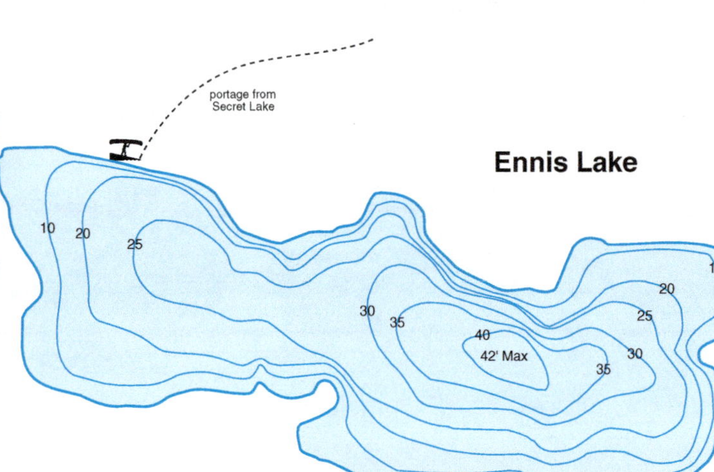

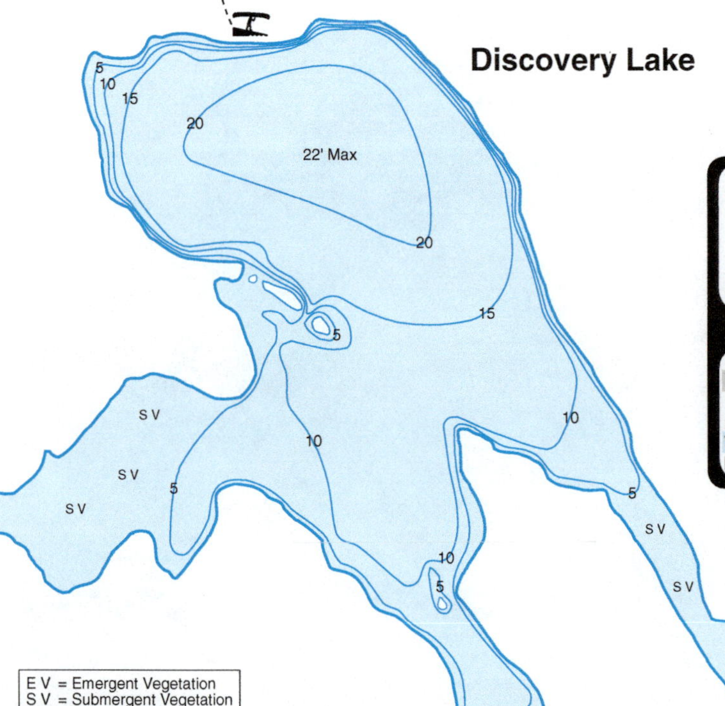

Discovery Lake, Lake County

Area map page / coordinates: 15 / B-4
Surface area / max depth: 30 acres / 22 feet
Accessibility: Carry-down off Moose Lake Road to Judd Lake; portage from Judd Lake to Discovery

NO RECORD OF STOCKING

LENGTH OF SELECTED SPECIES SAMPLED FROM ALL GEAR
Survey Date: 06/19/1980
Number of fish caught for the following length categories (inches):

species	0-5	6-8	9-11	12-14	15-19	20-24	25-29	>30	Total
Yellow Perch	5	31	3	2	-	-	-	-	41
Bluegill	10	1	-	-	-	-	-	-	11

E V = Emergent Vegetation
S V = Submergent Vegetation
F V = Floating Vegetation

NOT FOR NAVIGATION

Source: Minnesota Department of Natural Resources, USGS

Nickel Lake, Lake County

Area map page / coordinates: 14 / D-3
Surface area / max depth: 23 acres / 10 feet
Accessibility: Carry-down access (100 ft portage); Hwy. 1 to Spruce Road, east on Spruce Road 0.6 miles to trail

FISH STOCKING DATA

year	species	size	# released
12	Walleye	Fry	30,000
14	Walleye	Fry	25,000
15	Walleye	Fry	25,000

LENGTH OF SELECTED SPECIES SAMPLED FROM ALL GEAR
Survey Date: 06/28/2010
Number of fish caught for the following length categories (inches):

species	0-5	6-8	9-11	12-14	15-19	20-24	25-29	>30	Total
Walleye	-	109	17	93	21	-	-	-	240

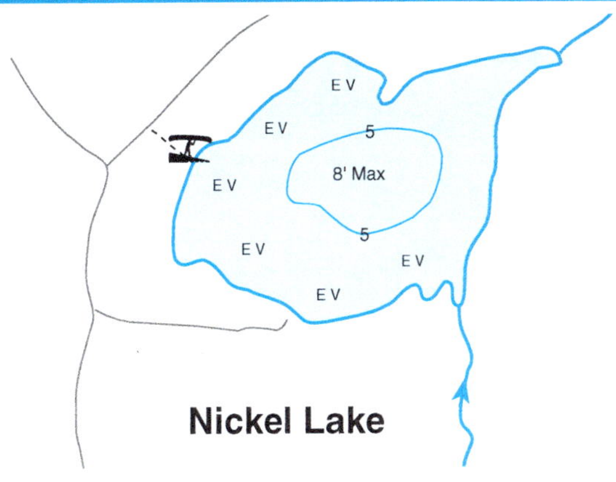

Norway Lake

Norway Lake, Lake County

Area map page / coordinates: 14 / E-3
Surface area / max depth: 12 acres / 19 feet
Accessibility: Carry-down access (200-yard portage) from USFS Rd. 173, north 4.4 miles on USFS Rd. 388

FISH STOCKING DATA

year	species	size	# released
13	Splake	Fingerling	847
14	Splake	Fingerling	903
15	Splake	Fingerling	996

LENGTH OF SELECTED SPECIES SAMPLED FROM ALL GEAR
Survey Date: 10/05/2011
Number of fish caught for the following length categories (inches):

species	0-5	6-8	9-11	12-14	15-19	20-24	25-29	>30	Total
Pearl Dace	-	1	-	-	-	-	-	-	1
Splake	-	6	21	24	8	-	-	-	59

August Lake

August Lake Road

FR 388

August Creek

August Lake, Lake County

Area map page / coordinates: 22 / A-3
Surface area / max depth: 229 acres / 19 feet
Accessibility: Carry-down access from August Lake Road (off USFS Rd. 388) to north shore

FISH STOCKING DATA

year	species	size	# released
12	Walleye	Fingerling	11,704
14	Walleye	Fingerling	14,997

LENGTH OF SELECTED SPECIES SAMPLED FROM ALL GEAR
Survey Date: 08/19/2013
Number of fish caught for the following length categories (inches):

species	0-5	6-8	9-11	12-14	15-19	20-24	25-29	>30	Total
Northern Pike	-	-	-	4	12	17	1	1	35
Walleye	-	10	9	16	9	3	-	-	47
Yellow Perch	4	18	-	-	-	-	-	-	22

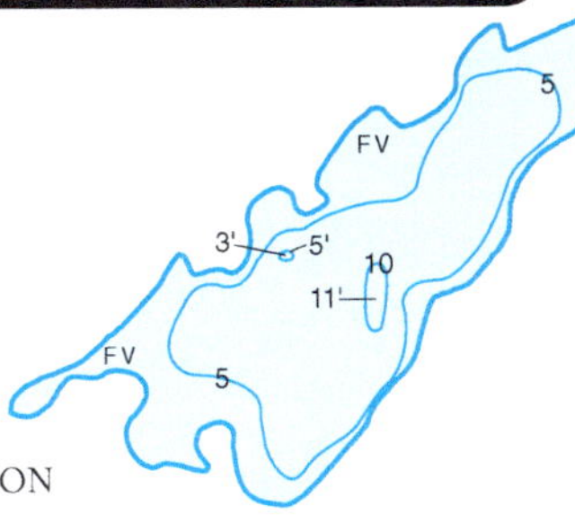

E V = Emergent Vegetation
S V = Submergent Vegetation
F V = Floating Vegetation
⁎ = Rocks

NOT FOR NAVIGATION

SNOWBANK LAKE *Lake County*

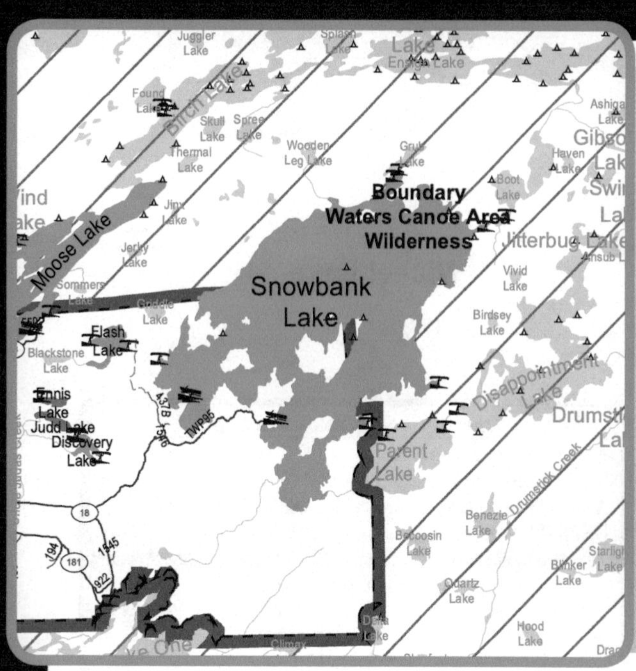

Area map page / coordinates: 15 / A,B-4,5

Watershed: Rainy headwaters

Surface water area / shorelength: 4,655 acres / 26.3 miles

Maximum / mean depth: 150 feet / NA

Water color / clarity: Clear / 19.0 ft. secchi (2010)

Shoreland zoning classification: Recreational development

Management class / Ecological type: Lake trout / trout

Accessibility: 1) Public access with concrete ramp past lodge on southwest corner

91° 27' 20" W / 47° 58' 33" N

Accessibility: 2) Public access with concrete ramp on south shore mid-lake;

91° 25' 56" W / 47° 58' 16" N

Accommodations: Resort, camping, boat rental

FISHING INFORMATION

Snowbank Lake is a 4,655-acre body of water littered with structure. The lake is located half in, and half out of the Boundary Waters. You'll need a day-use permit to fish the BWCA section, and you'll find a 25-horsepower motor restriction in place for the part of the lake within the B-Dub. Permits can be picked up at Skube's Bait & Tackle, 1810 E. Sheridan St., Ely, MN 55731, (218) 365-5358, or at the launch site.

Snowbank's main attraction, other than its scenic beauty, is its lake trout fishery. The lake contains a good, self-sustaining population of lakers, with some growing fairly large. Fishing for lake trout is popular both during the summer, when anglers troll for them over deep water, as well as in winter, when jigging around steep ledges is the technique of choice.

According to angler Dave Yapel, "The lake trout fishing can, at times, be productive. There are good numbers of nice-sized trout swimming around in there."

Walleye numbers are pretty good. Most aren't wall-hangers, but there are enough larger fish present that a trophy is a possibility. Walleyes are primarily targeted during the first part of the summer when they are still up shallow after spawning.

Snowbank boasts a unique northern pike fishery. Silver-phase northern pike are present here. And although normal-colored pike are the norm, this odd, light-colored phase is out there. Pike grow large here, as they prey on ciscoes.

Smallmouth fishing is good in Snowbank and even some largemouth bass inhabit the shallows.

Anglers focus on the deep holes **(Spot 1)** and steep north shore breaks **(Spot 2)** in pursuit of lake trout. The northern reaches of the lake are the primary laker spots, but some may also be taken around the humps and reefs near Harry's Island earlier in the year. North Bay **(Spot 3)** can also be productive.

Steep-dropping shorelines on the southeast end of the lake and on the north side of Harry's Island **(Spots 4)** can also produce lake trout. Try looking for walleyes at the humps **(Spots 5)** and narrows **(Spot 6)**. Look for that elusive silver pike in Pickerel Bay as well as normal-colored northerns and largemouth bass.

Smallmouth bass relate to the lake's abundant rock structure. Although they can be caught shallow, some large fish can be found deeper than you might think; sometimes in 50 feet of water or more.

Snowbank also has good numbers of eelpout, or burbot, and they grow fairly large. Eelpout are often caught in winter by lake trout anglers who leave a dead cisco on the bottom. These bottom-oriented predators are most active in winter, and although they are often thought of as scavengers, they will hit jigging lures intended for lake trout as well.

NET CATCH DATA

Date: 07/19/2010	Gill Nets		Trap Nets	
species	# per net	avg. fish weight (lbs.)	# per net	avg. fish weight (lbs.)
Burbot	1.35	1.40	-	-
Lake Trout	0.70	3.07	-	-
Largemouth Bass	-	-	1.60	0.55
Northern Pike	2.04	2.56	0.80	1.90
Rock Bass	2.78	0.22	20.47	0.19
Smallmouth Bass	2.04	1.02	1.60	0.30
Walleye	4.04	1.63	0.67	1.73
White Sucker	3.04	2.13	0.40	1.51
Yellow Perch	0.13	0.25	0.13	0.15

LENGTH OF SELECTED SPECIES SAMPLED FROM ALL GEAR

Number of fish caught for the following length categories (inches):

species	0-5	6-8	9-11	12-14	15-19	20-24	25-29	>30	Total
Burbot	-	-	-	5	19	7	-	-	31
Golden Shiner	-	1	-	-	-	-	-	-	1
Lake Trout	-	-	2	4	1	5	4	-	16
Largemouth Bass	-	5	15	4	-	-	-	-	24
Northern Pike	-	-	-	-	21	26	9	3	59
N. Pike (silver)	-	-	-	-	2	1	2	-	5
Rock Bass	174	191	-	-	-	-	-	-	365
Smallmouth Bass	-	30	21	12	8	-	-	-	71
Tullibee (Cisco)	-	41	17	9	-	-	-	-	67
Walleye	-	2	1	63	16	16	5	-	103
White Sucker	-	8	-	11	47	10	-	-	76
Yellow Perch	-	5	-	-	-	-	-	-	5

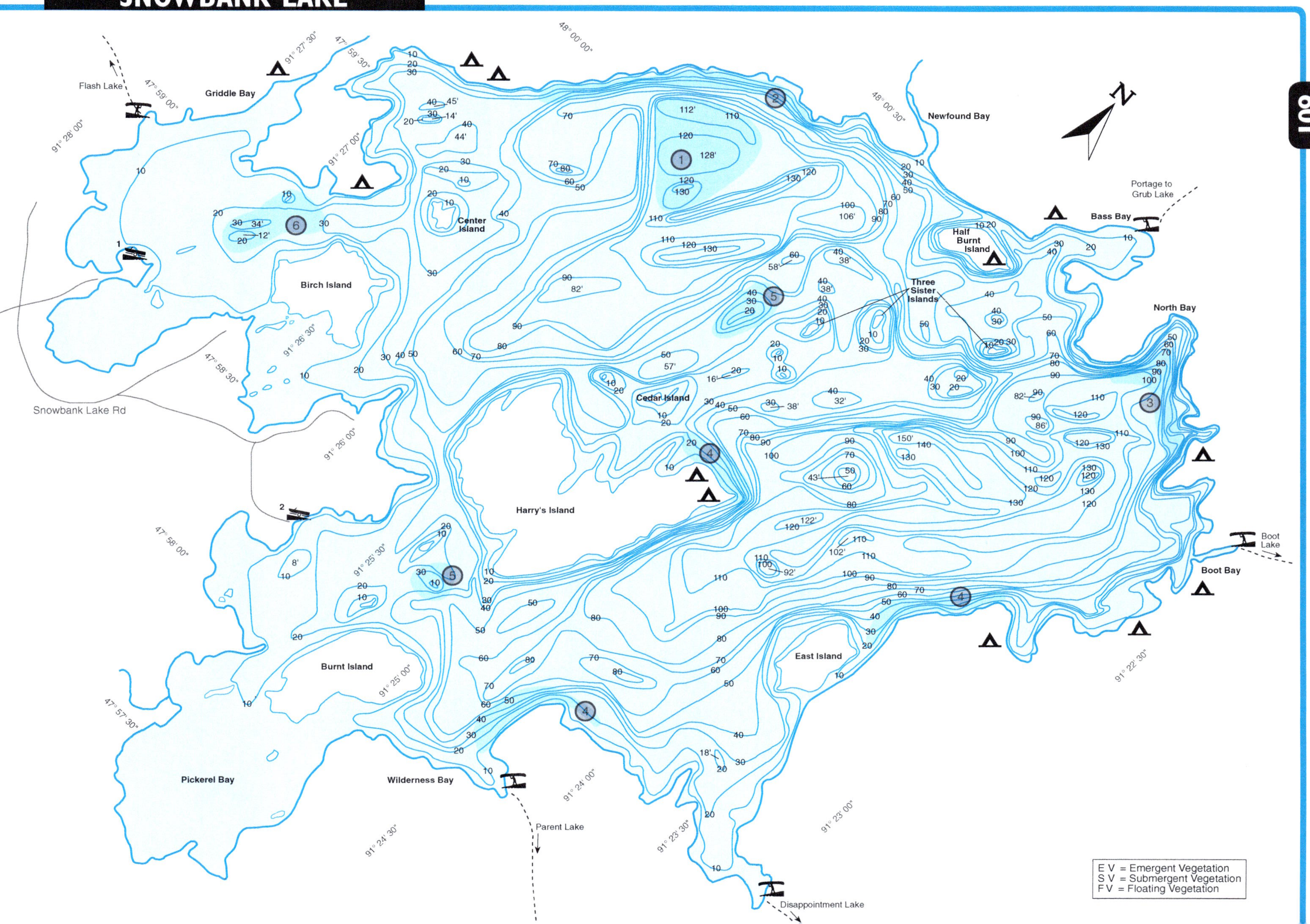

Source: Minnesota Department of Natural Resources, USGS

LAKE ISABELLA *Lake County*

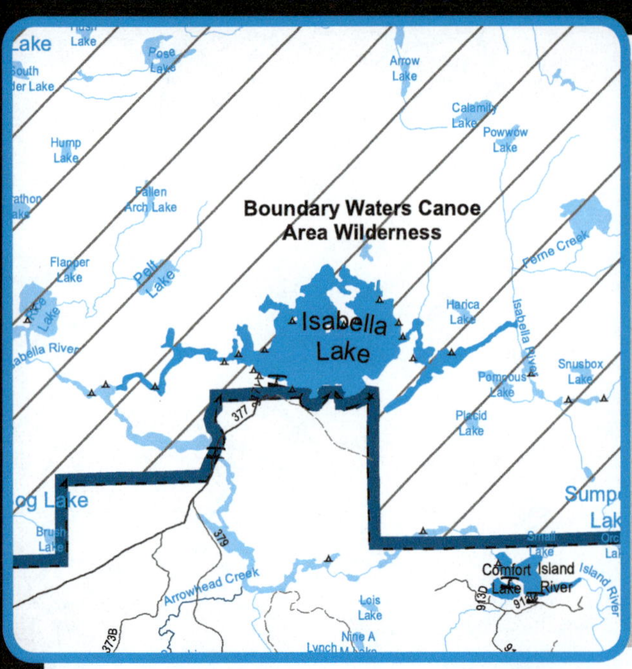

Area map page / coordinates: 15 / D,E-6 & 16 / D,E-1

Watershed: Rainy headwaters

Surface water area / shorelength: 1,257 acres / 4.0 miles

Maximum / mean depth: 19 feet / NA

Water color / clarity: Brown, bog stain / 9.0 ft. secchi (2006)

Shoreland zoning classification: Natural environment

Management class / Ecological type: Walleye /soft-water walley

Accessibility: Carry-down access (1,000 foot trail) from parking lot to southwest corner

91° 18' 10" W / 47° 48' 13" N

Accommodations: Camping, restrooms

FISHING INFORMATION

Lake Isabella, located just inside the Boundary Waters, north of Isabella holds a lot of walleyes and some impressive northern pike.

Al Anderson of the Finland Area DNR Fisheries Office, 6686 Hwy 1 Box 546, Finland MN, 55603, (218) 353-7591, says walleyes averaged 12.25 inches while the pike, down slightly from past surveys, averaged 23.25 inches in the last survey of Isabella Lake. The largest pike surveyed was just over 36 inches, but, Anderson explains, a lake with low numbers of northern pike and a quality forage base, such as lake whitefish, always has the potential to produce some trophy-sized northern pike.

The folks at the Knotted Pine Inn & Tavern, 9702 Highway 1, Isabella, MN 55607, (218) 323-7681, say the lake's walleyes are quite numerous and offer some good action, but a little sorting may be in order.

The latest survey did turn up some big pike, with a couple of them measuring more than 35 inches. That prey base that Anderson talked about is robust. Lake whitefish are present in above-average numbers. They certainly provide forage for Isabella's medium- and large-sized northern pike, as well as some of the lake's rare large walleyes. Fall netting of whitefish is allowed on Isabella, but very few anglers target this tasty species.

Perch inhabit the lake in average numbers, and although most are relatively small, there are some real giants pushing up to 13 inches.

The DNR also found largemouth bass and black crappies in the last survey for the first time. These fish apparently swam in via the Isabella River. The crappies that showed up were of good size.

Spring walleye fishing is good around the inlet on the lake's east shore **(Spot 1)**. Toss minnows on a jig here and around the island **(Spot 2)** just off the river mouth. Later in the year, action migrates to the mid-lake humps and islands **(Spots 3)**. Jig thes areas with minnows till about July 1 and with leeches thereafter.

Fish the shallow weed edges for small pike, but look to the deeper hole where ciscoes congregate for the real brutes. The weedbeds east of the bi island offer good northern pike cover and can be worked with spinner or weedless spoons.

No motors are allowed in this lake. The folks at the Knotted Pine In & Tavern have day-use permits.

NO RECORD OF STOCKING

NET CATCH DATA

Date: 09/05/2006	Gill Nets		Trap Nets	
species	# per net	avg. fish weight (lbs.)	# per net	avg. fish weight (lbs
Black Crappie	0.27	0.99	-	-
Lake Whitefish	5.40	0.73	-	-
Largemouth Bass	0.07	0.16	-	-
Northern Pike	2.67	3.39	-	-
Pumpkinseed	0.27	0.14	-	-
Rock Bass	1.00	0.27	-	-
Walleye	9.53	0.72	-	-
White Sucker	7.07	1.35	-	-
Yellow Perch	4.87	0.20	-	-

LENGTH OF SELECTED SPECIES SAMPLED FROM ALL GEAR

Number of fish caught for the following length categories (inches):

species	0-5	6-8	9-11	12-14	15-19	20-24	25-29	>30	Total
Black Crappie	-	-	4	-	-	-	-	-	4
Lake Whitefish	-	4	24	39	14	-	-	-	81
Largemouth Bass	-	1	-	-	-	-	-	-	1
Northern Pike	-	-	-	3	11	15	3	8	40
Pumpkinseed	4	-	-	-	-	-	-	-	4
Rock Bass	2	13	-	-	-	-	-	-	15
Walleye	-	2	43	55	17	3	1	-	143
White Sucker	-	20	16	22	47	1	-	-	106
Yellow Perch	12	52	7	2	-	-	-	-	73

LAKE ISABELLA

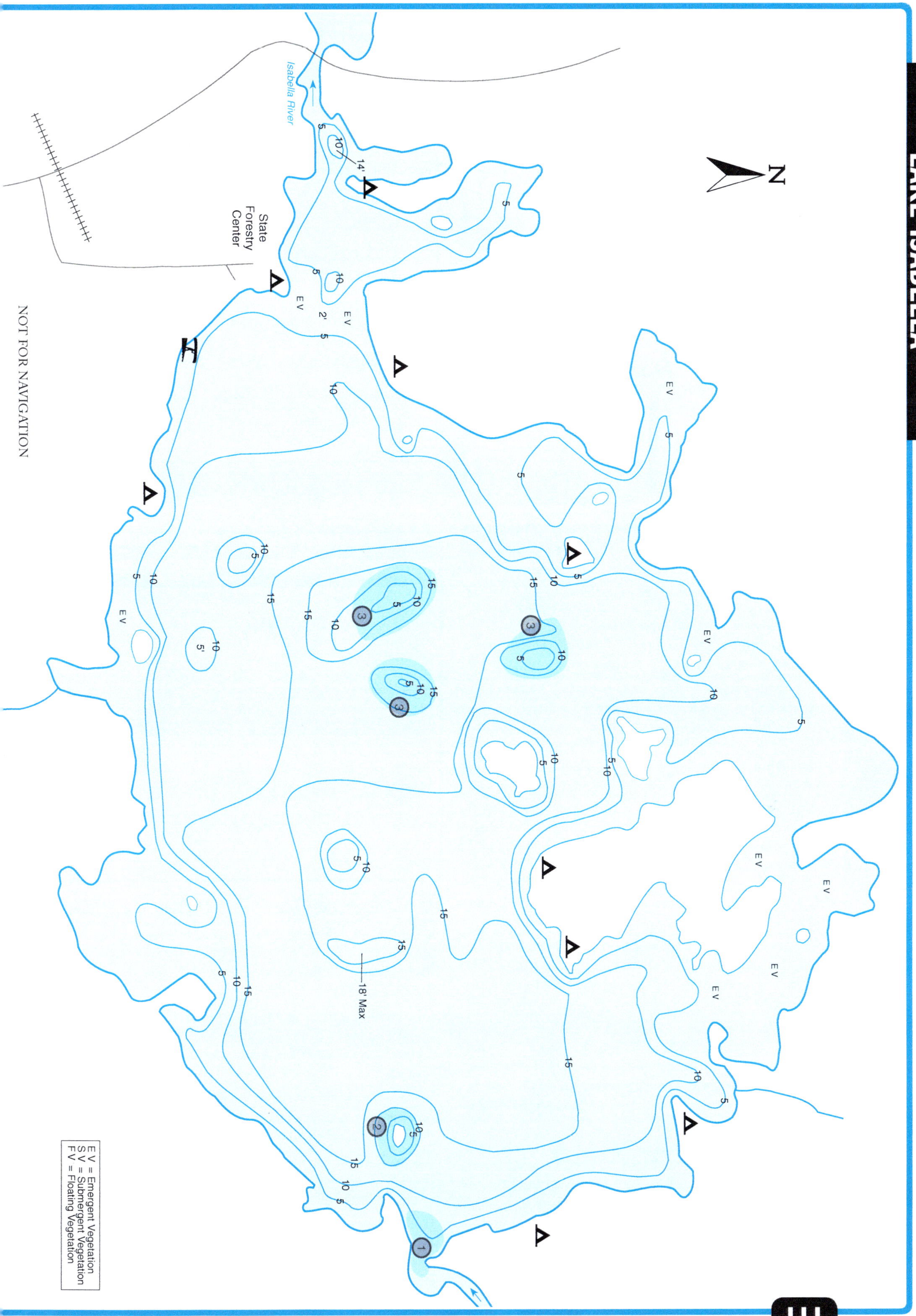

Isabella River

State Forestry Center

18' Max

NOT FOR NAVIGATION

EV = Emergent Vegetation
SV = Submergent Vegetation
FV = Floating Vegetation

Source: Minnesota Department of Natural Resources, USGS

KAWISHIWI LAKE *Lake County*

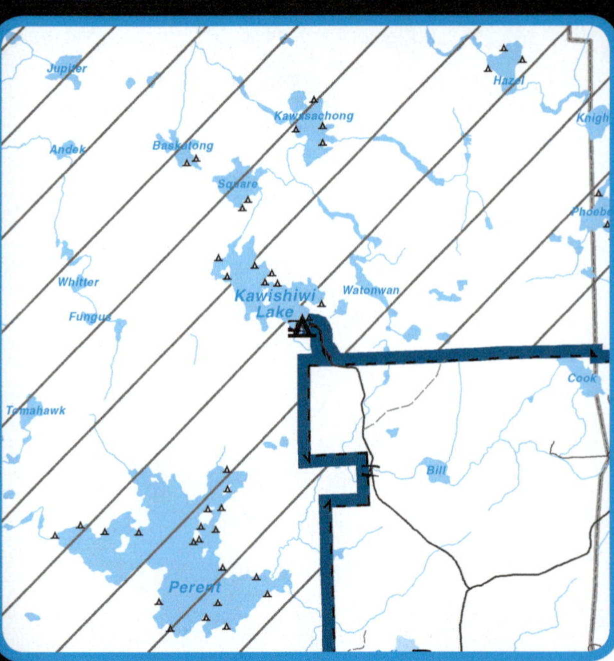

Area map page / coordinates: 16 / D-2,3

Watershed: Rainy headwaters

Surface water area / shorelength: 372 acres / 7.7 miles

Maximum / mean depth: 12 feet / 5 feet

Water color / clarity: Dark brown, bog stain / 7.5 ft. secchi (2010

Shoreland zoning classification: Natural environment

Management class / Ecological type: Walleye /soft-water walley

Accessibility: Paddle-in access from Square Lake to north shore; carry-down access on southeast shore at campground off FR 354

Accommodations: Camping, picnicking, restrooms

FISHING INFORMATION

Kawishiwi Lake is a popular BWCA entry point. The lake is reasonably convenient to access via a modest carry-down launch in the southeast corner that offers plenty of parking. There's a campground there, so you can stay awhile if you pick up the appropriate permit from the Forest Service. There are also several remote campsites scattered around the lake as well.

The lake has a pretty good fishery for walleyes, northern pike and yellow perch. The fishing is good enough to warrant a day trip or to spend some extra time fishing here before you continue on to your destination further into the Boundary Waters.

Walleye numbers are good in Kawishiwi Lake and the average size of these fish is excellent. Anglers will be happy to learn that in the latest DNR survey, more than half of the walleyes sampled were over 15 inches. This is much better than average, yet these results are typical for Kawishiwi. The lake's walleyes run large, although you won't find any trophies here.

It's just the opposite for northern pike. Here, you'll find a lot of hammer-handle northerns and nothing of any size. Still, they provide action and are always easier to catch than walleyes.

Yellow perch are also a bright spot here. Although their numbers are about average, their size structure is pretty good. Nearly half of the perch in the last DNR survey were 8 inches or larger, with the biggest just shy of the one-foot mark. These jumbo perch are a nice bonus for Kawishiwi's walleye anglers.

The folks at the Knotted Pine Inn & Tavern, 9702 Highway 1, Isabella, MN 55607, (218) 323-7681, say the fishing is pretty good and maybe just as good from shore as it is from a boat. Kawishiwi isn't very deep, with a maximum depth of 12 feet and an average depth of just 5 feet. Outside of points off shorelines and islands, there isn't a whole lot of structure. That means the fish have to make do with what's available. Fish in Kawishiwi relate to boulders, smaller rocks and an abundance of weeds. Find boulders, and you'll find walleyes. Fin weedbeds and you'll find northern pike and 'eyes. One exception is th "deep" hole. You'll find walleyes there in the summer, as the added dept provides more shade for their sensitive eyes.

For walleyes, try a jig and minnow. Remember, only preserved min nows are allowed in the Boundary Waters. Later in the year, switch t nightcrawlers or leeches – again under a bobber or dropped into the hol on a jig.

For northern pike, fish the weedlines with weedless spoons, spinnerbait or spinners. You may be able to get away with shallow-running crankbait if the weeds aren't too high.

Kawishiwi's jumbo perch will hit offerings intended for walleyes, some times to the chagrin of walleye purists. Search for them around the weed or try the deep hole.

There is a self-registration box at the landing for day-use anglers. Fc those seeking for a multi-day trip from May to September, you'll hav to apply for a permit. You can self-register for off-season camping at th landing.

NO RECORD OF STOCKING

NET CATCH DATA

Date: 09/13/2010	Gill Nets		Trap Nets	
species	# per net	avg. fish weight (lbs.)	# per net	avg. fish weight (lbs
Northern Pike	5.67	1.07	0.25	0.46
Rock Bass	0.67	0.22	0.25	0.13
Walleye	5.11	1.58	0.50	1.15
White Sucker	21.67	2.07	2.08	1.96
Yellow Perch	6.56	0.26	0.25	0.16

LENGTH OF SELECTED SPECIES SAMPLED FROM ALL GEAR

Number of fish caught for the following length categories (inches):

species	0-5	6-8	9-11	12-14	15-19	20-24	25-29	>30	Total
Northern Pike	-	-	7	6	29	12	-	-	54
Rock Bass	3	6	-	-	-	-	-	-	9
Walleye	-	-	2	21	24	4	1	-	52
White Sucker	-	2	14	16	179	9	-	-	220
Yellow Perch	9	35	18	-	-	-	-	-	62

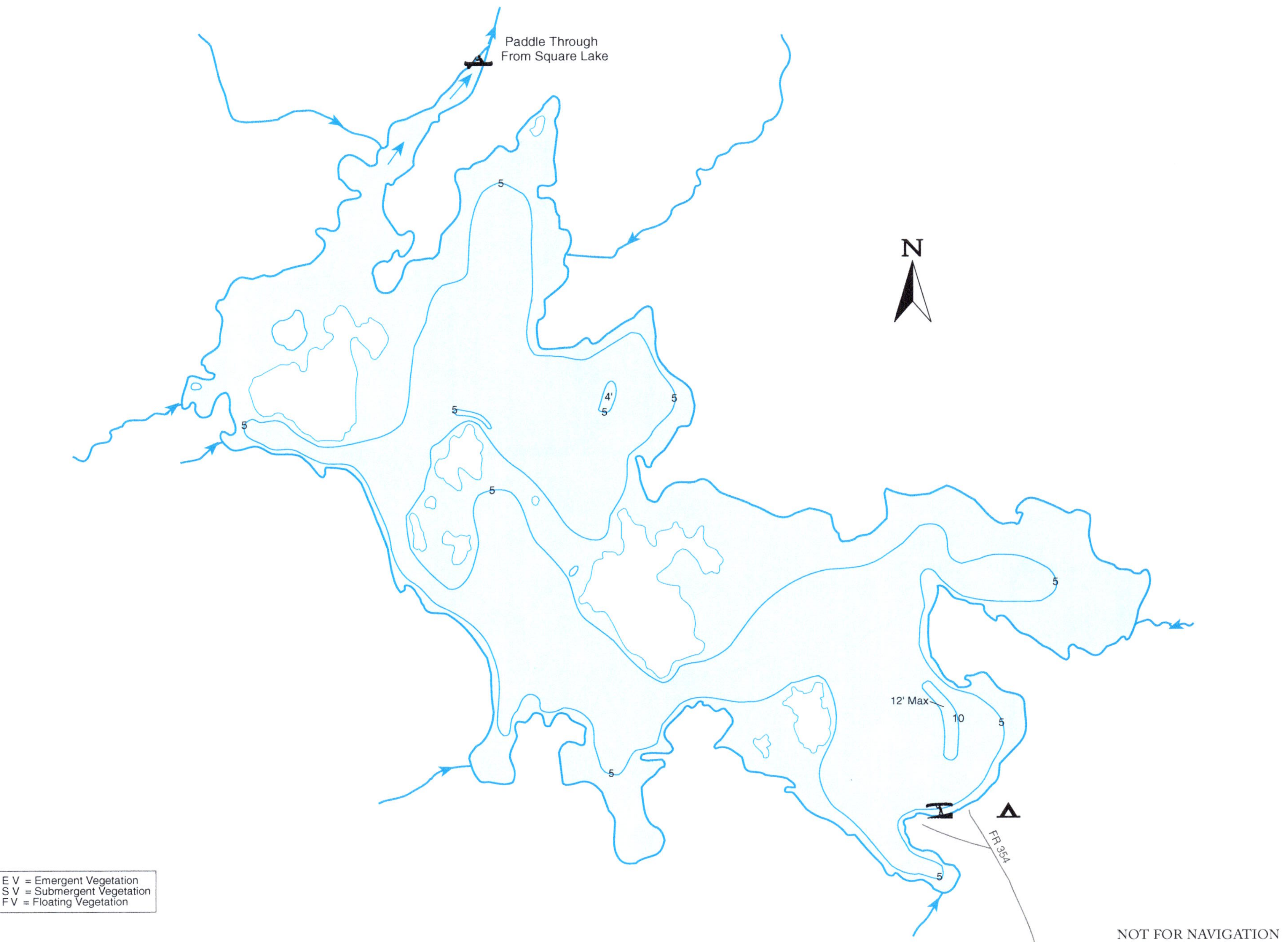

Source: Minnesota Department of Natural Resources, USGS

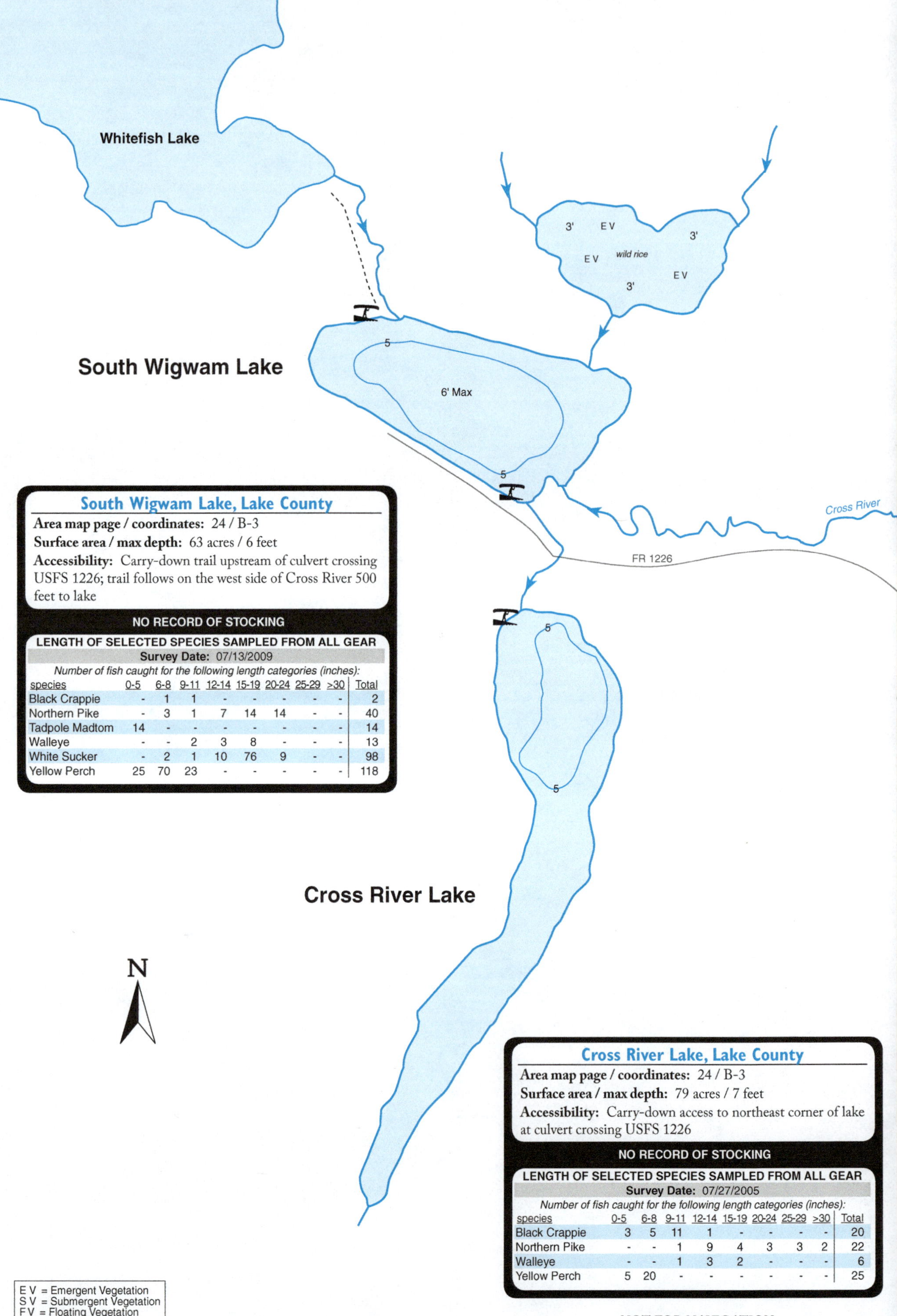

South Wigwam Lake, Lake County

Area map page / coordinates: 24 / B-3
Surface area / max depth: 63 acres / 6 feet
Accessibility: Carry-down trail upstream of culvert crossing USFS 1226; trail follows on the west side of Cross River 500 feet to lake

NO RECORD OF STOCKING

LENGTH OF SELECTED SPECIES SAMPLED FROM ALL GEAR
Survey Date: 07/13/2009
Number of fish caught for the following length categories (inches):

species	0-5	6-8	9-11	12-14	15-19	20-24	25-29	>30	Total
Black Crappie	-	1	1	-	-	-	-	-	2
Northern Pike	-	3	1	7	14	14	-	-	40
Tadpole Madtom	14	-	-	-	-	-	-	-	14
Walleye	-	-	2	3	8	-	-	-	13
White Sucker	-	2	1	10	76	9	-	-	98
Yellow Perch	25	70	23	-	-	-	-	-	118

Cross River Lake, Lake County

Area map page / coordinates: 24 / B-3
Surface area / max depth: 79 acres / 7 feet
Accessibility: Carry-down access to northeast corner of lake at culvert crossing USFS 1226

NO RECORD OF STOCKING

LENGTH OF SELECTED SPECIES SAMPLED FROM ALL GEAR
Survey Date: 07/27/2005
Number of fish caught for the following length categories (inches):

species	0-5	6-8	9-11	12-14	15-19	20-24	25-29	>30	Total
Black Crappie	3	5	11	1	-	-	-	-	20
Northern Pike	-	-	1	9	4	3	3	2	22
Walleye	-	-	1	3	2	-	-	-	6
Yellow Perch	5	20	-	-	-	-	-	-	25

Source: Minnesota Department of Natural Resources, USGS

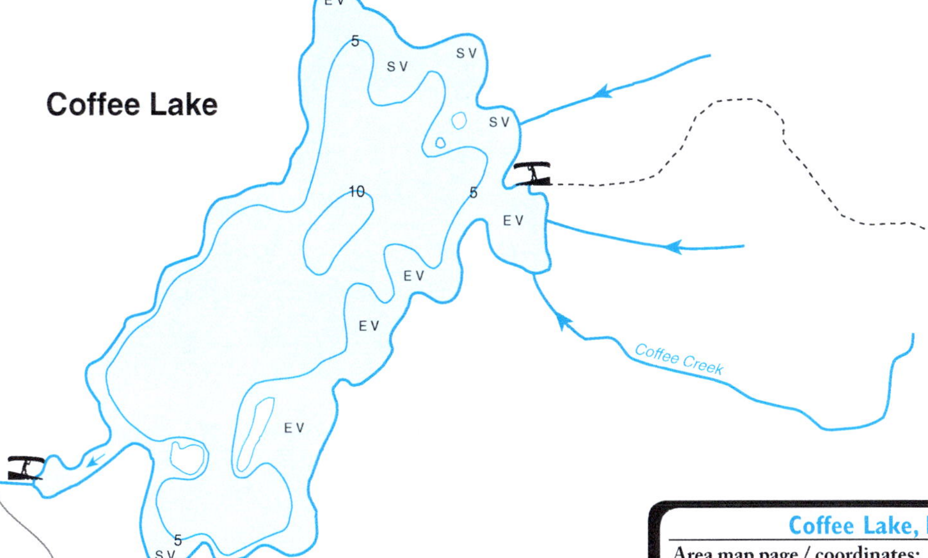

Coffee Lake, Lake County

Area map page / coordinates: 16 / E-3
Surface area / max depth: 129 acres / 11 feet
Accessibility: USFS logging road off Co. Rd. 7; 2.0 miles to the end of road, then 100 ft. portage to outlet on west shore

NO RECORD OF STOCKING

LENGTH OF SELECTED SPECIES SAMPLED FROM ALL GEAR

Survey Date: 08/28/2007

Number of fish caught for the following length categories (inches):

species	0-5	6-8	9-11	12-14	15-19	20-24	25-29	>30	Total
Northern Pike	-	-	1	-	5	15	1	-	22
Rock Bass	4	5	-	-	-	-	-	-	9
Walleye	-	-	6	7	8	3	-	-	24
White Sucker	-	3	11	1	35	7	-	-	57
Yellow Perch	2	28	-	-	-	-	-	-	30

N

Bone Lake

5 10 15 20 30 40 50 40 30 20 15 10 5

FR 357

Bone Lake, Lake County

Area map page / coordinates: 16 / E-3
Surface area / max depth: 43 acres / 51 feet
Accessibility: Carry-down access- from Co. Rd. 7, north 5.9 miles on USFS Road 357; continue north 2.3 miles on very rough logging road

FISH STOCKING DATA

year	species	size	# released
12	Rainbow Trout	Yearling	1,020
12	Splake	Fingerling	3,500
13	Rainbow Trout	Yearling	1,010
14	Rainbow Trout	Yearling	1,000
14	Splake	Fingerling	3,400
15	Rainbow Trout	Yearling	1,000

LENGTH OF SELECTED SPECIES SAMPLED FROM ALL GEAR

Survey Date: 08/16/201

Number of fish caught for the following length categories (inches):

species	0-5	6-8	9-11	12-14	15-19	20-24	25-29	>30	Total
Brown Trout	-	-	1	2	-	1	-	-	4
Golden Shiner	8	5	-	-	-	-	-	-	13
Rainbow Trout	-	2	2	1	-	-	-	-	5
Splake	-	8	110	8	4	-	-	-	130
White Sucker	-	59	180	18	1	-	-	-	258

NOT FOR NAVIGATION

SAWBILL LAKE *Cook County*

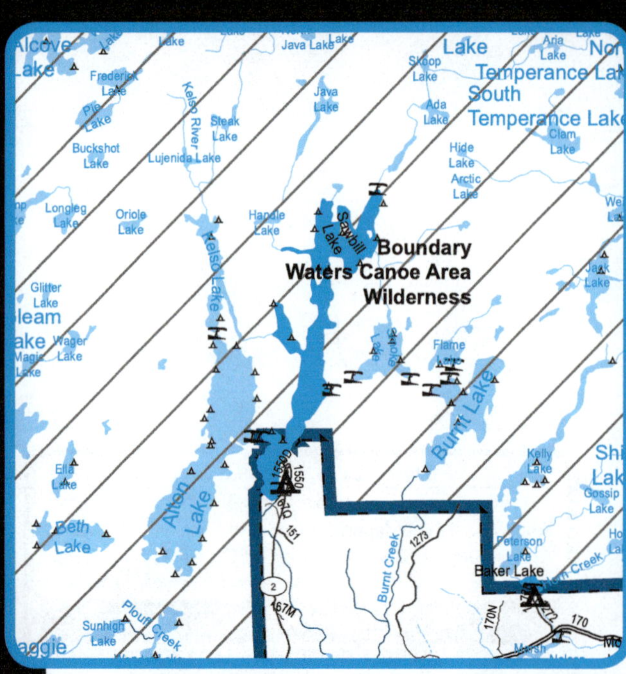

Area map page / coordinates: 17 / B,C-5

Watershed: Baptism-Brule

Surface water area / shorelength: 834 acres / 3.9 miles

Maximum / mean depth: 45 feet / 13 feet

Water color / clarity: Brown, bog stained / 7.5 ft. secchi (2013)

Shoreland zoning classification: Recreational development

Management class / Ecological type: Walleye / northern pike-sucker

Accessibility: Carry-down access through campground on south-east shore; portage to west shore from Alton Lake; portage from Smoke Lake to east shore, mid-lake (BWCAW: day-use permit required, no motors allowed)

Accommodations: Camping, picnicking, restrooms

FISHING INFORMATION

Lying partially within the Boundary Waters Canoe Area, Sawbill Lake is a fun lake to explore and it has a decent fishery. Because of its somewhat remote location, it offers a taste of a wilderness experience, yet still lets you return to your lodge at the end of the day if you choose. Sawbill Lake is also a major entry point for campers trekking into the Boundary Waters.

Walleye numbers aren't high in Sawbill, but they are decent. Through the years, walleyes have never been super-abundant, but they do all right and the population is self-sustaining. If there's an upside, it's that these fish grow faster than the area average.

The latest survey found northern pike numbers at high levels for Sawbill Lake, but still below average compared to other area lakes. Northern pike size is generally pretty small, with no fish even breaking the 25-inch mark in the latest DNR survey.

Smallmouth bass fishing may be the highlight of Sawbill Lake. The lake boasts a good bass population and growth rates are better than average. What's more, fish achieve good sizes here. You won't find an endless supply of 6- or 8-inchers like you do in some lakes. There are some real quality-sized bass here.

Local anglers say Sawbill is a better fishery than the survey numbers show. This lake is known as a good producer most of the year; you can fish it early or try later in the season and still boat fish

For early season walleyes, start at the inlets, tossing a preserved minnow on a jig. This technique works well off Java Creek on the northwest corner of the lake and in the bay in the northeast corner. The south shore of the big island **(Spot 1)**, near the lake's northern end, also is good when the wind is from the south or southwest. A bobber with a leech can be productive. Switch to jigs in yellow, pink or white later in the year and fish structure. The island complex just south of Java

NO RECORD OF STOCKING

NET CATCH DATA

Date: 09/09/2013	Gill Nets		Trap Nets	
species	# per net	avg. fish weight (lbs.)	# per net	avg. fish weight (lbs
Burbot	0.08	0.05	-	-
Cisco Species	0.08	3.54	-	-
Northern Pike	1.17	1.25	0.67	0.70
Rock Bass	1.67	0.32	0.33	0.27
Smallmouth Bass	0.58	1.60	0.07	0.74
Walleye	2.75	1.04	1.33	1.04
White Sucker	10.67	2.62	2.93	2.95
Yellow Perch	1.17	0.17	-	-

LENGTH OF SELECTED SPECIES SAMPLED FROM ALL GEAR

Number of fish caught for the following length categories (inches):

species	0-5	6-8	9-11	12-14	15-19	20-24	25-29	>30	Total
Burbot	1	-	-	-	-	-	-	-	1
Cisco Species	-	-	-	-	-	1	-	-	1
Northern Pike	-	-	-	9	12	3	-	-	24
Rock Bass	3	22	-	-	-	-	-	-	25
Smallmouth Bass	-	-	1	6	1	-	-	-	8
Walleye	-	4	7	29	9	4	-	-	53
White Sucker	-	-	8	10	115	38	-	-	171
Yellow Perch	2	10	-	-	-	-	-	-	12

Creek **(Spot 2)** deserves a good look, as does similar structure in the lake' northern lobe **(Spot 3)**.

You'll find smallies off of the lake's many bars and shorelines. There i no shortage of productive smallmouth bass water in Sawbill Lake. Cast small crankbait for them or fish with jigs and plastic grubs or even smal spinners. Smallies aren't too fussy. If it's in their face, they'll usually hi it.

Although northern pike aren't numerous, there are enough of them t be worth fishing. They'll usually be found prowling the weedlines. Cree mouths would certainly be worth a look for any larger fish, particularl early in the season. Spoons, spinners and crankbaits can all be produc tive.

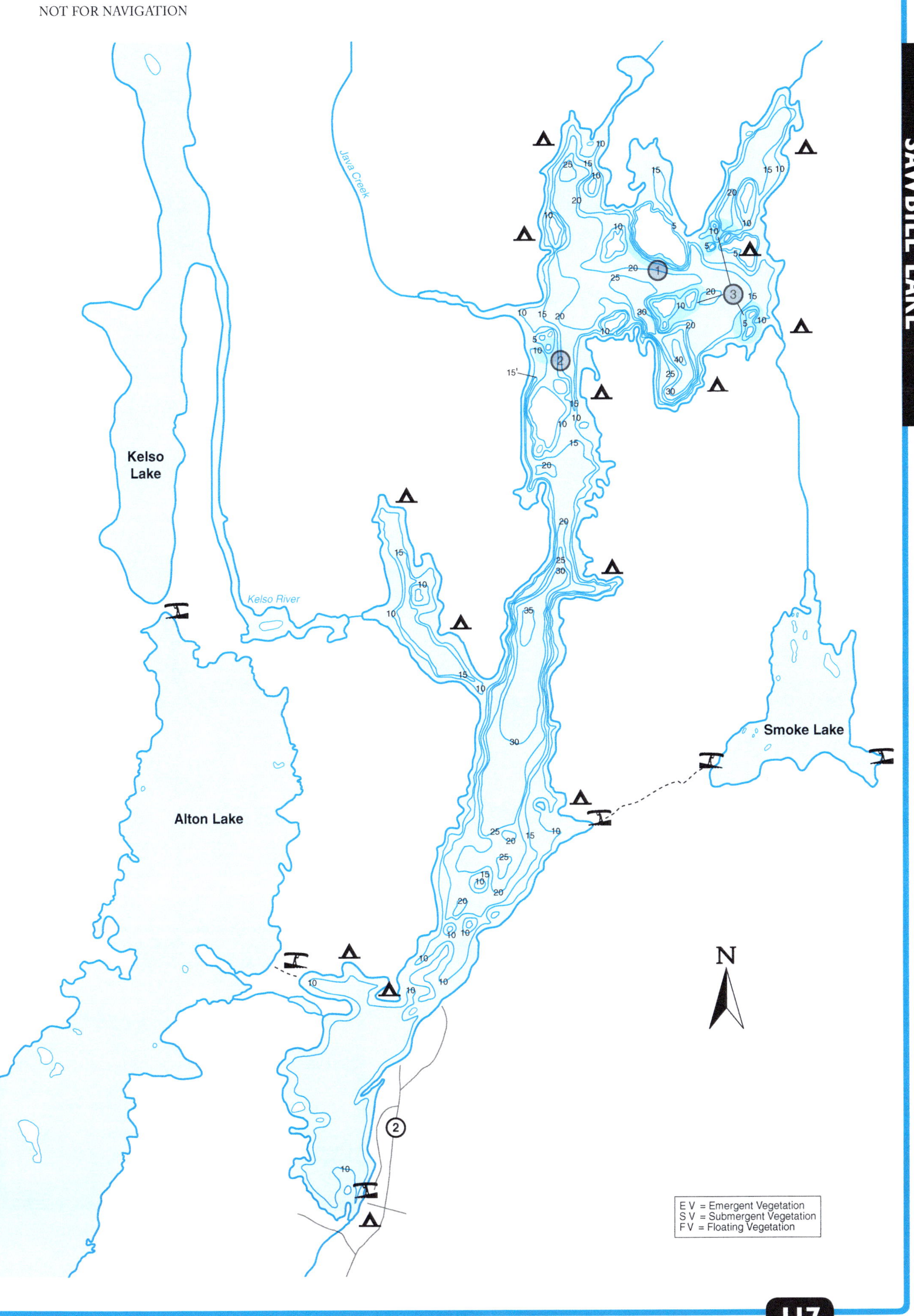

Source: Minnesota Department of Natural Resources, USGS

Pancore Lake, Cook County

Area map page / coordinates: 25 / A-6
Surface area / max depth: 31 acres / 38 feet
Accessibility: Carry-down access across public land from FR 338

FISH STOCKING DATA

year	species	size	# released
10	Splake	Fingerling	1,500
11	Splake	Fingerling	1,500
12	Splake	Fingerling	1,729
13	Brook Trout	Fingerling	1,300
14	Splake	Fingerling	1,500
15	Splake	Fingerling	1,500

LENGTH OF SELECTED SPECIES SAMPLED FROM ALL GEAR

Survey Date: 10/22/2012

Number of fish caught for the following length categories (inches):

species	0-5	6-8	9-11	12-14	15-19	20-24	25-29	>30	Total
Splake	-	-	5	3	5	-	-	-	13

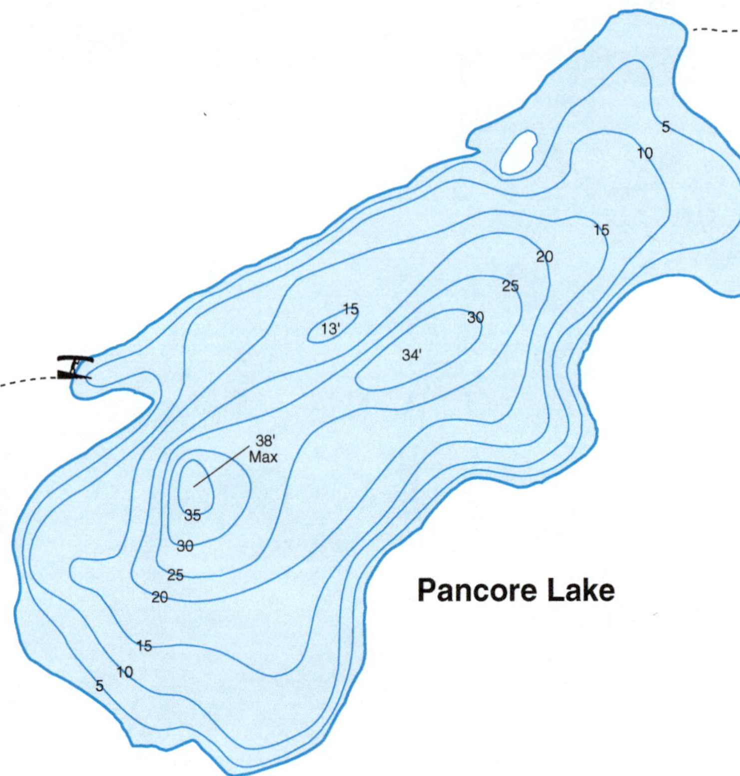

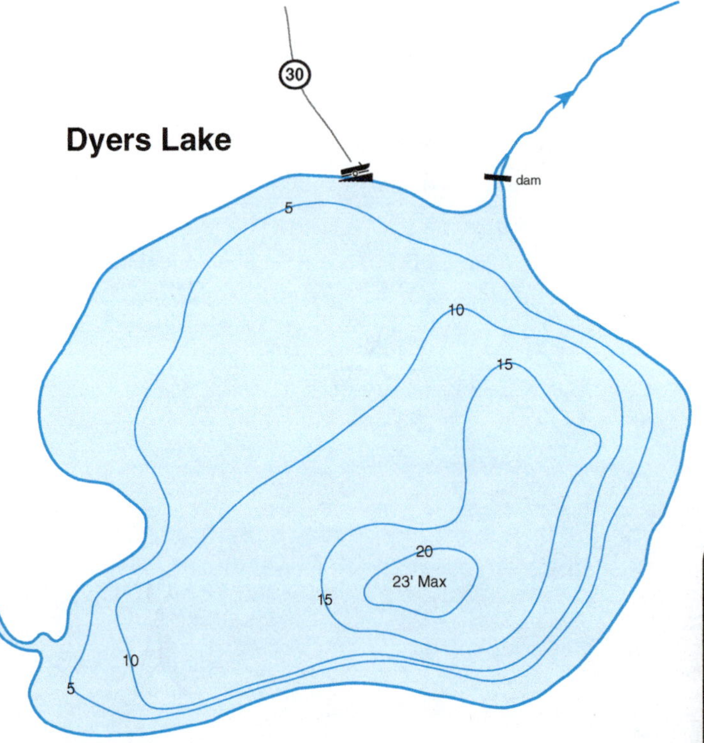

Dyers Lake, Cook County

Area map page / coordinates: 25 / E-4
Surface area / max depth: 69 acres / 23 feet
Accessibility: County-owned public access with earthen ramp on north shore off County Road 30; limited parking
90° 58' 51" W / 47° 31' 52" N

NO RECORD OF STOCKING

LENGTH OF SELECTED SPECIES SAMPLED FROM ALL GEAR

Survey Date: 06/09/2014

Number of fish caught for the following length categories (inches):

species	0-5	6-8	9-11	12-14	15-19	20-24	25-29	>30	Total
Black Crappie	410	317	1	2	-	-	-	-	730
Bluegill	64	81	1	-	-	-	-	-	146
Northern Pike	-	-	1	-	8	16	6	-	31
Pumpkinseed	31	-	-	-	-	-	-	-	31
Yellow Perch	9	30	2	-	-	-	-	-	41

NOT FOR NAVIGATION

Source: Minnesota Department of Natural Resources, USGS

Baker Lake

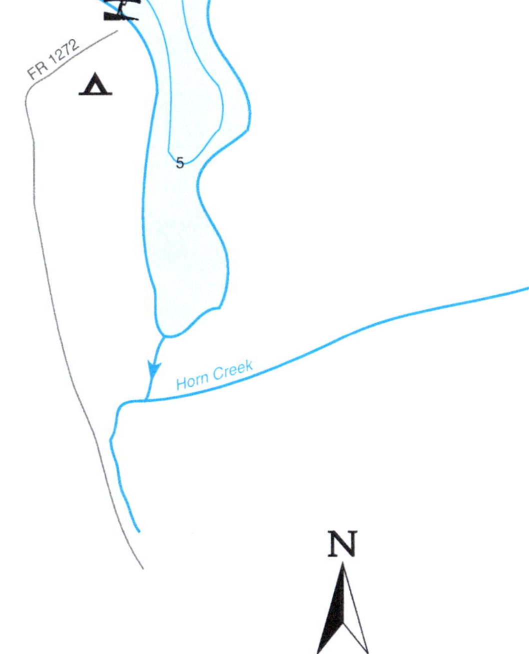

Baker Lake, Cook County

Area map page / coordinates: 17 / D-6
Surface area / max depth: 24 acres / 10 feet
Accessibility: Carry-down access to southwest shore off FR 1272; day-use permit required. No motors allowed.

NO RECORD OF STOCKING

LENGTH OF SELECTED SPECIES SAMPLED FROM ALL GEAR
Survey Date: 07/19/1990
Number of fish caught for the following length categories (inches):

species	0-5	6-8	9-11	12-14	15-19	20-24	25-29	>30	Total
Yellow Perch	11	55	6	-	-	-	-	-	72
Walleye	-	-	3	-	-	-	-	-	3
Northern Pike	-	-	1	2	-	-	-	-	3

Moore Lake, Cook County

Area map page / coordinates: 17 / D-6
Surface area / max depth: 61 acres / 8 feet
Accessibility: Carry-down access to north shore off FR 165

NO RECORD OF STOCKING

LENGTH OF SELECTED SPECIES SAMPLED FROM ALL GEAR
Survey Date: 06/21/2006
Number of fish caught for the following length categories (inches):

species	0-5	6-8	9-11	12-14	15-19	20-24	25-29	>30	Total
Hybrid Sunfish	1	-	-	-	-	-	-	-	1
Northern Pike	-	-	5	3	13	15	3	-	39
White Sucker	1	6	52	70	53	-	-	-	182
Yellow Perch	7	26	16	-	-	-	-	-	49

Moore Lake

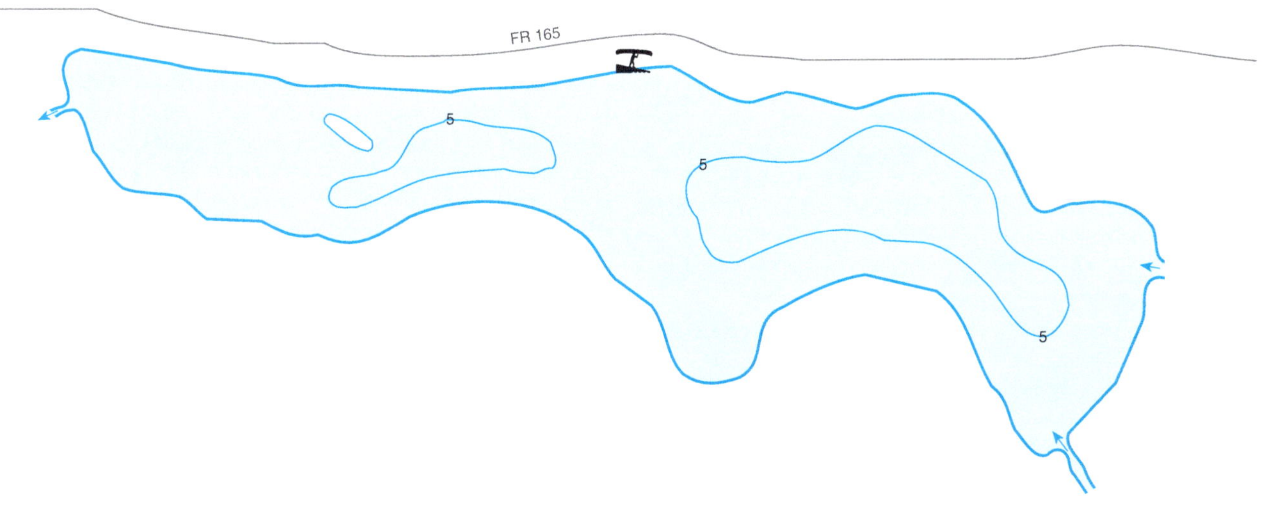

NOT FOR NAVIGATION

CRESCENT LAKE *Cook County*

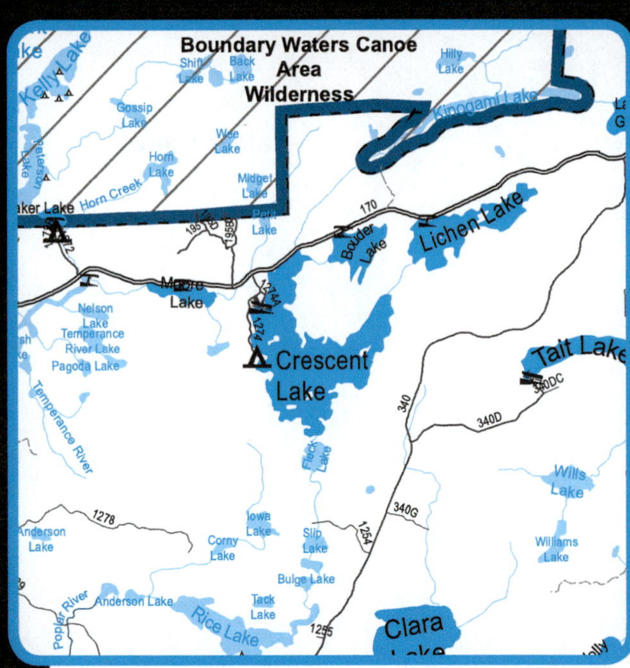

Area map page / coordinates: 17 / D-6

Watershed: Baptism-Brule

Surface water area / shorelength: 755 acres / 9.4 miles

Maximum / mean depth: 28 feet / 11 feet

Water color / clarity: Yellow-brown tint / 6.8 ft. secchi (2014)

Shoreland zoning classification: Natural environment

Management class / Ecological type: Walleye/ soft-water walley

Accessibility: USFS-owned public access with concrete ramp in campground on west shore off FR 1274; parking for 20 vehicles

90° 46' 18" W / 47° 49' 29" N

Accommodations: Camping, picnicking, restrooms

FISHING INFORMATION

Crescent Lake is a beautiful northwoods gem filled with rocky structure. There is a large National Forest campground on the lake that is quite popular, and thus, the lake gets more fishing pressure than many surrounding lakes. Still, thanks to its large size and robust walleye population, there is plenty of good fishing to be found in Crescent.

One interesting thing about the lake is the presence of muskies, which is a rarity in Cook County. This species was stocked back in the 1970s and they've taken hold. Unfortunately, that was in the infancy of the DNR's muskie stocking program, and the strain that was stocked was the Shoepack strain. This strain doesn't have nearly the same growth rate as the Leech Lake strain that is now being stocked in the state's muskie waters. Shoepack-strain muskies often top out in the low 30-inch-range, with a 40-incher a real giant. The good news is these fish are fairly willing biters, as far as muskies go.

The folks at Devil Track Resort, 205 Fireweed Lane, Grand Marais, MN 55604, (877) 387-9414, say the average size of walleyes in this lake is 12 to 14 inches and there are plenty of fish larger than that. Given their abundance, the chance of having a shore lunch at your campsite is pretty good, although don't expect a lot of large fillets.

Smallmouth bass showed up in DNR surveys for the first time in the late 1990s and are now well established. You'll likely tie into a lot of smallies while you're walleye fishing, particularly if you're using jigs with nightcrawlers or leeches. Smallmouth are slow-growing in Crescent and you'll find a lot of small fish.

The latest muskie numbers are good, with plenty of fish over 30 inches. Although you won't find any wall-hangers here, there are enough muskies here to warrant fishing for them and they are large enough to be exciting. Some naturally produced tiger muskies have also been observed, although northern pike numbers are low. Tiger muskies are northern pike/muskie hybrids.

NO RECORD OF STOCKING

NET CATCH DATA

Date: 07/07/2014	Gill Nets		Trap Nets	
species	# per net	avg. fish weight (lbs.)	# per net	avg. fish weight (lbs
Muskellunge	1.67	5.26	0.89	4.52
Northern Pike	0.33	0.85	-	-
Smallmouth Bass	0.22	0.11	0.78	0.24
Tiger Muskellunge	0.22	2.94	-	-
Walleye	6.22	0.98	1.00	2.82
White Sucker	3.11	1.37	-	-
Yellow Perch	8.00	0.11	0.11	0.07

LENGTH OF SELECTED SPECIES SAMPLED FROM ALL GEAR

Number of fish caught for the following length categories (inches):

species	0-5	6-8	9-11	12-14	15-19	20-24	25-29	>30	Total
Muskellunge	-	-	1	-	3	-	11	8	23
Northern Pike	-	-	-	1	2	-	-	-	3
Smallmouth Bass	2	7	-	-	-	-	-	-	9
Tiger Muskellunge	-	-	-	-	-	2	-	-	2
Walleye	-	1	25	21	10	6	2	-	65
White Sucker	-	8	4	2	12	2	-	-	28
Yellow Perch	42	29	1	-	-	-	-	-	72

Most anglers come to this rocky lake in search of walleyes, but don't b surprised to catch lots of smallmouth bass and even a stray muskellung There is an endless array of structure to fish, much of which is foun on no map. For walleyes, fish the windy sides of islands and points. Th islands just south of the boat landing **(Spot 1)** are a good starting poin Almost directly across the lake **(Spot 2)** a couple of small islands nea deep water are worth a look. Finally, on the south end is similar structur that holds walleyes **(Spot 3)**.

For muskies, try the back bays at the weed edges. They relate to roc reefs as well. Bucktails with bright blades will get some attention, as wi bright crankbaits.

Be careful when boating on Crescent. Despite its popularity, there ar many unmarked rock reefs that come up quickly from relatively dee water.

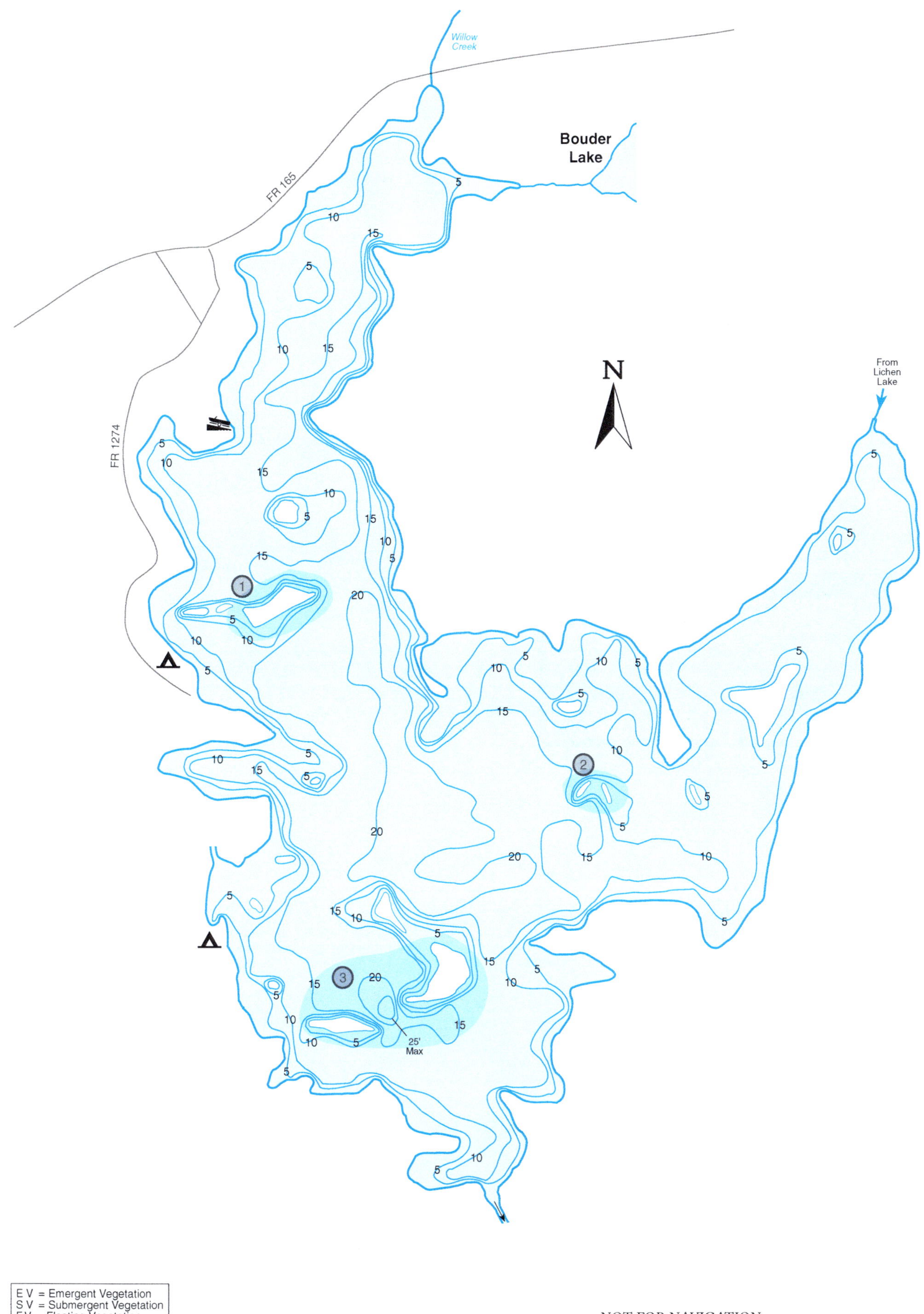

E V = Emergent Vegetation
S V = Submergent Vegetation
F V = Floating Vegetation

NOT FOR NAVIGATION

Source: Minnesota Department of Natural Resources, USGS

BOUDER LAKE

Bouder Lake, Cook County

Area map page / coordinates: 17 / D-6
Surface area / max depth: 136 acres / 17 feet
Accessibility: Carry-down access to north shore, off FR 165; parking for two vehicles. Navigable channel from Crescent

NO RECORD OF STOCKING

LENGTH OF SELECTED SPECIES SAMPLED FROM ALL GEAR
Survey Date: 06/30/2014
Number of fish caught for the following length categories (inches):

species	0-5	6-8	9-11	12-14	15-19	20-24	25-29	>30	Total
Muskellunge	-	-	-	-	1	10	12	3	26
Northern Pike	-	-	-	-	1	-	-	-	1
Pumpkinseed	3	-	-	-	-	-	-	-	3
Smallmouth Bass	-	1	1	1	-	-	-	-	3
Walleye	-	8	30	5	4	3	-	-	50
White Sucker	-	5	1	-	16	3	-	-	25
Yellow Perch	5	5	-	-	-	-	-	-	10

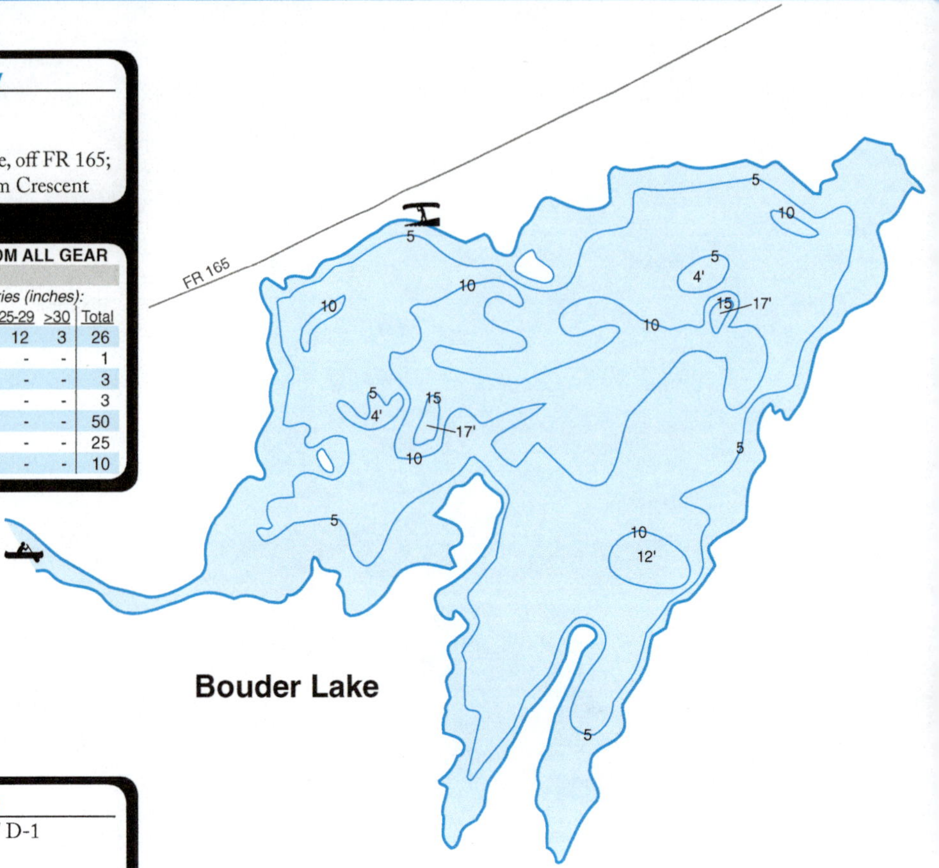

LICHEN LAKE

Lichen Lake, Cook County

Area map page / coordinates: 17 / D-6 & 18 / D-1
Surface area / max depth: 276 acres / 17 feet
Accessibility: Carry-down access to north shore off FR 165

NO RECORD OF STOCKING

LENGTH OF SELECTED SPECIES SAMPLED FROM ALL GEAR
Survey Date: 07/08/2014
Number of fish caught for the following length categories (inches):

species	0-5	6-8	9-11	12-14	15-19	20-24	25-29	>30	Total
Muskellunge	-	-	-	-	1	6	-	3	10
Smallmouth Bass	-	3	1	-	-	-	-	-	4
Walleye	-	15	7	29	5	1	-	-	57
White Sucker	-	1	2	1	12	-	-	-	16
Yellow Perch	2	15	1	-	-	-	-	-	18

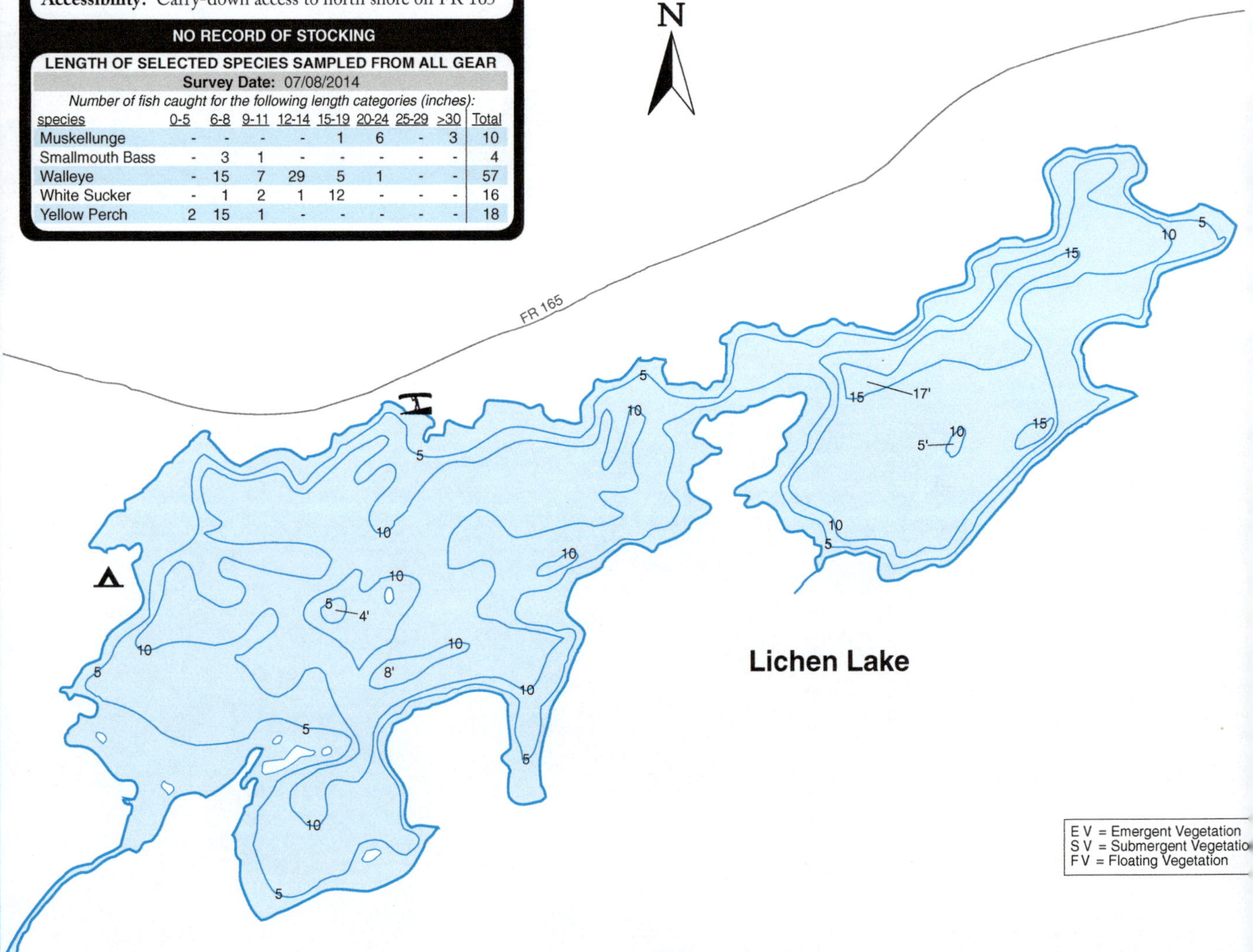

Tomash Lake, Cook County

Area map page / coordinates: 18 / C-2
Surface area / max depth: 96 acres / 5 feet
Accessibility: Carry-down access to west shore off Brule Lake Road

LAST RECORD OF STOCKING 1998 (WAE FRY)

LENGTH OF SELECTED SPECIES SAMPLED FROM ALL GEAR
Survey Date: 08/16/2000
Number of fish caught for the following length categories (inches):

species	0-5	6-8	9-11	12-14	15-19	20-24	25-29	>30	Total
Walleye	-	-	-	3	4	-	-	-	7
Yellow Perch	3	53	7	-	-	-	-	-	63

Tomash Lake

4'
4'
4'
4'

N

Lake Gust, Cook County

Area map page / coordinates: 18 / C,D-1
Surface area / max depth: 143 acres / 6 feet
Accessibility: Carry-down access to east shore from FR 153

NO RECORD OF STOCKING

LENGTH OF SELECTED SPECIES SAMPLED FROM ALL GEAR
Survey Date: 09/06/2011
Number of fish caught for the following length categories (inches):

species	0-5	6-8	9-11	12-14	15-19	20-24	25-29	>30	Total
Northern Pike	-	-	-	-	1	-	-	-	1
Smallmouth Bass	1	1	5	13	1	-	-	-	21
Walleye	-	1	7	18	37	-	-	-	63
White Sucker	-	1	6	7	4	-	-	-	18
Yellow Perch	-	8	7	-	-	-	-	-	15

Jock Mock Lake, Cook County

Area map page / coordinates: 18 / C-1
Surface area / max depth: 17 acres / 23 feet
Accessibility: Carry-down access to north shore off FR 153

NO RECORD OF STOCKING

LENGTH OF SELECTED SPECIES SAMPLED FROM ALL GEAR
Survey Date: 06/06/2011
Number of fish caught for the following length categories (inches):

species	0-5	6-8	9-11	12-14	15-19	20-24	25-29	>30	Total
Northern Pike	-	-	-	-	3	9	-	-	12
Smallmouth Bass	-	-	-	3	2	-	-	-	5
Walleye	-	-	-	-	4	3	1	-	8

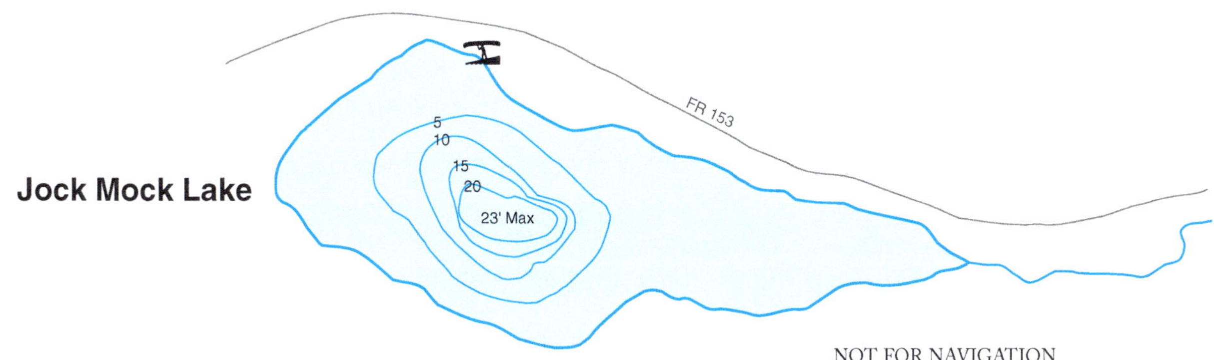

NOT FOR NAVIGATION

BRULE LAKE *Cook County*

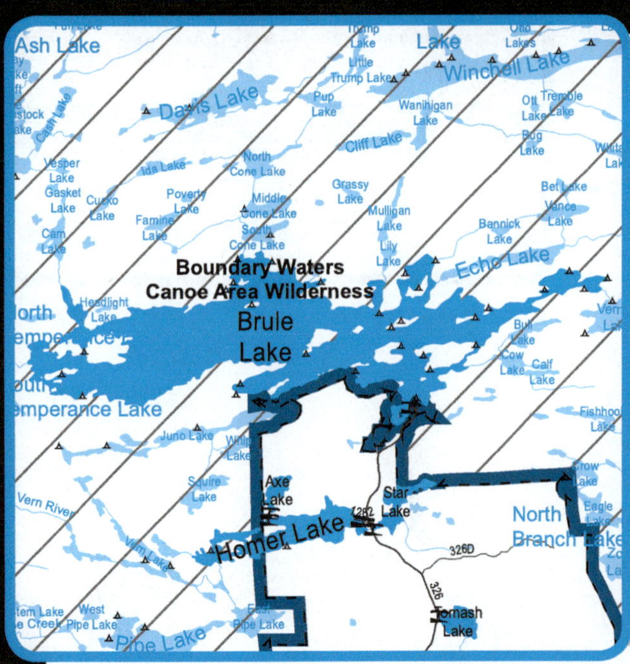

Area map page / coordinates: 17 / B-6 & 18 / B-1,2

Watershed: Baptism-Brule

Surface water area / shorelength: 4,272 acres / 23.6 miles

Maximum / mean depth: 78 feet / 35 feet

Water color / clarity: Light green to clear / 15.0 ft. secchi (2009)

Shoreland zoning classification: Natural environment

Management class / Ecological type: Walleye / trout

Accessibility: Carry-down access on southeast bay, 19 miles north of Lutsen, at the end of FR 326;
BWCAW day-use permit required; no motors allowed

90° 38' 41" W / 47° 55' 34" N

Accommodations: Camping, parking for 20 vehicles

FISHING INFORMATION

Steve Persons of DNR Fisheries, 1356 Hwy. 61, Grand Marais, MN 55604, (218) 387-3056, says before there were motor restrictions, Brule Lake was a tremendous walleye fishery. He believes it still is, but given its large size, anglers just don't fish it all that much. For anglers willing to go through a little effort, the reward could be a very good, largely untapped walleye fishery.

You'll find plenty of walleyes here with a good average size structure. A limiting factor for small walleyes is the low yellow perch population. Without adequate perch numbers as prey, young walleyes grow slowly. However, once these fish grow large enough, they can begin preying on Brule Lake's tullibee population. Tullibees are present in high numbers. They provide high-fat forage that sustains good growth rates for any fish large enough to prey on them, which would typically be walleyes and northern pike in Brule Lake.

Speaking of tullibees, they do grow large here and they are quite abundant. Anglers who fish deep water may stumble on some, but with non-motorized access only, it's likely there is very little fishing pressure on them. Netting is allowed in the fall for tullibees, but this sport doesn't attract much attention. Persons says in the summertime, large walleyes will feed on tullibees at 50-foot-plus depths.

Northern pike are common in Brule Lake, and although the last DNR assessment didn't look too impressive, there are probably some real brutes out there, given the abundance of tullibees and low fishing pressure.

Brule Lake offers a good fishery for smallmouth bass anglers. These fish grow quickly and tend to run fairly large. Their numbers appear to be on the rise.

Steep breaks form off the shoreline in several areas. These can be worked successfully for walleyes and bass. Other spots to try for walleyes include the two points that form the entrance to the two-fingered bay on the southeast end of the lake, not far from the boat landing **(Spots 1 and 2)**. Jigging the smal humps and islands near mid-lake **(Spot 3)** may also produce some fish The shallow structure just south of the islands in the lake's large north side bay **(Spot 4)** can also be productive.

Smallmouth can be found just about anywhere in Brule Lake. You can go wrong tossing a crankbait or jig to any rocky structure. Although mos fish will be found in relatively shallow areas, big smallies sometimes g deeper than you might think.

The best way to find a trophy-sized northern pike would be to tro deep-diving crankbaits in areas that hold tullibees. Try breaklines tha drop to deep slots that would concentrate fish.

If you want to try your hand at tullibees, seek out these deep slots o holes and vertically jig with a small spoon, or better yet, a small spoo with a tiny dropper jig and a waxworm a few inches below.

NO RECORD OF STOCKING

NET CATCH DATA

Date: 09/08/2009	Gill Nets		Trap Nets	
species	# per net	avg. fish weight (lbs.)	# per net	avg. fish weight (lbs.
Northern Pike	1.40	1.45	-	-
Smallmouth Bass	0.67	1.74	-	-
Tullibee (Cisco)	7.80	1.22	-	-
Walleye	3.53	1.12	-	-
White Sucker	3.27	3.27	-	-
Yellow Perch	0.40	0.13	-	-

LENGTH OF SELECTED SPECIES SAMPLED FROM ALL GEAR

Number of fish caught for the following length categories (inches):

species	0-5	6-8	9-11	12-14	15-19	20-24	25-29	>30	Total
Northern Pike	-	-	-	1	6	10	2	-	19
Smallmouth Bass	-	-	-	1	2	-	-	-	3
Tullibee (Cisco)	-	31	91	29	36	1	-	-	188
Walleye	-	1	7	10	31	6	-	-	55
White Sucker	-	1	-	4	21	23	-	-	49
Yellow Perch	-	6	-	-	-	-	-	-	6

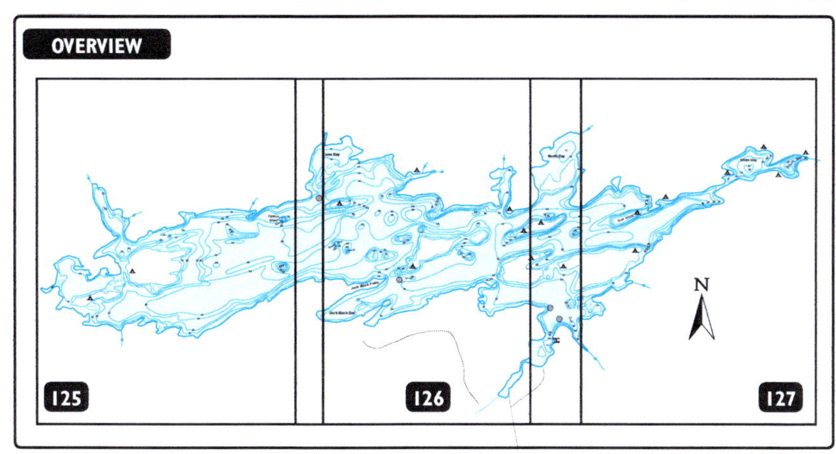

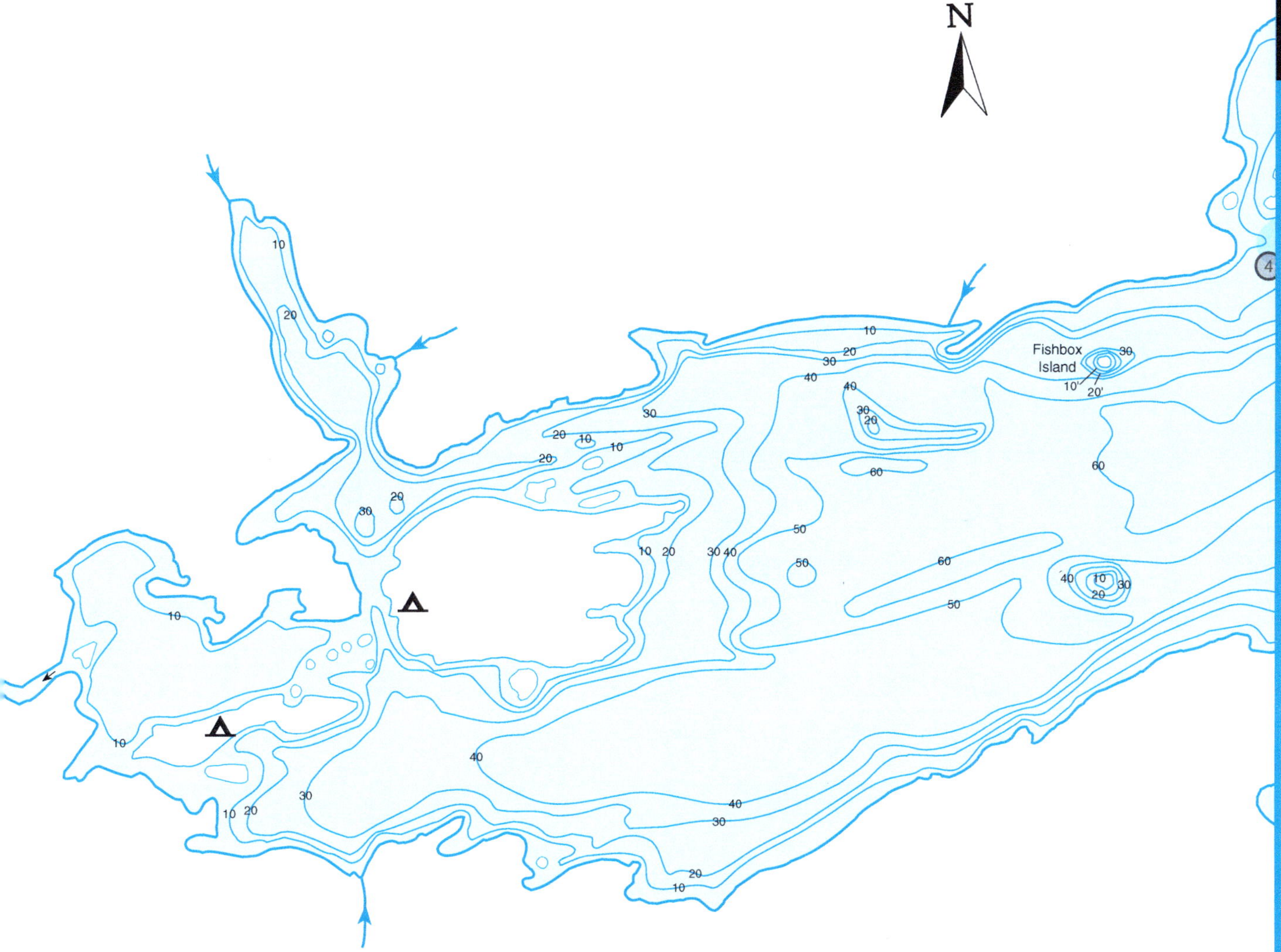

N

Fishbox Island

NOT FOR NAVIGATION

Source: Minnesota Department of Natural Resources, USGS

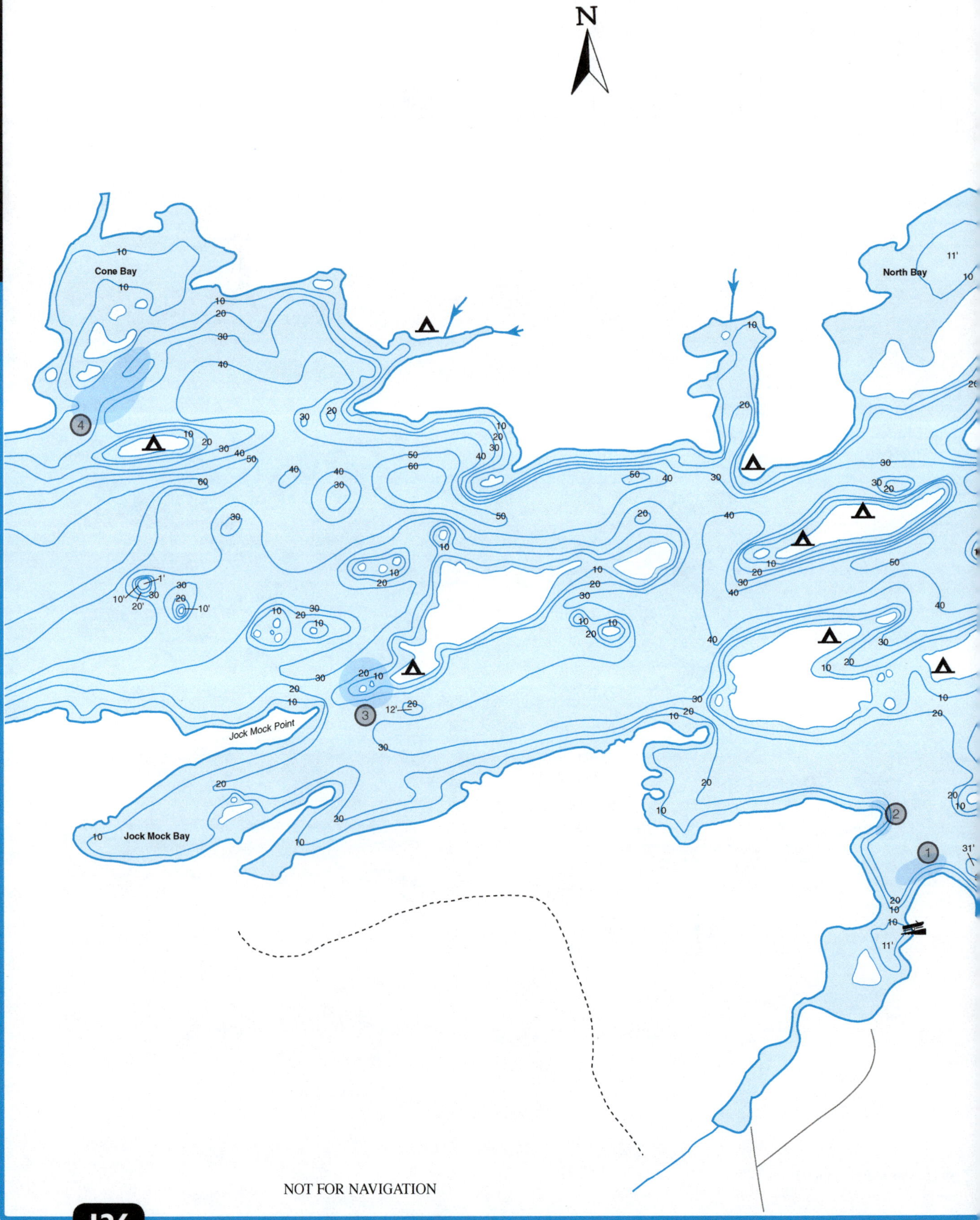

Cone Bay

North Bay

Jock Mock Point

Jock Mock Bay

NOT FOR NAVIGATION

Source: Minnesota Department of Natural Resources, USGS

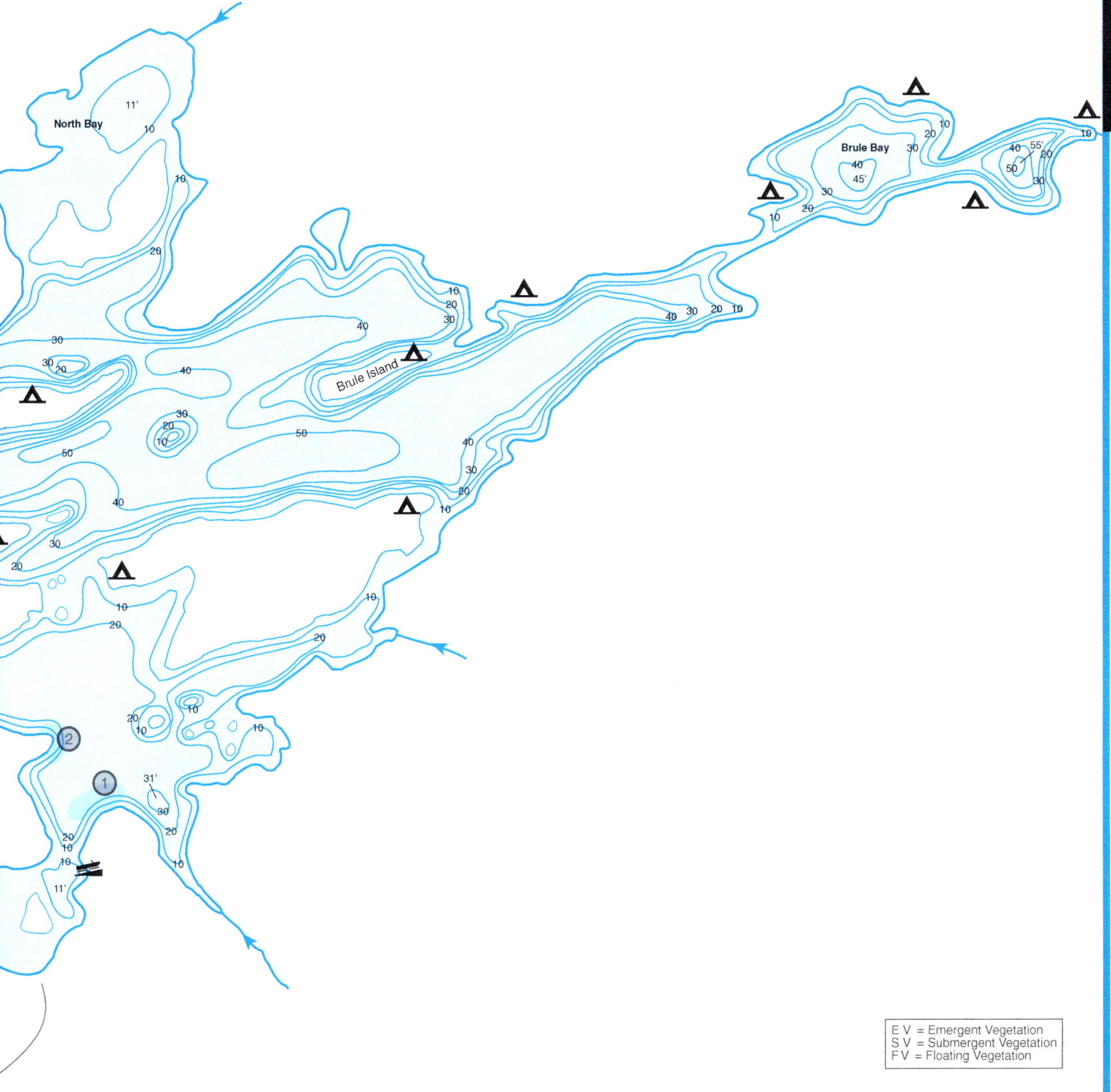

NOT FOR NAVIGATION

Source: Minnesota Department of Natural Resources, USGS

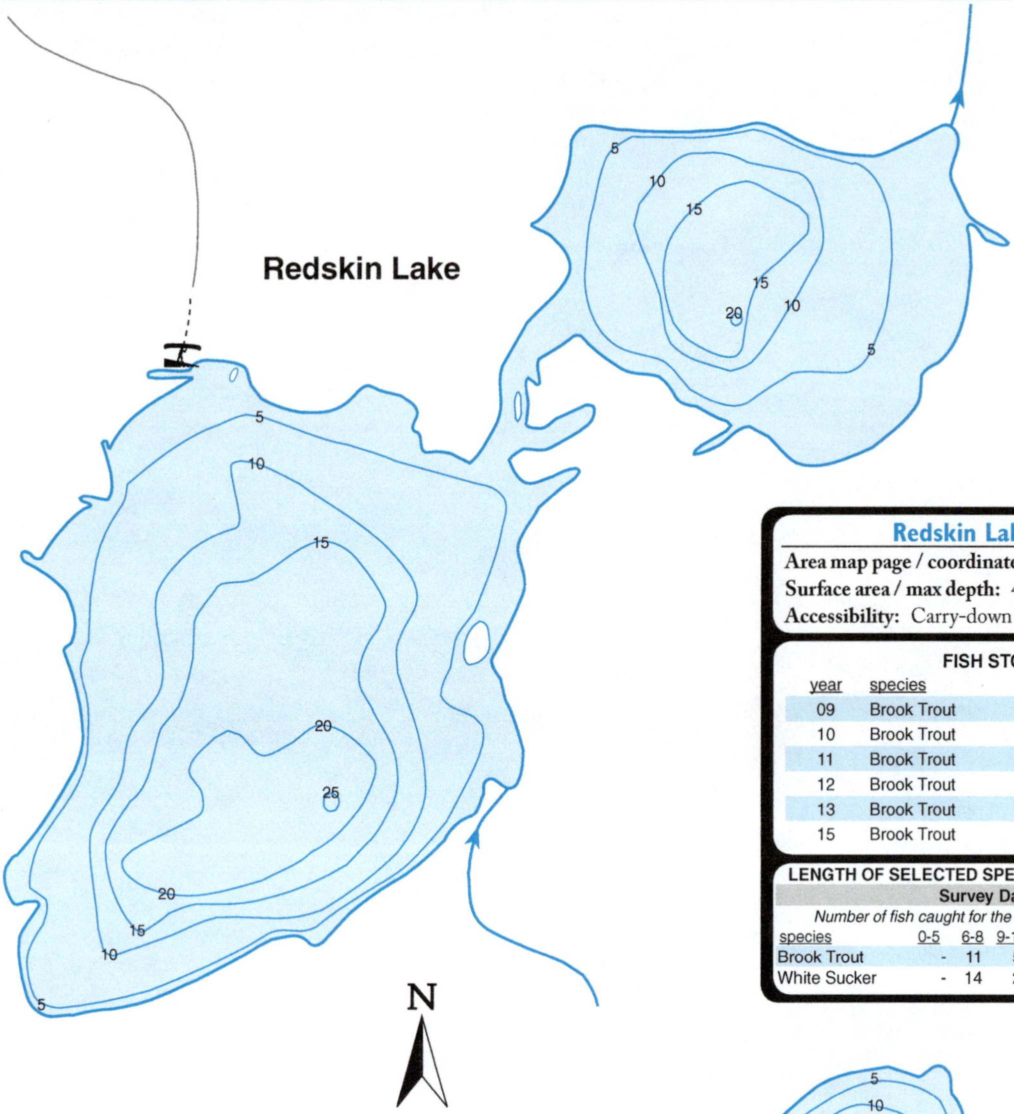

Redskin Lake

Redskin Lake, Lake County

Area map page / coordinates: 23 / C-6
Surface area / max depth: 43 acres / 25 feet
Accessibility: Carry-down access (500 feet) to north shore

FISH STOCKING DATA

year	species	size	# released
09	Brook Trout	Fingerling	2,026
10	Brook Trout	Fingerling	1,984
11	Brook Trout	Fingerling	2,000
12	Brook Trout	Fingerling	1,950
13	Brook Trout	Fingerling	2,000
15	Brook Trout	Fingerling	1,992

LENGTH OF SELECTED SPECIES SAMPLED FROM ALL GEAR
Survey Date: 09/13/2010
Number of fish caught for the following length categories (inches):

species	0-5	6-8	9-11	12-14	15-19	20-24	25-29	>30	Total
Brook Trout	-	11	5	5	-	-	-	-	21
White Sucker	-	14	2	-	4	-	-	-	20

N

Shoofly Lake, Lake County

Area map page / coordinates: 23 / C-6
Surface area / max depth: 10 acres / 25 feet
Accessibility: Carry-down access (425 foot trail, mostly bog) to southeast corner of lake; trail is 0.7 mile north on logging road off USFS Rd. 172

FISH STOCKING DATA

year	species	size	# released
08	Brook Trout	Fingerling	1,006
09	Brook Trout	Fingerling	1,013
10	Brook Trout	Fingerling	1,012
12	Brook Trout	Fingerling	500
13	Brook Trout	Fingerling	500
15	Brook Trout	Fingerling	500

LENGTH OF SELECTED SPECIES SAMPLED FROM ALL GEAR
Survey Date: 05/21/2008
Number of fish caught for the following length categories (inches):

species	0-5	6-8	9-11	12-14	15-19	20-24	25-29	>30	Total
Brook Trout	-	4	1	5	1	-	-	-	11

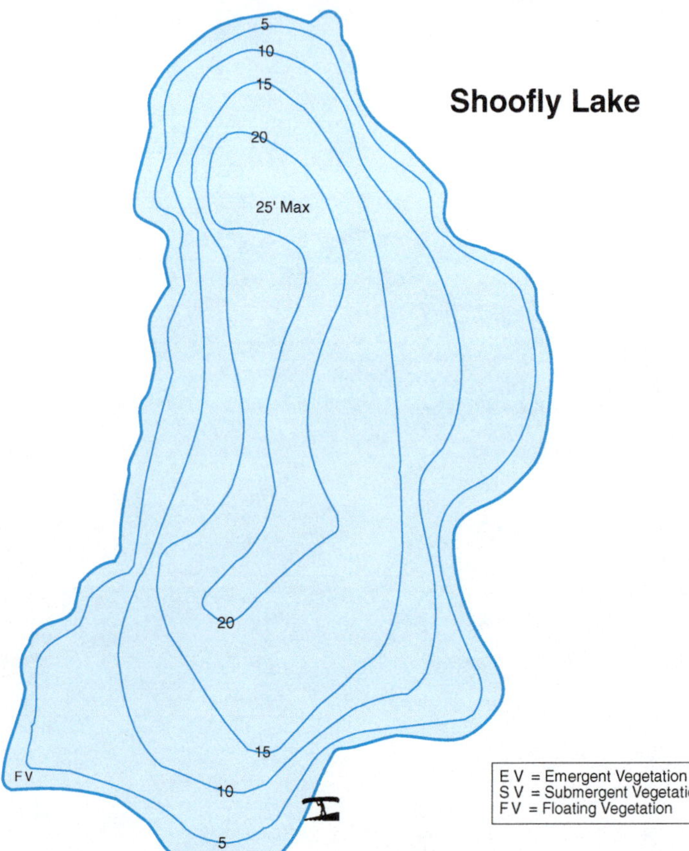

NOT FOR NAVIGATION

Source: Minnesota Department of Natural Resources, USGS

AXE LAKE

HOMER LAKE

STAR LAKE

NOT FOR NAVIGATION

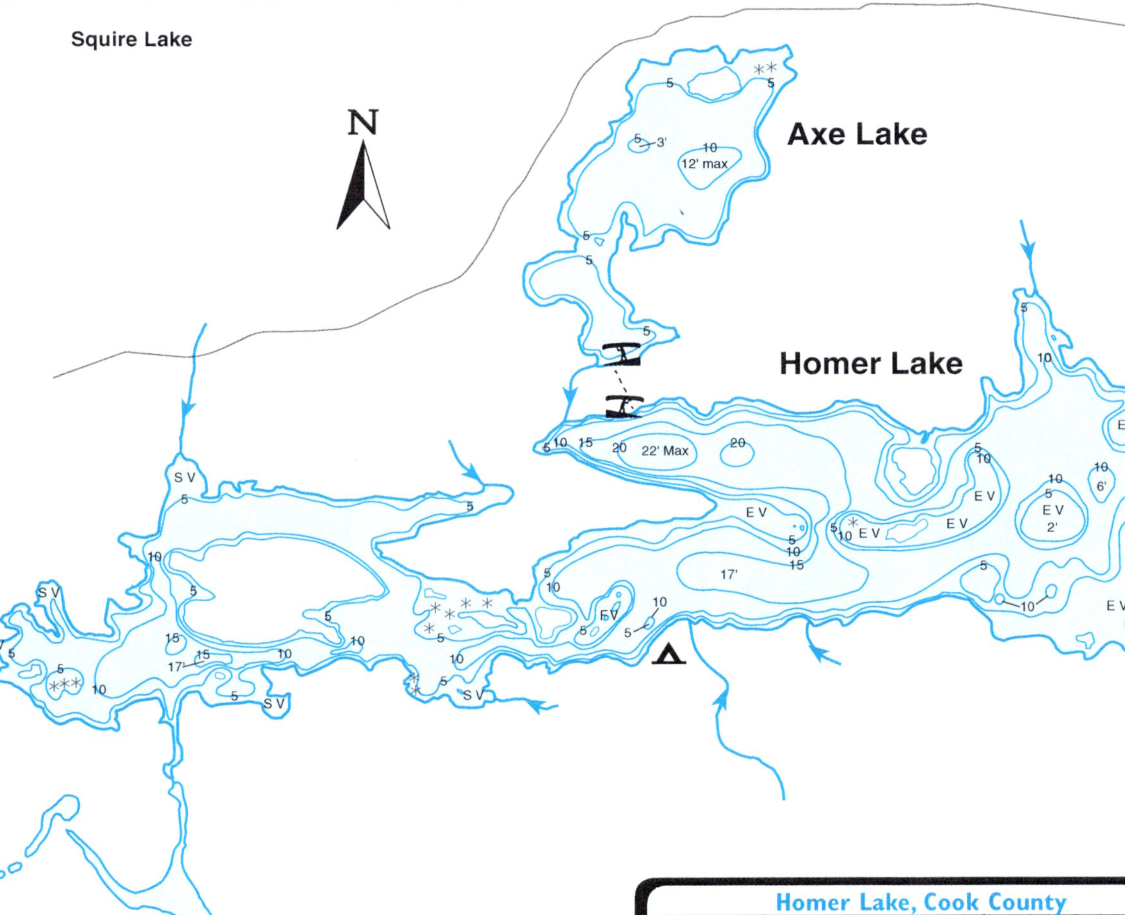

Axe Lake, Cook County

Area map page / coordinates: 18 / B,C-1
Surface area / max depth: 53 acres / 12 feet
Accessibility: Portage access from Homer Lake

FISH STOCKING DATA

year	species	size	# released
01	Walleye	Fry	50,000

LENGTH OF SELECTED SPECIES SAMPLED FROM ALL GEAR

Survey Date: 07/13/2000

Number of fish caught for the following length categories (inches):

species	0-5	6-8	9-11	12-14	15-19	20-24	25-29	>30	Total
Northern Pike	-	-	-	-	5	7	2	-	14
Walleye	-	-	1	2	6	-	-	-	9

Homer Lake, Cook County

Area map page / coordinates: 18 / B,C-1
Surface area / max depth: 443 acres / 22 feet
Accessibility: USFS-owned public access with concrete ramp on east shore, off FR 326 (Brule Lake Road); BWCAW- day-use permit required; no motors allowed.
90° 39' 36" W / 47° 54' 16" N

NO RECORD OF STOCKING

LENGTH OF SELECTED SPECIES SAMPLED FROM ALL GEAR

Survey Date: 07/12/2004

Number of fish caught for the following length categories (inches):

species	0-5	6-8	9-11	12-14	15-19	20-24	25-29	>30	Total
Northern Pike	-	-	2	-	12	5	1	-	20
Smallmouth Bass	-	-	2	2	1	-	-	-	5
Walleye	-	2	10	7	20	6	-	-	45
Yellow Perch	-	10	-	-	-	-	-	-	10

Star Lake, Cook County

Area map page / coordinates: 18 / B,C-1,2
Surface area / max depth: 120 acres / 13 feet
Accessibility: Carry-down access to west shore off FR 326

FISH STOCKING DATA

year	species	size	# released
09	Walleye	Fry	300,000
12	Walleye	Fry	280,000
13	Walleye	Fry	300,000

LENGTH OF SELECTED SPECIES SAMPLED FROM ALL GEAR

Survey Date: 06/13/2005

Number of fish caught for the following length categories (inches):

species	0-5	6-8	9-11	12-14	15-19	20-24	25-29	>30	Total
Northern Pike	-	-	1	2	26	1	-	-	30
Walleye	-	1	-	-	1	-	-	-	2
Yellow Perch	4	-	1	-	-	-	-	-	5

Source: Minnesota Department of Natural Resources, USGS

CASCADE LAKE
Cook County

Area map pg / coord: 18 / C-1,2

Watershed: Baptism-Brule

Surface area: 452 acres

Shorelength: 8.6 miles

Max / mean depth: 17 feet / 8 feet

Water color / clarity: Light brown / 7.7 ft. secchi (2012)

Shoreland zoning class: Nat. envt.

Mgmt class / Ecological type: Walleye / soft-water walleye

Accessibility: USFS-owned public access with gravel ramp on southeast bay; parking for 6 vehicles

90° 37' 50" W / 47° 51' 46" N

Accommodations: Resort, camping, restrooms

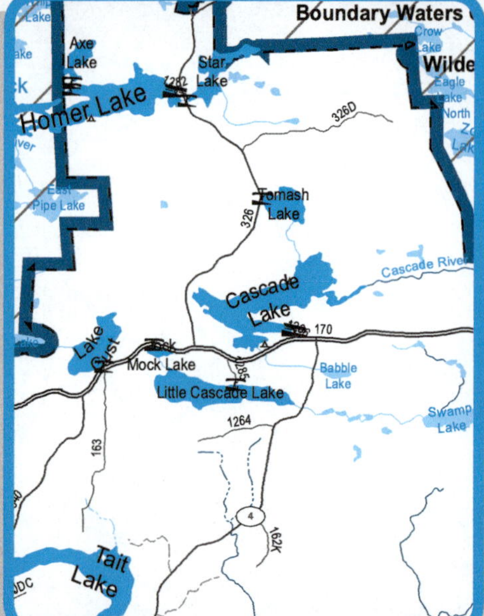

LITTLE CASCADE LAKE
Cook County

Area map pg / coord: 18 / C,D-1,2

Watershed: Baptism-Brule

Surface area: 262 acres

Shorelength: 4.4 miles

Max / mean depth: 9 feet / 6 feet

Water color / clarity: Brown stain / 5.0 ft. secchi (2012)

Shoreland zoning class: Nat. envt.

Mgmt class / Ecological type: Northern pike / northern pike-sucker

Accessibility: Carry-down access to north shore, off FR 153

Accommodations: None

Cascade Lake

NO RECORD OF STOCKING

NET CATCH DATA

Date: 08/27/2012	Gill Nets		Trap Nets	
species	# per net	avg. fish weight (lbs.)	# per net	avg. fish weight (lbs.)
Northern Pike	2.22	1.88	0.22	2.01
Walleye	9.11	1.62	0.33	1.30
White Sucker	10.22	2.82	1.11	2.42
Yellow Perch	3.11	0.11	0.44	0.07

LENGTH OF SELECTED SPECIES SAMPLED FROM ALL GEAR

Number of fish caught for the following length categories (inches):

species	0-5	6-8	9-11	12-14	15-19	20-24	25-29	>29	Total
Northern Pike	-	-	-	-	11	11	-	-	22
Walleye	-	2	12	13	54	4	-	-	85
White Sucker	-	1	-	15	79	7	-	-	102
Yellow Perch	16	16	-	-	-	-	-	-	32

Little Cascade Lake

NO RECORD OF STOCKING

NET CATCH DATA

Date: 06/11/2012	Gill Nets		Trap Nets	
species	# per net	avg. fish weight (lbs.)	# per net	avg. fish weight (lbs.)
Northern Pike	10.75	2.81	2.83	3.52
White Sucker	2.25	1.99	-	-
Yellow Perch	6.00	0.14	0.08	0.07

LENGTH OF SELECTED SPECIES SAMPLED FROM ALL GEAR

Number of fish caught for the following length categories (inches):

species	0-5	6-8	9-11	12-14	15-19	20-24	25-29	>29	Total
Northern Pike	-	-	-	-	5	54	18	-	77
White Sucker	-	-	1	2	6	-	-	-	9
Yellow Perch	6	19	-	-	-	-	-	-	25

FISHING INFORMATION

These two lakes offer decent fishing opportunities in an area scattered with great fishing lakes. Consequently, they don't get a ton of play, but, that doesn't mean you should ignore them, for each has something to offer.

In **Cascade Lake**, walleye numbers are very good, and the average size is fairly large. There are a lot of nice eaters in Cascade. There's also good action for northern pike, which the folks at Devil Track Resort, 205 Fireweed Lane, Grand Marais, MN 55604, (877) 387-9414, say average about 20 inches. But, every once in a while, you'll tie into one that's truly impressive.

Given Cascade's bog-stained, shallow water, it's a good lake to hit early in the season. Truthfully, the lake produces fairly well throughout the open-water season.

Among the places to try on this lake are the point with a deep hole off the end **(Spot 1)**. Jig this area late in the year for walleyes. Where the shallow southeast bay begins to break to deeper water **(Spot 2)** is a good place to find walleyes as well. The points with a deep slot in the center is a good funnel that concentrates walleyes **(Spot 3)**.

If you want to fish **Little Cascade**, you'll need to portage a canoe a little ways, but it's worth the trip if you want some fast northern pike action. There are a lot of them in this lake and the average size is actually pretty good. In fact, the DNR has implemented a special regulation on the lake to maintain and even improve the quality northern pike size. There is a protected slot on northern pike from 24 to 36 inches, with one over 36 inches allowed.

There isn't a whole lot of depth or structure to this lake, so you'll just have to cast to any weedbeds. The inlet and outlet creeks would also be worth a shot, but odds are, the pike are going to be everywhere in this 9-foot-deep lake. The aggressive fish will quickly let you know when you're in the right spot.

A good supply of white suckers and yellow perch keep the northerns fat and sassy. Oddly for lakes in this area, there are no known walleyes in Little Cascade.

Although perch numbers are decent, they aren't big enough to be worth trying for. The lake is a one-trick pony, and that pony has a long, green body with white spots and teeth.

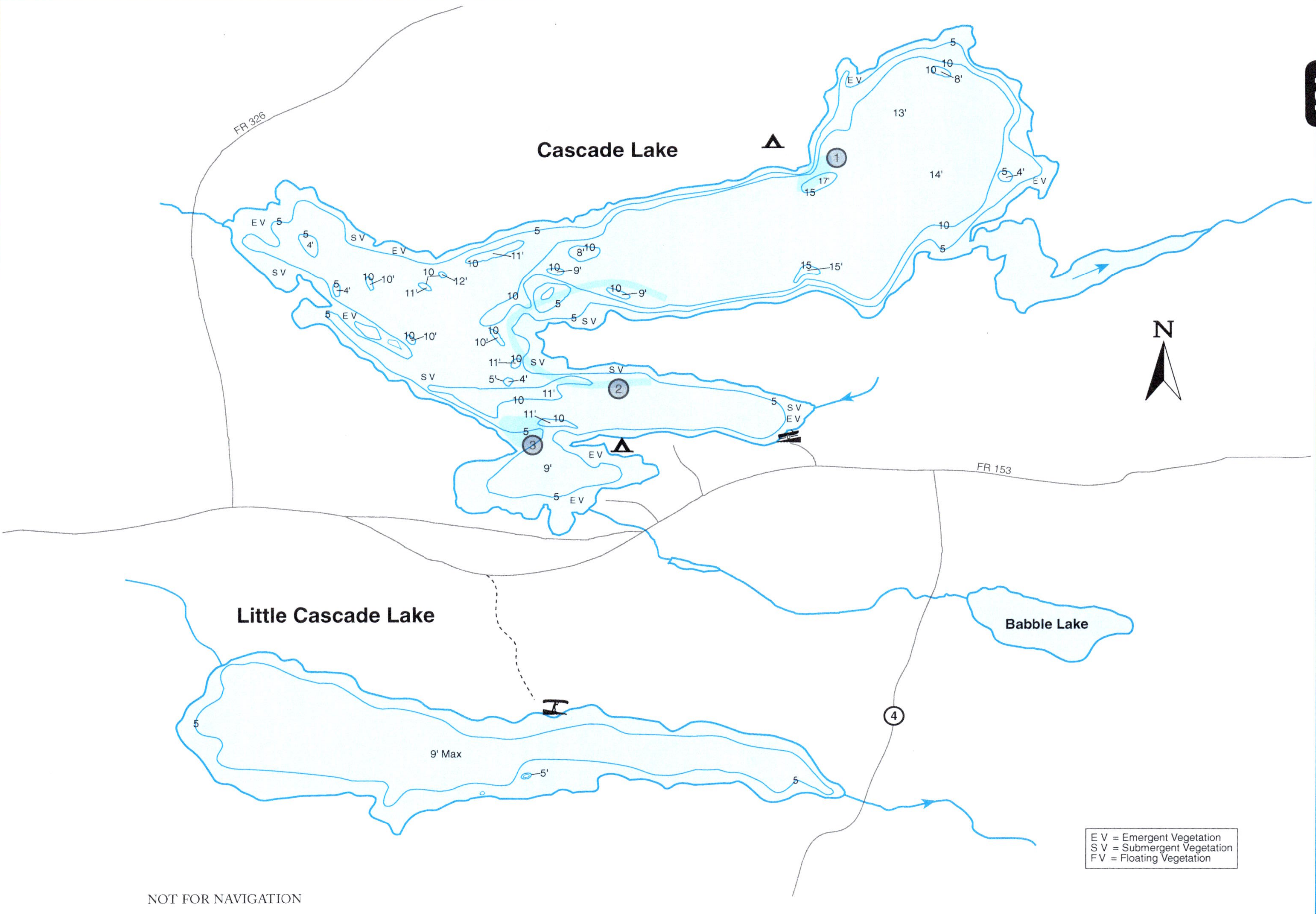
FR 326
Cascade Lake
FR 153
Little Cascade Lake
Babble Lake
9' Max
13'
14'
17'
N
4
E V = Emergent Vegetation
S V = Submergent Vegetation
F V = Floating Vegetation
NOT FOR NAVIGATION

Source: Minnesota Department of Natural Resources, USGS

TAIT LAKE *Cook County*

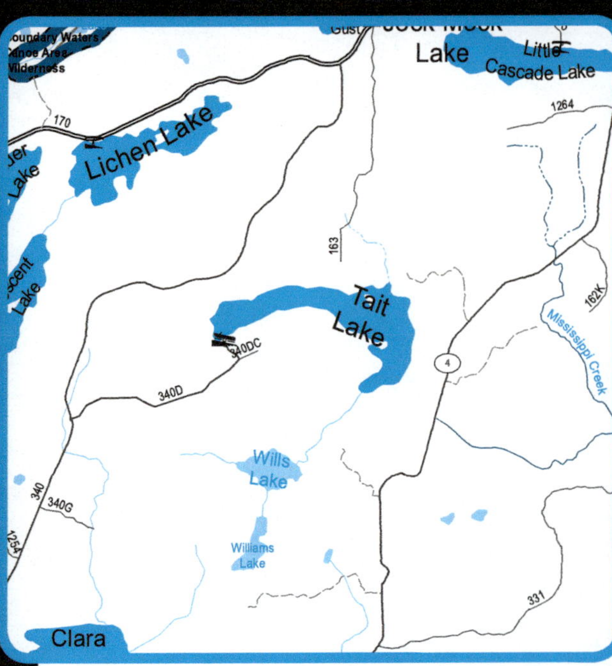

Area map page / coordinates: 18 / D-1

Watershed: Baptism-Brule

Surface water area / shorelength: 355 acres / 8.2 miles

Maximum / mean depth: 15 feet / 9 feet

Water color / clarity: Brown, bog stain / 7.9 ft. secchi (2013)

Shoreland zoning classification: Recreational development

Management class / Ecological type: Walleye-centrarchid/ northern pike-sucker

Accessibility: USFS-owned public access with concrete ramp on southwest shore, off FR 340

90° 42' 34" W / 47° 49' 12" N

Accommodations: Restrooms

FISHING INFORMATION

Tait Lake's moderately bog-stained waters harbor a fishery that's well worth an angler's time.

Although the lake contains a decent population of walleyes - all naturally produced - the population still falls short of the DNR's goal. Nonetheless, anglers will still find decent walleye numbers in Tait, with most of the fish falling solidly into the "good-eater" category.

Angler Jeff Herrick, owner of the Superior Bakery in the Tofte Holiday station, says the fishing is good on Tait Lake; maybe even better than the DNR survey shows. Herrick says walleyes average about 16 inches, and it's not hard to limit out on these tasty fish. Herrick suggests trying for them with a slip-bobber rig using minnows early in the season and switching to leeches around mid-summer.

Because of its dark water, the sun warms Tait relatively quickly. This causes it to turn on early, and since there isn't a ton of structure to be found in the lake and not much depth, locating fish shouldn't be too hard. A good spot to start walleye hunting in the spring is the first point east of the launch site, says Herrick. Work it well, paying most attention to the windward side. Moving farther east, try the points off the north and south shores where the lake bends and widens. Don't neglect the big points near the lake's southern end, either. Both can offer good opportunities, particularly the more northern one, with its relatively fast break to the "deep" hole. The bar off the tip of the island on the lake's north shore can also produce walleyes.

Tait has a low, but increasing northern pike population. Northern pike growth is fairly good, and you'll find some decent-sized pike in Tait, although it's doubtful you'll hook anything over 30 inches.

Because of the lack of structure in Tait, the best way to find pike is to troll for them, using perch-pattern crankbaits. Troll along the 10-foot break and you'll likely find fish. You can also find pike casting to the weedy bay on the west end and around th Tait River inlet and outlet.

The perch get pretty large in this lake; plenty big enough to fish fo The latest assessment, however, found the perch population to be dowr While that's bad news for anglers who like to add some bonus perch t their walleye catch, it may mean that the pike and walleyes - which pre on perch - are hungry and more willing to bite.

It's unusual for Cook County lakes to have much of a panfish fishery outside of yellow perch. However, there are plenty of pumpkinseeds i Tait, although they run very small. Bluegills have always been present i low numbers, but it appears their population may be growing. One fis in the latest survey even broke the 10-inch mark. Although there aren' enough 'gills to warrant fishing for them specifically, you never knov when a big bluegill will latch onto your walleye jig and nightcrawler.

NO RECORD OF STOCKING

NET CATCH DATA

Date: 07/15/2013

	Gill Nets		Trap Nets	
species	# per net	avg. fish weight (lbs.)	# per net	avg. fish weight (lbs
Bluegill	-	-	0.75	0.32
Northern Pike	2.11	1.81	1.33	1.44
Pumpkinseed	0.78	0.06	7.42	0.05
Walleye	4.33	1.06	3.33	1.39
White Sucker	4.44	2.01	0.08	1.65
Yellow Perch	2.11	0.29	0.42	0.10

LENGTH OF SELECTED SPECIES SAMPLED FROM ALL GEAR

Number of fish caught for the following length categories (inches):

species	0-5	6-8	9-11	12-14	15-19	20-24	25-29	>30	Total
Bluegill	6	2	1	-	-	-	-	-	9
Northern Pike	-	-	-	6	18	7	4	-	35
Pumpkinseed	93	-	-	-	-	-	-	-	93
Walleye	1	-	21	18	37	2	-	-	79
White Sucker	-	-	5	7	28	1	-	-	41
Yellow Perch	9	10	5	-	-	-	-	-	24

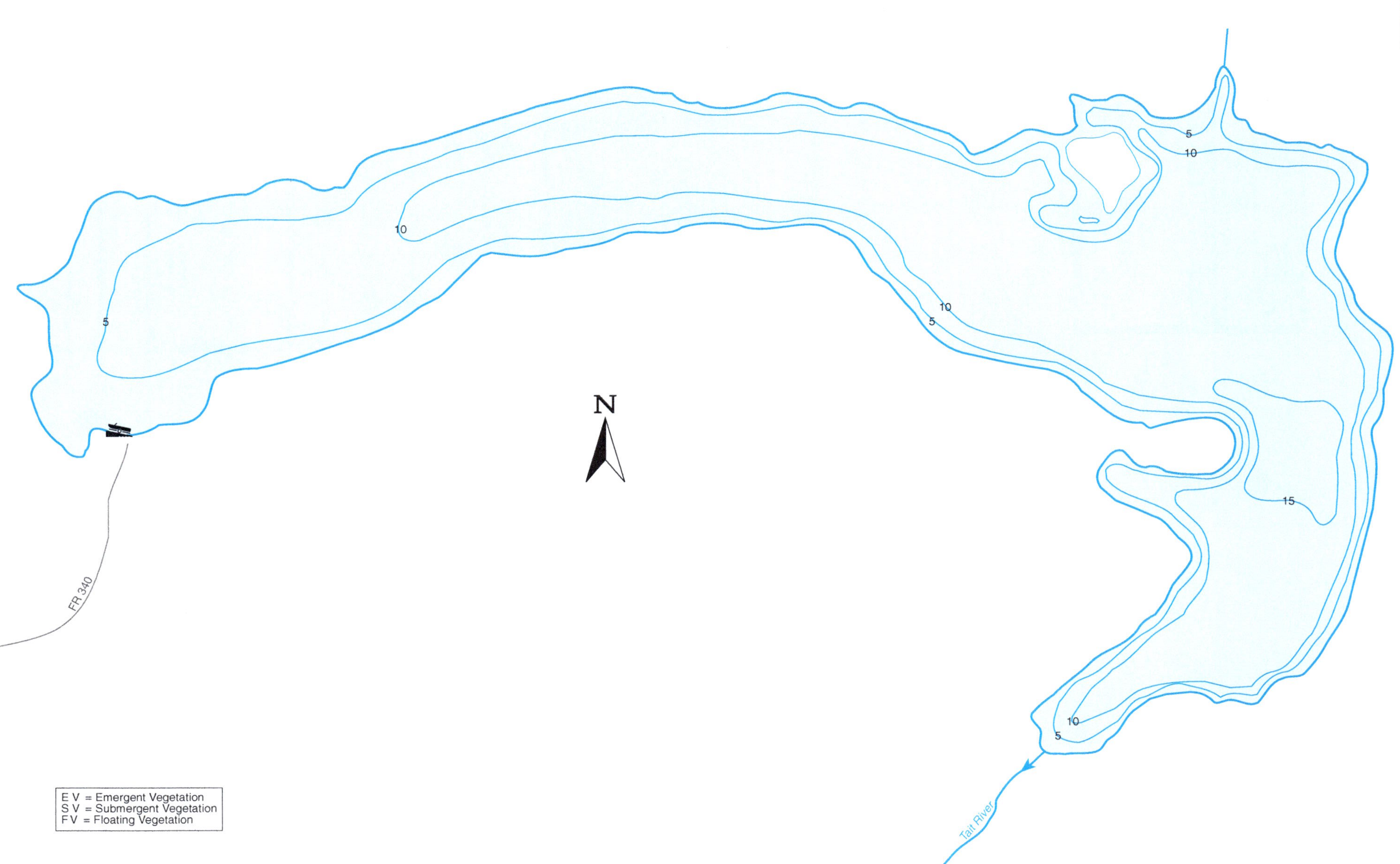

Source: Minnesota Department of Natural Resources, USGS

Binagami Lake, Cook County

Area map page / coordinates: 19 / C, D-5
Surface area / max depth: 117 acres / 21 feet
Accessibility: Carry-down access to east shore or southwest shore from FR 154

FISH STOCKING DATA

year	species	size	# released
15	Bluegill	Adult	592

LENGTH OF SELECTED SPECIES SAMPLED FROM ALL GEAR
Survey Date: 07/14/2014
Number of fish caught for the following length categories (inches):

species	0-5	6-8	9-11	12-14	15-19	20-24	25-29	>30	Total
Rock Bass	19	1	-	-	-	-	-	-	20
Walleye	-	-	13	-	5	2	-	-	20
White Sucker	-	-	5	-	33	13	-	-	51

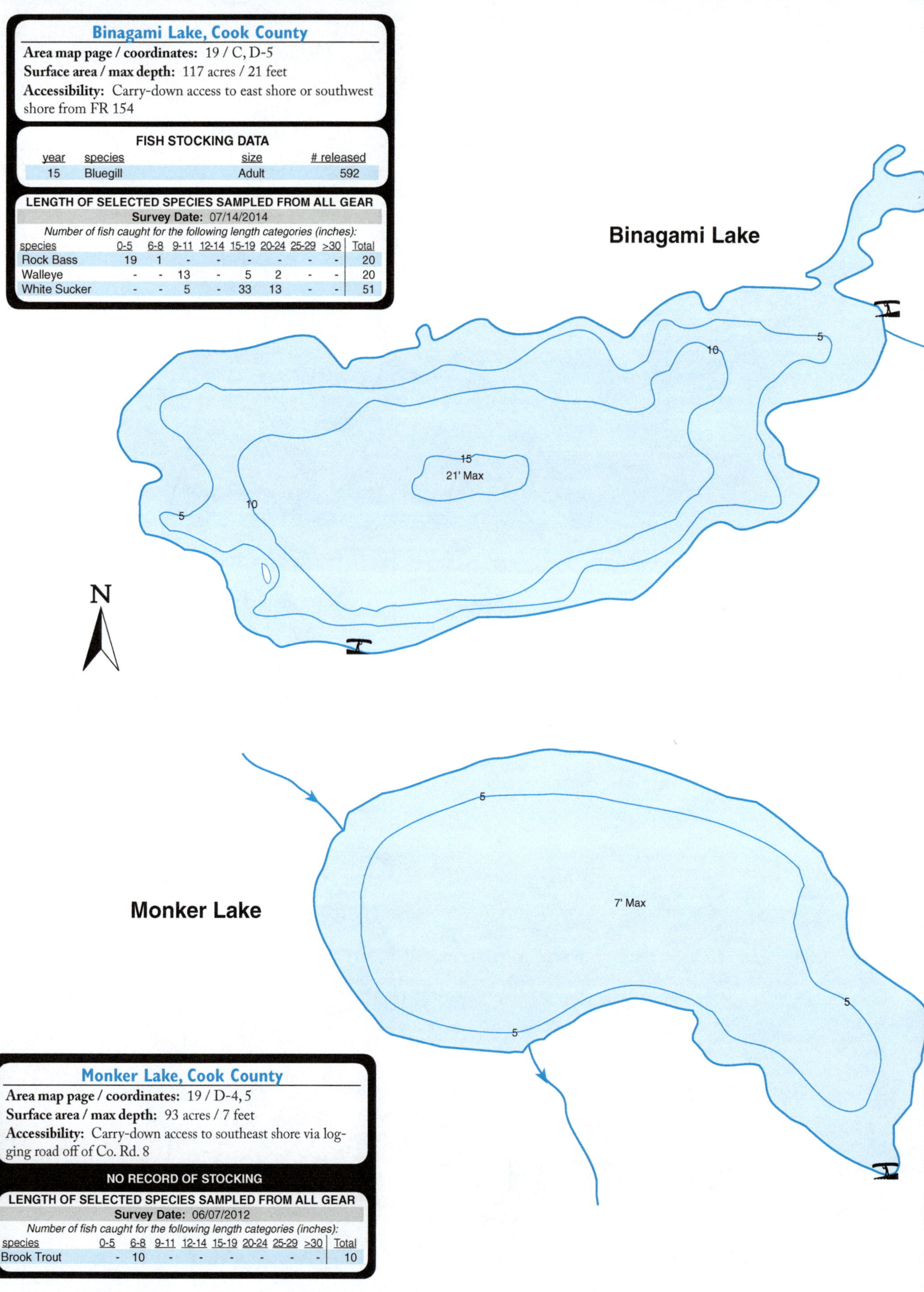

Monker Lake, Cook County

Area map page / coordinates: 19 / D-4, 5
Surface area / max depth: 93 acres / 7 feet
Accessibility: Carry-down access to southeast shore via logging road off of Co. Rd. 8

NO RECORD OF STOCKING

LENGTH OF SELECTED SPECIES SAMPLED FROM ALL GEAR
Survey Date: 06/07/2012
Number of fish caught for the following length categories (inches):

species	0-5	6-8	9-11	12-14	15-19	20-24	25-29	>30	Total
Brook Trout	-	10	-	-	-	-	-	-	10

NOT FOR NAVIGATION

Source: Minnesota Department of Natural Resources, USGS

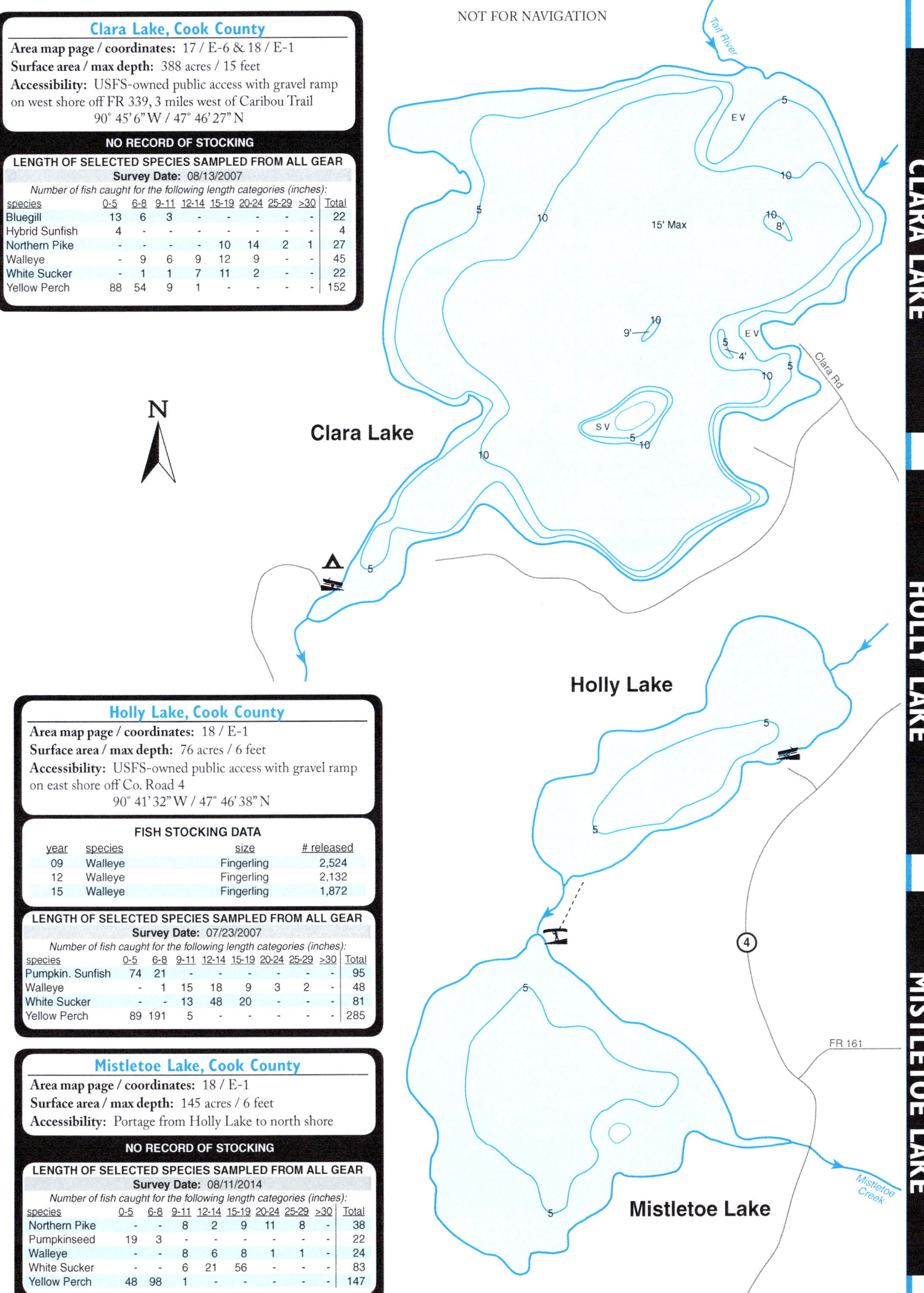

Clara Lake, Cook County

Area map page / coordinates: 17 / E-6 & 18 / E-1
Surface area / max depth: 388 acres / 15 feet
Accessibility: USFS-owned public access with gravel ramp on west shore off FR 339, 3 miles west of Caribou Trail
90° 45' 6" W / 47° 46' 27" N

NO RECORD OF STOCKING

LENGTH OF SELECTED SPECIES SAMPLED FROM ALL GEAR
Survey Date: 08/13/2007
Number of fish caught for the following length categories (inches):

species	0-5	6-8	9-11	12-14	15-19	20-24	25-29	>30	Total
Bluegill	13	6	3	-	-	-	-	-	22
Hybrid Sunfish	4	-	-	-	-	-	-	-	4
Northern Pike	-	-	-	-	10	14	2	1	27
Walleye	-	9	6	9	12	9	-	-	45
White Sucker	-	1	1	7	11	2	-	-	22
Yellow Perch	88	54	9	1	-	-	-	-	152

Holly Lake, Cook County

Area map page / coordinates: 18 / E-1
Surface area / max depth: 76 acres / 6 feet
Accessibility: USFS-owned public access with gravel ramp on east shore off Co. Road 4
90° 41' 32" W / 47° 46' 38" N

FISH STOCKING DATA

year	species	size	# released
09	Walleye	Fingerling	2,524
12	Walleye	Fingerling	2,132
15	Walleye	Fingerling	1,872

LENGTH OF SELECTED SPECIES SAMPLED FROM ALL GEAR
Survey Date: 07/23/2007
Number of fish caught for the following length categories (inches):

species	0-5	6-8	9-11	12-14	15-19	20-24	25-29	>30	Total
Pumpkin. Sunfish	74	21	-	-	-	-	-	-	95
Walleye	-	1	15	18	9	3	2	-	48
White Sucker	-	-	13	48	20	-	-	-	81
Yellow Perch	89	191	5	-	-	-	-	-	285

Mistletoe Lake, Cook County

Area map page / coordinates: 18 / E-1
Surface area / max depth: 145 acres / 6 feet
Accessibility: Portage from Holly Lake to north shore

NO RECORD OF STOCKING

LENGTH OF SELECTED SPECIES SAMPLED FROM ALL GEAR
Survey Date: 08/11/2014
Number of fish caught for the following length categories (inches):

species	0-5	6-8	9-11	12-14	15-19	20-24	25-29	>30	Total
Northern Pike	-	-	8	2	9	11	8	-	38
Pumpkinseed	19	3	-	-	-	-	-	-	22
Walleye	-	-	8	6	8	1	1	-	24
White Sucker	-	-	6	21	56	-	-	-	83
Yellow Perch	48	98	1	-	-	-	-	-	147

Source: Minnesota Department of Natural Resources, USGS

PIKE LAKE
Cook County

DEER YARD LAKE
Cook County

Area map pg / coord: 18 / E-2
Watershed: Baptism-Brule
Surface area: 814 acres
Shorelength: 8.5 miles
Max / mean depth: 45 feet / 23 feet
Water color / clarity: Clear / 18 ft. secchi (2009)
Shoreland zoning class: Rec. dev.
Mgmt class / Ecological type: Centrarchid / northern pike-sucker
Accessibility: 1) USFS-owned access with gravel ramp (poor and shallow) on east shore, off Co. Rd.
90° 33' 42" W / 47° 46' 14" N
Accessibility: 2) State-owned public access with concrete ramp off FR 332
90° 35' 25" W / 47° 45' 39" N
Accommodations: Resort

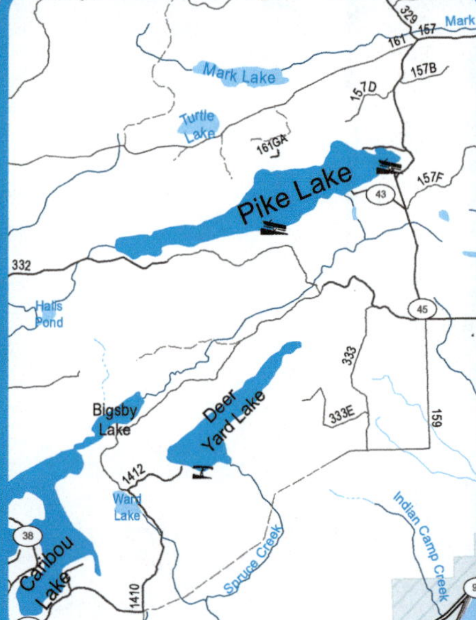

Area map pg / coord: 26 / A-2
Watershed: Baptism-Brule
Surface area: 343 acres
Shorelength: 4.8 miles
Max / mean depth: 20 feet / 14 feet
Water color / clarity: Green tint / 10 ft. secchi (2013)
Shoreland zoning class: Rec. dev.
Mgmt class / Ecological type: Walleye / northern pike - sucker
Accessibility: Carry-down access (125 feet) off FR 1412 to southwest shore
Accommodations: None

Pike Lake

NO RECORD OF STOCKING

NET CATCH DATA

Date: 07/20/2009	Gill Nets		Trap Nets	
species	# per net	avg. fish weight (lbs.)	# per net	avg. fish weight (lbs.)
Lake Whitefish	2.67	3.16	-	-
Northern Pike	1.33	2.17	-	-
Smallmouth Bass	2.33	1.21	1.42	0.74
Walleye	10.4	1.20	0.17	0.18
White Sucker	0.56	2.14	0.08	1.01
Yellow Perch	6.33	0.37	0.17	0.26

LENGTH OF SELECTED SPECIES SAMPLED FROM ALL GEAR

Number of fish caught for the following length categories (inches):

species	0-5	6-8	9-11	12-14	15-19	20-24	25-29	>29	Total
Lake Whitefish	-	-	-	1	14	9	-	-	24
Northern Pike	-	-	-	-	2	9	1	-	12
Smallmouth Bass	4	10	8	10	5	-	-	-	37
Walleye	-	3	16	38	29	4	-	-	90
White Sucker	-	-	-	1	5	-	-	-	6
Yellow Perch	1	24	29	-	-	-	-	-	54

Deer Yard Lake

NO RECORD OF STOCKING

NET CATCH DATA

Date: 07/22/2013	Gill Nets		Trap Nets	
species	# per net	avg. fish weight (lbs.)	# per net	avg. fish weight (lbs.)
Walleye	13.50	0.58	2.92	0.46
White Sucker	14.83	2.14	3.00	2.09

LENGTH OF SELECTED SPECIES SAMPLED FROM ALL GEAR

Number of fish caught for the following length categories (inches):

species	0-5	6-8	9-11	12-14	15-19	20-24	25-29	>29	Total
Walleye	-	19	66	22	8	-	1	-	116
White Sucker	-	-	6	14	93	12	-	-	125

FISHING INFORMATION

These two lakes are both full of walleyes, but that's about where their similarities end.

Pike Lake has a much more diverse fishery. It is also much deeper and clearer, and the lake's walleyes run much larger. The DNR's most recent survey showed the lake to be inhabited by pretty good numbers of 'eyes, with many fish of "eater" size.

Pike also has a very good smallmouth bass population. Not only will you find good numbers of these scrappers, you'll also find large fish in these clear waters.

Of course, Pike Lake also has northern pike. They grow large here, thanks to an abundance of perch and lake whitefish.

The perch fishing is also noteworthy. Pike's perch run big.

Anglers say the 'eyes average around 14 inches, and you can fill out on 16-inchers if you put in some effort. Larger ones don't come often, but there are fish up to 24 inches or so. Due to the clear water, fishing is best in the morning or evening. Places to try for 'eyes include a small trough on the lake's west end **(Spot 1)**. This should be worked with a minnow and slip bobber. The bay about midway up the lake's north shore is also good when the wind is blowing into the shore **(Spot 2)**. There are lots of rocks in this area. One angler says the bay on the lake's east end **(Spot 3)** also is good walleye country when there's been a west wind blowing for a few hours. Troll this bay with a Lindy rig with a minnow, leech or nightcrawler.

Deer Yard Lake offers high walleye numbers, but size is less impressive than in Pike Lake. The fish are slow-growing and most are pretty small. The most recent DNR survey showed walleye numbers were down slightly from their long-term average, but they were still very high.

The folks at Devil Track Resort, 205 Fireweed Lane, Grand Marais, MN 55604, (877) 387-9414, say you'll boat lots of fish on Deer Yard, but you'll have to do some sorting to limit out on anything sizeable. The fishing's pretty convenient. Anchor right off the landing **(Spot 1)** in 6 to 8 feet of water and drown a minnow under a slip bobber. Heading on up near the narrows on the lake's northeast end **(Spot 2)** may also yield some fish. Watch out, because there's a reef in this location **(Spot 3)** that tops out anywhere from 3 feet to 8 inches below the surface. Park your canoe near the reef and have at the walleyes.

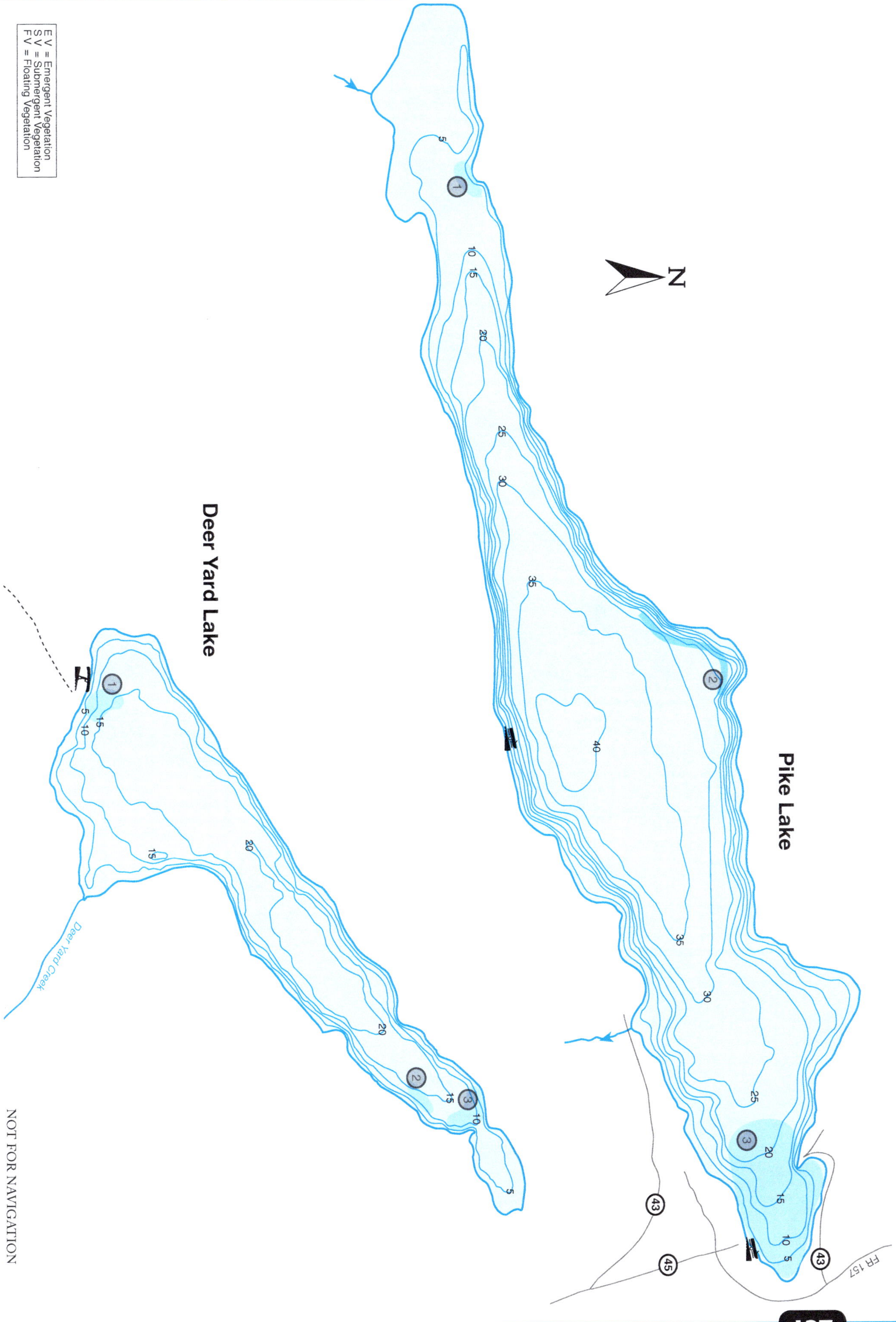

E V = Emergent Vegetation
S V = Submergent Vegetation
F V = Floating Vegetation

Pike Lake

Deer Yard Lake

Deer Yard Creek

N

43
45
43
FR 157

NOT FOR NAVIGATION

Source: Minnesota Department of Natural Resources, USGS

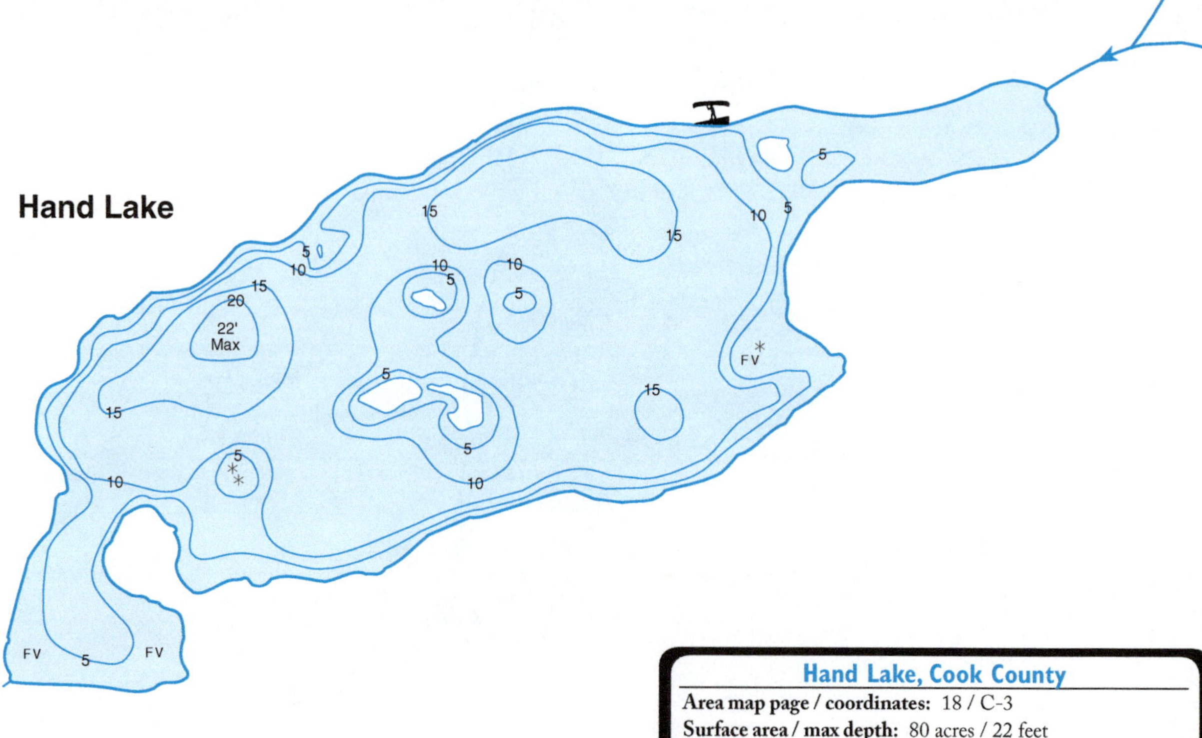

Hand Lake, Cook County

Area map page / coordinates: 18 / C-3
Surface area / max depth: 80 acres / 22 feet
Accessibility: Carry-down access to north shore off FR 323

NO RECORD OF STOCKING

LENGTH OF SELECTED SPECIES SAMPLED FROM ALL GEAR
Survey Date: 06/16/2010
Number of fish caught for the following length categories (inches):

species	0-5	6-8	9-11	12-14	15-19	20-24	25-29	>30	Total
Northern Pike	-	-	-	-	1	4	2	-	7
Walleye	-	-	-	10	5	3	-	-	18
Yellow Perch	-	2	-	-	-	-	-	-	2

McDonald Lake, Cook County

Area map page / coordinates: 18 / C-3
Surface area / max depth: 86 acres / 8 feet
Accessibility: Carry-down access to north shore off FR 153

NO RECORD OF STOCKING

LENGTH OF SELECTED SPECIES SAMPLED FROM ALL GEAR
Survey Date: 06/20/2007
Number of fish caught for the following length categories (inches):

species	0-5	6-8	9-11	12-14	15-19	20-24	25-29	>30	Total
Northern Pike	-	-	-	-	17	19	3	-	39
Smallmouth Bass	-	-	-	3	6	-	-	-	9
Walleye	-	-	-	-	3	-	-	-	3
White Sucker	-	-		1	1	13	-	-	15
Yellow Perch	2	-	2	1	-	-	-	-	5

FR 153

McDonald Lake

NOT FOR NAVIGATION

Source: Minnesota Department of Natural Resources, USGS

Bower Trout Lake, Cook County

Area map page / coordinates: 18 / B-3 & 19 / B-4
Surface area / max depth: 149 acres / 6 feet
Accessibility: Carry-down access to north shore off FR 152

NO RECORD OF STOCKING

LENGTH OF SELECTED SPECIES SAMPLED FROM ALL GEAR
Survey Date: 07/06/1989
Number of fish caught for the following length categories (inches):

species	0-5	6-8	9-11	12-14	15-19	20-24	25-29	>30	Total
Yellow Perch	5	10	2	-	-	-	-	-	17
Walleye	-	-	-	5	5	-	-	-	10
Smallmouth Bass	-	-	-	2	2	-	-	-	4
Northern Pike	-	-	3	5	2	-	-	-	10

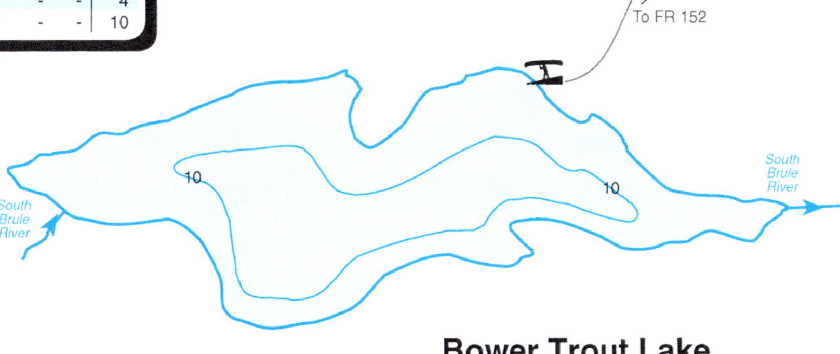

Bower Trout Lake

Ball Club Lake, Cook County

Area map page / coordinates: 18 / B-3
Surface area / max depth: 206 acres / 25 feet
Accessibility: USFS-owned public access with gravel ramp on southwest shore; parking for 6 vehicles
90° 30' 9" W / 47° 54' 47" N

FISH STOCKING DATA

year	species	size	# released
07	Walleye	Fingerling	2,590

LENGTH OF SELECTED SPECIES SAMPLED FROM ALL GEAR
Survey Date: 08/27/2012
Number of fish caught for the following length categories (inches):

species	0-5	6-8	9-11	12-14	15-19	20-24	25-29	>30	Total
Walleye	-	2	18	43	31	3	-	-	97
White Sucker	-	2	5	27	54	2	-	-	90
Yellow Perch	3	37	1	-	-	-	-	-	41

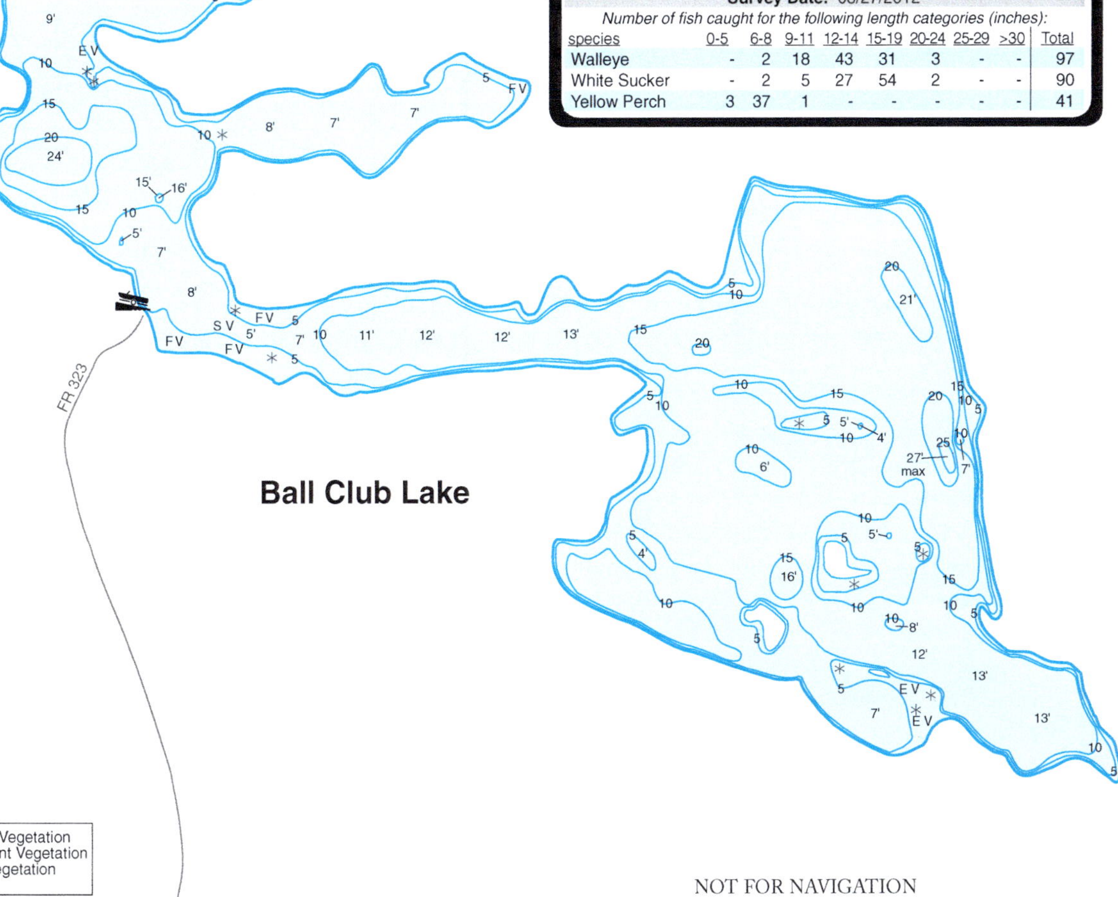

E V = Emergent Vegetation
S V = Submergent Vegetation
F V = Floating Vegetation
* = Rocks

NOT FOR NAVIGATION

Source: Minnesota Department of Natural Resources, USGS

TWO ISLAND LAKE *Cook County*

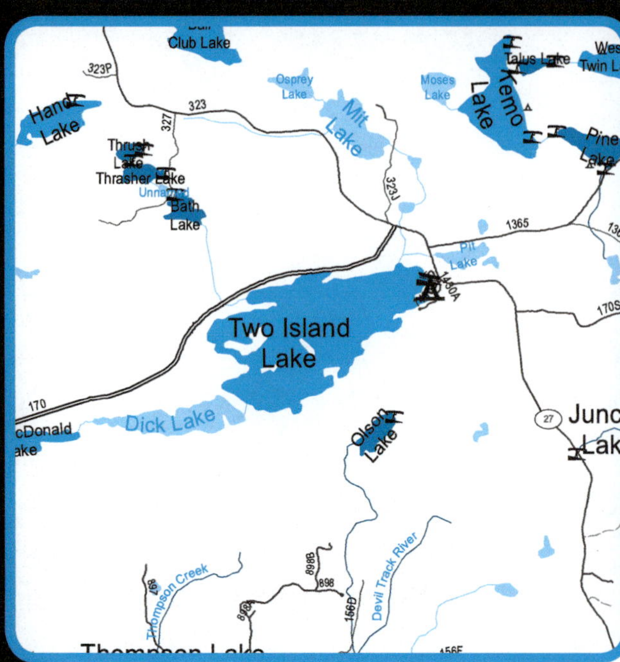

Area map page / coordinates: 18 / C-3 & 19 / C-4

Watershed: Baptism-Brule

Surface water area / shorelength: 754 acres / 5.8 miles

Maximum / mean depth: 27 feet / 10 feet

Water color / clarity: Light brown / 9.0 ft. secchi (2012)

Shoreland zoning classification: Natural environment

Management class / Ecological type: Walleye / northern pike-sucker

Accessibility: USFS-owned public access with concrete ramp in campground on northeast shore; parking for 15 vehicles

90° 26' 44" W / 47° 52' 49" N

Accommodations: Camping, picnicking, restrooms

FISHING INFORMATION

Despite its name, Two Island Lake is full of islands. And full of fish. Facilities on Two Island Lake are pretty decent as well. There's a Forest Service campground on the lake's eastern shore that sports a nice ramp suitable for moderate-sized boats.

The fishing, say locals, is pretty darn good. The folks at Devil Track Resort, 205 Fireweed Lane, Grand Marais, MN 55604, (877) 387-9414, say you'll find good numbers of nice walleyes, some fair northern pike, smallmouth bass and some bluegills.

Smallmouth and walleyes are the big attraction here. Bass fishing is very good, with plenty of fish to be caught and a good average size. The DNR is trying to improve the size of the smallies, or at least protect larger fish. Therefore, there is a special regulation in place that requires you to release any fish larger than 12 inches, except one bass over 20 inches is allowed. The folks at Devil Track Resort say bass aren't hard to catch. Just concentrate on the islands, rocks and reefs, casting a small crankbait or spinner to the shallows. It's not unusual to catch a bunch of these feisty fighters in a day.

The walleye population is in good shape and you'll find plenty of desirable-sized fish here. There is a nearly endless amount of structure to hold these fish.

The lake has a decent pike population - not too many and not too few. These fish have a nice average size and they grow quickly because of all the perch, walleyes and suckers present in Two Island.

The perch are generally on the small side, and although they aren't really of any interest to anglers, they are perfect snacks for that lake's predators.

You'll also find bluegills here, which is sort of an anomaly for area lakes. Some of these fish are of keeper size. There is also a fair number of pumpkinseed sunfish out there, but they are very small.

NO RECORD OF STOCKING

NET CATCH DATA

Date: 09/04/2012	Gill Nets		Trap Nets	
species	# per net	avg. fish weight (lbs.)	# per net	avg. fish weight (lbs
Bluegill	0.67	0.12	7.64	0.10
Northern Pike	2.44	2.25	0.64	1.95
Pumpkinseed	0.22	0.17	0.73	0.09
Smallmouth Bass	5.33	2.09	1.27	0.63
Walleye	5.89	1.24	1.73	1.71
White Sucker	2.56	3.07	1.09	3.63
Yellow Perch	6.00	0.16	0.55	0.17

LENGTH OF SELECTED SPECIES SAMPLED FROM ALL GEAR

Number of fish caught for the following length categories (inches):

species	0-5	6-8	9-11	12-14	15-19	20-24	25-29	>30	Total
Bluegill	72	18	-	-	-	-	-	-	90
Northern Pike	-	-	1	2	3	20	2	-	28
Pumpkinseed	10	-	-	-	-	-	-	-	10
Smallmouth Bass	5	12	2	11	32	-	-	-	62
Walleye	-	10	14	14	24	9	1	-	72
White Sucker	-	-	1	2	15	17	-	-	35
Yellow Perch	9	47	2	-	-	-	-	-	58

For walleyes, try the rocky area between two islands and an underwate point **(Spot 1)** by jigging or slip-bobber fishing with a fathead. A min now and a Beaver Flick, made and sold by the Beaver House Bait Shop 3 E. Wisconsin St., Grand Marais, MN 55604 (218) 387-2092, is also good choice for walleyes. Locals say these are maybe the best all-aroun bait for area walleyes and they can be trolled, cast or simply soaked unde a bobber. The tiny island **(Spot 2)**, which has a good weed edge is a excellent spot when there's a west wind. The rock off the hooked point o the lake's north shore **(Spot 3)** is also worth checking out. Last is a shal low area, which warms fast in the spring, develops good cabbage growt and is tailor-made for northern pike **(Spot 4)**. Locals say you can do we here with spoons, spinners or shallow-running crankbaits.

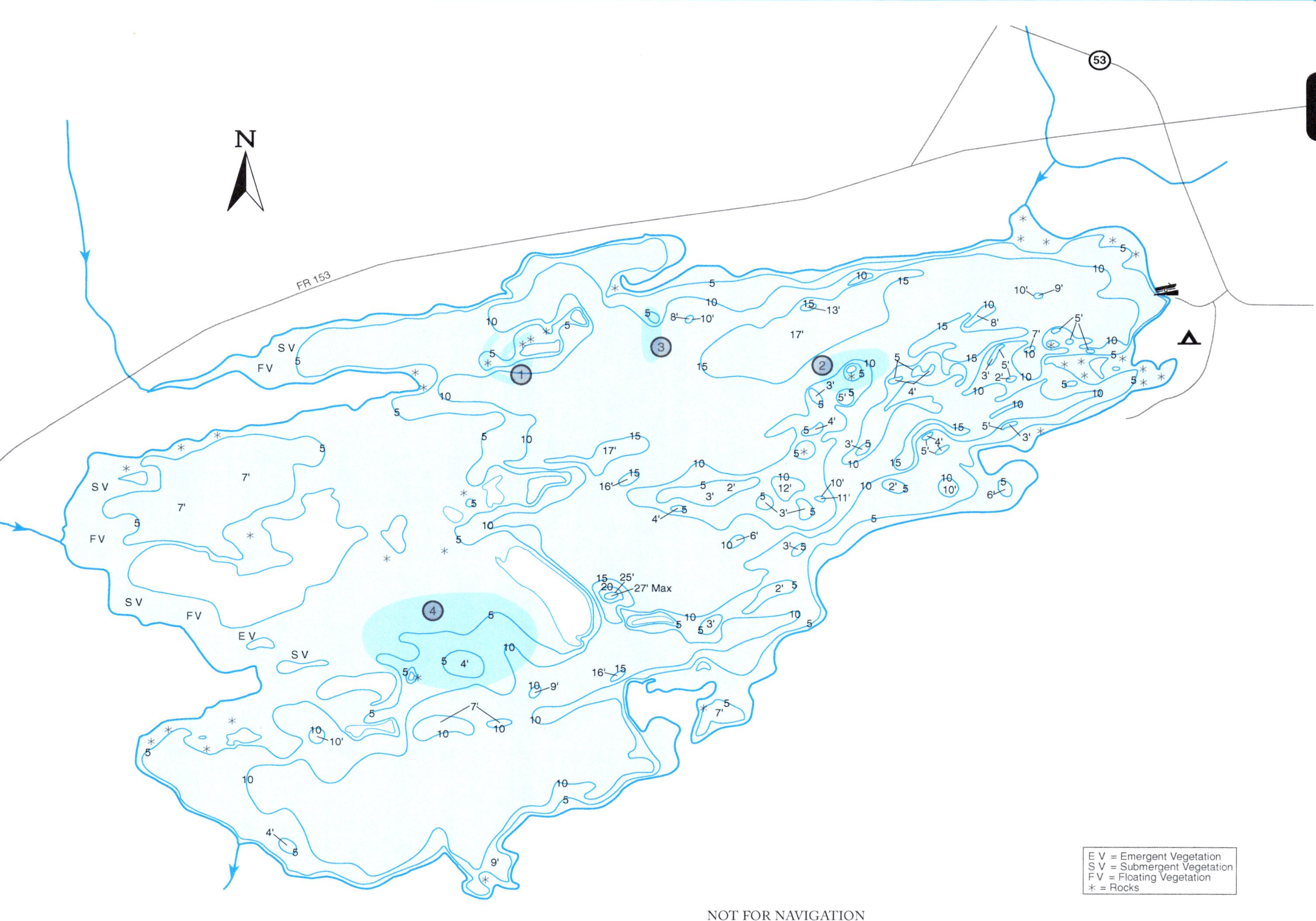

Source: Minnesota Department of Natural Resources, USGS

DEVIL TRACK LAKE *Cook County*

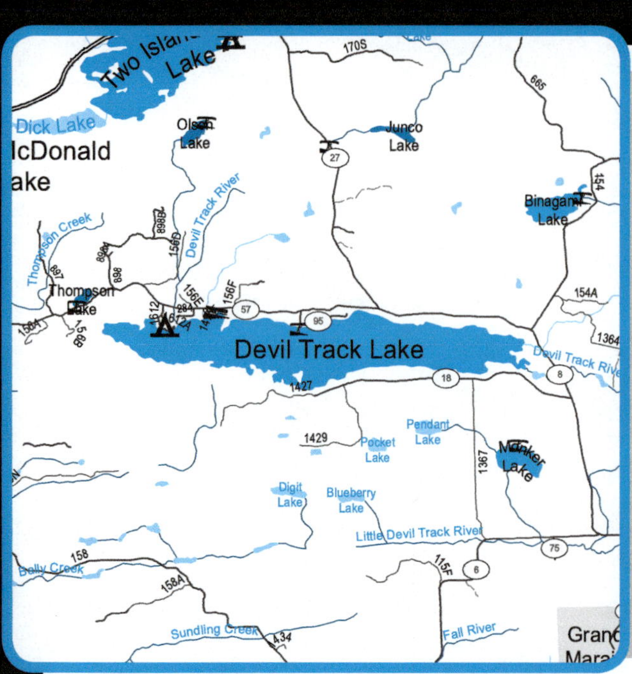

Area map page / coordinates: 18 / D-3 & 19 / D-4,5

Watershed: Baptism-Brule

Surface water area / shorelength: 1,868 acres / 13.0 miles

Maximum / mean depth: 50 feet / 24 feet

Water color / clarity: Brown, bog stain / 8.6 ft. secchi (2012)

Shoreland zoning classification: Recreational development

Management class / Ecological type: Walleye-centrarchid / soft-water walleye

Accessibility: USFS-owned public access with gravel ramp on north shore, off Hwy. 57; parking for 20 vehicles

90° 27' 6" W / 47° 49' 49" N

Accommodations: Seaplane dock with fueling facilities, resorts, boat rental, camping, picnicking, restrooms

FISHING INFORMATION

Devil Track Lake contains nearly 2,000 acres of dark water. It is located in Cook County just a bit north of Grand Marais. Although it's just off the Gunflint Trail, Devil Track is easy to reach and you'll find resorts and even a sea plane base here. Expect to find decent numbers of small walleyes, some northern pike and smallmouth bass.

The folks at Devil Track Resort, 205 Fireweed Lane, Grand Marais, MN 55604, (877) 387-9414, say this is a "consistent producer during open water. You can always find fish." The dark water allows the lake to warm fairly quickly, making it a good place to find hungry walleyes on opener.

The latest DNR survey found, as usual, a large amount of walleyes, but most of them were on the small side. This seems to be the pattern for Devil Track. Not surprisingly, the fish grow slowly here.

Smallmouth bass fishing can be very good on Devil Track, with high numbers of fish and a good overall size structure. You can have a field day casting for smallies here.

Pike numbers have been climbing and as the number of fish has risen, the average size has declined, despite the availability of yellow perch, white suckers and lake whitefish in the lake. No doubt some larger pike avoided survey nets as they cruise the depths in search of whitefish.

Not to be ignored are Devil Track's perch. Although it's a safe bet that no one comes to the lake specifically for perch, they can supplement your catch, as many of them run 8 inches or larger. They are sure to latch onto your walleye jig on occasion.

Walleyes can be caught off Sand Point on the north shore **(Spot 1)**. Work this with a minnow and slip bobber or a jig and minnow. Drifting or trolling a minnow on a Lindy rig will also do the trick. On the lake's eastern end is a point with a steady drop and some unmarked humps **(Spot 2)** that produce walleyes. The finger and a gradual drop on the lake's

FISH STOCKING DATA

year	species	size	# released
07	Brook Trout	Fingerling	1,500
09	Brook Trout	Fingerling	290
11	Walleye	Fingerling	21,580
13	Walleye	Fingerling	29,522

NET CATCH DATA

Date: 08/10/2009

	Gill Nets		Trap Nets	
species	# per net	avg. fish weight (lbs.)	# per net	avg. fish weight (lbs
Lake Whitefish	0.53	2.20	-	-
Northern Pike	1.07	1.68	1.13	1.08
Smallmouth Bass	3.07	1.63	1.00	0.32
Walleye	4.67	0.49	1.13	0.64
White Sucker	2.20	2.16	0.40	3.75
Yellow Perch	2.33	0.24	0.20	0.10

LENGTH OF SELECTED SPECIES SAMPLED FROM ALL GEAR

Number of fish caught for the following length categories (inches):

species	0-5	6-8	9-11	12-14	15-19	20-24	25-29	>30	Total
Green Sunfish	1	-	-	-	-	-	-	-	1
Lake Whitefish	-	-	2	-	2	4	-	-	8
Northern Pike	-	-	-	7	18	7	1	-	33
Smallmouth Bass	-	14	4	35	8	-	-	-	61
Walleye	-	32	17	31	4	-	1	-	85
White Sucker	-	1	5	5	20	8	-	-	39
Yellow Perch	9	19	8	-	-	-	-	-	36

north shore **(Spot 3)**, near the access/swimming beach, is good at dus if there's been a wind across it all day. The rocky area with small island near the lake's south shore **(Spot 4)** is smallmouth country. A variet of lures will catch bass, from jigs with live bait to spinners and sma crankbaits. For a real thrill, try working a topwater near any rock structur just before dark. Smallmouth bass action is good during the summer a the Junco Creek inlet **(Spot 5)**. The folks at the lodge say this is also consistent producer of walleyes, northern pike and whitefish. Anothe spot that's worth a look is the series of islands, humps, inside turns an fingers off the south shore about mid-lake **(Spot 6)**. Finally, investigat the humps, turns and fingers toward the lake's eastern end.

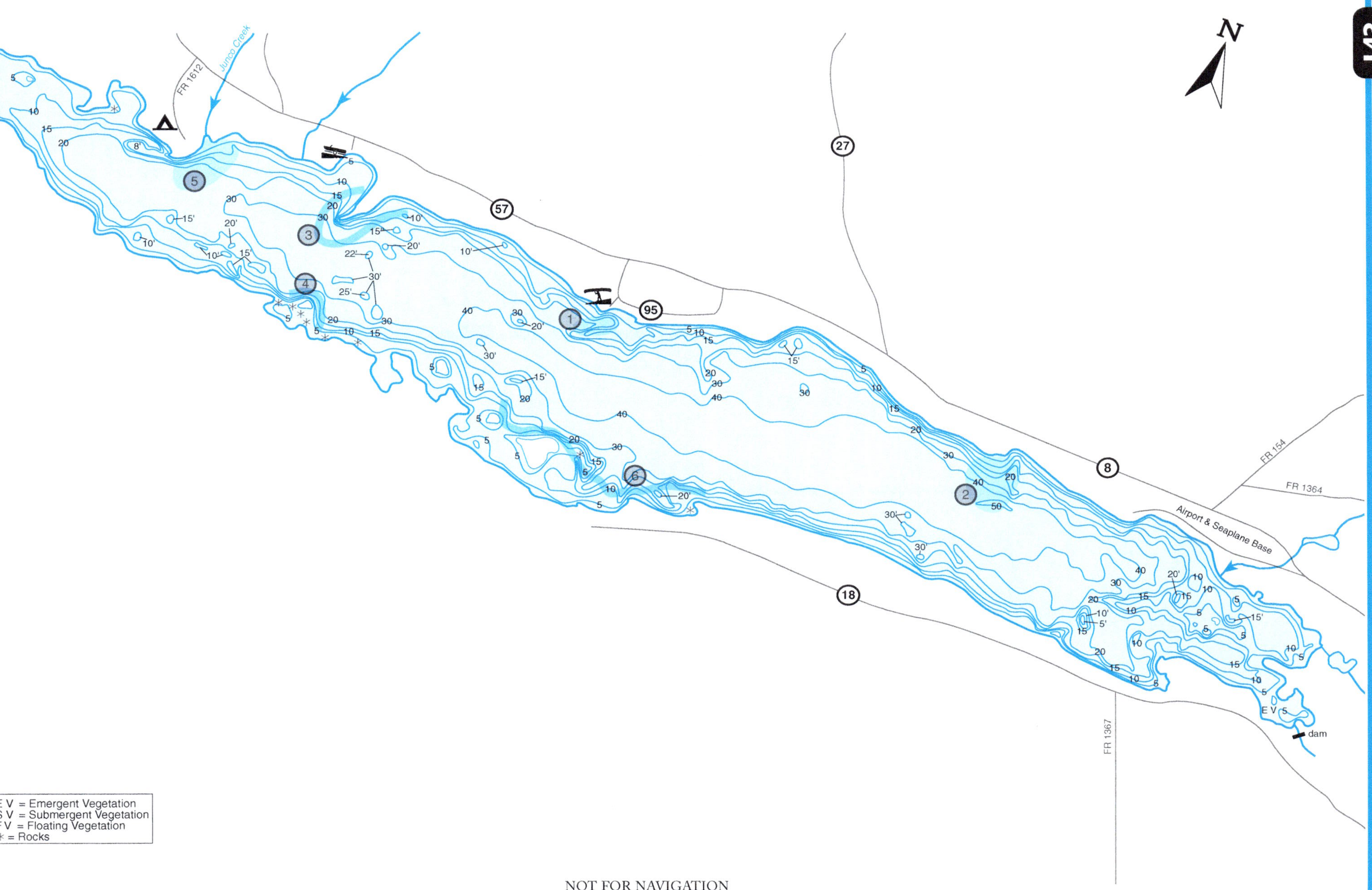

NOT FOR NAVIGATION

Source: Minnesota Department of Natural Resources, USGS

Thrush Lake, Cook County

Area map page / coordinates: 18 / C-3
Surface area / max depth: 15 acres / 48 feet
Accessibility: Carry-down access to northwest shore off FR 323

FISH STOCKING DATA

year	species	size	# released
10	Brook Trout	Fingerling	1,000
11	Brook Trout	Fingerling	1,000
12	Brook Trout	Fingerling	1,000
13	Brook Trout	Fingerling	1,000
14	Brook Trout	Fingerling	1,108
15	Brook Trout	Fingerling	1,000

LENGTH OF SELECTED SPECIES SAMPLED FROM ALL GEAR
Survey Date: 08/28/2006
Number of fish caught for the following length categories (inches):

species	0-5	6-8	9-11	12-14	15-19	20-24	25-29	>30	Total
Brook Trout	-	-	-	1	2	-	-	-	3

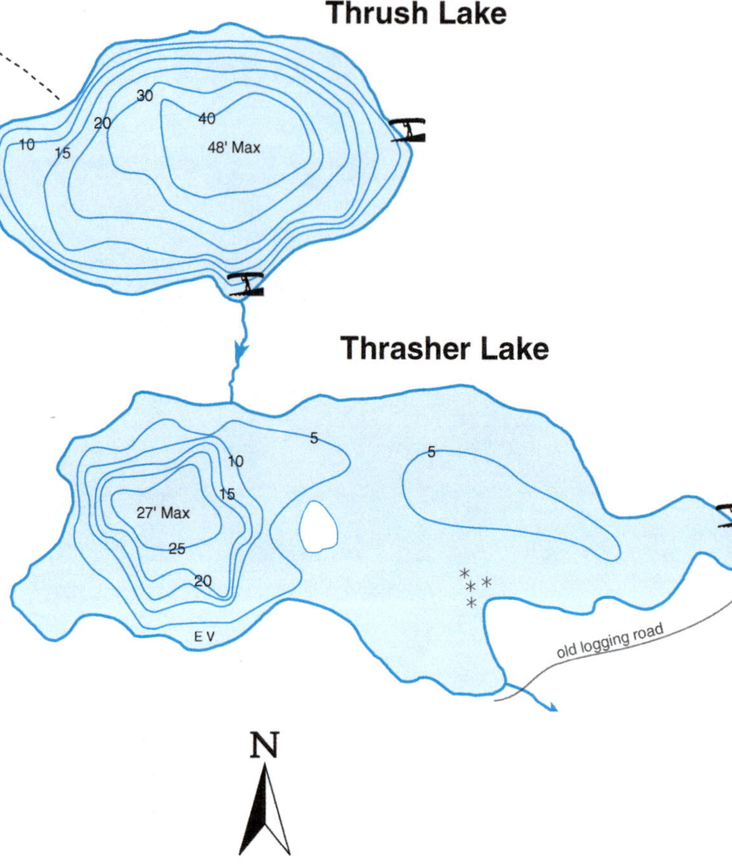

Thrasher Lake, Cook County

Area map page / coordinates: 18 / C-3
Surface area / max depth: 24 acres / 27 feet
Accessibility: Carry-down access to east shore off FR 323

FISH STOCKING DATA

year	species	size	# released
07	Splake	Fingerling	2,500
08	Splake	Fingerling	2,500
09	Splake	Fingerling	2,500
10	Splake	Fingerling	2,500
11	Splake	Fingerling	2,500
12	Splake	Fingerling	2,500
13	Splake	Fingerling	2,500
14	Splake	Fingerling	2,500
15	Splake	Fingerling	2,765

LENGTH OF SELECTED SPECIES SAMPLED FROM ALL GEAR
Survey Date: 06/13/2011
Number of fish caught for the following length categories (inches):

species	0-5	6-8	9-11	12-14	15-19	20-24	25-29	>30	Total
Splake	-	17	6	26	3	-	-	-	52

Bath Lake

5
10
15
20
23' Max
5
20
15
10
5
Less than 5'
Less than 5'

E V = Emergent Vegetation
S V = Submergent Vegetation
F V = Floating Vegetation
✳ = Rocks

Bath Lake, Cook County

Area map page / coordinates: 18 / C-3
Surface area / max depth: 28 acres / 23 feet
Accessibility: Carry-down access to northwest shore off FR 323

FISH STOCKING DATA

year	species	size	# released
10	Brook Trout	Fingerling	4,280
11	Brook Trout	Fingerling	3,645
12	Brook Trout	Fingerling	3,000
13	Brook Trout	Fingerling	3,000
14	Brook Trout	Fingerling	3,891
15	Brook Trout	Fingerling	3,000

LENGTH OF SELECTED SPECIES SAMPLED FROM ALL GEAR
Survey Date: 10/01/2013
Number of fish caught for the following length categories (inches):

species	0-5	6-8	9-11	12-14	15-19	20-24	25-29	>30	Total
Brook Trout	-	4	17	46	1	-	-	-	68
Splake	-	-	-	-	4	-	-	-	4

NOT FOR NAVIGATION

Source: Minnesota Department of Natural Resources, USGS

NOT FOR NAVIGATION

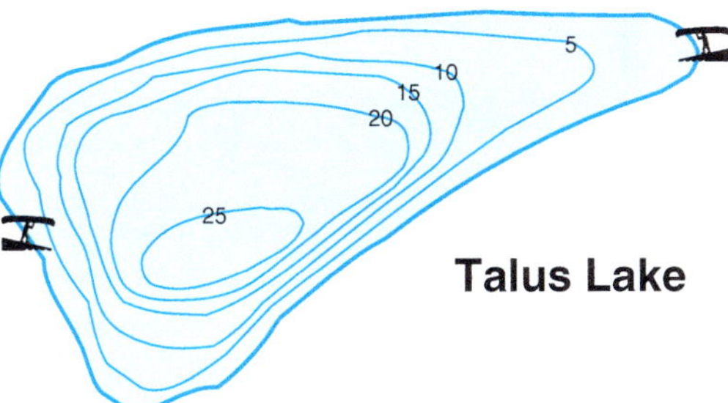

Talus Lake, Cook County

Area map page / coordinates: 19 / B-4
Surface area / max depth: 17 acres / 25 feet
Accessibility: Portage from West Twin Lake to east shore; Portage from Kemo Lake to west shore

FISH STOCKING DATA

year	species	size	# released
10	Rainbow Trout	Fingerling	1,452
11	Rainbow Trout	Fingerling	1,500
12	Rainbow Trout	Fingerling	1,500
13	Rainbow Trout	Fingerling	1,513
14	Rainbow Trout	Fingerling	1,520
15	Rainbow Trout	Fingerling	1,500

LENGTH OF SELECTED SPECIES SAMPLED FROM ALL GEAR

Survey Date: 06/04/2012

Number of fish caught for the following length categories (inches):

species	0-5	6-8	9-11	12-14	15-19	20-24	25-29	>30	Total
Rainbow Trout	-	3	-	7	3	-	-	-	13
White Sucker	-	-	2	18	32	-	-	-	52

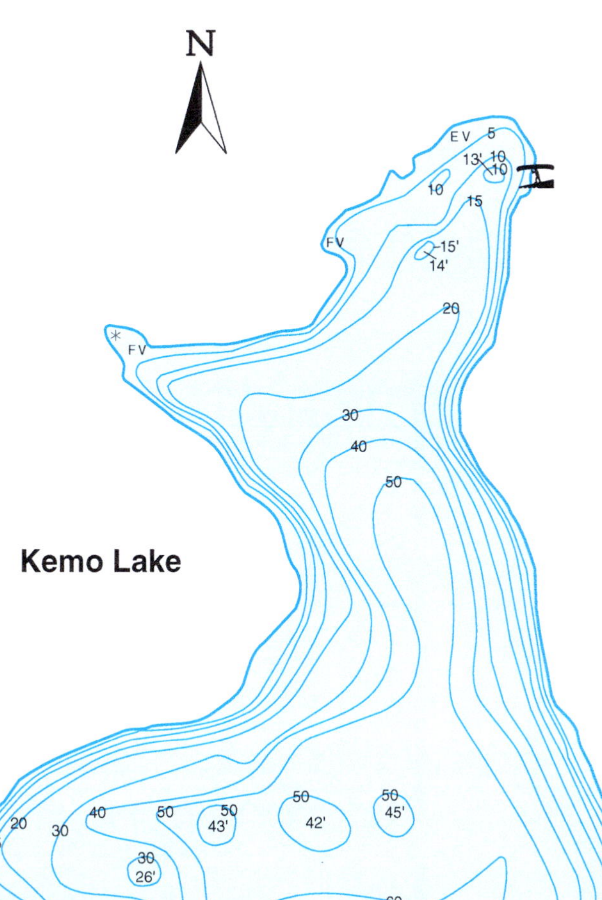

Kemo Lake, Cook County

Area map page / coordinates: 19 / B,C-4
Surface area / max depth: 189 acres / 68 feet
Accessibility: Carry-down access via Kemo Cutoff Road off FR 1365; or portage from Pine Lake or Talus Lake

FISH STOCKING DATA

year	species	size	# released
05	Lake Trout	Fingerling	7,190
07	Lake Trout	Fingerling	7,208
09	Lake Trout	Fingerling	7,176
13	Lake Trout	Fingerling	7,120

LENGTH OF SELECTED SPECIES SAMPLED FROM ALL GEAR

Survey Date: 07/23/2012

Number of fish caught for the following length categories (inches):

species	0-5	6-8	9-11	12-14	15-19	20-24	25-29	>30	Total
Lake Trout	-	5	11	9	5	3	-	-	33
Splake	-	1	1	-	-	-	-	-	2
White Sucker	-	11	18	3	-	-	-	-	32

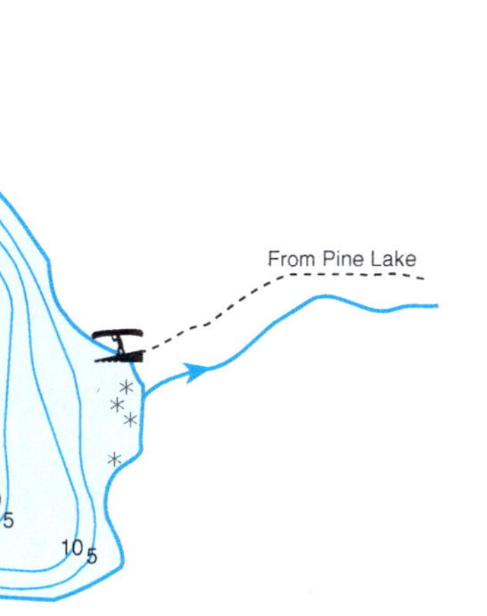

E V = Emergent Vegetation
S V = Submergent Vegetation
F V = Floating Vegetation
* = Rocks

Source: Minnesota Department of Natural Resources, USGS

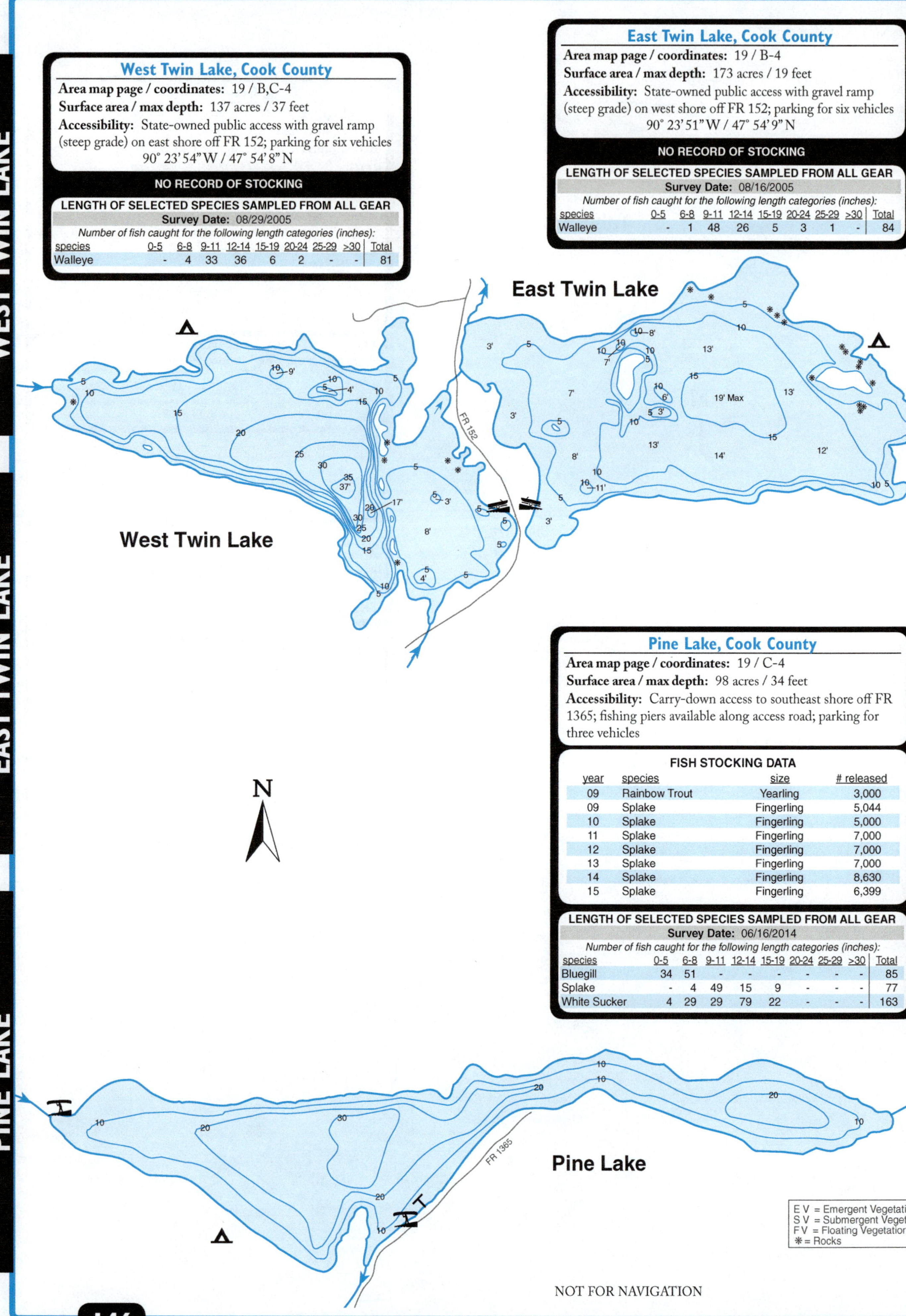

West Twin Lake, Cook County

Area map page / coordinates: 19 / B,C-4
Surface area / max depth: 137 acres / 37 feet
Accessibility: State-owned public access with gravel ramp (steep grade) on east shore off FR 152; parking for six vehicles
90° 23' 54" W / 47° 54' 8" N

NO RECORD OF STOCKING

LENGTH OF SELECTED SPECIES SAMPLED FROM ALL GEAR
Survey Date: 08/29/2005
Number of fish caught for the following length categories (inches):

species	0-5	6-8	9-11	12-14	15-19	20-24	25-29	>30	Total
Walleye	-	4	33	36	6	2	-	-	81

East Twin Lake, Cook County

Area map page / coordinates: 19 / B-4
Surface area / max depth: 173 acres / 19 feet
Accessibility: State-owned public access with gravel ramp (steep grade) on west shore off FR 152; parking for six vehicles
90° 23' 51" W / 47° 54' 9" N

NO RECORD OF STOCKING

LENGTH OF SELECTED SPECIES SAMPLED FROM ALL GEAR
Survey Date: 08/16/2005
Number of fish caught for the following length categories (inches):

species	0-5	6-8	9-11	12-14	15-19	20-24	25-29	>30	Total
Walleye	-	1	48	26	5	3	1	-	84

Pine Lake, Cook County

Area map page / coordinates: 19 / C-4
Surface area / max depth: 98 acres / 34 feet
Accessibility: Carry-down access to southeast shore off FR 1365; fishing piers available along access road; parking for three vehicles

FISH STOCKING DATA

year	species	size	# released
09	Rainbow Trout	Yearling	3,000
09	Splake	Fingerling	5,044
10	Splake	Fingerling	5,000
11	Splake	Fingerling	7,000
12	Splake	Fingerling	7,000
13	Splake	Fingerling	7,000
14	Splake	Fingerling	8,630
15	Splake	Fingerling	6,399

LENGTH OF SELECTED SPECIES SAMPLED FROM ALL GEAR
Survey Date: 06/16/2014
Number of fish caught for the following length categories (inches):

species	0-5	6-8	9-11	12-14	15-19	20-24	25-29	>30	Total
Bluegill	34	51	-	-	-	-	-	-	85
Splake	-	4	49	15	9	-	-	-	77
White Sucker	4	29	29	79	22	-	-	-	163

Source: Minnesota Department of Natural Resources, USGS

Olson Lake

Olson Lake, Cook County

Area map page / coordinates: 19 / C-4
Surface area / max depth: 34 acres / 18 feet
Accessibility: Portage access to northeast shore from campground site on Two Island Lake

FISH STOCKING DATA

year	species	size	# released
09	Rainbow Trout	Fingerling	1,500
10	Rainbow Trout	Fingerling	1,500
11	Rainbow Trout	Fingerling	1,493
12	Rainbow Trout	Fingerling	1,500
14	Rainbow Trout	Fingerling	1,500
15	Rainbow Trout	Fingerling	1,500

LENGTH OF SELECTED SPECIES SAMPLED FROM ALL GEAR
Not Available

27

5' Max

Junco Lake

Junco Lake, Cook County

Area map page / coordinates: 19 / C-4
Surface area / max depth: 41 acres / 5 feet
Accessibility: Carry-down access to west shore, north side of Junco Creek, off Hwy. 27

NO RECORD OF STOCKING

LENGTH OF SELECTED SPECIES SAMPLED FROM ALL GEAR
Survey Date: 06/04/2012
Number of fish caught for the following length categories (inches):

species	0-5	6-8	9-11	12-14	15-19	20-24	25-29	>30	Total
Brook Trout	-	9	9	-	-	-	-	-	18

Thompson Lake, Cook County

Area map page / coordinates: 18 / D-3
Surface area / max depth: 18 acres / 12 feet
Accessibility: Carry-down access to southwest shore off Hwy. 57; parking for three vehicles

FISH STOCKING DATA

year	species	size	# released
10	Rainbow Trout	Yearling	1,050
11	Brown Trout	Fingerling	1,000
11	Rainbow Trout	Yearling	1,050
12	Rainbow Trout	Yearling	1,050
13	Brown Trout	Fingerling	1,000
13	Rainbow Trout	Yearling	1,050
14	Rainbow Trout	Yearling	1,050
15	Brown Trout	Fingerling	1,000
15	Rainbow Trout	Yearling	1,048

LENGTH OF SELECTED SPECIES SAMPLED FROM ALL GEAR
Survey Date: 10/01/2012
Number of fish caught for the following length categories (inches):

species	0-5	6-8	9-11	12-14	15-19	20-24	25-29	>30	Total
Brown Trout	-	-	-	-	5	1	-	-	6
Rainbow Trout	-	-	9	24	-	-	-	-	33

N

Thompson Lake

NOT FOR NAVIGATION

Source: Minnesota Department of Natural Resources, USGS

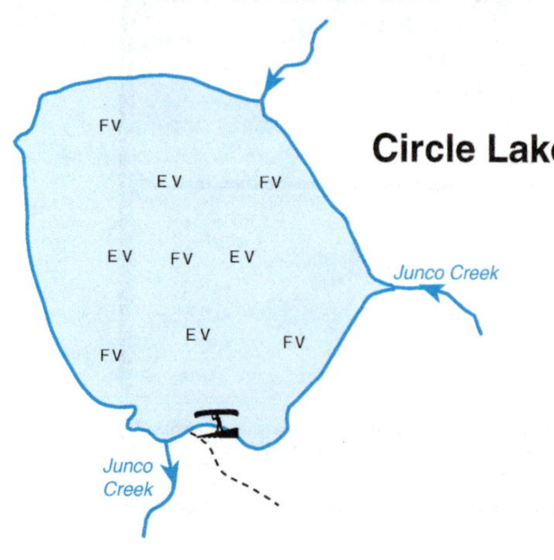

Circle Lake, Cook County

Area map page / coordinates: 19 / B-5
Surface area / max depth: 31 acres / 3 feet
Accessibility: Carry-down access to south shore off FR 1422

NO RECORD OF STOCKING

LENGTH OF SELECTED SPECIES SAMPLED FROM ALL GEAR
Survey Date: 07/18/1972
Number of fish caught for the following length categories (inches):

species	0-5	6-8	9-11	12-14	15-19	20-24	25-29	>30	Total
Brook Trout	-	-	1	-	-	-	-	-	1

Muckwa Lake, Cook County

Area map page / coordinates: 19 / B-5
Surface area / max depth: 41 acres / 25 feet
Accessibility: Portage access from Musquash Lake to southwest shore

FISH STOCKING DATA

year	species	size	# released
08	Rainbow Trout	Fingerling	3,075
09	Rainbow Trout	Fingerling	3,200
10	Rainbow Trout	Fingerling	2,905
11	Rainbow Trout	Fingerling	4,568
13	Rainbow Trout	Fingerling	4,000
15	Rainbow Trout	Fingerling	4,000

LENGTH OF SELECTED SPECIES SAMPLED FROM ALL GEAR
Survey Date: 07/28/2005
Number of fish caught for the following length categories (inches):

species	0-5	6-8	9-11	12-14	15-19	20-24	25-29	>30	Total
Rainbow Trout	-	-	2	2	4	4	-	-	12

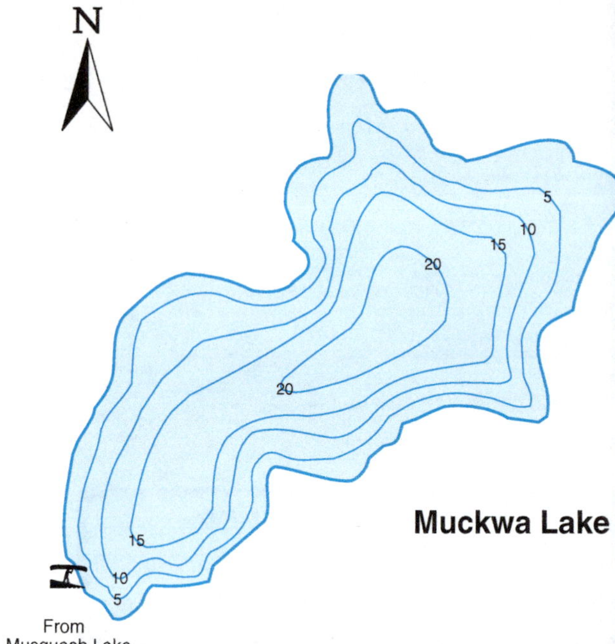

Musquash Lake

From
Muckwa Lake

FR 1422

Musquash Lake, Cook County

Area map page / coordinates: 19 / B-5
Surface area / max depth: 131 acres / 26 feet
Accessibility: Carry-down access to south shore off FR 1422

FISH STOCKING DATA

year	species	size	# released
10	Splake	Fingerling	9,000
11	Splake	Fingerling	6,000
12	Splake	Fingerling	4,724
13	Splake	Fingerling	6,000
14	Splake	Fingerling	6,000
15	Splake	Fingerling	6,000

LENGTH OF SELECTED SPECIES SAMPLED FROM ALL GEAR
Survey Date: 07/28/2008
Number of fish caught for the following length categories (inches):

species	0-5	6-8	9-11	12-14	15-19	20-24	25-29	>30	Total
Splake	-	16	10	20	12	-	-	-	58
White Sucker	-	87	85	39	44	-	-	-	255

NOT FOR NAVIGATION

Source: Minnesota Department of Natural Resources, USGS

Northern Light Lake, Cook County

Area map page / coordinates: 19 / B, C-5,6
Surface area / max depth: 453 acres / 7 feet
Accessibility: State-owned public access with gravel ramp upriver on the Brule River; parking for six vehicles
90° 16' 0" W / 47° 54' 37" N

NO RECORD OF STOCKING

LENGTH OF SELECTED SPECIES SAMPLED FROM ALL GEAR
Survey Date: 07/09/2007
Number of fish caught for the following length categories (inches):

species	0-5	6-8	9-11	12-14	15-19	20-24	25-29	>30	Total
Northern Pike	-	-	4	5	8	7	3	1	28
Pumpkin. Sunfish	7	11	-	-	-	-	-	-	18
Smallmouth Bass	-	-	-	2	2	-	-	-	4
Walleye	-	1	1	2	7	2	1	-	14
Yellow Perch	17	45	20	-	-	-	-	-	82

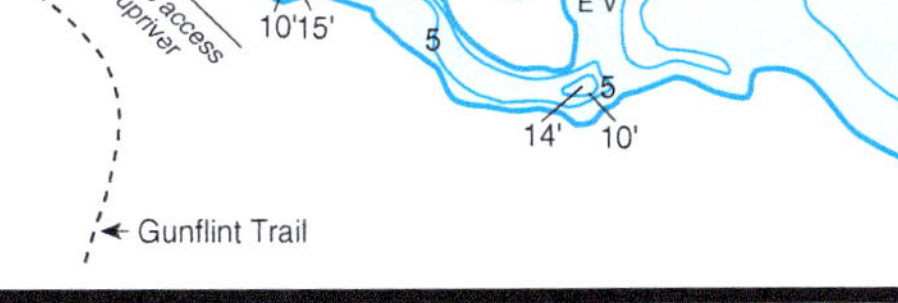

Pine Mountain Lake, Cook County

Area map page / coordinates: 19 / B, C-5
Surface area / max depth: 103 acres / 30 feet
Access: Carry-down access to northeast shore off FR 1310

FISH STOCKING DATA

year	species	size	# released
10	Brown Trout	Yearling	1,600
10	Splake	Fingerling	7,900
11	Splake	Fingerling	6,410
12	Splake	Fingerling	6,000
13	Splake	Fingerling	6,000
14	Splake	Fingerling	6,000
15	Splake	Fingerling	6,083

LENGTH OF SELECTED SPECIES SAMPLED FROM ALL GEAR
Survey Date: 10/02/2002
Number of fish caught for the following length categories (inches):

species	0-5	6-8	9-11	12-14	15-19	20-24	25-29	>30	Total
Brook Trout	-	7	30	15	7	-	-	-	59
Splake	1	2	-	-	-	-	-	-	3

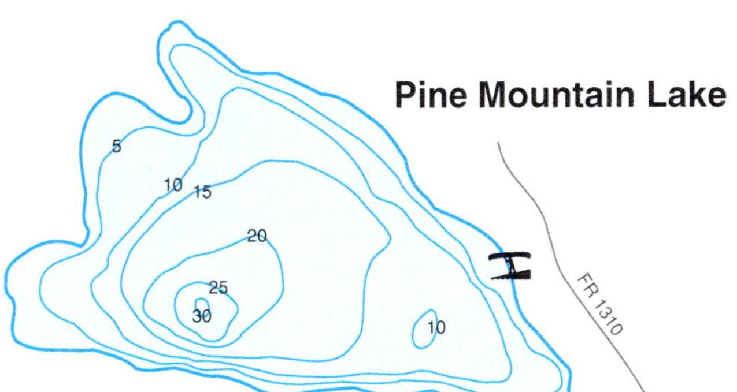

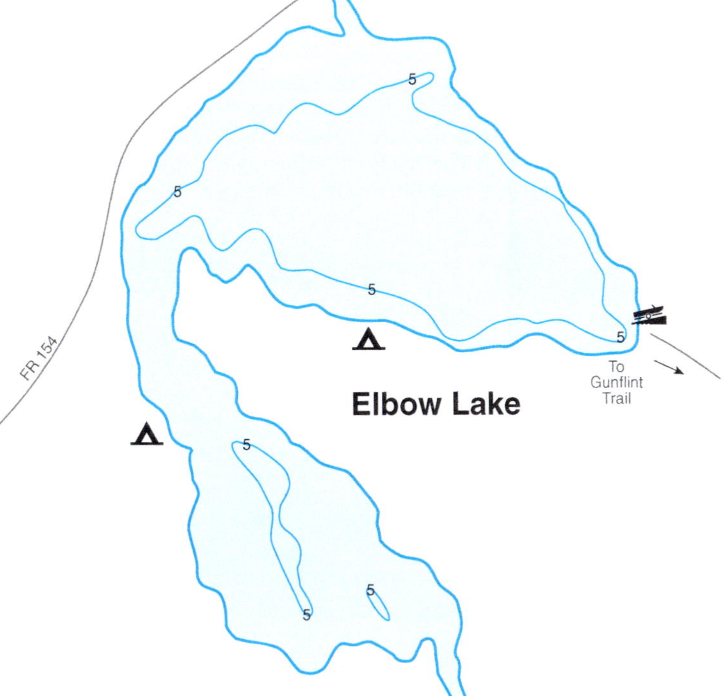

Elbow Lake, Cook County

Area map page / coordinates: 19 / C-5
Surface area / max depth: 408 acres / 9 feet
Accessibility: State-owned public access with concrete ramp on east shore of north basin; parking for 20 vehicles
90° 17' 7" W / 47° 51' 39" N

FISH STOCKING DATA

year	species	size	# released
07	Bluegill	Adult	3,892
09	Bluegill	Adult	3,430

LENGTH OF SELECTED SPECIES SAMPLED FROM ALL GEAR
Survey Date: 08/30/2010
Number of fish caught for the following length categories (inches):

species	0-5	6-8	9-11	12-14	15-19	20-24	25-29	>30	Total
Bluegill	-	5	1	-	-	-	-	-	6
Northern Pike	-	-	2	1	7	3	-	-	13
Walleye	-	-	2	30	12	6	1	-	51
White Sucker	-	-	-	-	30	14	-	-	44
Yellow Perch	26	230	16	1	-	-	-	-	273

NOT FOR NAVIGATION

Source: Minnesota Department of Natural Resources, USGS

Mink Lake, Cook County

Area map page / coordinates: 19 / C-6
Surface area / max depth: 57 acres / 15 feet
Accessibility: Carry-down access to east shore off FR 140; fishing pier; parking for 30 cars; roadside access on FR 140

FISH STOCKING DATA

year	species	size	# released
10	Rainbow Trout	Yearling	2,499
10	Splake	Fingerling	7,673
11	Rainbow Trout	Yearling	2,500
11	Splake	Fingerling	5,500
12	Rainbow Trout	Yearling	2,500
12	Splake	Fingerling	5,000
13	Rainbow Trout	Yearling	2,499
14	Rainbow Trout	Yearling	2,500
15	Rainbow Trout	Yearling	857
15	Rainbow Trout	Yearling	1,655
15	Splake	Fingerling	5,056

LENGTH OF SELECTED SPECIES SAMPLED FROM ALL GEAR
Survey Date: 09/25/2013
Number of fish caught for the following length categories (inches):

species	0-5	6-8	9-11	12-14	15-19	20-24	25-29	>30	Total
Rainbow Trout	-	-	2	-	-	-	-	-	2
Splake	-	-	3	-	-	-	-	-	3
Yellow Perch	3	304	-	-	-	-	-	-	307

Boys Lake, Cook County

Area map page / coordinates: 19 / C-6
Surface area / max depth: 24 acres / 13 feet
Accessibility: Carry-down access to south shore from gravel pit off FR 140

FISH STOCKING DATA

year	species	size	# released
08	Rainbow Trout	Fingerling	1,200
09	Rainbow Trout	Fingerling	1,200
10	Rainbow Trout	Fingerling	1,200
11	Rainbow Trout	Fingerling	1,200
15	Brook Trout	Fingerling	2,713
15	Brook Trout	Yearling	500

LENGTH OF SELECTED SPECIES SAMPLED FROM ALL GEAR
Survey Date: 09/23/2013
Number of fish caught for the following length categories (inches):

species	0-5	6-8	9-11	12-14	15-19	20-24	25-29	>30	Total
Brook Trout	1	1	11	5	1	-	-	-	19
Yellow Perch	2	24	5	1	-	-	-	-	32

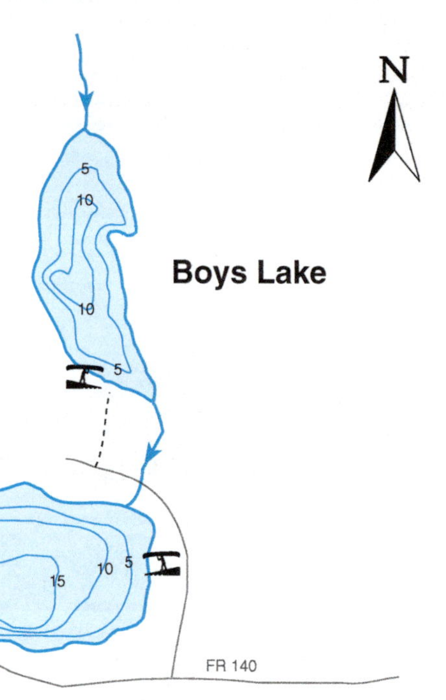

Kimball Lake

5
10
15
16' Max
10
5

Kimball Lake, Cook County

Area map page / coordinates: 19 / C-6
Surface area / max depth: 77 acres / 16 feet
Accessibility: USFS-owned public access with gravel ramp on east shore; parking for 5 vehicles
90° 13' 42" W / 47° 51' 49" N

FISH STOCKING DATA

year	species	size	# released
10	Rainbow Trout	Yearling	4,500
11	Brown Trout	Fingerling	2,000
11	Rainbow Trout	Yearling	4,500
12	Rainbow Trout	Yearling	4,500
13	Rainbow Trout	Yearling	4,500
14	Rainbow Trout	Yearling	4,494
15	Rainbow Trout	Yearling	4,542

LENGTH OF SELECTED SPECIES SAMPLED FROM ALL GEAR
Survey Date: 09/30/2013
Number of fish caught for the following length categories (inches):

species	0-5	6-8	9-11	12-14	15-19	20-24	25-29	>30	Total
Brown Trout	-	-	-	-	1	-	-	-	1
Golden Shiner	-	-	-	-	-	-	-	-	-
Rainbow Trout	-	-	2	2	-	-	-	-	4
Rock Bass	67	7	2	-	-	-	-	-	76
Splake	-	-	-	1	-	-	-	-	1
Yellow Perch	-	10	5	-	-	-	-	-	15

NOT FOR NAVIGATION

Source: Minnesota Department of Natural Resources, USGS

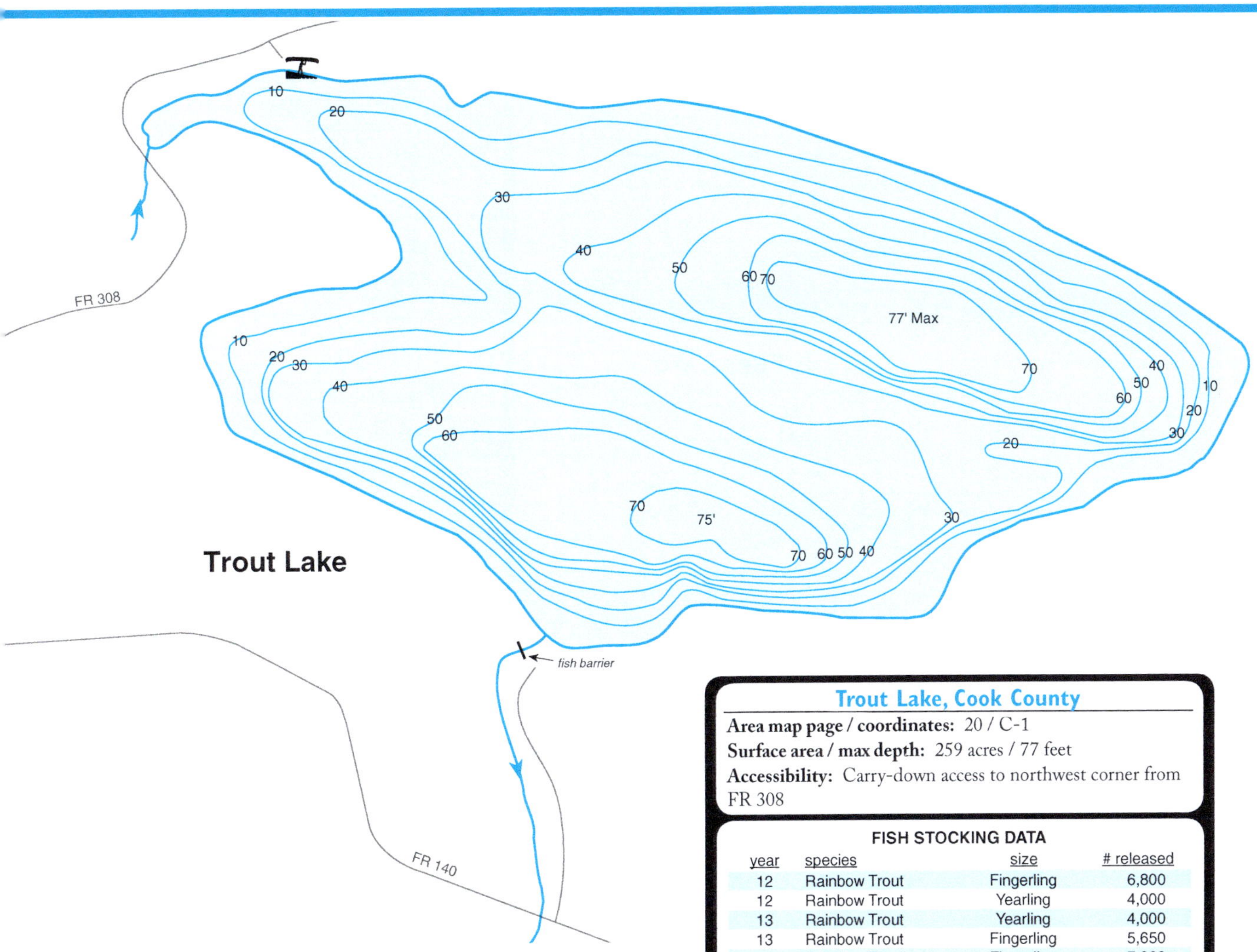

FR 308

77' Max

75'

Trout Lake

fish barrier

FR 140

N

Trout Lake, Cook County

Area map page / coordinates: 20 / C-1
Surface area / max depth: 259 acres / 77 feet
Accessibility: Carry-down access to northwest corner from FR 308

FISH STOCKING DATA

year	species	size	# released
12	Rainbow Trout	Fingerling	6,800
12	Rainbow Trout	Yearling	4,000
13	Rainbow Trout	Yearling	4,000
13	Rainbow Trout	Fingerling	5,650
14	Rainbow Trout	Fingerling	7,000
14	Rainbow Trout	Yearling	3,996
15	Rainbow Trout	Fingerling	7,000
15	Rainbow Trout	Yearling	4,004

LENGTH OF SELECTED SPECIES SAMPLED FROM ALL GEAR

Survey Date: 07/22/2013

Number of fish caught for the following length categories (inches):

species	0-5	6-8	9-11	12-14	15-19	20-24	25-29	>30	Total
Brook Trout	-	2	1	-	-	-	-	-	3
Lake Trout	-	-	8	14	-	3	1	-	26
Rainbow Smelt	-	16	-	-	-	-	-	-	16
Rainbow Trout	-	-	3	-	-	-	-	-	3
Yellow Perch	13	79	8	-	-	-	-	-	100

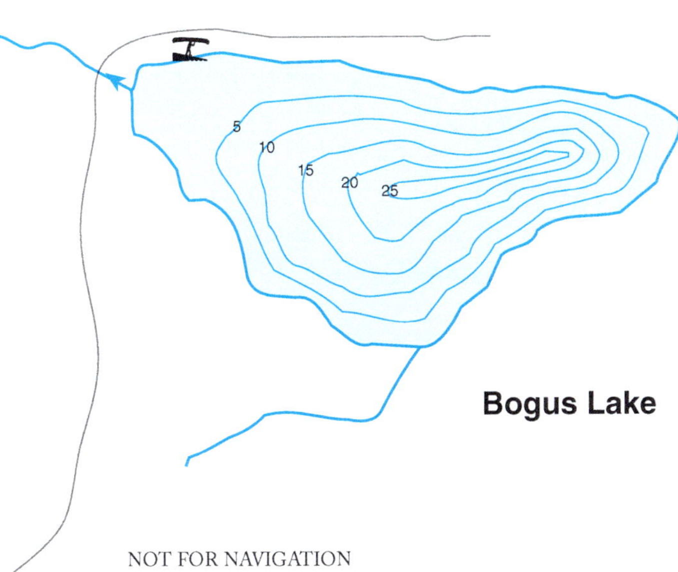

NOT FOR NAVIGATION

Bogus Lake, Cook County

Area map page / coordinates: 20 / C-1
Surface area / max depth: 18 acres / 25 feet
Accessibility: Carry-down access to north shore off FR 140

FISH STOCKING DATA

year	species	size	# released
10	Splake	Fingerling	2,500
11	Splake	Fingerling	2,500
12	Splake	Fingerling	2,500
13	Splake	Fingerling	2,500
14	Splake	Fingerling	2,500
15	Splake	Fingerling	2,528

LENGTH OF SELECTED SPECIES SAMPLED FROM ALL GEAR

Survey Date: 10/01/2007

Number of fish caught for the following length categories (inches):

species	0-5	6-8	9-11	12-14	15-19	20-24	25-29	>30	Total
Splake	-	-	17	22	5	-	-	-	44

Esther Lake

Esther Lake, Cook County

Area map page / coordinates: 20 / A-1
Surface area / max depth: 78 acres / 35 feet
Accessibility: State-owned public access with gravel ramp on northeast shore, off Co. Rd. 16; parking for four vehicles
90° 6' 31" W / 47° 58' 53" N

FISH STOCKING DATA

year	species	size	# released
10	Rainbow Trout	Yearling	3,000
10	Splake	Fingerling	2,000
11	Brown Trout	Yearling	800
11	Rainbow Trout	Yearling	3,000
11	Splake	Fingerling	2,000
12	Splake	Fingerling	4,000
13	Splake	Fingerling	4,000
14	Splake	Fingerling	6,217
15	Splake	Fingerling	4,069

LENGTH OF SELECTED SPECIES SAMPLED FROM ALL GEAR
Survey Date: 09/20/2011
Number of fish caught for the following length categories (inches):

species	0-5	6-8	9-11	12-14	15-19	20-24	25-29	>30	Total
Brown Trout	-	-	2	-	-	-	-	-	2
Rainbow Trout	-	-	9	2	-	-	-	-	11
Splake	-	8	19	7	2	-	-	-	36
White Sucker	-	1	13	57	4	-	-	-	75

N

Chester Lake, Cook County

Area map page / coordinates: 20 / A-2
Surface area / max depth: 52 acres / 35 feet
Accessibility: Carry-down access (10 yards) to north shore; parking for four vehicles

FISH STOCKING DATA

year	species	size	# released
11	Brown Trout	Yearling	800
13	Brown Trout	Yearling	800
15	Brown Trout	Yearling	800

LENGTH OF SELECTED SPECIES SAMPLED FROM ALL GEAR
Survey Date: 09/22/2014
Number of fish caught for the following length categories (inches):

species	0-5	6-8	9-11	12-14	15-19	20-24	25-29	>30	Total
Brown Trout	-	-	-	1	2	1	-	-	4
Rainbow Smelt	3	-	-	-	-	-	-	-	3
White Sucker	-	9	12	6	7	-	-	-	34

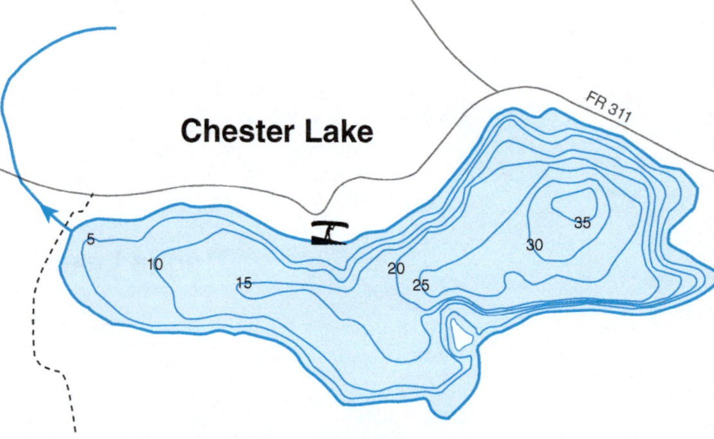

NOT FOR NAVIGATION

Source: Minnesota Department of Natural Resources, USGS

Margaret Lake

29' Max

Margaret Lake, Cook County

Area map page / coordinates: 10 / A-2
Surface area / max depth: 6 acres / 29 feet
Accessibility: Carry-down access trail from old logging road that starts near north end of gravel pit, just south of Portage Brook crossing of Arrowhead Trail

FISH STOCKING DATA

year	species	size	# released
06	Brook Trout	Fingerling	504
08	Brook Trout	Fingerling	750
10	Brook Trout	Fingerling	750
12	Brook Trout	Fingerling	750
14	Brook Trout	Fingerling	829

LENGTH OF SELECTED SPECIES SAMPLED FROM ALL GEAR
Survey Date: 09/17/2013
Number of fish caught for the following length categories (inches):

species	0-5	6-8	9-11	12-14	15-19	20-24	25-29	>30	Total
Brook Trout	-	10	-	3	1	-	-	-	14
White Sucker	-	7	6	2	-	-	-	-	15

Loft Lake, Cook County

Area map page / coordinates: 12 / E-2
Surface area / max depth: 14 acres / 48 feet
Accessibility: Carry-down access to northeast shore off FR 313; parking for one vehicle

FISH STOCKING DATA

year	species	size	# released
10	Brook Trout	Fingerling	1,427
12	Brook Trout	Fingerling	1,000
14	Brook Trout	Fingerling	1,297

LENGTH OF SELECTED SPECIES SAMPLED FROM ALL GEAR
Survey Date: 09/08/2014
Number of fish caught for the following length categories (inches):

species	0-5	6-8	9-11	12-14	15-19	20-24	25-29	>30	Total
Brook Trout	-	-	13	15	-	-	-	-	28

Loft Lake

Otter Lake

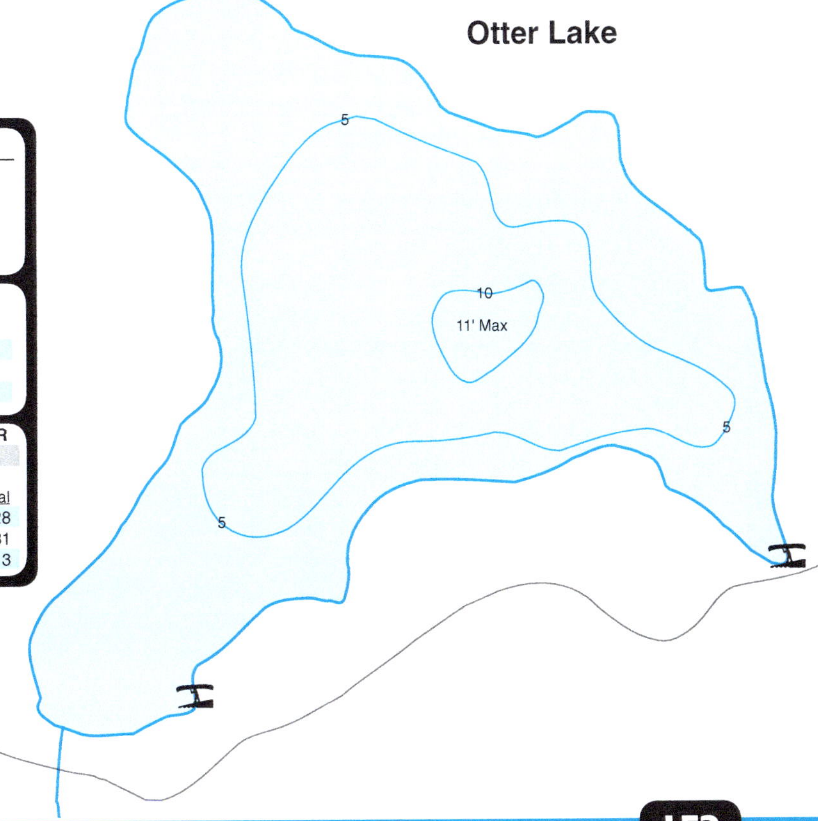

Otter Lake, Cook County

Area map page / coordinates: 20 / A-2, 3
Surface area / max depth: 75 acres / 11 feet
Accessibility: Carry-down access sites on southwest and southeast shores

FISH STOCKING DATA

year	species	size	# released
11	Walleye	Fry	150,000
14	Walleye	Fry	75,000
15	Walleye	Fry	75,000

LENGTH OF SELECTED SPECIES SAMPLED FROM ALL GEAR
Survey Date: 07/07/2014
Number of fish caught for the following length categories (inches):

species	0-5	6-8	9-11	12-14	15-19	20-24	25-29	>30	Total
Northern Pike	-	-	7	1	16	4	-	-	28
Walleye	-	-	-	2	27	2	-	-	31
Yellow Perch	-	3	-	-	-	-	-	-	3

Source: Minnesota Department of Natural Resources, USGS

TOM LAKE *Cook County*

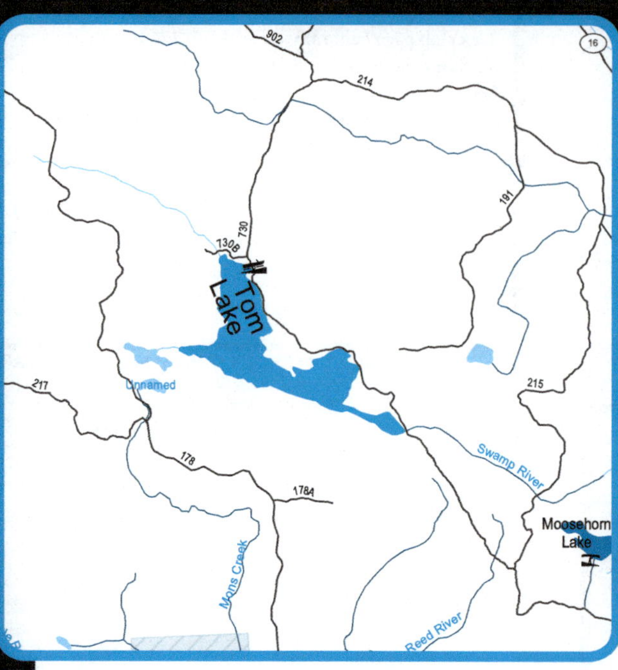

Area map page / coordinates: 20 / B-2

Watershed: Baptism-Brule

Surface water area / shorelength: 404 acres / 7.0 miles

Maximum / mean depth: 35 feet / 13 feet

Water color / clarity: Green tint / 7.5 ft. secchi (2013)

Shoreland zoning classification: Recreational development

Mgmt. class / Ecological type: Walleye / northern pike-sucker

Accessibility: State-owned public access with concrete ramp on northeast shore; parking for five vehicles

90° 3' 48" W / 47° 55' 55" N

Accommodations: Camping, picnicking, restrooms

FISHING INFORMATION

Tom Lake offers the usual mix of species for lakes up in the Arrowhead. You'll also find some large eelpout and lake whitefish.

Getting your presentation noticed on Tom Lake can be a bit difficult come mid-summer, as a light algae bloom clouds the water somewhat. Despite the algae, secchi disk readings still read 7.5 feet, which is better than many bog-stained bodies of water.

You'll find quite a few walleyes in Tom Lake, and although many are on the smaller end of the spectrum, there are actually some pretty good-sized walleyes swimming around in these waters. The fish grow relatively quickly here, thanks to a decent perch population.

Northern pike are scarce in Tom Lake, if you can believe it. The lake has had a reputation for low pike numbers for years, although the northern population has mild ups and downs. The low pike density doesn't usually bother walleye die-hards.

Perch numbers have increased, perhaps due to the decline of northern pike numbers. However, most of these fall short of "keeper" status.

Tom Lake also has good numbers of lake whitefish. In fact, the most recent DNR survey revealed the highest population ever observed of this pelagic species in Tom Lake. There are some really nice whitefish here. They are so big, you might have trouble fitting them into your smoker!

Some eelpout also show up in DNR surveys of this lake. This unsightly, albeit tasty, fish is seldom targeted, but they grow to nice sizes here.

You'll find walleyes in their typical haunts – in the shallows early and on deeper structure later in the season. The lake's western shoreline, with its broad point and relatively quick break **(Spot 1)**, can be an excellent producer of walleyes. It's best fished in an east or southeast wind – something that happens with some frequency in the area around Lake Superior.

NO RECORD OF STOCKING

NET CATCH DATA

Date: 07/08/2013	Gill Nets		Trap Nets	
species	# per net	avg. fish weight (lbs.)	# per net	avg. fish weight (lbs.)
Burbot	1.00	1.52	0.08	2.28
Lake Whitefish	5.00	2.39	-	-
Northern Pike	-	-	0.08	0.89
Walleye	3.11	0.74	3.75	1.27
White Sucker	3.44	2.19	6.83	1.63
Yellow Perch	1.67	0.32	2.67	0.13

LENGTH OF SELECTED SPECIES SAMPLED FROM ALL GEAR

Number of fish caught for the following length categories (inches):

species	0-5	6-8	9-11	12-14	15-19	20-24	25-29	>30	Total
Burbot	-	-	-	2	4	4	-	-	10
Lake Whitefish	-	-	8	7	8	21	-	-	44
Northern Pike	-	-	-	-	1	-	-	-	1
Walleye	-	3	22	28	13	7	-	-	73
White Sucker	-	10	12	14	69	8	-	-	113
Yellow Perch	15	26	6	-	-	-	-	-	47

The points off the east shore **(Spots 2)**, quickly dropping southwest shore **(Spot 3)** and the bar opposite the east-shore point **(Spot 4)** should also get a look.

Finding lake whitefish shouldn't be too hard on Tom Lake. You can pretty much rule out the shallow, eastern end of the lake. Look for whitefish in the lake's deepest hole and in the deep, narrow slots to the east and west of there. The best way to target them is the same in summer or winter: jig for them with a small spoon. Even better, attach a small dropper jig and a waxworm a couple inches below the spoon. The flash brings them in from a distance and the small bait gets bit because whitefish have small mouths and are primarily insect eaters anyway. These fish are impressive fighters and you if you find one, you'll usually find more, although you may have to hop around to stay with the school.

There is a small campground and a nice concrete boat ramp on the north shore.

TOM LAKE

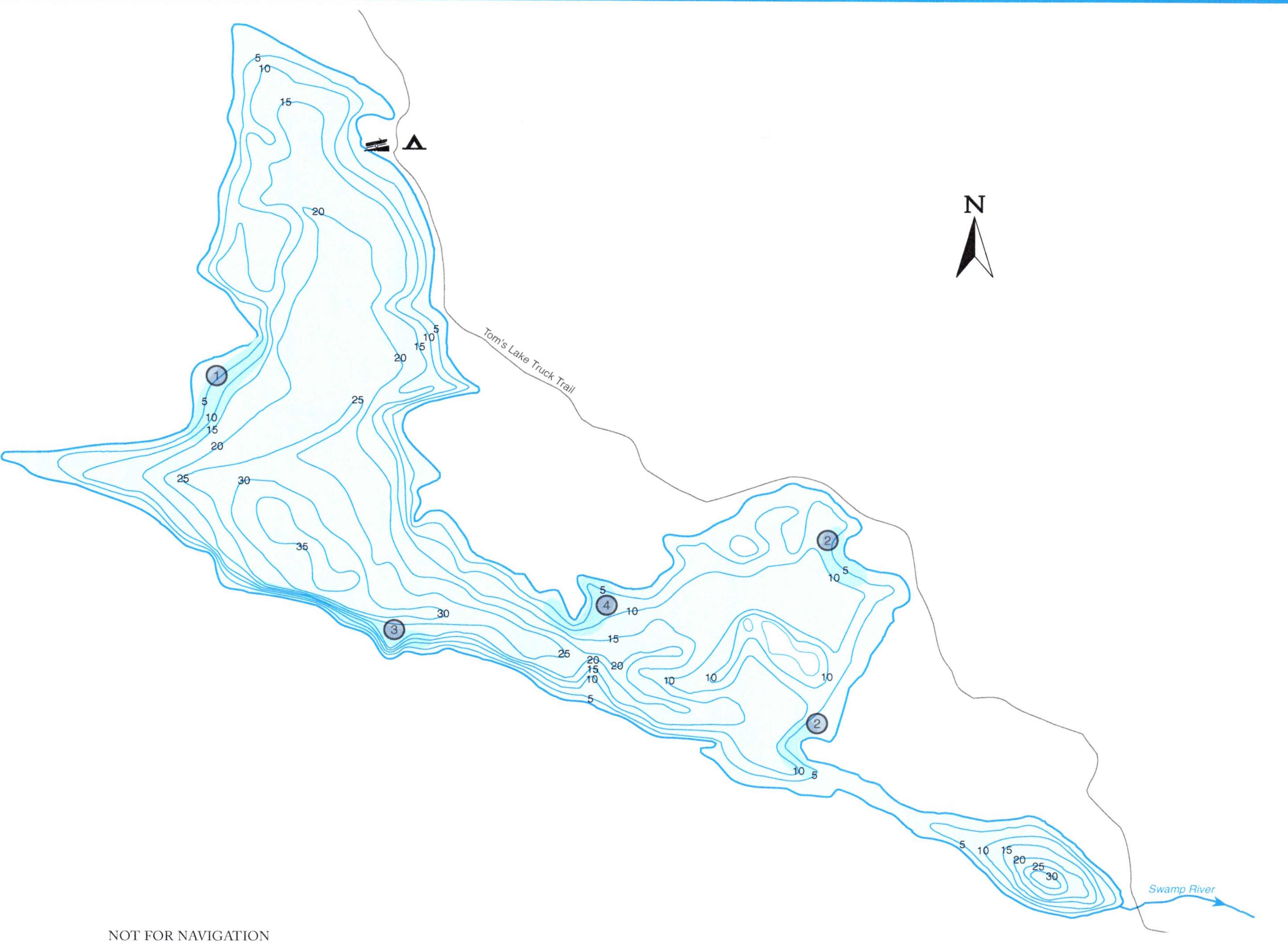

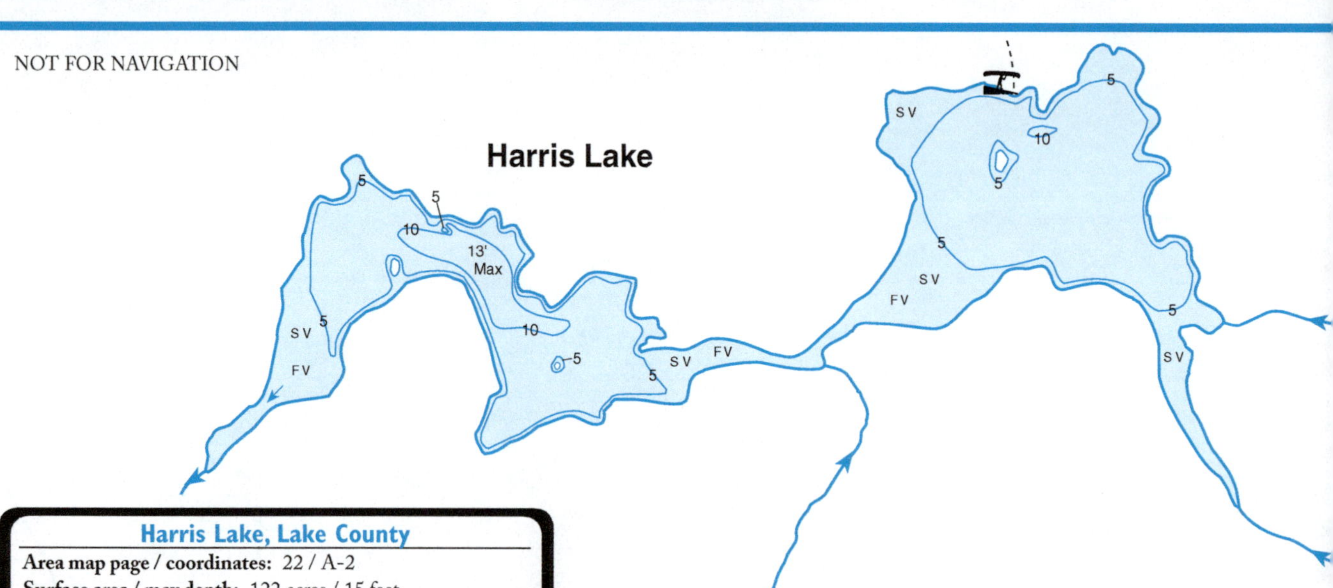

Harris Lake, Lake County

Area map page / coordinates: 22 / A-2
Surface area / max depth: 122 acres / 15 feet
Accessibility: Carry-down access; from Hwy. 1 take logging road (very rough) one mile to east bay of lake

NO RECORD OF STOCKING

LENGTH OF SELECTED SPECIES SAMPLED FROM ALL GEAR
Survey Date: 07/08/2013
Number of fish caught for the following length categories (inches):

species	0-5	6-8	9-11	12-14	15-19	20-24	25-29	>30	Total
Bluegill	7	-	-	-	-	-	-	-	7
Hybrid Sunfish	1	-	-	-	-	-	-	-	1
Muskellunge	-	-	-	-	-	3	14	2	19
Pumpkinseed	2	-	-	-	-	-	-	-	2
Walleye	-	7	16	28	21	4	2	-	78
White Sucker	-	-	1	-	-	-	-	-	1
Yellow Perch	12	20	-	-	-	-	-	-	32

Gypsy Lake, Lake County

Area map page / coordinates: 22 / B-2
Surface area / max depth: 15 acres / 18 feet
Accessibility: Carry-down access (200-yard portage) from FR 424

FISH STOCKING DATA

year	species	size	# released
Annual	Brook Trout	Fingerling	~ 2,000

LENGTH OF SELECTED SPECIES SAMPLED FROM ALL GEAR
Survey Date: 06/18/2013
Number of fish caught for the following length categories (inches):

species	0-5	6-8	9-11	12-14	15-19	20-24	25-29	>30	Total
Brook Trout	-	30	-	2	-	-	-	-	32

Beaver Hut Lake, Lake County

Area map page / coordinates: 22 / A-2
Surface area / max depth: 55 acres / 20 feet
Accessibility: 2 carry-down accesses via logging roads off Stony Spur Trail; map at Finland DNR Fisheries Office

FISH STOCKING DATA

year	species	size	# released
11	Splake	Fingerling	2,975
12	Splake	Fingerling	1,955
13	Splake	Fingerling	1,170
14	Splake	Fingerling	2,852
15	Splake	Fingerling	2,963

LENGTH OF SELECTED SPECIES SAMPLED FROM ALL GEAR
Survey Date: 09/27/2010
Number of fish caught for the following length categories (inches):

species	0-5	6-8	9-11	12-14	15-19	20-24	25-29	>30	Total
Green Sunfish	7	-	-	-	-	-	-	-	7
Splake	-	1	4	5	5	-	-	-	15
White Sucker	-	36	80	122	19	-	-	-	257
Yellow Perch	3	3	7	2	-	-	-	-	15

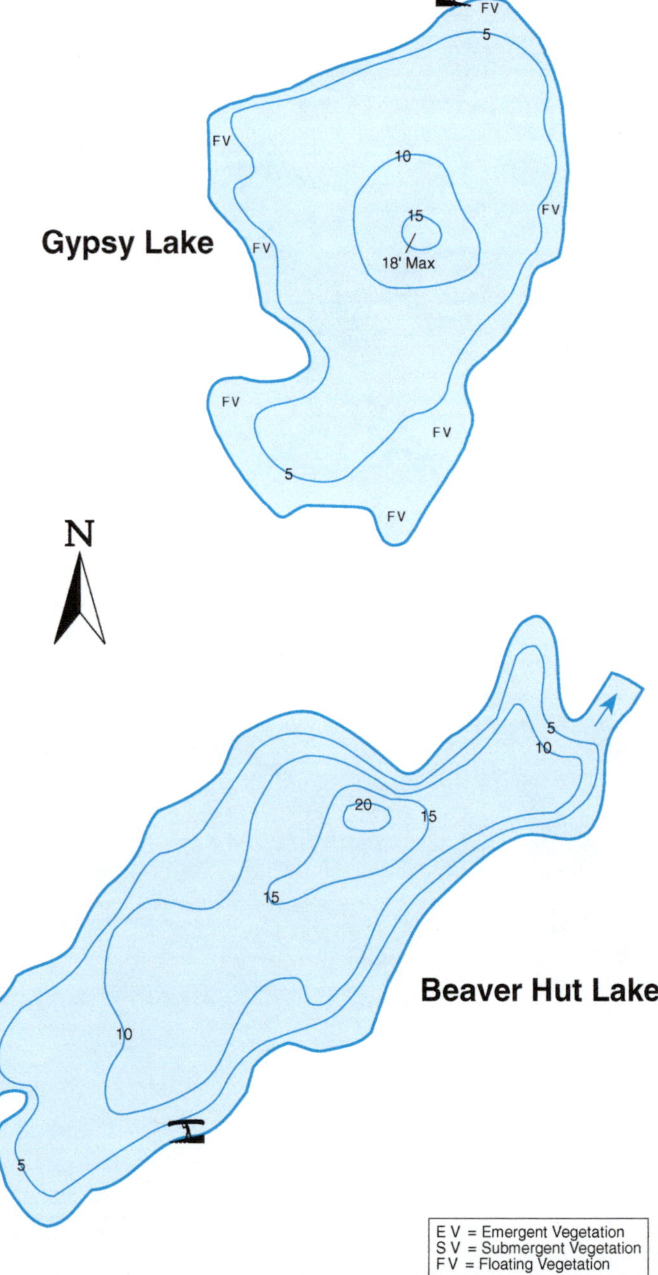

Source: Minnesota Department of Natural Resources, USGS

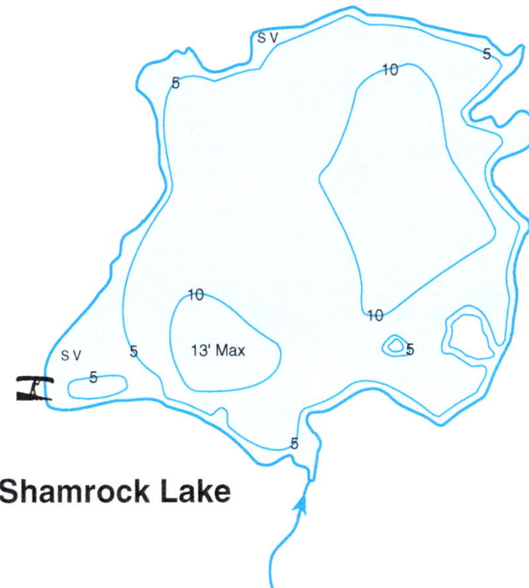

Shamrock Lake, Lake County

Area map page / coordinates: 22 / A,B-3
Surface area / max depth: 56 acres / 13 feet
Accessibility: Carry-down access via 600-foot marked trail off FR 386 to southwest corner of lake

FISH STOCKING DATA

year	species	size	# released
02	Black Crappie	Fingerling	210

LENGTH OF SELECTED SPECIES SAMPLED FROM ALL GEAR
Survey Date: 08/08/2006
Number of fish caught for the following length categories (inches):

species	0-5	6-8	9-11	12-14	15-19	20-24	25-29	>30	Total
Bluegill	33	11	1	-	-	-	-	-	45
Largemouth Bass	9	3	1	8	-	-	-	-	22

N

Dunnigan Lake, Lake County

Area map page / coordinates: 22 / B-3
Surface area / max depth: 81 acres / 14 feet
Accessibility: Carry-down access to south shore from Hwy. 1

FISH STOCKING DATA

year	species	size	# released
12	Walleye	Fingerling	2,668
13	Walleye	Fingerling	2,675

LENGTH OF SELECTED SPECIES SAMPLED FROM ALL GEAR
Survey Date: 08/22/2011
Number of fish caught for the following length categories (inches):

species	0-5	6-8	9-11	12-14	15-19	20-24	25-29	>30	Total
Bluegill	3	-	-	-	-	-	-	-	3
Rock Bass	4	12	-	-	-	-	-	-	16
Smallmouth Bass	14	19	8	7	-	-	-	-	48
Walleye	-	-	1	-	5	2	-	-	8

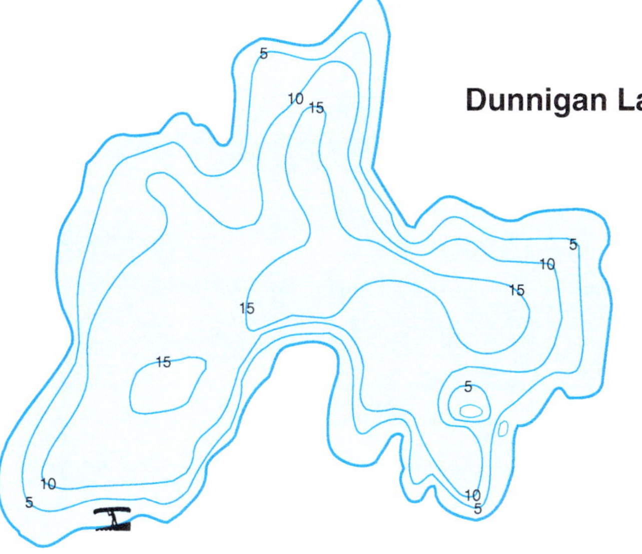

Slate Lake, Lake County

Area map page / coordinates: 22 / B-3
Surface area / max depth: 293 acres / 10 feet
Accessibility: Access off Hwy. 1 bridge right-of-way, up Stony River to Slate Lake

NO RECORD OF STOCKING

LENGTH OF SELECTED SPECIES SAMPLED FROM ALL GEAR
Survey Date: 07/07/2014
Number of fish caught for the following length categories (inches):

species	0-5	6-8	9-11	12-14	15-19	20-24	25-29	>30	Total
Bluegill	-	1	6	-	-	-	-	-	7
Northern Pike	-	-	5	5	9	3	2	1	25
Rock Bass	4	1	1	-	-	-	-	-	6
Smallmouth Bass	-	-	-	2	5	-	-	-	7
Walleye	-	8	14	5	4	1	1	-	33
White Sucker	-	1	13	27	49	1	-	-	91
Yellow Perch	15	32	12	-	-	-	-	-	59

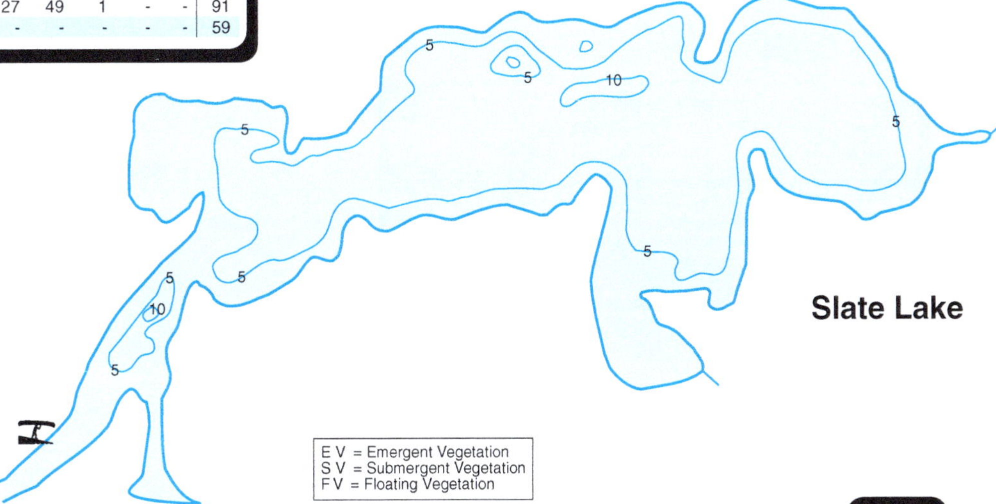

Source: Minnesota Department of Natural Resources, USGS

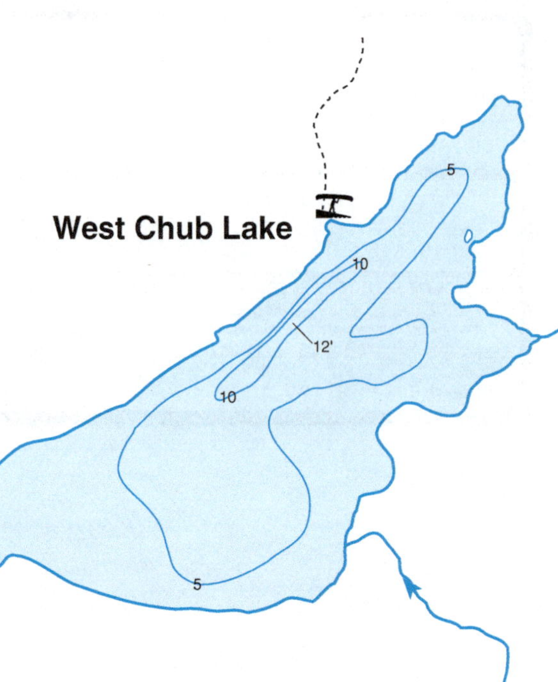

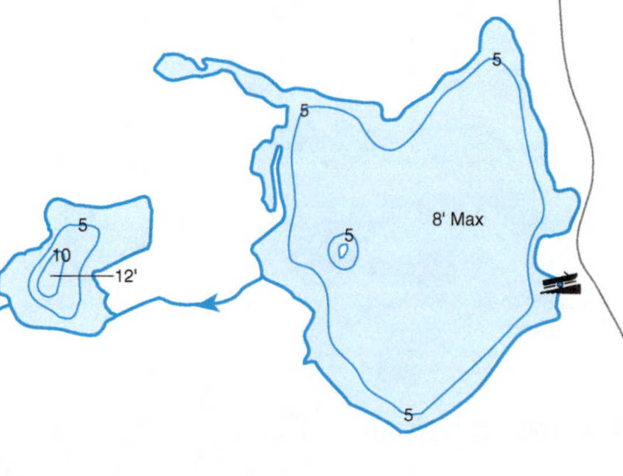

Chub Lakes, Lake County

Area map page / coordinates: 22 / B-2,3
Surface area: West = 114 acres / East = 63 acres
Accessibility: Gravel boat launch on east shore of East Chub Lake; access to West Chub is limited to snowmobile, ski or snowshoe from East Chub in winter, 0.4 mile across bog and small lake to east shore of lake
91° 37' 7" W / 47° 40' 39" N (East Chub launch)

NO RECORD OF STOCKING

LENGTH OF SELECTED SPECIES SAMPLED FROM ALL GEAR
EAST CHUB - Survey Date: 06/11/2012
Number of fish caught for the following length categories (inches):

species	0-5	6-8	9-11	12-14	15-19	20-24	25-29	>30	Total
Northern Pike	-	-	-	-	23	40	10	-	73
Pumpkinseed	18	-	-	-	-	-	-	-	18
White Sucker	-	-	2	3	25	-	-	-	30
Yellow Perch	29	60	2	-	-	-	-	-	91

LENGTH OF SELECTED SPECIES SAMPLED FROM ALL GEAR
WEST CHUB - Survey Date: 06/28/1999
Number of fish caught for the following length categories (inches):

species	0-5	6-8	9-11	12-14	15-19	20-24	25-29	>30	Total
Bluegill	18	25	6	-	-	-	-	-	49
Northern Pike	-	-	2	6	53	22	1	-	84
Pumpkin. Sunfish	8	2	-	-	-	-	-	-	10
Yellow Perch	96	245	47	-	-	-	-	-	388

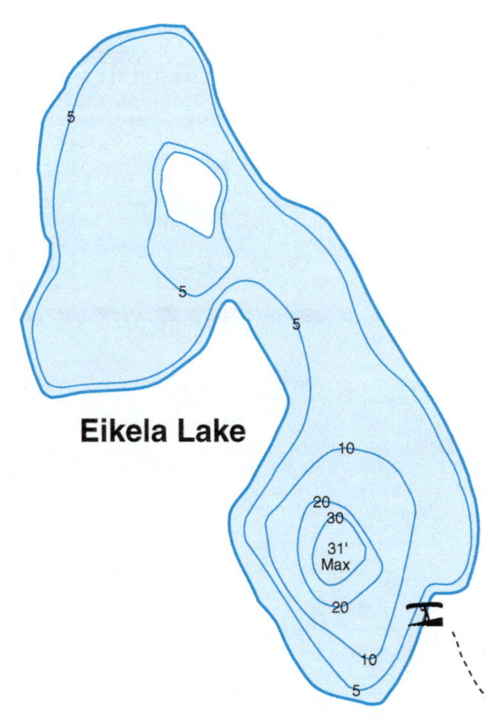

Eikala Lake, Lake County

Area map page / coordinates: 22 / B-3
Surface area / max depth: 9 acres / 31 feet
Accessibility: Carry-down access (1/4 mile portage); off Hwy. 1 take logging road for 1.3 miles then across bog to southeast shore

FISH STOCKING DATA

year	species	size	# released
Annual	Brook Trout	Fingerling	~500

LENGTH OF SELECTED SPECIES SAMPLED FROM ALL GEAR
Survey Date: 09/09/2009
Number of fish caught for the following length categories (inches):

species	0-5	6-8	9-11	12-14	15-19	20-24	25-29	>30	Total
Brook Trout	-	3	1	2	3	-	-	-	9

Source: Minnesota Department of Natural Resources, USGS

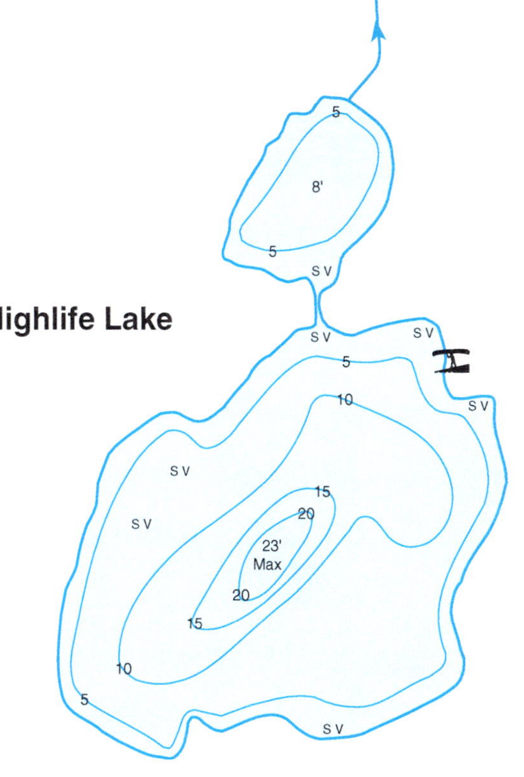

Highlife Lake, Lake County

Area map page / coordinates: 22 / B-3
Surface area / max depth: 20 acres / 23 feet
Accessibility: Carry-down access to northeast shore; Hwy. 1 to very rough logging road about 500' north of East Chub Lake access; then 325 feet east of logging road, go north one mile to end

FISH STOCKING DATA

year	species	size	# released
07	Brook Trout	Yearling	751

LENGTH OF SELECTED SPECIES SAMPLED FROM ALL GEAR
Survey Date: 09/22/2008
Number of fish caught for the following length categories (inches):

species	0-5	6-8	9-11	12-14	15-19	20-24	25-29	>30	Total
Brook Trout	-	-	1	3	-	-	-	-	4
Bluegill	6	10	-	-	-	-	-	-	16
Pumpkin. Sunfish	6	-	-	-	-	-	-	-	6
Yellow Perch	2	5	-	-	-	-	-	-	7

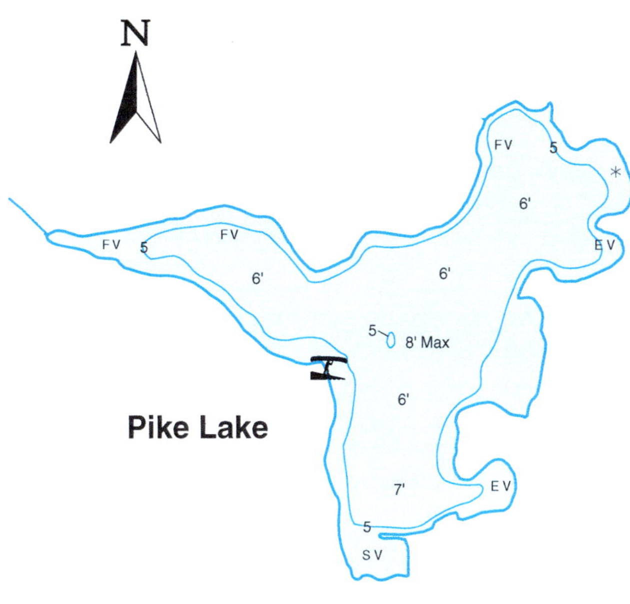

Pike Lake, Lake County

Area map page / coordinates: 22 / B-3 & 23 / B-4
Surface area / max depth: 74 acres / 8 feet
Accessibility: Carry-down access (1,500 ft. trail) from logging road off FR 1491 to southwest shore of lake

NO RECORD OF STOCKING

LENGTH OF SELECTED SPECIES SAMPLED FROM ALL GEAR
Survey Date: 08/13/2003
Number of fish caught for the following length categories (inches):

species	0-5	6-8	9-11	12-14	15-19	20-24	25-29	>30	Total
Largemouth Bass	-	-	1	-	1	-	-	-	2
Northern Pike	-	-	-	1	4	15	3	-	23
Yellow Perch	2	33	1	-	-	-	-	-	36

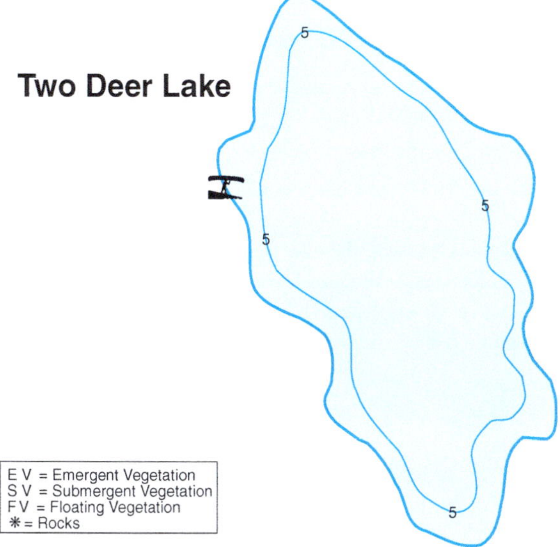

Two Deer Lake, Lake County

Area map page / coordinates: 22 / B-3
Surface area / max depth: 45 acres / 7 feet
Accessibility: Carry-down access (200 feet down steep hill) to west shore; Hwy. 1 to FR 1491, limited parking

NO RECORD OF STOCKING

LENGTH OF SELECTED SPECIES SAMPLED FROM ALL GEAR
Survey Date: 06/27/2011
Number of fish caught for the following length categories (inches):

species	0-5	6-8	9-11	12-14	15-19	20-24	25-29	>30	Total
Largemouth Bass	1	-	1	-	2	-	-	-	4
Northern Pike	-	-	1	2	3	12	13	2	33
Pumpkinseed	1	2	-	-	-	-	-	-	3
White Sucker	-	28	38	4	9	1	-	-	80
Yellow Perch	37	197	1	-	-	-	-	-	235

NOT FOR NAVIGATION

NORTH McDOUGAL MIDDLE McDOUGAL SOUTH McDOUGA

Lake County *Lake County* *Lake County*

	NORTH MCDOUGAL	MIDDLE MCDOUGAL	SOUTH MCDOUGAL
Area map pg / coord:	22, 23 / C-3, 4	22, 23/C-3, 4	22, 23/C, D-3, 4
Watershed:	Rainy headwaters	Rainy headwaters	Rainy headwaters
Surface area:	273 acres	104 acres	287 acres
Shorelength:	4.8 miles	0.6 miles	4.4 miles
Max / mean depth:	13 ft. / NA	7 ft. / NA	7 ft. / NA
Water color / clarity:	4.3 ft. secchi (2009)	5.0 ft. secchi (2009)	3.5 ft. secchi (2009)
Accessibility:	USFS-owned public access with concrete ramp on northeast shore, at campground off Hwy. 1; via navigable channel to Middle and South McDougal Lakes 91° 32' 13" W 47° 38' 19" N		
Accommodations:	Camping, restrooms	None	None

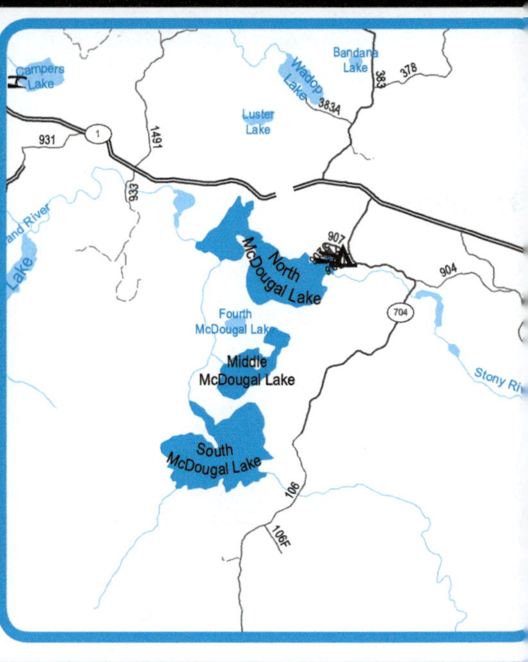

North McDougal Lake

NO RECORD OF STOCKING

LENGTH OF SELECTED SPECIES SAMPLED FROM ALL GEAR

Survey Date: 07/20/2009

Number of fish caught for the following length categories (inches):

species	0-5	6-8	9-11	12-14	15-19	20-24	25-29	>29	Total
Bluegill	-	12	1	-	-	-	-	-	13
Northern Pike	-	-	3	2	13	6	2	2	28
Walleye	-	2	20	3	4	1	2	-	32
Yellow Perch	11	33	13	-	-	-	-	-	58

Middle McDougal Lake

NO RECORD OF STOCKING

LENGTH OF SELECTED SPECIES SAMPLED FROM ALL GEAR

Survey Date: 07/20/2009

Number of fish caught for the following length categories (inches):

species	0-5	6-8	9-11	12-14	15-19	20-24	25-29	>29	Total
Bluegill	1	133	1	-	-	-	-	-	135
Northern Pike	-	1	2	4	6	2	-	-	15
Walleye	-	-	7	4	4	1	-	-	16
Yellow Perch	21	22	3	-	-	-	-	-	46

South McDougal Lake

NO RECORD OF STOCKING

LENGTH OF SELECTED SPECIES SAMPLED FROM ALL GEAR

Survey Date: 08/17/2009

Number of fish caught for the following length categories (inches):

species	0-5	6-8	9-11	12-14	15-19	20-24	25-29	>29	Total
Bluegill	-	3	-	-	-	-	-	-	3
Northern Pike	-	-	6	4	13	4	1	-	29
Walleye	-	9	26	13	4	3	1	-	56
Yellow Perch	10	19	7	-	-	-	-	-	36

FISHING INFORMATION

These three Isabella-area lakes have similar northern pike, walleye and perch fisheries. They're not destination fishing waters, but they are a nice place to spend a weekend camping and doing a little fishing on the side.

North McDougal is the most accessible of the three, with a concrete launch ramp, restrooms and a USFS campground. Because the lake is so shallow, averaging maybe 6 or 7 feet, it warms early in the spring, making it a good early season walleye destination. The lake has a decent walleye population, but walleyes run small. The folks at the Knotted Pine Inn & Tavern, 9702 Highway 1, Isabella, MN 55607 (218) 323-7681, say the best spot to try for early walleyes is in the southwest, at the Stony River inlet. The lake also has northern pike, and although they, too, average on the small side, there are some large fish out there. One bright spot here is the yellow perch fishing. They tend to have a pretty nice average size and can be a bonus for walleye anglers. Smallmouth bass showed up in the chain a few years back. Not much is known about their population here so far, as they are too smart to be easily caught in DNR nets, but there are certainly some large bass here.

Middle McDougal is a shallow body of water up the Stony River from North McDougal. It is the weediest of the three lakes and provides good nursery areas for small fish in the chain. This is a good place to try for panfish. Bluegills showed up a few years back in the McDougal lakes and there are some good-sized 'gills here, as well as some nice perch. You'll find walleyes and northern pike as well in this shallow little lake.

South McDougal has a similar fishery to the other lakes. Expect to find large numbers of walleyes here, with most of them running pretty small. It's pretty much the same story with northern pike: lots of small fish. However, every once in a while, a 5-pound walleye or a 10-pound northern shows up. The lake also has yellow perch, and although they aren't super-abundant, the ones present are often fairly large, often running 9 or 10 inches or even larger. Bluegills are also present here as well.

Anglers should be careful when navigating on these shallow lakes. There are lots of boulders that can do some real damage to your motor. Boulders are often difficult to see in the dark water.

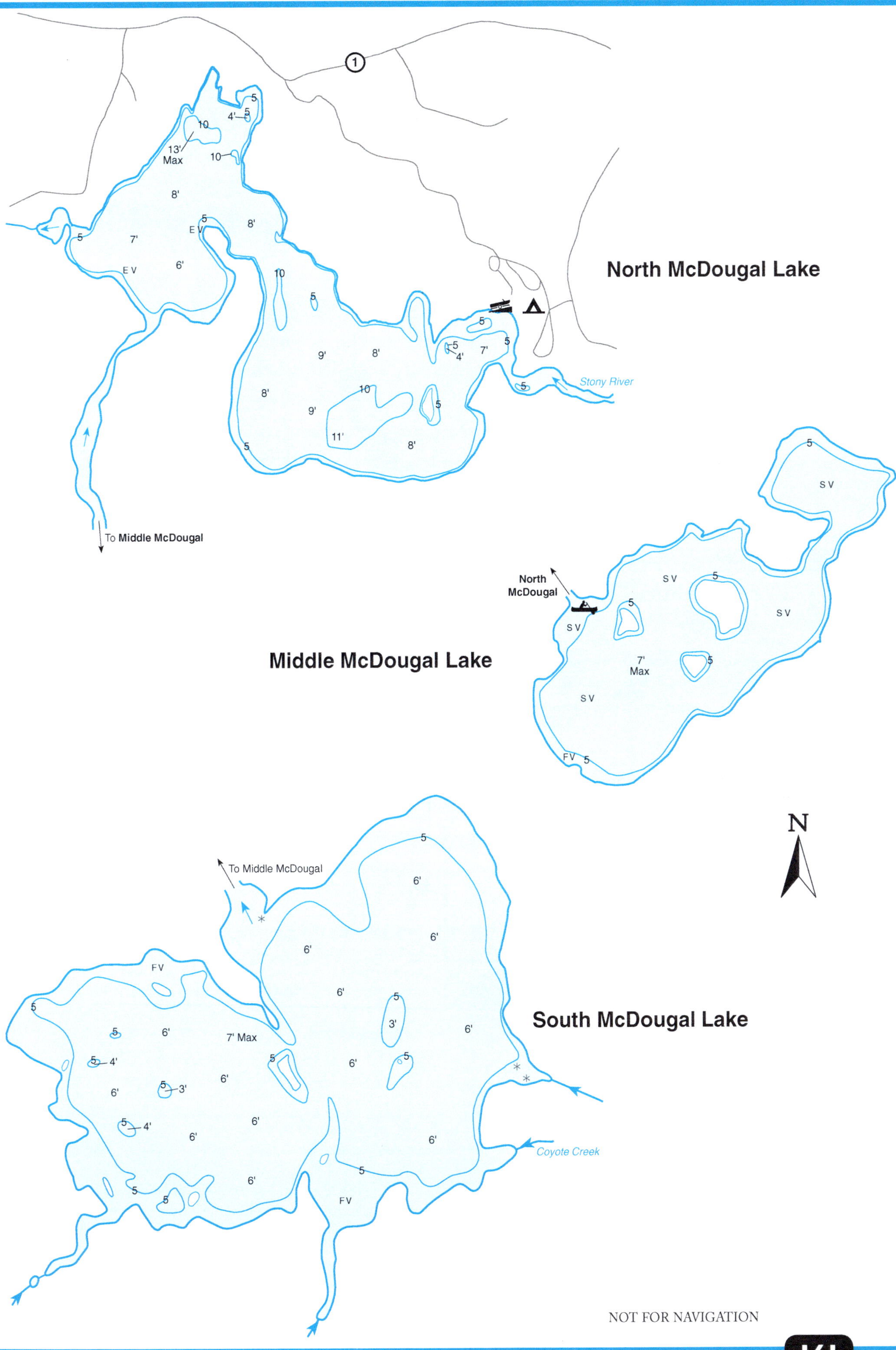

Source: Minnesota Department of Natural Resources, USGS

SAND LAKE

Lake County

Area map pg / coord: 22 / D-2

Watershed: Rainy headwaters

Surface area: 486 acres

Shorelength: 7.2 miles

Max / mean depth: 11 feet / 7 feet

Water color / clarity: Brown / 4.2 ft. secchi (2014)

Shoreland zoning class: Rec. dev.

Mgmt class / Ecological type: Walleye / soft-water walleye

Accessibility: Carry-down access at campground on east shore, 0.5 mile west off County Hwy. 2

91° 39' 55" W / 47° 35' 7" N

Accommodations: Camping, picnicking, restrooms

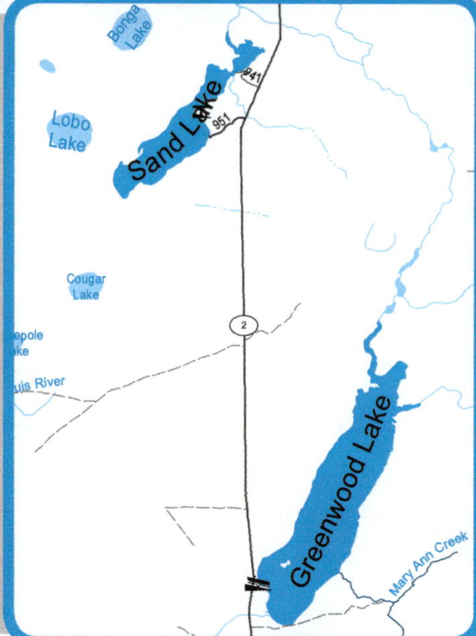

GREENWOOD LAKE

Lake County

Area map pg / coord: 22/E-3, 28/A-2

Watershed: Rainy headwaters

Surface area: 1,329 acres

Shorelength: 9.1 miles

Max / mean depth: 7 feet / NA

Water color / clarity: Brown, bog stain / 4.2 ft. secchi (2009)

Shoreland zoning class: Nat. envt.

Mgmt class / Ecological type: Walleye-centrarchid/soft-water walleye

Accessibility: State-owned public access with concrete ramp on southwest shore

91° 39' 9" W / 47° 30' 17" N

Accommodations: Dock

Sand Lake

FISH STOCKING DATA

year	species	size	# released
08	Walleye	Fry	500,000
09	Walleye	Fry	500,000
12	Walleye	Fry	500,000
13	Walleye	Fry	500,000

NET CATCH DATA

Date: 08/11/2014	Gill Nets		Trap Nets	
species	# per net	avg. fish weight (lbs.)	# per net	avg. fish weight (lbs.)
Bluegill	-	-	0.33	0.33
Northern Pike	0.33	1.18	0.44	0.94
Walleye	11.11	0.44	0.56	1.07
White Sucker	7.56	1.53	0.56	2.50
Yellow Perch	3.67	0.15	0.22	0.08

LENGTH OF SELECTED SPECIES SAMPLED FROM ALL GEAR

Number of fish caught for the following length categories (inches):

species	0-5	6-8	9-11	12-14	15-19	20-24	25-29	>29	Total
Bluegill	-	3	-	-	-	-	-	-	3
Northern Pike	-	-	1	1	3	1	-	-	6
Walleye	-	40	30	30	4	1	-	-	105
White Sucker	-	6	16	18	29	2	-	-	71
Yellow Perch	12	22	1	-	-	-	-	-	35

Greenwood Lake

NO RECORD OF STOCKING

NET CATCH DATA

Date: 08/04/2009	Gill Nets		Trap Nets	
species	# per net	avg. fish weight (lbs.)	# per net	avg. fish weight (lbs.)
Northern Pike	4.2	1.62	1.8	0.91
Walleye	12.7	0.77	1.1	1.59
White Sucker	6.6	2.15	1.1	2.81
Yellow Perch	11.3	0.23	2.7	0.24

LENGTH OF SELECTED SPECIES SAMPLED FROM ALL GEAR

Number of fish caught for the following length categories (inches):

species	0-5	6-8	9-11	12-14	15-19	20-24	25-29	>29	Total
Northern Pike	-	1	4	17	28	14	5	2	72
Walleye	-	7	86	35	30	8	-	-	166
White Sucker	-	4	2	11	69	6	-	-	92
Yellow Perch	19	124	25	-	-	-	-	-	168

FISHING INFORMATION

These two shallow lakes west of Isabella on Highway 2 are in the middle of nowhere and offer some pretty scenic fishing.

Sand Lake has a high walleye population, but you'll find that most of the walleyes are pretty small. The lake gets regular walleye fry stocking, which accounts for most of the fish that appear in DNR surveys. Most of the fish that turned up in the latest survey were below keeper size. Northern pike numbers in the last survey were very low and the fish caught were small. Perch numbers were also lower than expected, although they could rebound quickly, given low northern pike abundance. Sand was stocked with bluegills some years back, and although numbers are low, there are some plate-sized gills out there. Thus, there is a five-fish limit on bluegills in place on Sand Lake.

For walleyes, try trolling with shallow-running crankbaits or use a jig and minnow or leech off the points and the steeply dropping west shoreline. For northern pike, troll crankbaits outside the weed edges or cast spoons or spinners to weedy areas. Worm chunks fished along the weeds will take perch and bluegills. Use fluorescent or glow colors in these dark-stained waters.

Greenwood Lake is an expansive, shallow lake that is dotted by erratic boulders, so use caution here. The rocks are tough to see in the bog-stained water. Greenwood has a pretty good fishery for walleyes, northern pike and yellow perch. Like on Sand, the walleyes tend to be small, although they probably average a little larger here than they do on Sand Lake. Working the rocks is the way to find walleyes. The folks at Knotted Pine Inn & Tavern, 9702 Highway 1, Isabella, MN 55607, (218) 323-7681, say walleyes average 1 1/2 pounds or so and they recommend trolling shorelines early and the lake's center during warmer weather. Bright fluorescent colors are the ticket in this tea-colored water. Northern pike are found here in a mix of sizes, with some decent-sized fish feeding on the lake's abundant perch supply. Some of these perch are pretty decent as well.

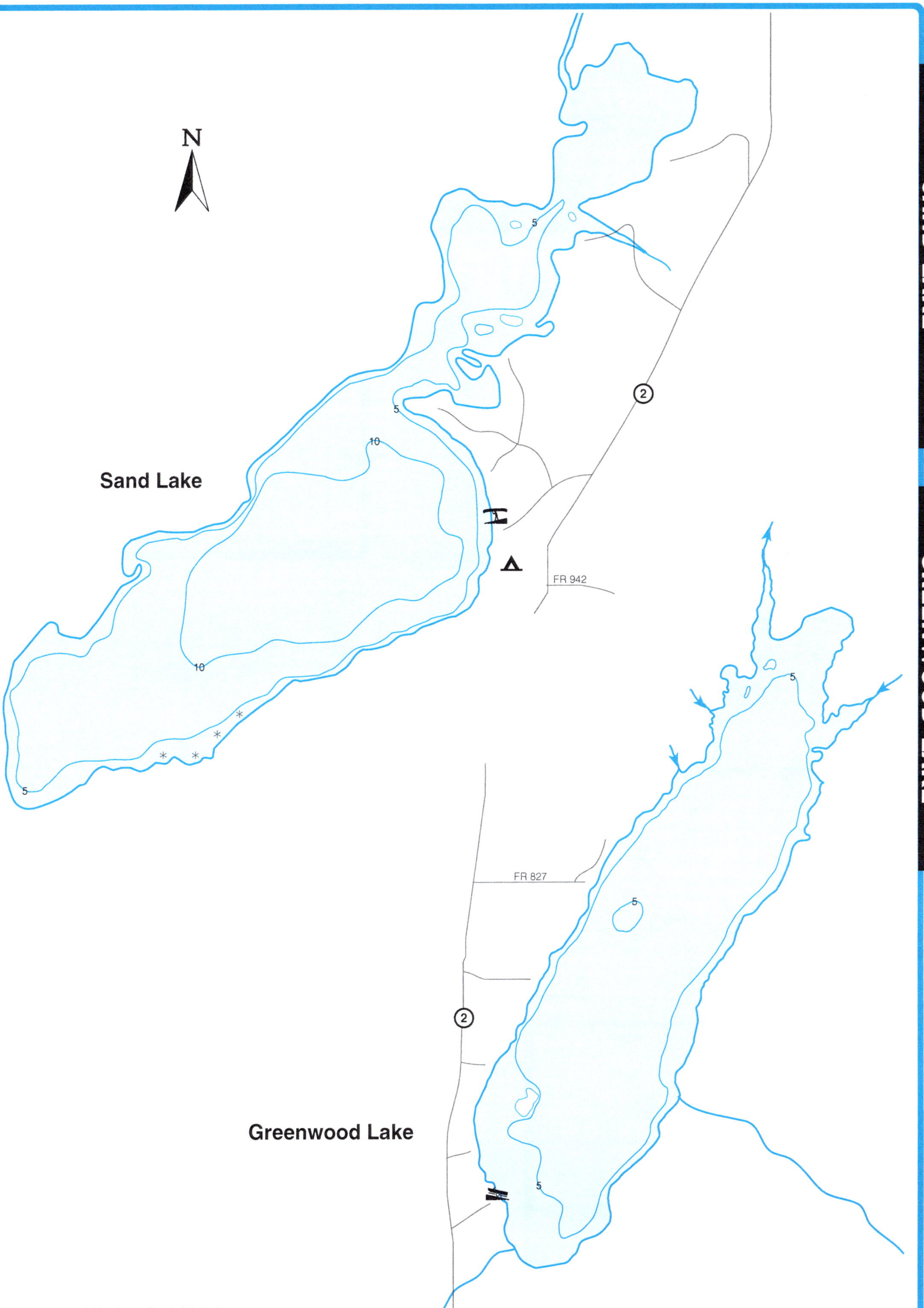

NOT FOR NAVIGATION

Source: Minnesota Department of Natural Resources, USGS

GRASS LAKE
SURPRISE LAKE
DRAGON LAKE
BEETLE LAKE

Grass Lake, Lake County

Area map page / coordinates: 23 / B-4
Surface area / max depth: 27 acres / 9 feet
Accessibility: Carry-down from FR 383 to south shore
91° 31' 56" W / 47° 42' 15" N

NO RECORD OF STOCKING

LENGTH OF SELECTED SPECIES SAMPLED FROM ALL GEAR
Survey Date: 07/15/2013
Number of fish caught for the following length categories (inches):

species	0-5	6-8	9-11	12-14	15-19	20-24	25-29	>30	Total
Bluegill	4	-	-	-	-	-	-	-	4
Largemouth Bass	2	-	-	-	-	-	-	-	2
Northern Pike	-	4	7	6	4	7	8	1	37
Pumpkin. Sunfish	11	-	-	-	-	-	-	-	11
White Sucker	-	1	12	6	5	3	-	-	27
Yellow Perch	38	20	-	-	-	-	-	-	58

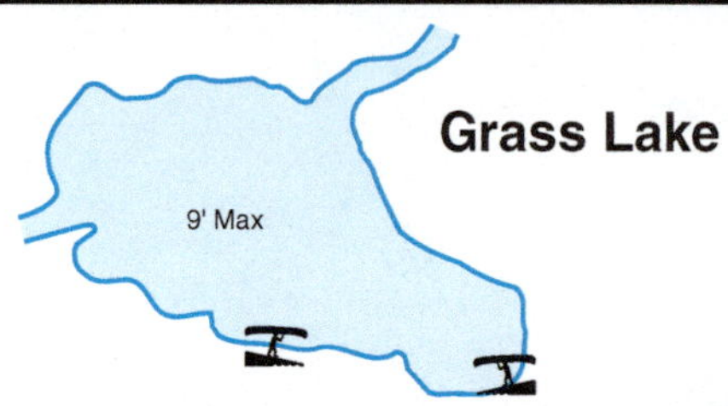

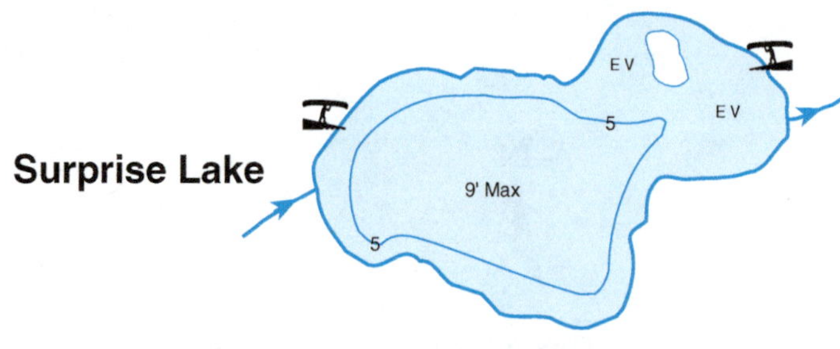

Surprise Lake, Lake County

Area map page / coordinates: 23 / B-4
Surface area / max depth: 38 acres / 9 feet
Accessibility: An unsigned access road off FR 386 through a logged area, passes within 50 ft. of the northeast shore
91° 31' 7" W / 47° 42' 35" N

NO RECORD OF STOCKING

LENGTH OF SELECTED SPECIES SAMPLED FROM ALL GEAR
Survey Date: 06/15/2010
Number of fish caught for the following length categories (inches):

species	0-5	6-8	9-11	12-14	15-19	20-24	25-29	>30	Total
Black Crappie	2	-	1	-	-	-	-	-	3
Largemouth Bass	-	-	-	-	2	-	-	-	2
Northern Pike	-	-	-	1	11	11	2	1	26
Pumpkin. Sunfish	4	-	-	-	-	-	-	-	4
Walleye	-	-	-	-	7	3	3	-	13
White Sucker	-	2	-	13	26	2	-	-	43
Yellow Perch	4	17	-	-	-	-	-	-	21

Dragon Lake, Lake County

Area map page / coordinates: 23 / B-4
Surface area / max depth: 79 acres / 15 feet
Accessibility: Carry-down access at the end of a road to the west shore; 75-foot steep trail down a hill to shoreline
91° 30' 49" W / 47° 41' 56" N

NO RECORD OF STOCKING

LENGTH OF SELECTED SPECIES SAMPLED FROM ALL GEAR
Survey Date: 06/21/2010
Number of fish caught for the following length categories (inches):

species	0-5	6-8	9-11	12-14	15-19	20-24	25-29	>30	Total
Black Crappie	-	-	5	-	-	-	-	-	5
Northern Pike	1	-	1	2	13	5	1	2	25
Walleye	-	2	2	3	8	2	-	-	17
White Sucker	-	-	-	8	66	-	-	-	74
Yellow Perch	15	13	-	-	-	-	-	-	28

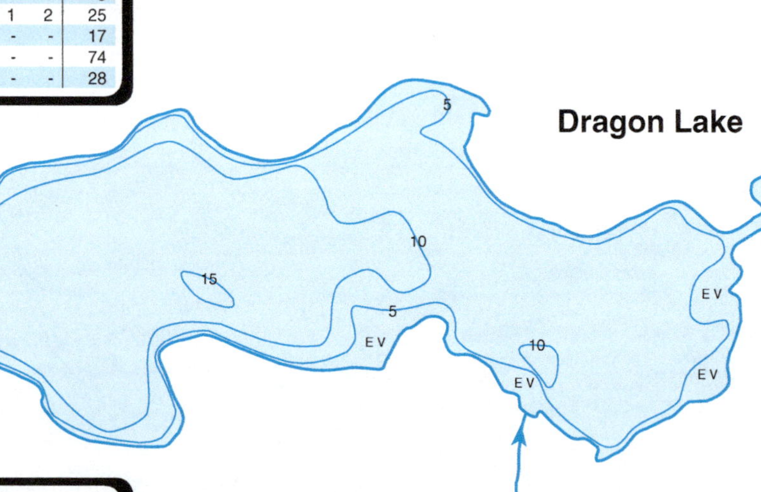

Beetle Lake, Lake County

Area map page / coordinates: 23 / B-4
Surface area / max depth: 29 acres / 26 feet
Accessibility: Carry-down trail from FR 383 to shallow bay on northwest shore
91° 31' 36" W / 47° 41' 49" N

FISH STOCKING DATA

year	species	size	# released
Annual	Brook Trout	Yearling	~ 650

LENGTH OF SELECTED SPECIES SAMPLED FROM ALL GEAR
Survey Date: 09/15/2014
Number of fish caught for the following length categories (inches):

species	0-5	6-8	9-11	12-14	15-19	20-24	25-29	>30	Total
Brook Trout	-	-	2	1	1	-	-	-	4

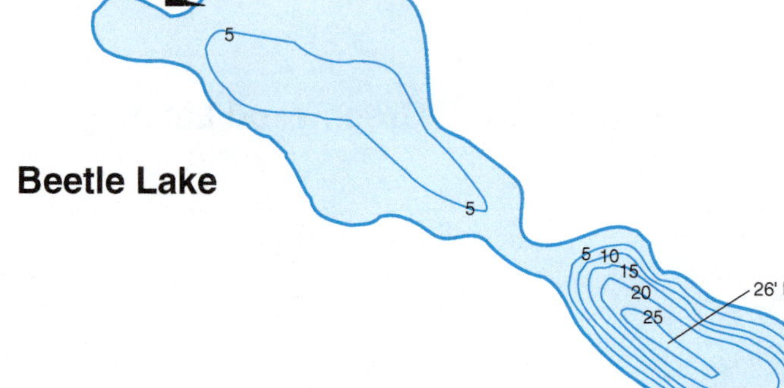

NOT FOR NAVIGATION

Source: Minnesota Department of Natural Resources, USGS

PALOMAR KNOT

A popular and easy to tie knot for small terminal tackle connections. It is one of the few recommended knots for use with braided lines.

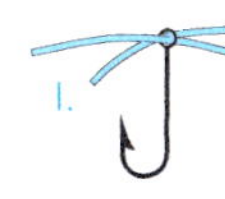

1. Double 4 to 6 inches of line and pass loop through eye of hook or lure.

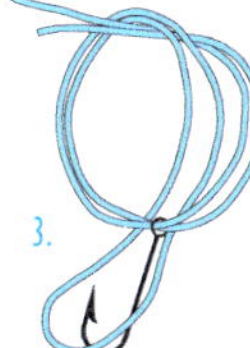

3. Holding overhand knot between thumb and forefinger, pass loop of line over hook or lure.

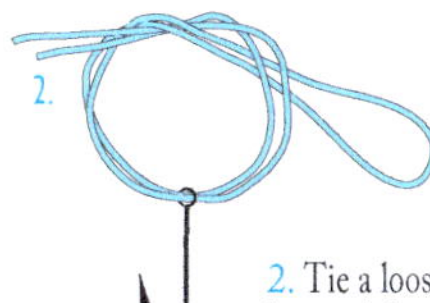

2. Tie a loose overhand knot in doubled line with hook hanging from bottom.

4. Pull both standing line and tag end to tighten knot down onto eye. Clip tag end.

IMPROVED CLINCH KNOT

This knot has become one of the most popular knots for tying terminal tackle connections. It is quick and easy to tie and is strong and reliable. However, it is not recommended for use with braided lines.

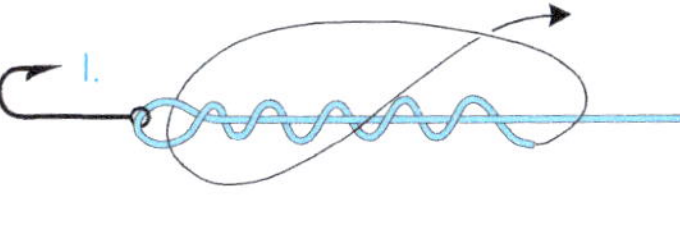

1. Thread end of line through eye of hook or lure. Double back and make 5 or more turns around the standing line. Bring the end of the line through the first loop formed behind the eye, then through the big loop.

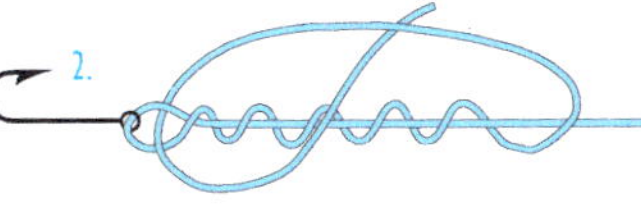

2. Wet knot and pull slightly on the tag end to draw up coils.

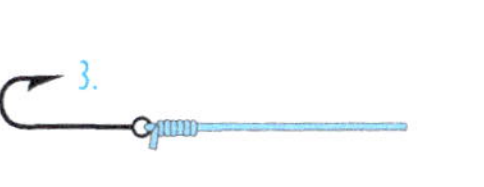

3. Pull on the standing line to form knot with coils pressed neatly together. Slide tight against eye and clip tag end.

BLOOD KNOT

Use this knot to join sections of leader or line together. It works best with lines of approximately equal diameter.

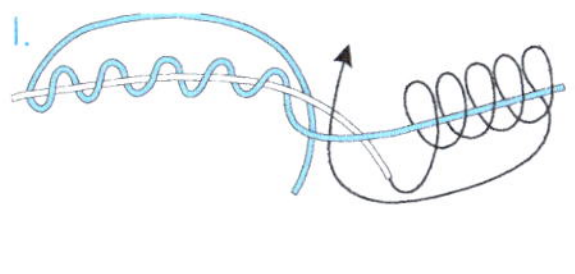

1. Overlap ends of lines to be joined. Twist one around the other making 5 turns. Bring tag end back between the two lines. Repeat with other end, wrapping in opposite direction the same number of turns.

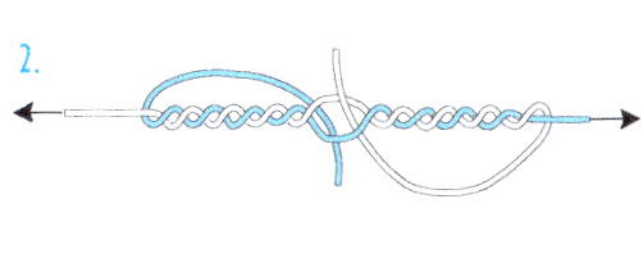

2. Slowly pull lines or leaders in opposite directions. Turns will wrap and gather.

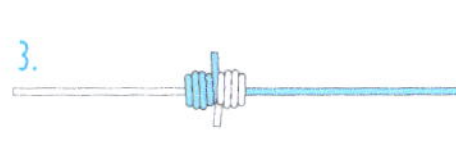

3. Pull tight and clip ends closely.

SAN DIEGO JAM KNOT

This knot can be tied with confidence in braided and monofilament line, but works exceptionally well with fluorocarbon line.

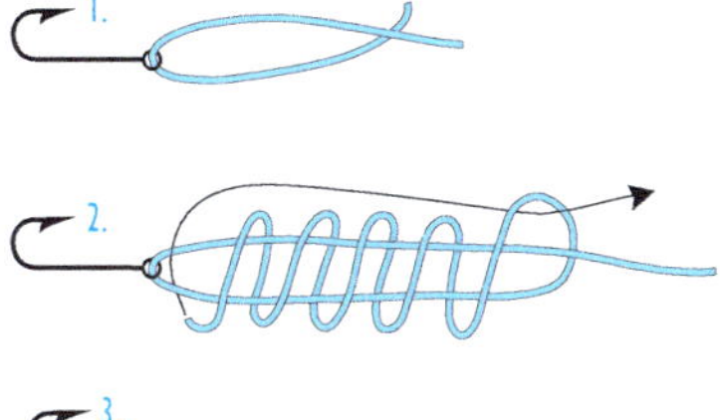

1. Pass line through hook or lure. Let a heavy lure hang down or pinch hook between little finger and palm of opposite hand.

2. Loop tag end over index finger and make 7 wraps (5 with heavy line) around the double line, then feed tag end between double lines below last wrap and bring back through loop made by index finger.

3. Moisten lines and pull tag end tight. Slide knot down to eye and tighten.

When tying knots, there are some important things to remember:

- Make sure you have enough wraps on your knot.
- Use a fingernail clipper to trim your knots.
- Trim knots to about 1/4" in length unless it's a knot that travels through the guides — the extra bit of line may hold the knot if it slips.
- Make sure knot wraps are lying cleanly inline, overlapping line will cut your knot strength.
- Wet your knots before cinching tight and make sure you pull knots tight with firm, even pressure. Jerking to tighten knots compromises the strength and integrity of the line.
- Most monofilament line will deteriorate when exposed to sunlight. In order to maintain maximum strength, change line often. Good line and a strong knot are your link to the fish of a lifetime.

Finding the right line:

There are only a few different types of fishing lines available: superlines, fluorocarbon, monofilament and trolling line. It is important to choose the right line for your fishing needs.

Superline: tough, minimal stretch, thin diameter line. The minimal line stretch gives anglers increased sensitivity to detect strikes and more frequent hook sets. Superlines offer excellent knot strength. When in doubt, use a Palomar knot. Great in heavy cover situations. Also an excellent choice for jerkbaits.

Fluorocarbon: line of choice by many anglers today and virtually invisible in the water. It has minimal line stretch, quick sink rate and great abrasion resistance. It also resists UV rays so it won't break down as quickly as monofilament. This line is ideal for flipping or pitching and a good choice for finesse presentations. It can also be used for trolling.

Monofilament: the most recommended line for beginning anglers. It casts well and is easier to work with for knot tying. This is the past and present go-to workhorse of the fishing industry. It is easy to cut but is more abrasion prone. It stretches under strain causing it to dampen or absorb light strikes so you may not feel them. Manufacturing methods with added coating and other improvements are making it even more abrasion resistant, thinner and sensitive.

Trolling Lines: specifically for trolling presentations and deeper water fishing. Trolling line features colored sections that help you gauge the amount of line you've let out (color changes every 10 yards). It may also feature a lead-core center, which allows you to present baits at specific depths. The uniformity of the weight gives smooth presentation of baits and also tracks boat movement extremely well.

GEGOKA LAKE

Lake County

Area map pg / coord: 23 / C-4

Watershed: Rainy headwaters

Surface area: 145 acres

Shorelength: 4.9 miles

Max / mean depth: 10 feet / 4 feet

Water color / clarity: Dark / 6.5 ft. secchi (2011)

Shoreland zoning class: Rec. dev.

Mgmt class / Ecological type: Walleye

Accessibility: USFS-owned public access with gravel ramp on south shore

91° 28' 33" W / 47° 38' 57" N

Accommodations: Camping, picnicking

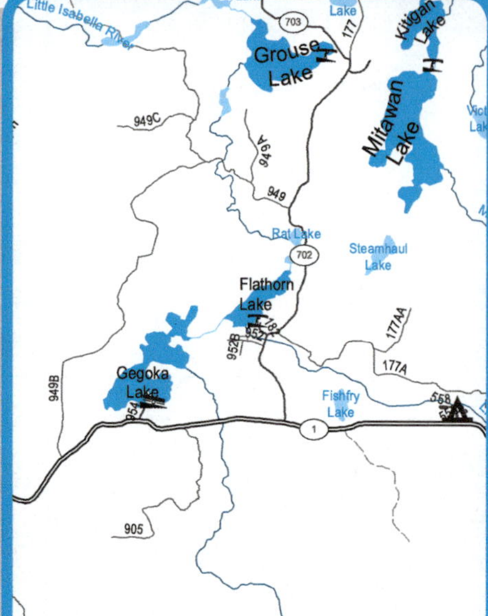

FLATHORN LAKE

Lake County

Area map pg / coord: 23 / C-5

Watershed: Rainy headwaters

Surface area: 52 acres

Shorelength: NA

Max / mean depth: 13 feet / NA

Water color / clarity: Dark / 7.5 ft. secchi (2006)

Shoreland zoning class: NA

Mgmt class / Ecological type: NA

Accessibility: Carry-down access to south shore off FR 177

91° 27' 28" W / 47° 39' 28" N

Accommodations: Picnicking, restrooms, beach

Gegoka Lake

NO RECORD OF STOCKING

NET CATCH DATA

Date: 07/25/2011

	Gill Nets		Trap Nets	
species	# per net	avg. fish weight (lbs.)	# per net	avg. fish weight (lbs.)
Bluegill	-	-	0.33	0.98
Northern Pike	7.25	2.74	1.00	0.29
Pumpkinseed	1.50	0.27	2.67	0.16
Rock Bass	0.50	-	0.11	0.34
Walleye	6.00	1.56	0.22	3.11
White Sucker	14.75	1.47	3.11	2.02
Yellow Perch	26.75	0.19	1.89	0.22

LENGTH OF SELECTED SPECIES SAMPLED FROM ALL GEAR

Number of fish caught for the following length categories (inches):

species	0-5	6-8	9-11	12-14	15-19	20-24	25-29	>29	Total
Bluegill	-	-	3	-	-	-	-	-	3
Northern Pike	-	2	8	11	8	1	3	4	37
Pumpkinseed	15	13	-	-	-	-	-	-	28
Rock Bass	-	1	-	-	-	-	-	-	1
Walleye	-	-	8	6	6	5	1	-	26
White Sucker	-	4	14	18	44	5	-	-	85
Yellow Perch	14	96	11	-	-	-	-	-	121

Flathorn Lake

NO RECORD OF STOCKING

NET CATCH DATA

Date: 06/27/2006

	Gill Nets		Trap Nets	
species	# per net	avg. fish weight (lbs.)	# per net	avg. fish weight (lbs.)
Northern Pike	4.3	2.06	1.0	1.24
Pumpkinseed Sunfish	12.0	0.15	13.0	0.17
Rock Bass	0.3	0.09	0.9	0.30
Walleye	2.0	2.36	0.1	2.54
White Sucker	27.3	1.50	4.5	1.66
Yellow Perch	11.7	0.14	1.9	0.14

LENGTH OF SELECTED SPECIES SAMPLED FROM ALL GEAR

Number of fish caught for the following length categories (inches):

species	0-5	6-8	9-11	12-14	15-19	20-24	25-29	>29	Total
Northern Pike	-	1	-	2	11	7	2	-	23
Pumpkin. Sunfish	93	73	-	-	-	-	-	-	166
Rock Bass	2	8	-	-	-	-	-	-	10
Walleye	-	-	-	-	6	1	-	-	7
Yellow Perch	20	30	4	-	-	-	-	-	54

FISHING INFORMATION

These two little lakes north of Isabella offer a smorgasbord of fishing options. You'll find everything here from panfish to walleyes and northern pike.

Gegoka offers anglers a chance at largemouth bass, walleyes, northern pike, bluegills and perch. The walleyes are present in good numbers and their size is larger than average. The same can be said for northern pike, with several fish topping 30 inches in this small lake. Bluegills were first stocked here in 2000 to meet the growing demand for this fishery in the Finland area. Reproduction is sporadic, but there are some really impressive bluegills here. Average yellow perch size is good too, with fish over 11 inches found in the last DNR survey. Anglers will also find some good-sized largemouth bass in Gegoka.

For walleyes, work the long point on the lake's south shore near the boat access and at the mouth of the channel on the opposite shore. There is a rock pile in this area that can often yield a walleye or two.

Flathorn offers decent fishing for northern pike, walleyes and panfish. Northern pike do well here. They are found in about average numbers and about average size. Walleyes are few and far between. A small population maintains itself through natural reproduction. Although you won't find a lot of walleyes here, the ones you do find are typically large. Yellow perch numbers are good, and although most are small, there are some larger ones within the population. Bluegill numbers appear to be expanding. They are likely swimming in from neighboring Gegoka Lake.

There are plenty of weedy areas to cast for northern pike in this shallow lake. Walleyes will be a bit tougher to find, but they may strike crankbaits or other lures intended for pike. Small worm chunks will tempt both bluegills and perch.

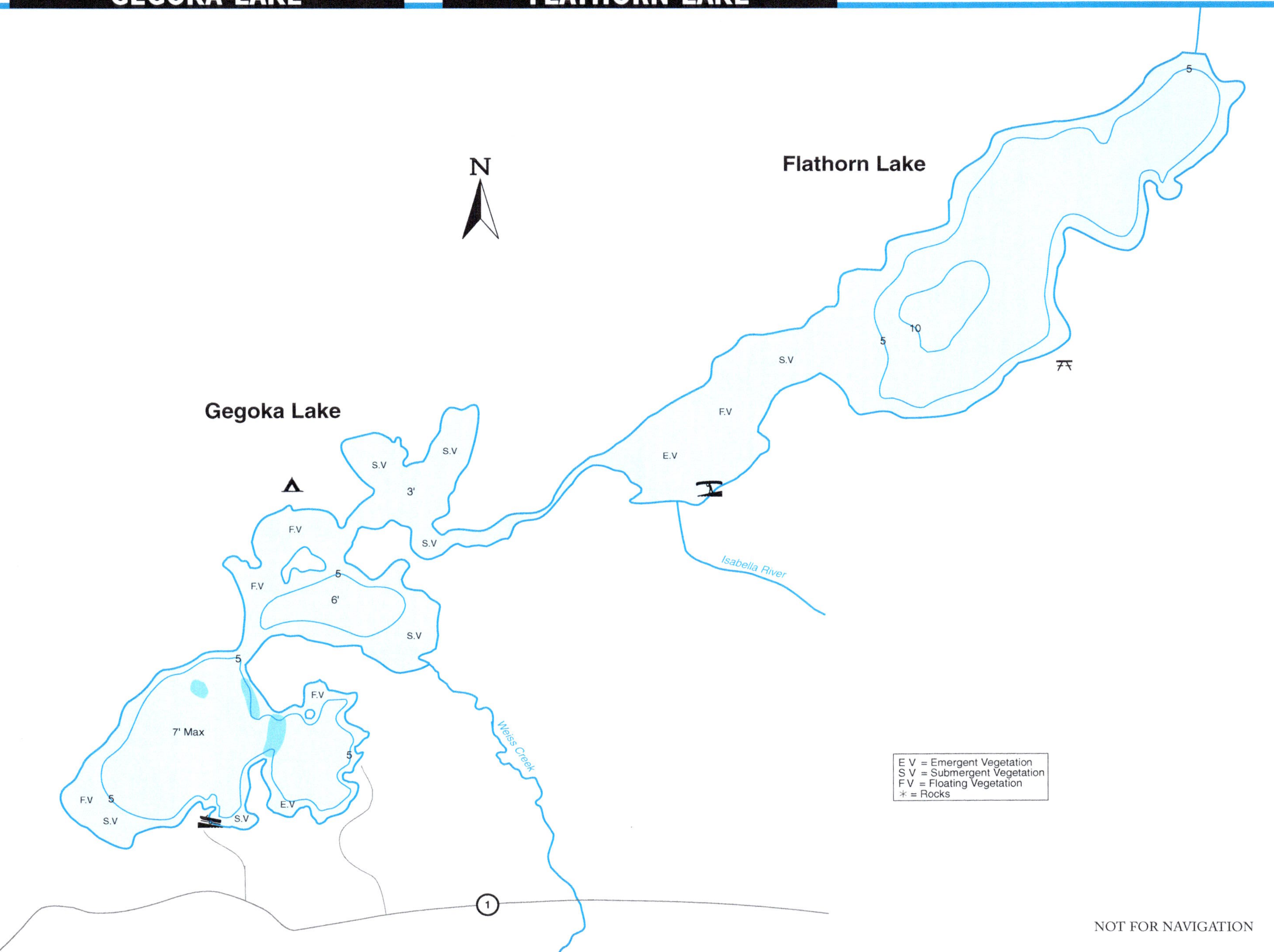

Source: Minnesota Department of Natural Resources, USGS

INGA LAKE
Lake County

GROUSE LAKE
Lake County

Area map pg / coord: 23 / B-5

Watershed: Rainy headwaters

Surface area: 41 acres

Shorelength: 1.0 mile

Max / mean depth: 6 feet / 5 feet

Water color / clarity: Brown / 4.0 ft. secchi (2006)

Shoreland zoning class: Nat. envt.

Mgmt class / Ecological type: Northern pike / northern pike-sucker

Accessibility: Carry-down access from FR 177 to logging road. Carry-down access at Inga Creek north of lake.

91° 26' 4" W / 47° 42' 36" N

Accommodations: None

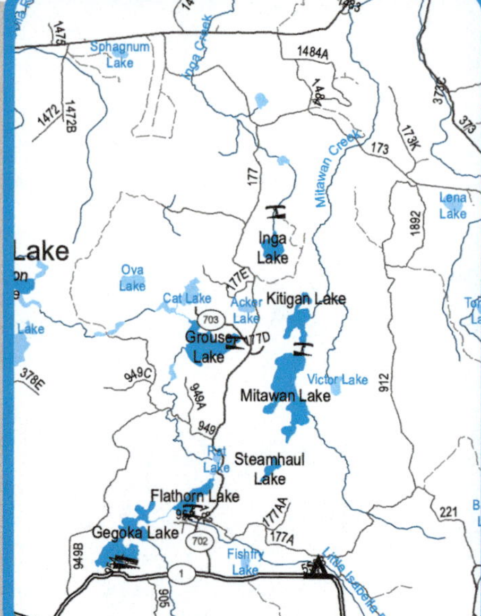

Area map pg / coord: 23 / B-5

Watershed: Rainy headwaters

Surface area: 119 acres

Shorelength: 2.7 miles

Max / mean depth: 11 feet / NA

Water color / clarity: Brown / 7.5 ft. secchi (2008)

Shoreland zoning class: Rec. dev.

Mgmt class / Ecological type: Walleye / soft-water walleye

Accessibility: Carry-down access from Grouse Lake Road to east shore

91° 26' 42" W / 47° 41' 14" N

Accommodations: None

NO RECORD OF STOCKING

NET CATCH DATA

Date: 06/27/2006	Gill Nets		Trap Nets	
species	# per net	avg. fish weight (lbs.)	# per net	avg. fish weight (lbs.)
Common Shiner	0.5	0.04	-	-
Northern Pike	14.5	2.55	-	-
Yellow Perch	1.0	0.08	-	-

LENGTH OF SELECTED SPECIES SAMPLED FROM ALL GEAR

Number of fish caught for the following length categories (inches):

species	0-5	6-8	9-11	12-14	15-19	20-24	25-29	>29	Total
Common Shiner	1	-	-	-	-	-	-	-	1
Northern Pike	-	-	-	3	2	20	4	-	29
Yellow Perch	-	2	-	-	-	-	-	-	2

NO RECORD OF STOCKING

NET CATCH DATA

Date: 07/28/2008	Gill Nets		Trap Nets	
species	# per net	avg. fish weight (lbs.)	# per net	avg. fish weight (lbs.)
Black Crappie	0.5	0.31	1.2	0.47
Bluegill	0.2	0.12	1.9	0.26
Northern Pike	4.2	2.01	1.4	1.59
Pumpkinseed Sunfish	-	-	1.3	0.14
Rock Bass	0.2	0.17	0.2	0.08
Walleye	5.2	1.0	0.8	1.98
White Sucker	19.2	1.66	2.7	2.33
Yellow Perch	6.3	0.11	1.6	0.09

LENGTH OF SELECTED SPECIES SAMPLED FROM ALL GEAR

Number of fish caught for the following length categories (inches):

species	0-5	6-8	9-11	12-14	15-19	20-24	25-29	>29	Total
Black Crappie	4	4	4	2	-	-	-	-	14
Bluegill	10	7	1	-	-	-	-	-	18
Northern Pike	-	-	-	1	13	21	3	-	38
Pumpkin. Sunfish	9	2	-	-	-	-	-	-	11
Rock Bass	2	1	-	-	-	-	-	-	3
Walleye	-	5	9	11	11	2	-	-	38
Yellow Perch	36	15	-	-	-	-	-	-	52

FISHING INFORMATION

These are two little lakes in the middle of nowhere north of Isabella. They are lightly fished and each offers something of interest to the angler.

Inga Lake is a northern pike and yellow perch fishery, and since locals typically aren't heavily into pike fishing, you may have this little lake to yourself. The pike population is quite high, and yet size is pretty good, with fish averaging around the 22- to 25-inch mark.

At 41 acres and with a maximum depth of 6 feet, finding fish shouldn't be too hard. Keep a spinner, spoon, crankbait - just about anything - above the weeds and you'll encounter some pike.

The folks at the Knotted Pine Inn & Tavern, 9702 Hwy. 1, Isabella, MN 55607, (218) 323-7681, say **Grouse Lake** is known mainly for its walleyes. Walleye numbers in Grouse are pretty good. You'll find a mix of both eaters and small fish here. The lake also offers good fishing for moderate-sized northern pike and large panfish. Although crappie numbers are low, they run nice, with some crappies topping 12 inches here. Bluegill numbers are a little higher than crappies, and there are some decent-sized fish here as well. Yellow perch tend to run pretty small. There are also some largemouth bass here and a lone smallmouth showed up for the first time in the last DNR survey. Size for both bass species is pretty good.

Grouse Lake is shallow and doesn't contain a lot of structure. There are plenty of weeds, however, and this is the place to find fish. In the spring, anglers can find good action for walleyes and perch around the Little Isabella River inlet on the west shore. Any developing weedbeds also deserve your attention. Later, work a shallow-running crankbait, spoon or spinner around the emergent weedbed near the lake's center. The narrows near the boat access might be worth a try as well, as fish would be concentrated here. The 10-foot-deep "hole" just south of the river inlet on the west shore also offers some possibilities for mid-summer fishing. It might also be worth a look for some of the lake's big crappies in winter. Due to the lake's shallow nature, you might just have to resort to casting or trolling crankbaits down the center of the lake until you find some walleyes.

NOT FOR NAVIGATION

Source: Minnesota Department of Natural Resources, USGS

KITIGAN LAKE

Lake County

Area map pg / coord: 23 / B-5

Watershed: Rainy headwaters

Surface area: 69 acres

Shorelength: 2.6 miles

Max / mean depth: 8 feet / 4 feet

Water color / clarity: Clear / NA

Shoreland zoning class: Rec. dev.

Mgmt class / Ecological type: Walleye / northern pike-sucker

Accessibility: Carry-down off FR 177 (Mitawan Lake Road) at culvert between Mitawan and Kitigan Lakes

91° 25' 37" W / 47° 41' 9" N

Accommodations: None

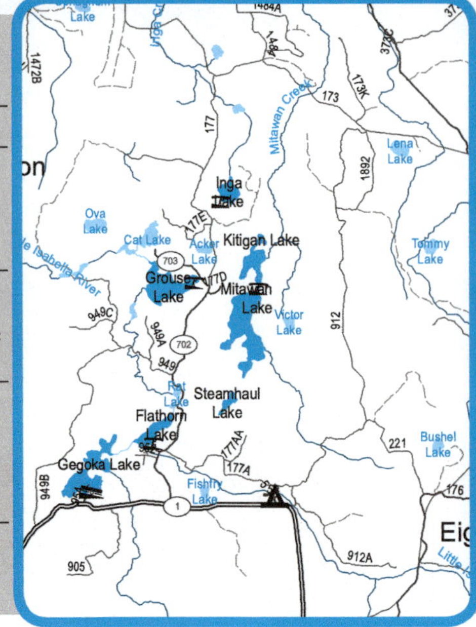

MITAWAN LAKE

Lake County

Area map pg / coord: 23 / B-5

Watershed: Rainy headwaters

Surface area: 185 acres

Shorelength: 4.3 miles

Max / mean depth: 24 feet / 13 feet

Water color / clarity: Clear / 15.0 ft. secchi (2002)

Shoreland zoning class: Rec. dev.

Mgmt class / Ecological type: Walleye / northern pike-sucker

Accessibility: Carry-down off FR 177 (Mitawan Lake Road) at culvert between Mitawan and Kitigan Lakes

91° 25' 37" W / 47° 41' 9" N

Accommodations: None

Kitigan Lake

NO RECORD OF STOCKING

NET CATCH DATA

Date: 08/16/2004	Gill Nets		Trap Nets	
species	# per net	avg. fish weight (lbs.)	# per net	avg. fish weight (lbs.)
Bluegill	2.7	0.36	9.0	0.42
Largemouth Bass	2.0	1.50	0.3	0.13
Northern Pike	7.7	3.10	0.3	2.49
Rock Bass	0.3	0.34	1.3	0.22
Smallmouth Bass	0.3	1.77	-	-
Walleye	2.7	1.92	0.8	0.63
White Sucker	1.3	ND	0.5	0.83
Yellow Perch	24.3	0.17	1.2	0.19

LENGTH OF SELECTED SPECIES SAMPLED FROM ALL GEAR

Number of fish caught for the following length categories (inches):

species	0-5	6-8	9-11	12-14	15-19	20-24	25-29	>29	Total
Bluegill	5	53	4	-	-	-	-	-	62
Largemouth Bass	1	1	2	2	2	-	-	-	8
Northern Pike	-	-	-	1	5	14	3	2	25
Rock Bass	3	6	-	-	-	-	-	-	9
Smallmouth Bass	-	-	-	1	-	-	-	-	1
Walleye	-	2	1	2	7	1	-	-	13
Yellow Perch	3	66	10	-	-	-	-	-	79

Mitawan Lake

NO RECORD OF STOCKING

NET CATCH DATA

Date: 08/06/2002	Gill Nets		Trap Nets	
species	# per net	avg. fish weight (lbs.)	# per net	avg. fish weight (lbs.)
Bluegill	-	-	0.8	0.39
Largemouth Bass	0.2	0.18	0.2	0.02
Northern Pike	2.3	2.92	0.4	2.86
Rock Bass	0.7	0.17	1.2	0.21
Smallmouth Bass	1.3	2.19	0.4	0.11
Walleye	7.3	1.98	1.7	1.39
White Sucker	14.0	1.99	1.0	3.11
Yellow Perch	4.2	0.15	0.6	0.09

LENGTH OF SELECTED SPECIES SAMPLED FROM ALL GEAR

Number of fish caught for the following length categories (inches):

species	0-5	6-8	9-11	12-14	15-19	20-24	25-29	>29	Total
Bluegill	2	4	1	-	-	-	-	-	7
Largemouth Bass	2	1	-	-	-	-	-	-	3
Northern Pike	-	-	2	-	2	9	3	2	18
Rock Bass	9	5	1	-	-	-	-	-	15
Smallmouth Bass	4	1	-	2	5	-	-	-	12
Walleye	-	5	8	11	19	13	3	-	59
Yellow Perch	6	23	1	-	-	-	-	-	30

FISHING INFORMATION

These two northern Minnesota lakes contain a typical Arrowhead fishery of northern pike, walleyes, smallmouth and largemouth bass and some panfish.

Kitigan has a good walleye population with a nice overall average size. Pike numbers are high and the average size is fairly high, with some fish topping 10 pounds. You'll also find some large bluegills here. There are lots of perch, although most are below keeper size. Both largemouth and smallmouth bass inhabit Kitigan Lake.

The rock pile next to the larger island is worth a look for walleyes. Any of the weedy areas should hold largemouth bass and northern pike. Check the weed edges for bluegills and perch.

The larger of the two lakes, **Mitawan** also has an unimproved, carry-down access on its north shore. The folks at the Knotted Pine Inn & Tavern, 9702 Highway 1, Isabella, MN 55607, (218) 323-7681, say the lake has a nice population of gamefish and some panfish opportunities as well. Walleye numbers are good and their size is pretty big. Northern pike have a high average size here as well. You'll also find some nice bluegills, largemouth bass and smallmouth bass. Overall, it's got some pretty good fishing and the rough access really limits fishing pressure.

For walleyes, try off the point on the lake's south shore. The steeply dropping east shoreline is also worth a look, as is the small point and rock pile off the lake's northwest shore.

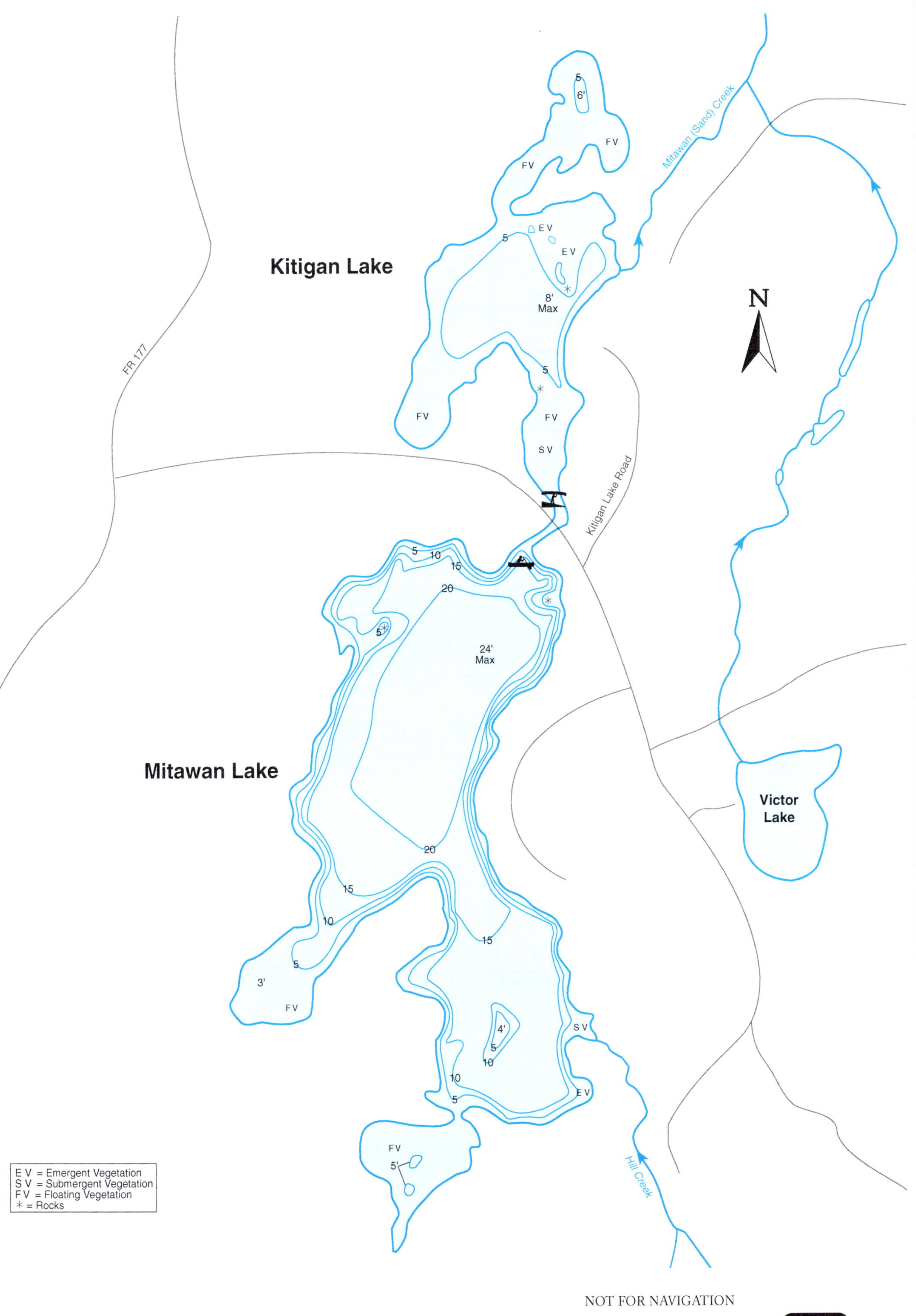

Source: Minnesota Department of Natural Resources, USGS

Eighteen Lake, Lake County

Area map page / coordinates: 23 / C-6
Surface area / max depth: 102 acres / 12 feet
Accessibility: Carry-down access to east shore off FR 369

FISH STOCKING DATA

year	species	size	# released
12	Walleye	Fingerling	5,564
14	Walleye	Fingerling	5,640
14	Walleye	Adult	19
14	Walleye	Fingerling	5,143

LENGTH OF SELECTED SPECIES SAMPLED FROM ALL GEAR
Survey Date: 07/27/2009
Number of fish caught for the following length categories (inches):

species	0-5	6-8	9-11	12-14	15-19	20-24	25-29	>30	Total
Walleye	-	5	1	26	13	2	-	-	47
Yellow Perch	11	21	2	-	-	-	-	-	34

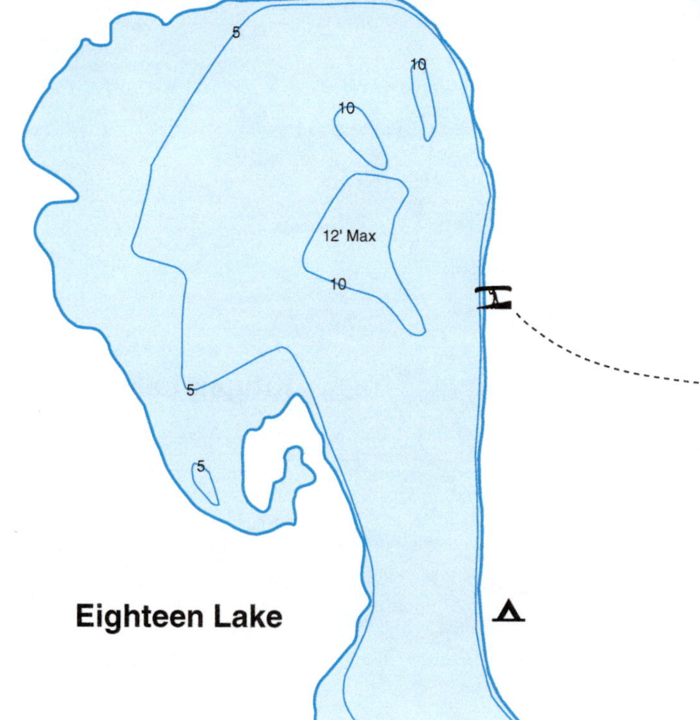

Delay Lake

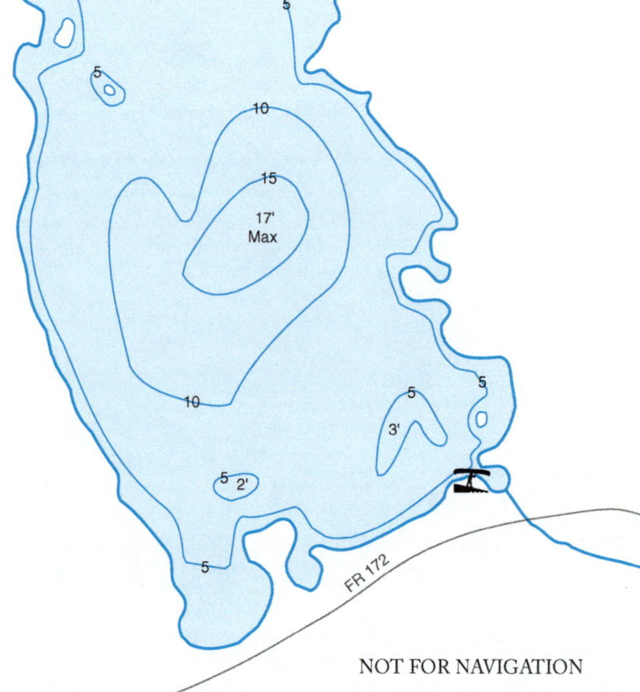

Delay Lake, Lake County

Area map page / coordinates: 23 / C-6
Surface area / max depth: 104 acres / 17 feet
Accessibility: Carry-down access to southeast corner near outlet off FR 172

FISH STOCKING DATA

year	species	size	# released
08	Walleye	Fingerling	1,663
09	Walleye	Fingerling	2,443
12	Walleye	Fingerling	3,190
13	Walleye	Fingerling	3,140

LENGTH OF SELECTED SPECIES SAMPLED FROM ALL GEAR
Survey Date: 08/05/2008
Number of fish caught for the following length categories (inches):

species	0-5	6-8	9-11	12-14	15-19	20-24	25-29	>30	Total
Northern Pike	-	-	-	-	1	1	6	3	11
Rock Bass	5	4	-	-	-	-	-	-	9
Smallmouth Bass	-	8	11	3	4	-	-	-	26
Walleye	-	3	5	13	10	13	-	-	44
Yellow Perch	1	21	7	-	-	-	-	-	29

Source: Minnesota Department of Natural Resources, USGS

Spear Lake, Lake County

Area map page / coordinates: 23 / C-6
Surface area / max depth: 8 acres / 4 feet
Accessibility: Carry-down access; from FR 369, go east about 0.5 mile, then south about 200 yards to lake

NO RECORD OF STOCKING

LENGTH OF SELECTED SPECIES SAMPLED FROM ALL GEAR
Survey Date: 06/27/1990
Number of fish caught for the following length categories (inches):

species	0-5	6-8	9-11	12-14	15-19	20-24	25-29	>30	Total
Yellow Perch	3	20	-	-	-	-	-	-	23
Brook Trout	-	4	1	-	-	-	-	-	5

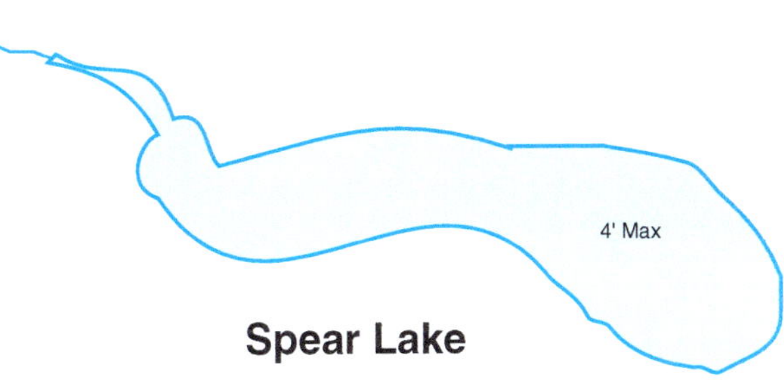

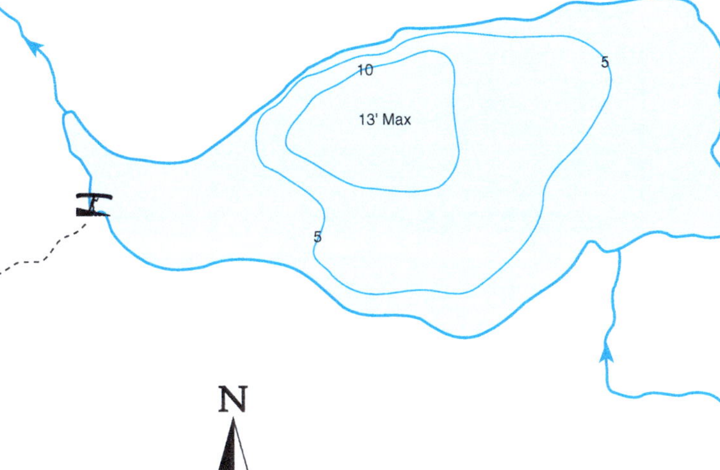

Trappers Lake, Lake County

Area map page / coordinates: 23 / C-6
Surface area / max depth: 19 acres / 13 feet
Accessibility: Carry-down access (0.25-mile portage) from FR 369 to the west shore

FISH STOCKING DATA

year	species	size	# released
01	Brook Trout	Fingerling	1,504
03	Brook Trout	Fingerling	1,499
05	Brook Trout	Fingerling	1,500
07	Brook Trout	Fingerling	1,500

LENGTH OF SELECTED SPECIES SAMPLED FROM ALL GEAR
Survey Date: 06/24/2008
Number of fish caught for the following length categories (inches):

species	0-5	6-8	9-11	12-14	15-19	20-24	25-29	>30	Total
Brook Trout	1	8	9	-	-	-	-	-	18

Weapon Lake, Lake County

Area map page / coordinates: 23 / C-6
Surface area / max depth: 7 acres / 4 feet
Accessibility: Carry-down access (0.4-mile portage) east of FR 369 near Trappers Creek

NO RECORD OF STOCKING

LENGTH OF SELECTED SPECIES SAMPLED FROM ALL GEAR
Survey Date: 07/15/2013
Number of fish caught for the following length categories (inches):

species	0-5	6-8	9-11	12-14	15-19	20-24	25-29	>30	Total
White Sucker	-	6	6	-	-	-	-	-	12

NOT FOR NAVIGATION

DUMBBELL LAKE *Lake County*

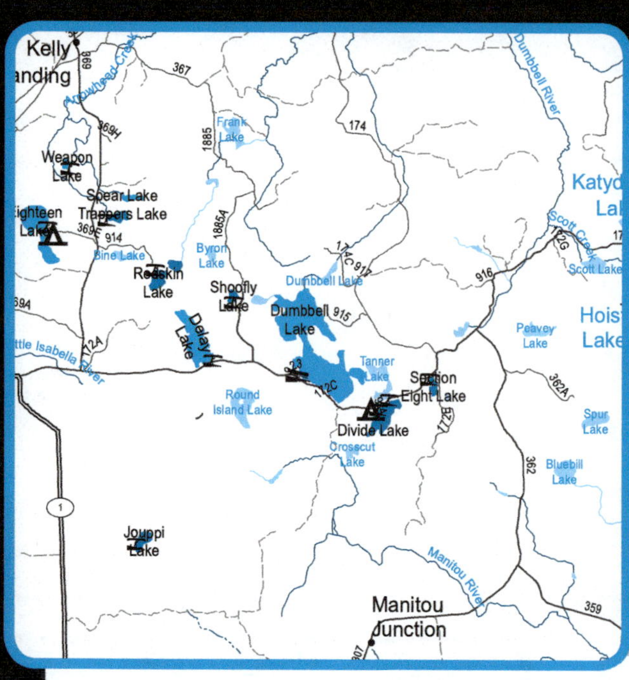

Area map page / coordinates: 24 / C-1

Watershed: Rainy headwaters

Surface water area / shorelength: 406 acres / 7.5 miles

Maximum / mean depth: 40 feet / 18 feet

Water color / clarity: Light green / 9.0-ft. secchi (2009)

Shoreland zoning classification: Recreational development

Management class / Ecological type: Walleye /soft-water walley

Accessibility: USFS-owned public access with concrete ramp on west shore off USFS Rd. 172

91° 16' 37" W / 47° 37' 0" N

Accommodations: Airplane dock, fishing pier, picnicking, camping, restrooms

FISHING INFORMATION

The Arrowhead region of Minnesota is chiefly known for its walleyes, northern pike and smallmouth bass, but as the old saying goes, there are exceptions to every rule.

Years ago, the DNR stocked muskies in Dumbbell Lake. The Arrowhead has very few muskie lakes, and none of them contain native populations. Dumbbell's muskies feasted on the lake's walleyes, perch and smallmouth bass and are now thriving. According to the folks at Muskie Doom Guide Service, (218) 491-3277, muskiedoom.com, you won't find a lake anywhere with the sheer number of muskies this lake contains. It's not uncommon to have 15 to 30 follows a day. The downside is muskies are small here. You'll find a lot of fish in the 28- to 34-inch range. A 40-incher is a monster by Dumbbell standards. The folks at Muskie Doom say because these fish run small, downsize your lures. A number 4 or 5 spinner is perfect medicine for Dumbbell muskies. Due to the number of muskies you will encounter in a day of fishing, it's a great place to go if you're an aspiring muskie angler. You'll get plenty of practice doing Figure 8s. However, the high muskie population may spoil you. Try fishing muskies here on a sunny day when you have the best chance of seeing follows.

Walleye numbers are very high on Dumbbell, but most of them are small. There are plenty of rock reefs that hold walleyes. A jig or Lindy rig with live bait will catch fish. You'll probably have to sort through a lot of smaller fish to get some keepers.

You'll find lots of smallmouth bass in Dumbbell, but these fish are generally of the 6- to 8-inch variety. They are often a nuisance to walleye anglers fishing with leeches or nightcrawlers.

Yellow perch numbers are high, but most tend to be small. These fish serve as great muskie forage.

The lake is loaded with structure and you could find a muskie almost anywhere, holding in weeds or on rocks. These rocks are the places to find smallmouth and walleyes as well.

FISH STOCKING DATA

year	species	size	# released
07	Walleye	Fry	250,000
08	Walleye	Fry	550,000
10	Brook Trout	Fingerling	2,867
11	Walleye	Fry	500,000
12	Walleye	Fry	500,000
15	Walleye	Fry	500,000

NET CATCH DATA

Date: 08/10/2009

	Gill Nets		Trap Nets	
species	# per net	avg. fish weight (lbs.)	# per net	avg. fish weight (lbs.
Muskellunge	1.8	5.96	0.3	5.87
Rock Bass	7.6	0.20	2.7	0.13
Smallmouth Bass	1.0	0.16	0.4	0.13
Walleye	16.1	0.61	-	-
White Sucker	0.8	0.60	0.2	0.74
Yellow Perch	9.0	0.11	1.1	0.11

LENGTH OF SELECTED SPECIES SAMPLED FROM ALL GEAR

Number of fish caught for the following length categories (inches):

species	0-5	6-8	9-11	12-14	15-19	20-24	25-29	>30	Total
Muskellunge	-	-	-	-	1	-	7	10	18
Rock Bass	47	38	-	-	-	-	-	-	85
Smallmouth Bass	4	8	-	-	-	-	-	-	12
Walleye	-	20	76	20	9	3	1	-	129
Yellow Perch	43	39	-	-	-	-	-	-	82

One good spot is located just to the left of the boat access. Three finger converge just south of the lake's center, and these should all be worked fo smallies and walleyes. The one jutting out from the east shore deserve the most attention. Any humps are worth a look as well, as are the side of the rock islands.

Boaters need to be extremely careful when navigating on Dumbbel Rocks thrust up everywhere. Even when you think you're safe in 40 fee of water on the south end, you'll suddenly find a rock reef jutting up to 5 feet! Many of these hazards are not marked. Go slowly until you learn the lake a little and stick to your tracklines when cruising.

The lake has some very nice campsites and receives relatively littl fishing pressure.

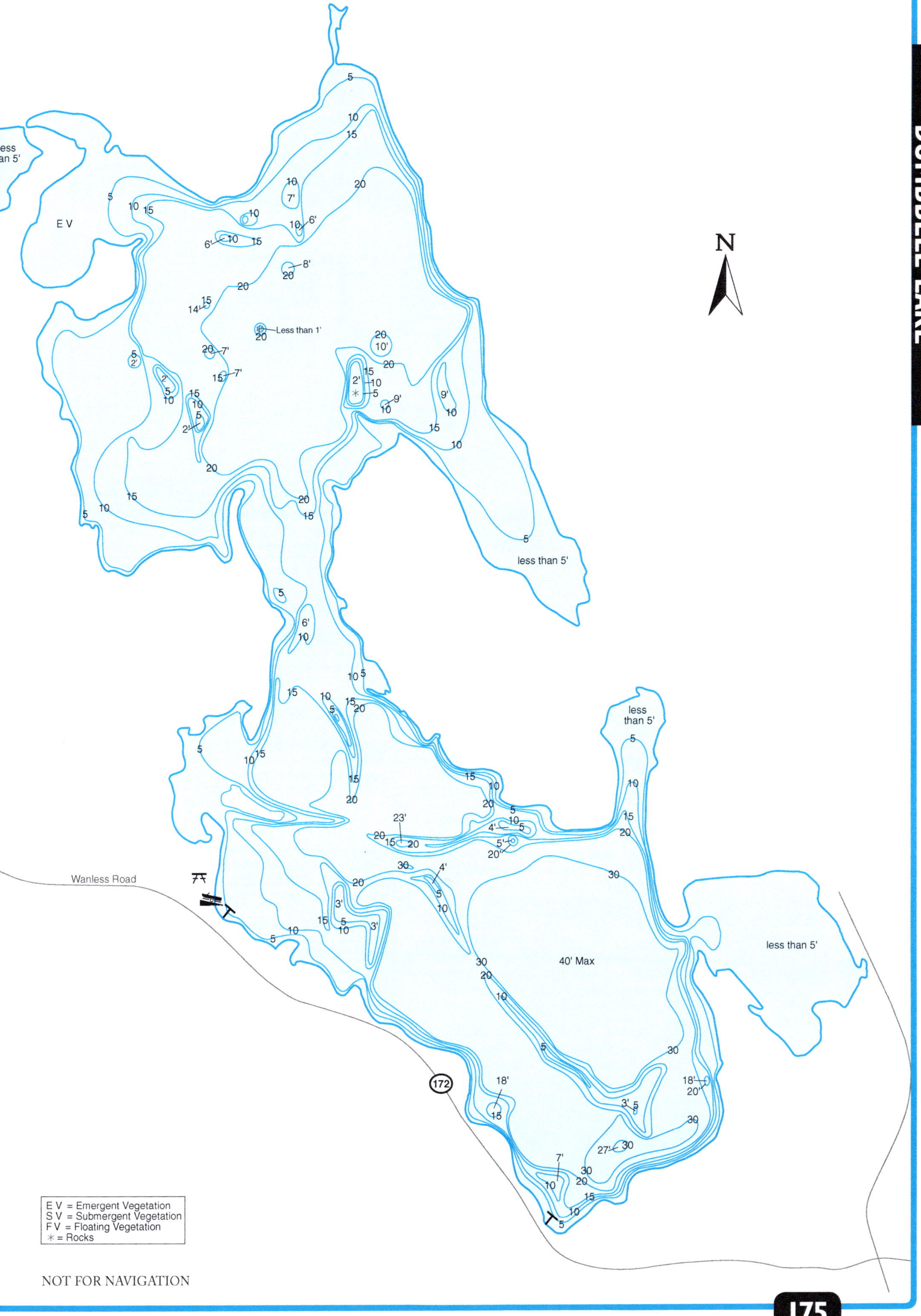

Source: Minnesota Department of Natural Resources, USGS

JOUPPI LAKE
Lake County

DIVIDE LAKE
Lake County

SECTION 8 LAKE
Lake County

	JOUPPI	DIVIDE	SECTION 8
Area map pg / coord:	23 / D-6	24 / C,D-1	24 / C-1
Watershed:	Baptism-Brule	Baptism-Brule	Baptism-Brule
Surface area:	6 acres	61 acres	5 acres
Shorelength:	0.5 mile	1.8 miles	0.4 mile
Max / mean depth:	19 ft. / NA	22 ft. / 14 ft.	24 ft. / NA
Water color / clarity:	Brown stain / 4.4 ft. secchi (2010)	Clear / 11.7 ft. secchi (2011)	Clear / 10.9 ft. secchi (2009)
Shoreland zoning class:	NA	Nat. envt.	Nat. envt.
Management class:	NA	Stream trout	NA
Ecological type:	NA	Unclassified	NA
Accessibility:	Carry-down from logging road to west shore of lake	Carry-down access at campground on north shore off FR 172	Carry-down access via 200-foot trail across bog to north shore
Accommodations:	None	Camping, restrooms	None

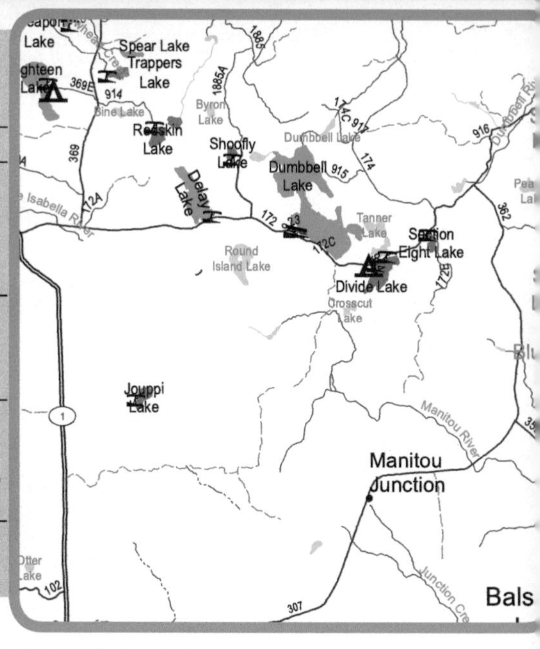

Jouppi Lake

FISH STOCKING DATA

year	species	size	# released
07	Brook Trout	Fingerling	1,250
09	Brook Trout	Yearling	499
10	Brook Trout	Yearling	500
11	Brook Trout	Yearling	500
12	Brook Trout	Yearling	500
13	Brook Trout	Yearling	500
14	Brook Trout	Yearling	500
15	Brook Trout	Yearling	500

LENGTH OF SELECTED SPECIES SAMPLED FROM ALL GEAR

NOT AVAILABLE

Divide Lake

FISH STOCKING DATA

year	species	size	# released
10	Rainbow Trout	Yearling	2,004
10	Splake	Fingerling	4,003
11	Rainbow Trout	Yearling	1,984
11	Splake	Fingerling	3,010
12	Rainbow Trout	Yearling	1,965
12	Splake	Fingerling	2,998
13	Rainbow Trout	Yearling	2,019
13	Splake	Fingerling	2,535
14	Rainbow Trout	Yearling	1,999
14	Splake	Fingerling	2,900
15	Rainbow Trout	Yearling	1,995
15	Splake	Fingerling	3,000

LENGTH OF SELECTED SPECIES SAMPLED FROM ALL GEAR

Survey Date: 06/13/2011

Number of fish caught for the following length categories (inches):

species	0-5	6-8	9-11	12-14	15-19	20-24	25-29	>29	Total
Rainbow Trout	-	12	23	2	-	-	-	-	37
Splake	1	46	13	29	6	-	-	-	95

Section 8 Lake

FISH STOCKING DATA

year	species	size	# released
10	Brook Trout	Yearling	150
11	Brook Trout	Yearling	150
12	Brook Trout	Yearling	165
13	Brook Trout	Yearling	149
14	Brook Trout	Yearling	300
15	Brook Trout	Yearling	298

LENGTH OF SELECTED SPECIES SAMPLED FROM ALL GEAR

Survey Date: 09/29/2009

Number of fish caught for the following length categories (inches):

species	0-5	6-8	9-11	12-14	15-19	20-24	25-29	>29	Total
Brook Trout	-	-	7	4	-	-	-	-	11

FISHING INFORMATION

These three Isabella-area lakes are designated trout lakes.

Divide is the largest of the three lakes. The folks at the Knotted Pine Inn & Tavern, 9702 Highway 1, Isabella, MN 55607, (218) 323-7681, say you'll find pretty decent rainbow trout in these 61 acres of clear water. Divide Lake is one of the more popular trout lakes in the area because the DNR stocks both rainbow trout and splake in it on an annual basis. Still, you'll find plenty of fish to go around. Most of the trout you'll catch average around 10 inches, although some larger specimens do turn up once in a while. The access is carry down and there is a U.S. Forest Service campground with three campsites, restroom facilities and a pump with fresh water. A separate parking area is located further down FR 172.

At only 6 acres, **Jouppi** is much tinier than Divide. Jouppi is stocked with about 500 yearling brook trout on an annual basis. For only 6 acres that's . . . well, you do the math. It should be noted that this small bog lake has low oxygen levels in the deeper areas. So how does a cold-water fish like a brook trout survive? Al Anderson of Finland Area Fisheries, 6686 Hwy 1 Box 546, Finland, MN 55603, says these fish seek shade under the floating bog around the edges of the lake. Fishing deep water and the bottom is usually a waste of time. Try a worm suspended below a bobber. Most brookies average around 9 inches, with some 12-inchers caught on occasion.

Section 8 Lake is stocked with yearling brook trout on an annual basis. The lake is close to the road, so it gets some decent fishing pressure. A recent survey found these fish to average 11 inches, with fish up to 14 inches a possibility. The lake does winterkill occasionally, but it is simply restocked the following year. The lake's brookies will hit a variety of presentations, including worms, spinners and tiny crankbaits. For some real fun, try casting for them with dry flies.

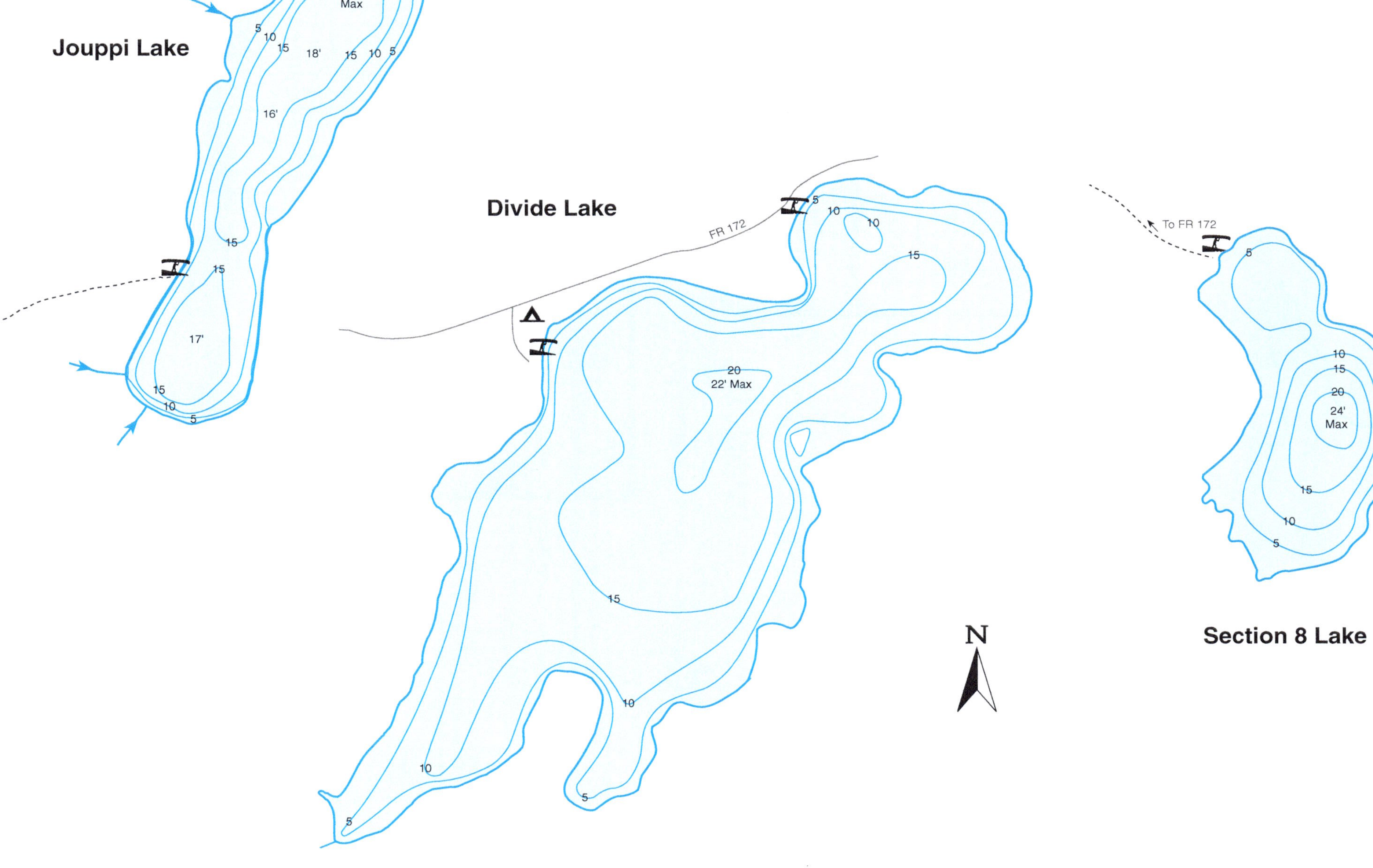

Source: Minnesota Department of Natural Resources, USGS

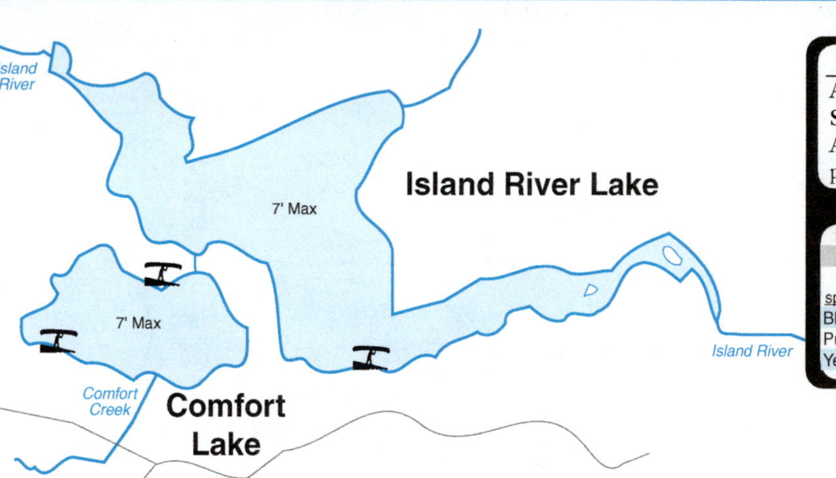

Island River Lake, Lake County

Area map page / coordinates: 16 / E-1
Surface area / max depth: 81 acres / 7 feet
Accessibility: Carry-down access from end of FR 913; portage from Comfort Lake

NO RECORD OF STOCKING

LENGTH OF SELECTED SPECIES SAMPLED FROM ALL GEAR
Survey Date: 08/31/2009
Number of fish caught for the following length categories (inches):

species	0-5	6-8	9-11	12-14	15-19	20-24	25-29	>30	Total
Black Crappie	-	1	6	9	-	-	-	-	17
Pumpkin. Sunfish	-	1	-	1	-	-	-	-	2
Yellow Perch	11	33	3	-	-	-	-	-	47

Comfort Lake, Lake County

Area map page / coordinates: 16 / E-1
Surface area / max depth: 38 acres / 7 feet
Accessibility: Portage access from FR 913 to southwest shore

NO RECORD OF STOCKING

LENGTH OF SELECTED SPECIES SAMPLED FROM ALL GEAR
Survey Date: 07/09/1984
Number of fish caught for the following length categories (inches):

species	0-5	6-8	9-11	12-14	15-19	20-24	25-29	>30	Total
Northern Pike	-	-	4	7	4	-	-	-	15
Walleye	-	3	-	2	-	-	-	-	5
Yellow Perch	3	20	1	-	-	-	-	-	24

Section 29 Lake, Lake County

Area map page / coordinates: 24 / A-1
Surface area / max depth: 97 acres / 20 feet
Accessibility: USFS-owned public access with gravel ramp on southeast shore of north basin, 0.2 mile off FR 356
91° 14' 22" W / 47° 44' 30" N

FISH STOCKING DATA

year	species	size	# released
08	Walleye	Yearling	4
08	Walleye	Fingerling	5,680
10	Walleye	Adult	67
10	Walleye	Fingerling	6,384
12	Walleye	Fingerling	4,176
14	Walleye	Fingerling	1,920
14	Walleye	Fingerling	3,739

LENGTH OF SELECTED SPECIES SAMPLED FROM ALL GEAR
Survey Date: 07/23/2012
Number of fish caught for the following length categories (inches):

species	0-5	6-8	9-11	12-14	15-19	20-24	25-29	>30	Total
Northern Pike	-	-	3	3	11	9	1	-	27
Pumpkinseed	19	-	-	-	-	-	-	-	19
Walleye	-	-	10	5	9	-	-	-	24
Yellow Perch	12	14	-	-	-	-	-	-	26

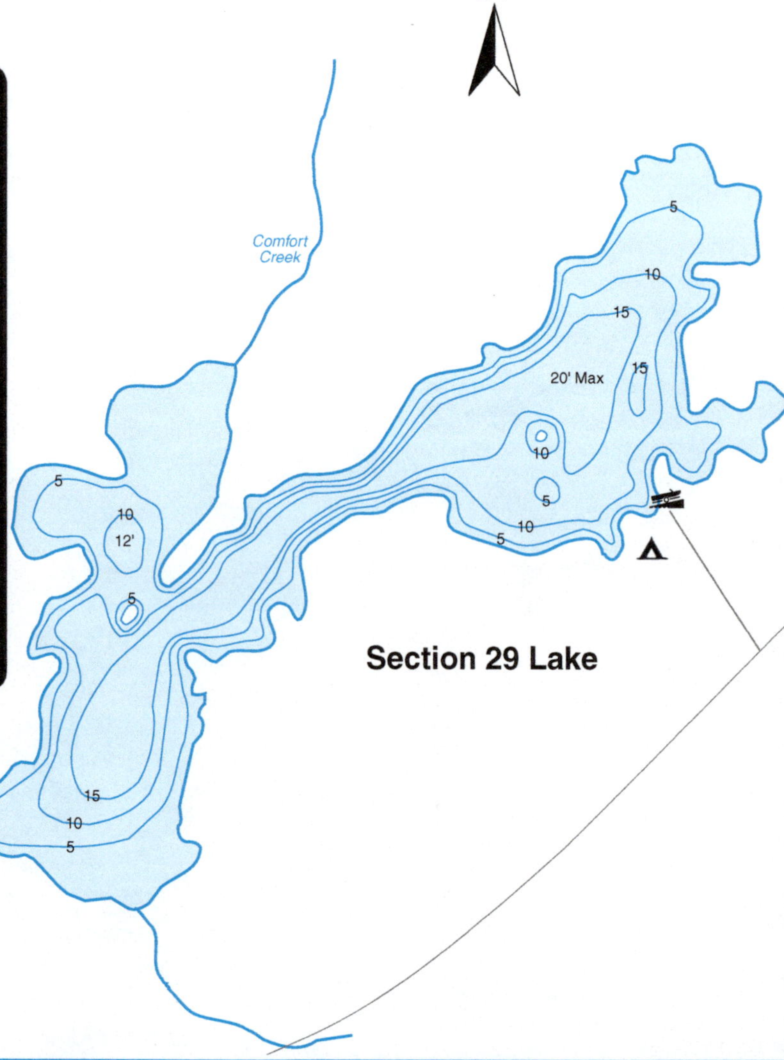

NOT FOR NAVIGATION

Source: Minnesota Department of Natural Resources, USGS

Bunny Lake, Lake County

Area map page / coordinates: 24 / A-1
Surface area / max depth: 39 acres / 6 feet
Accessibility: Portage from Sylvania Lake to south shore

NO RECORD OF STOCKING

LENGTH OF SELECTED SPECIES SAMPLED FROM ALL GEAR
Survey Date: 07/09/2012
Number of fish caught for the following length categories (inches):

species	0-5	6-8	9-11	12-14	15-19	20-24	25-29	>30	Total
Northern Pike	-	-	5	2	8	5	1	-	21
Yellow Perch	7	4	4	-	-	-	-	-	15

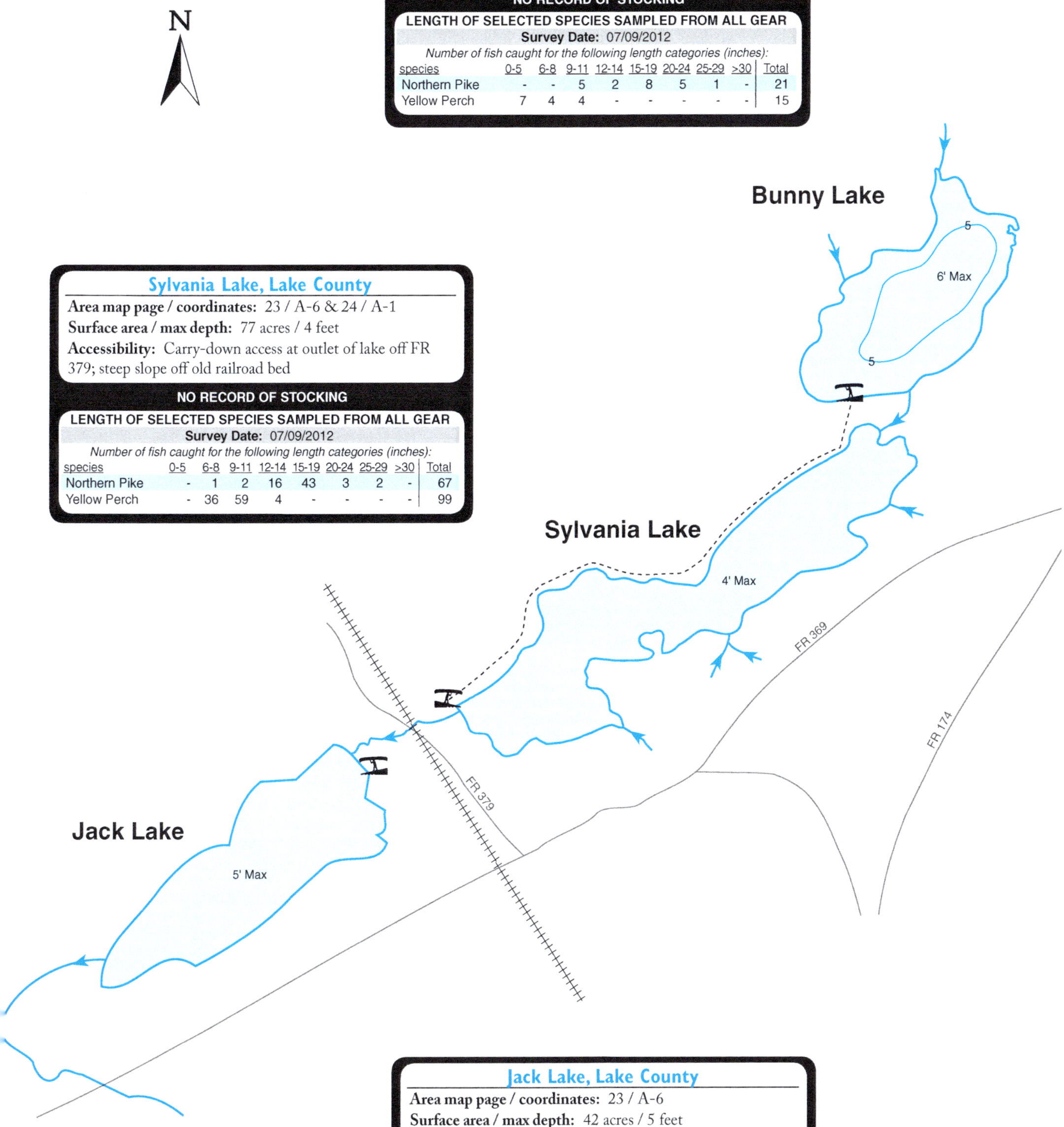

N

Bunny Lake

6' Max

5

5

Sylvania Lake, Lake County

Area map page / coordinates: 23 / A-6 & 24 / A-1
Surface area / max depth: 77 acres / 4 feet
Accessibility: Carry-down access at outlet of lake off FR 379; steep slope off old railroad bed

NO RECORD OF STOCKING

LENGTH OF SELECTED SPECIES SAMPLED FROM ALL GEAR
Survey Date: 07/09/2012
Number of fish caught for the following length categories (inches):

species	0-5	6-8	9-11	12-14	15-19	20-24	25-29	>30	Total
Northern Pike	-	1	2	16	43	3	2	-	67
Yellow Perch	-	36	59	4	-	-	-	-	99

Sylvania Lake

4' Max

FR 369

FR 174

FR 379

Jack Lake

5' Max

Jack Lake, Lake County

Area map page / coordinates: 23 / A-6
Surface area / max depth: 42 acres / 5 feet
Accessibility: Carry-down access off FR 379, downstream 700 feet to Jack Lake

NO RECORD OF STOCKING

LENGTH OF SELECTED SPECIES SAMPLED FROM ALL GEAR
Survey Date: 07/21/1997
Number of fish caught for the following length categories (inches):

species	0-5	6-8	9-11	12-14	15-19	20-24	25-29	>30	Total
Northern Pike	-	-	2	5	3	2	-	-	12
Yellow Perch	2	62	29	-	-	-	-	-	93

NOT FOR NAVIGATION

Homestead Lake, Lake County

Area map page / coordinates: 24 / C-2
Surface area / max depth: 44 acres / 7 feet
Accessibility: Carry-down via small unmarked road to the lake's east bay

FISH STOCKING DATA

year	species	size	# released
01	Muskellunge	Adult	128
03	Muskellunge	Adult	33

LENGTH OF SELECTED SPECIES SAMPLED FROM ALL GEAR
Survey Date: 07/21/2014
Number of fish caught for the following length categories (inches):

species	0-5	6-8	9-11	12-14	15-19	20-24	25-29	>30	Total
Muskellunge	-	-	-	2	3	15	6	-	26
Pumpkinseed	16	-	-	-	-	-	-	-	16
Yellow Perch	28	14	-	-	-	-	-	-	42

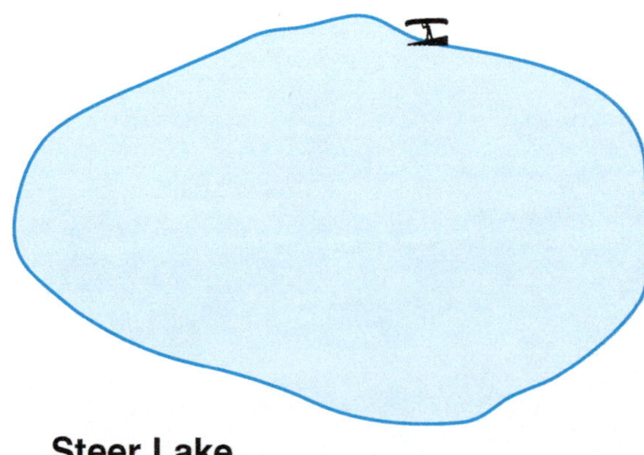

Steer Lake

Steer Lake, Lake County

Area map page / coordinates: 24 / C-2
Surface area / max depth: 4 acres / 24 feet
Accessibility: Carry-down access via marked 0.5-mile trail from Cty. Rd. 7 to north shore; also via marked 1.3 mile trail from Hogback Lake to northwest shore

FISH STOCKING DATA

year	species	size	# released
10	Brook Trout	Fingerling	1,135
11	Brook Trout	Fingerling	490
12	Brook Trout	Fingerling	500
13	Brook Trout	Fingerling	500
15	Brook Trout	Fingerling	500

LENGTH OF SELECTED SPECIES SAMPLED FROM ALL GEAR
Survey Date: 06/29/2009
Number of fish caught for the following length categories (inches):

species	0-5	6-8	9-11	12-14	15-19	20-24	25-29	>30	Total
Brook Trout	-	14	-	1	-	-	-	-	15
White Sucker	-	14	5	2	2	-	-	-	23

NOT FOR NAVIGATION

Source: Minnesota Department of Natural Resources, USGS

NOT FOR NAVIGATION

Elixir Lake, Lake County

Area map page / coordinates: 24 / C-2
Surface area / max depth: 19 acres / 8 feet
Accessibility: Carry-down access off FR 172 to east shore

NO RECORD OF STOCKING

LENGTH OF SELECTED SPECIES SAMPLED FROM ALL GEAR
Survey Date: 06/27/2001
Number of fish caught for the following length categories (inches):

species	0-5	6-8	9-11	12-14	15-19	20-24	25-29	>30	Total
Northern Pike	-	-	-	-	3	1	-	1	5
Yellow Perch	18	6	-	-	-	-	-	-	24

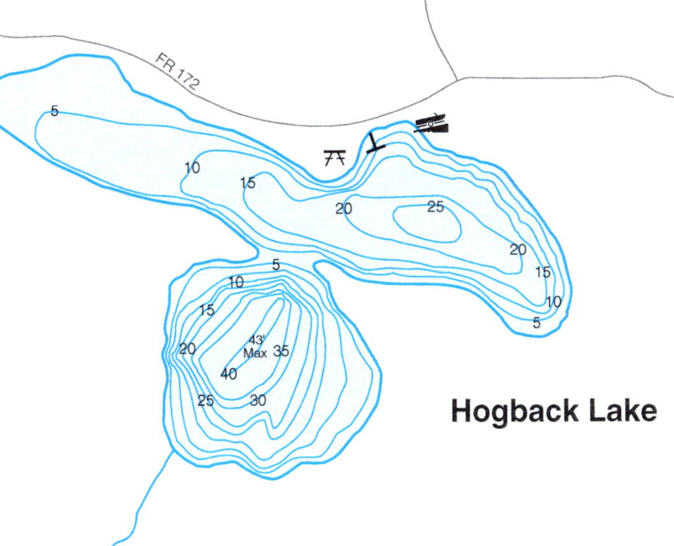

Hogback Lake, Lake County

Area map page / coordinates: 24 / C-2
Surface area / max depth: 40 acres / 43 feet
Accessibility: Public access with gravel ramp on north shore; ADA fishing pier, camping and picnic area at site

FISH STOCKING DATA

year	species	size	# released
11	Rainbow Trout	Yearling	1,013
11	Splake	Fingerling	3,995
12	Rainbow Trout	Yearling	1,002
12	Splake	Fingerling	4,011
13	Rainbow Trout	Yearling	1,001
13	Splake	Fingerling	3,507
14	Rainbow Trout	Yearling	999
14	Splake	Fingerling	3,955
15	Rainbow Trout	Yearling	1,000
15	Splake	Fingerling	3,984

LENGTH OF SELECTED SPECIES SAMPLED FROM ALL GEAR
Survey Date: 06/20/2011
Number of fish caught for the following length categories (inches):

species	0-5	6-8	9-11	12-14	15-19	20-24	25-29	>30	Total
Rainbow Trout	-	-	28	-	3	1	-	-	32
Splake	2	36	9	2	3	1	-	-	53

Scarp (Cliff) Lake, Lake County

Area map page / coordinates: 24 / C-2
Surface area / max depth: 39 acres / 15 feet
Accessibility: Portage from east shore of south basin of Hogback Lake

FISH STOCKING DATA

year	species	size	# released
11	Rainbow Trout	Yearling	1,061
12	Rainbow Trout	Yearling	1,071
13	Rainbow Trout	Yearling	1,063
14	Rainbow Trout	Yearling	1,049
15	Rainbow Trout	Yearling	1,050

LENGTH OF SELECTED SPECIES SAMPLED FROM ALL GEAR
Survey Date: 08/08/2013
Number of fish caught for the following length categories (inches):

species	0-5	6-8	9-11	12-14	15-19	20-24	25-29	>30	Total
Rainbow Trout	-	-	8	25	2	-	-	-	35

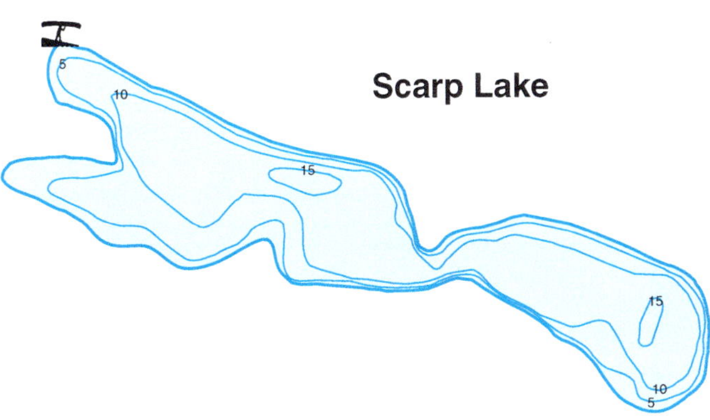

Source: Minnesota Department of Natural Resources, USGS

CROOKED LAKE

Lake County

Area map pg / coord: 24 / C,D-3
Watershed: Baptism-Brule
Surface area: 272 acres
Shorelength: 6.1 miles
Max / mean depth: 18 feet / 4 feet
Water color / clarity: Green tint / 12.0 ft. secchi (2014)
Shoreland zoning class: Rec. dev.
Mgmt class / Ecological type: Walleye / soft-water walleye
Accessibility: USFS-owned public access with concrete ramp on northwest shore of main lake, off FR 358

91° 4' 25" W / 47° 36' 33" N

Accommodations: Resort, boat rental, camping, picnicking, restrooms

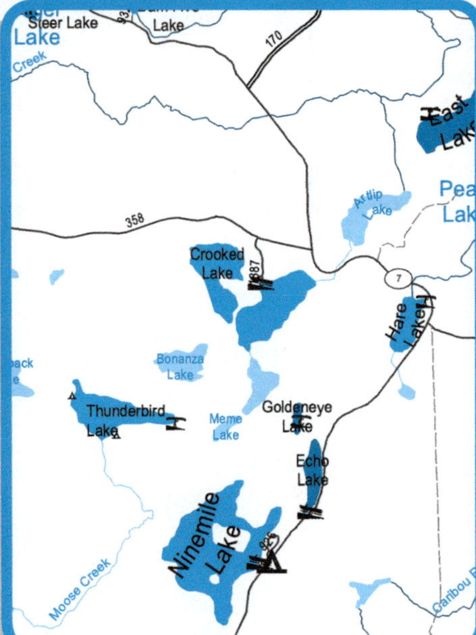

FISH STOCKING DATA			
year	species	size	# released
14	Walleye	Fingerling	5,013
14	Walleye	Fingerling	180
15	Walleye	Fingerling	2,865
15	Walleye	Adult	3

NET CATCH DATA — Date: 07/28/2014

	Gill Nets		Trap Nets	
species	# per net	avg. fish weight (lbs.)	# per net	avg. fish weight (lbs.)
Muskellunge	0.50	7.72	-	-
Northern Pike	1.17	4.20	0.44	2.05
Smallmouth Bass	5.17	0.77	6.00	0.34
Walleye	17.0	0.96	0.89	1.59
White Sucker	7.50	2.41	-	-
Yellow Perch	8.33	0.20	0.11	0.55

LENGTH OF SELECTED SPECIES SAMPLED FROM ALL GEAR

Number of fish caught for the following length categories (inches):

species	0-5	6-8	9-11	12-14	15-19	20-24	25-29	>29	Total
Muskellunge	-	-	-	-	-	-	2	1	3
Northern Pike	-	-	-	1	1	5	2	2	11
Smallmouth Bass	18	35	19	8	5	-	-	-	85
Walleye	-	7	39	29	32	3	-	-	110
White Sucker	-	1	1	4	32	7	-	-	45
Yellow Perch	10	31	10	-	-	-	-	-	51

THUNDERBIRD LAKE

Lake County

Area map pg / coord: 24 / D-2,3
Watershed: Baptism-Brule
Surface area: 97 acres
Shorelength: 2.3 miles
Max / mean depth: 18 feet / 7 feet
Water color / clarity: Brown stain / 4.5 ft. secchi (2013)
Shoreland zoning class: Nat. envt.
Mgmt class / Ecological type: Walleye / northern pike-sucker
Accessibility: Carry-in to NE corner of lake. From trailhead off Thunder Road, go NW 0.75 miles on trail to lake
Accommodations: Camping, picnicking, restrooms

FISH STOCKING DATA			
year	species	size	# released
10	Walleye	Adult	45
10	Walleye	Fingerling	3,690
13	Walleye	Fingerling	2,737

NET CATCH DATA — Date: 08/12/2013

	Gill Nets		Trap Nets	
species	# per net	avg. fish weight (lbs.)	# per net	avg. fish weight (lbs.)
Northern Pike	0.50	3.12	-	-
Pumpkinseed	0.50	0.05	-	-
Walleye	9.00	0.78	-	-
White Sucker	12.2	1.37	-	-
Yellow Perch	1.17	0.19	-	-

LENGTH OF SELECTED SPECIES SAMPLED FROM ALL GEAR

Number of fish caught for the following length categories (inches):

species	0-5	6-8	9-11	12-14	15-19	20-24	25-29	>29	Total
Northern Pike	-	-	-	-	-	2	1	-	3
Pumpkinseed	3	-	-	-	-	-	-	-	3
Walleye	-	5	31	8	6	2	2	-	54
White Sucker	-	2	12	32	27	-	-	-	73
Yellow Perch	-	7	-	-	-	-	-	-	7

FISHING INFORMATION

Located east of Finland, these two lakes offer varied angling opportunities.

Crooked Lake is one of the few muskellunge waters in Lake County. Shoepack-strain muskies were stocked here in the late 1970s and have maintained a population. Locals say they are relatively easy to catch, but they don't grow very large. Most top out around 28 to 30 inches. The largest the DNR has ever sampled in this lake - in nearly 40 years - was 39 inches. As a result, you don't need muskie lures the size of a chunk of firewood. Smaller lures get the nod for these smaller fish. Walleyes are numerous, although they're not overly large, with a pound being about average. The lake's main lobe is the place to look for walleyes. Smallmouth bass numbers are pretty high and there are some good-sized bass to be found. Northern pike showed up a few years back and have now become established, although their numbers remain low. Muskie numbers have fallen since pike were discovered, perhaps coincidentally, perhaps not. There are some decent-sized pike out there that can match those Shoepack-strain muskies inch for inch.

Thunderbird is for the adventurous angler. You'll have to portage a canoe to reach the lake. Thunderbird holds walleyes, northern pike and perch, with the walleyes being the main draw. These fish are fairly numerous, and although they are stocked here, there is pretty good natural reproduction as well. Most fish are on the small side, but there are some big ones hiding here, too. Northern pike numbers are on the low side, but a few larger fish are present. Yellow perch are too small to interest anglers, but do provide a good forage base for the lake's walleyes and northern pike.

For 'eyes, try fishing early in the year near the inlet in the northwest corner. In summer, try the sharp break off the north shore and the bar pointing northwest above the Moose Creek inlet on the lake's south side. The water is moderately bog-stained, so expect daytime action. For northerns, try the shallow east and west ends of the lake, or anywhere you find weeds.

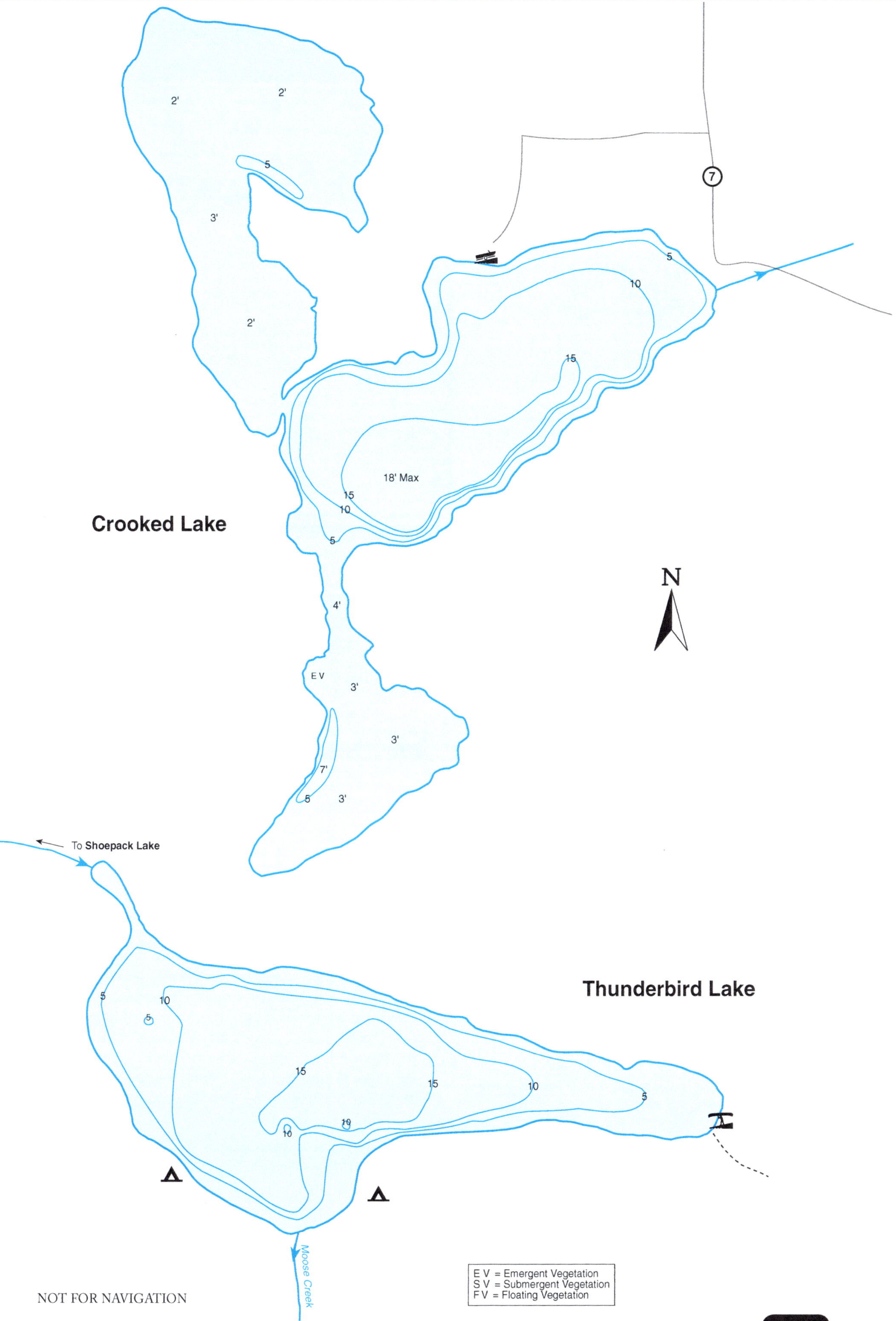

Source: Minnesota Department of Natural Resources, USGS

NINEMILE LAKE *Lake County*

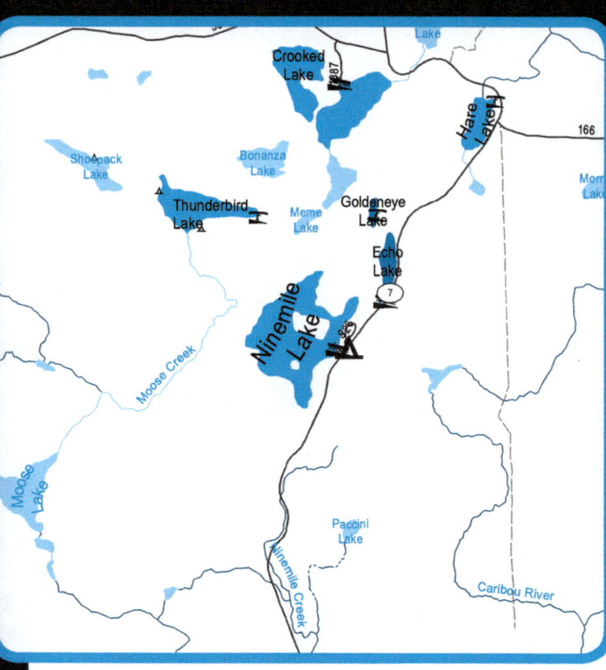

Area map page / coordinates: 24 / D-3

Watershed: Baptism-Brule

Surface water area / shorelength: 297 acres / 4.0 miles

Maximum / mean depth: 40 feet / 7 feet

Water color / clarity: Green tint / 8.0 ft. secchi (2013)

Shoreland zoning classification: Recreational development

Management class / Ecological type: Walleye /soft-water walleye

Accessibility: USFS-owned public access with concrete ramp on east shore in campground off County Road 7

91° 4' 32" W / 47° 34' 40" N

Accommodations: Picnicking, camping, restrooms

FISH STOCKING DATA

year	species	size	# released
13	Walleye	Fry	150,000
14	Walleye	Fry	288,000

NET CATCH DATA

Date: 07/22/2013	Gill Nets		Trap Nets	
species	# per net	avg. fish weight (lbs.)	# per net	avg. fish weight (lbs.)
Bluegill	-	-	0.17	0.07
Northern Pike	13.50	1.77	0.83	2.19
Walleye	2.50	2.14	0.33	3.43
White Sucker	23.00	2.22	0.33	2.73
Yellow Perch	39.00	0.19	-	-

LENGTH OF SELECTED SPECIES SAMPLED FROM ALL GEAR

Number of fish caught for the following length categories (inches):

species	0-5	6-8	9-11	12-14	15-19	20-24	25-29	>30	Total
Bluegill	1	-	-	-	-	-	-	-	1
Northern Pike	1	-	2	10	34	28	8	1	84
Walleye	-	-	-	3	11	2	1	-	17
White Sucker	-	5	1	29	89	16	-	-	140
Yellow Perch	55	157	19	-	-	-	-	-	231

FISHING INFORMATION

Ninemile is a pretty decent lake. It has good access, with a concrete boat launch, which is somewhat of a rarity in this relatively remote location. There is also a nice Forest Service campground here, with 24 campsites and some basic amenities. The lake also has a pretty good fishery for walleyes, northern pike and yellow perch.

Walleye numbers are good here in general, however, a fish kill occurred following the severe winter of 2013, and walleyes and several other fish species were found dead that spring. That's why walleyes were stocked here recently, to rebuild the population following the winterkill event. Otherwise, Ninemile's fishery is maintained entirely through natural reproduction.

Obviously, following the winterkill, walleye numbers were lower than usual, however, some fish certainly survived. Most of the walleyes that showed up in the subsequent DNR survey were good-sized fish.

Northern pike numbers were high, even following the winterkill. However, pike are fairly tolerant of low oxygen levels and survive these events much better than species such as bluegills, crappies and walleyes. Overall pike size was generally pretty small, although one fish just over 30 inches was captured in the DNR assessment.

There are a lot of yellow perch here, which provide good forage for pike and walleyes. Most of them are pretty small and they can certainly annoy live-bait anglers. However, some nicer perch are out there and you may get a few if you have the patience to deal with numerous small fish.

Bluegills, black crappies and smallmouth bass are also present in Ninemile. Although their numbers were either low or nonexistent in the last DNR survey, all three species were found dead on the shoreline following the winterkill. There are certainly some survivors of these species still out there, and no doubt they are rebuilding their populations.

The folks at the Knotted Pine Inn & Tavern, 9702 Highway 1, Isabella MN 55607, (218) 323-7681, say Ninemile is fairly clear, but due to it shallow nature, it still warms quickly. Therefore, it's a good lake to fish early in the season. For walleyes, minnows on a Lindy rig or soaked under a slip bobber will work. Switch to leeches later in the season. Early on you'll find fish near the 5-foot contour, off the large island's southwest side **(Spot 1)**. Also try the hole off the northeast tip of that island **(Spot 2)**. Jigging the drop to the lake's deep hole off the small point on the southern island **(Spot 3)** could also produce some fish.

For northerns, your best success will come in the shallow, weedy bay year-round. Toss spoons, spinnerbaits or shallow-running crankbaits for pike.

If you want to weed through some small yellow perch, try fishing the weedlines. Using minnows rather than worms may high-grade your catch to some extent, but sometimes even small perch can be pretty ambitious.

NOT FOR NAVIGATION

Source: Minnesota Department of Natural Resources, USGS

Goldeneye Lake, Lake County

Area map page / coordinates: 24 / D-3
Surface area / max depth: 10 acres / 19 feet
Accessibility: Carry-down access from Cty. Rd. 7 (0.25-mile, steep grade) to east shore of lake

FISH STOCKING DATA

year	species	size	# released
08	Brook Trout	Fingerling	763
09	Brook Trout	Fingerling	746
10	Brook Trout	Fingerling	793
11	Brook Trout	Fingerling	750
13	Brook Trout	Fingerling	750
15	Brook Trout	Fingerling	747

LENGTH OF SELECTED SPECIES SAMPLED FROM ALL GEAR

Survey Date: 06/16/2014

Number of fish caught for the following length categories (inches):

species	0-5	6-8	9-11	12-14	15-19	20-24	25-29	>30	Total
Brook Trout	1	4	1	5	-	-	-	-	11

Echo Lake, Lake County

Area map page / coordinates: 24 / D-3
Surface area / max depth: 42 acres / 61 feet
Accessibility: County-owned public access with gravel ramp on south shore off Cty. Rd. 7
91° 3' 58" W / 47° 35' 0" N

FISH STOCKING DATA

year	species	size	# released
11	Rainbow Trout	Yearling	3,029
11	Splake	Fingerling	2,535
12	Rainbow Trout	Yearling	3,010
12	Splake	Fingerling	2,506
13	Rainbow Trout	Yearling	3,029
13	Rainbow Trout	Adult	146
13	Splake	Fingerling	1,717
14	Rainbow Trout	Yearling	3,001
14	Splake	Fingerling	2,470
15	Rainbow Trout	Fingerling	1,011
15	Rainbow Trout	Yearling	3,005
15	Splake	Fingerling	2,500

LENGTH OF SELECTED SPECIES SAMPLED FROM ALL GEAR

Survey Date: 09/23/2013

Number of fish caught for the following length categories (inches):

species	0-5	6-8	9-11	12-14	15-19	20-24	25-29	>30	Total
Rainbow Trout	-	-	18	28	5	-	-	-	51
Splake	2	20	20	13	-	1	-	-	56

Goldeneye Lake

19' Max

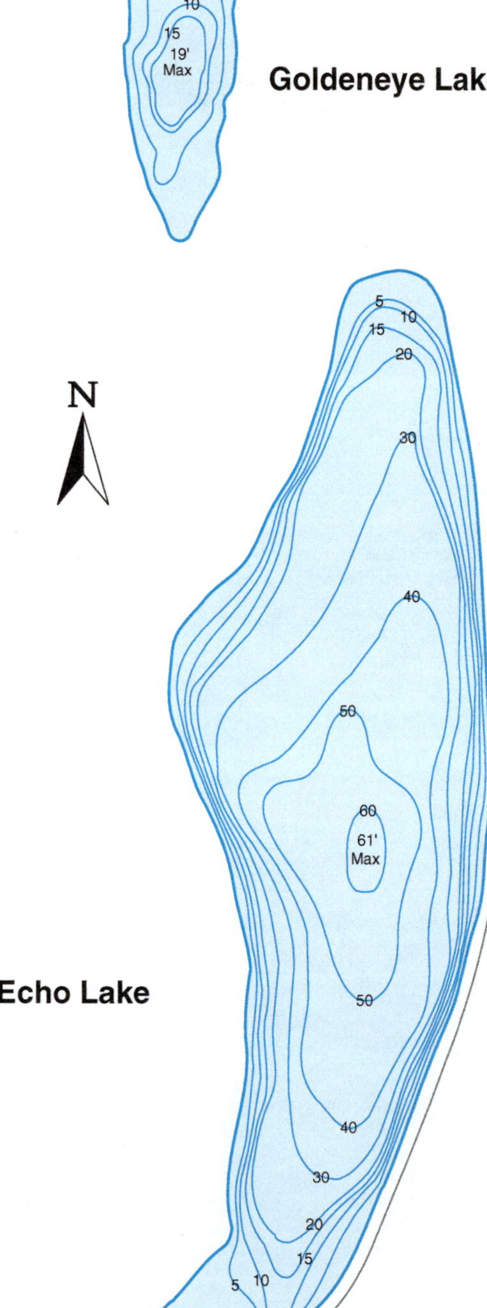

Ninemile Lake

E V = Emergent Vegetation
S V = Submergent Vegetation
F V = Floating Vegetation

NOT FOR NAVIGATION

Source: Minnesota Department of Natural Resources, USGS

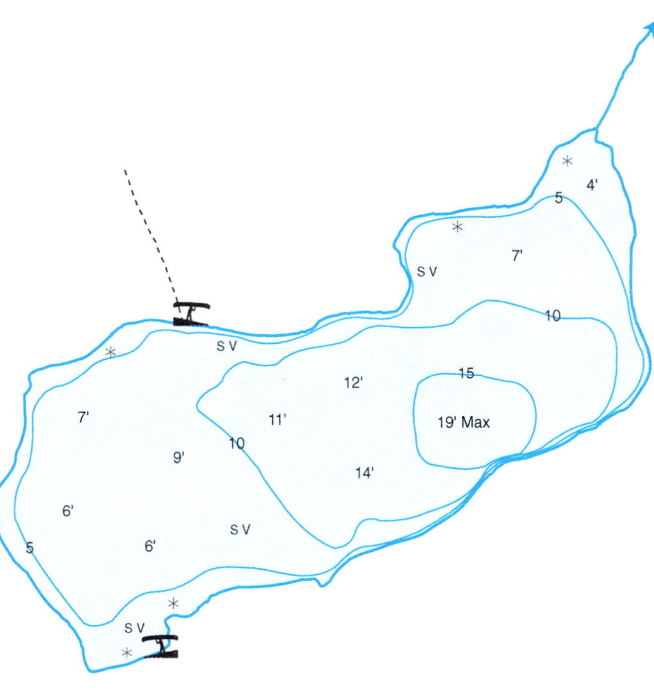

East Lake

East Lake, Lake County

Area map page / coordinates: 24 / C-3
Surface area / max depth: 82 acres / 18 feet
Accessibility: Carry-down access (1,000 yards) to southwest corner from FR 1849; also from Houghtaling Creek, midway along the north shore (330 yards, unmarked)

FISH STOCKING DATA

year	species	size	# released
09	Brook Trout	Fingerling	3,534
09	Brown Trout	Yearling	1,198
10	Brook Trout	Fingerling	2,646
11	Brook Trout	Fingerling	1,740
12	Brook Trout	Fingerling	1,750
13	Brook Trout	Fingerling	1,899
15	Brook Trout	Yearling	999

LENGTH OF SELECTED SPECIES SAMPLED FROM ALL GEAR

Survey Date: 09/18/2012

Number of fish caught for the following length categories (inches):

species	0-5	6-8	9-11	12-14	15-19	20-24	25-29	>30	Total
Brook Trout	-	1	1	5	-	-	-	-	7
Brown Trout	-	-	-	-	5	-	-	-	5
Yellow Perch	12	75	1	-	-	-	-	-	88

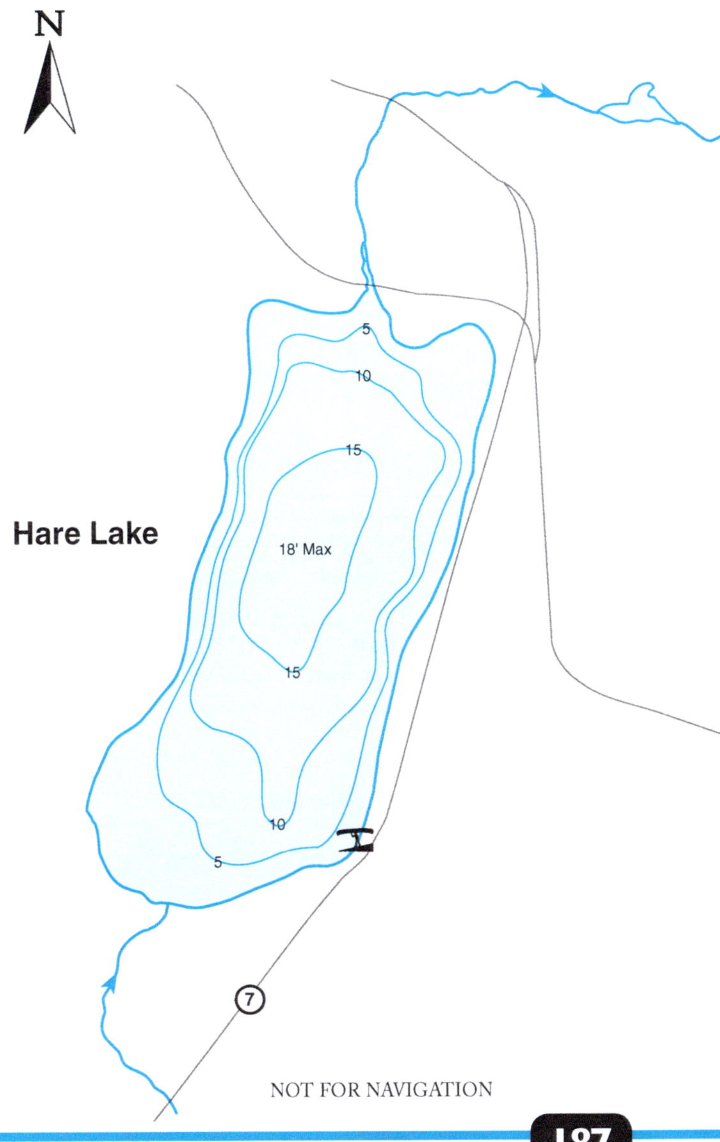

Hare Lake

Hare Lake, Lake County

Area map page / coordinates: 24 / C,D-3
Surface area / max depth: 48 acres / 22 feet
Accessibility: County-owned gravel ramp on southeast shore off Hwy. 7

FISH STOCKING DATA

year	species	size	# released
10	Brook Trout	Adult	424
10	Brook Trout	Yearling	2,001
11	Brook Trout	Yearling	1,998
12	Brook Trout	Yearling	2,025
13	Brook Trout	Yearling	2,072
14	Brook Trout	Yearling	2,000
15	Brook Trout	Yearling	1,679

LENGTH OF SELECTED SPECIES SAMPLED FROM ALL GEAR

Survey Date: 10/07/2014

Number of fish caught for the following length categories (inches):

species	0-5	6-8	9-11	12-14	15-19	20-24	25-29	>30	Total
Brook Trout	-	1	-	-	-	-	-	-	1
White Sucker	1	257	50	4	1	-	-	-	313
Yellow Perch	18	18	3	-	-	-	-	-	39

DAM 5 LAKE

Lake County

Area map pg / coord: 24 / C-2,3
Watershed: Rainy headwaters
Surface area: 78 acres
Shorelength: 2.2 miles
Max / mean depth: 38 feet / 13 feet
Water color / clarity: Clear / 13.5 ft. secchi (2010)
Shoreland zoning class: Nat. envt.
Mgmt class / Ecological type: Walleye / soft-water walleye
Accessibility: 1) Carry-down access off Cty. Rd. 7 to west shore (steep hill)
91° 6' 15" W / 47° 38' 44" N
Accessibility: 2) USFS-owned public access with earthen ramp on southern tip of lake, off County Road 7
91° 5' 41" W / 48° 38' 24" N
Accommodations: Camping

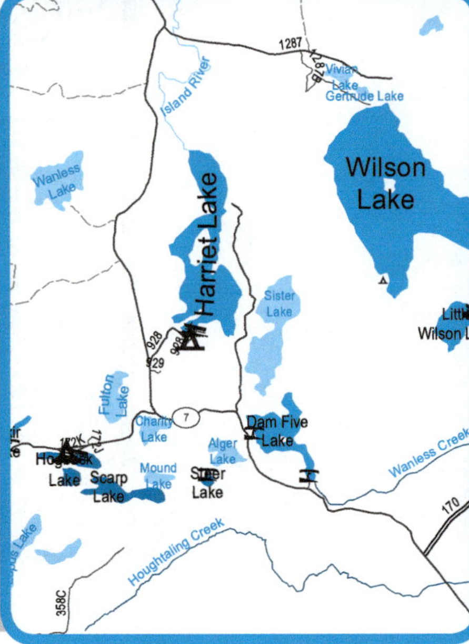

FISH STOCKING DATA			
year	species	size	# released
07	Walleye	Adult	80
07	Walleye	Fingerling	12,815
09	Walleye	Fingerling	4,579
11	Walleye	Fingerling	3,285
14	Walleye	Fry	64,000

NET CATCH DATA

Date: 07/19/2010	Gill Nets		Trap Nets	
species	# per net	avg. fish weight (lbs.)	# per net	avg. fish weight (lbs.)
Northern Pike	1.25	1.60	-	-
Walleye	4.50	0.75	0.56	0.92
White Sucker	17.0	2.28	1.44	2.61
Yellow Perch	0.50	0.13	-	-

LENGTH OF SELECTED SPECIES SAMPLED FROM ALL GEAR

Number of fish caught for the following length categories (inches):

species	0-5	6-8	9-11	12-14	15-19	20-24	25-29	>29	Total
Northern Pike	-	-	-	3	-	-	1	-	4
Walleye	-	3	3	13	4	-	-	-	23
White Sucker	-	1	-	1	75	4	-	-	81
Yellow Perch	-	2	-	-	-	-	-	-	2

FISHING INFORMATION

Dam 5 Lake is still in a state of flux from when a dam washed out in 2001. Since then, lake levels have dropped, then gradually returned to near normal. Still, these fluctuating levels affected spawning habitat, which just doesn't reform overnight. Northern pike and walleye populations have been especially affected.

Walleye stocking has been aimed at helping this species recover. Walleyes are present in above-average numbers and the population is mostly maintained through stocking.

You'll also find a few northern pike and small largemouth bass and yellow perch.

When fishing Dam 5, concentrate on the deep sides of the islands and the lake's steeply dropping north shore for walleyes. Jig/minnow combos or a minnow under a slip bobber should work. Look for the lake's limited number of northern pike around the lake's weedlines, working the shallows early in the season.

HARRIET LAKE

Lake County

Area map pg / coord: 24 / B,C-2
Watershed: Rainy headwaters
Surface area: 265 acres
Shorelength: 5.9 miles
Max / mean depth: 37 feet / 12 feet
Water color / clarity: Clear / 11.0 ft. secchi (2009)
Shoreland zoning class: Rec. dev.
Mgmt class / Ecological type: Walleye-centrarchid / soft-water walleye
Accessibility: USFS-owned public access with concrete ramp on southwest shore, off County Road 7
91° 6' 51" W / 47° 39' 27" N
Accommodations: Campground, restrooms

NO RECORD OF STOCKING

NET CATCH DATA

Date: 07/27/2009	Gill Nets		Trap Nets	
species	# per net	avg. fish weight (lbs.)	# per net	avg. fish weight (lbs.)
Black Crappie	-	-	0.3	1.07
Northern Pike	3.2	1.27	1.6	1.09
Walleye	16.0	1.10	0.9	0.74
White Sucker	11.3	2.30	2.2	2.48
Yellow Perch	7.5	0.13	2.1	0.12

LENGTH OF SELECTED SPECIES SAMPLED FROM ALL GEAR

Number of fish caught for the following length categories (inches):

species	0-5	6-8	9-11	12-14	15-19	20-24	25-29	>29	Total
Black Crappie	-	1	1	1	-	-	-	-	3
Northern Pike	-	-	2	3	18	9	1	-	33
Walleye	-	5	40	30	22	6	1	-	104
White Sucker	-	4	1	3	76	4	-	-	88
Yellow Perch	24	40	-	-	-	-	-	-	64

Harriet Lake is a good place to spend a weekend. It has a nice campground and restroom facilities and some pretty good walleye fishing.

Walleye numbers are above average, and the average size is respectable at just under 14 inches.

Northern pike abundance is pretty high, but average size is small. Still, there is a chance you might luck into a big northern here. Past assessments have occasionally turned up a real lunker.

Harriet has a lot of yellow perch, but they're small. There are a few crappies here and they do grow large if you can find them.

The saddle between the two points **(Spot 1)** offers good structure and is the most obvious place to concentrate your walleye efforts.

The access to Harriet is via a concrete ramp. There is free camping in the grassy area nearby.

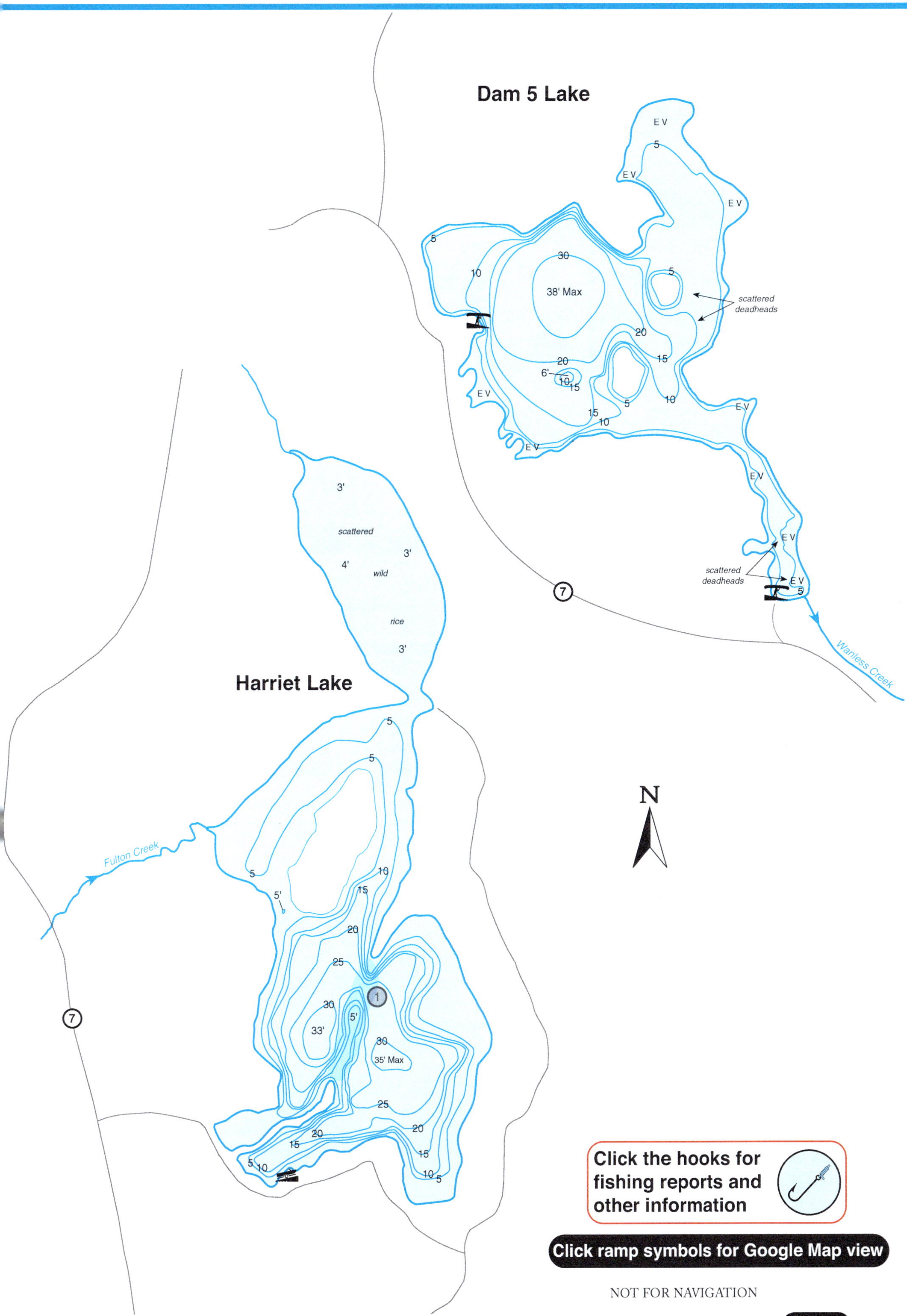

Dam 5 Lake

EV
5
EV
EV
5
30
10
38' Max
5
scattered deadheads
20
15
20
6'
10
15
EV
5
10
15
10
EV
EV
EV
EV
scattered deadheads
EV
5
7
Wanless Creek

Harriet Lake

3'
scattered
3'
4'
wild
rice
3'
5
5
Fulton Creek
5
10
5'
15
20
25
1
30
5'
33'
30
35' Max
7
25
20
20
15
15
5
10
10
5

N

Click the hooks for fishing reports and other information

Click ramp symbols for Google Map view

NOT FOR NAVIGATION

Source: Minnesota Department of Natural Resources, USGS

WILSON LAKE

Lake County

Area map pg / coord: 24 / B-3

Watershed: Baptism-Brule

Surface area: 650 acres

Shorelength: 7.1 miles

Max / mean depth: 53 feet / 30 feet

Water color / clarity: Clear / 18.0 feet secchi (2011)

Shoreland zoning class: Rec. dev.

Mgmt class / Ecological type: Walleye / soft-water walleye

Accessibility: USFS-owned public access with concrete ramp on south shore

91° 3' 39" W / 47° 39' 39" N

Accommodations: Camping, restrooms

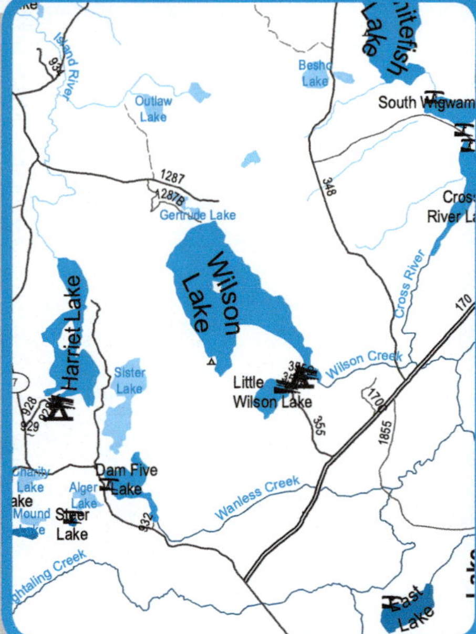

NO RECORD OF STOCKING

NET CATCH DATA				
Date: 08/01/2011	Gill Nets		Trap Nets	
species	# per net	avg. fish weight (lbs.)	# per net	avg. fish weight (lbs.)
Northern Pike	1.33	3.13	0.08	0.12
Walleye	27.3	1.24	0.33	1.97
White Sucker	9.78	1.80	-	-
Yellow Perch	20.0	0.21	3.50	0.14

LENGTH OF SELECTED SPECIES SAMPLED FROM ALL GEAR

Number of fish caught for the following length categories (inches):

species	0-5	6-8	9-11	12-14	15-19	20-24	25-29	>29	Total
Northern Pike	-	1	-	1	3	4	2	1	12
Walleye	-	26	23	92	85	15	1	-	242
White Sucker	-	4	18	14	37	8	-	-	81
Yellow Perch	35	150	32	1	-	-	-	-	218

FISHING INFORMATION

Wilson Lake offers anglers a quality walleye fishery in a scenic, remote setting. And with a concrete launch, you won't have any trouble getting to those walleyes.

According to the folks at Muskie Doom Guide Service, (218) 491-3277, www.muskiedoom.com, Wilson has an abundance of good-sized walleyes. The lake is very clear, making it a low-light fishery. You'll find a lot of desirable-sized walleyes in the 14- to 16-inch range, with the chance to hook into something pretty decent as well. Bait choices for walleyes are pretty typical for the area. Drifting a Lindy rig with live bait is highly effective. The lake is full of good walleye spots. The sunken islands are worth a look, as are the steep-dropping shorelines. Any underwater points you can find are worth a drift as well.

There's also a decent fishery for yellow perch. Although most of the perch you'll encounter on Wilson Lake will be small, there are some definite keepers out there as well. Perch are often caught incidentally while Lindy rigging with nightcrawlers.

Northern pike are present here, but don't expect to tangle with too many. The size structure of the ones you'll find is generally pretty good.

There is a four-site campground near the boat launch on Wilson Lake. There is also an isolated boat-in campsite on the southwest corner with a latrine.

The folks at Muskie Doom recommend going slowly until you learn the lake. There are lots of rocks in the shallow bay near the access and the broad, shallow shelves around both the large and tiny islands come out much farther than you might think.

Little Wilson is a smaller, less-complex version of its larger sibling. Anglers will find a lot of nice walleyes in this little lake. There are lots of yellow perch and just a few northern pike. White sucker numbers are very high in both of these lakes. Maximum depth is 22 feet, and there isn't a lot of structure, although there are a lot of boulders in the shallows near the access.

LITTLE WILSON LAKE

Lake County

Area map pg / coord: 244 / B,C-3

Watershed: Baptism-Brule

Surface area: 54 acres

Shorelength: NA

Max / mean depth: 22 feet / NA

Water color / clarity: Brown tint / 9.6 ft. secchi (2012)

Shoreland zoning class: Nat. envt.

Mgmt class / Ecological type: Walleye / northern pike - sucker

Accessibility: USFS-owned public access with small gravel launch on northeast corner

91° 3' 54" W / 47° 39' 32" N

Accommodations: Camping

FISH STOCKING DATA

year	species	size	# released
08	Walleye	Fry	45,000
09	Walleye	Fry	45,000
12	Walleye	Fry	45,000
13	Walleye	Fry	42,500

NET CATCH DATA				
Date: 07/16/2012	Gill Nets		Trap Nets	
species	# per net	avg. fish weight (lbs.)	# per net	avg. fish weight (lbs.)
Northern Pike	0.67	1.14	0.22	1.85
Walleye	9.67	1.51	0.89	1.52
White Sucker	14.0	1.04	0.78	1.69
Yellow Perch	5.00	0.12	9.22	0.14

LENGTH OF SELECTED SPECIES SAMPLED FROM ALL GEAR

Number of fish caught for the following length categories (inches):

species	0-5	6-8	9-11	12-14	15-19	20-24	25-29	>29	Total
Northern Pike	-	-	-	-	3	1	-	-	4
Walleye	-	-	-	17	16	4	-	-	37
White Sucker	-	6	19	5	17	1	-	-	48
Yellow Perch	36	57	1	-	-	-	-	-	94

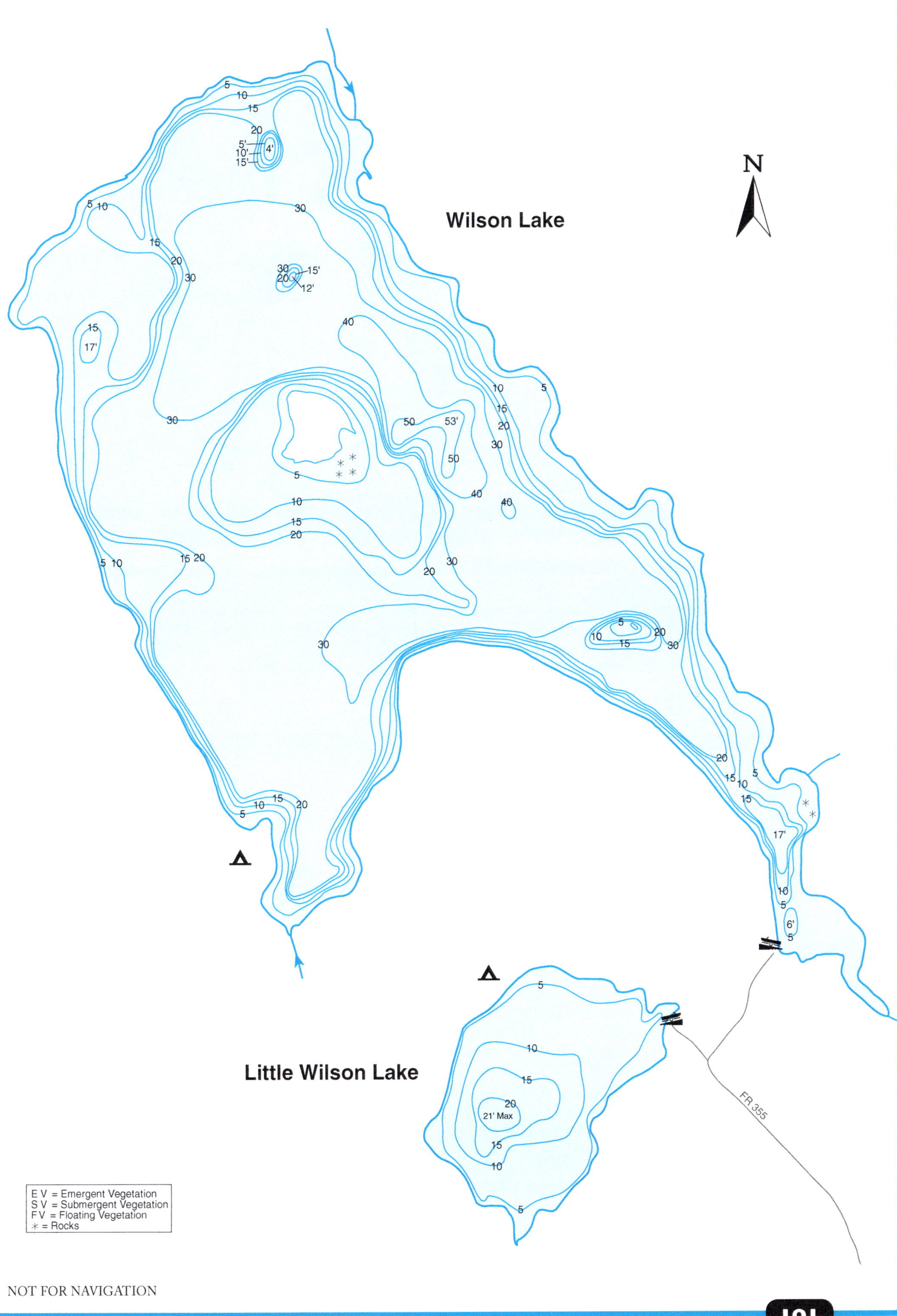

NOT FOR NAVIGATION

Source: Minnesota Department of Natural Resources, USGS

SILVER ISLAND LAKE

Lake County

Area map pg / coord: 24 / A-2

Watershed: Rainy headwaters

Surface area: 1,239 acres

Shorelength: 13.7 miles

Max / mean depth: 16 feet / 8 feet

Water color / clarity: Brown bog stain / 5.3 ft. secchi (2012)

Shoreland zoning class: Nat. envt.

Mgmt class / Ecological type: Walleye / soft-water walleye

Accessibility: USFS-owned public access with concrete ramp on southwest shore at campground

91° 8' 56" W / 47° 43' 30" N

Accommodations: Picnicking, camping, restrooms

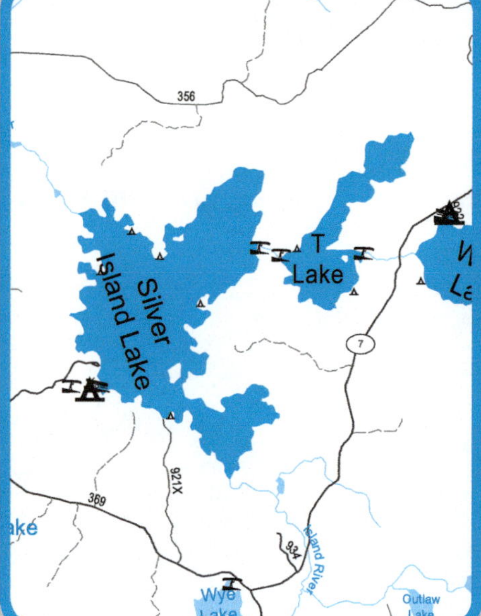

"T" LAKE

Lake County

Area map pg / coord: 24 / A-2,3

Watershed: Rainy headwaters

Surface area: 295 acres

Shorelength: 5.3 miles

Max / mean depth: 15 feet / 5 feet

Water color / clarity: Brown stain / 7.0 ft. secchi (2011)

Shoreland zoning class: Nat. envt.

Mgmt class / Ecological type: Walleye / soft-water walleye

Accessibility: Carry-down access (0.5-mile portage) from Co. Road 7; also portage (0.2 mile) from northeast shore of Silver Island to west shore of T

Accommodations: Picnicking, camping, restrooms

Silver Island Lake

NO RECORD OF STOCKING

NET CATCH DATA

Date: 07/16/2012

	Gill Nets		Trap Nets	
species	# per net	avg. fish weight (lbs.)	# per net	avg. fish weight (lbs.)
Lake Whitefish	3.11	1.89	-	-
Northern Pike	4.22	1.33	0.50	1.25
Pumpkinseed	0.11	0.35	0.33	0.09
Rock Bass	0.78	0.35	0.17	0.09
Walleye	15.4	0.95	1.00	1.77
White Sucker	14.3	1.15	3.17	1.85
Yellow Perch	12.6	0.19	1.42	0.22

LENGTH OF SELECTED SPECIES SAMPLED FROM ALL GEAR

Number of fish caught for the following length categories (inches):

species	0-5	6-8	9-11	12-14	15-19	20-24	25-29	>29	Total
Lake Whitefish	-	2	-	4	22	-	-	-	28
Northern Pike	-	-	-	10	21	13	-	-	44
Pumpkinseed	4	1	-	-	-	-	-	-	5
Rock Bass	3	6	-	-	-	-	-	-	9
Walleye	-	7	31	71	35	7	-	-	151
White Sucker	-	11	41	38	76	1	-	-	167
Yellow Perch	24	88	14	-	-	-	-	-	126

"T" Lake

NO RECORD OF STOCKING

NET CATCH DATA

Date: 07/25/2011

	Gill Nets		Trap Nets	
species	# per net	avg. fish weight (lbs.)	# per net	avg. fish weight (lbs.)
Black Crappie	2.50	0.69	-	-
Northern Pike	2.83	1.27	-	-
Rock Bass	0.50	0.38	-	-
Walleye	6.17	0.80	-	-
White Sucker	8.83	1.51	-	-
Yellow Perch	16.3	0.20	-	-

LENGTH OF SELECTED SPECIES SAMPLED FROM ALL GEAR

Number of fish caught for the following length categories (inches):

species	0-5	6-8	9-11	12-14	15-19	20-24	25-29	>29	Total
Black Crappie	5	-	6	4	-	-	-	-	15
Northern Pike	-	-	-	4	8	4	1	-	17
Rock Bass	-	2	-	-	-	-	-	-	2
Walleye	-	1	10	20	5	1	-	-	37
White Sucker	-	5	6	13	28	1	-	-	53
Yellow Perch	26	60	10	-	-	-	-	-	96

FISHING INFORMATION

Silver Island is a pretty interesting lake with lots of structure and a diverse fishery. The lake holds black crappies, northern pike, yellow perch, walleyes, largemouth bass and lake whitefish. The lake is best known for its abundant walleyes. You'll find lots of them - many of them good eaters - in the lake's abundant rocky areas. Northern pike numbers are fairly high, and although few large pike are showing up in DNR surveys, they're probably out there, given the presence of lake whitefish. This species is present, despite the lake only being 15 feet at the deepest. There are some large whitefish here. There are some really nice black crappies in Silver Island Lake as well, and largemouth bass somehow made their way into the lake recently.

Silver Island Lake has good access and accommodations, with a concrete ramp, dock and campground with restrooms. Plus, there are several remote campsites scattered around the lake. Shore-fishing is available at several locations.

The water is stained, with a visibility of just 5 feet. The darkness of the water, coupled with the lake's relatively shallow depth, mean early warming. That dark water also conceals the boulders that abound in this lake. Be careful.

T Lake is similar to Silver Island, but in a smaller version. Eater-size walleyes are common, along with small northern pike and crappies. There are some pretty nice crappies here. Yellow perch are abundant, but you'll have to do some sorting to find some keepers.

Access to T is via a portage from Silver Island or a half-mile portage from Highway 7. There is parking at the road for portagers. T has a couple water-access campsites if you want to make a weekend out of it.

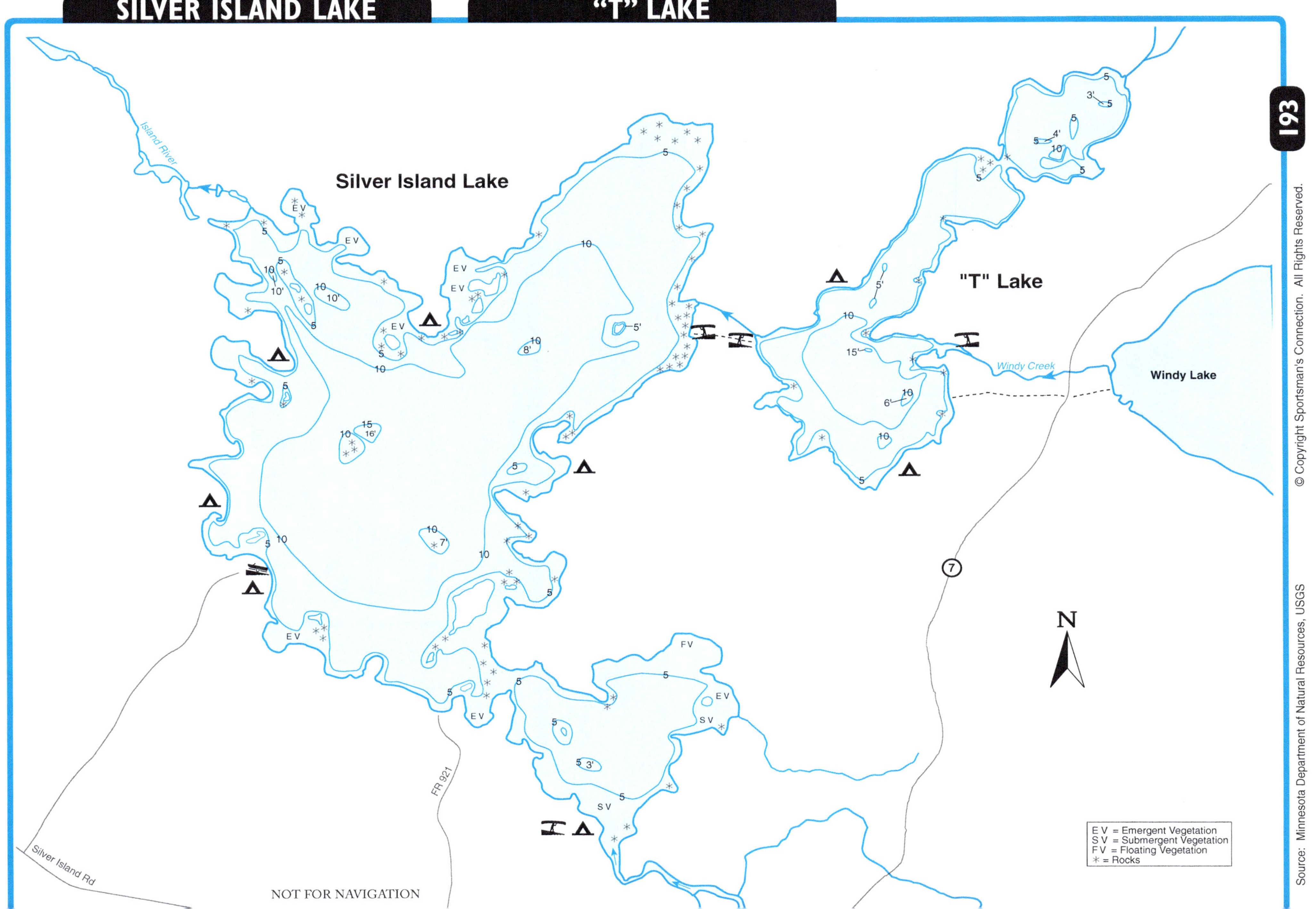

Source: Minnesota Department of Natural Resources, USGS

WHITEFISH LAKE

Lake County

Area map pg / coord: 24 / A,B-3

Watershed: Baptism-Brule

Surface area: 345 acres

Shorelength: 3.5 miles

Max / mean depth: 49 feet / 15 feet

Water color / clarity: Clear / 19.0 ft. secchi (2010)

Shoreland zoning class: Rec. dev.

Mgmt class / Ecological type: Walleye / soft-water walleye

Accessibility: Carry-down access at campground on northwest shore; portages from Elbow Lake (65 rods) and South Wigwam Lake (20 rods)

91° 2' 40" W / 47° 43' 6" N

Accommodations: Camping, restrooms

NO RECORD OF STOCKING

NET CATCH DATA

Date: 08/09/2010	Gill Nets		Trap Nets	
species	# per net	avg. fish weight (lbs.)	# per net	avg. fish weight (lbs.)
Northern Pike	3.00	3.79	0.11	0.16
Walleye	35.2	1.20	3.33	1.00
White Sucker	9.17	2.12	0.11	0.36
Yellow Perch	7.33	0.24	0.22	0.06

LENGTH OF SELECTED SPECIES SAMPLED FROM ALL GEAR

Number of fish caught for the following length categories (inches):

species	0-5	6-8	9-11	12-14	15-19	20-24	25-29	>29	Total
Northern Pike	-	1	-	2	3	8	2	3	19
Walleye	-	7	21	138	57	17	1	-	241
White Sucker	-	2	9	8	29	6	-	-	54
Yellow Perch	3	31	12	-	-	-	-	-	46

WINDY LAKE

Lake County

Area map pg / coord: 24 / A-3

Watershed: Rainy headwaters

Surface area: 456 acres

Shorelength: 5.1 miles

Max / mean depth: 39 feet / 16 feet

Water color / clarity: Brown / 9.1 ft. secchi (2012)

Shoreland zoning class: Rec. dev.

Mgmt class / Ecological type: Walleye / soft-water walleye

Accessibility: USFS-owned public access with concrete ramp on northwest shore

91° 5' 13" W / 47° 44' 36" N

Accommodations: Camping, restrooms

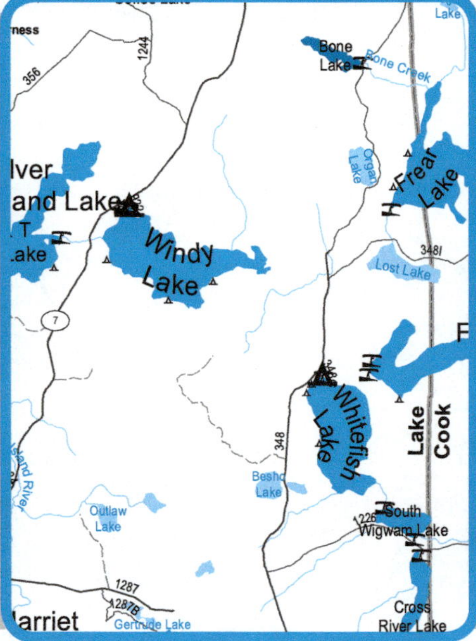

NO RECORD OF STOCKING

NET CATCH DATA

Date: 08/13/2012	Gill Nets		Trap Nets	
species	# per net	avg. fish weight (lbs.)	# per net	avg. fish weight (lbs.)
Lake Whitefish	9.50	0.67	-	-
Northern Pike	0.62	3.83	0.78	0.97
Pumpkinseed	-	-	0.11	0.07
Rock Bass	2.12	0.46	0.78	0.42
Walleye	15.0	0.64	0.67	0.66
White Sucker	8.38	1.38	0.33	1.59
Yellow Perch	3.62	0.15	0.33	0.10

LENGTH OF SELECTED SPECIES SAMPLED FROM ALL GEAR

Number of fish caught for the following length categories (inches):

species	0-5	6-8	9-11	12-14	15-19	20-24	25-29	>29	Total
Lake Whitefish	-	4	5	64	3	-	-	-	76
Northern Pike	-	2	1	1	3	4	-	1	12
Pumpkinseed	1	-	-	-	-	-	-	-	1
Rock Bass	1	19	4	-	-	-	-	-	24
Walleye	-	12	53	43	17	1	-	-	126
White Sucker	-	4	19	19	28	-	-	-	70
Yellow Perch	12	20	-	-	-	-	-	-	32

FISHING INFORMATION

Looking for a pair of walleye lakes that really rock? You may have found them. These two Finland-area lakes provide some quality fishing for walleyes.

Anglers who want to fish **Whitefish Lake** will have to portage, but don't let that stand in the way of a nice stringer of walleyes. There are three ways to get to the lake. Two are short portages from other lakes, but the easiest is a short carry-down access from a small campground.

The last survey of the lake showed really good numbers of walleyes, with a pretty good average size as well. Northern pike numbers are good, and many are fair-sized, with multiple fish in the last assessment topping 30 inches. Yellow perch fishing can be good as well. Although you'll find your typical small perch, some of them grow pretty nice.

In the spring, concentrate your efforts near the creek inlet in the southwest corner or on the shallow flats nearby. A minnow on a Lindy rig will do nicely. This same area is also a good bet for the lake's northern pike. As the water warms, anglers will want to follow the walleyes deeper. The steeply dropping east shore is a good bet, as is the inside turn off the west shore at mid-lake. There's good water clarity in Whitefish Lake, so the best walleye bite will likely be during low-light conditions.

Windy Lake offers a daytime alternative for walleye anglers. Its water is much darker than that of neighboring Whitefish, so anglers have better luck catching walleyes here during the day. Like on Whitefish, there are a lot of walleyes here as well, however, they run a little smaller.

Anglers will also find low numbers of northern pike, small perch and a healthy population of lake whitefish.

A small creek enters in the northeast and another exits in the west. Anglers may want to try around these areas in the spring for walleyes. Later, head for the lake's numerous points, bars and rock piles, making sure to bring lots of jigs, minnows and leeches.

There is a campground at the access on Whitefish and both lakes have remote, boat-in campsites.

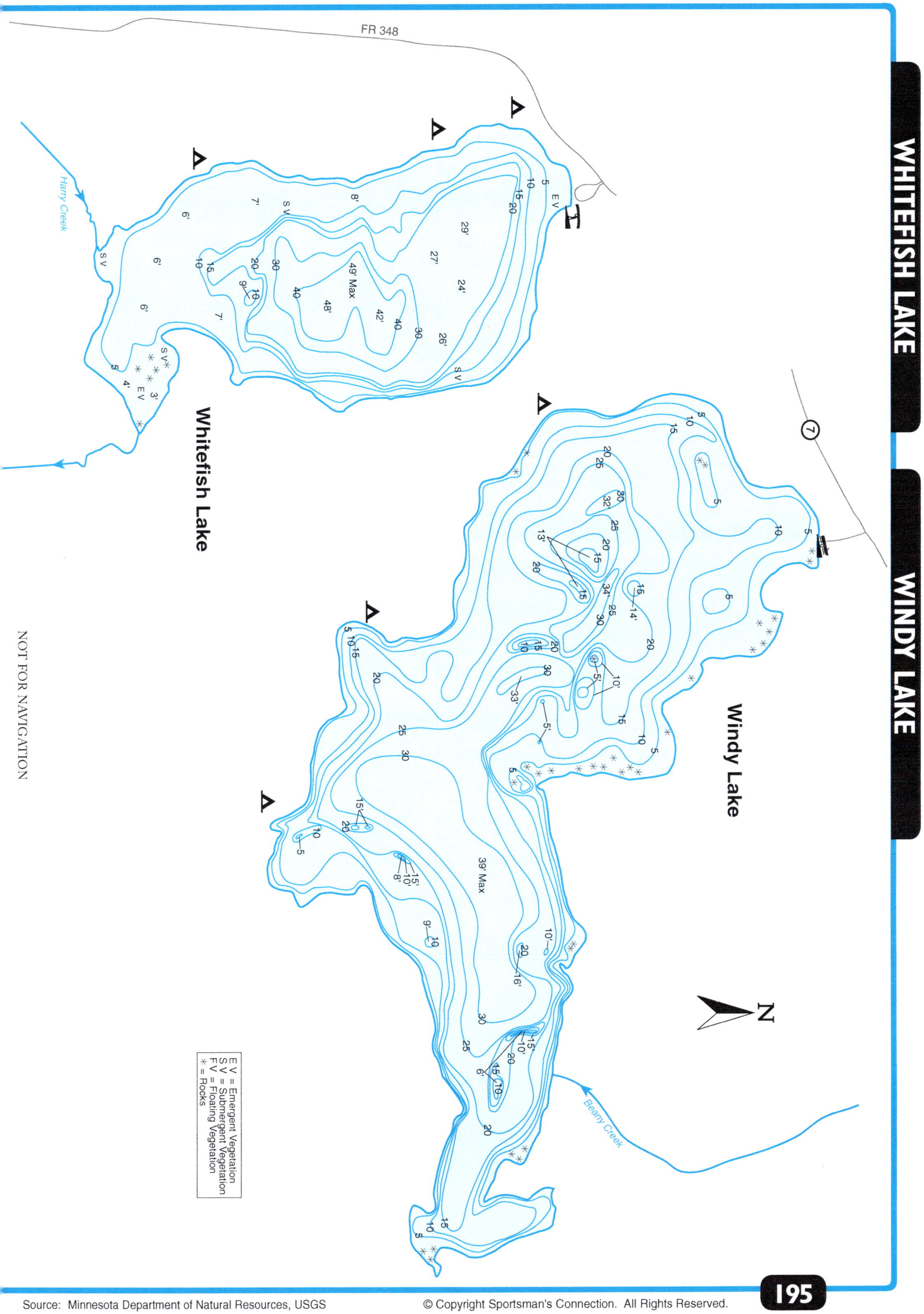

WHITEFISH LAKE

WINDY LAKE

FR 348

Harry Creek

Whitefish Lake

49' Max

Windy Lake

39' Max

Beany Creek

N

E V = Emergent Vegetation
S V = Submergent Vegetation
F V = Floating Vegetation
✳ = Rocks

NOT FOR NAVIGATION

Source: Minnesota Department of Natural Resources, USGS

FREAR LAKE
Cook County

Area map pg / coord: 24/A-3, 25/A-4

Watershed: Baptism-Brule

Surface area: 317 acres

Shorelength: 5.1 miles

Max / mean depth: 17 feet / 8 feet

Water color / clarity: Light brown / 7.3 ft. secchi (1998)

Shoreland zoning class: Nat. envt.

Mgmt class / Ecological type: Walleye / northern pike - sucker

Accessibility: Portage from USFS Rd. 357 (1/4 mile) to southwest corner of lake; portage from Lost Lake (120 rods) portage from Timber Lake (130 rods)

Accommodations: Camping

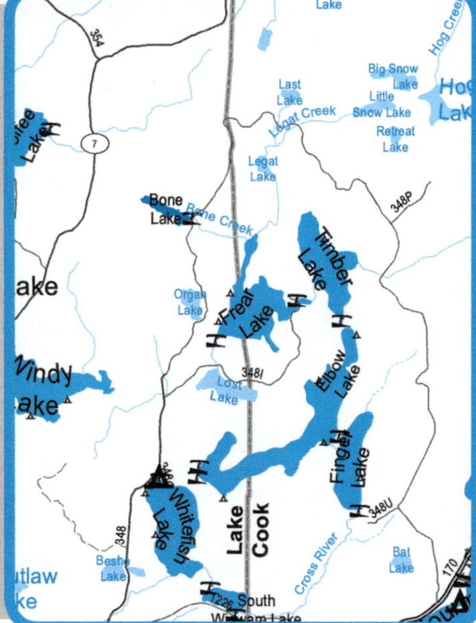

NO RECORD OF STOCKING

NET CATCH DATA

Date: 08/03/2009

species	Gill Nets # per net	Gill Nets avg. fish weight (lbs.)	Trap Nets # per net	Trap Nets avg. fish weight (lbs.)
Northern Pike	2.5	2.05	-	-
Walleye	18.0	1.14	-	-
White Sucker	11.0	2.81	-	-
Yellow Perch	0.7	0.10	-	-

LENGTH OF SELECTED SPECIES SAMPLED FROM ALL GEAR

Number of fish caught for the following length categories (inches):

species	0-5	6-8	9-11	12-14	15-19	20-24	25-29	>29	Total
Northern Pike	-	-	-	-	4	11	-	-	15
Walleye	-	3	16	49	37	3	-	-	108
White Sucker	-	-	9	6	31	20	-	-	66
Yellow Perch	2	2	-	-	-	-	-	-	4

TIMBER LAKE
Cook County

Area map pg / coord: 25 / A-4

Watershed: Baptism-Brule

Surface area: 278 acres

Shorelength: 3.5 miles

Max / mean depth: 12 feet / 7 feet

Water color / clarity: Brown / 7.0 ft. secchi (2009)

Shoreland zoning class: Nat. envt.

Mgmt class / Ecological type: Walleye / soft-water walleye

Accessibility: Portage from Frear Lake (130 rods); portage from Elbow Lake (40 rods)

Accommodations: Camping

NO RECORD OF STOCKING

NET CATCH DATA

Date: 08/24/2009

species	Gill Nets # per net	Gill Nets avg. fish weight (lbs.)	Trap Nets # per net	Trap Nets avg. fish weight (lbs.)
Northern Pike	1.3	3.28	-	-
Walleye	8.0	0.92	-	-
White Sucker	13.3	2.49	-	-
Yellow Perch	1.3	0.30	-	-

LENGTH OF SELECTED SPECIES SAMPLED FROM ALL GEAR

Number of fish caught for the following length categories (inches):

species	0-5	6-8	9-11	12-14	15-19	20-24	25-29	>29	Total
Northern Pike	-	-	-	-	-	5	3	-	8
Walleye	-	-	16	18	12	2	-	-	48
White Sucker	-	3	2	12	50	12	-	-	80
Yellow Perch	1	5	2	-	-	-	-	-	8

FISHING INFORMATION

These two lakes, along with Lost, Elbow, Finger and Whitefish, make up the Timber-Frear Canoe Route. This chain of lakes gives visitors a Boundary Waters-like experience, without the need for permits or restrictions on motors, although the accesses make use of a large boat and motor difficult. Visitors will find remote boat-in campsites and plenty of solitude.

Frear Lake has multiple access sites, none of which are particularly easy to navigate. A few portage routes are available, or you may be able to drive down Forest Road 1271 and put in at Timber Creek, depending on how rough the road is.

Angler Jeff Herrick, owner of Superior Bakery, says Frear is a walleye and northern pike lake. Action on Frear is pretty good throughout the open-water season, says Herrick. It's not very deep, so its clear water warms relatively fast. Minnows are the ticket early. Fish them either on a jig or drift or troll with a Lindy rig. As the water warms – maybe around July 1 – a switch to a leech may be in order. Locals say walleyes can be pretty picky, so you might have to switch back and forth between minnows and leeches for a time in mid-summer. Try fishing around the inlets early, but don't overlook the point on the lake's south end, which is probably the best overall spot for walleyes. The big, broad peninsula that forms the eastern bay, the inside turn on the northeast shore, the small point on the north end and the eastern bay can all be good walleye producers as well.

Spoons and spinners should work for northern pike. Cast around the shallows early in the season, switching to deeper weedlines when the water warms.

Timber Lake offers northerns, walleyes and yellow perch. This lake is also good all year. Walleye numbers are bountiful and average size is good, although these fish tend to grow slowly. There aren't a whole lot of northern pike here, but the ones you do find are often decent-sized. Yellow perch numbers are relatively low, but there are a few keeper-sized ones out there.

Herrick says he prefers Lindy rigs with leeches for Timber Lake's walleyes. The big point on the west shore is the most well-known spot for walleyes, but the bar almost directly across the lake on the east shore is a close second. The inside turn in the bay just north of that bar and the steep drop off the western shoreline also deserve a look.

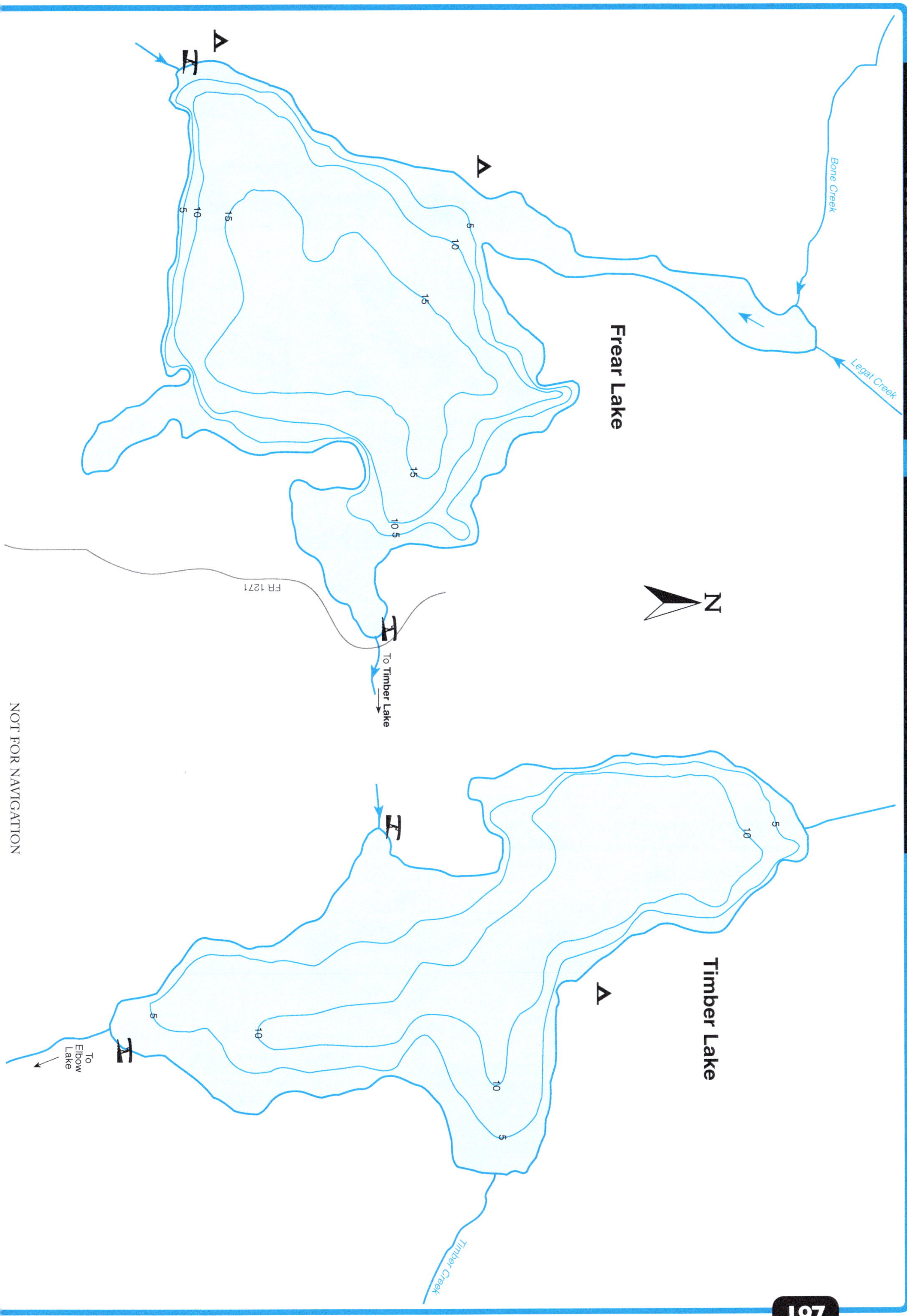

Source: Minnesota Department of Natural Resources, USGS

ELBOW LAKE

Cook County

Area map pg / coord: 24/A-3, 25/A-4

Watershed: Baptism-Brule

Surface area: 528 acres

Shorelength: 6.0 miles

Max / mean depth: 23 feet / 5 feet

Water color / clarity: Light brown stain / 9.5 ft. secchi (2009)

Shoreland zoning class: Nat. envt.

Mgmt class / Ecological type: Walleye / northern pike-sucker

Accessibility: Portage from Timber Lake (40 rods); portage from Finger Lake (30 rods) portage from Lost Lake (160 rods); portage from Whitefish Lake (60 rods)

Accommodations: Camping

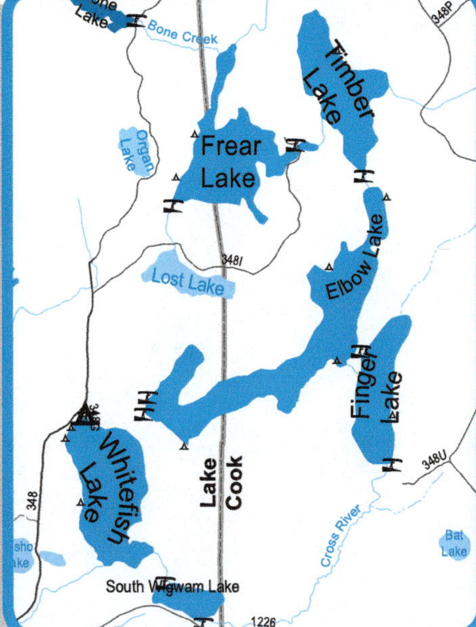

FINGER LAKE

Cook County

Area map pg / coord: 25 / A-4

Watershed: Baptism-Brule

Surface area: 204 acres

Shorelength: 2.7 miles

Max / mean depth: 14 feet / 7 feet

Water color / clarity: Brown stain / 4.0 ft. secchi (2011)

Shoreland zoning class: Nat. envt.

Mgmt class / Ecological type: Walleye/ soft-water walleye

Accessibility: Portage access from Elbow Lake (30 rods) Canoe-in access from Cross River off FR 1225

Accommodations: Camping

Elbow Lake

NO RECORD OF STOCKING

NET CATCH DATA

Date: 08/17/2009

species	Gill Nets # per net	Gill Nets avg. fish weight (lbs.)	Trap Nets # per net	Trap Nets avg. fish weight (lbs.)
Yellow Perch	1.8	1.69	-	-
White Sucker	25.3	0.71	-	-
Walleye	2.2	2.72	-	-
Northern Pike	2.7	0.26	-	-

LENGTH OF SELECTED SPECIES SAMPLED FROM ALL GEAR

Number of fish caught for the following length categories (inches):

species	0-5	6-8	9-11	12-14	15-19	20-24	25-29	>29	Total
Northern Pike	-	-	-	-	6	4	1	-	11
Walleye	-	2	52	80	16	2	-	-	152
Yellow Perch	-	11	5	-	-	-	-	-	16

Finger Lake

FISH STOCKING DATA

year	species	size	# released
10	Walleye	Fry	200,000
11	Walleye	Fry	200,000
14	Walleye	Fry	200,000
15	Walleye	Fry	200,000

NET CATCH DATA

Date: 08/15/2011

species	Gill Nets # per net	Gill Nets avg. fish weight (lbs.)	Trap Nets # per net	Trap Nets avg. fish weight (lbs.)
Black Crappie	0.83	0.08	-	-
Northern Pike	2.33	1.63	0.89	1.02
Walleye	10.5	1.04	0.11	1.59
White Sucker	20.5	2.52	0.33	1.51
Yellow Perch	1.33	0.39	0.33	0.08

LENGTH OF SELECTED SPECIES SAMPLED FROM ALL GEAR

Number of fish caught for the following length categories (inches):

species	0-5	6-8	9-11	12-14	15-19	20-24	25-29	>29	Total
Black Crappie	5	-	-	-	-	-	-	-	5
Northern Pike	-	1	-	2	15	3	1	-	22
Walleye	-	4	4	27	28	1	-	-	64
White Sucker	-	2	10	7	86	21	-	-	126
Yellow Perch	2	2	7	-	-	-	-	-	11

FISHING INFORMATION

Elbow and Finger are two more appendages of the Timber-Frear Canoe Route.

Elbow is not only the larger of these two, but it probably has better fishing. A local angler says it's a good lake throughout the year for walleyes, and there are also northern pike and yellow perch.

The walleyes aren't huge, averaging about a pound or so, but there are plenty of them. Most are on the small end of keeper range, but they fry up just fine.

The perch population isn't real high, but local anglers say they're pretty nice. Small minnows will do nicely and you can often catch decent perch while using live bait for walleyes.

The fishing for northerns is pretty standard. Use spinnerbaits and spoons tossed to weed edges or any structure you can find.

For walleyes, use jigs tipped with minnows in the spring, but carry some leeches from July on as the fish may have a picky palate. Another local favorite is the Beaver Flick, which is made and sold by The Beaver House in Grand Marais. This little flicker spinner gives added attraction to your minnow.

Look for walleyes near the point by the creek outlet to Finger Lake **(Spot 1)**. The broad point near the narrows **(Spot 2)** on the lake's northern end and the 12-foot-deep "hole" on the lake's western shore **(Spot 3)** may also yield walleyes.

Nearby **Finger Lake** is accessible via portage from Elbow Lake or by paddling on Cross River from a put-in on Forest Road 1225.

The lake doesn't get much fishing pressure, although it does support a decent population of walleyes, northern pike and yellow perch. Black crappies showed up in lakes along the Cross River just a few years back. Walleye fry are stocked regularly.

Locals say there are quite a few small walleyes, but there are some larger ones as well. The lake doesn't have a whole lot of structure. The creek inlets on the north and west shores are spots to try early in the season. Later, you might want to switch to the east shore's moderately quick drop or the 13-foot-deep "hole" in the middle.

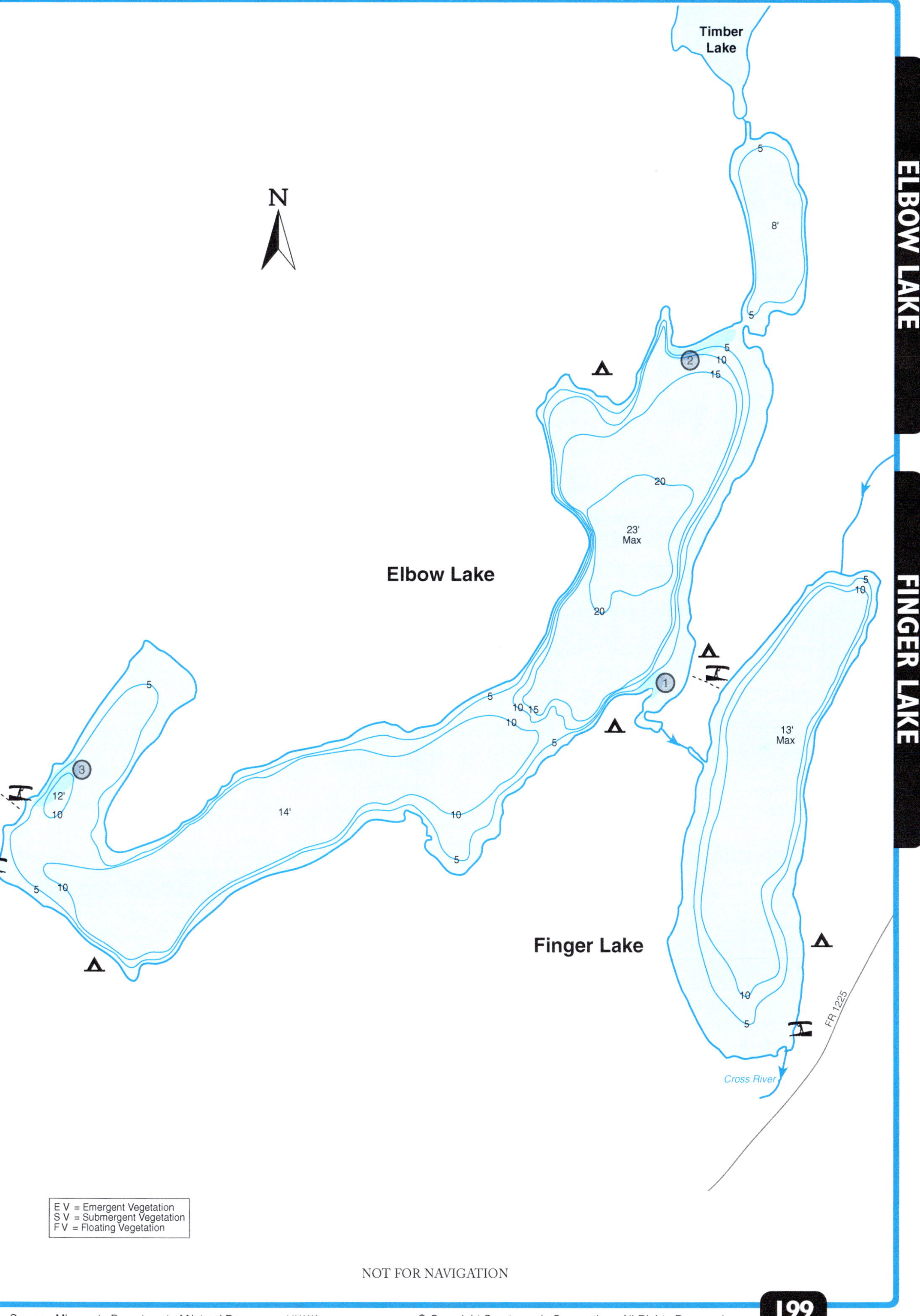

NOT FOR NAVIGATION

TOOHEY LAKE

Cook County

Area map pg / coord: 25 / A-4

Watershed: Baptism-Brule

Surface area: 369 acres

Shorelength: 3.3 miles

Max / mean depth: 11 feet / 9 feet

Water color / clarity: Brown, bog stain / 5.6 ft. secchi (2012)

Shoreland zoning class: Nat. envt.

Mgmt class / Ecological type: Walleye / soft-water walleye

Accessibility: USFS-owned public access with gravel ramp in campground on south shore off FR 170

90° 57' 12" W / 47° 42' 48" N

Accommodations: Camping, picnicking, restrooms

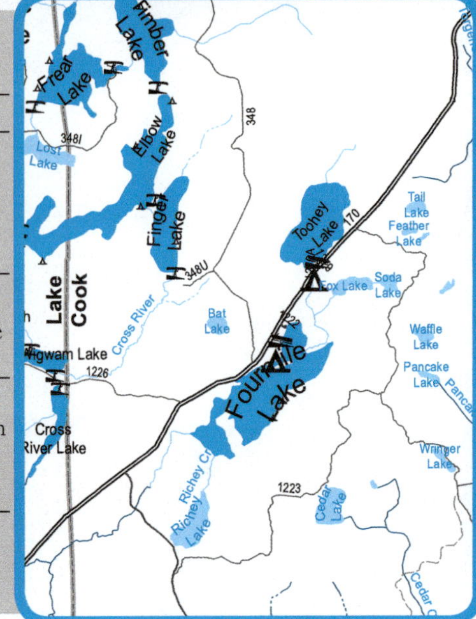

NO RECORD OF STOCKING

NET CATCH DATA				
Date: 08/06/2012	Gill Nets		Trap Nets	
species	# per net	avg. fish weight (lbs.)	# per net	avg. fish weight (lbs.)
Northern Pike	1.00	0.71	0.44	0.57
Walleye	41.00	0.99	2.00	1.09
White Sucker	1.40	1.76	0.11	2.54
Yellow Perch	20.60	0.39	2.67	0.28

LENGTH OF SELECTED SPECIES SAMPLED FROM ALL GEAR

Number of fish caught for the following length categories (inches):

species	0-5	6-8	9-11	12-14	15-19	20-24	25-29	>29	Total
Northern Pike	-	-	1	6	2	-	-	-	9
Walleye	1	6	41	79	94	-	1	-	222
White Sucker	-	-	1	1	6	-	-	-	8
Yellow Perch	7	59	53	7	-	-	-	-	126

FOURMILE LAKE

Cook County

Area map pg / coord: 25 / B-4

Watershed: Baptism-Brule

Surface area: 593 acres

Shorelength: 7.0 miles

Max / mean depth: 20 feet / 10 feet

Water color / clarity: Dark brown, bog stained / 6.3 ft. secchi (2011)

Shoreland zoning class: Nat. envt.

Mgmt class / Ecological type: Walleye / soft-water walleye

Accessibility: USFS-owned public access with concrete ramp at campground on northwest shore, off FR 170

90° 57' 49" W / 47° 41' 59" N

Accommodations: Camping, picnicking, restrooms

NO RECORD OF STOCKING

NET CATCH DATA				
Date: 08/22/2011	Gill Nets		Trap Nets	
species	# per net	avg. fish weight (lbs.)	# per net	avg. fish weight (lbs.)
Black Crappie	1.78	0.37	1.00	0.97
Northern Pike	0.44	1.45	0.67	0.91
Walleye	17.11	1.04	1.56	1.57
White Sucker	7.78	2.17	1.00	3.04
Yellow Perch	3.00	0.62	0.44	0.33

LENGTH OF SELECTED SPECIES SAMPLED FROM ALL GEAR

Number of fish caught for the following length categories (inches):

species	0-5	6-8	9-11	12-14	15-19	20-24	25-29	>29	Total
Black Crappie	11	1	9	4	-	-	-	-	25
Northern Pike	-	1	-	1	5	3	-	-	10
Walleye	1	7	27	70	56	7	-	-	168
White Sucker	-	4	4	5	59	7	-	-	79
Yellow Perch	2	2	27	-	-	-	-	-	31

FISHING INFORMATION

Anglers looking for good numbers of walleyes may just want to make a stop at **Toohey Lake**. This lake consistently produces high numbers of good-sized walleyes and large perch, with few northern pike to bite you off.

There isn't a lot of depth or structure to the lake, and that makes what there is quite important. The series of points along the eastern shore are said to be the best spots on the lake. Make sure to check out the island and it's 11-foot-deep hole to the west. The edges of the bulrush beds hold fish, particularly perch and pike. Angler Jeff Herrick suggests fishing walleyes with stickbaits or live-bait rigs. This is a good early season lake, but it offers some ice action as well.

There's a boat ramp for access, but visiting anglers should be forewarned that it's very shallow and you may have to muscle your boat off and back onto your trailer. The lake also has a small campground and restrooms near the outlet of Toohey Creek.

Fourmile Lake also holds very good numbers of walleyes and perch, but also has black crappies, some of which make it to slab proportions.

The walleye population is self-sustaining, and Herrick says numbers, as well as size, are pretty good. The lake is a good early season lake, although anglers will find good action throughout the open-water season, as well as a decent winter walleye bite.

Anglers will find some good structure in Fourmile, even though it isn't very deep. The many humps and holes, as well as the adjacent edges, are all worth a look. Fishing the windward side of structure is always a solid plan.

The bar and accompanying weedbed off the southern tip of the big island is probably the best spot on the lake to fish, says Herrick, but the series of underwater points and inside turns off the lake's eastern shore also deserve a look.

Fish the 'eyes with slip-bobbers and minnows, leeches or crawlers. At first ice, use a jigging spoon or jigging Rapala tipped with a minnow head. When fish are a bit more finicky, a shiner under a tip-up or deadstick can also be productive.

The launch site is nice with a good concrete ramp.

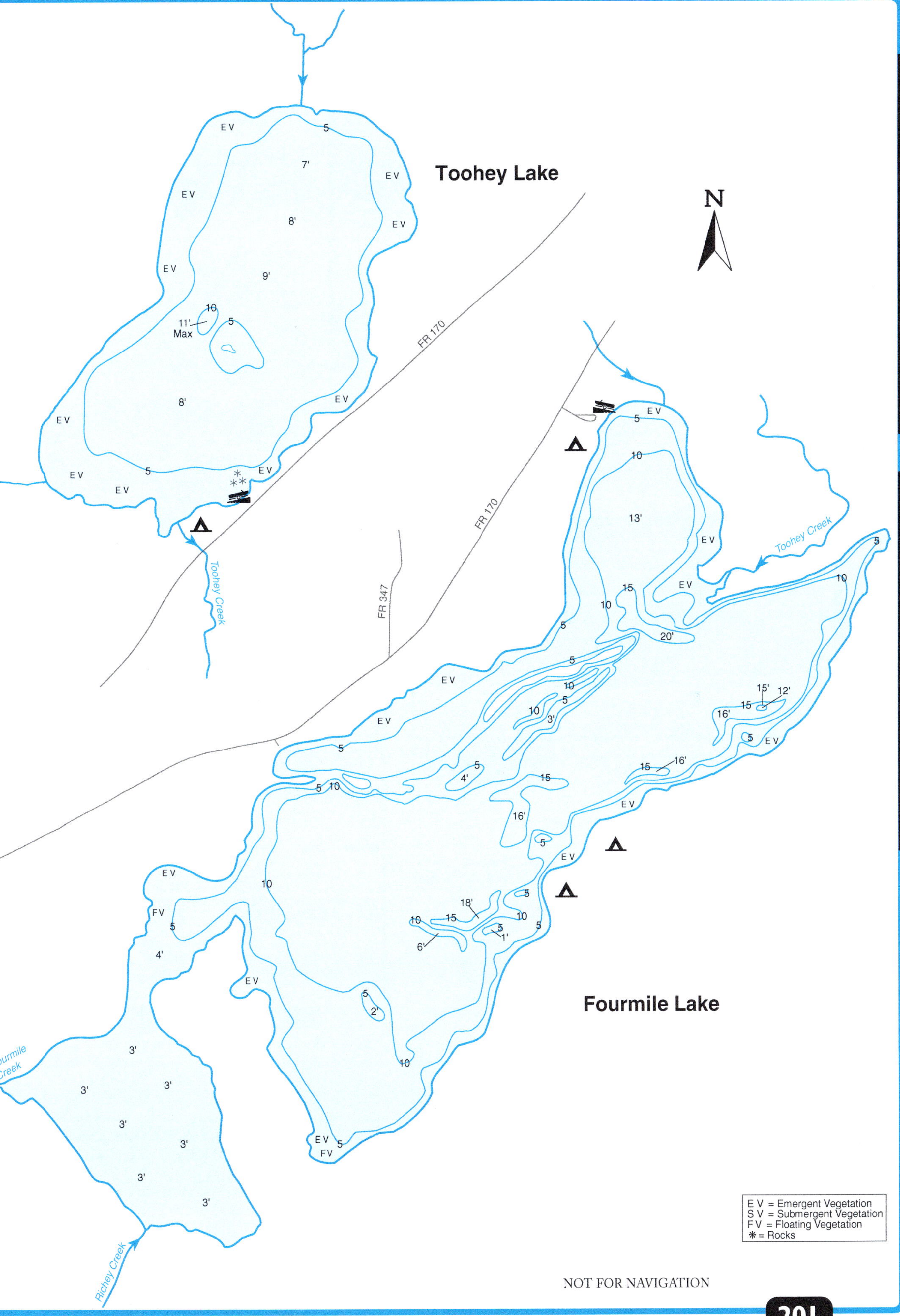

Source: Minnesota Department of Natural Resources, USGS

WHITE PINE LAKE — Cook County

CHRISTINE LAKE — Cook County

BARKER LAKE — Cook County

	WHITE PINE	CHRISTINE	BARKER
Area map pg / coord:	25 / A-6	26 / A-1	25/B-6, 26/B-1
Watershed:	Baptism-Brule	Baptism-Brule	Baptism-Brule
Surface area:	346 acres	195 acres	149 acres
Shorelength:	5.2 miles	3.4 miles	3.2 miles
Max / mean depth:	10 ft. / 4 ft.	7 ft. / 5 ft.	15 ft. / 7 ft.
Water color / clarity:	Brown tint / 4.3 ft. secchi (2012)	Brown tint / 7.0 ft. secchi (2001)	Brown stain / 3.0 ft. secchi (2013)
Shoreland zoning class:	Rec. dev.	Rec. dev.	Nat. envt.
Management class:	Walleye	Centrarchid	Walleye
Ecological type:	Northern pike-sucker	Northern pike-sucker	Soft-water walleye
Accessibility:	USFS-owned public access with concrete ramp on south shore 90° 44' 52" W 47° 44' 22" N	State-owned public access with gravel ramp on west shore 90° 44' 8" W 47° 44' 10" N	Carry-down access to east shore; parking for five vehicles
Accommodations:	Camping, pier	None	None

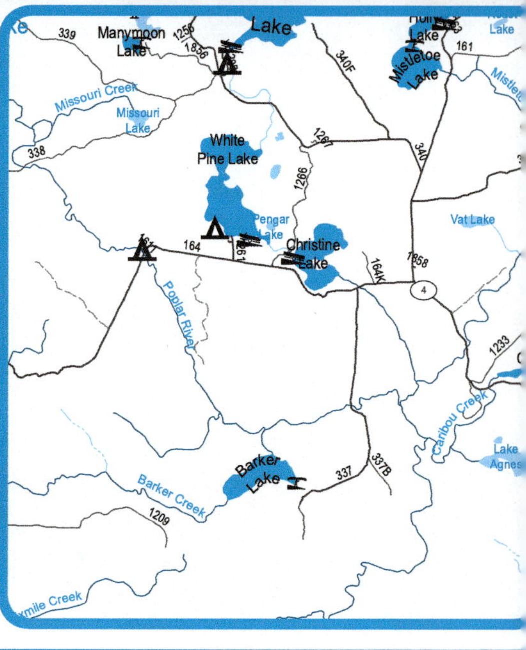

White Pine Lake

NO RECORD OF STOCKING

LENGTH OF SELECTED SPECIES SAMPLED FROM ALL GEAR

Survey Date: 09/10/2012

Number of fish caught for the following length categories (inches):

species	0-5	6-8	9-11	12-14	15-19	20-24	25-29	>29	Total
Bluegill	8	4	1	-	-	-	-	-	13
Northern Pike	-	-	3	5	11	14	3	1	37
Pumpkinseed	13	1	-	-	-	-	-	-	14
Walleye	-	-	1	3	1	4	2	-	11
White Sucker	-	2	-	3	10	-	-	-	15
Yellow Perch	19	46	70	3	-	-	-	-	138

Christine Lake

NO RECORD OF STOCKING

LENGTH OF SELECTED SPECIES SAMPLED FROM ALL GEAR

Survey Date: 07/23/2001

Number of fish caught for the following length categories (inches):

species	0-5	6-8	9-11	12-14	15-19	20-24	25-29	>29	Total
Bluegill	43	6	1	-	-	-	-	-	50
Northern Pike	-	1	5	6	9	10	4	2	37
Pumpkin. Sunfish	102	8	-	-	-	-	-	-	110
Walleye	-	-	-	2	4	5	1	-	12
Yellow Perch	14	37	30	2	-	-	-	-	83

Barker Lake

FISH STOCKING DATA

year	species	size	# released
00	Walleye	Fry	140,000

LENGTH OF SELECTED SPECIES SAMPLED FROM ALL GEAR

Survey Date: 09/04/2013

Number of fish caught for the following length categories (inches):

species	0-5	6-8	9-11	12-14	15-19	20-24	25-29	>29	Total
Black Crappie	1	1	1	-	-	-	-	-	3
Northern Pike	-	-	-	-	4	2	-	-	6
Pumpkinseed	1	-	-	-	-	-	-	-	1
Walleye	3	11	9	6	1	1	-	-	31
White Sucker	-	-	-	17	5	-	-	-	22
Yellow Perch	9	13	2	-	-	-	-	-	24

FISHING INFORMATION

These three Lutsen-area lakes contain similar fisheries. In **White Pine**, expect to find walleyes, northern pike, nice-sized perch, bluegills and, according to angler Jeff Herrick, who owns the Superior Bakery at the Holiday station in Tofte, some smallmouth bass. He says the walleyes are nice and they offer some good action in this stained body of water.

Anglers will find the narrows between the two sections of the lake to be the best spot. Herrick says he likes live bait soaked under slip bobbers. Minnows will work fine well into June; then switch over to leeches and crawlers. Casting stickbaits over emerging vegetation can also produce early in the season. As the season advances, the lake weeds up heavily, so you'll want to do most of your fishing before August.

Christine Lake, Herrick says, is another good early season lake for walleyes. Like White Pine, it also sports northern pike, bluegills and yellow perch. Northerns have good size structure, with some good eaters and some larger fish in the mix as well. Perch have a similar quality size distribution, with good numbers of 9- to 10-inch keepers and the occasional 12-inch jumbo. Walleyes numbers aren't particularly high, but some larger fish are present. There are a pretty decent number of both bluegills and pumpkinseeds here, and some of these sunfish reach keeper size. Casting a stickbait in Christine Lake is a sure way to get bit, most likely by pike, but you might hook an aggressive walleye as well.

The lake's gravel ramp is located on the west shore.

Barker Lake is known for big northern pike, "eater-size" walleyes, decent perch and crappies. The latter, says Herrick, are few in number but big in size. A 12-incher isn't out of the question. Walleyes are fairly abundant - even more abundant now than when they were stocked years ago - but most are on the small side. This lake is bowl-shaped and offers no typical walleye structure. An angler's best bet, says Herrick, is to troll with stickbaits and when you find some fish, stop and start drowning a minnow or leech under a slip bobber. Northerns can be found inhabiting the weedlines. Perch run decent and there are a few smallmouth bass present.

Anglers will be relegated to a carry-down access at the end of a trail on the lake's east shore.

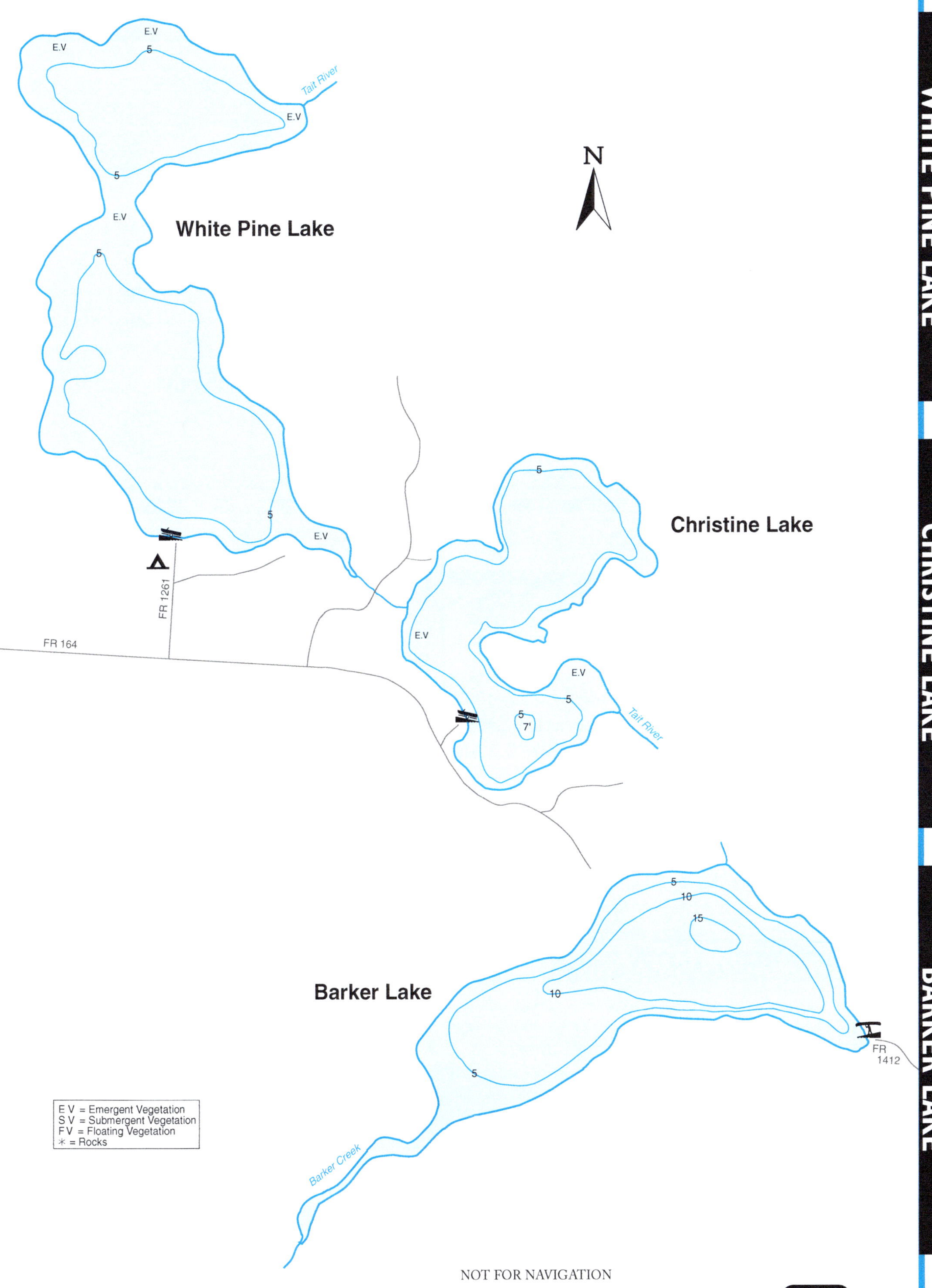

NOT FOR NAVIGATION

Source: Minnesota Department of Natural Resources, USGS

CARIBOU LAKE

Cook County

Area map pg / coord: 26/A,B-1,2

Watershed: Baptism-Brule

Surface area: 721 acres

Shorelength: 10.4 miles

Max / mean depth: 30 feet / 13 feet

Water color / clarity: Yellow-green / 7.8 ft. secchi (2014)

Shoreland zoning class: Rec. dev.

Mgmt class / Ecological type: Walleye / northern pike - sucker

Accessibility: State-owned public access with concrete ramp on west shore of middle basin, off Co. Rd. 4; parking for five vehicles

90° 39' 56" W / 47° 42' 27" N

Accommodations: Resort

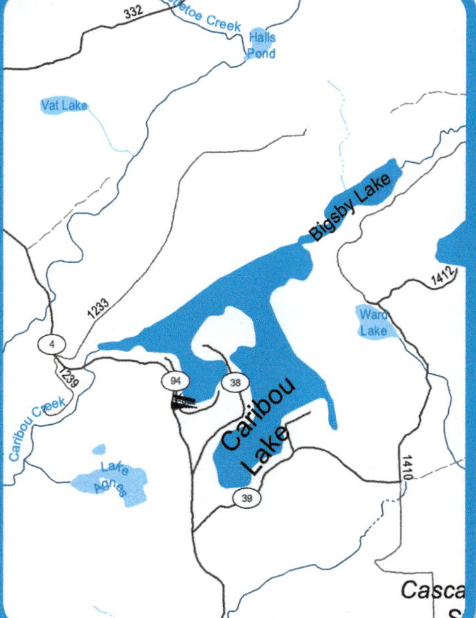

BIGSBY LAKE

Cook County

Area map pg / coord: 26 / A-2

Watershed: Baptism-Brule

Surface area: 90 acres

Shorelength: NA

Max / mean depth: 4 feet / NA

Water color / clarity: Brown, bog stained / 4.0 ft. secchi (1998)

Shoreland zoning class: Nat. envt.

Mgmt class / Ecological type: NA / NA

Accessibility: Via navigable channel from Caribou Lake (ramp on Caribou)

Accommodations: None

Caribou Lake

FISH STOCKING DATA

year	species	size	# released
07	Walleye	Fry	440,000
09	Walleye	Fry	440,000

NET CATCH DATA

Date: 07/21/2014

	Gill Nets		Trap Nets	
species	# per net	avg. fish weight (lbs.)	# per net	avg. fish weight (lbs.)
Black Crappie	-	-	0.11	1.55
Bluegill	-	-	2.00	0.21
Northern Pike	1.44	1.91	0.56	2.39
Smallmouth Bass	-	-	0.44	0.33
Walleye	6.67	0.77	0.56	1.53
White Sucker	3.22	2.09	0.22	1.33
Yellow Perch	2.44	0.08	0.33	0.08

LENGTH OF SELECTED SPECIES SAMPLED FROM ALL GEAR

Number of fish caught for the following length categories (inches):

species	0-5	6-8	9-11	12-14	15-19	20-24	25-29	>29	Total
Black Crappie	-	-	-	1	-	-	-	-	1
Bluegill	8	9	1	-	-	-	-	-	18
Northern Pike	-	-	1	-	9	6	1	1	18
Smallmouth Bass	-	2	2	-	-	-	-	-	4
Walleye	-	17	23	10	12	3	-	-	65
White Sucker	-	3	4	7	13	4	-	-	31
Yellow Perch	22	3	-	-	-	-	-	-	25

Bigsby Lake

NO RECORD OF STOCKING

NET CATCH DATA

Date: 06/29/1998

	Gill Nets		Trap Nets	
species	# per net	avg. fish weight (lbs.)	# per net	avg. fish weight (lbs.)
Northern Pike	15.0	1.19	2.7	1.19
Smallmouth Bass	0.3	2.50	0.2	1.32
Walleye	2.3	2.08	1.7	2.06
Yellow Perch	11.3	0.26	0.3	0.37

LENGTH OF SELECTED SPECIES SAMPLED FROM ALL GEAR

Number of fish caught for the following length categories (inches):

species	0-5	6-8	9-11	12-14	15-19	20-24	25-29	>29	Total
Northern Pike	-	-	5	7	35	14	-	-	61
Smallmouth Bass	-	-	-	1	1	-	-	-	2
Walleye	-	1	-	-	13	3	-	-	17
Yellow Perch	4	22	10	-	-	-	-	-	36

FISHING INFORMATION

Caribou Lake is home to northern pike, smallmouth bass, yellow perch and walleyes. You'll even find some bluegills and crappies here, which is relatively uncommon for area lakes.

Walleyes are of primary interest to most anglers here and their numbers are good. However, they are down from what they were a few years back and below the DNR's goal for this lake, which has more development and more fishing pressure than most lakes in the area. Walleyes are stocked sometimes, but the population is composed almost entirely of naturally produced fish. One local angler says the 'eyes are not only numerous, but nice as well. It's not unusual, he says, to limit out on 16-inch fish or to tie into something larger.

Northern pike numbers are decent here, and you'll find some quality-sized pike here. Both northern pike and walleyes grow faster than average in Caribou.

Perch are generally small. Bluegills and crappies reach good size, but the trick might be in finding them, because neither is found here in very large numbers. Smallmouth bass are present here as well, although their numbers are down from what they were in the early 2000s.

The shallows around the Caribou Creek inlet and outlet **(Spots 1)** are good spring walleye spots. Later, troll the eastern shore of the large peninsula **(Spot 2)** near the lake's center or work the steep drops **(Spots 3)** off the east, south and west shores.

Bigsby is more a bay on Caribou than a separate lake; it's accessed via a channel in the northeast section of Caribou Lake. Its shallow depth and several inlets make it a place to try in the spring for walleyes, northern pike, perch and smallmouth bass. There's little in the way of structure, so the fishing is pretty straightforward: cast or troll shallow-running crankbaits or drift through the lake with a slip bobber and minnow.

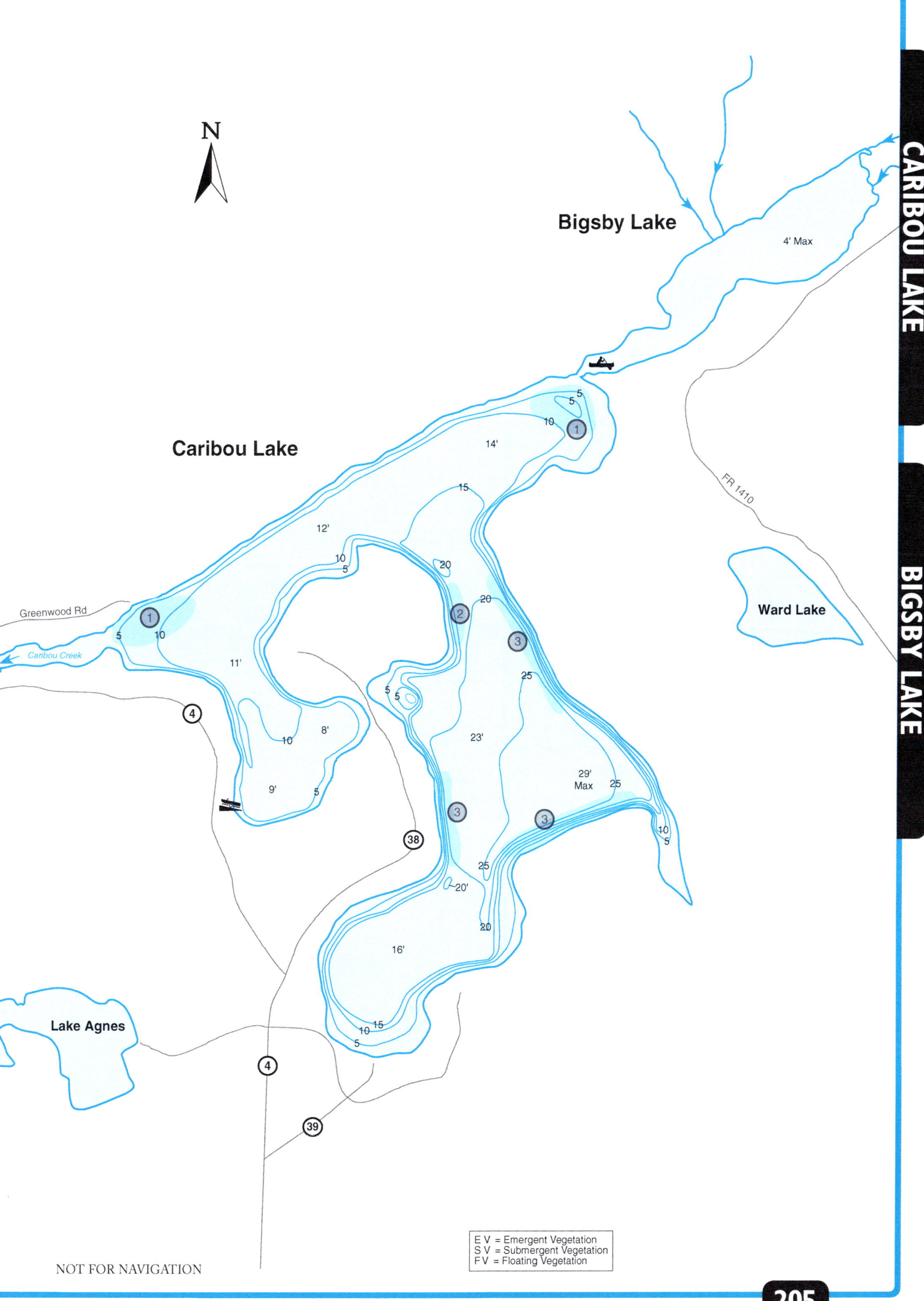

Source: Minnesota Department of Natural Resources, USGS

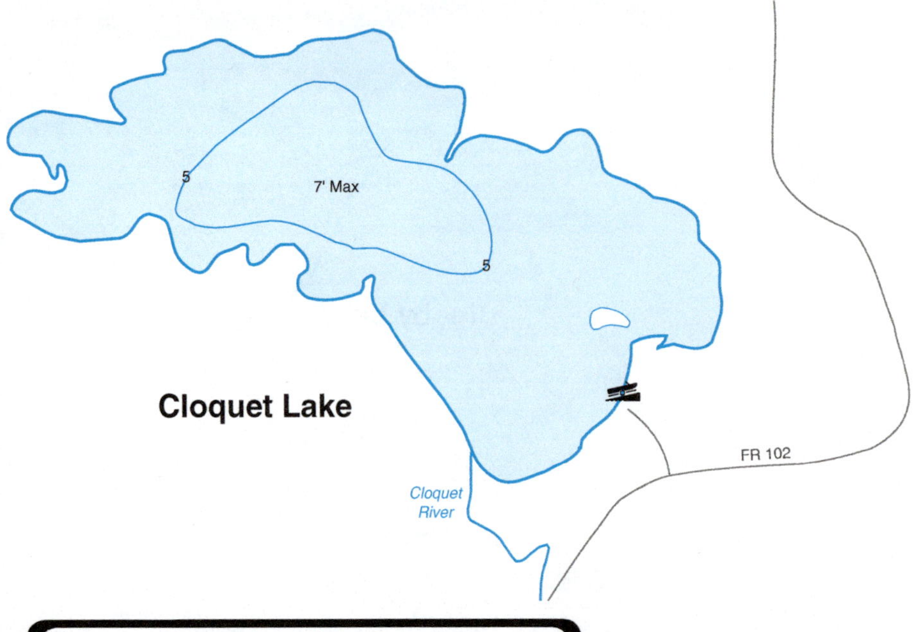

Cloquet Lake, Lake County

Area map page / coordinates: 28 / B-4
Surface area / max depth: 183 acres / 7 feet
Accessibility: USFS-owned public access with gravel ramp (suitable for smaller boats) on southeast shore
91° 29' 8" W / 47° 25' 51" N

FISH STOCKING DATA

year	species	size	# released
11	Walleye	Fingerling	2,344
12	Walleye	Fingerling	3,973
15	Walleye	Fingerling	2,050

LENGTH OF SELECTED SPECIES SAMPLED FROM ALL GEAR

Survey Date: 08/23/2010

Number of fish caught for the following length categories (inches):

species	0-5	6-8	9-11	12-14	15-19	20-24	25-29	>30	Total
Northern Pike	-	-	-	5	35	2	-	2	44
Walleye	-	-	4	-	16	6	1	-	27
White Sucker	-	-	1	-	20	2	-	-	23
Yellow Perch	3	6	34	2	-	-	-	-	45

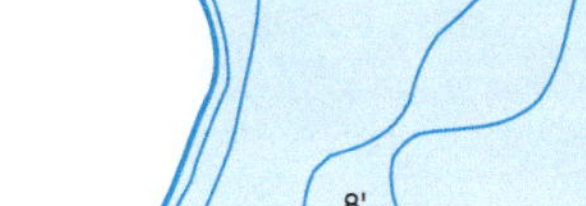

Sullivan Lake, Lake County

Area map page / coordinates: 28 / C-2
Surface area / max depth: 53 acres / 8 feet
Accessibility: State-owned public access with earthen ramp on northwest shore in campground, 1/4 mile south of Co. Rd. 15
91° 40' 12" W / 47° 22' 52" N

FISH STOCKING DATA

year	species	size	# released
05	Bluegill	Adult	300

LENGTH OF SELECTED SPECIES SAMPLED FROM ALL GEAR

Survey Date: 06/02/2008

Number of fish caught for the following length categories (inches):

species	0-5	6-8	9-11	12-14	15-19	20-24	25-29	>30	Total
Northern Pike	-	-	-	4	7	7	6	2	26
Yellow Perch	4	65	48	2	-	-	-	-	119

Source: Minnesota Department of Natural Resources, USGS

NOT FOR NAVIGATION

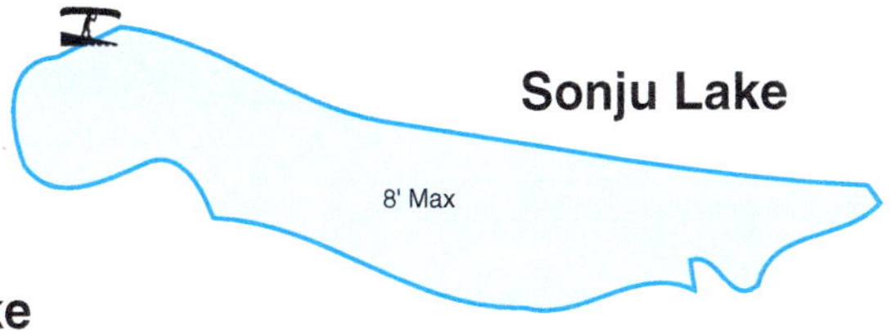

Sonju Lake

8' Max

Balsam Lake

Less than 4' throughout

5

Less than 4' throughout

3'

15

10

16'

15

5

F.V

Sonju Lake, Lake County

Area map page / coordinates: 30 / A-1

Surface area / max depth: 37 acres / 8 feet

Accessibility: Carry-down access to northwest shore from Sonju Lake Road (30 yard portage)

FISH STOCKING DATA

year	species	size	# released
10	Brook Trout	Yearling	799
11	Brook Trout	Adult	331
11	Brook Trout	Yearling	751
12	Brook Trout	Yearling	1,020
13	Brook Trout	Yearling	1,000
14	Brook Trout	Yearling	600

LENGTH OF SELECTED SPECIES SAMPLED FROM ALL GEAR

Survey Date: 09/24/2012

Number of fish caught for the following length categories (inches):

species	0-5	6-8	9-11	12-14	15-19	20-24	25-29	>30	Total
Brown Trout	-	7	6	-	-	-	-	-	13

BALSAM LAKE

Cramer Lake

4' Max

Balsam Lake, Lake County

Area map page / coordinates: 24 / E-1,2

Surface area / max depth: 225 acres / 18 feet

Accessibility: Carry-down access to south shore

NO RECORD OF STOCKING

LENGTH OF SELECTED SPECIES SAMPLED FROM ALL GEAR

Survey Date: 06/19/2000

Number of fish caught for the following length categories (inches):

species	0-5	6-8	9-11	12-14	15-19	20-24	25-29	>30	Total
Brook Trout	4	43	4	15	7	-	-	-	73

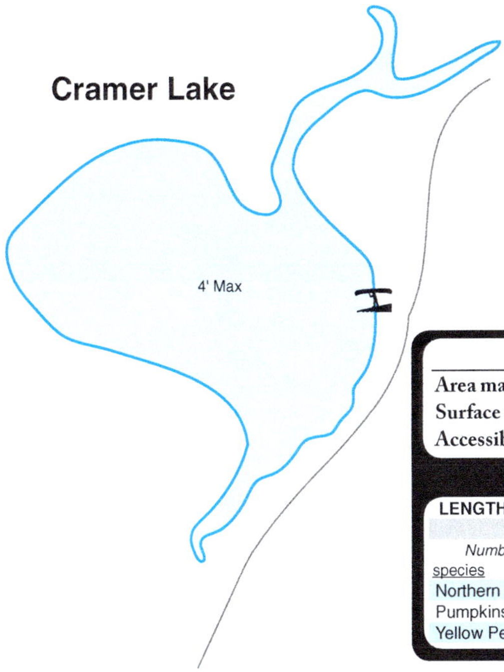

CRAMER LAKE

Cramer Lake, Lake County

Area map page / coordinates: 24 / E-3

Surface area / max depth: 68 acres / 4 feet

Accessibility: Carry-down access to east shore

NO RECORD OF STOCKING

LENGTH OF SELECTED SPECIES SAMPLED FROM ALL GEAR

Survey Date: 07/06/2010

Number of fish caught for the following length categories (inches):

species	0-5	6-8	9-11	12-14	15-19	20-24	25-29	>30	Total
Northern Pike	-	-	3	3	26	7	5	1	45
Pumpkinseed	110	1	-	-	-	-	-	-	111
Yellow Perch	12	19	6	-	-	-	-	-	37

N

10

20

30

Benson Lake, Lake County

Area map page / coordinates: 30 / A-2

Surface area / max depth: 19 acres / 36 feet

Accessibility: Carry-down access to northwest shore via the Crosby-Manitou State Park entrance road; vehicle permit required

FISH STOCKING DATA

year	species	size	# released
10	Splake	Fingerling	2,499
11	Splake	Fingerling	2,610
12	Splake	Fingerling	2,496
13	Splake	Fingerling	1,734
14	Splake	Fingerling	2,420
15	Splake	Fingerling	2,500

LENGTH OF SELECTED SPECIES SAMPLED FROM ALL GEAR

Survey Date: 09/22/2014

Number of fish caught for the following length categories (inches):

species	0-5	6-8	9-11	12-14	15-19	20-24	25-29	>30	Total
Splake	2	12	4	13	10	-	-	-	41

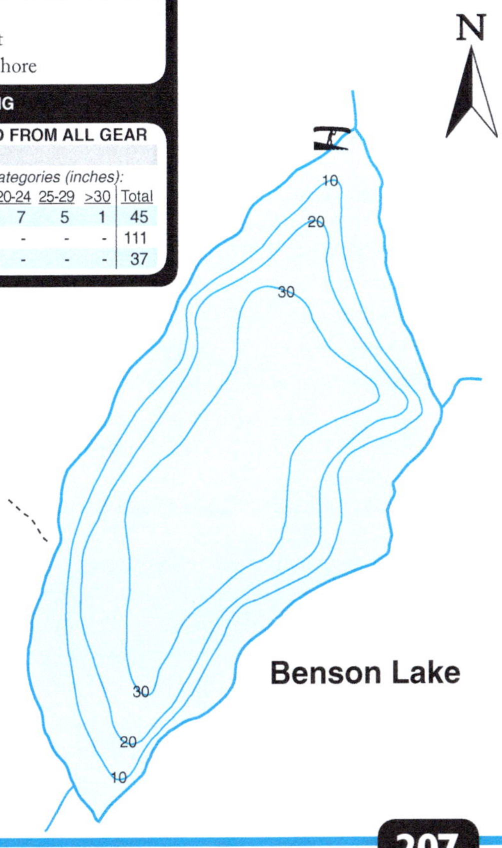

Benson Lake

30

20

10

BENSON LAKE

Source: Minnesota Department of Natural Resources, USGS

LAX LAKE *Lake County*

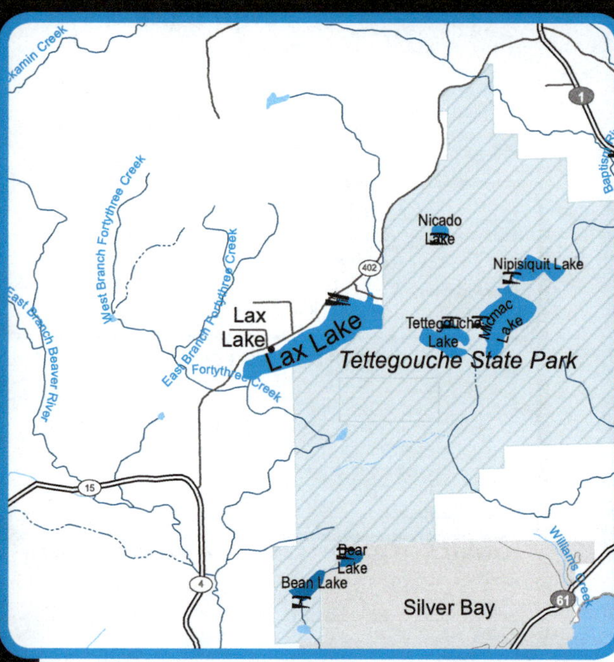

Area map page / coordinates: 29 / D-6 & 30 / D-1

Watershed: Beaver-Lester

Surface water area / shorelength: 295 acres / 3.8 miles

Maximum / mean depth: 35 feet / 10 feet

Water color / clarity: Light brown tint / 10.1 ft. secchi (2014)

Shoreland zoning classification: General development

Management class / Ecological type: Walleye /soft-water walley

Accessibility: State-owned public access with concrete ramp on north shore, off County Road 4

91° 17' 35" W / 47° 21' 5" N

Accommodations: Resort, boat rental, fishing pier, camping, restrooms

FISHING INFORMATION

Lax is one of the better-known lakes in Lake County. It spreads its 295 acres of slightly brown-stained water across the wooded landscape north of Silver Bay, just outside the western boundary of Tettegouche State Park. The lake is rather heavily developed, with private cabins taking up much of the shoreline. Naturally, Lax receives a lot of fishing pressure, but with the help of DNR stocking efforts, it keeps on producing.

Walleye numbers have been on a downward trend, so the DNR is now stocking fingerlings annually to help remedy the situation. Most of the walleyes sampled correlate to years in which fish were stocked, so although natural reproduction isn't great, at least it appears the stocked fingerlings are surviving.

Lax is a popular destination for panfish anglers. The lake holds a high number of bluegills and a pretty good crappie population. Most of the bluegills are on the small side, with some nice fish caught on occasion. The crappies can get fairly large, but a lot of them get cropped off because of the lake's heavy fishing pressure.

This may be one of the better largemouth bass lakes in the area. The average bass size just keeps going up, and there are fish knocking on the 20-inch mark.

The folks at the Knotted Pine Inn & Tavern, 9702 Highway 1, Isabella, MN 55607, (218) 323-7681, say most anglers target walleyes on this lake, focusing on the shallows near the Nicado Creek inlet **(Spot 1)** and around the little hump **(Spot 2)** on the lake's east end in late May. Later, the 'eyes will head deep in search of cooler temperatures. Anglers will find them at the steep break on the lake's south shore **(Spot 3)** during the day, returning to the shallows in the evening to dine on perch. Offer them minnows until June, switching to crawlers and leeches thereafter.

Northern pike will also be in the shallows early, where they should respond to artificials. Later, try for them at the weedlines using crankbaits, spoons or spinners.

FISH STOCKING DATA

year	species	size	# released
08	Walleye	Fingerling	5,722
09	Walleye	Fingerling	4,926
12	Walleye	Fingerling	5,423
12	Walleye	Fingerling	58
13	Walleye	Fingerling	6,303
15	Walleye	Fingerling	2,873

NET CATCH DATA

Date: 08/14/2006

	Gill Nets		Trap Nets	
species	# per net	avg. fish weight (lbs.)	# per net	avg. fish weight (lbs
Black Crappie	3.50	0.28	0.78	0.34
Bluegill	9.17	0.22	27.44	0.13
Hybrid Sunfish	0.17	0.05	0.33	0.06
Largemouth Bass	0.67	2.12	-	-
Northern Pike	4.83	2.56	0.67	1.25
Pumpkinseed	0.67	0.07	3.44	0.11
Walleye	2.17	2.21	0.22	1.18
White Sucker	3.17	2.09	-	-
Yellow Perch	2.33	0.12	0.22	0.07

LENGTH OF SELECTED SPECIES SAMPLED FROM ALL GEAR

Number of fish caught for the following length categories (inches):

species	0-5	6-8	9-11	12-14	15-19	20-24	25-29	>30	Total
Black Crappie	4	23	1	-	-	-	-	-	28
Bluegill	174	127	1	-	-	-	-	-	302
Hybrid Sunfish	4	-	-	-	-	-	-	-	4
Largemouth Bass	-	-	-	-	4	-	-	-	4
Northern Pike	-	-	-	-	20	7	7	1	35
Pumpkinseed	30	5	-	-	-	-	-	-	35
Walleye	-	-	3	1	7	3	1	-	15
White Sucker	-	-	1	5	11	2	-	-	19
Yellow Perch	7	7	-	-	-	-	-	-	14

Look for bass around the shallow, weedy areas, particularly at the cree inlet and outlet. These same areas will also hold the lake's abundan bluegills.

There is a good public access site on the lake's north end, off Count Road 4.

Source: Minnesota Department of Natural Resources, USGS

Tettegouche Lake, Lake County

Area map page / coordinates: 30 / D-1
Surface area / max depth: 67 acres / 20 feet
Accessibility: From Co. Rd. 4 use the Tettegouche State Park service road; portage 1.25 miles on marked trail to north shore of lake

NO RECORD OF STOCKING

LENGTH OF SELECTED SPECIES SAMPLED FROM ALL GEAR
Survey Date: 06/25/2012
Number of fish caught for the following length categories (inches):

species	0-5	6-8	9-11	12-14	15-19	20-24	25-29	>30	Total
Northern Pike	-	-	1	1	7	27	5	-	41
Yellow Perch	-	3	-	-	-	-	-	-	3

Bean Lake, Lake County

Area map page / coordinates: 29 / D-6
Surface area / max depth: 30 acres / 26 feet
Accessibility: Carry-down access to south shore, about 60 feet east of outlet

FISH STOCKING DATA

year	species	size	# released
13	Rainbow Trout	Yearling	1,001
13	Splake	Fingerling	1,684
14	Rainbow Trout	Yearling	1,000
15	Rainbow Trout	Yearling	1,000
15	Splake	Fingerling	1,985

LENGTH OF SELECTED SPECIES SAMPLED FROM ALL GEAR
Survey Date: 06/24/2013
Number of fish caught for the following length categories (inches):

species	0-5	6-8	9-11	12-14	15-19	20-24	25-29	>30	Total
Rainbow Trout	-	-	8	-	2	-	-	-	10
Splake	-	-	3	13	-	-	-	-	16

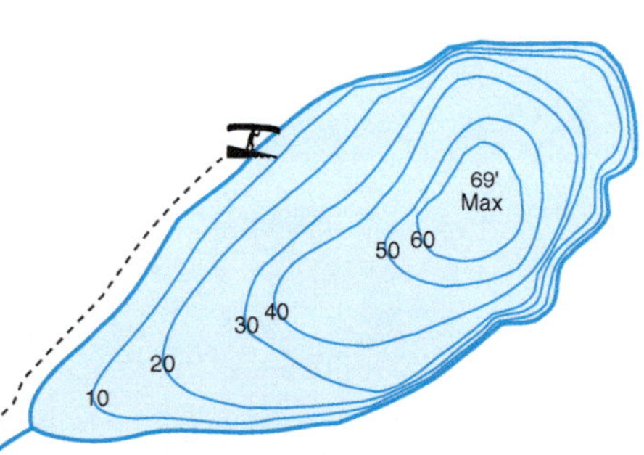

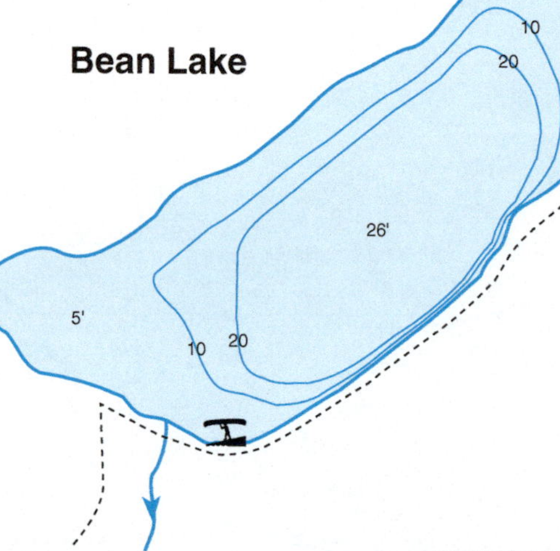

Bear Lake, Lake County

Area map page / coordinates: 30 / D-1
Surface area / max depth: 17 acres / 69 feet
Accessibility: Carry-down access from Superior Hiking Trail, which runs along cliff above the lake; portage access from Bean Lake

FISH STOCKING DATA

year	species	size	# released
07	Splake	Fingerling	2,001
09	Splake	Fingerling	1,997
11	Splake	Fingerling	2,150
13	Splake	Fingerling	1,680
15	Splake	Fingerling	2,000

LENGTH OF SELECTED SPECIES SAMPLED FROM ALL GEAR
Survey Date: 07/01/2013
Number of fish caught for the following length categories (inches):

species	0-5	6-8	9-11	12-14	15-19	20-24	25-29	>30	Total
Lake Trout	-	-	-	-	-	-	2	-	2
Splake	-	1	25	9	-	2	-	-	37

NOT FOR NAVIGATION

Source: Minnesota Department of Natural Resources, USGS

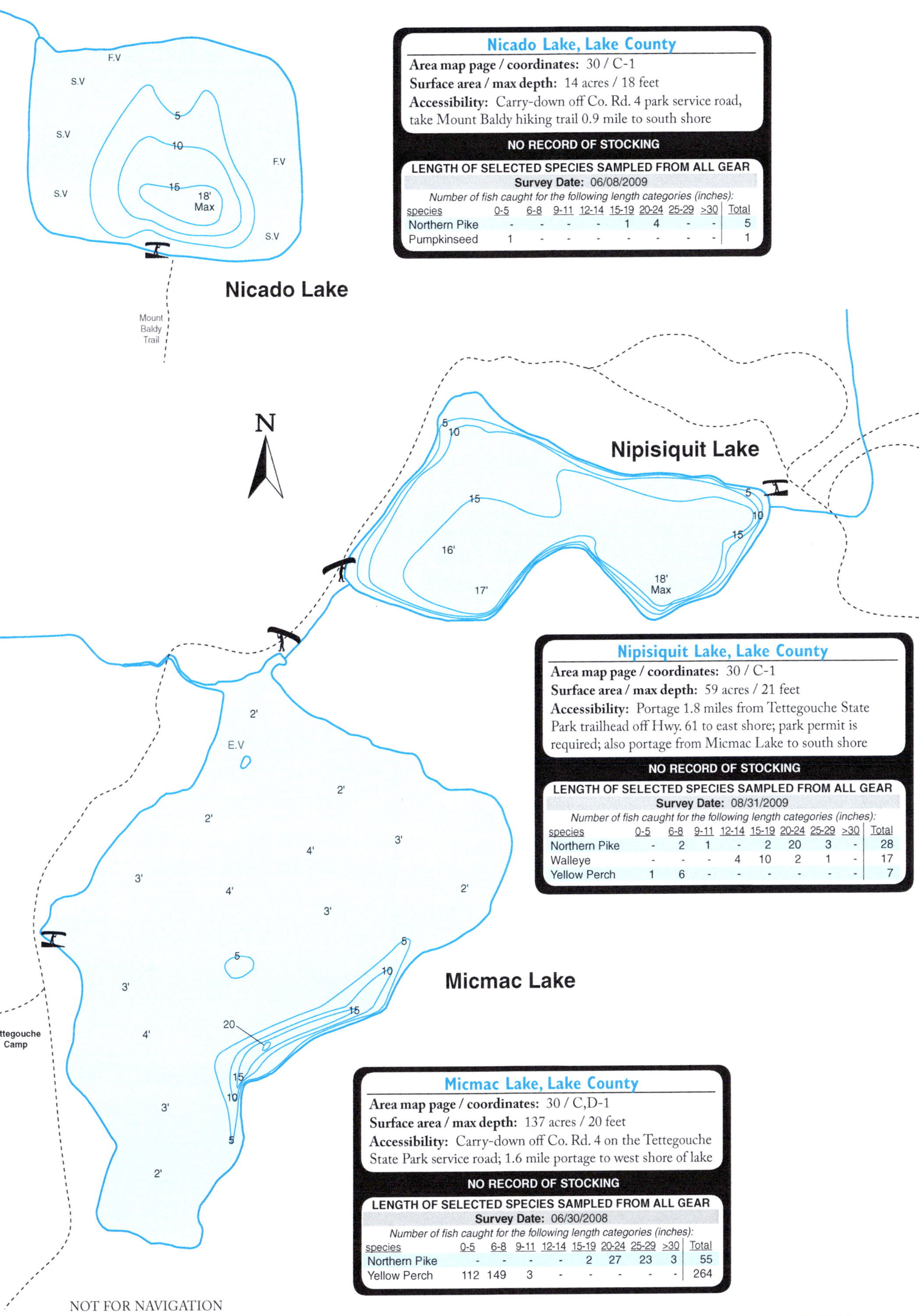

Nicado Lake, Lake County

Area map page / coordinates: 30 / C-1
Surface area / max depth: 14 acres / 18 feet
Accessibility: Carry-down off Co. Rd. 4 park service road, take Mount Baldy hiking trail 0.9 mile to south shore

NO RECORD OF STOCKING

LENGTH OF SELECTED SPECIES SAMPLED FROM ALL GEAR
Survey Date: 06/08/2009
Number of fish caught for the following length categories (inches):

species	0-5	6-8	9-11	12-14	15-19	20-24	25-29	>30	Total
Northern Pike	-	-	-	-	1	4	-	-	5
Pumpkinseed	1	-	-	-	-	-	-	-	1

Nipisiquit Lake, Lake County

Area map page / coordinates: 30 / C-1
Surface area / max depth: 59 acres / 21 feet
Accessibility: Portage 1.8 miles from Tettegouche State Park trailhead off Hwy. 61 to east shore; park permit is required; also portage from Micmac Lake to south shore

NO RECORD OF STOCKING

LENGTH OF SELECTED SPECIES SAMPLED FROM ALL GEAR
Survey Date: 08/31/2009
Number of fish caught for the following length categories (inches):

species	0-5	6-8	9-11	12-14	15-19	20-24	25-29	>30	Total
Northern Pike	-	2	1	-	2	20	3	-	28
Walleye	-	-	-	4	10	2	1	-	17
Yellow Perch	1	6	-	-	-	-	-	-	7

Micmac Lake, Lake County

Area map page / coordinates: 30 / C,D-1
Surface area / max depth: 137 acres / 20 feet
Accessibility: Carry-down off Co. Rd. 4 on the Tettegouche State Park service road; 1.6 mile portage to west shore of lake

NO RECORD OF STOCKING

LENGTH OF SELECTED SPECIES SAMPLED FROM ALL GEAR
Survey Date: 06/30/2008
Number of fish caught for the following length categories (inches):

species	0-5	6-8	9-11	12-14	15-19	20-24	25-29	>30	Total
Northern Pike	-	-	-	-	2	27	23	3	55
Yellow Perch	112	149	3	-	-	-	-	-	264

CHRISTIANSON LAKE
Lake County

THOMAS LAKE
Lake County

STEWART LAKE
Lake County

	CHRISTIANSON	THOMAS	STEWART
Area map pg / coord:	28/E-2, 32/A-2	32 / A-2	32 / B-1, 2
Watershed:		Beaver-Lester, Cloquet	
Surface area:	158 acres	148 acres	238 acres
Shorelength:	2.6 miles	2.0 miles	3.2 miles
Max / mean depth:	8 ft. / 5 ft.	20 ft. / 11 ft.	20 ft. / 7 ft.
Water color / clarity:	Brown / 4.3 ft. secchi (1981)	NA / 3.0 ft. secchi (1999)	NA / 13.0 ft. secchi (2014)
Shoreland zoning class:	Rec. dev.	Rec. dev.	Nat. envt.
Management class:	Centrarchid	Walleye	Walleye
Ecological type:	Centrarchid	Northern pike-sucker	Northern pike-sucker
Accessibility:	Public access with gravel ramp on east shore, off Cty. Rd. 202	Carry-down access to northwest shore	County-owned public access with concrete ramp on south shore
	91° 40' 10" W 47° 15' 23" N	N / W	91° 45' 15" W 47° 11' 0" N
Accommodations:	None	None	None

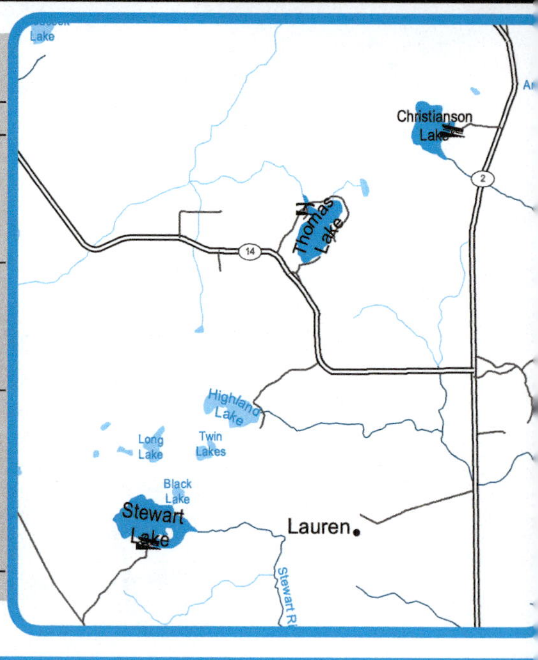

Christianson Lake

NO RECORD OF STOCKING

LENGTH OF SELECTED SPECIES SAMPLED FROM ALL GEAR

Survey Date: 08/24/1981

Number of fish caught for the following length categories (inches):

species	0-5	6-8	9-11	12-14	15-19	20-24	25-29	>29	Total
Black Crappie	2	1	32	2	-	-	-	-	37
Northern Pike	-	-	2	1	-	-	5	-	8
Pumpkin. Sunfish	21	1	-	-	-	-	-	-	22
Yellow Perch	19	134	5	-	-	-	-	-	158

Thomas Lake

NO RECORD OF STOCKING

LENGTH OF SELECTED SPECIES SAMPLED FROM ALL GEAR

Survey Date: 07/27/1999

Number of fish caught for the following length categories (inches):

species	0-5	6-8	9-11	12-14	15-19	20-24	25-29	>29	Total
Black Bullhead	5	52	29	1	-	-	-	-	87
Black Crappie	40	69	14	1	-	-	-	-	124
Bluegill	17	6	-	-	-	-	-	-	23
Largemouth Bass	-	-	-	-	1	-	-	-	1
Northern Pike	-	-	-	2	4	16	6	3	31
Pumpkin. Sunfish	15	-	-	-	-	-	-	-	15
Rock Bass	-	1	-	-	-	-	-	-	1
Walleye	-	-	-	-	-	1	-	-	1
Yellow Perch	58	48	-	-	-	-	-	-	106

Stewart Lake

NO RECORD OF STOCKING

LENGTH OF SELECTED SPECIES SAMPLED FROM ALL GEAR

Survey Date: 07/28/2014

Number of fish caught for the following length categories (inches):

species	0-5	6-8	9-11	12-14	15-19	20-24	25-29	>29	Total
Black Crappie	3	7	18	-	-	-	-	-	28
Bluegill	46	66	11	-	-	-	-	-	123
Hybrid Sunfish	1	-	-	-	-	-	-	-	1
Northern Pike	1	1	2	10	22	14	5	7	62
Pumpkinseed	206	95	-	-	-	-	-	-	301
Walleye	-	-	3	4	5	2	1	-	15
White Sucker	-	-	1	2	12	1	-	-	16
Yellow Perch	23	139	61	2	-	-	-	-	225

FISHING INFORMATION

Christianson Lake is known for northern pike, some of which occasionally hit the 20-pound mark. Crappies can also be found here in decent sizes. Perch are abundant, but you'll have to do a lot of sorting to find some keepers. Small minnows or waxies on small jigs work just fine for the crappies. Concentrate your efforts on the weeds for the pike. The lake is relatively featureless, so look for weed pockets. Christianson is a popular winter fishing destination.

Thomas Lake offers a few walleyes, good numbers of northern pike, crappies, bluegills and largemouth bass. Locals say this is one of the better crappie lakes in the area, with fish present in all sizes. Although most northern pike are about average size, there are a few good-sized pike found here. The point on the lake's east side, near the 20-foot hole, is the place to try for crappies, both in mid-summer and in winter. For northern pike, it's hard to beat the weedbeds near the rock pile and off the north side of the point. Locals often fish from shore at the shoreline access site with a bobber and large minnows for pike.

The lake is mostly private. Carry-down access is at the bridge on County Road 141. Since the access is difficult, anglers fish Thomas mostly in the winter.

Stewart Lake is probably the best of the bunch. It has good numbers of walleyes, northern pike, perch, crappies and bluegills. The folks at Muskie Doom Guide Service, (218) 491-3277, www.muskiedoom.com say there are some really nice 'gills here, with 10-inch slabs present. There are also some nice crappies. Walleyes come in all sizes, some of them large, but many are a nice eating size. Northern pike also run large here, with a decent population of large pike over 30 inches. There are some pretty good perch swimming around here as well. Stewart is a quality fishing lake, despite fairly heavy fishing pressure.

For walleyes, the folks at Muskie Doom recommend fishing the rocky slopes around the small, round island straight north of the boat landing. The rocky drops northeast of the lake's deep hole are also worth a look.

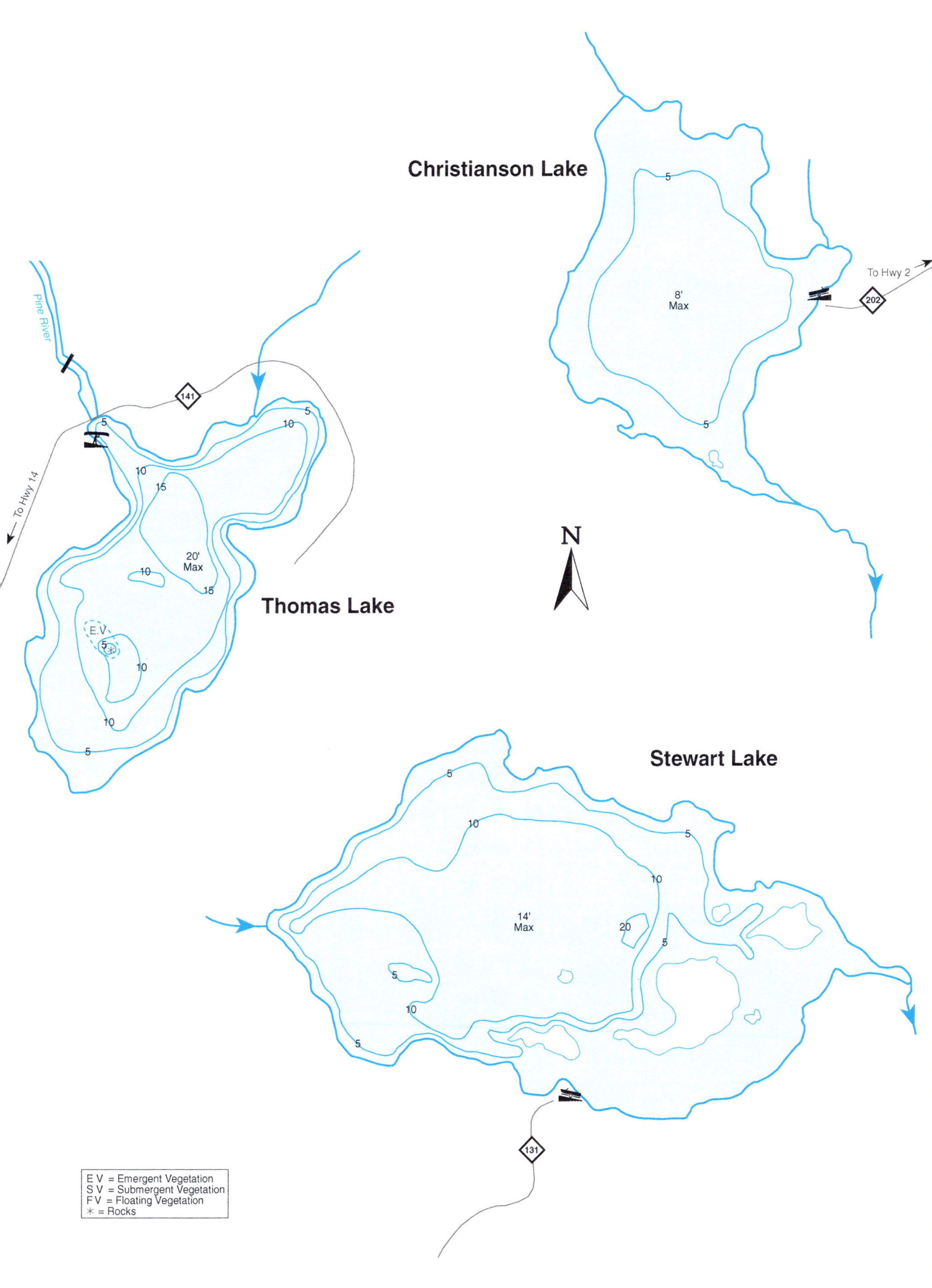

CHRISTIANSON LAKE

THOMAS LAKE

STEWART LAKE

Source: Minnesota Department of Natural Resources, USGS

ISLE ROYALE

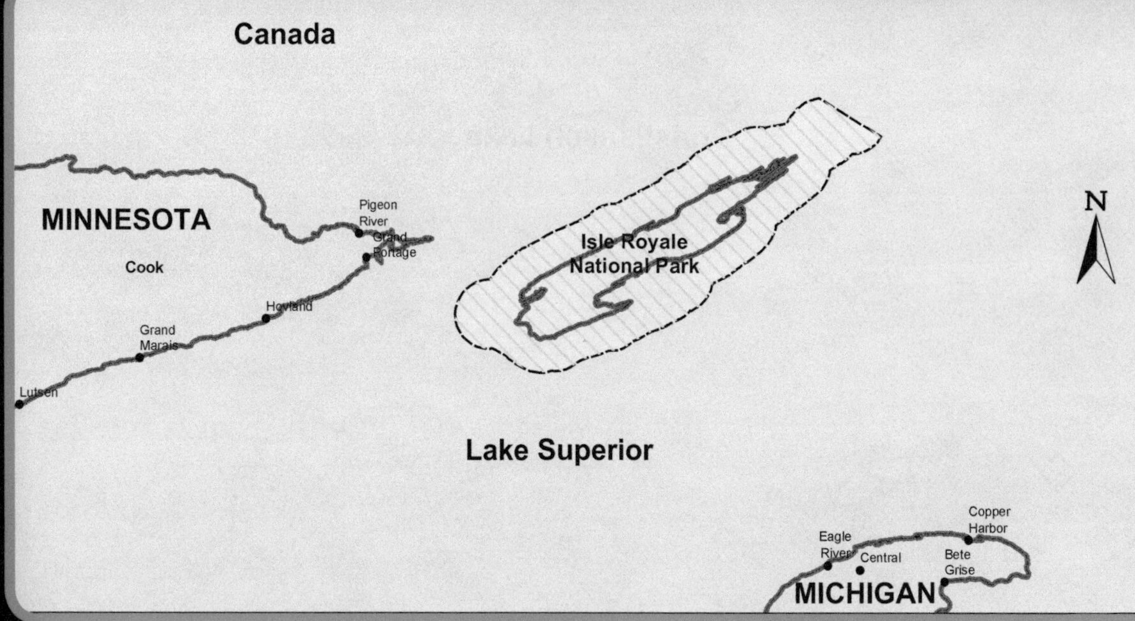

Lake Elevation, Area, Maximum Depth					Species Present					
Lake Name	Page #	Lake Elevation (feet)	Lake Area (acres)	Max Depth (ft)	Brook Trout	Lake Trout	Northern Pike	Yellow Perch	Walleye	Pumpkinseed
Ahmik	223	632.2	25.4	11.0			•	•		
Amygdaloid	222	613.5	26.7	29.0						
Angleworm	222	789.0	124.5	27.6			•	•		
Beaver	222	679.1	49.6	17.0			•	•		
Benson	222-223	787.1	59.5	12.5				•		
Chickenbone	222	3.9	228.7	21.0			•	•	•	•
Desor	221	854.0	1,056.7	46.0	Δ					
Dustin	222	649.6	10.9	20.0			•	•	•	
Epidote	223	620.1	3.2	13.0			•	•		
Eva	222	614.2	43.5	21.0			•	•		
Feldtman	220	660.1	458.9	9.0			•	•		
Forbes	223	774.3	16.8	19.0				•		
George	222	669.0	9.4	8.9			•	•		
Halloran	221	656.2	191.2	8.9			•	•		
Harvey	222	762.1	136.8	13.1				•		
Hatchet	221-222	754.3	122.5	17.1	Δ					
Hidden	223									
Intermediate	222	675.9	174.9	22.0			•	•		
John	223	643.0	8.2	18.0			•	•		
Lesage	222	732.9	111.2	21.0			•	•		
Linklater	222	729.0	42.7	19.7			•	•		
Livermore	222	699.1	74.3	18.0			•	•		
Mason	222	610.2	56.3	27.9			•	•		•
McDonald	222	698.8	36.6	13.1			•	•		
Mud	221	-	-	3.0			•			
Otter	222	698.8	49.9	14.0			•	•		
Patterson	223	623.4	24.9	11.8			•	•		
Richie	222	628.0	534.0	35.0			•	•		•
Sargent	222	695.5	354.2	45.0			•	•		•
Scholts	222	669.3	5.7	5.0			•	•		
Shesheeb	222	728.3	28.4	18.0			•	•		
Siskiwit	221-222	659.4	4038.9	150.9		•	•	•		
Wagejo	222	751.0	15.1	7.2			•	•		
Whittlesey	222	682.4	160.6	25.0			•	•	•	

Δ = Brook Trout formerly present

FISHING INFORMATION

Isle Royale is the largest island in Lake Superior. It measures 45 miles long and 9 miles wide. The big island is surrounded by dozens of smaller islands. Isle Royale National Park, which consists of Isle Royale, the smaller islands around it and the waters of Lake Superior extending 4.5 miles from the islands in all directions, encompasses a total of 894 square miles. Of this, 209 square miles is land and the rest is water.

Isle Royale is located in the northwestern part of Lake Superior, approximately 22 miles from the Canadian shore and from Grand Portage, Minn., and 55 miles from Michigan's Keweenaw peninsula.

Isle Royale National Park was established in 1940. The park was designated as part of the National Wilderness Preservation System in 1976, under the Wilderness Act, and remains today as an example of primitive America. In fact, 99 percent of the park's land area is designated as wilderness. In 1981, Isle Royale was designated an International Biosphere Reserve by the United Nations, giving it global scientific and educational significance. Accessible only by boat or float plane, Isle Royale is relatively untouched by direct outside influences and serves as a living laboratory.

The park is open from mid-April though October. Visitors are required to pay a nominal National Park Service day use fee. Boat and seaplane services run from early May through October. With fewer than 20,000 visitors annually, Isle Royale is the least-visited national park, but the one with the largest number of repeat visitors. More people visit Yellowstone National Park in a day than visit Isle Royale in a year. Due to its location, it is not an easy place to go to, and a visit takes some planning. Once you get to the island, there's very little available in the way of facilities or services, so you must take everything you need — including food — with you.

Visitors to Isle Royale could take their own boats, but due to Lake Superior's unpredictability and the possibility of severe weather, the following transportation services may be a better option.

Grand Portage - Isle Royale Transportation Line operates out of Grand Portage, Minn. You can contact them at (651) 653-5872 (November through April) or at (218) 475-0024 during the summer months. www.grand-isle-royale.com

The Isle Royale Line provides ferry service from Copper Harbor, Mich. Contact them at (906) 289-4437 or www.isleroyale.com.

The National Park Service offers ferry transportation via the Ranger III out of Houghton, Mich. Contact the park office at (906) 482-0984 or www.nps.gov/isro/planyourvisit/ranger-iii.htm.

Isle Royale Seaplanes flies sea planes daily from the Houghton County airport to Isle Royale. For information call (906) 483-4991 or visit www.isleroyaleseaplanes.com.

Cont'd on page 216

ISLE ROYALE MILEAGE CHART

Site	Grace Island	Beaver Island CG	Windigo	Siskiwit CG	Hay Bay CG	Malone Bay	Isle Royale Light	Chippewa Harbor CG	Middle Island Passage	Moskey Basin CG	Daisy Farm CG	Caribou Island CG	Mott Island	Three Mile CG	Tooker's Island CG	Rock Harbor Lodge	Raspberry Island	Hidden Lake	Duncan Narrows CG	Duncan Bay CG	Belle Isle CG	Birch Island CG	McCargoe Cove CG	Todd Harbor CG	Huginnin Cove
Grace Island	-	3	4	28	26	29	28	36	43	46	43	43	43	46	47	48	49	50	46	49	41	31	33	34	5
Beaver Island CG	3	-	1	31	29	32	31	39	46	49	46	46	49	49	50	51	52	52	48	51	43	33	35	26	7
Windigo	4	1	-	32	30	33	32	40	47	50	47	47	48	50	51	52	53	53	49	52	44	34	36	27	8
Siskiwit CG	28	31	32	-	6	11	12	20	26	29	26	26	27	29	30	31	32	36	40	43	45	51	53	60	33
Hay Bay CG	26	29	30	6	-	7	9	16	23	26	23	23	24	26	27	29	29	32	36	39	41	47	49	56	31
Malone Bay	29	32	33	11	7	-	3	10	17	20	17	17	18	20	21	22	23	26	30	33	35	41	43	50	34
Isle Royale Light	28	31	32	12	9	3	-	9	15	18	15	15	16	18	19	20	21	24	28	31	33	39	41	48	53
Chippewa Harbor CG	36	39	40	20	16	10	9	-	7	10	7	7	8	10	11	12	13	16	20	23	25	31	33	40	41
Middle Island Passage	43	46	47	26	23	17	15	7	-	3	1	1	2	4	5	6	7	9	13	16	18	24	26	33	48
Moskey Basin CG	46	49	50	29	6	20	18	10	3	-	3	4	5	7	8	9	10	13	17	20	22	28	30	37	51
Daisy Farm CG	43	46	47	26	23	17	15	7	1	3	-	1	2	4	5	6	7	10	14	17	19	25	27	3	48
Caribou Island CG	43	46	47	26	23	17	15	7	1	4	1	-	1	3	4	5	6	9	13	16	18	24	26	33	48
Mott Island	43	49	48	27	24	18	16	8	2	5	2	1	-	2	3	4	5	8	12	15	11	23	25	32	47
Three Mile CG	46	49	50	29	26	20	18	10	4	7	4	3	2	-	1	2	3	6	10	13	15	21	23	30	49
Tooker's Island CG	47	50	51	30	27	21	19	11	5	8	5	4	3	1	-	2	2	5	9	12	14	20	22	29	48
Rock Harbor Lodge	48	51	52	31	29	22	20	12	6	9	6	5	4	2	2	-	1	4	8	11	13	19	21	28	47
Raspberry Island	49	52	53	32	29	23	21	13	7	10	7	6	5	3	2	1	-	3	7	10	12	18	20	27	46
Hidden Lake	50	52	53	36	32	26	24	16	99	13	10	8	8	6	5	4	3	-	6	9	12	18	19	28	45
Duncan Narrows CG	46	48	49	40	36	30	28	20	13	17	14	13	12	10	9	8	7	6	-	3	9	14	16	24	43
Duncan Bay CG	49	51	52	43	39	33	31	23	16	20	17	16	15	13	12	11	10	9	3	-	12	17	19	27	46
Belle Isle CG	41	43	44	45	41	35	33	25	18	22	19	18	11	15	14	13	12	12	9	12	-	7	9	15	38
Birch Island CG	31	33	34	51	47	41	39	31	24	28	25	24	23	21	20	19	18	18	14	17	7	-	2	9	26
McCargoe Cove CG	33	35	36	53	49	43	41	33	26	30	27	26	25	23	22	21	20	19	16	19	9	2	-	11	28
Todd Harbor CG	34	26	27	60	56	50	48	40	33	37	34	33	32	30	29	28	27	28	24	27	15	9	11	-	19
Huginnin Cove	5	7	8	33	31	54	53	41	48	51	48	48	47	49	48	47	46	45	43	46	38	26	28	19	-

NAVIGATION AIDS

MAFOR CODE (Marine Weather Forecast)

G = Forecast Period	D = Wind Direction	Fm = Wind Force	W1 = Forecast
0 = Begin period	0 = Calm	0 = 0 to 10 knots	0 = Moderate or good visibility, more than 3 nautical miles
1 = 3 hours	1 = Northeast	1 = 11 to 16 knots	1 = Risk of accumulation of ice on super-structures
2 = 6 hours	2 = East	2 = 12 to 21 knots	2 = Strong risk of accumulation of ice on superstructure
3 = 9 hours	3 = Southeast	3 = 22 to 27 knots	3 = Mist (visibility ship to ship to 3 nautical miles)
4 = 12 hours	4 = South	4 = 28 to 33 knots	4 = Fog (visibility less than 5/8 nautical miles)
5 = 18 hours	5 = Southwest	5 = 34 to 40 knots	5 = Drizzle
6 = 24 hours	6 = West	6 = 41 to 47 knots	6 = Rain
7 = 48 hours	7 = Northwest	7 = 48 to 55 knots	7 = Snow, or rain and snow
8 = 72 hours	8 = North	8 = 56 to 63 knots	8 = Squally weather with or without showers
9 = Occasionally	9 = Variable	9 = Over 64 knots	9 = Thunderstorms

Useful Radio Frequencies

Channel	Proper Use
16	DISTRESS, ship to ship / shore hailing
6	Hailing Intership (safety only)
22A	Communication with U.S. Coast Guard
68, 69, 70, 78A	Non-commercial intership and ship to coast
162.550 MHz, 162.400 MHz, 162.475 MHz	NOAA Weather broadcast
24, 25, 26, 27, 28, 84, 85, 86	Ship to public coast

Above is a list of some radio frequencies you may find useful while cruising Lake Superior. Ranger stations at Mott Island and Windigo monitor channel 16 during normal business hours. The National Park Service uses Channel 68 and 9 as the park's working channels.

TRAIL MILEAGE BETWEEN ISLE ROYALE CAMPGROUNDS

Campground	Chickenbone E	Chickenbone W	Chippewa Harbor	Daisy Farm	Desor North	Desor South	Feldtmann Lake	Hatchet Lake	Huginnin Cove	Island Mine	Lake Richie	Lane Cove	Little Todd	Malone Bay	McCargoe Cove	Moskey Basin	Rock Harbor	Siskiwit Bay	Three Mile	Todd Harbor	Washington Channel
Chickenbone E	-	1.8	9.3	6.1	19.6	16.4	35.8	9.3	30.3	21.3	5.0	10.9	15.6	19.6	2.1	7.3	13.3	25.7	10.5	8.7	27.1
Chickenbone W	1.8	-	7.9	7.9	19.8	15.0	34.4	7.9	29.1	19.9	3.6	12.7	16.2	18.2	2.7	5.9	14.8	24.3	12.5	9.3	25.7
Chippewa Harbor	9.3	7.9	-	9.7	27.3	22.5	42.0	15.2	36.4	27.2	4.3	16.6	22.6	25.7	10.6	6.2	16.8	31.6	14.1	17.3	33.0
Daisy Farm	6.1	7.9	9.7	-	26.0	22.5	41.9	15.4	37.3	27.4	5.8	6.9	21.5	27.2	8.2	3.9	7.1	31.8	4.4	14.9	33.2
Desor North	19.6	19.8	27.3	26.0	-	20.0	21.4	12.3	14.4	18.6	23.0	30.8	5.7	23.2	18.0	25.3	33.1	23.0	30.4	11.4	12.6
Desor South	16.4	15.0	22.5	22.5	20.0	-	20.1	8.1	14.7	5.5	18.2	27.3	15.5	10.8	17.7	20.5	29.4	9.9	26.7	11.8	11.3
Feldtmann Lake	35.8	34.4	42.0	41.9	21.4	20.1	-	27.6	12.8	14.6	37.8	46.7	26.1	30.3	37.1	40.1	49.0	10.3	46.3	31.8	8.8
Hatchet Lake	9.3	7.9	15.2	15.4	12.3	8.1	27.6	-	25.7	13.0	11.1	20.2	7.8	11.3	10.7	13.4	22.3	17.4	19.8	4.1	18.8
Huginnin Cove	30.3	29.1	36.4	37.3	14.4	14.7	12.8	25.7	-	10.0	32.3	41.2	19.1	24.9	31.8	34.6	44.4	14.4	41.7	24.8	4.0
Island Mine	21.3	19.9	27.2	27.4	18.6	5.5	14.6	13.0	10.0	-	23.1	32.2	20.4	15.7	22.6	25.4	34.3	4.4	31.6	16.7	6.6
Lake Richie	5.0	3.6	4.3	5.8	23.0	18.2	37.8	11.1	32.3	23.1	-	12.7	18.5	21.4	6.3	2.3	12.9	27.5	10.2	13.0	28.9
Lane Cove	10.9	12.7	16.6	6.9	30.8	27.3	46.7	20.2	41.2	32.2	12.7	-	26.5	30.5	13.0	10.8	6.9	36.6	4.6	19.5	38.3
Little Todd	15.6	16.2	22.6	21.5	5.7	15.5	26.1	7.8	19.1	20.4	18.5	26.5	-	18.7	13.5	22.1	28.6	24.8	25.9	7.0	17.3
Malone Bay	19.6	18.2	25.7	27.2	23.2	10.8	30.3	11.3	24.9	15.7	21.4	30.5	18.7	-	20.9	23.7	34.3	20.1	31.6	15.0	21.5
McCargoe Cove	2.1	2.7	10.6	8.2	18.0	17.7	37.1	10.7	31.8	22.6	6.3	13.0	13.5	20.9	-	8.4	15.3	27.0	12.6	6.7	28.4
Moskey Basin	7.3	5.9	6.2	3.9	25.3	20.5	40.1	13.4	34.6	25.4	2.3	10.8	22.1	23.7	8.4	-	11.0	29.8	8.3	15.1	31.0
Rock Harbor	13.3	14.8	16.8	7.1	33.1	29.4	49.0	22.3	44.4	34.3	12.9	6.9	28.6	34.3	15.3	11.0	-	38.7	2.7	22.2	40.1
Siskiwit Bay	25.7	24.3	31.6	31.8	23.0	9.9	10.3	17.4	14.4	4.4	27.5	36.6	24.8	20.1	27.0	29.8	38.7	-	36.0	21.1	11.0
Three Mile	10.5	12.5	14.1	4.4	30.4	26.7	46.3	19.8	41.7	31.6	10.2	4.6	25.9	31.6	12.6	8.3	2.7	36.0	-	19.5	37.8
Todd Harbor	8.7	9.3	17.3	14.9	11.4	11.8	31.8	4.1	24.8	16.7	13.0	19.5	7.0	15.0	6.7	15.1	22.2	21.1	19.5	-	23.0
Washington Creek	27.1	25.7	33.0	33.2	12.0	11.3	8.8	18.8	4.0	6.6	28.9	38.3	17.3	21.5	28.4	31.0	40.1	11.0	37.8	23.0	-

Cont'd from page 214

There are more than 165 miles of hiking trails on the island, and these range from easy to difficult. The steep terrain of the Greenstone Ridge can make hiking difficult on some trails. You'll also find more than 35 campgrounds to accommodate campers.

Wildlife abounds here, and the relationship between the island's moose and wolves is world famous. Moose swam to the island, probably from the Canadian mainland, sometime in the early 1900s. They found abundant food and no predators, and their population grew rapidly. Then, during a severe winter in the late 1940s, a rare ice bridge formed between Isle Royale and the Canadian mainland and a pack of wolves found their way to the island. The interaction between wolves and moose on Isle Royale has been intensely studied for more than 50 years, making it the longest-running study of large predator and prey relationships in the world.

In addition to moose and wolves, the island holds a large population of red foxes, as well as red squirrels, beavers, mink, snowshoe hares, both blue and gray jays, cormorants, and various species of ducks, woodpeckers and songbirds.

Fishing Isle Royale's Inland Lakes

Fishing the inland lakes of Isle Royale can be a true adventure. Not only is it difficult simply to reach the island, but once there, you'll have to hike to a lake, portaging a canoe if you wish. Most lakes are lightly fished, and some rarely see anglers, due to their remote location. These wilderness lakes truly are wild, and most are largely unchanged from the time when man first explored the island. In fact, a fishery assessment conducted in the mid-1990s found much the same results as the original assessment conducted in 1929. Special regulations – such as the prohibition of natural bait and motors – as well as the remoteness of the lakes, have helped maintain these unique fisheries. Most of the island's 40+ lakes have fish, with northern pike and yellow perch being the most common species. Walleyes, pumpkinseed sunfish and lake trout are also found in some waters, while brook trout inhabit the island's streams.

The National Park Service regulates the inland fishery on Isle Royale, and no fishing license is required to fish inland lakes and streams. Only artificial baits and lures may be used. No live or dead minnows, worms, leeches, insects or fish eggs may be used. Michigan fishing seasons, size and possession limits apply, with the exception of park-specific restrictions for brook trout. Check with a ranger for additional information.

Most inland fishing is done by canoe or kayak, as the shorelines of most lakes have a large amount of forest vegetation, making shore fishing impractical. Wading anglers will find action along the edges of lakes. A few lakes are accessible to shore fishing, and some lakes have docks. However, Jay Glase, a National Park Service fisheries biologist, noted that anglers who fish from canoes and kayaks tend to be more successful than shore-bound anglers.

Glase said the fishing is generally good on most waters within Isle Royale, but it varies from lake to lake. On some waters, anglers may catch fish seemingly on every cast, although these fish may be small. He said anglers can expect to find lots of fish, but not necessarily large fish. However, he said some lunkers are available, and every year people catch big fish. As would be expected, Glase said anglers who can get into the remote lakes will find some of the best fishing.

Northern pike are the most common fish species in the inland lakes. Most lakes have little fishing pressure, so fish populations are high. Average pike size is 3 to 4 pounds, with some fish measuring 40 inches and nearing 20 pounds caught every year. Some of the best pike lakes are Chickenbone, Feldtman, Intermediate, Richie, Siskiwit, Wagejo and Whittlesey.

Most of the pike lakes also contain perch – a primary food source for pike. It makes sense that perch-colored lures are often effective for pike. Spoons like the Johnson Silver Minnow and Dardevle are effective, but the Dardevle tends to snag in the weedy areas pike inhabit. Spinnerbaits are very effective in weedy areas. If you're targeting perch, try casting small jigs with twister tails.

Only a few lakes have walleyes: Chickenbone, Dustin and Whittlesey. Walleye fishing can be as a simple as casting a jig with a twister tail. If you can get over a rocky point or hump in a canoe, fish the jig vertically, bouncing it just off the bottom.

Although the Lake Superior waters surrounding Isle Royale are known as a top lake trout destination, Siskiwit Lake ¬– the largest lake on the island – also has lake trout. These lurkers of the deep are very difficult to find, except in the spring when they can be found in shallow water and again in the fall when they move close to shore to spawn. In summer, they tend to suspend over deep water, making them difficult to locate with the primitive equipment anglers can carry into the park.

A handful of streams have brook trout. Although fishing for brookies is allowed, it is strictly catch and release. The Big and Little Siskiwit rivers have spring runs of steelhead. The fish bunch up below the falls, offering

Cont'd on page 218

#	pg	Description	Lat	Long
1		Voyageurs Marina	47°57'74	89°39'18
2		Grand Portage Marina	47°57'36	89°41'19
3		Turning Point to Hat Point	47°57'55	89°39'54
4		between Hat Pt. and Bell	47°57'15	89°38'57
5		Thunder Bay, Welcome Island, S buoy	48°20'40	89°08'85
6		Abeam Pie Island on east	48°16'29	89°01'80
7		Abeam Augus Island on NE	48°14'43	88°59'36
8		Amygdaloid Channel, SW end	48°17'80	88°40'00
9		Grand Marais, mid-channel between break-water	47°44'37	90°20'26
10		Turning Point to go north	47°44'10	90°20'38
11		Eagle Harbor, Abeam Gong	47°29'88	88°09'53
12		Abeam Copper Harbor, channel bell	47°28'70	87°51'87
13		Keweenaw entrance, mid-channel	47°14'50	88°37'85
14	220	Turning point into North Gap	47°53'89	89°13'48
15	220	North Gap	47°53'65	89°13'35
16	220	North Gap / Wash. Harbor	47°53'39	89°13'23
17	220	Mid-channel, W. Beaver Island	47°54'04	89°11'13
18	220	S of W end Beaver Island	47°54'19	89°10'42
19	220	Turning point to go up North Shore	47°54'33	89°13'95
20	220	Abeam McGinty Cove	47°55'37	89°12'40
21	220	Abeam Huginnin Cove	47°56'30	89°10'66
22	220	Abeam Finlander Reef	47°58'99	89°05'51
23	221	Abeam Gull Rocks	48°01'19	88°57'19
24	222	Abeam Todd Harbor	48°03'63	88°50'04
25	222	Abeam Kamloops Point	48°05'17	88°45'35
26	222	Hawk Island to S	48°06'18	88°43'18
27	222	Abeam McCargo Cove	48°06'98	88°41'40
28	222	Abeam East Round Island	48°07'62	88°40'00
29	222	Abeam Amygdaloid Ranger Station	48°08'06	88°39'24
30	223	Abeam Amygdaloid NE end	48°09'34	88°35'50
31	223	Abeam to E from W end Cpt Kidd Island	48°09'57	88°34'62
32	223	N ent Dead Horse Rocks Narrows	48°09'35	88°34'42
33	223	S ent Dead Horse Rocks Narrows	48°09'23	88°34'30
34	223	Belle Isle Dock	48°09'06	88°35'24
35	223	Turning Point 1.5 mile W of Locke Pt	48°11'24	88°29'50
36	223	Entrance Duncan Bay	48°11'48	88°26'35
37	223	E of Duncan Bay Narrows	48°10'48	88°28'02
38	223	begin Duncan Narrows	48°10'25	88°28'56
39	223	Abeam NE Blake Point	48°11'58	88°25'20
40	223	E-NE Blake Point Turning Point	48°11'66	88°24'67
41	223	Turning Point N Govt Island	48°11'07	88°25'12
42	223	mid-channel NW Tobin Harbor	48°10'22	88°26'80
43	223	Turning Point NE Scoville Point	48°09'92	88°26'42
44	223	Abeam NW end Gull Rock	48°09'43	88°26'66
45	223	Abeam to S of Scoville Point	48°09'66	88°26'88
46	223	Abeam Rock Harbor Lodge Bay	48°08'45	88°29'08
47	223	Abeam Mott Island Govt Dock	48°06'56	88°32'94
48	223	N entrance Middle Isle Passage	48°05'72	88°34'64
49	223	Abeam Daisy Farm Dock	48°05'35	88°35'52
50	223	W end Moskey Basin Narrows	48°04'75	88°36'87
51	222	Moskey Basin Dock	48°03'90	88°38'56
52	223	S entrance Middle Isle Passage	48°05'52	88°34'38
53	223	Abeam Conglomerate Bay	48°04'87	88°34'20
54	223	Abeam Mine Point	48°04'32	88°34'02
55	223	Abeam Saginaw Point	48°03'52	88°34'36
56	223	Abeam Epidote Mine	48°02'37	88°36'48
57	222	Abeam Chippewa Harbor	48°01'49	88°38'16
58	222	Abeam Blueberry Cove	48°00'45	88°40'38
59	222	Abeam Schooner Island	47°58'83	88°44'97
60	222	Turning Point	47°58'34	88°47'62
61	222	NE end Malone Bay Channel	47°58'78	88°48'45
62	222	West End, Malone Bay	47°58'35	88°50'40
63	221	Hopkins Harbor	47°58'12	88°50'40
64	222	Abeam Malone Bay Channel	47°57'65	88°46'30
65	221	Turning Point	47°57'76	88°51'16
66	221	Spruce Point	47°56'84	88°53'47
67	221	Hay Bay	47°56'69	88°54'42
68	221	Abeam Hay Bay Dock	47°56'09	88°56'44
69	221	Abeam Point Houghton, N ent to Houghton Passage	47°54'28	88°53'30
70	221	S ent Houghton Passage	47°53'78	88°53'18
71	221	Abeam Isle Royale Light	47°56'48	88°45'32
72		Abeam Harlem Reef Buoy	47°53'90	89°50'00

#	pg	Description	Lat	Long
73		Abeam Houghton Passage	47°53'13	88°53'06
74	221	Abeam McCormick Rocks	47°52'10	88°57'31
75	221	Abeam SW Point McCormick Reef	47°50'78	89°01'77
76	221	Long Point	47°49'56	89°07'16
77	220	Turning Point	47°49'23	89°09'00
78	220	Abeam The Head	47°49'23	89°09'88
79	220	Rainbow Point	47°49'77	89°11'84
80	220	Cumberland Point	47°51'13	89°14'71
81	220	Abeam Middle Point	47°52'09	89°13'72
82	220	North Grace Harbor	47°52'97	89°12'46
83	220	Grace Island Narrows	47°53'15	89°12'69
84	220	Turn Pt, W Grace Narrows	47°53'20	89°12'77
85	220	Gap to/from Grace Harbor	47°53'25	89°13'03
86	220	Abeam N mid-point Wash Island	47°52'74	89°15'40
87		mile south lighthouse	47°51'20	89°18'91
88		mile south of buoy	47°51'10	89°19'22
89		one mile SW of lighthouse	47°51'41	89°19'76
90		23 ft. SW of lighthouse	47°51'67	89°19'64
91		14 ft. S of lighthouse	47°51'77	89°18'85
92		11 ft. reef, E lighthouse	47°51'95	89°18'43
93		1/4 mile NE lighthouse	47°52'22	89°18'61
94		1 mile NE lighthouse	47°52'57	89°17'94
95		0.8 mile NE lighthouse	47°52'58	89°18'18
96		1.4 mile NE lighthouse	47°52'75	89°17'40
97	220	SW end Johns Reef	47°52'98	89°15'10
98		0.6 mile N lighthouse	47°53'08	89°18'80
99		22 ft. reef, 0.4 NW light	47°52'29	89°19'09
100		Rock of Ages Lighthouse	47°51'97	89°18'88
101		Fishermans Reef	47°46'80	89°24'72
102		SW reef, off North Rock	47°51'78	89°16'92
103	220	SW end South Rock	47°51'71	89°16'27
104	220	SW Bottle 1	47°51'95	89°16'20
105	220	between Johns & Booth Islands	47°53'07	89°14'10
106	221	SW end McCormick Reef	47°51'09	89°01'96
107	221	rocky point, SW McCormick Rock	47°52'06	88°58'03
108	221	NE McCormick Rocks Reef	47°52'66	88°56'35
109	221	Little Boat Harbor Reef	47°52'90	88°56'05
110	221	SW end Harlem Reef	47°53'98	88°50'70
111	221	SW San Antonio Reef	47°54'31	88°51'04
112	221	mid-point, Inner Reef	47°54'94	88°51'24
113	221	NW Point Hay	47°56'50	88°54'73
114	221	Butterfield Shoal	47°56'90	88°52'61
115	221	West Lump Reef	47°57'52	88°50'96
116	222	17 ft. reef, S. Ross Island	47°58'39	88°46'87
117		NE end Taylor Reef	47°56'12	88°46'88°
118		SW end Long Island Reef	47°55'39	88°49'92
119		SW Menagerie Island	47°56'63	88°46'33
120	222	Glenlyon Shoal	47°57'10	88°44'90
121	222	18 Reef, NE Glenlyon Shoal	47°57'34	88°44'15
122		0.4 mile NE Five Foot Reef	48°11'54	88°23'82
123		Five Foot Reef	48°11'33	88°24'22
124	223	East Blake Point	48°11'52	88°25'00
125		E of Passage Island Light	48°13'34	88°21'16
126		NE of N end Passage Island	4314'44	88°19'82
127		Gull Islands	48°15'71	88°15'97
128		Gull Island Reef, E. 11/4 mile	48°15'60	88°14'08
129		Gull Island Reef, SE 0.5 mile	48°15'36	88°15'74
130		Gull Island Reef, NW 0.8 mile	48°16'17	88°17'30
131		Gull Island Reef, NW 1.4 mile	48°16'64	88°17'60
132		Gull Island Reef, N 1.4 mile	48°16'82	88°16'97
133		Gull Island Reef, NW 2.3 mile	48°16'60	88°19'00
134		Bateau Rock	48°1617	88°06'59
135		Bateau Rock, W Reef	48°16'18	88°07'14
136		Bateau Rock, NW Reef	48°16'64	88°07'36
137	223	Congdon Shoal	48°11'59	88°30'79
138	223	NW of Steamboat Island	48°10'88	88°32'00
139	222	Ollies Dogs Rocks	48°07'00	88°42'81
140	222	W of Kamloops Point	48°05'11	88°46'22
141	222	W ent/Mid Harbor/Todd Harbor	48°03'42	88°49'66
142	220	Finlander Reef, east end	47°58'49	89°05'30
143	220	Finland Reef, west end	47°58'37	89°05'52
144	223	middle of Canoe Rocks	48°11'87	88°29'83

Gray shading indicates point that does not appear on the map pages.

ISLE ROYALE

Cont'd from page 216

great fishing. Hikers carrying a light rod and reel or a fly-fishing outfit will often be surprised at what they come across in the island's streams.

Fishing Lake Superior

According to Don Szczech, charter captain of All-Out Charters, the lake trout fishing around Isle Royale is "if not the best, within a percent or two of being the best in all of Lake Superior." Szczech should know, because he's been fishing Lake Superior for decades and is the last active charter captain fishing around Isle Royale.

Not only are the lake trout abundant; they are large, too. "Every time you put a line in the water you've got a chance of getting one over 30 (pounds)," Szczech said. During the 2006 season, his clients landed 10 fish over 30 pounds. Most days someone catches a 20-pounder, with the average fish running 8 to 12 pounds. Unless an angler is getting a fish mounted, Szczech encourages anglers to release fish over 15 pounds.

Szczech credits the great fishery largely to the incredible structure found around Isle Royale. There are literally hundreds of excellent fishing areas around the island, and every time he ventures out, Szczech says he finds more new places that aren't marked on maps. The area has numerous rock reefs and humps that can rise from 400 feet up to 2 feet in the matter of a couple boat lengths. As such, there is plenty of habitat for fish and their prey, but navigation can be extremely dangerous.

The lack of fishing pressure also plays a role in the area's fantastic fishing. There was never much commercial fishing in the area, and few people are willing to make the long trek from the mainland to fish. Szczech noted that in about the last five years, more recreational boaters have ventured across the sometimes treacherous waters of Lake Superior to fish, but many days you'll never see another fishing boat.

Trolling is the most common method of fishing for lakers. Szczech usually trolls spoons from 1.8 to 2.2 mph. Most fishing is done close to bottom. Shelf edges and deep-water breaks are the best places to look for lakers. Typically in spring, Szczech targets the 150- to 200-foot depths. In summer, he'll fish in 100 to 150 feet of water. He moves shallower in fall, as lake trout prepare for spawning. Sometimes he'll use J-Plugs on outriggers trolled along the edges of rock reefs in 20 to 30 feet of water in fall. At this time of year, fishing can be great, and Szczech says it would be possible to catch 150 fish per day sometimes in September and October; the trick is being able to get out on the water, as the weather can be rough at this time of year.

If Szczech finds fish on a piece of structure, he may try jigging for them if the water is relatively calm and allows him to maintain a vertical presentation. On a really calm day, he can get away with a ¾-ounce jig. On a rough day when fishing deep water, he may use up to a 5-ounce jig. He tips them with herring or a strip of fish belly. White, pink and chartreuse are some of the most productive colors, but color isn't all that important. "Lake trout are pretty aggressive," Szczech said. "If you find fish, you're going to catch them."

When jigging, Szczech likes to work up the side of the structure, fish the top, and then go back over the other edge. The hookset is critical when jigging. It takes some real power to adequately set the hook on a big fish in more than 100 feet of water. Szczech uses a stiff, medium-heavy saltwater rod and a spinning reel. Using fishing line with minimal stretch is critical.

Szczech noted that most people targeting lake trout fish in August, but he said they don't realize the fishing is good all season. Szczech usually fishes from May to mid-October.

Although lake trout are the biggest draw for anglers fishing the outlying waters of Isle Royale, the steelhead fishing can be good as well. Szczech said these trout average 6 to 8 pounds. Ten-pounders are common, and his clients take fish up to 14 pounds. Szczech trolls a bit faster for steelhead – 3.5 to 4 mph – and fishes closer to shore. Generally the best fishing is in 20 feet of water or less. Szczech trolls along the shore, looking for temperature breaks, which are the real key to finding fish, especially if you can find a 10- to 15-degree break. Other things to look for are scum/bug lines and flocks of seagulls congregating over the water, feeding on injured baitfish. Szczech trolls spoons or stickbaits using planer boards. He runs the lures 150 to 200 feet behind the boat during the summer.

Although there are salmon in the area, Szczech says the fish are hard to pin down and he doesn't target them specifically. Plus they are a bit fussier when it comes to lure selection. The salmon are usually just a bonus fish.

The Michigan DNR regulates fishing within the Lake Superior waters of Isle Royale National Park and a Michigan fishing license is required. The daily bag limit is five trout and salmon, but no more than three can be trout.

If you've got the ambition and are looking for an adventure, give Isle Royale charter fishing a try. Szczech may have summed it up best: "I fished from Lake Michigan to Manitoba regularly, and once I fished there (Isle Royale), I never went anywhere else. There's no other place like it."

Greenstones in Isle Royale National Park

What is a Greenstone?

That's a good question. On Isle Royale, greenstone has two entirely different meanings. Hiking along Isle Royale's loftiest ridge, you might encounter an outcropping of basalt with a greenish hue. Welcome to Greenstone Ridge, backbone of Isle Royale and its highest and longest ridge. Running more than 40 miles along the ridge, the Greenstone Trail provides excellent island-wide views. The ridge is named for the color of the underlying Greenstone Flow. This basalt flow is up to 800 feet thick and extends deep under Lake Superior in a continuous flow which reappears 50 miles later, on the Keweenaw Peninsula in Michigan. It is one of the earth's largest and thickest lava flows.

Strolling along a pebble beach on Isle Royale, you might stoop down and find a pea-sized greenish pebble amongst myriad other stones. Upon closer examination, you may be looking at the mineral pumpellyite, the "Isle Royale Greenstone" and Michigan's state gemstone. Chlorastrolite, which means "green star stone," is uncommon outside of Isle Royale. Chlorastrolite originates in lava flow cavities, is weathered out, and then is washed out into Lake Superior and sometimes wave-washed onto beaches. These stones usually show a mosaic or segmented pattern of "facets," sometimes called "turtleback." The facets are symbolic of the many faces Isle Royale's wilderness shows. As with the greenstone, each facet is unique and integral to the whole. And just as untrammeled land across the face of the United States was once much more common, so were greenstones and related minerals on Isle Royale beaches and under Lake Superior.

In summer of 1997, in a remote campground, Rangers found ten large zip lock bags filled with over 300 pieces of datolite (a semi-precious gemstone) that two individuals had collected from Isle Royale's Lake Superior waters. A reexamination by the U. S. Attorney's office and Interior Department lawyers of mineral collection laws revealed that the submerged Lake Superior minerals are afforded the same protection under Park Service-wide regulations that protect all natural, cultural, archeological and mineral resources. What this means is that the traditional use of beach combing, looking for greenstones, agates, and other mineral can continue, but visitors will not be permitted to collect and keep them. Instead, visitors can enjoy their discoveries via photographs, drawings and memories. Many old time collectors admit that the quantity and quality of minerals have become scarcer due to years of collection. This new protection ensures that these nonrenewable resources will continue to be seen and may even increase through storm deposition, allowing for generations yet unborn to enjoy them.

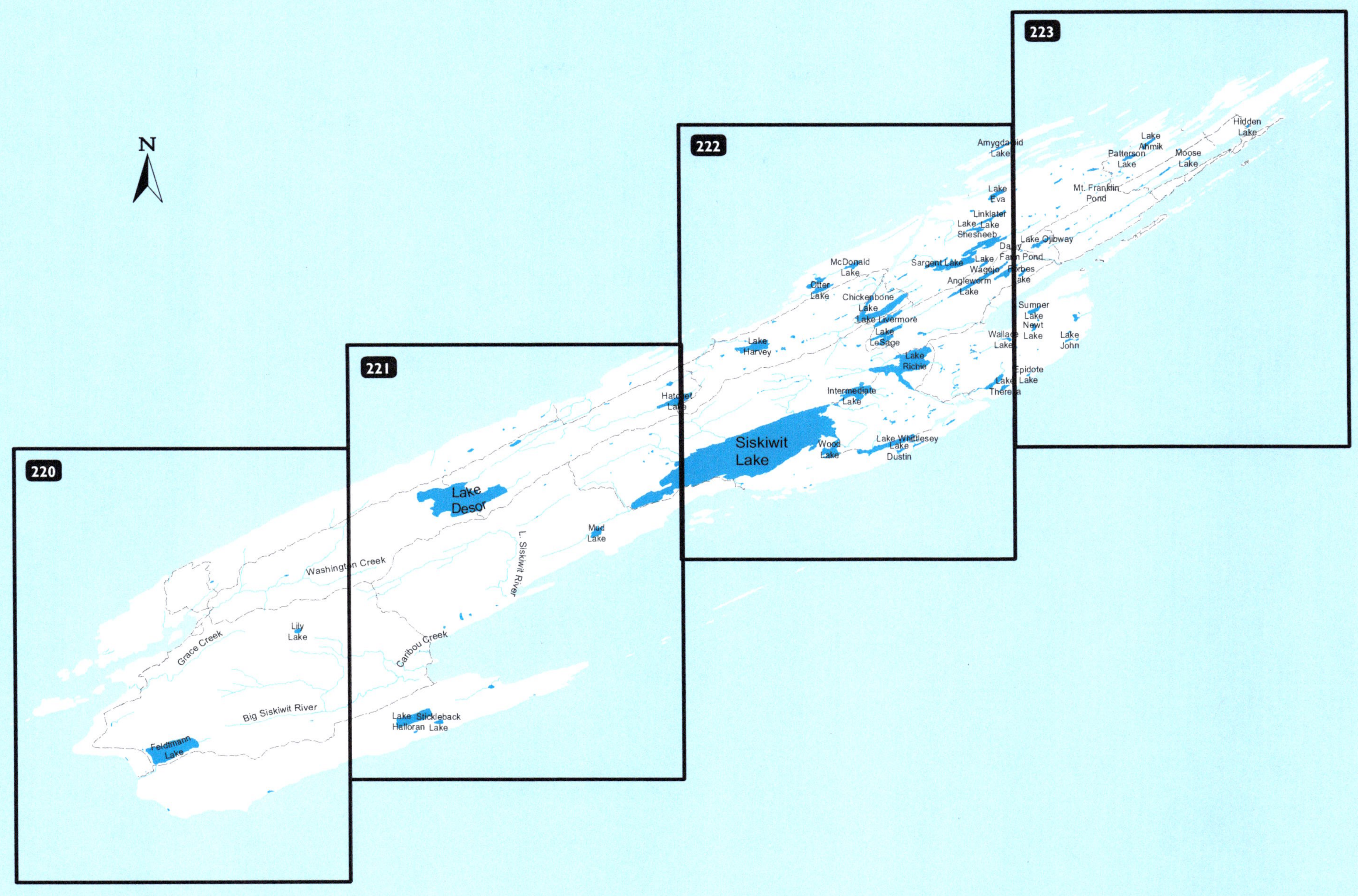
N
220
221
222
223
Feldtmann Lake
Grace Creek
Big Siskiwit River
Lily Lake
Washington Creek
Caribou Creek
Lake Stickleback
Halloran Lake
Lake Desor
L. Siskiwit River
Mud Lake
Hatchet Lake
Siskiwit Lake
Wood Lake
Lake Whittlesey
Lake Dustin
Intermediate Lake
Lake Harvey
Otter Lake
McDonald Lake
Chickenbone Lake
Lake Livermore
Lake LeSage
Lake Richie
Sargent Lake
Lake Wagejo
Angleworm Lake
Linklater Lake
Lake Shesheeb
Lake Eva
Amygdaloid Lake
Lake Ojibway
Farm Pond
Forbes Lake
Sumner Lake
Newt Lake
Wallace Lake
Lake John
Epidote Lake
Lake Theresa
Mt. Franklin Pond
Patterson Lake
Lake Ahmik
Moose Lake
Hidden Lake

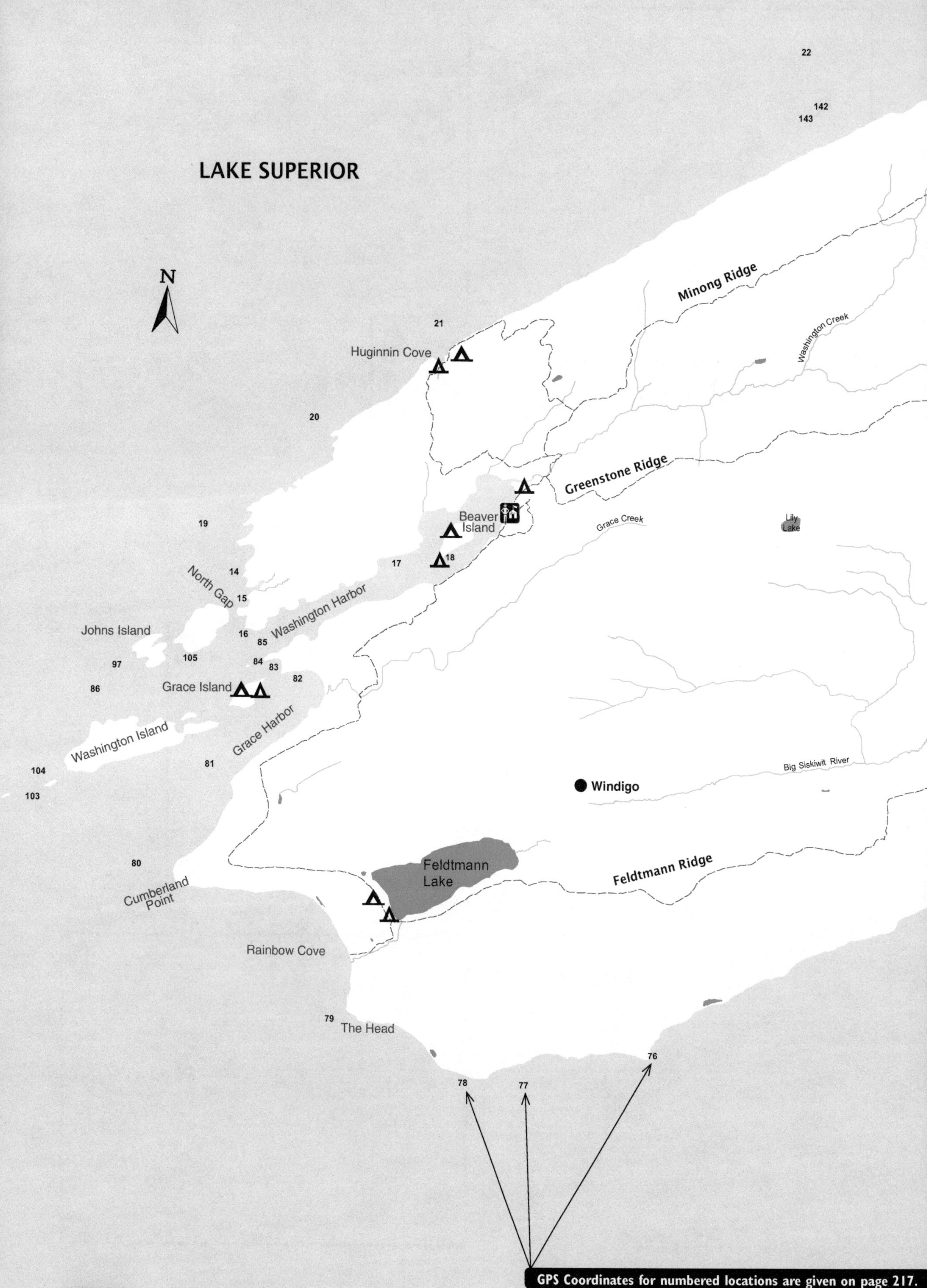

GPS Coordinates for numbered locations are given on page 217.

Source: National Park Service, USGS

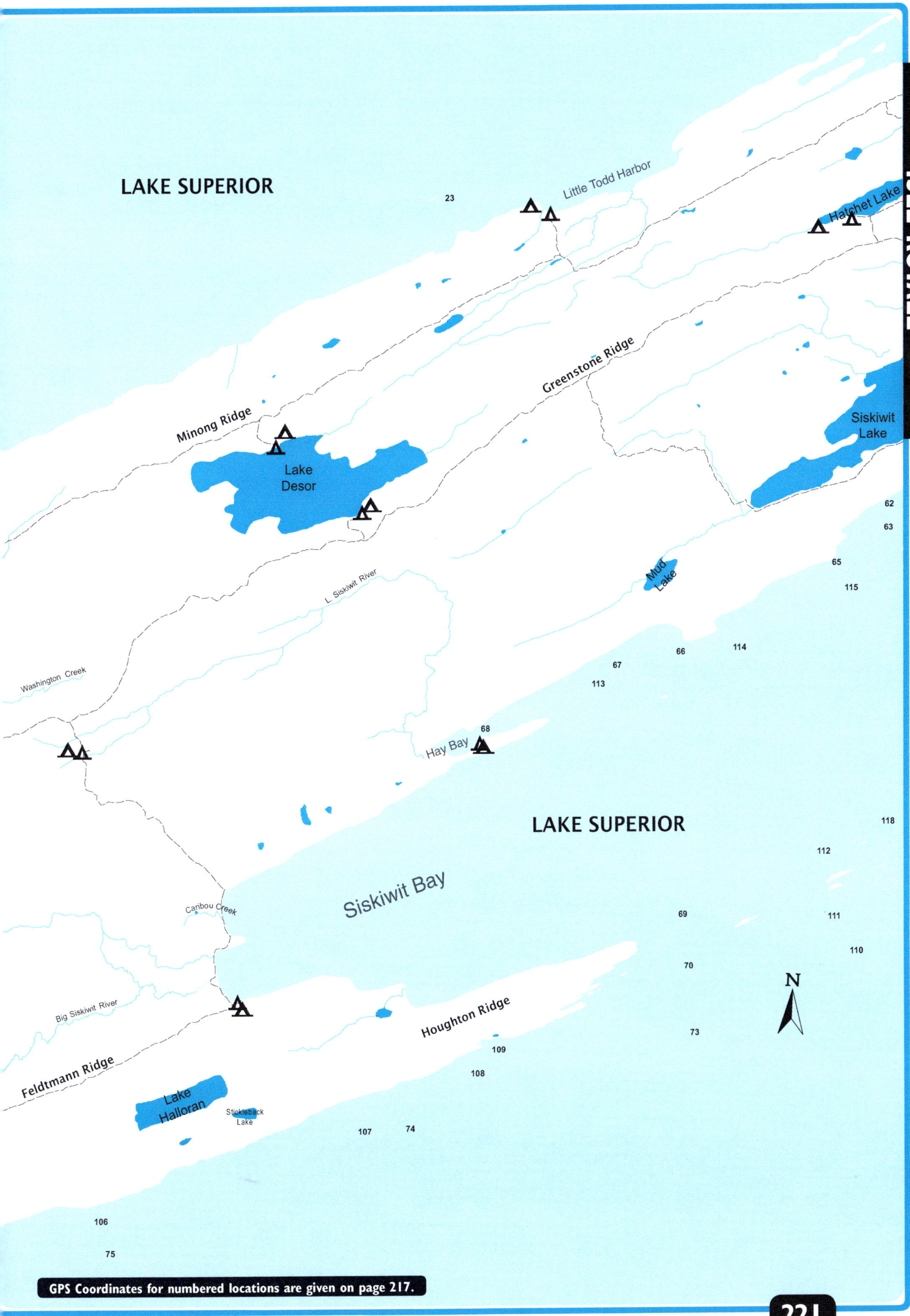

LAKE SUPERIOR

Little Todd Harbor

23

Hatchet Lake

Minong Ridge

Greenstone Ridge

Lake Desor

Siskiwit Lake

62

63

65

115

Mud Lake

L. Siskiwit River

Washington Creek

66

114

67

113

68

Hay Bay

LAKE SUPERIOR

118

112

Siskiwit Bay

Caribou Creek

69

111

110

70

N

Big Siskiwit River

Houghton Ridge

73

109

108

Feldtmann Ridge

Lake Halloran

Stickleback Lake

107

74

106

75

GPS Coordinates for numbered locations are given on page 217.

Source: National Park Service, USGS

GPS Coordinates for numbered locations are given on page 217.

Source: National Park Service, USGS

GPS Coordinates for numbered locations are given on page 217.

Source: National Park Service, USGS

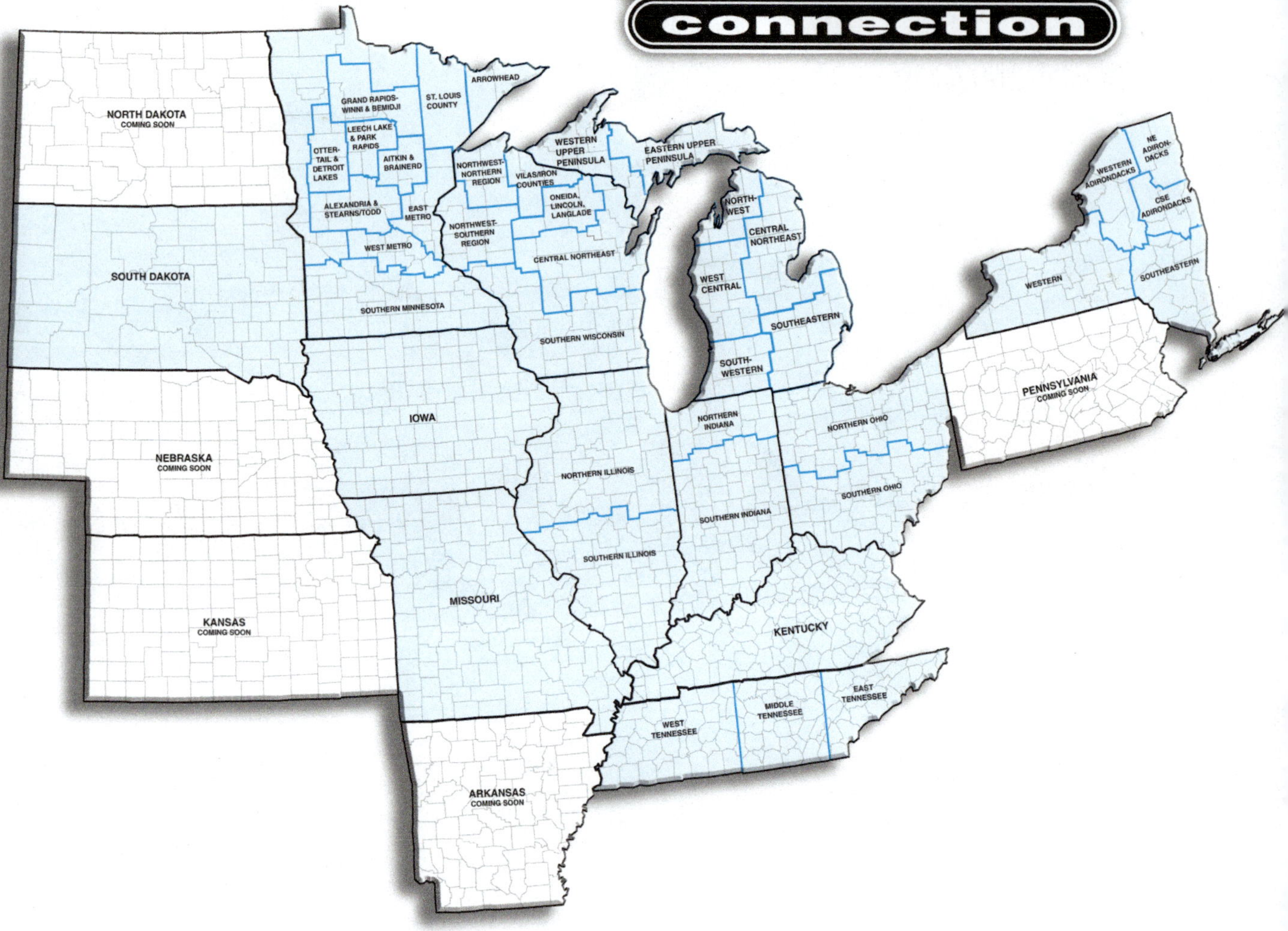